D0190692

Talleyrand

Also by Robin Harris

Dubrovnik: A History

Valois Guyenne: A Study of Politics, Government and
Society in Late Medieval France

Talleyrand

Betrayer and Saviour of France

ROBIN HARRIS

JOHN MURRAY

© Robin Harris 2007

First published in Great Britain in 2007 by John Murray (Publishers)
A division of Hodder Headline

The right of Robin Harris to be identified as the Author of the Work has been asserted by
him in accordance with the Copyright, Designs and Patents Act 1988.

I

All rights reserved. Apart from any use permitted under UK copyright law no part of this
publication may be reproduced, stored in a retrieval system, or transmitted, in any form or by any
means, without the prior written permission of the publisher, nor be otherwise circulated in any
form of binding or cover other than that in which it is published and without a similar condition
being imposed on the subsequent purchaser.

A CIP catalogue record for this title is available from the British Library

ISBN 978-0-7195-6486-4

Typeset in 11.5/14 Monotype Bembo by Servis Filmsetting Ltd, Manchester

Printed and bound in Great Britain by William Clowes Ltd, Beccles, Suffolk

Hodder Headline policy is to use papers that are natural, renewable and recyclable products and
made from wood grown in sustainable forests. The logging and manufacturing processes are
expected to conform to the environmental regulations of the country of origin.

John Murray (Publishers)
338 Euston Road
London NW1 3BH

Contents

Illustrations	vii
Preface	ix
1. A Vocation of Convenience	1
2. The Path to Preferment	15
3. Bishop and Revolutionary	37
4. Apprentice Diplomat	57
5. Exile	70
6. The Directory	87
7. Bonaparte's Foreign Minister	110
8. Political Fortunes	131
9. Re-shaping Europe	153
10. The Business of Pleasure	171
11. Treason and Disgrace	185
12. Régime Change	209
13. The Congress of Vienna	234
14. President of the Council	257
15. Opposition and Vindication	273
16. Ambassador in London	294
17. The Final Curtain	308
18. Politician, Diplomat, Statesman	327
Chronology	339
Notes	349
Bibliography	408
Index	419

Illustrations

1. Talleyrand in his official dress of Imperial *Grand Chambellan*, painting by Pierre-Paul Prud'hon (1807)
2. Madame Grand, the future princesse de Bénévent, painting by Élisabeth Vigée-Lebrun (1783)
3. 'Boney and Tally' (Bonaparte and Talleyrand), cartoon by James Gillray (1803)
4. *Le Sacre* (Napoleon's Coronation as Emperor of the French), detail, painting by David (1804)
5. Joseph Fouché, duc d'Otrante, anonymous lithograph
6. Tsar Alexander I of Russia, painting by François Gérard (1814)
7. Louis XVIII, painting by Antoine-Jean Gros (*c.*1814)
8. *L'Homme aux six têtes* (The Man with Six Heads), anonymous cartoon (1815)
9. *Le Congrès de Vienne* (The Congress of Vienna), lithograph after the painting by Jean-Baptiste Isabey (1819)
10. Dorothée, duchesse de Dino, engraving by Jean-Baptiste Isabey after the painting by François Gérard (1824), from the collection of André Beau
11. Talleyrand, lithograph by François-Séraphin Delpech from a drawing by Zèphirin Belliard (1824)
12. *The Lame Leading the Blind* (Talleyrand and Palmerston), cartoon by John Doyle (1832)
13. Talleyrand, painting by Ary Scheffer (1828)
14. Talleyrand, lithograph by 'Alfred Croquis' i.e. Daniel Maclise (*c.*1833)
15. Château of Valençay: a view of the keep (*donjon*)
16. Château of Valençay: a view, up from the Nahon valley and the road to Châteauroux, of the two right-angled wings of the château

Photographic acknowledgements:
Courtesy André Beau: 10; Bridgeman Art Library: 1 (Musée Carnavalet, Paris), 4 (Musée du Louvre, Paris), 6 (Musée du Louvre, Paris), 9 (Bibliothèque Nationale de France), 13 (Musée Condé, Chantilly); British Library: 12; National Portrait Gallery, London: 3, 8; Metropolitan Museum of Art, New York, Bequest of Edward S. Harkness, 1940 (50.135.2) Photo © Metropolitan Museum of Art: 2; © Photo Réunion des Musées Nationaux: 5 (© droits reservés), 7 (© Gérard Blot); Bibliothèque Nationale de France, 11; British Library: 14; Culture Espaces: 15, 16

Preface

I have often myself seen [Talleyrand] smile at the idea of anyone attempting his autobiography (Colmache, Talleyrand's private secretary)[1]

DESPITE THAT, NO excuses are needed for writing a biography of Charles-Maurice de Talleyrand – especially one in English. The English have generally been more sympathetic to Talleyrand than have his compatriots. Talleyrand's first serious English biographer, Lytton Bulwer, writing towards the end of the nineteenth century, doubted 'whether his character has ever been fairly given, or is at this moment justly appreciated'.[2] Others have agreed. Duff Cooper's splendid study of 1932, frequently reissued, is still the most readable, and it is no less favourable in its judgements.[3] The later, longer biography by Jack Bernard is somewhat marred by lack of reference to sources, which is more important in Talleyrand's case than most, since so many apocryphal stories circulated, even in his lifetime. Both Cooper and Bernard also take what he says in his memoirs with too few grains of salt.[4]

Naturally, French biographies of Talleyrand abound.[5] But two are outstanding, and any book – in any language – is to some extent written in their shadow. Until recently, the classic work was the multi-volume *opus* of Georges Lacour-Gayet, published between 1928 and 1934.[6] Paradoxically, perhaps, the more that Lacour-Gayet studied his subject the less regard he seems to have developed for him. The result is a largely negative assessment of Talleyrand the statesman, albeit a certain sympathy for Talleyrand the man.[7] Since Lacour-Gayet's work appeared, important reassessments have been made, for example, by Philip Dwyer, who argues for a more consistent, even a principled Talleyrand lurking behind the cynical façade.[8]

But the fine biography by Emmanuel de Waresquiel, *Talleyrand, le Prince immobile*, which appeared in 2003, constitutes nothing short of a historiographical revolution.[9] For Waresquiel, Talleyrand's wisdom stems from the fact that he has a unique understanding of the events of his time.[10] Moreover, this Talleyrand – as the subtitle implies – is remarkably consistent and coherent in his political views, despite the twists and turns of self-interest and expediency over a long career. Waresquiel has also sought to restore the reputation of Talleyrand as an international statesman. What seemed to earlier generations of Frenchmen a failure to guard against the threat of an aggressive Germany now looks more like a far-sighted appreciation of the importance of achieving order and balance in Europe.

In the pages that follow I shall examine and qualify some of these judgements, including that of Talleyrand's statesmanship, which is perhaps over-favourably – and anachronistically – regarded in the new era of European integration.[11] Suffice it now to say the following. I would agree, as Waresquiel argues, that Talleyrand's social outlook and political views were in many respects formed under the last period of the *ancien régime* and the beginnings of the Revolution. I do not believe, however, that his attitudes were then fixed into immobility. Talleyrand was always a liberal, but he started as a liberal utopian and he finished as a liberal conservative. He had always enjoyed cultivated living, but as he grew older he increasingly saw the importance of culture itself. He was always conscious of his birth, but in old age he wrote with conviction of the benefits of social hierarchy. And in one respect his views did change still more fundamentally: as regards religion; for while the former bishop of Autun retained the reputation of a libertine to the end, he died, with his own kind of sincerity and to the amazement and annoyance of friends and enemies alike, in the arms of the Church – though, naturally, on very much his own terms.

One other book deserves a particular mention here – Talleyrand's own memoirs. Unlike his modern biographers, the Prince felt no pressing need to tell the truth, let alone the whole truth. The memoirs are a work of self-justification and, even then, as much a commentary on events as a personal statement. When they first appeared in 1891, there was a sense of disappointment at how little they revealed that was obviously new. Moreover, they had been subject to extensive editorial amendments by Talleyrand's secretary, Bacourt. Yet the memoirs are of great importance for three reasons. First, despite attempts at various times to suggest otherwise, they are authentic. Talleyrand read sections out to his friends during his lifetime, and people later remembered seeing the large exercise books in which he had written down his thoughts. A few fragments in his own hand remain. Second, the memoirs reveal what he thought of himself and what he wanted others to think of him. This makes them almost, if not quite, as important as they would be if they were always true to the facts. Finally, and beyond the strict scope of history or even biography, the memoirs are important as a text for all those interested in wider questions of political thought. Some sections, such as those commenting upon the underlying causes of the French Revolution, upon American society, upon the flaws of Napoleon's statesmanship, and upon the case for opportunistic pragmatism in times of political upheaval, deserve a status that they have never been accorded.[12]

In the course of writing this book, my judgements on Talleyrand varied from time to time before becoming settled. But at the end I am left with the strong impression of a man quite unlike any other then or since. He can be categorized by types: renegade priest, libidinous libertine, cynical opportunist; or, on the other hand, principled liberal, wise statesman, loyal and loving friend. The categories have their place, but he fits into too many, combines too many opposites. Moreover, he delighted in self-concealment as much as he strove for recognition. What he says of himself is rarely a help. What others say is more useful but it too reflects the impression he wanted to give. Mirrors always distort. To get to the bottom of his character is, in one sense, futile, because there is no bottom, though there is plenty of character. Talleyrand's personality is as multi-layered as one of his chef Carême's *millefeuille* pastries. Fortunately, the paradoxes are no less delicate or delicious.

The sources that proved of direct use in the writing of this book are listed in the Bibliography. The great majority are printed. The Napoleonic and Restoration eras are well served both by published correspondence and by memoirs, the latter often based on shrewd observation and usually very well written, though naturally of differing degrees of authority and truthfulness. (An invaluable guide is provided by Jean Tulard in his *Nouvelle Bibliographie critique des mémoires sur l'époque napoléonienne* (Geneva: Droz, 1991).)

By contrast, manuscript sources for Talleyrand's life and work are less revealing, because of the vicissitudes of their history. The Talleyrand papers were originally divided between the archives kept at the château of Broglie and those at the castle of Sagan in Silesia/Poland (which came from the duchesse de Dino). The latter were destroyed during the Second World War, though earlier copies of some letters survived and have been published. The Broglie collection itself was dispersed. Some of this material is now in private hands; some was acquired and used by Michel Poniatowski. A substantial part was later repurchased by descendants of the Talleyrand family, and is not now accessible. The undispersed Broglie archives had been extensively exploited by Lacour-Gayet, while other private archives have most recently been explored by Waresquiel. Perhaps the most valuable unpublished material to which reference is made in these pages are the 140 letters from Talleyrand deriving from the Holland House collection and now kept at the British Library.

The translations in this book are all mine, and they are necessarily numerous. They are also inevitably unsatisfactory. Talleyrand was known for his *bons mots* which he polished extensively, considering expression at least as important as content. He revelled in puns, both good and not so good, and even by the standards of his own day, he employed a concentrated, opaque, ambiguous style. How much more must it perplex the twenty-first-century British reader? As usual, Talleyrand perfectly expressed the problem: 'Translations augment the faults of a work and spoil its beauty.'[13] Unfortunately, he offered no solution.

I wish, finally, to thank those who made this book possible: in France, the staff of the Archives nationales, the Bibliothèque nationale (Manuscripts – *site* Richelieu, and Printed Material – *site* Mitterrand), and the Ministry of Foreign Affairs archives; in England, the staff of the British Library and the London Library. I benefited from the advice of M. André Beau, with his encyclopaedic knowledge of Talleyrand and of Valençay. I am also grateful to Dr Robert Tombs for reading the typescript and offering many helpful suggestions. The illustrations of Valençay are provided by kind permission of Culture Espaces.

I

A Vocation of Convenience

CHARLES-MAURICE DE Talleyrand-Périgord was born on 2 February 1754 at the house that his family rented in Paris in the rue Garancière. The child was baptized the same day at the neighbouring church of Saint-Sulpice. Charles-Maurice's parents would have five children – four boys and a girl – and he was the second son. With the death of his infant elder brother three years later, Charles-Maurice would also – for a time – become heir to the family fortune. The latter, however, was distinctly modest. This fact would have a profound impact on the young man's outlook.[1]

His parents had to keep up, as Talleyrand records in his memoirs, a 'position at court'.[2] It was a distinguished one and, as such, it was in a long line of similar service. Charles-Maurice's father, Charles-Daniel, comte de Talleyrand-Périgord, was a colonel in the grenadiers of France. The child's paternal grandfather, Daniel-Marie-Anne, comte de Grignols, known as 'marquis de Talleyrand-Périgord', had been killed at the siege of Tournai in 1745. Charles-Maurice's god-father and paternal uncle, Gabriel-Marie, comte de Périgord, another soldier, enjoyed the ancient title of menin de Mgr. le Dauphin.[3]

The Talleyrands were acutely conscious of their social pre-eminence, and this may well have been heightened by unseemly public doubts which were raised about their origins. The family claimed to be descended from the ancient feudal counts of Périgord. A historical anecdote has the tenth-century count, Aldebert, rudely demonstrating his independence at the expense of Hugh Capet, founder of the French Capetian dynasty. To the King's sharp rebuke, 'Who made you count?' Aldebert insolently replied: 'And who made you King?' An echo of this tradition of unbending family pride is to be found in the Talleyrand family motto, written in the old Périgordin patois, *Re que diou* ('Nothing except God'). This can be interpreted either as an expression of piety or of pride. It was the second sense that was current, and it would certainly apply in the case of Charles-Maurice.

The Talleyrand family claim was given the seal of royal approval by letters of Louis XIII dated 6 September 1613. These erected the castellany of Grignols in Bazadais into a county and the castellany of Excideuil in Périgord into a marquisate, in favour of Daniel de Talleyrand, prince de Chalais. In doing so, the King recognized Daniel as issue in the direct line of the old counts of Périgord.[4]

But, in actual fact, the claim was historically false. The Talleyrands did not descend from the Périgords, but rather from the Grignols family, who were numbered among the counts' vassals. They appear to have adopted the name of Talleyrand (spelled in various fashions) at the end of the fifteenth century.[5]

This was privately understood by the leading eighteenth-century royal genealogists. Indeed, there can be little doubt that as intelligent and inquisitive a man as Charles-Maurice de Talleyrand privately understood it too. But that did not prevent his taking pride in the allegedly ancient lineage of his family. He does so in his memoirs. And he did so in characteristic fashion during his political life. He would, for example, privately despise the new titles handed out by Napoleon. To one member of the old nobility who had expressed pleasure at becoming a count, Talleyrand sarcastically expressed the hope that he would soon become a baron. Publicly addressed as 'Highness' in view of his own newly acquired title of 'Prince', Charles-Maurice would demur in apparent modesty, observing that he was 'less', before quietly adding, in allusion to his family origins, 'and perhaps I am more.'[6]

Charles-Maurice vigorously defended his family's claim to ancient nobility to the very end of his life. When requesting from Charles X the revival of his grandfather's title of marquis de Talleyrand on behalf of his great-nephew in 1836, the old Prince arranged for the appearance of a pamphlet giving his own preferred view of the genealogical evidence. It was promptly attacked in another pamphlet.[7]

Given the number of dubious genealogical claims that had been authorized in the seventeenth and eighteenth centuries, there was no risk that the myth of the Talleyrand family's origins would be officially exploded. Talleyrand was, however, the butt of sarcasm from Louis

XVIII on the matter. The King liked to observe: 'The Talleyrands are only wrong about one letter in their pretensions: they are from [du] not of [de] Périgord.'[8]

On his mother's side, Charles-Maurice was also blessed with distinguished aristocratic connections. Alexandrine-Victoire-Éléonore was the daughter of Joseph-François de Damas, marquis d'Antigny – dead in 1736 – and of Marie-Judith, only daughter of the comte de Commarin. But here too money did not match status. The marriage was far from making up for the comte de Talleyrand's relative indigence for a man of his rank. Alexandrine brought with her a dowry of 12,600 livres of *rentes* secured on her family's lands – an extremely modest sum for such a union.[9] Soon after the marriage, which was celebrated at Saint-Sulpice in 1751, her mother, Mme d'Antigny, withdrew to her estates in Burgundy, leaving the young couple to their own devices in the house that she had rented in the rue Garancière.

The Talleyrands duly appeared at court, where Alexandrine was attached to the household of the Dauphine. But these advantages also incurred expenditure. Her husband's family, always conscious of appearances, insisted that the couple acquire horses. Alexandrine, for her part, wanted more fashionable dresses. And debts had to be paid. In every case, pleas for financial assistance were despatched to Mme d'Antigny.

Alexandrine bore her first child, Alexandre-François-Jacques, on 18 January 1752. In July the following year she wrote to tell her mother that she was pregnant again – this time with Charles-Maurice.[10] It was an occasion for more financial solicitation. The expectant mother complained that unless whatever was required for childbirth was promptly sent from Commarin she would be forced to imitate the Virgin Mary's predicament in Bethlehem.[11]

Charles-Maurice was not in the end born in a barn. But forced to live beyond their means by their social and political duties, both mother and father would always be anxious about money. This may have contributed to a certain amount of cheese-paring when arrangements were made for the child's upbringing. On top of that, both parents had to spend far more time away from home – on the King's and the court's business – than modern child psychologists would consider desirable. In any case, the attitudes adopted by aristocratic parents towards their children at this time were typically – and again judged by today's standards – harsh, remote and materialistic.

Charles-Maurice's infant elder brother was boarded out in 1756, only to die of smallpox the following year. This in itself could have worked to the younger sibling's advantage, since he would thus become presumptive heir to his father, the comte de Talleyrand. But other circumstances prevented that outcome; and since these were retailed, distorted and exploited by Charles-Maurice in future years – since, indeed, they became part of the carefully constructed Talleyrand legend – they deserve closer investigation.

At the start of his short character study of Talleyrand, his sometime political collaborator, the writer Benjamin Constant, crisply asserts: 'What decided M. de Talleyrand's character was his feet.'[12] Charles-Maurice was born with a severely deformed right foot, as is testified by medical examination of the orthopaedic shoes preserved at the château of Valençay. These reveal that Talleyrand's left foot was flat and elongated and that his right – the one that troubled him throughout his life – was short, round and stunted. These are classic symptoms of *talipes equinovarus*, a handicap that ran in the Talleyrand family. A painting of Charles-Maurice's uncle, Gabriel-Marie, showing his club foot with none of the delicate optical illusion adopted for the Prince's own later portraits, decisively confirms the fact.[13]

Talleyrand himself devised a different, more self-serving and less humiliating story. He then repeated it – as did his friends on his behalf – throughout his life.[14] Finally, and for the benefit of future generations, he incorporated it in his memoirs in the following passage:

> The fashion for parental care had not yet arrived: the fashion was quite different during my childhood; so I was left for several years in a suburb of Paris. At four I was still there. It was at this age that the woman in whose house I was boarding let me fall from the top of a chest of drawers. I dislocated my foot. For several months she said nothing. It was only noticed when they arrived to send me to Périgord, to the house of Mme de Chalais, my [great-]grandmother, who asked me about it. . . .The accident I had suffered was by then too old to remedy; the other foot too, which had had to support the weight of my body during the early period of pain, had been weakened. I remained with a limp.

This accident influenced the whole of the rest of my life: it is what persuaded my parents that I could not be a soldier, or at least succeed in that field, and so led them to push me towards another profession [i.e. the priesthood]. That seemed to them to be more favourable to the family. For in the great noble houses it was the family that was loved much more than individuals, and above all more than young individuals whom they did not yet know. I do not like to dwell on this idea. . .I leave it.[15]

But he never did leave it. He returned to it again and again. It became an explanation, an excuse, a justification, a proof of his exceptional ability to overcome hardship. It is easy, of course, to imagine why a handsome, energetic young man might wish to explain away his handicap by a putative early accident rather than by the cruel, mysterious processes of heredity. Charles-Maurice had, though, a deeper reason to feel embittered. This was because from some time after the birth of his younger brother, Archambaud, in 1762, he would no longer be regarded as his father's heir on account of this disability. Instead, as he would lament ceaselessly and publicly in later years, he was destined for the Church. Continuing resentment at Archambaud's preference and at his own effective disinheritance – including disinheritance, be it noted, from the fortune of his beloved great-grandmother, the princesse de Chalais – is the best explanation for Charles-Maurice's absence from the celebration of Archambaud's highly remunerative marriage in 1779.[16]

Talleyrand went much further, however, in elaborating his alleged childhood hardships, of which the story of his fall from a chest of drawers and his resultant limp was just the most dramatic episode. In 1758, and probably for the best of reasons, the young and sickly Charles-Maurice was sent by his parents to stay with Mme de Chalais at her château in Périgord. He was accompanied by the family governess, Mlle Charlemagne, and he remained there about eighteen months.

The account of the period in his memoirs is uncharacteristically lyrical. Indeed, it seems more suited to the pen of Talleyrand's future enemy Chateaubriand.[17] Charles-Maurice depicts a rural nobility on the eve of the Revolution fulfilling its ancient obligations with grace and charity. Mme de Chalais is shown surrounded by members of the local nobility as by 'a kind of court.' After Sunday mass, neighbouring peasants who are in need of help are shown, one by one, into her presence. Seated in the great hall of the château on a velvet-covered armchair, with the young Talleyrand beside her, the appropriate *châtelaine* indicates to one of the assembled gentry where precisely the remedy is to be found. The peasants finally depart, not only with their medication but with a little gift, or at least with some words of consolation.

Charles-Maurice thus formed an early appreciation of the ancient ties that united the Talleyrands with their tenants. Looking back on this experience, he concluded: 'The time that I spent at Chalais made a deep impression on me.'[18]

The attractive portrayal of his great-grandmother's behaviour is also intended, of course, to highlight the unfavourable contrast with that of Charles-Maurice's own parents. The memoirs continue much in the same vein. They recount how the carriage that finally arrived to bring Charles-Maurice back from Chalais to the capital did not take him, once in Paris, to see his parents, but rather straight to the Collège d'Harcourt for the start of his formal education.[19] This, at least, is demonstrably untrue. In fact, two years elapsed between his leaving Chalais and going to school.

Talleyrand never stopped lamenting the way he was supposedly treated at this tender age. Many years later his political collaborator, Étienne Dumont de Genève, would recall: 'I have often heard him say that, rejected by his parents as a miserable specimen of a good-for-nothing, he had developed as a child a silent, sombre disposition. He had never slept under the same roof as his father or mother.'[20]

Whatever Charles-Maurice's real or invented feelings about seeing so little of his family, as soon as he was in a position to exercise charm over his peers his prospects improved. Beginning school thus marked the start of something still more important: the growth of Talleyrand's friendships. Much later in his life, the Prince would be taken to task by a royalist critic, the baron de Vitrolles, for the lack of true friends upon whom he could rely.[21] But, to the extent that this was a fair observation at all, it only reflected the degree to which Talleyrand's own fabled tergiversations had by then made him an object of distrust. Charles-Maurice valued friendship and was, after a fashion, true to his friends.

At the Collège d'Harcourt he made contact with Augus[t] Choiseul-Gouffier, the future travel writer and ambassado[r] Constantinople, of whom Talleyrand writes that he had 'share[d] _... still shares all the worries, all the pleasures, all the plans, that have agitated my soul in the course of my life', and (later) that 'M. de Choiseul is the man whom I have most loved.'[22] Charles-Maurice's tutor at the Collège was the abbé Hardi, for whom the child never conceived much respect. Hardi would take him once a week for an excruciatingly formal interview with the boy's parents.

Three years into his schooling, Charles-Maurice developed small-pox and was promptly, and doubtless prudently, sent away to be kept and (after the fashion of the time) treated in isolation by a nurse who lived in the rue Saint-Jacques. While there he reflected on his situation: 'I was twelve; during my convalescence, I was astonished at my position. The little interest that anyone took in my illness, my entry into the college without having seen my parents and other depressing memories wounded my heart. I felt isolated, without any support, constantly forced back on myself. I do not complain . . .'[23] Talleyrand continues with one of the most elegantly cruel passages that any memoirist ever devoted to his parents: 'I have since understood that my parents, having determined, according to what they understood as the family interest, to lead me towards a state for which I showed no inclination, distrusted their courage in executing this plan if they saw me too often. This fear is evidence of a tenderness, for which I like to be grateful.'[24]

Talleyrand would have two more clerics as tutors during his remaining time at the Collège. The first, a M. Hulot, went mad. The second, a M. Langlois, who would later help raise Charles-Maurice's two brothers and who was an extreme snob, became a great favourite and would remain under the statesman's protection. The old abbé, until the end of his days, still dressed in the style of the *ancien régime*, regarded the magnificent Hôtel Talleyrand in the rue Saint-Florentin as his home.[25]

Charles-Maurice was soon, however, to mix in much more distinguished ecclesiastical company than at the Collège, for it had been decided – as the earlier passage shows – that he was now destined for high office in the Church. Accordingly, with the end of his studies and at the age of fifteen, in 1769 Charles-Maurice was sent on an extended visit to Reims, where his uncle Alexandre-Angélique was currently coadjutor to the archbishop. The latter, Charles-Antoine, comte de La Roche-Aymon, grand almoner of France and soon to receive his cardinal's hat, was one of the great princes of the French Church. Reims itself, as the first archdiocese of France and scene of the sacramental coronation of successive French monarchs, was a rich prize, and the fact of being episcopal coadjutor meant that it would, sooner or later, fall into the hands of Alexandre-Angélique de Talleyrand. Charles-Maurice spent a year there. To judge from his account, he was unimpressed by the luxurious lifestyle, the pomp and all the other advantages which his family had hoped would nourish within him an ambition for ecclesiastical preferment. He was, though, persuaded to read the memoirs of previous great ecclesiastical politicians, such as the cardinals de Retz and de Richelieu. And perhaps this did have some effect in opening up the more congenial prospect of political advancement through the Church.

In the end, alone and unsupported in resistance to the plans that had been made for him, 'my worn-out spirit yielded: I allowed myself to be led to the seminary of Saint-Sulpice.'[26] Or at least that is how Talleyrand during his later life, and in his memoirs, portrayed matters. But if such an account contains some of the truth, it is not the unvarnished truth, let alone the whole truth; nor should this be a source of surprise, since as the historian Sainte-Beuve acidly but accurately notes: 'as soon as [Talleyrand] had the slightest interest in doing so, it was his custom to lie.'[27]

It would certainly be in the Prince's interests to portray himself as a passive victim when explaining away his early choice of an ecclesiastical career. It would be useful when convincing his Revolutionary masters of his credentials as a politician, and afterwards in convincing the Directory of his acceptability as a minister. It would be still more important many years later in excusing his abandonment of holy orders and other unacceptable behaviour to the restored Bourbons and the papacy.

Not that the practice of sending physically disabled members of noble families into the Church was unusual. Of Talleyrand's later clerical contemporaries, the bishop of Comminges, Charles d'Osmond de Médavy, endured the misfortune of having one leg three inches shorter than the other. The bishop of Saint-Dié, Barthélemy de Chaumont de la Galaizière, was an even more prominent case. He was, for the times, a giant of a man – six feet tall – and strong and burly. Apparently, he would have liked to be a colonel in the *carabiniers*. But his appearance was deformed, and his clerical career decided, by one huge eye, like that of the Cyclops, which altogether dwarfed the other.[28]

It is also perfectly possible that Talleyrand's accounts of his dislike of a clerical career are accurate, in so far as they reflect his tastes and sentiments. But that is not at all to say that he was a mere pawn in the process. And in any case at very few points in Charles-Maurice's long life did sentiment overcome calculation in determining his course of action.

Moreover, the fact remains that had Talleyrand chosen firmly to resist a clerical career he could have done so successfully, just as, for example, his contemporaries Turgot, Chateaubriand and Fouché did.[29] In December 1769 Talleyrand's mother wrote to her own mother that her son was 'very happy with his new [clerical] estate'.[30] This may have been wishful thinking. But Charles-Maurice was surely by now keenly aware that the episcopate represented a short and well-travelled route to power and wealth. It was not just the young man's club foot that was the consideration here: still more important was the need to acquire a position of influence through which to supplement his own and his branch of the family's mediocre means. And in reaching this judgement at least as important as Talleyrand's parents was probably his uncle (his father's younger brother), Alexandre-Angélique.

The French Church of the day was dominated by the great aristocratic families. This was in part the result of historic Gallicanism – the doctrine that powers of ecclesiastical appointment, decision-making and jurisdiction should rest with the King of France and the French secular courts and not with the Pope. Royal patronage in the later eighteenth century was increasingly exercised in all fields on behalf of the nobility. As is usually the case, the extension of secular control in spiritual matters led over time to a lessening of zeal. This did not mean that the French Church on the eve of the Revolution was universally corrupt. There were, indeed, pockets of notable holiness – for example, among some monastic houses of the enclosed orders. But by the time that Charles-Maurice de Talleyrand-Périgord was a candidate for holy orders these were widely understood as a conventional path to material advancement. The spirit of the French Church would only begin to change in reaction to the Revolutionary persecution, before being transformed by a vigorous Catholic revival under the Restoration.

In the circumstances prevailing in the 1760s and 1770s it was, therefore, quite natural for the Talleyrand family to look to ecclesiastical spoils; and it was equally natural for Alexandre-Angélique to seek to create his own ecclesiastical dynasty, as did many of his peers. In any case, Charles-Maurice's uncle may well already have discerned in his young nephew early evidence of the administrative talents required to run the archdiocese of Reims, once Alexandre-Angélique himself succeeded the elderly Mgr de La Roche-Aymon.[31]

It was during his year at Reims that young Charles-Maurice first began to wear the soutane – symbolic proof that he had personally accepted a clerical career. Mme de Genlis, the celebrated memoirist, popular novelist and mistress of the then duc de Chartres (who would succeed his father as duc d'Orléans in 1785) – a woman who would figure large in Charles-Maurice's life – first encountered him at this time. She noted: 'He limped a bit; he was pale and silent; but I found his face very pleasant and he had a watchful manner that impressed me.'[32] The seeds of a future attraction were sown.

Charles-Maurice's entry at the age of sixteen, in 1770, into the seminary of Saint-Sulpice in Paris set him formally on the path to the priesthood. Saint-Sulpice consisted of four separate communities of which the most important was the *grand séminaire*, where the young Talleyrand was to reside and pursue his studies. The complex had been built in the seventeenth century under the inspiration of M. Olier, founder of the Sulpicians.[33] The buildings then occupied the space of today's place Saint-Sulpice, blocking much of the view of the great church of the same name. Saint-Sulpice was, of course, already well known to Charles-Maurice, who had been baptized there, doubtless worshipped there, and for some years lived close by. The fact that by now his family had moved to a house in the rue Saint-Dominique perhaps removed one influence that might have inhibited the young seminarian's enjoyment of life's more basic pleasures.[34]

The notoriety that Talleyrand gained at this time for his carousing became inextricably linked with his public personality in later life. It was faithfully retailed by the duchesse d'Abrantès, never one to pass up a good story: 'His strength, it is said, was miraculous. He would spend two or three nights in succession without sleeping. He would have to appear on the fourth morning with all his faculties, serious and alert. He would sleep for an hour, having taken a bath, and appeared as fit in mind and body as if he had just spent six weeks on retreat at La Trappe.'[35]

Charles-Maurice's stamina was real, as he would show. But many stories of his philanderings at this time were doubtless exaggerated. Some, indeed, seem to be entirely invented, like the one that circulated during his lifetime and according to which he seduced three young sisters in succession. One allegedly died, one went mad, and the third went into a convent before also dying.[36]

A more romantic and less improbable account has him falling in love with a well-known actress, Louise Contat, who performed in productions for the Orléans family's theatre at Issy. Talleyrand would, apparently, climb the seminary wall and hitch a lift on the back of a carriage, returning to bed in time for matins. If true, this places Charles-Maurice in good company: Mlle Contat would also be the mistress of Louis XVI's youngest brother, the comte d'Artois, to whom she bore a son.[37]

These accounts seem to have circulated with Talleyrand's own blessing. He always enjoyed boasting of his conquests, even in circumstances that some of his hearers must have considered in doubtful taste.[38] Talleyrand includes one such amorous episode in his memoirs:

> I had reached an age of mysterious revelations of the soul and the passions, the moment in life when all one's faculties are active and over-flowing. On several occasions, I had noticed in one of the chapels of the church of Saint-Sulpice a beautiful young person whose simple and modest manner pleased me greatly . . . One day, when she was leaving the church, heavy rain gave me the courage to offer to take her back to her home, if she did not live too far away. She accepted half my

umbrella. I brought her to the rue Férou where she was lodging; she allowed me to go upstairs with her, and with no embarrassment, like a very pure young person, she asked me to return. I was there every three or four days, later more often. Her parents had made her, despite her wishes, become an actress; and, despite my own wishes, I was at the seminary. This domination exercised for the sake of interest over her, and for the sake of ambition over me, established between us a confidence without reserve.[39]

This touching narrative concerns, in fact, the actress Dorothée Luzy, who first performed at the Comédie-Française in 1763. She was seven years Talleyrand's senior and was living, in the rue Férou, in a house provided by her long-standing lover, a M. Landry, a royal financial official, to whom she bore several children. Her relationship with Charles-Maurice lasted two years.[40]

In his memoirs, Talleyrand paints a dark and dismal picture of life at the seminary. Indeed, the account of his romance with Dorothée Luzy appears as a single bright incident in the otherwise unrelieved gloom. He was, it seems, as much the classically misunderstood young man as any rebel without a cause. His superiors and his colleagues considered him haughty and disdainful, but in truth he was just 'a good young man, extremely unhappy and angry inside.'[41] His free time was largely spent in the great library of Saint-Sulpice, enriched thirty years earlier with the collection of Cardinal Fleury. Here Charles-Maurice's voracious reading concentrated on history, poetry, biography and travelogues, and he indulged his taste for the dramatic and the dangerous. He educated himself using this material, but absorbing it from his own viewpoint. In fact, he read as a Revolutionary − as other future Revolutionaries were, doubtless, reading at this time. He later noted: 'In this way my ideas remained my own: the books provided illumination, but they never held sway over me.'[42]

Yet to judge from Talleyrand's own words on other occasions, this bleak description of life at the seminary can be no more than part of the truth. As an old man he often told his private secretary, Colmache, that the days he had spent alone reading in the seminary library had been the happiest of his life.[43] He never showed signs of bitterness towards either his former superiors or his former fellow seminarians, and at the height of his influence he saw three of the latter given bishoprics. He also invited M. Émery, the reforming superior of Saint-Sulpice, to dine with him at the Ministry of Foreign Affairs. (His guest later returned the favour with the gift of a signed letter from Fénelon.) Still more significant, because more public, were Talleyrand's words in 1821 in his eulogy of his former director at the seminary, the Senator-bishop Bourlier of Évreux. He went out of his way to extol the education received at Saint-Sulpice and to praise the Sulpicians.[44] He once told comte Alexis de Noailles, who accompanied him to the Congress of Vienna in 1814: 'When I want to be happy, I think of Saint-Sulpice.'[45] But perhaps that was hyperbole. By contrast, his assertions in a letter to Mme Gentil de Chavagnac of October 1827, reacting to stories circulating about his behaviour at the seminary, are certainly false. He told her that he had spent his days walking alone around the courtyard, brooding like 'a little Bonaparte', and that his only departure from the path of moral rectitude was a fleeting (and unfulfilled) visit with a friend to some houses of ill repute.[46] The truth probably lies somewhere between the two conflicting versions, one of unrelieved drudgery and the other of delightful debauchery. While at the time the study of theology – and what little effort he made to keep to the rules of the seminary – was doubtless uncongenial to him, in later life he realized that he had gained from the experience. He also came to appreciate the merits, or at least the utility, of many of those with whom he associated. This was surely enough to sweeten the memory.

Despite his preferred image of cultivated lethargy, Talleyrand was never an intellectual sluggard, and there is no reason to suppose that he was remiss in his studies at Saint-Sulpice. Each day for five years he had to attend lectures at the theology faculty of the Sorbonne. At the end of that time, he had to pass examinations in philosophy and theology before being admitted – on 22 September 1774 – to defend his thesis for a period of five hours before nine professors. The thesis itself, written in Latin, was entitled *Quaenam est scientia quam custodient labia sacerdotis?* ('What knowledge is guarded by the lips of the priest?'). Talleyrand was duly awarded his baccalauréat. Three months earlier he had also received the minor ecclesiastical orders of porter, lector, exorcist and acolyte. His career was thus progressing as envisaged.

But at this stage there seems to have occurred some trouble in Talleyrand's affairs and in his usual equilibrium. He did not complete the full period of residence at Saint-Sulpice. It is possible that he was removed because of an infraction of discipline that even the indulgent authorities at the seminary would not overlook. In any case, by the time he was received to the order of sub-deacon – on 1 April 1775 in the Paris church of Saint-Nicolas-du-Chardonnet – he was no longer resident at the seminary. Contemporaries bear witness to Talleyrand's ill-humour at the time. One source has him say: 'They want to make a priest of me. Well, you will see that they will make a ghastly one. But I limp, I am a younger son. There is no way of pulling back from my destiny.'[47] Perhaps conscience still pricked on occasion, even though ambition for advancement prevailed.

Charles-Maurice could henceforth look to his uncle as benefactor. Having reached the sub-diaconate, the abbé de Périgord, as the young Talleyrand was known, was now able to accept a benefice in the parish church of the Sainte-Vierge in Reims. He was also incorporated into the archdiocese as a member of the cathedral chapter, though he continued to live, and greatly to enjoy himself, in Paris.

Reims was about to become the focus of more than the abbé de Périgord's somewhat restless attention, however, for on Sunday, 11 June that year the solemn coronation of Louis XVI took place in its cathedral. It was only natural that Charles-Maurice should attend. The officiating prelate was the cardinal of La Roche-Aymon, archbishop of Reims, and at his side was his coadjutor, Alexandre-Angélique. The abbé de Périgord's father, the comte de Talleyrand, was one of the *seigneurs otages de la Sainte Ampoule*.[48] It was their honoured role to protect, with their lives if necessary, the phial of holy chrism oil with which the monarch would be anointed. Talleyrand would many years later recall his impressions: it was 'the most moving ceremony' he ever witnessed; everything had conspired to make it so, 'beautiful weather. . .magnificence, reverence and gaiety.'[49]

And, of course, there were attractive women to ogle in the congregation: 'It is from the coronation of Louis XVI that date my relations with several women whose advantages in different ways rendered them remarkable, and whose friendship has not for a single moment failed to add charm to my life. It is of Mme la duchesse de Luynes, Mme la duchesse de Fitz-James, and Mme la vicomtesse de Laval that I wish to speak.'[50]

2

The Path to Preferment

THE ABBÉ DE Périgord now took his first steps along the pathway
of ecclesiastical promotion. He would soon give unmistakable
signs of those political and administrative aptitudes that rendered him
indispensable to different masters in his future career. But he was
lucky, all the same, that the opportunity came so soon and that his
uncle's powerful patronage allowed him to take advantage of it.

A general assembly of the French clergy was summoned at the
start of the new reign, officially in order to welcome Louis XVI's
accession, but in practice to vote the expected subsidy to an increasingly cash-strapped monarchy. The fiscal and representative arrangements relating to the clergy in France were by now well developed.
In exchange for agreeing to provide the required subsidies –
tithes and so-called 'free gifts' (*dons gratuits*) – the clergy secured
their immunities and insisted upon a regular representation of their
grievances.

The deputies who served in these general assemblies were elected
by sixteen provincial assemblies. Each province sent two deputies of
the 'first order' – that is bishops – and two from the 'second order' –
that is the other clerics. The abbé de Périgord was selected, doubtless
at his uncle's command, as a deputy of the second order from the
province of Reims. More importantly, the cardinal archbishop of
Reims, Mgr de La Roche-Aymon, who had been appointed president of the forthcoming assembly, also chose Talleyrand as one of its
two 'promoters' – again reflecting his coadjutor's influence. These
promoters were expected to assist the president and to prepare the
agenda and other papers for the assembly's debates. But their activities
were, in fact, more far-reaching than that, because they were also
expected to present their conclusions on vexed issues of the day to the

assembly for its deliberation. At the age of twenty-one, and with no previous experience of such matters at all, this must have represented a stimulating challenge to the young Talleyrand.

On 13 December 1775, after five months of work, and having organized the collection of money for the royal coffers and submitted remonstrances on subjects ranging from evil books, to teachers' morals, to unseemly Protestant displays – none of which one imagines would have greatly worried the abbé de Périgord in a personal capacity – the doors of the monastery of the Grands-Augustins finally closed, and the assembly dispersed.[1] The young promoter's skills were evidently appreciated, as his uncle was able to obtain for him the much more important position of agent general of the clergy for the next general assembly, which was due in 1780.

Alexandre-Angélique had already been active on his nephew's behalf in other respects. He set out to ensure that Charles-Maurice's income was raised to the level expected of a future prelate. In September, the abbé de Périgord received by royal nomination the great Augustinian abbey of Saint-Denis in Reims. Officially, it was worth 18,000 livres a year, but its real value, like that of other important French benefices of the day, was a good deal more. This was a swift advance for one who was still four years away from the priesthood and had barely reached the age of majority.[2]

But it was also necessary to move further along more conventional routes of promotion. Since April 1775, Charles-Maurice had been enrolled at the Sorbonne to obtain his licentiate in theology. The candidates had to defend three theses, of which the third was the most demanding: this examination took place in the great hall of the Sorbonne and lasted for twelve hours. On 2 March 1778 the abbé de Périgord underwent this test successfully, which brought the period of his formal education to an end. As he says in his memoirs: 'On leaving the Sorbonne, I was at last under my own, free and exclusive direction.'[3] He would make the most of it.

Talleyrand had already settled into comfortable lodgings. He had no hesitation in continuing his preference for Paris rather than Reims (the benefices he received there were held *in commendam*, that is as an absentee). He lived in a small, charming, two-storey house in Bellechasse, a quiet district, still full of convents and secluded gardens, rented from the canonesses of the Holy Sepulchre, known as the 'nuns of Bellechasse.' Charles-Maurice's first priority was to form a library.[4]

Talleyrand loved his books, but he felt able to part with them if the price was right. Indeed, he assembled his libraries with a view to their worth, and they would prove a particularly useful source of funds when life was hard. He sold his libraries on three occasions: in 1793 in London, in 1811 in Paris, and in 1816 again in London. Talleyrand was not fastidious in his literary taste. His friend (and rival in love), the visiting American Gouverneur Morris, was lent a book by the abbé de Périgord in January 1790 entitled *Le Portier des Chartreux* ('The Carthusians' Porter'). Even Morris found it shockingly obscene.[5] Talleyrand used his library, in later life at least, as a kind of prop for seductive, entertaining conversation, as Mme de Coigny observed: 'No one can converse in a library like M. de Talleyrand. He takes the books, leaves them, disagrees with them, abandons them, only in order to pick them up again, and questions them as if they were alive. And this exercise, by endowing his mind with the profundity and the experience of centuries, bestows on the written works a grace that their authors often lacked.'[6]

The house at Bellechasse was, above all, intended as somewhere for the abbé de Périgord to receive his friends. It was a pleasure he had already indulged during his time at the Sorbonne. In 1776 his grandmother sent him a consignment of wine from Burgundy, and in the abbé's temporary absence the bottles were stored in the university cellars. His old governess, Mlle Charlemagne, who sent back reports on his conduct, noted in a letter to the marquise d'Antigny: 'I am afraid that if the wine is very good it will not last long. M. l'abbé is very generous, and he will want to entertain his friends with it.'[7]

Naturally, the names of those who frequented Bellechasse changed as Talleyrand's interests, fortunes and contacts also changed. But a few were particularly close. The abbé de Périgord was delighted to renew contact with his old school friend Choiseul-Gouffier, of whose 'noble, good, trusting, sincere' character the memoirs paint a delicate portrait. The two friends combined in May 1779 to equip a privateer operating out of Brest.[8] As a diplomat and distinguished traveller, Choiseul-Gouffier would often be abroad, causing Talleyrand to complain: '[Choiseul-Gouffier] has friends, he loves them, he wishes their happiness, he would do good by them, but he manages extra-ordinarily well to go without seeing them.'[9] Charles-Maurice wrote to his friend in 1787, when Choiseul-Gouffier was ambassador at Constantinople: 'I want you to receive a word from me to tell you that with all my soul and at every moment of my life – happy, or vexing, or even unhappy – I love you more than anything in the world. Farewell. Write me just four lines: but write to me.'[10]

Choiseul-Gouffier would go into exile in Russia in 1789 and returned to France only in 1802, financially ruined. But before leaving for home he received from Talleyrand, now Foreign Minister, a warm, reassuring letter: 'Our old friendship is my sweetest memory. . .We have the loss of eighteen years of confidences to make up. . .It is enough to say that the interests that you recommend to me in your letter will be the object of all my attention, before as after your return.'[11] The friendship would continue, despite political upheavals, until Choiseul-Gouffier's death in 1817.

One other friend receives special mention – and slightly more caustic observations – in the memoirs. Louis de Narbonne was widely said to be Louis XV's illegitimate son. A man of passion, the future lover of both the vicomtesse de Laval and Mme de Staël, Narbonne would serve briefly as Minister of War, before barely escaping with his life into exile. He would later serve Napoleon as his aide-de-camp. Talleyrand enjoyed his company but, by the time the memoirist came to provide his word-portrait, the one-time friend had become a polit-ical rival, which shows in some refined character assassination con-cealed as appreciation: 'M. de Narbonne . . . has a politeness without nuance; his gaiety often compromises good taste; and his character does not inspire the confidence that intimacy demands.'[12]

The gatherings at Bellechasse had a distinct political atmosphere, consisting of a group of formidable individuals who, like Talleyrand, would play a large role in the fortunes of France. Among the most notable was Armand de Gontaut, duc de Lauzun, later duc de Biron, a man seven years older than Charles-Maurice. A strong supporter of the duc d'Orléans at the Estates General, he later became commander-in-chief of French forces on the Rhine, and was subsequently arrested and guillotined in 1793. Talleyrand was always fond of him, describing his friend as 'brave, romantic, generous, witty.'[13] But despite their mutual fascination, the impulsive soldier and the shrewd churchman-politician were as different in character as in their fate.

A still more important and influential figure who came regularly to Bellechasse was the banker Isaac Panchaud, a Swiss resident in Paris, a financial theorist as well as practised speculator, and the abbé de Périgord's mentor in such matters. There also appeared at Charles-Maurice's table Pierre Dupont de Nemours. He was a noted member of the 'physiocrat' school of economists, to whose theories Talleyrand himself more or less subscribed.[14] Dupont de Nemours was an associate of Panchaud's, and a future colleague of Talleyrand in the service of Calonne. He narrowly escaped death during the Terror.[15]

The most famous of the abbé de Périgord's guests, however, was undoubtedly Mirabeau, who for a time under the Constituent Assembly would be effective political master of France. Mirabeau hardly merits a word in Talleyrand's memoirs. He seems to have been introduced to the abbé de Périgord in 1785, probably by Panchaud.[16] The two men became close political colleagues and they enjoyed a somewhat uneasy friendship. It was Talleyrand who punctured Mirabeau's vanity, when the latter had been listing the various attributes required of the perfect minister.

'All this is true,' interrupted Talleyrand. 'But you have omitted one of his qualities.'

Mirabeau: 'No – surely? What do you mean?'

'Should he not', replied Charles-Maurice, 'be very much pitted with the small pox?'

(Mirabeau's face was deeply pock-marked as a result of contracting that disease.)

Talleyrand waited on Mirabeau at his deathbed; he read out the speech that the orator had intended to give to the Assembly; and he delivered the eulogy at Saint-Eustache.[17] Towards the end of his life, the Prince would recall with emotion his memories of the 'giant Mirabeau.' He apparently subscribed to the commonly held view that he had been poisoned and considered that the present generation – that of Louis-Philippe – undervalued Mirabeau's historical importance.[18]

Violence and untimely death would thus affect several of those who joined the abbé de Périgord at his Bellechasse retreat. But for now life was undoubtedly sweet for the ambitious, optimistic group who met there – as, indeed, it was for much of upper-class society in Paris. It was of this period that Talleyrand would later famously tell Guizot: 'Those who did not live during the years close to 1789 do not know the pleasure of living.'[19]

There would, though, have been little such pleasure for the abbé de Périgord if his only companions had been men. He loved women and he was extremely attractive to them. The painter Mme Vigée-Lebrun, who met him at this time in her studio in the company of Chamfort, recalled: 'His face was gracious, his cheeks very round, and although he had a limp he was nonetheless very elegant.'[20] Charles-Maurice had an irresistible sweetness of expression which, along with his light blue eyes, pale complexion, flowing golden locks and delicate snub nose, was suited to entrance the opposite sex.[21] A full, surprisingly deep voice removed any impression of frivolity or effeminacy and could convey, when he chose, strength and gravity. He was also quite tall for the times in which he lived: five feet five and a half inches. In all respects, he was, in fact, well placed to hold his own in the company of the handsome, irreverent young clerics who, with their lay coun-terparts, were made very welcome by the great ladies of Paris.

During the years of Louis XV's long reign, as Talleyrand observes, the Parisian *salons* had acquired a political as well as a social function as places where those who wished to advance themselves through high office or state patronage would congregate. An entertaining, if perhaps apocryphal, anecdote has it that some time before the death of the old King (10 May 1774), the abbé de Périgord, Choiseul-Gouffier, Lauzun and Narbonne were all together with the royal mis-tress, Mme du Barry, in her boudoir. While the three others retailed their amorous conquests, the abbé de Périgord remained silent. Intrigued, their hostess asked him to speak about his own successes.

But the young cleric merely sighed and said, 'Ah! Madame, I have had a sad thought.'

'But what is it?' she insisted.

'It is that Paris is a city in which it is a lot easier to get women than abbeys.'

He was, as a result, given two benefices.[22]

Talleyrand moved in what he described as 'society', or sometimes '*la grande société*', and in such a milieu he felt at home. He was not only seductive, but was also capable of sustaining a friendship after – and even without – seduction. It was in the company of women that he made his most useful contacts and that he developed the finesse and charm to exploit them. Claire de Rémusat would note that women had much more influence over him than men.[23] And he, for his part, as she also noted, knew how to treat women properly; in marked contrast, for example, to Napoleon, who adored, wept, bullied and complained, but never knew how to behave in a woman's presence.

An insight into why women loved Charles-Maurice, and why they became his friends, is provided by a pen-portrait of 'Clari' (Mme de Rémusat) that he composed some years later during a boring session of the Napoleonic Senate:

> Clari is not what they call a beauty. Everyone agrees that she is a nice woman. She is twenty-eight or twenty-nine years old. She is no more nor less fresh than one should be at twenty-eight. Her figure is good, her manner is simple and gracious. Clari is not thin. She is no weaker than is required to be delicate. Her complexion is not dazzling. But it has the special advantage of seeming to be whiter, the brighter the sunlight. Is that perhaps the symbol of Clari herself, who, the more that you get to know her, seems better and more lovable? Clari has big black eyes. Long lashes give her a mixture of tenderness and vivacity, which is noticeable even when she is quiet and not seeking to express herself. But those moments are rare. Lots of ideas, an acute perception, constant kindness are expressed in her gaze.[24]

Among the *salons* frequented by the abbé de Périgord was that of Louise de Rohan, comtesse de Brionne. He would write near the end of his life that he had passed the pleasantest days of his youth at her house. He also came to know her two daughters – the princesse de Carignan and the princesse de Lorraine – and also the comtesse's daughter-in-law, the princesse de Vaudémont. The latter would be one of his dearest friends for the next fifty years.[25]

The *salon* of the marquise de Montesson was of special political significance because it brought him into contact with the circle of the duc d'Orléans, whom she had, in fact, secretly married. Parties were given both in the Palais-Royal and at Mme de Montesson's home in the rue de Provence. She was a great theatre buff, and Talleyrand mentions in his memoirs her 'theatre [where] there was a box for the rather dissipated clergy', such as the archbishop of Toulouse, the bishop of Rodez, the archbishop of Narbonne, the bishop of Comminges – and, of course, the abbé de Périgord.[26] The Orléans connection would be of great importance to Talleyrand's fortunes.

But time was now pressing. In order to take up his designated position as agent general of the assembly of the French clergy in 1780, the abbé de Périgord had first to be ordained as priest. He naturally chose to be incardinated into the diocese of his uncle. (Alexandre-Angélique had, on the death of the cardinal de La Roche-Aymon, succeeded to the archbishopric of Reims in 1777.) On 17 September 1779 Charles-Maurice thus received the diaconate from the bishop of Beauvais, one of his uncle's suffragans. Finally, on 18 December that year, and at the age of twenty-five, Charles-Maurice was ordained to the priesthood.

Talleyrand's latest biographer is inclined to dismiss, on this as on other occasions, any evidence to suggest that the young man was subject to psychological crises about his vocation. According to both the morals and the philosophical outlook then prevailing among the aristocratic clergy the abbé de Périgord would not have been alone in making light of his vows. Indeed, whether the ordinand at this stage even believed in God at all, let alone the God of the Catholic doctrine to which he was meant to subscribe, is unclear. But this does not fully describe his attitude. On occasion, his approach was not just ambiguous but also uneasy. Perhaps it was merely an innate dislike of hypocrisy. Perhaps it was more. On the eve of his priestly ordination, Choiseul-Gouffier apparently found him in tears and close to despair. But the future priest rebuffed every attempt to make him change his mind. 'No,' he said. 'It is too late; there is no going back.'[27] So the ceremony went ahead as planned, performed by the bishop of Noyon, another suffragan of his uncle, in the archbishop's chapel in Reims.

On 19 December Talleyrand was appointed vicar general – that is effective administrator – of Alexandre-Angélique's diocese. On the same day, the fourth Sunday of Advent, the newly ordained priest said his first mass. His parents were both present.[28] Whatever crisis had erupted for a moment in the abbé de Périgord's soul had been stilled. His life of self-indulgence and self-promotion resumed as normal.

There was, in fact, no time for the new vicar general to come to terms with his diocesan responsibilities, even had he wished to do so, because the assembly of the French clergy would soon be meeting. It did so under the presidency of the cardinal de La Rochefoucauld, arch-bishop of Rouen, on 29 May. Having completed its deliberations and prepared its remonstrances, the members were solemnly received by the King on 8 October. Three days later it held its final session. Only now would the serious work of the two agents general really begin.[29]

The agent generalship was a choice appointment. The salary of 20,000 livres a year for a five-year term was comparable to that of a bishop. But it brought with it no diocesan chores; it had the benefit of residence in Paris; and it involved close contact with many of the most influential figures of the day. Moreover, it was assumed that the post brought with it subsequent – though as Talleyrand was to dis-cover not necessarily immediate – promotion to the episcopate. That said, the job was certainly no sinecure. The agents general had at their disposal a modest bureaucracy, the most important division of which was the secretariat. But a high degree of personal direction was involved if business was to be transacted promptly and effectively.[30]

The agents general had to oversee the collection and use of Church revenues, to uphold Church rights, and to manage the central Church archives. But because the first two of these tasks were so broad, they found themselves in regular relations with government at all levels, including the highest. They were allowed to attend full meetings of the Royal Council. Moreover, in 1776 the King formally gave 'the agents general of his clergy, present and future, permission to attend the *bureaux* [departments] of his council, where are discussed matters in which the clergy may have an interest, in order to make, if they judge it necessary, their observations, as they do at the [full] council'.[31] The post of agent general, therefore, allowed its holder not just to observe but to intervene in the work of government. It was as near to ministerial office as anyone could come without royal appointment.

In practice, these responsibilities fell almost entirely upon the shoulders of the abbé de Périgord, rather than his colleague. The abbé de Boisgelin was in some respects not so different from Charles-Maurice. He too had been a beneficiary of powerful patronage – in this case that of his uncle, the archbishop of Aix. His family, like Talleyrand's, hoped that the agent generalship would lead to a swift episcopal appointment. But the abbé de Boisgelin, unlike the abbé de Périgord, had failed to respect the proprieties. Even in late eighteenth-century France, the indiscreet abbé being caught with his lover (and Louis XV's former mistress) Mme de Cavanac *in flagrante delicto* by her outraged husband was a source of public scandal: in fact, it precluded his ever becoming a bishop.[32] But, for Talleyrand, his colleague's obsession with Mme de Cavanac ensured that there was no real competitor for whatever reputation was to be won as a successful agent general.

The abbé de Périgord's secretariat was headed by Henri-Gabriel Duchesne, the first of a long line of capable bureaucrats whose loyalty and effort Talleyrand would know how to inspire. But the young agent general worked ferociously hard himself. He examined bundles of letters on every subject, assimilated their contents, and wrote down his comments and instructions in the margins. He penned personal replies to the hundreds of memoranda that arrived on his desk from the dioceses and he encouraged the clergy to approach him to discuss their cases and their problems.[33]

Talleyrand also now revealed for the first time another trait that would serve him well: the shrewd use of previously acquired relationships when seeking out collaborators in different fields. Thus both the abbé (future bishop) Bourlier and the abbé (and also future bishop) Mannay, who had been his tutors at Saint-Sulpice, joined Talleyrand's little team. The abbé (and, again, future bishop) Duvoisin had been a professor at the Sorbonne where he had probably come to know his young master as a student. He too was put to good use. The abbé Desrenaudes had received his licentiate of theology at the Sorbonne at the same time as Charles-Maurice. Of him the memoirs note that he was not in the 'same line' as the others – that is he was not marked out for ecclesiastical promotion. Instead, Desrenaudes would be closely linked to Talleyrand for the next twenty years and would come to be considered his all-purpose *homme de confiance*.[34]

Inevitably, much of what fell to the abbé de Périgord to resolve was without enduring significance, but he demonstrated a distinctive taste for reform and concern with justice. And while these preoccupations doubtless reflect the rationalizing spirit of the time, they also provide a signpost to the statesman's own future interests. For example, the agent general recommended that the basic salary of the poorest clergy should be raised in line with the intentions of an earlier law of 1768. This clearly desirable measure remained, though, without effect.

Talleyrand would recall in his memoirs another attempt to rectify hardship. This was his proposal, devised after a visit to Brittany where he had noticed the number of widows – and the abbé de Périgord was, one would imagine, a keen observer of eligible women. But these were not eligible, which was the problem. The Church decreed that when a sailor was apparently lost at sea his spouse should not be permitted to remarry, unless there were proof of his death. The abbé de Périgord tried in vain to have this harsh requirement modified.[35]

As agent general, Charles-Maurice was a resolute and effective defender of clerical privilege. In 1785 he presented a memorandum arguing that the Church could never be and had never been vassal to the King. Needless to say, this high doctrine of clerical rights was completely at odds with the arguments he would put in future years for the despoliation of Church lands – as was pointed out forcefully in the National Assembly in October 1789.[36]

Talleyrand's work as agent general culminated in a well-received report to the new assembly of the French clergy that met in 1785. It was very comprehensive and consisted of 324 pages of text, 17 pages of contents, and no fewer than 568 pages of appendices. Moreover, its drafting was obviously the work of the abbé de Talleyrand and his assiduous team, rather than of his lethargic, love-struck colleague.[37]

During his time as agent general Talleyrand had given ample proof of his abilities. He had, as a result, every right to expect that he would imminently be rewarded with a bishopric. But he was to be disappointed. And the cost of disappointing Talleyrand would usually prove greater than that of satisfying him. Many years later he observed that he brought misfortune upon the governments that neglected him. This contained more than an element of truth.[38]

The abbé de Périgord's ecclesiastical ambitions may have been frustrated for a while. But in other respects he had spent his time profitably. Talleyrand had, for example, made political contacts. One of these was the duc de Choiseul, uncle of his great friend.[39] Choiseul was of no immediate practical help, for he was now in disgrace; but he was a fund of political wisdom and experience. He had effectively governed France for twelve years before being ousted in a court coup and exiled to his estates at Chanteloup. There he liked to entertain his friends and, more discreetly, to welcome up-and-coming figures on the contemporary political scene, such as the abbé de Périgord, whom the old statesman received in 1784. The two were joined by a young professor at the French Oratory (and Talleyrand's future collaborator), Maurice Blanc d'Hauterive, as they strolled around the garden. Choiseul told the abbé de Périgord that there would be no more churchmen in charge of the government: the days of Richelieu, Mazarin, Dubois and Fleury were over. This meant that Charles-Maurice could at best hope to be an ambassador; Hauterive himself was about to join the staff of Choiseul-Gouffier in Constantinople. More generally, Choiseul gave his views of how a minister should behave: 'In my government, I always had others work more than I did myself. One must not get snowed under with papers; one must find someone to deal with them. . .A minister who goes out in society can at any moment be alerted to some danger, even at a party; what will he learn if he locks himself away permanently in his office?'[40]

Talleyrand would take both pieces of advice: the first directly by becoming a layman, and the second indirectly by making good use of draughtsmen and other underlings, so that he himself could pick up and disseminate useful gossip in society. It might therefore be imagined that Talleyrand would have been grateful to Choiseul, but this would be to misunderstand him. As in the case of the duc d'Orléans, the very similarities of character seem to have provoked resentment. And perhaps there was some professional jealousy at work as well.

Talleyrand in his pen-portrait of Choiseul, written between 1811 and 1816, described him as frivolous and shallow.[41] Choiseul, he alleged, was mainly concerned with maintaining the favour of Mme de Pompadour. He had failed to think through the implications of the 'diplomatic revolution' of 1756, which initiated the Franco-Austrian axis that dominated foreign policy until the Revolution. Above all, Charles-Maurice blamed Choiseul for not preventing the first partition of Poland in 1772 which, he always maintained, initiated the radical imbalance of Europe. He greatly preferred the model of Cardinal Fleury as Chief Minister, who between 1724 and 1742 had

ensured peace abroad and a degree of harmony at home, thus allowing the country's economic recovery.[42]

Charles-Maurice's interest in politics was not, however, mainly
historical but, rather, contemporary and very practical. His attempts
to build a political career were at this stage inextricably connected
with his desire to make money, and in this respect his talents were
admirably suited to the political circumstances of the day. The French
government's financial straits offered opportunities for speculation, as
did industrial and commercial growth inside and outside France. It
was an age when bankers and their associates were able to exert great
influence, not just through providing or securing credit but also as
advisers on public finance.

Isaac Panchaud's name has already been mentioned. Panchaud,
Talleyrand and their group undertook the same speculative investments in coal mines, peat extraction and above all on the money
markets. To carry out successfully the business of currency speculation, accurate and timely information was vital: hence the group's
interest in politics and especially foreign affairs.[43]

One notable manifestation of this was Mirabeau's mission to Berlin
in 1786–7. Mirabeau himself, though gregarious and observant, was in
some respects an unsuitable diplomat-cum-spy, being also undisciplined
and indiscreet. Talleyrand counter-balanced these defects, acting as his
controller in Paris, and rewriting Mirabeau's reports before they were
passed on to ministers. And behind Talleyrand, somewhere in the
shadows, stood Panchaud. Mirabeau was expected to give advice on
opportunities for investment and Panchaud would advise on the practicalities.[44] Unfortunately, Mirabeau's vanity was even greater than his
usefulness and when he subsequently found himself passed over for
preferment, he published the whole correspondence. This caused a
serious rift with Charles-Maurice, not healed until both were elected
to the Estates General. The correspondence contains, among other
embarrassing titbits, memoranda drawn up by Talleyrand for potential
foreign investors on government securities and the impact of the
Franco-British commercial treaty of 1786.[45]

The latter is, however, a reminder that those gathered around
Panchaud were not simply interested in lining their pockets: they also
had clear ideas about wider economic policy. The Panchaud group

were strong advocates of a policy of peace and free trade with Britain. This anglophile, free-trading view of international relations would in the years to come find one of its most ardent and eloquent advocates in Charles-Maurice de Talleyrand, though at this stage, as he modestly admits, he was merely an apprentice in economics.

The treaty itself was not, in political terms at least, a success: the interests favouring protection were too powerful. Much the same could be said of Panchaud's other *idée fixe*, which was the need to reform French public finances through the amortization of national debt by means of a *caisse d'escompte* or discount bank.[46] Talleyrand recalls Panchaud repeatedly telling Calonne, the new controller general of the finances,[47] and indeed anyone else who would listen, that in the present state of Europe, whichever of the two countries, France or England, followed exactly his plan of amortization would see off the other.[48] As with the Franco-British free trade treaty, the banker was right in theory. In practice, however, the conjuncture of a deep-seated political crisis with an immediate financial crisis put such obviously sensible solutions beyond reach.

This, indeed, was why another of Panchaud's earlier financial schemes – the creation of a more modest *caisse d'escompte* in 1776 – had run into difficulties. Turgot, a serious economic reformer of the physiocrat school and the late *ancien régime*'s most able Finance Minister, was then controller general.[49] Despite Panchaud's pressure, the *caisse* was only permitted to discount commercial and financial instruments, not to amortize state debt, which negated a large part of its purpose. More seriously, however, it soon became far too close for financial comfort to the near bankrupt royal treasury. In 1783 this resulted in a full-scale crisis.

The crisis itself was temporarily averted as the authorities stepped in, but the value of the bills issued by the *caisse* fell sharply. The Church held a substantial number of these bills and this gave the abbé de Périgord the *locus* to intervene in his capacity as the clergy's agent general. When a commission was appointed to reform the *caisse d'escompte*, Charles-Maurice was named as one of its eleven members, along with Panchaud.

A general meeting of the shareholders of the *caisse* was summoned for 22 October in order to hear about the proposed changes to the institution's statutes. The introductory address was given by Charles-Maurice and it made a powerful impression. When he came to write his memoirs, he recognized the occasion as marking the start of his public career. One banker from Geneva rushed up afterwards, grasped Talleyrand's hand and begged to have a copy, so moved had he been by the agent general's remarks about promptly honouring bills of exchange.

Talleyrand's speech reflects his settled view of the supreme importance of confidence in financial matters. He argued that if the public finances enjoyed a secure credit, anything was possible. It followed – and this was a subject to which he would return even more insistently under the Revolution – that nothing should be done to forfeit that credit.[50]

Talleyrand's performance may have helped bring him to the notice of Calonne, since at some point Charles-Maurice, along with his mentor Panchaud and Mirabeau, began to constitute the minister's team of informal advisers. Their relationship with Calonne seems at first to have centred on a secret scheme to create (another) *caisse d'amortissement*.[51] For Talleyrand, though, it meant that he was finally inside the workings of government.

In fact, Talleyrand thought Calonne lazy and superficial and he despised him, as he had despised Choiseul, for being too much a courtier and too little a statesman.[52] But he agreed entirely with the ambitious plans for financial reform that Calonne proposed in 1786. Radical action was long overdue. For three years, the controller general had signally failed to establish a grip on the public finances, with the result that the government's credit was all but exhausted.

Calonne's approach had all the merits, as well as all the defects, of rationalization. As such, it was entirely in tune with the spirit of the times. The government proposed in the short run to stabilize the debt by the sale of royal domain, with the proceeds going towards debt amortization, and by a new loan. But underpinning this were sweeping changes, mooted many times before but never undertaken, to abolish all fiscal privileges and remove obstacles to internal free trade, particularly the politically sensitive trade in grain. A new tax called the *subvention territoriale* would be levied on all landowners, replacing the old *vingtièmes* with their numerous exemptions. *Corvée* (forced labour) would be abolished. The *gabelle* (salt tax) would be more fairly distributed. Regional representative assemblies would be instituted. And in order to gain consent for these reforming measures, without falling foul of the traditionally obstructive *parlements* on the one hand or being forced to summon an Estates General on the other, an Assembly of Notables was to be convoked.

Calonne believed that this gathering would prove amenable. Quite why he or Talleyrand or the other enthusiasts for reform thought so, given the fiscal and other sacrifices that those summoned would have to make, is unclear. But it must be one of the few times in his life that the charge of naïveté can with justice be levelled at Talleyrand: for the outcome was disastrous.

Sloppy preparation was certainly part of the problem, as he relates. Just a week before the assembly was due to meet, he received a note from Calonne urgently asking him to come to Versailles and join an ad hoc group to edit the documents that had to be presented. Hardly any of the required preparatory work had been done. Talleyrand's own assignment was to draft the memorandum and part of the law on liberalizing the grain market. He also worked on the question of the debts of the clergy, which he had already considered, and that of the *corvée*, which must have been quite new to him. Acting as a kind of proto-civil service, the group managed to complete within a few days tasks that should have been undertaken over months.

If the proposals were to be taken seriously at all, however, they must be known to enjoy Louis XVI's committed personal support. And at first they did. But a few days before the assembly opened, the death of Louis's closest confidant among the ministers, the comte de Vergennes, who had also firmly backed Calonne, began the all too easy process of weakening the King's resolve. The storm that the proposals themselves provoked, and the resultant ripples within the court, achieved the rest.

Yet when he wrote to Choiseul-Gouffier on 4 April, enclosing a copy of Calonne's speeches to the assembly, Charles-Maurice was still full of optimism. He thought that Calonne should have made greater efforts to publicize his proposals and he acknowledged the scale of the opposition, but he was convinced of speedy success: 'It seems impossible that the King should not support [Calonne]: a fortnight more and he will have won.'[53] But this was a complete misjudgement. Louis

dismissed his minister and exiled him to Lorraine. The cardinal archbishop of Toulouse, Loménie de Brienne, a favourite of the Queen,
was put in charge of the royal finances. The Assembly of Notables
concluded its obstructive work on 25 May. The Paris *parlement* led ever
louder demands for an Estates General.

The crisis was rapidly becoming less a matter of finance, more a
matter of high politics. Although Charles-Maurice was no longer one
of the government's advisers, having lost his position with the fall of
Calonne, he was a close observer of events. The account in his
memoirs reveals his contempt for the inconsistent policies, alternating
between unnecessary concessions and brittle assertiveness, that finally
undid the monarchy. What the memoirs do not reveal, however, is the
degree to which – as an associate of the duc d'Orléans, who was by
now increasingly manipulating the opposition – the author was personally part of the plotting.[54]

Loménie de Brienne now attempted to win back the ground that
had been lost. Large economies in government expenditure were
made. But the crisis continued to grow. The nobility and the clergy
resisted all new impositions. From every side, and with differing purposes (and in some cases a large degree of cynicism), the calls for an
Estates General mounted.

Charles-Maurice will have hoped that the cardinal's fall would
provide an opportunity for him and his friends to return to the centre
of affairs. But he was disappointed. On 25 August 1788 the King
reluctantly reappointed Necker.[55] And far from being favourable to
Charles-Maurice, the new government had no time for him at all.
Talleyrand would repay Necker amply for the insult. But that would
have to wait.

At this point, however, it is necessary to turn back and consider
Charles-Maurice's parallel and equally stalled ecclesiastical career. The
problem was simple. Despite his aristocratic background, despite his
charm, despite a formidable array of political contacts, and despite his
proven technical brilliance as financial adviser and administrator, he
found himself shunned by the court. The principal reason had
nothing to do with his reputation for immorality, but was rather his
unfortunate connections, particularly those with the Rohan-Lorraine
family.

In 1784 Mme de Brionne had made a serious if bizarre attempt to secure the abbé de Périgord a cardinal's hat. She wrote to her friend (the Lutheran Protestant) Gustav III, King of Sweden, who was on holiday in Italy, asking him to intervene on Charles-Maurice's behalf with Pope Pius VI. Her letter spoke enthusiastically of her protégé's 'birth, personal qualities, talents'. Such a favour would also, though, require support from the King of France. At this point the question of a cardinal's hat for Charles-Maurice became lost in the crisis of the 'affair of the necklace', which now engulfed the court.

In January 1785 the Prince-cardinal Louis de Rohan, grand almoner of France and thus France's senior churchman, was duped into purchasing a magnificent necklace, originally intended for Mme du Barry. He hoped to employ it as a lavish gift to Marie-Antoinette in order to win her favour. He even believed that he had received her encouragement, although in fact the Queen knew nothing of the proposal. The whole affair was the brainchild of an adventuress known as the comtesse de La Motte, whose associates preyed on Rohan's gullibility to have the necklace given over to them. They then promptly escaped with it to London. The matter came to light when the jewellers who had the made the piece, and who had not been paid, presented their bill to the Queen, who in turn brought the matter before her husband. In the ensuing scandal it was, in the long run, the monarchy that suffered most. But the immediate result was the trial and punishment of cardinal de Rohan in the summer of 1786, and his whole family also fell into deep disgrace. This included Charles-Maurice's friend, the comtesse de Brionne, who fearlessly if imprudently acted as her cousin's leading supporter.

In such circumstances, there was no possibility of Talleyrand escaping acute royal disfavour. Nor is there evidence that he made any particular attempt to do so. He apparently told a vulgar joke about the Queen in the very public and very provocative environs of the Palais-Royal.[56] But his close association with the circle that gravitated around the duc d'Orléans would already have marked him out in the eyes of the court as a dangerous member of the opposition.[57]

The abbé de Périgord's introduction into the Orléans circle probably came through the *salon* of the sophisticated comtesse de Boufflers, who acted as the companion of the old duchesse d'Orléans.

It was by a quick-witted answer at the comtesse's house in Auteuil that Charles-Maurice first made his social mark.[58]

Of the women who moved within the circle of the Palais-Royal, the already mentioned Mme de Genlis was certainly Charles-Maurice's closest friend. She was a beauty as well as a blue stocking, with all the accomplishments required of the *salon*: she talked well; she sang beautifully; she was a fine actress; she played the harp better, it is said, than anyone of her day. She had made her appearance at the Palais-Royal as the animator of the duchesse de Chartres's *salon* and turned it, in the discriminating eyes of the duchess d'Abrantès, into the 'pleasantest in Paris'.[59] She soon became the duc's principal mistress and was charged with bringing up his three children. From 1777 she lived at Bellechasse just a stone's throw from Charles-Maurice, of whom she was certainly an early mistress. Her memoirs reveal a lasting affection for him and she would complain that 'his enemies have not done justice to his goodness of heart'.[60] Talleyrand would reciprocate the affection with various acts of kindness. But these did not preclude one cutting observation in his memoirs: 'M. le duc [de Chartres, later d'Orléans] found her charming, told her so, and soon received a hearing; for Mme de Genlis, in order to avoid the scandal of coquettishness, has always yielded readily.'[61]

Talleyrand may not have participated in the orgies for which the duc was notorious, but he did share two of his mistresses. He would also play cards with d'Orléans at the Palais-Royal and at his house in the parc Monceau: gambling was already one of the young cleric's passions. For a decade, he would be close to Philippe Égalité, as d'Orléans was known at the high point of his fragile popularity. The group contained many of Talleyrand's friends – Lauzun, Mirabeau, Narbonne, Liancourt, Chamfort and Laclos among others.

Another powerful tie between Talleyrand and the duc d'Orléans, and indeed with many of the Orléans circle, was in all probability freemasonry. It is not quite certain that Charles-Maurice was a mason, but the likelihood is strong. He seems to have been initiated by the duc as *premier surveillant* ('first warden') of a masonic lodge that d'Orléans established in Paris in 1786.[62] That did not prevent Talleyrand in his memoirs from mocking what he considered the duc's ridiculous pride in being grand master of France's Grand-Orient lodge.[63]

Talleyrand's biographical essay on the duc, now included in the memoirs, was originally intended to be published separately, when Charles-Maurice was in exile in England in 1792. Prepared with the help of his friend Beaumetz, its purpose was the very practical one of raising much needed cash. The depiction is not just unflattering but malicious: the duc had, apparently, a 'dry heart'; he had been so morally corrupted that he could 'love no one'; he achieved little or nothing in his life because of his weakness of character. Philippe Égalité's importance lies, according to his jaundiced biographer, in the degree to which he represented the 'relaxation of the public and private morals' of the day. The hypocritical final flourish, conveying a certain lack of self-knowledge, is typical of Talleyrand in his worst moments.[64]

In any case, as an associate both of the Rohan-Lorraine family and of the duc d'Orléans, the young abbé de Périgord's opportunities for promotion were for a time doubly blighted. His uncle's influence could not prevail against such court disfavour. Charles-Maurice thus had to wait three full years for his bishopric. Moreover, he did not want or expect just any bishopric. As an ambitious would-be ecclesiastical statesman, Talleyrand wanted a wealthy diocese and one of political significance, with its own provincial assembly.[65]

The month of December 1786 found Charles-Maurice in a state of hopeful expectation that he might soon be appointed archbishop of Bourges, for he had learned that the incumbent was gravely ill. Talleyrand described it to Mirabeau as a 'fine position', predicting that the archbishop would be dead within two or three weeks. This was premature. In April 1787, though, the archbishop's health suddenly grew worse. Charles-Maurice was again full of excitement at the prospect and informed Choiseul-Gouffier that the archbishop appeared to be in his death throes. He thought that the archbishopric would be his, and not even the influential administrator of the *feuille des bénéfices*, Alexandre de Marbeuf, bishop of Autun, whose hostility to Talleyrand reflected that of the court, would be able to stop him. But although the archbishop of Bourges duly breathed his last in September, the bishop of Nancy was appointed to fill the vacancy. Talleyrand wrote bitterly to his friend: 'Nothing that I want turns out as I would like. . .But that will change.' And it soon did.[66]

In May 1788 the archbishop of Lyon suddenly died. Talleyrand was again passed over in favour of one of the archbishop's suffragans, the bishop of Autun. On the face of it, Charles-Maurice's chances of filling the latter's shoes did not seem high. But another death came to the rescue. Talleyrand's father fell mortally ill. On his deathbed, thinking as any Talleyrand would about the honour and income of the family, Charles-Daniel asked the King for a bishopric for his son. Louis consented. The anecdotes surrounding this event are probably baseless, but they do revealingly reflect the hostility that followed Talleyrand throughout his later career. It was said that Charles-Maurice's mother, knowing of her son's unsuitability, intervened to try to persuade the King to withdraw his consent. Louis XVI allegedly justified his decision, while acknowledging the candidate's deficiencies, with the remark: 'That will put him right.'

In any event, the royal warrant of nomination issued on 2 November announced that, 'well informed of the good life, morals, piety, doctrine, great sufficiency and other virtuous and commendable qualities' of Charles-Maurice de Talleyrand-Périgord, vicar-general of Reims, the King had granted him the bishopric of Autun. Charles-Daniel died two days later.[67]

The bishopric was worth the relatively modest sum of 22,000 livres a year, but it came with an annual pension of 3,000 livres, payable for life. More importantly, on 3 December Talleyrand was granted by the King the abbey of Celles in Poitou, on the 'presentation' of Louis's youngest brother, the comte d'Artois. This benefice was worth 12,000 livres annually. The decision was also an early indication that Charles-Maurice was now restored to a measure of court favour, and that this extended beyond the King himself.

Talleyrand undertook the prescribed retreat at the Sulpicians' novitiate house at Issy under the direction of M. Émery, the congregation's superior. It was in the chapel there that Charles-Maurice was consecrated bishop on 4 January 1789. The ceremony was performed by Louis-André de Grimaldi, bishop of Noyon, who had nine years earlier ordained Charles-Maurice to the priesthood, assisted by the bishops of Béziers and Saint-Dié.

According to M. Émery, Charles-Maurice now underwent a further crisis. When the oil of unction was placed on his hands, he became pale and ill and the ceremony had to be halted. But after a few minutes he composed himself and it went ahead as planned.[68] Talleyrand's family, including his uncle the archbishop of Reims, were absent: they were, doubtless, still mourning the comte de Talleyrand. Ten days later, the new bishop of Autun addressed a lengthy letter, full of worthy and affectionate sentiments, to the faithful of his diocese. He claimed to have them constantly in mind. He even declared, in a passage as mawkish as it must have been unconvincing, that as he wept at the bedside of his dying father, he had looked forward to finding consolation in Autun, the Burgundian homeland of his mother.[69] In the event, Charles-Maurice so contained his longing that he did not see Autun for another two months.

The paths of political advance and ecclesiastical promotion had at last converged. Necker, with an excessively high regard for his ability to direct popular sentiment, had on his return to power persuaded the King to summon an Estates General. On 24 January a royal decree established arrangements for the forthcoming elections. The procedure would begin in March. It was clearly now time for the bishop of Autun to take a closer interest in his diocese.

3

Bishop and Revolutionary

❦

O N THURSDAY, 12 March 1789 Charles-Maurice arrived for the first time in Autun and the following Sunday formally took possession of the see. He had already taken a solemn oath, at the time of his consecration, not to alienate property belonging to the bishopric. He now swore 'to observe inviolate and to defend all the privileges, liberties, franchises, immunities, exceptions, rights and customs of the church of Autun'.[1] There is no evidence that he felt any scruples when he later flagrantly broke these undertakings. But then Talleyrand always took a light view of oaths.

In any case, the new bishop's attention was focused on politics. More than 200 clergy would soon gather for the purpose of electing the ecclesiastical representative of the *bailliage* to the forthcoming Estates General. It was by no means a foregone conclusion that an incoming bishop would emerge as victorious. Charles-Maurice accordingly set about political seduction on a grand scale. His vicars-general were sent out to neighbouring towns and villages to prepare opinion, while the bishop himself entertained lavishly in his palace. The cathedral chapter were soon won over and the humbler clergy followed their lead.[2]

Charles-Maurice's early political aptitude and sophistication can be judged from the *cahiers de doléances* that emerged from the assembly's deliberations, which closely reflected the bishop's own distinctive views. True, some of the remonstrances he would privately have found less agreeable – such as that 'the Catholic, Apostolic, Roman religion be declared the sole religion of state and that all other public cults be prohibited for ever' – but in other respects he persuaded his colleagues to adopt much of his own group's programme of reform. Thus the clergy 'submitted with pleasure to all taxes as well as all public obligations converted into taxation'. It defended its privileges against arbitrary authority, but it recognized 'none before the Nation'. Similarly, it urged an increase in the basic clerical salary, the *portion congrue*, which was, of course, another of Charles-Maurice's causes.[3]

Talleyrand's speech to the gathering was later published. It was devoted to the large political issues – those that, in the clerical *cahiers* themselves, figured under the rubric of 'general affairs of the nation'. Even in summary, the impression is of a mature and coherent programme of reform. Talleyrand emphasizes the need for the Estates General to exercise, like the (unmentioned) British Parliament, control over its deliberations. He calls for 'a charter or declaration of rights', which would be an interest during most of his political career. He asserts that the 'nation' alone has the right to make laws and to levy and regulate the expenditure of taxes. Talleyrand's preoccupation with the right to private property is evident. Echoing Locke, he states that this right is 'natural' and prior to human society. But in a passage that should have given his audience some indigestible food for thought, he draws attention to certain alleged property which is 'abusive'. Such false property must be at the nation's disposition, though there must be recompense for those who lose out. No one, except perhaps the speaker, will have interpreted this as adumbrating the confiscation of Church lands.

Talleyrand then forcefully states a principle which, as events would demonstrate, was of more importance to him than it was to the chief architects of the Revolution: 'What individual liberty demands of every citizen will be respected or re-established by the Estates General. Beyond the law, all are free. No one can be deprived of liberty, even for a time, except by law, and never by an arbitrary order.'[4] Charles-Maurice demands a reform of the criminal code, restriction of the death penalty, *habeas corpus*, trial by one's peers, freedom from censorship, and protection against the interception of mail. The programme is a comprehensive if ambitious one for the entrenchment of individual liberty in France on the pattern that reformers admired across the Channel, but going in some respects beyond it.[5]

The final section of Talleyrand's speech dealt with the financial crisis, about which he had expert knowledge. The notable omission, of course, is any mention of Church property, but in other respects the proposals are frank and practical. Although he initially pays lip service to the universally popular notion that no new taxes are required to cover the deficit, he soon moves on to discuss how revenues should, in fact, be raised. They should be levied on the basis of the real economy (which as a physiocrat he primarily interpreted as agricultural land). All tax privileges must be abolished. Burdensome dues should be transmuted into tax. A full assessment of the wealth of the kingdom should be made. And all the facts and figures about the finances must be made public to the Estates General. Yet, with a characteristic touch of prudence, Talleyrand warns against unnecessary disruption and against the 'seductive but perhaps chimerical idea of a single, uniform tax in all the realm'.[6]

On the following day (2 April), Talleyrand was overwhelmingly elected as clerical representative to the Estates General. It was time to return to Paris. The bishop decided to avoid the liturgically taxing celebrations of the Easter Vigil and departed early on Saturday morning (12 April).[7] It was his last episcopal visitation. He would spend a mere twenty-two months as Autun's bishop. And if his sudden departure surprised his clergy now, they would soon have cause to be more astonished still.

Charles-Maurice's speech to the clergy of Autun shows that he had been thinking out his programme for months; and he had not been alone. Since at least the previous autumn, he had been a member of one of the many political dining clubs that met in Paris at this time of political ferment. The group that became known as the 'Society of Thirty' (Société des Trente) met three times a week at the house of Adrien Duport in the Marais district. The membership included, besides Charles-Maurice and Duport, many of the figures who would dominate the early stages of the forthcoming Revolution – notably Mirabeau, Lafayette, the abbé Sieyès and Alexandre Lameth. As events unfolded, it became clear that within the ranks of the society there were different views which would crystallize into different factions. In December 1789 Duport and Lameth left to found the more radical Jacobin Club.

Mirabeau described the society as 'a conspiracy of well-intentioned men'. In fact, it was a looser group than that: regular members could bring politically sympathetic guests. The immediate purpose was to coordinate the campaign for the election of reformist deputies to the

Estates General. The original programme, before ideological fissures appeared, was to create a constitutional monarchy of the kind prevailing in Britain, and to achieve the sort of liberal reforms that Talleyrand outlined to the clergy of Autun. It was the vehicle by which the so-called Patriot Party, of which Charles-Maurice was acknowledged as a leading member, very successfully advanced their aims and interests.[8]

The account in Talleyrand's memoirs of the period that now began is of more interest for what it reveals of his later (more conservative) views than of his thought and emotions at the time. He criticizes – in language that unconsciously echoes Burke's remarks in his *Reflections* – the quality of the deputies of the Third Estate (the commoners), who were elected as a result of Necker's decision that the number should be set at 600. As a result, there were too many lawyers, 'a kind of men whose habits of mind, being the necessary consequence of their profession, generally make them extremely dangerous'.[9] More important, by choosing twice as many deputies of the Third as of the First and Second Estates (the clergy and the nobility) the government implicitly accepted the greater importance of the Third. This paved the way for the uniting of the three orders, and also ensured that in the resulting National Assembly nobles and clergy would be outvoted.

Talleyrand does not discuss the links that bound him now, as earlier, to the duc d'Orleáns. Yet the duc was at this stage the indispensable patron not just of Talleyrand and Mirabeau, but also of Sieyès and most of the other reformist politicians. In February the Club de Valois had opened in the precincts of the Palais-Royal. Talleyrand and his colleagues were members. Another informal group called the Société du Palais-Royal met in the Café de Foy. It too was Orléanist. Pamphlets wrote of an Orléanist 'slate' and Talleyrand's name figured prominently.[10]

It is difficult at this stage to distinguish Talleyrand's personality and opinions from those of the wider political group of which he was a part. So the subsequent recollection of the playwright, and aide to Napoleon, Antoine-Vincent Arnault is especially important:

> In June 1789, when I was walking around the stretch of water called des Suisses at Versailles, I had noticed someone sitting alone and looking philosophical under a tree, *lentus in ombra* [lying in the shade]. He seemed plunged in meditation and more concerned with his own

ideas than other people's, although he had a book in his hand.[11] His face, which was not without charm, had struck me, all the same, less by its attractions than by its expression, by a certain mixture of nonchalance and malice which gave it a particular character – that of the head of an angel animated by the spirit of the devil. It was evidently that of a man of fashion, a man more accustomed to preoccupy others than to be preoccupied with them, a man who, despite his youth, was already sated with worldly pleasures. I would have ascribed that face to a First Page or a favoured colonel, if the hairstyle and the bands had not told me that it belonged to a cleric, and if the pectoral cross had not proved that this was a prelate.[12]

It was, of course, none other than the bishop of Autun.

Equally revealing, however, is the earliest assessment of Talleyrand's qualities as a politician, contained in a satirical assessment of the main Revolutionary figures. Here Charles-Maurice appears under the pseudonym of 'Amène':

> The first means of [Amène's] success is an excellent mind. Judging men with indulgence and events with *sang-froid*, he has that moderation which is the true characteristic of wisdom. . .Amène does not dream of building in a day the edifice of a great reputation. . .But he will attain all he wants, because he will seize the opportunities that are numerous for anyone who does not abuse his luck. Each step will be marked by the development of his talents, and going from success to success, he will gather the votes that summon a man to all the high positions that come vacant.

Yet, by the side of this commendable shrewdness, there is also a suggestion of a certain weakness of character, perhaps a lack of revolutionary grit: 'Amène yields to circumstances, to reason, and thinks one can offer some sacrifices to peace without abandoning the principles that he makes the basis of his morality and his conduct.'[13]

It was a surprisingly accurate summary of Charles-Maurice's political personality, though he had a greater reserve of ruthlessness than the author imagined. He demonstrated it as he manoeuvred between forces and events during that turbulent summer.

On 17 June, on a motion from the abbé Sieyès, the Third Estate declared itself the 'National Assembly'. But would the other Estates now join them? To do so would be to provide a probably irresistible momentum for sweeping change, perhaps even revolution. To resist would be to rely on a notoriously weak royal authority and an archaic constitutional formula for succour.

Talleyrand was one of the few who grasped what was at stake. He may not have thought that there was much hope of resisting the tide. And, contrary to the impression he gives in his memoirs, he probably did not greatly want to resist it at this stage. But such dangerous circumstances offered unique opportunities for self-advancement. As a cool-headed gambler, he was not averse to taking the risk.

That calculation surely explains the contact which Charles-Maurice and his circle now initiated with the court. In June and July, while acting as cheerleaders and on occasion initiators of the Revolution, they were in secret negotiations to abort it. The account in Talleyrand's memoirs of these transactions could perhaps be dismissed as a mendacious invention or at least gross exaggeration, devised to burnish his reputation when the Revolution was discredited. But the business is confirmed from other sources – including the royalist Vitrolles – and at least some of it became public, to Charles-Maurice's great discomfort.[14]

Talleyrand's plan was for a coup. The Estates General would be summarily dissolved. A British-style Upper House of Peers would be instituted in place of the Second Estate. The Third Estate would be transformed into a House of Commons. Presumably, the clergy would have had no place in this arrangement, though perhaps it was envisaged that some prelates would appear in the Upper House. Irrespective of the merits or practicability of this scheme, it had one great advantage in the eyes of Talleyrand and his friends: it required that control of the government be handed over to them, if the plan had any hope of accomplishment. This was more or less the project for which the monarchists, led by Jean-Joseph Mounier, would argue in the debates of that August. But by then Charles-Maurice, though he voted for the proposal, had already decided that the King and the court had no stomach for the fight.

Initially, and perhaps because of the intimidating presence of his uncle Alexandre-Angélique, he held his peace, though he was seen plotting with his colleagues as the tension grew.[15] But once the movement began among the clergy to unite with the Third Estate,

Charles-Maurice was one of the first bishops who, on 26 June, went to join the self-declared National Assembly.

Moreover, it was he who, on 7 July, cut the Gordian knot that bound the deputies in the Assembly to the provinces that had elected them, by proposing the annulment of the *mandats impératifs*, that is the precise instructions, they had received. In fact, Sieyès persuaded the Assembly that a motion on the subject was unnecessary in the light of the actions already taken. But the bishop of Autun's stock had risen greatly.

As a result, a week later Charles-Maurice was nominated as the first of eight members of the new Committee of the Constitution. And when it was renewed on 15 September he was again a member. In this capacity, he prepared and had adopted the celebrated Article 6, beginning: 'The Law is the expression of the General Will.'[16]

In early July popular sentiment was agitated to fever pitch by talk of a military *coup de main* aimed at the monarchy's chief critics. The King's dismissal of Necker on 12 July added to the alarm and prompted a deputation from the National Assembly, which met with a stony royal response. Charles-Maurice hated Necker and undoubtedly approved of Louis's decision. He had already counselled a coup and would again. But he now bent to the prevailing wind and agreed to draft and then read out the text of a formal protest about the crisis. Paris was by now in the throes of disorder. On 14 July a mob broke into the fortress of the Bastille and carried its governor's head away on a pike.

The true face of the Revolution was glimpsed. And we may be sure that Charles-Maurice was among those who liked it least.[17] He now prudently sought to help restore order, while at the same helping himself to whatever benefits disorder happened to bring with it. He had retained a foothold at court through his friendship with the duc de Liancourt, Louis's trusted (but liberal-minded) Grand Master of the Wardrobe. It was almost certainly the latter's influence that persuaded the King to turn to Charles-Maurice to write the speech that Louis delivered to the Assembly on 15 July.[18] It was the sort of exercise at which Talleyrand excelled. The later elegant and somewhat unctuous style is already evident in the King's declaration: 'The head of the nation comes with confidence amid its representatives to bear witness to them of his sorrow, and to invite them to find the means to restore order and calm. . .I know that some have dared to publish that your persons were at risk. Is it, therefore, necessary to reassure you about such culpable rumours, contradicted in advance by my known character?'[19]

The response was tumultuous applause. No one ever gained greater – albeit temporary – advantage from a reputation for weakness than did Louis XVI by the pen of Talleyrand. And, naturally, when it was necessary to appoint a delegation from the National Assembly to try to restore calm to Paris, the bishop of Autun figured as a prominent member.

But Charles-Maurice's private thoughts were less of reconciliation than of action. He now made his last attempt before the Emigration of much of the high nobility to persuade the King to accomplish the constitutional coup he had been advising. It was on the night of 16–17 July and, as previously, the comte d'Artois was the intermediary. The discussion lasted for over two hours. In the wake of the recent bloody disorder, Talleyrand had no hesitation in counselling the use of force. Artois then went away to speak to the King. But he returned to say that Louis would rather yield than risk further bloodshed. Artois added that he himself would leave France in the morning. The memoirs record Charles-Maurice's characteristic response:

'Then, Monseigneur, it therefore remains only for each of us to think of his own interests, since the King and the princes desert theirs and those of the monarchy.'

'Indeed,' replied Artois. 'That is what I advise you to do. Whatever happens, I shall never be able to blame you. Count always on my friendship.'

But when he came to write his account of these events, Charles-Maurice also appended his judgement on them; in doing so, he sought to justify his conduct to future generations: 'I resolved, therefore, not to leave France until forced to do so by danger to my person; to do nothing to provoke it; not to struggle against the torrent which it was necessary to let pass; but to hold myself in a situation and in reach to help save what could be saved; not to raise any obstacle against that opportunity, and to reserve myself for it.'[20] As a manifesto for all those politicians down the ages who have favoured compromise over sacrifice, the formulation cannot be bettered. Whether it properly explains the motivations of Charles-Maurice de Talleyrand, now or later, is more questionable.

Charles-Maurice's abiding interest in public affairs lay, though, in finance. Here, too, his desire for order and the sound basis for public credit that is its manifestation are evident. On 27 August he supported the raising of a new state loan. But he did so in terms designed to bring home to the Assembly the reality of the financial crisis and the need for rigour. Four times he repeated the phrase, 'credit is destroyed', before urging the need to re-establish it. Equally, he warned against the state 'breaking the engagements that it has solemnly contracted' with the *rentiers* who had acquired its debt. He argued that Britain enjoyed lower interest rates than France, not because of its wealth but because of its orderly finances. He called for a great national effort to follow that example, involving the summons of provincial assemblies to secure tax payments and the appointment of a special national committee to oversee the budget.[21]

This was not, though, the sort of message that the hot-heads of the National Assembly were interested in hearing. Significantly, three days later the bishop of Autun failed in a bid to become President of the Assembly. Late that summer – when France was swept by the mass panic known as the Grande Peur – it must have been apparent to Charles-Maurice that the skills he possessed were more suited to resolving the problems of government than to manipulating popular passions. His speeches, for example, read as powerful instruments of argument. But his voice, his bearing, above all the inescapable traits that came with his aristocratic background, were unsuited to mass oratory. His contemporaries thought him a poor speaker.[22] His genuine concern for the national finances and his need for a sweeping gesture that would secure him popular support were probably of equal importance in deciding him to propose, on 10 October, the confiscation of Church property.

The opening of his speech is arresting: 'The state has for a long while been in the grip of the greatest necessity. All of us know that. Great measures are, therefore, needed to provide for it.'

Charles-Maurice's arguments are couched mainly in financial terms.[23] But they must also be set against the historical background of several centuries of attempts by kings, Gallican theorists and anticlerical laymen to seize Church land.[24] Talleyrand borrows the arguments advanced, for example, by Turgot in his famous article on 'foundations' in the *Encyclopédie*. Thus the bishop of Autun observes that the Church does not, strictly speaking, own its property at all. Such property is merely held in trust in exchange for certain services, both religious and philanthropic. If the state should take on these responsibilities it could also legitimately confiscate the assets – which would henceforth be considered *biens nationaux* – in order to pay for them. He stresses that this measure 'can be allied with a severe respect for property': otherwise he 'would reject it'. Finally, each holder of a benefice must be ensured an 'honest subsistence' – at least 1,200 livres.

The speech is a masterpiece of lucid figuring. Charles-Maurice envisages that all the real estate of the Church should be sold. Its capital value would be some 2.1 billion livres and its annual revenues worth about 70 million. In order to overcome the problem of a lack of available cash to purchase this land, it must be used directly to pay off public debt. The state's creditors will be able to acquire in quittance of their loan the corresponding revenue from this nationalized property. Other charges upon it would be the reimbursement of state office-holders whose offices were to be suppressed, the reduction in the *gabelle*, and, of course, the maintenance of the clergy. Not only would the deficit be extinguished, so would future demands on state revenues.[25]

But he was to be proved wrong by events. The confiscation of Church property, like other such confiscations, proved no answer to the state's financial deficit: it would, instead, be used, through the irresponsible issue of paper money, to stoke inflation and destroy, not build, the stable credit that was its goal. And meanwhile the deficit expanded, not shrank.

Did Talleyrand at the time grasp the full significance of his actions? At one level, of course, he did. A passage in a letter that he wrote on 9 October to Mme de Brionne reveals his thinking about the future:

> The Revolution that is taking place in France is indispensable in the order of things in which we live, and this Revolution will finish up by being useful. The unhappiness and the troubles of today stem from what some have done to hold it back and others to accelerate it . . .

People still entertain illusions that have become culpable, people cherish chimeras in order to console themselves for the painful truths that cannot be resisted.[26]

Beyond all this he knew the value of having a bishop, rather than a layman, propose the despoliation of the Church; and by so obviously breaking ranks he knew that he could expect to be treated as a hero by the left in the Assembly.[27] But he was beginning to feel distinctly queasy at the socially disruptive aspects of the Revolution. A few days earlier a mob of Parisians had marched on Versailles, demanding the return of the royal family to Paris. In this tense political climate Charles-Maurice needed popularity, and he had certainly found the means to acquire it. His speech was received with 'very great applause', and 1,200 copies were quickly published.[28] Mirabeau then supported the proposal, subject to a technical amendment of the motion, and it thus became the basis of the law effecting confiscation.

Charles-Maurice must have known that he would be vilified by the right, by much of the clergy, and by loyal Catholic opinion. He found some formidable opponents in the Assembly itself, like that tough, eloquent royalist the abbé Maury, who used to go about armed with a pair of pistols.[29] Nor did the clergy of his diocese remain silent. On 24 October, the chapter of Autun met and prepared a formal protest, which was widely supported by curés and religious alike and sent to the National Assembly. In April the following year another clash occurred. The Assembly debated a motion from a Carthusian that Catholicism be declared 'the religion of the nation, and the only authorized cult'. It was defeated by another motion from the duc de La Rochefoucauld, which prompted more outrage on the right. A protestation supporting the role of the Church was then drawn up and signed by 144 members of the clergy. Charles-Maurice was among those who did not sign. News of this was greeted with indignation in Autun. In May the chapter met to subscribe to the protestation; they urged their bishop to append his signature and then to present their declaration to the Assembly. Talleyrand wrote back a flippant letter saying that he was 'completely decided never to sign [the protestation]', because he considered the document inopportune and unnecessary.[30]

He will have expected much of this, and he will have presumed that condemnation from Rome would follow too. But perhaps he underestimated the staying power of his enemies, who would pursue him to the grave and beyond.

The bishop of Autun already enjoyed a bad reputation, as sexually immoral and financially dishonest. When suggestions began to appear that he might be invited to join the government, he was roundly denounced 'for [his] scandalous immorality, for disgraceful speculation, for boundless ambition'. But this was not, in fact, worse than was said of others in the front rank of public affairs. From the time of his motion on Church property, however, disapproval of these traditional, *ancien régime* vices was incorporated into and overshadowed by the blackest of reputations. Talleyrand was henceforth depicted as a perjured and treacherous turncoat cleric, whose character was not just weak but wicked, and whose motives were not just selfish but diabolic.[31]

Charles-Maurice sought to rebut the attacks on his motives and prepared a speech to do so. Not being called to speak in the session of 2 November, he had the text printed and distributed. It begins defensively: 'I am perhaps the only one of my estate who upholds here the principles opposed to its interests. If I mount this tribune, it is not without feeling all the difficulties of my position.' But he then proceeded to tell the clergy some brutal home truths. He reminded them that they were no longer a separate order. Their tithes had been suppressed. Those who retained landed property had a duty to those who had lost their income. The nation could be relied upon to provide whatever was needed for the Church. Warming to his theme, Charles-Maurice argued that their lot would even be improved by his measure: 'By being paid by the nation, the clergy will be no less revered by the people. . .It is by ceasing to be a corporation [*corps*], that eternal object of envy, that the clergy will become a collection of citizens, the object of eternal gratitude.'[32]

Again, he was wrong. Anticlericalism, which was the driving passion behind confiscation, was not abated but rather increased. It would soon take the form of anti-Catholic persecution. Talleyrand's initiative would thus contribute to the social anarchy of which he, as a moderate and as an aristocrat (albeit a religious sceptic), so heartily disapproved.

He continued to take a close interest in public finances. In November 1789 he was appointed to report on the *caisse d'escompte*. The following month he delivered a long speech criticizing the proposal to set up a National Bank. It was widely seen as an attack on Necker and was, as a result, badly received. Charles-Maurice's ambition to enter the government was too well known, and his own reputation too stained, for him to be entirely credible.[33]

That said, his arguments were sound and prescient, especially those against the issue of non-convertible paper money. The only consequence, he warned, would be the disappearance of silver and gold coin. In an echo of Gresham's Law, he argued that bad money was bound to drive out good, and that the result would be economic disruption, as confidence in paper diminished and its value accordingly fell. The only way to restore credit was to attack the source of the problem, which was the public debt. As soon as confidence was regained in the willingness and ability to repay it, cheap and plentiful credit would be restored, and the current dearth of gold and silver coin would be at an end.[34]

Yet the seductive appeal of printing money, rather than tackling the underlying deficit, was too great to be overcome by such analysis. The result was the disastrous development of the *assignats* – in theory based upon the nationalized Church property, but in practice an inflationary device to cheat the state's creditors.

In April 1790 Charles-Maurice argued forcefully against the issue of 400 million *assignats*. These would lose their value and there was nothing that could prevent it, for 'the sovereign can never arbitrarily decide the value of currency'.[35] The first *tranche* of *assignats* was, in fact, quickly snapped up. And, as with all such inflationary boosts, the true cost was not immediately apparent. In September Charles-Maurice returned to the charge in similar language, when it was proposed to issue another 2 billion. But the argument again fell on deaf ears.

Yet Talleyrand still had his uses. He was a known moderate and a skilled draughtsman. In February 1790 he was, therefore, asked to compose and deliver an 'Address from the National Assembly to the French People', designed to justify to an increasingly unhappy nation the changes that the Revolutionaries in Paris had introduced.

Alongside the overblown list of achievements are to be found some more unusual features that suggest the author's personal imprint. For example, there is the odd admission that debates in the Assembly had often been 'tumultuous' and 'impetuous', to such an extent that these had 'pained' even the nation's representatives. Thus Charles-Maurice expressed his contempt for the brawling demagogy he had been forced to witness. Equally characteristic is a stern passage urging the country to act in an orderly manner: 'Distrust impetuous vivacity; above all fear acts of violence – for all disorder is fatal to liberty. You cherish that liberty; you now possess it; show yourselves worthy to keep it.'[36]

In March 1790 Charles-Maurice proposed a motion for the reform of weights and measures. It was the kind of technical question which – with his dislike of jargon and his intellectual lucidity – he was ideally equipped to expound.[37] The project was typical of the liberal rationalism of which Charles-Maurice, admirer of the physiocrats and the (less radical) *philosophes*, was such a faithful proponent. The metric system would provide the basis of the new reform. The precise measurement should be established in joint experimentation by the French Académie des Sciences and the British Royal Academy. He optimistically concluded: 'Perhaps it is even permitted to see in the cooperation of the two nations, interrogating nature together in order to obtain an important result, the principle of a political union operating through the mediation of science.'[38]

Even less is to be gleaned from his memoirs about Charles-Maurice's personal than his political life during this period. So nothing but a later disobliging mention refers to the beautiful Adélaïde de Flahaut, with whom he was now living in a close, passionate relationship from about 1780. The comtesse de Flahaut, *née* Filleul, was, in truth, the illegitimate daughter of Étienne-Michel Bouret, Louis XV's very rich *trésorier général*. She married in 1779 the much older comte de La Billarderie, whose brother held a prestigious post at court. These connections allowed her to live off pensions from the King, from Monsieur (the future Louis XVIII) and from the comte d'Artois (the future Charles X). Through her brother-in-law she enjoyed the right to live in an apartment in the Louvre, and it was here that she entertained Charles-Maurice.[39]

Neither the bishop of Autun nor his mistress was by inclination sexually exclusive. Thus during the Revolutionary years of Charles-Maurice's politicking the couple's mutual friend – and Adélaïde's occasional if obsessive lover – the visiting American, Gouverneur Morris, lived with them, and took notes of private and public events in his diary.[40] The apartment in the Louvre was, indeed, the scene of constant political scheming. 'The Bishop' (as Morris referred to Charles-Maurice) discussed there his motion on Church property, his financial ideas and, above all, his ambitions to enter the government – for these were always lurking behind each apparently unconnected initiative.[41]

Morris hated leaving Adélaïde in the company of Charles-Maurice, who had the habit of arriving at the most inconvenient moments and then staying on until the other man was compelled to depart, and thus, as he wrote, 'risque heroically the chances of cuckoldom'.[42] The American had high hopes, which were not in the end disappointed, that Charles-Maurice would transfer his attentions to Necker's daughter, Germaine de Staël. Indeed, he went so far as to ask her to let him know about the Bishop's successes, so that he could relay them to Adélaïde. So the odd *ménage* continued. Friendship of a sort, political like-mindedness and a shared desire to exploit every financial opportunity helped keep the two men together.[43] And both of them looked after Adélaïde, whose health was often precarious. Morris noted on one occasion: 'Madame being ill, I find her feet in warm water, and when she is about to take them out, one of her women employed in that operation, the Bishop employs himself in warming her bed, and I look on. It is curious enough to see a Reverend father of the Church engaged in this pious operation.'[44]

Charles-Maurice, who never seems to have suffered much from sexual jealousy, evidently played his part with good humour. The Bishop had, in any case, a greater hold over his mistress than Morris could match, for he was the father of her child.[45] Charles de Flahaut – the Christian name an implicit acceptance by Charles-Maurice of his paternity – was born on 21 April 1785. Charles was the first (though probably not the last) of Talleyrand's illegitimate children, and the only son.

Talleyrand's clerical status was no great impediment to his personal life. Moreover, he still had some credit as the most prominent renegade prelate. On 7 June he proposed on behalf of the Committee of the Constitution that the anniversary of 14 July should be marked by a special public mass in honour of the 'Federation' of France. This Messe de la Fédération should be held in the Champs-de-Mars. Naturally enough, it being a very political affair, no prelate more suitable than himself could be found to celebrate it. Unfortunately, he had had little experience of the liturgy. A colourful, and even credible, anecdote describes the bishop of Autun practising the required ritual at home, using the chimney piece as an altar, with Mirabeau acting as server. When the latter raised the bishop's chasuble at the elevation, Charles-Maurice's dog Pirame leapt on him, barking loudly. Whether accurate or not, the story accurately portrays the frivolous, indeed blasphemous, attitude with which the Revolution's favourite prelate approached his religious duty.[46] This is confirmed by another anecdote retailed by Talleyrand's future colleague Pasquier, who had heard it many times from Lafayette. When the solemnly vested bishop of Autun, approaching the high altar the following day, passed by Lafayette resplendent in his National Guard uniform, he muttered to him: 'Don't make me laugh!'[47]

Arnault did not yet know Talleyrand by sight. But he was among the congregation of some 500,000 who that day were assembled in the rain on the Champ-de-Mars. A huge altar had been erected in the middle of the open space. He watched as a prelate advanced towards it, mitre on head and crosier in hand, 'not with the firmest of tread but with a firm countenance, a bishop who, with truly patriotic generosity, cast streams of holy water and blessings upon the people, the army and also the court. "It's the abbé de Périgord, it's the abbé de Talleyrand, it's the bishop of Autun," people said.' Arnault then remembered the unknown cleric he had seen in Versailles a year earlier.[48]

Charles-Maurice told Adélaïde that he considered the occasion 'ridiculous'. Sieyès had speculated that no more than 500 of the huge crowd were actually Christians. Talleyrand considered that the figure was too large – which he regretted, because he thought the fear of hell was socially useful.[49] But while the two cynical clerics exchanged quips about it, the Mass of the Federation was a noteworthy political success. And if what he told Vitrolles many years later can be believed, the bishop of Autun followed his public triumph with a prolonged session of heavy and successful gambling:

> There were then two gambling houses in Paris. Before dinner I went to one and, *ma foi!*, fortune was mine: I broke the bank. I carried away more gold than my pockets could hold, without counting the bills of the *caisse d'escompte*, and I took it all to the house of Mme de Laval, where I dined. In the evening, I went to the other game with every confidence of winning. I broke the bank there too. I came back once more to Mme de Laval's in order to show her the gold and the bills. I was covered in them. Even my hat was full.[50]

But Talleyrand's episcopal status would shortly involve him in an enterprise whose consequences would haunt him until the end of his life: the establishment of the Civil Constitution of the Clergy. In his memoirs he deliberately minimizes his part in the affair, and with good reason. After several months of debate, the measure was finally promulgated by the National Assembly in August, and in November the Assembly imposed the fatal clause requiring all clerics to take an oath of loyalty. After a month of vain delay, Louis XVI accepted the measure. Sixty clerics, led by the abbé Grégoire, took the oath on the first day, as did Charles-Maurice, without any publicity, on the next (28 December). He felt no scruples, and he had the utmost contempt for those who evinced any. He wrote to Adélaïde: 'I am tired of all the cavilling about the oath required by the Assembly. If my brothers in Jesus Christ were not mad, they would follow my example.'[51] In similar vein, he would pour scorn on those prelates who had the day before (4 January) publicly refused the oath in the Assembly: 'The hypocrites! They have really created a fine masterpiece! You will doubtless have noticed how studied their speeches were and how affected their resignation. . .They well knew that they were running no great risk in exchanging their episcopal mitres for a sham martyrdom.'[52]

Naturally, his enemies in the diocese of Autun were becoming incandescent. At one level, the diocesan administrative machine had continued to function. On the day he celebrated mass in the Champs-de-Mars, the bishop of Autun thoughtfully addressed a letter to his flock urging them to reform their 'moral depravity' and 'irreligion' to win back God's favour for France. But when the clergy of the diocese received a letter from him defending the Civil Constitution as a return to the 'most pure laws of the Church', and urging them to take the oath as he had, there was an outburst of recrimination. The majority eventually followed his example, but the recalcitrant minority sent him a letter that began, 'your apostasy has surprised no one'.[53] And nor should it have done.

Discord in distant Autun could safely be ignored. But as one of only seven bishops to take the oath, it was much more difficult for Charles-Maurice to forget ecclesiastical matters in general, as he by now certainly wished. On 13 January 1791 Charles-Maurice sent his resignation as bishop of Autun to the King. It was duly accepted on 22 January. Doubtless he felt liberated, and for once the memoirs acquire an authentic contemporary note: '[I] submitted my resignation from the bishopric of Autun, and my only thought was of distancing myself from the first career I had pursued. I placed myself at the disposal of events, and provided that I remained French, everything suited me. The Revolution promised new destinies for the nation; I followed in its steps and I shared its fortunes.'[54]

Yet if he imagined that he was truly free of his clerical past, he would soon be disillusioned. Talleyrand clearly thought of his episcopal office as an office of state that could be taken up or laid down at will. Indeed, that is precisely how on 20 January he explained the matter to the administrators of the district of Autun: he had resigned, he told them, simply because retaining his bishopric was incompatible with his recent election as one of the administrators of the district of Paris.[55] But, of course, that is not how Catholic theology, or the Pope, viewed it.

Nor did it suit the interests of the state itself at this point to regard Talleyrand's bishopric in this fashion. This was because the refusal to take the oath by the great majority of the bishops – including Charles-Maurice's uncle, the archbishop of Reims – and their consequent removal from their sees, threatened to render the Constitutional Church stillborn. New bishops had to be consecrated if there were to continue to be new priests. And no priests, no Church – or rather simply an underground Catholic Church supported by Rome and the

Emigration. So the former bishop of Autun had briefly to be called back into service.

In his memoirs, Talleyrand absurdly claims that he agreed to consecrate new schismatic bishops in order to prevent France from falling into Presbyterianism. But, in fact, he had little choice. Even the juror bishops were most unwilling to consecrate, knowing the drastic ecclesiastical penalties that the perpetuation of schism traditionally incurred from the Holy See.

So on 24 February the bishop of Autun, assisted by two bishops without dioceses in France, Gobel, coadjutor of the bishop of Basel and Miroudot, bishop of Babylon, consecrated bishops for the vacant sees of Quimper and Soissons. In fact, during February and March he would perform canonical confirmations of fifteen others, including Gobel as archbishop of Paris.[56] It was, however, the first consecration, of 24 February, which provoked in Charles-Maurice another psychological crisis, though he subsequently sought to disguise it.

In 1792, and in order to while away the tedium of the journey from London to Paris, Talleyrand told a colleague about these events. On the eve of the planned consecrations, the bishop of Autun apparently discovered that each of his episcopal collaborators had developed an attack of nerves and that they intended to pull out. In order to force their hand, he threatened first one and then the other that he would shoot himself with a little pistol that he brandished: at this, both agreed to continue. The consecrations were accordingly performed in the Oratorian chapel in the rue Saint-Honoré.[57] But the truth is rather different, as Gouverneur Morris reveals. It was, in fact, Talleyrand, not his fellow bishops, who fell into terror for his life, presumably from assassination by a Catholic loyalist. Charles-Maurice went into hiding before the consecration. He made out his will and left it for Mme de Flahaut with a note which suggested to her that he was planning suicide. Naturally, he afterwards laughed it all off as a misunderstanding.[58]

Charles-Maurice adopted a similar tone of mockery in response to the inevitable papal condemnation of his actions. On 11 March Pius VI in the brief *Quod Aliquantum* expressed his sorrow that the bishop of Autun had taken the oath to the Civil Constitution. On 13 April in the brief *Charitas*, the (now former) bishop was suspended from his episcopal functions and was given forty days' grace after which he would suffer all the penalties of excommunication. Charles-Maurice gave no direct reply. But in a letter to his friend Lauzun he wrote: 'You know the news – excommunication. Come and console me over supper. Everyone is going to refuse me fire and water: so this evening we shall have only cold meats and *vin frappé*.'[59]

Soon, however, the Revolution would take a direction that, for Charles-Maurice among others, was no laughing matter.

4

Apprentice Diplomat

BY THE SPRING of 1791, unencumbered with even the lightest
duties from his now abandoned bishopric, Charles–Maurice was
at last free to pursue his public career. Unfortunately, the political
climate was no longer propitious for moderates, technical experts or,
indeed, men of peace of any description. Talleyrand revealingly confessed to Morris that he had accepted his appointment as an administrator of the Paris *département*, because this was the 'only door now
open'.[1] He was, in fact, one of a group of 'Constitutionalists', that is
constitutional monarchists, elected at the time, including Sieyès,
La Rochefoucauld and Mirabeau. He had also been trying to make
financial provision for eventualities, telling Adélaïde that he was planning to place funds abroad 'in case of shipwreck'.[2]

On 2 April the political world was shaken by news of the death of
Mirabeau. Talleyrand had, of course, known of its imminence. He
had been with Mirabeau at the start of his final illness and had seen
him on his deathbed. He had heard the dying man's fateful warning
that he took with him to the grave 'the last shreds of the monarchy'.[3]
It was in answer to a question from Charles–Maurice that Mirabeau,
now unable to speak, wrote down his last poignant words: 'It is time
to sleep.'[4] (It went the rounds of Paris that the former bishop of Autun
was a 'confessor worthy of the penitent'.)[5]

But was he much moved by the death of his old friend and rival?
Perhaps not. He had drily remarked to Dumont, on leaving
Mirabeau's room, that the dead man had 'dramatized his death'.[6] Nor
did that drama prevent Charles–Maurice from quickly calculating
what advantage might be gained. When Morris told him that there
was now a political vacancy that he should strive to fill, he replied
that his thoughts were already running along the same lines.[7] Yet the

problems in doing so were, in fact, insuperable. Unlike Mirabeau, Talleyrand was no popular orator. The two men's views might coincide; their characters and accomplishments were profoundly different. Talleyrand was a counsellor not a leader. This might not of itself have proved fatal, if Louis XVI were someone who could appreciate and act upon good counsel. But then, had he been so, the monarchy's circumstances would never, as Dumont observed, have reached their perilous state.[8]

For the last six months of his life, Mirabeau had been seeking to gain control of the government, not in order to advance the Revolution but to halt and in certain respects reverse it. He was as serious as Charles-Maurice about the need to restore order, by force if necessary, while there was still time to save the monarchy.[9] Talleyrand later recalled his friend saying scornfully to some zealous anti-monarchists that even if the monarchy were abolished, France would still not be ready for a republic, though perhaps it would for a 'Commonwealth' – that is a military dictatorship on the model of Cromwell's England.[10]

It was, therefore, very much in pursuit of the programme espoused by Mirabeau that Talleyrand now, once again, secretly approached the royal court. His earlier intermediary, the comte d'Artois, was no longer available, since he was now an *émigré*. As a result the initiative was undertaken through Arnaud de Laporte, *intendant* of the royal civil list, a potential source of financial subsidy and thus precisely the kind of contact that best suited Charles-Maurice in all respects. The details are hazy. Talleyrand says nothing in his memoirs. Indeed, when in exile he mendaciously denied that he had had any such dealings at all. But the evidence is clear; and it would prove damning, despite his protestations. After the abolition of the monarchy, the so-called 'iron cupboard' in the Tuileries was opened to reveal bundles of incriminating papers, some of which concerned Charles-Maurice. On 16 April Laporte is shown there complaining that Talleyrand and his friends had failed to fulfil the agreements they had made. Worse still, on 22 April Laporte sent a note to the King from the bishop of Autun; the note itself, as Charles-Maurice would later point out, was missing, but the covering letter clearly reveals the contents. It speaks of Talleyrand as wishing 'to serve Your Majesty. [He] has had me say that Your Majesty could test his zeal and his trustworthiness by showing him some points that you would like, either from the *département* [of Paris] or from the National Assembly. If he succeeds in having executed what you lay down, you will have proof of his zeal.'[11]

Another note of 3 May, also found in the iron cupboard, informed Louis that the bishop of Autun was going to make a speech in the Assembly on religion and even appended a summary.[12] It seems that Talleyrand used the religious question to try to gain influence with the King. His speech of 7 May, therefore, struck an interesting balance. It justified all the measures that had been taken in connection with the Civil Constitution of the Clergy, declared that there was no schism, and appealed (in traditional Gallican fashion) to a future and better informed Pope than Pius VI. But it defended the relatively liberal attitude taken by the Paris *département* towards the non-juror ('refractory') clergy, allowing them at least limited use of churches. With some boldness, Talleyrand claimed for the non-jurors the full rights of freedom of conscience guaranteed by the Declaration of the Rights of Man in the new Constitution, which he, of course, had helped write.[13]

Talleyrand's negotiations with the court yielded nothing. But the legacy of Mirabeau, even if it would not lead Charles-Maurice to the heights of power, still conveyed some benefits. So he succeeded to the places vacated by Mirabeau's death on both the Diplomatic Committee of the Assembly and the Directory of the *département* of Paris. The second of these posts was both more important and more politically sensitive, and thus dangerous, as Charles-Maurice would discover. But for the moment it reinforced his position.

On 20 June the royal family attempted to flee France, but were arrested at Varennes. The monarchy itself was now openly attacked. Charles-Maurice finally gave up on seeking advancement for himself from that quarter, though he continued to fight to preserve the institution. When the Jacobin Club broke up in July, on the issue of Louis XVI's dethronement, he would be among those who left behind the Revolutionary minority to set up the (Constitutionalist) Feuillants Club.[14]

At the same time, Charles-Maurice continued to adopt the safe but dull expedient of placing his technical expertise at the service of the state. In September he presented a lengthy report on public education to the Assembly. Like his earlier initiative for the reform of weights and measures, the report has acquired historical significance because of what followed it – in this case, the modern secular, centralized French education system. Unlike Talleyrand's earlier contributions, it bears few of his own distinctive stylistic marks, and it may be assumed that alongside the distinguished experts whose assistance he admitted he also employed a large team of draughtsmen. In the new dispensation, education in France will be universal, for both sexes and at all ages. At its heart will be knowledge of the French Constitution. And at the head of the whole structure will be an Institut national, which 'unites all [and] perfects all'.[15] Charles-Maurice's association with the Institut (under its different appellations) would be of some importance in his future career. For now, the report merely burnished his reforming credentials at a useful juncture.

This was all the more important because, with the new Constitution accepted and promulgated, the National or Constituent Assembly (Constituante) was dissolved at the end of September and yielded its place to a new and short-lived Legislative Assembly (Législative). Charles-Maurice was not a member of the new body. Like all members of the Constituante he was prevented from standing in the elections. Still more frustrating, the retiring deputies were forbidden from undertaking any public functions for two years. He was, of course, still a member of the Paris Directory, but trying to control the passions of the Paris mob, while watching others exercise the great offices of state, held few attractions. Such were the circumstances in which the future international statesman made his first foray into diplomacy.

In the memoirs, Talleyrand gives his own account:

The [Feuillant] government of the day, of which M. Necker was no longer a part, felt that it was useful for the monarchy to contact the main courts of Europe to ask that some of them should not take up arms and that the others should disarm. The leaders of the second [Legislative] Assembly, known under the name of Girondins, had demanded this move, persuaded as they were that it would not be accepted by the royal government. They were wrong. M. de Lessart, at that time Minister of Foreign Affairs, seized upon the idea and proposed that I should go to England for this purpose. I wanted to get away for a while; I was tired, disgusted, and although I knew well that this mission had little chance of success, I accepted.[16]

But, as is frequently the case, Talleyrand's version conceals as much as it reveals. The government's motive for sending him to England was, indeed, to try to prevent a general European coalition forming against France. It is also easy to understand why he might have been bored enough to accept the mission. But the prospects of securing British neutrality, perhaps even benevolent neutrality, were not as remote as he suggests. Moreover, Charles-Maurice arrived in London with a separate, unofficial agenda to press.

Of the Feuillant government ministers, only Narbonne, Minister for War, knew about Talleyrand's secret mission. Extraordinarily, Lessart was altogether unaware of it. The Foreign Minister was simply intent on obtaining reassurances that Britain would stay out of any forthcoming war with Austria. But a group of French and English bankers wanted to go far beyond this, extending the Franco-British commercial treaty of 1786 and consolidating it into a political alliance. Charles-Maurice acted as an adviser to one of these, Barthélemy Hüber, a director of the French East India Company (the Compagnie des Indes) and the Paris agent of the London bankers Bourdieu, Choller and Bourdieu. The plan centred initially on the island of Tobago, which had been ceded to France in 1783, but which was also encumbered with a large debt to London bankers that the French government had not paid. These London financiers, after fruitless litigation, now offered £200,000 in order to secure the retrocession of Tobago to Britain. (Charles-Maurice's commission was £40,000, which he used to speculate on property in the – then undeveloped – Champs-Élysées.)

Hüber and Talleyrand also hoped to have France grant substantial interests to the British in the Île de Bourbon (today's Réunion) in exchange for a loan of £50 million from Britain and a further loan from Holland, secured on shares in the *caisse d'escompte* and the Compagnie des Indes. The final step envisaged was still more ambitious. Britain was to abandon its alliance with the Habsburg Emperor while France was to renounce the so-called Family Pact with the other branch of the Bourbon family ruling Spain. Both powers would then set about 'liberating' Spanish colonies in the New World to their mutual commercial profit. This final goal would find its way into Talleyrand's diplomatic strategy on future occasions. At this stage, however, the whole grand scheme proved unworkable, mainly because of the uncontrollable Revolution that was taking place in France.[17]

Charles-Maurice left Paris on 14 January 1792, stayed a few days in Dover, and arrived in London ten days later. He was accompanied by his friend the duc de Biron, who had been sent by Narbonne to buy horses for the army. His presence, though, turned out to be a mixed blessing. Nor was the atmosphere politically friendly. As Charles-Maurice complained to Lessart, the English press were already reporting that he had been snubbed in meetings with both Pitt and the British Foreign Secretary, Lord Grenville. In fact, he had as yet been unable to see either. The Whig opposition, though, quickly sought him out.[18] And this too was a mixed blessing.

Talleyrand's position was difficult. Dumont later thought that one problem was his manner. In diplomatic dealings he was cold, reserved and almost silent on first acquaintance. The English, who even then had strong preconceived impressions of what Frenchmen were supposed to be like, were disappointed, because they did not find in Charles-Maurice 'the vivacity, nor the familiarity, nor the indiscretion, nor the gaiety' they expected.[19] He was soon showing symptoms of the frustration that is the lot of ambassadors left devoid of regular instructions. He complained that his letters to Paris went unanswered. But, then, some of his ideas were not very realistic, for example his suggestion that the despatch of a squadron of the French navy would force the British to negotiate. The situation was now also greatly complicated by the arrest of his colleague Biron for debts in connection with the horses he had purchased. Attempts to plead diplomatic immunity failed. Talleyrand was convinced that French royalist *émigrés* in London were behind it all, and had to agree to pay £2,000 of the debt incurred. To make his mood worse, he found himself traduced in the French press.[20]

Although he was not about to tell the French Foreign Minister, Talleyrand had, in fact, been coldly received in London. Lord Grenville apparently considered him 'deep and dangerous'. Pitt's treatment, when they met, was particularly hurtful. Charles-Maurice had spent six weeks with him in the summer of 1783, when Pitt took advantage of the peace with France and of the Commons recess to come with his friends Eliot and Wilberforce over to Reims in order to learn French.[21] Charles-Maurice had even made available to these English guests his own apartment in the abbey of Saint-Thierry, where he regularly lived with his uncle, the archbishop. But when they now met again, Pitt made no reference to their earlier acquaintance and engaged in only the most cursory conversation. Many years later, such ingratitude still rankled.[22] Charles-Maurice's presentation at court was, if anything, even more humiliating. George III paid almost no attention to him at all, and the Queen just turned her back. This, of course, set a trend. Talleyrand found himself excluded from polite society, except that of the opposition – and those contacts, which excited government suspicion, made his diplomatic position yet more difficult.[23]

Charles-Maurice's mood improved, however, once he finally managed to have a long discussion with Lord Grenville; though whether Grenville's own mood was improved by his interlocutor's manner is more doubtful, for he had to listen to a lengthy speech, and was even on several occasions told not to interrupt.[24]

Talleyrand denied that France was in a state of anarchy. There was bound to be some agitation after the great Revolution of three years previously. But order was emerging. Turning to the threat which some in Britain believed was posed by the Revolution, he explicitly rejected any idea of propagandizing by France. Indeed, he claimed that Frenchmen would 'never cease to see in [the English] our elders in liberty and our models in its defence'.

Finally, addressing the secret orders he had received, Charles-Maurice spoke warmly about the mutual harmony that should exist between Britain and France. Only prejudice had divided the two countries. Shared economic interests would in the long run bring them together. He would like to see each power guarantee the other's possessions throughout the world. Above all, Britain's interests lay in a long period of peace, because, he reminded Grenville, 'peace is the soul of your trade and your credit, and credit is the soul of your state'.[25]

This account comes from his despatch to Lessart and was thus subject to self-interested polishing. But the ideas it contains are clearly Talleyrand's own, rather than those of the French government of the day. Indeed, they were, in part, addressed to that government – as much a tutorial in diplomatic strategy and tactics as an informative despatch. This fact was not lost on Lessart, who wrote back objecting to much of what his unofficial envoy had said. The Foreign Minister had also somehow learned that Talleyrand had in mind the retrocession of Tobago. Charles-Maurice responded by saying that he had not proposed such a move but thought it valuable if it led to an extension of £3 or £4 million credit, which would strengthen the French exchange rate.[26]

Grenville's own reply, when it came, was friendly but non-committal. Britain had no wish, he said, to profit from France's problems. But he could give no reply to Charles-Maurice's specific points because of the envoy's unofficial status. Talleyrand believed that this was true and not just an excuse. He remained optimistic, because Britain wanted peace so as to reduce its taxes and its debt. He thought that even should French troops enter the Netherlands, Britain would escape from its obligations under the Hague Treaty of 1790 and avoid declaring war. (In this he was too sanguine.) He added that France must now urgently send an officially accredited ambassador with powers to negotiate. And he impertinently warned Lessart that he could find himself in trouble if he failed to do so.[27] The threat was superfluous. By the time his letter to Lessart arrived, the minister had been removed from office and was under arrest.

Even before the change, Talleyrand had been planning to return to Paris. He now arrived on 10 March 1792 to find his friend Narbonne removed from the Ministry of War and General Dumouriez installed at Foreign Affairs. With the Girondins in the ascendant, European war was fast approaching. Paradoxically, the immediate result meant that greater importance was attached to the peace mission, because of the urgent necessity of ensuring British neutrality.

Charles-Maurice's visit to Paris lasted six weeks. He had brought back from London two Swiss advisers: Étienne Dumont, who was in the service of the Whig magnate, the Marquis of Lansdowne, and his associate Jacques-Antoine Du Roveray, who usefully was on good terms with the Girondin leaders Brissot and Clavière.[28] Unfortunately, Du Roveray fell seriously ill and was confined to bed for a month. Meanwhile, Dumont had to kick his heels, with little or no sight of Talleyrand, who plunged into intensive politicking. This was necessary in order to neutralize the prejudices that leading Girondins held against him. He was successful. They quickly had to accept that he was the best available candidate to direct the mission. A suitable front man as formal ambassador was also needed. François de Chauvelin was finally selected for the role and, being young and ambitious, was initially keen to accept. But as it became clear that he would have to take instructions from Talleyrand and be subject to strict surveillance by his colleagues, the nominee developed a bad case of pique. Eventually, Dumouriez gave them all twenty-four hours to leave Paris. Otherwise, he threatened, another mission would be appointed.

Thus chastened, the delegation, travelling in two carriages, departed at four o'clock the next morning. With Talleyrand, Chauvelin, Du Roveray and Dumont went a number of others. Dominique-Joseph Garat had acquired public recognition by his reports on the proceedings of the National Assembly in the *Journal de Paris*; he was also a would-be historian, which may have provided the main incentive for his participation. Above all, he was a wit, and that, it seems, was why Charles-Maurice wanted him along.[29] Charles-Frédéric (Karl-Friedrich) Reinhard acted as secretary to the mission. He was a Protestant ex-cleric from Württemberg and this was his first foray into French diplomacy. It was also his first contact with Charles-Maurice, and he would remain over many years the latter's confidant and collaborator. One other member of the group deserves mention. Desrenaudes, who had known Charles-Maurice since the latter's time at the seminary, accompanied the mission and did whatever secret business was required of him.[30]

It was Chauvelin who arrived in England first, on Friday, 27 April, to take up residence in Portman Square, where his main initial concern was to retrieve some of his belongings detained by the zealous British customs. Two days later the rest of the party appeared. It was arranged that Chauvelin would formally present his credentials at court on 2 May.[31]

Before his departure, Talleyrand had obtained from Louis XVI, and probably drafted for his signature, a warm letter of personal recommendation addressed to George III. It did not even mention Chauvelin by name but emphasized instead the primacy of Talleyrand. Louis, it said, 'placed the highest importance on the success of the [proposed] alliance'.[32] Unfortunately, the good effect of this letter was diminished by the fact that it was widely published in French newspapers before it was received by the British monarch – to Talleyrand's great annoyance.[33]

There were other irritations too. The French found themselves subject to a host of minor snubs, and on occasion responded in kind. One day at court, Pitt placed himself between Chauvelin and George III, so that the King would not have to acknowledge him. Chauvelin then deliberately trod on Pitt's foot, forcing him to back away. What seemed the excessive size of the mission provoked adverse comment in the British press, which speculated that Charles-Maurice and his colleagues would try to spread Revolutionary propaganda. British supporters of the mission were sympathetic but divided in their counsels as to what to do. Sir Samuel Romilly, the liberal-minded law reformer, suggested a public disclaimer and a threat of legal action.[34] More realistically, Lansdowne recommended that the French try to rise above it all.

Talleyrand was disturbed by the political implications of such hostility. He accordingly wrote (in the name of Chauvelin) a long despatch to Dumouriez, urging the French government to recognize once and for all that no revolution was imminent across the Channel, and to act accordingly. He complained that the task of his mission was made immeasurably harder by widespread suspicion that its purpose was to destabilize Britain. Unhelpful articles in the French press and reports of disorder in Paris fed these fears and so played into the hands of those hostile to France.[35]

Despite this, the mission could claim some success. Britain promised to fulfil the terms of the existing trade treaty and to remain neutral in the war between Austria and France. In fact, Talleyrand's main concern was now what was happening back in France, where his and his fellow moderates' prospects were looking ever bleaker. He was denounced by name in the French press as part of an Orléanist faction out to betray the country.[36] On 20 June a mob invaded the Tuileries and laid hands on the King. Having gained permission to return for consultations – there was now a new Foreign Minister, the marquis de Chambonas – Charles–Maurice left London on 6 July.

He walked straight into a new crisis. Shortly before his return to Paris, the Directory of the *département* of Paris had declared the suspension of the city's mayor, Pétion, for his complicity in the events of 20 June. This provoked the fury of the left. Under mob pressure, the decision was humiliatingly reversed by the Legislative Assembly on 13 July. It was a crushing defeat for Talleyrand and his colleagues. But there was worse. Knowing where Talleyrand's sympathies lay, the Queen publicly displayed her favour towards him at the Feast of the Federation. This confirmed the left's suspicions.[37] His political position was impossible, so on 20 July he resigned from the Paris Directory.

By now the imminent threat posed by foreign armies dominated politics. And the real threat from abroad fuelled imagined threats at home. The Legislative Assembly voted itself emergency powers. On 25 July the mainland European powers solemnly declared war on France. Under more mob pressure, the Assembly voted on 10 August to establish a republic. Two days later the royal family was incarcerated in the Temple prison. Contradictory rumours later circulated about Charles–Maurice's conduct at this time. One account (which is certainly false) has him secretly counselling the Bourbons' imprisonment. In truth, he was on the fringe of attempts to engineer their escape, planned by his friend Liancourt and others.[38] But Talleyrand's main preoccupation by now was self-preservation, and that meant departure from France.

Not for the first time, the memoirs give a somewhat misleading account:

> After the day of 10 August 1792, I asked the provisional executive authorities for a temporary mission to London. I chose as the objective of this mission a scientific question in which I had to some extent the right to involve myself, because it related to a proposal that I had earlier made to the Constituent Assembly. It was about the establishment throughout the realm of a uniform system of weights and measures. Once the accuracy of this system had been verified by the

scientists of the whole of Europe, it could subsequently have been generally adopted. So it was useful to consult with England about this objective.

My real aim was to leave France, where it seemed to me futile and even dangerous to remain. But I did not want to leave except with a regular passport, so that I did not close for ever the door on my return.[39]

The second part of this assertion is true. But the suggestion that he sought, let alone obtained, an official commission to discuss weights and measures with the British appears baseless. It is also odd; for, by the time he came to write his memoirs, he needed no excuse for his departure to escape the approaching Terror. On this, as on other occasions, he simply became so accustomed to repeating a convenient lie that he ceased to be aware of the truth.[40]

Charles-Maurice was very fortunate that one of his colleagues and collaborators on the Paris Directory had been Danton, who was now Minister of Justice and effective head of the government.[41] But Danton was not going to risk his reputation by entrusting such a suspect figure with an official mission. Nor was he going to deliver up the precious passport without exacting a price. It was, therefore, almost certainly as a *quid pro quo* that Talleyrand drafted the memorandum that was issued by the government on 18 August for use by its envoys with foreign powers, particularly Britain, justifying the destruction of the monarchy.

It is not a very convincing article of propaganda, which is hardly surprising since its author would not himself have been convinced. The document lays all the blame on the former King for having undermined the Constitution. In response to such bad faith, the people of Paris had, therefore, bravely stormed the Tuileries. It also includes a provocative comparison between the overthrow of the Bourbons and the British Glorious Revolution of 1688.[42] But it doubly served Talleyrand's purpose, if not that of France, because it helped get him out of the country and in time he would use his authorship of the tract to prove his Republican credentials.[43]

As the allies advanced, tension in Paris heightened. Charles-Maurice pressed the authorities as hard as he dared in order to obtain his passport. Barère would recall encountering him at half past eleven at night on 31 August at the Ministry of Justice in the place Vendôme. He was wearing his hat, coat, buckskin breeches and boots, evidently ready to depart on a journey. Talleyrand explained, disingenuously, that he was due to leave the next morning for London on an official mission and that Danton was to give him his papers.[44] But the meeting, when it finally took place, was evidently to no avail. There was, of course, no mission; and for the moment there were no papers authorizing his departure either.

Those who could do so were now leaving. To his credit, Charles-Maurice still spared a thought for his friends. After the disorders of 10 August, he had his carriage transport Narbonne and Beaumetz around Paris during daylight hours, taking them to different locations each evening. Eventually, with the assistance of Mme de Staël, they managed to get out of the city, Narbonne posing as a cart driver and Beaumetz as a victualler.[45] On 2 September – the first day of the September Massacres – Charles-Maurice also urged Gouverneur Morris to leave Paris. A few days later, he repeated the advice: he professed no confidence that the Duke of Brunswick's approaching army would manage to take the city, and in this he was proved right.[46]

At last, the passport arrived. On 10 September, Charles-Maurice departed. He could now afford to make a leisurely journey, the immediate crisis having passed, and he finally arrived in London on 18 September. He had encountered en route large numbers of priests, also fleeing the country. He noted in a letter to his friend and long-time financial collaborator, Maximilien Radix de Sainte-Foy, that these clergy were already sustained by money from England, and he correctly deduced that the British would now use every means to achieve the overthrow of the French régime.[47] That, though, would soon cease to be his concern.

5

Exile

～～

TALLEYRAND'S CIRCUMSTANCES IN London were not initially dis-
pleasing. He moved into Herring House, 11/12 Kensington
Square, where an old friend and former lover, Charlotte de La
Châtre, kept house for him. He did not lack congenial company.
During his earlier mission he had come to enjoy the friendship of
Whig politicians and the patronage of the Marquis of Lansdowne,
and these sympathizers continued to stand by him. He was also one
of a large expatriate community, as London was now receiving the
second wave of exiles from the Revolution. These liberal monarchists, or Constitutionalists, were viewed with the greatest disfavour
by the first-wave *émigrés* and their Tory patrons. They were also the
object of distinct suspicion by the bulk of the population, which
increased with the news of atrocities from France. These pressures,
though, only reinforced the mutual friendships and solidarity of the
liberal exiles.

Mme de La Châtre was passionately in love with another political
refugee, the marquis de Jaucourt, who had managed to flee to
Switzerland thanks to Mme de Staël, before joining the group in
London. So too, of course, had Narbonne and Beaumetz. Both came
straight to Kensington Square on their arrival in England.

Other friends and political allies of Charles-Maurice arrived as
well. Liancourt, his main supporter in the old royal court – and future
comrade in his American exile – was one of these. The political moderate, playwright and future academician and philanthropist, the
marquis de Lally-Tollendal, was another. Mathieu de Montmorency,
the son of Charles-Maurice's old friend the vicomtesse de Laval, had
been an early radical, on the left of the National Assembly, but he, too,
now fled the storm. In London, Montmorency was passing through

an uncharacteristic phase of level-headedness: later he would become an ultra-royalist reactionary.

As well as the men, an array of beautiful and sophisticated women were members of the group, among them Adélaïde de Flahaut. She had, it seems, fallen out of love with Charles-Maurice, but they were still friends, their common interest now centring on their son Charles, who accompanied his mother on her journey. Having escaped from Paris thanks to the intervention of John Petty, Earl of Wycombe, son of the Marquis of Lansdowne, it was natural that she should spend a good deal of time with her new friend on his father's estates. (Both were at different times her lovers.) That other former lover, Charles-Maurice, was also a frequent visitor to Bowood. He spent his days fishing or correcting the text of Adélaïde's novel, *Adèle de Senanges*. But Kensington Square was the social centre of the group. Sometimes as many as eighteen would sit down to dinner there, to discuss politics and swap information about absent and endangered friends.[1]

Charles-Maurice had no plans to remain a permanent exile, and had taken great trouble to leave France with the blessing of the authorities. He even hoped to retain some political influence. So that November he composed a long memorandum which was sent not only to the French Foreign Ministry but also to Danton. As the first of the (rather few) serious analyses that reveal Talleyrand's thinking about foreign relations, it is of considerable importance. It is essentially an extended essay on the application of what can be termed a liberal theory of foreign policy to the circumstances of Revolutionary France.

Talleyrand offers a radically new conception of alliances and treaties, in which these instruments of policy are drained of aggressive purpose and become, instead, the means of promoting the seminal ideas of 1789. As in his later diplomatic thinking, he advocates restraint, moderation and limits:

> If France contracts alliances, it will. . .not be for its own interest, but for that of the states that it has liberated or which it wishes to liberate. It will be in order to hasten the complete development of the great system of the emancipation of peoples. That is where the unique purpose of its present policy should reside, because it is there that resides the true principle of the general and immutable interest of the human race. . .

France must, therefore, remain circumscribed within its proper limits. It owes this to its glory, to its justice, to its reason, to its interest, and to the interest of those who will be free because of it.

. . .Of all the parts of the old system, that which is most in contradiction with our laws, our opinions and our new customs – that of which, in consequence, the traces ought to fade with every passing day – is the matter of alliances. . .It has finally been learned that the true primacy, the only one that is useful and rational, the only one that suits men who are free and enlightened, is to be master in one's own domain, and never to have the ridiculous pretension to be master in another's.[2]

Equally characteristic of Talleyrand's thinking is his emphasis on the relationship between economics and power, and specifically the importance of trade in assessing long-term strategic interests:

The only relationships that France can, therefore, at this moment seek to undertake and to expand with England are industrial and commercial. [But beyond that], one other object of the greatest importance, not just for France and England, but for the interests of the New and the Old Worlds, must focus the two countries' attention and unite their common efforts. That is the independence of the Spanish colonies in Peru, Mexico etc. The vessels of France and England together will go and open up – in the Pacific, in the South Seas and in the South Atlantic – free trade with this immense part of the West Indies.[3]

But by the time the memorandum came to be considered, its author's political reputation in Paris was in ruins. He had been implicated, as has already been mentioned, by highly incriminating documents discovered in Louis XVI's safe. This damning information was relayed to the Convention by Roland, one of the signatories of Charles-Maurice's passport for London and now Minister of the Interior. On 5 December he was declared under accusation as a traitor and his papers were sealed.

Charles-Maurice fought back. A letter from Talleyrand, 'former bishop of Autun to his fellow citizens', dated 12 December from London, was accordingly posted up in Paris in the form of a placard. It was also included on 24 December in *Le Moniteur universel*, the official journal of public record. Charles-Maurice flatly denied all that he had read in the decree about his purported relations with the court.

He brazenly affirmed: 'I have never had any sort of relations, direct or indirect, either with the King or M. Laporte.' In support of its author's Revolutionary and anti-monarchist credentials, the letter included an extract from the address to the King that he had drawn up on 19 April 1791, urging Louis to rid himself of the services of non-juror priests. Charles-Maurice also denied the accusation that he had paid for his passport. That denial, at least, may have been true.[4]

All these efforts were in vain. The following August, an official list of *émigrés* was issued and Talleyrand's name was on it. So were other members of his family, including his mother and his uncle, Alexandre-Angélique. The police were ordered to arrest him if he set foot in France. His Paris lodgings were searched, but revealed nothing of interest. Talleyrand and the French Revolution had definitively parted company.

The moment was a decisive one in the development of his political opinions. He had never, of course, been an unqualified proponent of Revolution. He believed in social order. His culture, his assumptions, his view of himself, all ensured that he could never accept levelling. He was, indeed, the personification of social hierarchy. Yet he was thoroughly imbued with the spirit of the French Enlightenment. In his youth he had met Voltaire and admired him, and he continued to sing his praises to the end of his days. If some of the other *philosophes* incurred his criticism it was more because of their naïveté than their views. They had failed to grasp that ideas have consequences, and so they had undermined order, as Voltaire (he argued) had not.[5] So despite his painful experiences at the hands of the Revolutionary fanatics, he would never be driven to become a reactionary. He would remain a liberal, or at least a liberal conservative, to the end.[6]

But he was appalled by the Revolution, which he now saw in a new light. That autumn he laid bare his feelings in a letter to Lansdowne: 'Those [in France] who remain faithful to Liberty, despite the mask of blood and mud with which atrocious blackguards have concealed her features, are very few. . .From the leaders of the Jacobins, who bow down before butchers, to the most honest citizens, there is nothing today but a chain of baseness and lies, whose first link is lost in the mud.'[7]

Talleyrand's hostility to the régime in France was now heartily reciprocated, which meant that it was more necessary than ever to ensure the favour of the authorities in Britain. On 1 January 1793 he wrote at some length to the Foreign Office to explain what he was doing on British soil. He said that he was involved in no political business, was attached to no party, and was in search only of peace and security, being unable to return home. He was also in England, he explained, in order to oversee the sale of his library, which had been shipped over earlier from France. The sale itself took place in April, but the proceeds did not match his expectations, and they certainly could not sustain a fashionable existence in London. He reluctantly decided that it was not worth publishing the Life of the duc d'Orléans on which he had been working. Potentially more lucrative was the project on which he drew up a memorandum at about this time, for an Indian Bank to be established in Paris. It was intended to attract the funds of British nabobs grown rich in the subcontinent. Naturally, though, such a scheme was impossible in current circumstances, and in fact it remained unfulfilled.[8]

Charles-Maurice was not alone among the exiles in feeling the pinch. The French, accordingly, took to spending time outside London, and were a source of great curiosity to their neighbours. Fanny Burney records in her diary learning, in May 1792, of a group of early arrivals: it was the household of the duc d'Orléans, of which the centre was Mme de Genlis.[9] By September the trickle had become a flood. Fanny's sister, Susanna Phillips, found that Juniper Hall, near the village of Mickleham in Surrey, had been taken by a group comprising the marquise de La Châtre and her son, Narbonne, Montmorency and Jaucourt; and several more were said to be on their way.[10] In November Mrs Phillips made her first visits to Juniper Hall and was immediately charmed by the occupants. The following month she met Talleyrand, who had accepted that he would not now be able to return to France.[11]

Yet his eyes remained focused on events there. When he went to partake of frugal suppers with Mme de Genlis and the Orléans entourage, the talk always returned to the horrors that their mutual friends were undergoing at home.[12] Indeed, by now, the French royal family's sufferings preoccupied everyone. Towards the end of January 1793 news was received at Juniper Hall of the King's execution. The little French colony felt a sense of shame and depression. Narbonne had been planning to return to Paris to testify in his own and Louis's defence. Talleyrand had not. He had no taste for whimsical gallantry.

The news that Mme de Staël would soon be joining her friends in England momentarily raised his spirits. He wrote to her in January: 'If I ever dare to speak of happiness, I am very sure that it will be with you.'[13] She, for her part, was more apprehensive, worrying about what her former lover, Charles-Maurice, might say to the current object of her passion, Narbonne.[14] By February, though, she was effectively presiding over the group. Its members were also by now 'bosom friends' with Fanny Burney and her sister. The Gallic charm did its work: 'There can be nothing imagined more charming, more fascinating, than this colony: between their sufferings and their *agreements* they occupy us almost wholly.'[15] In fact, two very potent sources of attraction were at play. On the one hand, there was the budding relationship between Fanny and her future husband, Alexandre d'Arblay. On the other, there was the seductive personality of Talleyrand.

Not unusually, Fanny Burney's first impression of Charles-Maurice was rather unfavourable, though she acknowledged his intellect. He was 'a man of admirable conversation, quick, terse, *fin*, and yet deep, to the extreme of those four words'.[16] Mme de Staël asked in a whisper how Fanny liked him. 'Not very much,' she replied, 'but I do not know him.' Germaine assured her that he was 'the best of men'. Fanny was soon convinced: 'It is inconceivable what a convert M. de Talleyrand has made of me; I think him now one of the first members, and one of the most charming, of this exquisite set. . .His powers of entertainment are astonishing, both in information and in raillery.'[17]

But no amount of persiflage could disguise the seriousness of the political situation. The execution of Louis XVI was quickly followed by France's declaration of war on Great Britain and Holland. Plots and stratagems were soon afoot aimed at overthrowing the French Revolutionary government.

Talleyrand was quite optimistic about schisms opening up in the ranks of the Revolutionaries, though not, it seems, to the point of acting with imprudence. As he explained to Susanna Phillips: 'To take a side, we ought first to know whether that which would suit us will be strong enough to justify the hope of success, without which it would be silly to side with any party.' But he laughingly added that he would like to fight and 'to thrash those beggarly rascals soundly'.[18]

At the end of August Toulon surrendered to the British fleet. Narbonne, Talleyrand and Mme de Staël all hoped that the seizure of this great naval port could be used as a means to establish a rival centre of authority to Paris. Talleyrand argued the need to establish an assembly there. The government under his scheme, would, naturally enough, consist of the Constitutionalist Party. But, in practice, they could only wait on events, which were directed by a British government that had no faith in the liberal *émigrés*. Talleyrand became quite obsessed with Toulon. Even Narbonne spoke mockingly about 'the Bishop's thousand and one plans'.[19]

But, now and later, Charles-Maurice's understanding of French political realities was remarkably sound. He did not believe in a régime imposed by force alone. As he wrote to Germaine de Staël:

> It is from inside France that can come the only force able to achieve the great objective that the powers have to set themselves. . .People keep on saying that the Constitutionalists do not have a party in France. But France itself, apart from the leaders of the Revolution, is their party. . . The powers, by openly declaring themselves for the Constitution, would not henceforth have much fighting to do, and would have in the very bosom of France thousands of men to help them.[20]

However, no one was listening and events moved quickly. Paris fell into the grip of the Terror. France became a Revolutionary dictatorship where all power resided with the leaders of the Committee of Public Safety. Charles-Maurice gave up hope of a return of the Bourbons. In November he wrote to Mme de Staël the revealing, if hardly prophetic, words: 'The house of Bourbon is finished, as far as France is concerned. There is something to think about.'[21]

Talleyrand's own prospects also looked bleak. He thought that he would have to leave England, but he could not decide whether to seek to join Germaine de Staël in Switzerland.[22] The decision was taken out of his hands. On 28 January 1794 two men arrived at five o'clock in the evening and informed him that, under the terms of the previous year's Alien Act, he was to be expelled from Britain. He had just five days in which to leave the country. In writing to Mme de Staël, he blamed the Emperor of Austria and the King of Prussia for his fate, while in his memoirs he points his finger at the *émigrés*.[23] He persuaded the liberal (and gullible) Lord Lansdowne that it was a plot by exiled French clerics, who could not 'pardon in a bishop a desire to promote the general freedom of public worship'.[24] In any case, it amounted to much the same thing. Despite his bitterness, he put a brave face on it all. Narbonne observed that 'nothing equals [Talleyrand's] calm, his courage, almost his cheerfulness'.[25] He himself wrote: 'At the age of thirty-nine I am beginning a new life, for it is life that I want; I love my friends too much to have other ideas.'[26] Nor were those friends in any happier position. The vicomtesse de Laval had been arrested. Before leaving, he urged Germaine de Staël to do whatever she could to help get her out of 'our horrible France'.[27]

Reviewing the options, he concluded that Europe was too dangerous for him; he would seek haven in the United States. But before accepting the inevitable, he fought a vigorous battle to have the order for his expulsion withdrawn. He wrote to William Windham at the Home Office demanding to know the specifics of the accusation against him.[28] The next day, he sent a further letter to Pitt asking for an explanation, protesting that he had done nothing wrong. He received no reply. So, on 1 February, he asked instead for a suspension of the order for a fortnight, until he could leave on the *William Penn* for Philadelphia. The reprieve was granted; though, because of contrary winds, the ship did not actually set sail until 2 March.

America was not without its attractions. In a letter to Fanny Burney, Charles-Maurice revealed that he intended to improve his English there: and he seems, indeed, to have done so very effectively.[29] Otherwise, though: 'I do not know how long I shall stay in America. If something reasonable and stable should be restored for our unhappy country, I would come back. If Europe is ruined in the next campaign, I shall prepare places of asylum in America for all my friends.'[30]

In later years, Talleyrand made light of the wrench of his departure. He would recall how his loyal Gascon valet, Courtiade, on being told that his master must leave at once and the servant catch the next ship, point blank refused. The problem turned out to be that Talleyrand's best shirts and muslin cravats were with the launderers. 'How in heaven's name,' demanded Courtiade, 'will you be able to make an appearance without them, and in a foreign country too?'[31]

Talleyrand was also accompanied on his journey by Beaumetz, who was determined to make his fortune in the New World. Unfortunately, he turned out to be less adept at this than his travelling companion, and also seems to have suffered a nervous breakdown.[32]

The *William Penn* ran into a violent storm two days out and had to put in for shelter to the Cornish port of Falmouth. Here Talleyrand found himself staying in the same inn as an American, who he initially hoped might provide him with useful introductions. But his fellow guest turned out to be Benedict Arnold, detested as a traitor by all Americans.[33] It was not an encouraging portent. The weather now abated and the *William Penn* left port once more; but, as she headed out into the Atlantic, the going was still rough. For ten days, Charles-Maurice was seasick, before suddenly finding his sea legs. Indeed, he never lost them and even began to enjoy the experience of maritime solitude. On arriving at the mouth of the Delaware River, after thirty-eight days at sea, he wondered whether to continue his journey aboard another ship bound for Calcutta. But it could not take him; and so he and his companions finally disembarked in Philadelphia.[34]

Talleyrand's reputation had preceded him, and for the most part it was not of assistance. True, he was able to send to President Washington a flattering letter of introduction from Lord Lansdowne. But Washington had also received, two years earlier, from Gouverneur Morris, another letter that was more to the point. It described Talleyrand and his friends as notoriously immoral.[35] Despite intercession from the US Secretary of the Treasury, Alexander Hamilton, with whom Talleyrand quickly struck up a close friendship, Washington would not receive him.[36] It was a question of politics. The United States was keen not to annoy the French government; and France was bitterly hostile to Charles-Maurice, even in his distant exile. Indeed, the French ambassador, Joseph Fauchet, had made strong representations on the matter, and continued to put the worst possible gloss on Talleyrand's and Beaumetz's activities.[37]

Fortunately, other Frenchmen were more welcoming – and none more so than Médéric Moreau de Saint-Méry. Originally hailing from the French West Indies, he had been a prominent Revolutionary politician, in Paris and then in the Constituent Assembly, before fleeing France for America in November 1793. After spending some time as a shipping agent first in Norfolk and then in New York, he moved with his family to Philadelphia in October 1794 and started up a newsagents and printers. By chance, he was visiting Philadelphia that May when he saw two men waving wildly at him from a carriage. It turned out to be Talleyrand and Beaumetz. Moreau de Saint-Méry went back to dine with them and they were joined by other political exiles and friends: the marquis de Blacons, the vicomte de Noailles and Omer Talon. Outside, a violent thunderstorm seemed to recall the dangers that they had all escaped.[38]

The French were everywhere. Talleyrand and Beaumetz rented a house in New York that summer. Being just off Broadway, it was well placed to allow them and their guests to watch the 4 July parade. Taking part was a contingent of Revolutionaries, who sang the 'Marseillaise'. The marchers spotted Talleyrand and his friends at the window and shouted insults.[39] Fortunately, the French consul in New York, Antoine de La Forest, was much more friendly and would become Charles-Maurice's political collaborator. Talleyrand was also visited by Hauterive, who had been dismissed as consul as politically suspect and had turned his hand to market gardening.[40] He would become Talleyrand's principal aide in the Ministry of Foreign Affairs.

Among the little group of spectators on that 4 July was also the Dutchman, Theophilus Cazenove, an agent of the Holland Land Company, which bought up land in the state of New York. Talleyrand was already into the business and tried to interest Mme de Staël's rich friends in investing.[41] He himself had mixed with familiarity in the *salons* of Whig magnates with men whose pockets bulged with riches emanating from British India, and he had well-established European banking contacts.[42] Charles-Maurice initially concentrated on persuading potential investors that they would be better indulging in speculation on the exchanges than on land purchase. But they were unconvinced.[43]

More ingenious was the scheme that Talleyrand and Beaumetz proposed to Cazenove in June 1794, a development of the earlier plan for a Paris-based Indian Bank, through which the funds of English nabobs could be used to finance trade with India. Now, however, the discontented nabobs – who, according to Charles-Maurice, were 'the only rich democrats in England' – were to be induced to acquire land in America. This offered them a way to establish their social status and to make their purchases secretly. Perhaps the Indian princes themselves might like to come and settle? Talleyrand offered his services as an agent to go and find out.[44]

As this (stillborn) scheme shows, Talleyrand was by now more interested in land acquisition. He soon had a further incentive to be so. Cazenove learned that rival bankers were interested in purchasing land in Maine (still part of the state of Massachusetts). He, therefore, suggested that Talleyrand and Beaumetz should accompany the Dutchman Jan Huidekoper to view the territory. That September saw the group (which also included Courtiade) heading inland on horseback; Charles-Maurice had a special saddle designed to make it easier to cope with his bad foot. They ascended rivers in canoes, examining the shore, talking to whatever inhabitants they found. Talleyrand was favourably impressed – at least with the commercial potential. Maine was fertile. There were abundant vegetable and cereal crops, though long, cold winters made rearing livestock difficult. Portland, the capital, Charles-Maurice liked greatly. It was attractively located, both accessible and defensible, and already a busy little entrepôt. He was, however, much less favourably disposed towards the inhabitants, whom he considered 'indolent and grasping'. Everything was low and primitive, and the economy amounted to a 'web of reciprocal frauds'.[45]

On returning to Boston, Talleyrand immediately prepared to undertake a further expedition, this time into the north-west of the state of New York, the territory lying between Albany and the Great Lakes. The three principals and Talleyrand's faithful servant were now accompanied by a British speculator and former Indian official, Thomas Law. On 9 October they set off by boat up the Hudson River and arrived without mishap in Albany, where they were entertained by General Schuyler, one of the wealthiest citizens.[46]

Their host was a generous man who had earlier befriended the marquis and marquise de La Tour du Pin-Gouvernet, on their arrival as exiles from Revolutionary France. Talleyrand and the La Tour du Pins had followed each other's movements at a distance for some while, but had never so far managed to meet up. Charles-Maurice was extremely fond of Henriette de La Tour du Pin, though he retained her friendship by knowing the limits she placed on flirtation. In a letter to Germaine de Staël, who certainly entertained no such scruples, he joked that the La Tour du Pins had made an excellent impression in Boston because, in common with the rest of this uxorious society, they shared the same bedroom – a peculiarity that he thought most amusing.[47]

General Schuyler was able now to tell Charles-Maurice where his friends were living. La Tour du Pin had purchased the lease of a house and estate near Troy, four miles from Albany, and, until they could move in, the family were renting a log cabin nearby. Here, the marquise turned her hand with facility to being a farmer's wife. And, naturally, as a French woman, and although she had a servant, she herself took charge of the cooking. One day, she was outside in the courtyard chopping up a leg of mutton to prepare *brochettes*. Suddenly, behind her she heard a loud voice saying in French: 'No one could skewer a leg of mutton with greater majesty.' It was Talleyrand, accompanied by Beaumetz. They had come to invite her and her husband to dinner at Schuyler's. And because Charles-Maurice was so amused to see his aristocratic friend tackling her leg of mutton, she insisted that they come back to eat the kebabs next day, which they did.

At Schuyler's, both good and bad news awaited them. From the *Gazette*, they learned of the overthrow of Robespierre. Charles-Maurice hoped that this meant that his imprisoned sister-in-law, the comtesse de Périgord, had escaped the scaffold. But later, while looking through earlier numbers, he found that she was among the last victims of the Terror, which greatly upset him.[48]

It was necessary, though, to press on with the expedition before winter closed in. They now made their way up the Mohawk towards Lake Oneida. The river itself was not at this time fully navigable. The settler population was sparse, the farms small, the climate harsh and unhealthy, and there was also a substantial Indian population. None of this made for good business prospects. The party turned back before reaching Niagara Falls, so there was no scenic drama to compensate for the general deprivation.[49]

Talleyrand's work of exploration and assessment was not much rewarded. Despite his later boasts, he lived modestly, or even frugally, during his time in America.[50] He did, though, make a healthy gain from one transaction. In 1796 he made a conditional purchase of 100,000 acres of land in Pennsylvania for ten shillings an acre from the American speculator Robert Morris.[51] It was to be paid for in fifteen months' time, if it could be re-sold in France. It duly was, and Talleyrand, by now back in Paris, seems to have made a 100 per cent profit.[52]

Charles-Maurice was a shrewd observer of America. He was unimpressed by Philadelphia, despite its veneer of sophistication. By contrast, New York, with its 'good and convenient harbour' and 'its central position', had in his view 'decisive advantages'.[53] History has, of course, proved him right. Similarly, he grasped that a shortage of population was the decisive factor holding back the United States. But it would be remedied. As he notes in his memoirs: 'You do not take a step [in the United States] without being convinced that the irresistible advance of nature intends an immense population should one day animate this mass of inert land.'[54] The following century's European immigration would provide that.

Where Chateaubriand three years earlier had found material for his novels about the noble savage, Talleyrand saw opportunities for profit and pictured settlements and towns appearing in the wilderness.[55] But both men brought with them a recognizably European disdain for the explicit materialism they encountered. Chateaubriand complained of the inequality, frivolity, luxury and gambling that he discovered in Philadelphia.[56] Talleyrand, for whom those particular manifestations of materialism were less objectionable, complained about the way in which a man's wealth in the New World was the only determinant of his social standing. He discovered, to his surprise, that for Americans living in the back lands the prospect of meeting a well-known tycoon was more attractive than that of meeting General Washington. And he was shocked by the way in which works of art went unappreciated, as when he witnessed, in Robert Morris's house, the owner's ugly, coarse hat placed on a table of delicate Sèvres porcelain.[57]

What was required, Talleyrand believed, to give weight, stability and unity to America as an emerging nation was systematic agriculture, with the regular habits and social ties that it always created. He even went so far as to enunciate a more questionable principle: 'Agriculture is not invasive: it establishes. Commerce has the spirit of conquest: it wants to expand.'[58]

More obviously well founded were Talleyrand's observations on the Anglo-American relationship. He first formulated his thoughts in a letter to Lansdowne of 1 February 1795. These were then developed in the lecture he delivered in April 1797 to the Institut national on his return to Paris.

Charles-Maurice began with a paradox. The Americans were very sympathetic to the French, who had helped them in their War of Independence. And within the limits of formal neutrality, they supported France in its current struggle with Britain. Despite that, the European traveller finds that 'America is completely English: that is to say that England has every advantage over France in drawing from the United States all the benefit that one nation can draw from the existence of another.' There were two reasons for this: 'inclination and interest'. On the first, the common language was a crucial factor. It gave Britain what he termed a 'right of ownership over all the inclinations of the Americans in a manner that is irresistible'. So did the similarity between the British and American constitutions, judicial usage and even the style of political debate. Moreover, by a different route – that of economic interest – the political élite of America, who had led the revolt against Britain and thus might be supposed to be by inclination enduringly anti-British, were also drawn to the mother country. This was because the former colonies remained heavily dependent on Britain for imports. And that in turn reflected the strength of British industry, the extent of British capital, and the scope of British credit.

In writing to Lansdowne, Talleyrand blamed British policy over the previous century for dissipating these advantages through the contempt that British governments had shown to the colonists.[59] But in his lecture in Paris he drew a rather different conclusion. He observed that after the Revolutionary War Britain had quickly reopened its trade with the former colonies and that the spirit of commerce had overcome the spirit of war. The classical liberal theme of the importance of free trade in establishing political harmony, though little appreciated in France (then or since), was already a favourite of his, and one to which he would return.[60]

During the emptier periods of his life in America, Charles-Maurice had also turned his mind to more utopian projects. He toyed with the conception of a universal international order, based on mutual respect for the rights of nations and on unfettered free trade. But he found an opponent in his friend Hamilton, and the decision of the American Congress to impose new tariffs brought home to him the difficulties of such schemes.[61]

Life in Philadelphia was by now not too unpleasant for Talleyrand. He felt at ease, and he even shocked prudish opinion by strolling around with a Negro girl on his arm. He also adopted a stray dog – dogs as well as women would always play a part in his life.[62] But the expatriate existence was, above all, made tolerable by the presence of so many French friends. From October 1794, when Moreau de Saint-Méry set up his bookshop and printers in Philadelphia, they had a regular meeting place where the discussion was always about France. Every evening, Charles-Maurice would come round to Moreau's office. A frugal supper would be served, at which Moreau confined himself to rice pudding while Talleyrand ate nothing, but drank his host's Madeira, which was (when dry) one of his favourites. The Moreau family and other French friends – such as Blacons, Talon, Noailles and the great travel writer Volney – would appear, and the conversation would become increasingly lively and noisy.[63] Blacons used to address Talleyrand as 'Monseigneur', as if he were still a bishop, and receive a few playful slaps in exchange. When at last it was time to go, Charles-Maurice would regularly find a reason to prolong the evening, until firmly reminded by Moreau's wife that though he could lie in bed until midday her husband had to be up to open the shop at seven o'clock.[64]

Yet this little French home-from-home was no substitute for the real thing. With the fall of Robespierre in the coup of 9 Thermidor Year II (27 July 1794) had appeared a glimmer of hope for the liberal exiles. Every journal arriving from France was eagerly read. Talleyrand learned while in New York, from a newspaper that Moreau sent, that on 4 September the Convention had formally revoked the accusations against him.[65] In his memoirs, he claims that his authorization to return to France was received 'without any solicitation' on his part.[66] But this is quite untrue.

On 16 June 1795 he had signed a long petition to the Convention, rehearsing the arguments he had previously used concerning his record and the circumstances of his departure from France, and seeking permission to return. Three copies were sent, respectively to Mme de Staël, to her friend and Talleyrand's future patron Paul Barras, and to Desrenaudes.[67] The latter added some explanatory notes and presented it to the Convention on 27 August. It was duly printed in *Le Moniteur*. Germaine lobbied furiously on her friend's behalf.

The political climate was in any case favourable. On 11 August Talleyrand's future collaborator Roederer had published a pamphlet calling for the return of those exiles who had not actually fought against France. Still more important was the intervention of Tallien, whose role in the overthrow of Robespierre had gained him great kudos.[68] On 30 August Tallien named Charles-Maurice in a speech as one of those unjustly appearing on the list of *émigrés*. There was now a growing body of opinion favourable to a return of the liberal exiles, but it was still vitally important to pick the right advocate of Charles-Maurice's cause before the Convention.

The choice finally fell on Marie-Joseph Chénier, a poet-politician in good standing with the left.[69] He was no natural admirer of Talleyrand. But Germaine de Staël worked on Chénier's mistress, Eugénie de La Bouchardie, who fired him up to go to the Convention on 4 September and deliver a passionate speech in defence of Talleyrand. Its high point was: 'I claim from you Talleyrand-Périgord, I claim him in the name of his numerous services, I claim him in the name of the Republic that he can again serve by his talents and his labours.' Chénier would soon repent of his encomium and give literary form to his spite. But for now the orator's enthusiasm was infectious. His peroration was cheered to the rafters; others intervened to support the proposal; the original accusation was revoked; Talleyrand's name was struck from the list of *émigrés*. He was at last permitted to return to France.[70]

The letter that Talleyrand now wrote to the French Foreign Minister expressed as much indignation at what he had had to suffer as gratitude for his recall. It smacks of a manifesto and implies a job application.[71] In fact, Talleyrand decided to postpone his departure until the following spring. One reason was the weather: a winter crossing would have been treacherous. Even when conditions improved, there was a dearth of ships coming from Europe on which he could obtain a return passage,[72] added to which some American captains were apparently uneasy about having him on board.[73] But there were also political reasons to wait. He rightly judged that events were moving in his direction in Paris. A new Constitution was ratified. Effective power passed to a five-man executive or Directory, of whom the shrewdest and soon the most influential member was Barras.

On 13 June 1796 Talleyrand finally left America on a Danish ship, *Den Nye Prove*, bound for Hamburg. He had carefully selected his destination. Hamburg would be full of French exiles; it was a banking centre where he could renew old contacts and organize lines of credit; it would allow him to establish in his own time the way back to favour. Moreau de Saint-Méry was sad to see him go as the two men had become close and would remain so. Charles-Maurice took with him 200 copies of Moreau's geographical essay on San Domingo, to be sold in Europe. He even offered to take Moreau's son and place him in some good position; the boy's mother, however, thought the enterprise too risky. On his arrival in France, Talleyrand would correspond as regularly as he could and when Moreau and his family themselves returned, he did all he could to advance their interests.[74]

But Charles-Maurice did not keep up with all his fellow exiles. When Blacons, back in France and crippled by debt, asked for a modest place, Talleyrand, now in office, never even replied to the request. Blacons committed suicide. When informed of the tragedy, Talleyrand yawned and murmured, 'Poor Blacons!'[75] Beaumetz, who had been his comrade through all those months, seems finally to have lost his senses and considered killing Charles-Maurice by throwing him off the Battery in New York. He then departed with a new wife to India, where he died a few years later in poverty.[76]

As for Talleyrand, after delays in the Delaware, he landed in Hamburg at the end of July 1796. His travels were finally over.

6

The Directory

━◆━

THE HAMBURG THAT Talleyrand found in August 1796 was full of intrigues; and so, despite falling ill for a fortnight with a high fever, he was in his element. He was in no hurry to reach Paris, where he felt 'there was too much movement to learn about France'.[1] There was an Orléanist faction there, but its importance was exaggerated. D'Orléans himself (the future King Louis-Philippe) was but a 'poor instrument', he observed in correspondence with Moreau: and, in any case, the duc had decided to leave Europe for the United States. The various *émigrés* were almost all desperate to return to France. The colours of the Republic were in fashion, and he took to wearing them himself.[2]

On his departure from Hamburg, Talleyrand passed through Bremen, Amsterdam and Brussels – looking up acquaintances, assessing financial opportunities – before entering France.[3] He finally arrived in Paris on 20 September, to take up temporary residence in the house of his old friend Mme de Boufflers at Auteuil. Here he found himself reintroduced into the company of still more friends, including Germaine de Staël and her latest escort, the young writer and would-be politician, Benjamin Constant.[4] Both would prove indispensable in the ambitious strategy of self-promotion upon which Charles-Maurice now embarked.

Leading political circles were soon aware of Talleyrand's return, but he had nonetheless to re-establish his reputation as a serious candidate for office. The Institut national des Sciences et des Arts, to which he had been elected in 1795, when still in America, provided a useful forum. On 4 April 1797 he delivered a public lecture there, on 'Trade Relations between the United States and England'. Its themes – outlined earlier – reflected his experience in the United States. His message for France was that a liberal polity and economy were the best means of promoting harmony and prosperity. But the lecture's political purpose lay in its demonstration of the speaker's own breadth of outlook, expertise and elegance of expression – all of which were greatly applauded, and later extolled in the press.[5]

Talleyrand delivered a second lecture to the Institut, on 3 July, concerning the 'Advantages to be drawn from New Colonies in Present Circumstances'. His starting point was that of contemporary France, a country recovering from the effects of a great Revolution which had left many individuals agitated, discontented and rancorous. These people, he suggested, needed for their own sakes, and above all for the sake of France, to find new scope for their energy. This could best be provided by emigration. But the existing French colonies in the New World had no future, threatened as they were by Britain. Economics was against the New World too, for in future Negro slaves were unlikely to be available to provide the labour for colonial exploitation. The colonies of tomorrow had, therefore, to be established along new lines and in new regions. They must be settled by the best, not the worst, inhabitants of the motherland. They should be based upon industries that complemented the French economy. They had to feel bound to France by mutual interest, enjoying the advantages of free trade and lightly administered government. There must be 'no domination, no monopoly; always the force that protects, never that which grabs'. Such 'justice, [and] benevolence' would be the 'source of mutual prosperity'. The new colonies had to enjoy a warm climate, benefit from productive soil, and be sufficiently close to France. This pointed to the coasts of Africa and, specifically, to Egypt.

The practicalities of this new colonialism did not receive much attention from the speaker on this occasion. How to subdue and pacify the indigenous population did not figure at all. Although understandable, given the nature of the occasion, the omission also reflected Charles-Maurice's lack of practical sense in military matters. It was a recurrent failing, not least in the forthcoming enterprise of Egypt.[6]

He had considered delivering a third lecture, this time on the influence of 'Society' – that is, of the *salons* and those who gathered in them – upon recent French history. It was a theme that interested him. But his friends, probably wisely, persuaded him against it. Revolutionary resentments were still too fresh.[7]

In any case, he had already acquired public notice. Not all of it, however, was beneficial. Rumours circulated that he was in direct negotiation with the agents of the comte de Provence (Louis XVIII) to sell out the Republic. The public letter he wrote to denounce the slanders and call for action against the slanderers seems to have been misjudged. Some of those who had worked hardest for his return had now turned against him. Chénier acidly commented that 'having been an anarchist and an *Orléaniste*, and not having been able to be a *Robespierriste*, because Maximilien [Robespierre] would not have anything to do with him, [Talleyrand] had become a *Directoiriste*, while waiting to be whatever would be in power later'.[8]

For now, though, it was on the Directory that he concentrated. The Directors received regular reports on his activity. Talleyrand, therefore, spoke prudently when in company. For example, at a dinner where most of those present deplored the severity shown towards the *émigrés*, Talleyrand expressed the contrary view: that they should be kept under the closest observation. But he was critical of the serving Foreign Minister, Charles Delacroix, whom Charles-Maurice was now anxious to replace.[9]

Of the five-man Directory, only one, Barras, was well disposed towards him.[10] Having played a crucial role in overthrowing Robespierre, Barras wanted the support of able moderates like Talleyrand. But the other Directors were in varying degrees hostile. Jean-François Reubell, a loud-mouthed Jacobin from Colmar, was the most passionately opposed.[11] Louis-Marie La Révellière-Lépaux was less easy to pigeon-hole. He too was of the left, but personally timid. He was also intellectually pretentious and proud to be the founder of the pseudo-religion of 'theophilanthropy'. An anecdote – probably untrue, but doubtless reflecting what Talleyrand had said in private – concerns the former bishop of Autun's reaction to a lecture by La Révellière-Lépaux to the Institut. Charles-Maurice allegedly said: 'As for me, I have just one observation to make to you. Jesus Christ, in order to found his religion, was crucified and rose from the dead. You should have tried to do the same.'[12]

The fourth Director, Lazare Carnot, a principled Republican, did not like or trust Talleyrand either. The fifth Director, Letourneur de La Manche, primarily a military man like Carnot, was of no great significance and would, in any case, soon be replaced by François de Barthélemy. Barras was, therefore, the key to Charles-Maurice's future and thus became the focus of the aspirant minister's efforts.

The Directory was chronically unstable, threatened from both left and right. In September 1796 it had successfully crushed the far left followers of Babeuf. But it was soon faced by real and putative threats from the right.

In the spring of 1797 there were elections to the two legislative councils, the Cinq-Cents and the Anciens. These councils had been fairly evenly divided between the two parties of '*constitutionnels*' and '*directoriaux*', the former emphasizing the necessity to respect the Constitution, and thus limit the Directory's authority, the latter supporting the Directors. The *constitutionnels* were not, though, of one mind. A minority covertly favoured a return of the Bourbons, and they now received a large increase in support. The possibility of a monarchist coup became a topic of fevered discussion.[13] In May the legislators appointed Barthélemy, a well-known royalist, to succeed Letourneur as Director. In these circumstances, Barras urgently needed to mobilize support from moderates of all kinds to resist the increasingly monarchist *constitutionnels*. So while the monarchists gathered in the Club de Chichy, Talleyrand and his allies were encouraged to found the Cercle Constitutionel. The Cercle met in the rue de Lille, in the old Hôtel Montmorency, and included, apart from Charles-Maurice, such luminaries as Sieyès, Constant, Garat, Chénier, Merlin de Douai and Generals Jourdan and Kléber. The group published a journal called *Le Conservateur*, to which Talleyrand contributed his thoughts on foreign policy – another indicator of his ambitions.[14]

He had hoped to contribute more practically in this area, but he was frustrated. The first contacts were due to be made at Lille with a view to the negotiation of peace with Britain, and Delacroix proposed to add Talleyrand and his associate Maret to the delegation. But Reubell, who had responsibility within the Directory for foreign affairs, resisted the appointment. Only Barthélemy supported it.

Talleyrand's prospects of promotion had, in fact, suddenly improved. Delacroix was by now seriously and very publicly ill: his stomach was swollen by a huge tumour, which Mme de Staël unkindly said made him look like a 'pregnant old woman'.[15] Rumours about a successor multiplied. Germaine de Staël was Talleyrand's chief lobbyist, pestering Barras shamelessly on his behalf. In his memoirs, Talleyrand suggests that she did so without his involvement.[16] But this is clearly untrue. Every morning, Benjamin Constant, who was deputed by his lover to assist in the campaign, planned the day's tactics with Charles-Maurice. Barras found himself approached from all sorts of different quarters; his friends suddenly conceived the need to send him notes urging Talleyrand's claims. Mme de Staël told him that Charles-Maurice had threatened to commit suicide if he were not made a minister.[17]

One of Talleyrand's most frequently quoted observations is that 'in matters of importance one must get the women going'.[18] And on this occasion, at least, he did just that. But an event that he records in his memoirs, and which is as subtly damning of Barras as Barras more crudely is of him, also helped. Invited to the Director's country house at Suresnes, Talleyrand was waiting for Barras when the latter's young aide (in fact, as the memoirs accurately imply, his boyfriend) was drowned in the Seine. On his return and learning the news, Barras broke down, clasped Talleyrand to his bosom, poured out his woes and insisted that the two men dine together and then return to Paris. Charles-Maurice was in short order appointed Minister of Foreign Affairs.[19]

In reality, the political situation was at least as important as all these personal interventions in securing Talleyrand's appointment.[20] July 1797 saw the power struggle between the Directory and the faction dominating the councils reach a peak. Within the Directory itself, it took the form of hostile manoeuvring in which Barras, Reubell and La Revellière-Lépeaux were pitted against Barthélemy and Carnot. The immediate occasion was the appointment of ministers. There were five ministerial positions to fill, and, despite the fact that Reubell hated Talleyrand, he was finally prepared to accept Barras's nominee to Foreign Affairs in exchange for others advanced by himself and La Revellière-Lépeaux. As Barras put it, the appointment 'slipped in during the fight'. Barras's own account of how Talleyrand received the news has become part of the legend. Charles-Maurice was apparently at the theatre when he learned of the decision. In the carriage back to the Luxembourg Palace, he sat between Boniface de Castellane and Benjamin Constant, squeezing their knees in his excitement, and repeating: 'We've a position! We must make an immense fortune, an immense fortune, an immense fortune. . .'[21]

Charles-Maurice required all his composure in dealing with the Directory, where bitter wrangling, threats and even blows took the place of reasoned discussion. As he says in his memoirs: 'Everything was violent and, as a result, nothing could be durable.'[22] Reubell referred to his Foreign Minister as the 'prototype of treason and corruption' and as a 'powdered lackey of the old régime'. The Directors mocked Charles-Maurice's exaggerated attempts to demonstrate his Republican zeal. Most humiliating of all, Reubell went out of his way to highlight the minister's incompetence, posing difficult questions. On one occasion he sent him to an adjoining room, like a naughty schoolboy, to prepare a reply, which Charles-Maurice still could not or would not provide.[23]

Barras's account, relishing his enemy's humiliations, does not reveal the substance of the disagreements between Talleyrand and the Directors, but they all seem to have related to means, timing or tactics. The Foreign Minister was, in any case, in no position to dictate or even direct policy. Like his predecessor, he found that the important decisions were made by the Directors themselves. It was his job to put them into effect, and otherwise to deal with passports, visas and suchlike minutiae.[24] Yet, for all that, the Foreign Minister did what he could to influence events.

An early opportunity came with the continuing Anglo-French peace negotiations at Lille, which had begun a fortnight before Talleyrand's appointment as Foreign Minister. His arrival on the scene was welcomed by Barthélemy and Carnot, and indeed by the British, as increasing the likelihood of a successful outcome. A vigorous secret diplomacy was undertaken. It had the added attraction of permitting Talleyrand to speculate to advantage on the exchanges, through his inside knowledge of political developments.[25]

Talleyrand's fundamental approach was to force France's allies, the (Dutch) Batavian Republic and Spain, to make sufficient concessions to the British in order to secure peace, while ensuring that French dominance in Europe went unchallenged. After some difficulty, notably with Reubell, he won the Directors round. But the violent rows that took the place of policy discussions within the Directorate constantly threatened to throw the strategy off course. On one occasion the Prussian minister, Sandoz-Rollin, witnessed the usually unflappable Talleyrand greatly agitated after seeing Barras and Carnot fly at each other and having to be pulled apart by the other Directors.[26]

With the ascendancy of the left and the crushing of the peace party that resulted from the coup of 18 Fructidor (4 September 1797) the possibilities of peace evaporated. Talleyrand's secret diplomacy came to an abrupt end. His main concern now was to cover his tracks and protect his job.

Talleyrand survived as Foreign Minister. He had secured his position by cannily supporting the victors of 18 Fructidor.

The coup had been planned by Barras. The required military threat was then supplied by troops under the command of Augereau, acting as General Bonaparte's agent. But Talleyrand also played his subtle part, with Mme de Staël and Benjamin Constant, working to undermine political support for the opposition.[27] Apparently, he even expressed disappointment that the principals of the alleged royalist *putsch* had been deported rather than executed. But, then, words came cheap. Sadly, they were not sufficient to gain Talleyrand the prize on which he had set his sights, that is membership of the Directory. Despite appeals to Barras, it was not Charles-Maurice but Merlin de Douai and François de Neufchâteau who were selected to fill the two vacancies.[28]

Talleyrand also secured his position by establishing a close relationship with Napoleon Bonaparte. He had written personally to inform Bonaparte of his appointment as Foreign Minister: 'I have the honour to announce to you, General, that the Directory has appointed me Minister of External Relations. Justly intimidated by the responsibilities whose perilous importance I know, I need to reassure myself by the recollection of what your glory brings, in means and capacity, to the [current] negotiations. The name alone of Bonaparte is a help that smooths out every obstacle.'[29]

Bonaparte hastened to reply in equally flattering terms: 'The choice that the government has made of you to be Minister of External

Relations honours its discernment. It finds in you great talents, a refined sense of civic duty, someone with no connection to the excesses that have dishonoured the Revolution.'[30]

The new Foreign Minister had taken over his post mid-way between the preliminary negotiations with Austria at Leoben in April and the final Treaty of Campo-Formio in October 1797. The coup of 18 Fructidor might have been expected to increase French intransigence, and in dealings with Britain it did so. But the balance between civilians and the military had also shifted in the latter's favour, and Bonaparte, for his own reasons, intended to demonstrate his power through magnanimity. He, therefore, imposed terms on the Austrians that were more generous than the Directors wanted, and which included cession to Austria of the territory of the old Venetian Republic. Bonaparte then informed Talleyrand that, without reference to Paris, he had gone ahead and signed the treaty. This, of course, was bold to the point of insubordination and, as he acknowledged, the general foresaw sharp criticism from his detractors of the terms.[31] He was clearly hoping that Talleyrand would win over the Directory. Nor was he disappointed.

Bonaparte despatched the treaty to Paris with two aides, General Berthier and the civilian Gaspard Monge, along with a large consignment of works of art plundered from Italy. Charles-Maurice greeted them in a flowery speech, exalting Bonaparte's and the Army of Italy's achievements. A majority of the Directors grudgingly accepted the fait accompli, and the treaty was duly ratified.[32] The minister wrote back a flattering letter of congratulation. This, Talleyrand declared, was a 'Peace à la Bonaparte'. The Directory was happy, the public delighted. There would perhaps be 'some whining from the Italians' (over Venice), but no one cared about that. 'Farewell, Peacemaker-General!'[33]

The Peacemaker-General and Talleyrand had not yet met. But they had, within limits, begun to trust one another. Both had developed a deep scorn for the Directory, but neither had any wish to risk a Bourbon restoration. So, despite their shared dislike of Jacobinism in all its forms, they had supported Barras and the left against Carnot, Barthélemy and the right. Their cooperation seems, indeed, to have been very close. A well-informed visitor to Bonaparte, Miot de

Mélito, French ambassador to Piedmont, thought that 'Talleyrand [had been] the main intermediary in relations' between the general and the organizers of the Directorial coup. Bonaparte certainly entertained a high view of the Foreign Minister; he had spent much of a journey from Milan to Lake Maggiore extolling Talleyrand's wit and capacity. Joséphine joined in the praise.[34]

Napoleon had also let Talleyrand into his thinking about the constitutional changes to which his mind was turning. Shortly before 18 Brumaire he wrote Charles-Maurice a long letter, whose style resembles that of a precocious schoolboy hoping to win his master's praise, but which also reveals the extent of the author's ambitions: 'Despite our pride, our thousand-and-one pamphlets, our garrulous and endless speeches, we are still very ignorant of political and moral science. We have not yet defined what is meant by executive, legislative and judicial power. Montesquieu gave us false definitions. . . The organization of the French people has, therefore, hardly been outlined.'[35]

Having spent just five days at the peace negotiations at Rastadt, Bonaparte now returned to Paris, arriving in the afternoon of 5 December accompanied by Generals Berthier and Championnet. He saw Barras that evening. But he also sent his aide-de-camp to the Ministry of Foreign Affairs. It was arranged that he would be received there the following morning at eleven o'clock. Talleyrand summoned his friends and acquaintances to this semi-official reception. Among these was Mme de Staël, who had conceived a burning enthusiasm to meet the military hero of the hour. When he arrived, however, Bonaparte proved to be much more interested in talking to the explorer Bougainville than to her.[36]

Charles-Maurice recalled years later the impression that Napoleon had made upon him:

> He seemed to me to have a charming face; twenty battles won go so well with youth, with a fine gaze, with a certain pallor, and with a kind of exhaustion. We went into my office. The conversation was, on his part, conducted in full confidence. He spoke very graciously of my appointment to the Ministry of External Affairs and insisted on the pleasure he had in corresponding with someone of a different sort than the Directors. Without much transition, he said: 'You are the

95

nephew of the archbishop of Reims, who is with Louis XVIII.' (I noticed at the time that he did not say the comte de Lille.) And he added: 'I, too, have an uncle who is archdeacon in Corsica; it is he who raised me; it is like being a bishop in France.' We soon returned to the *salon*.[37]

Viewed on one level, it is a pleasant enough scene. And perhaps there was a glow of mutual attraction between two such different characters, each able to appreciate the virtuosity of the other. But when Napoleon, in a manner at once arrogant and naïve, compared his own lineage with that of Charles-Maurice de Talleyrand-Périgord, he exposed a weakness: the young general was a snob. And in recalling the exchange, Talleyrand exposes, too, his reaction: he despised Napoleon for his *petit bourgeois* snobbery.

The friendly relations that Charles-Maurice enjoyed with Bonaparte made it all the more appropriate to give him a leading role at the Directory's reception for the general. Barras told him that the Directors wanted to downplay the military aspects of the occasion and, knowing that Talleyrand had 'tact', he asked him to deliver the opening speech. Charles-Maurice replied that he knew how to deal with military men, and went away to prepare.

On 10 December, at midday, artillery fire announced the start of the parade to the main courtyard of the Luxembourg Palace, which had been magnificently decorated. The Directors and members of the diplomatic corps took their seats. Huge crowds blocked the surrounding paths, and people hung out of the windows for a better view. Bonaparte then appeared, accompanied by the Minister of War, and, naturally, the Minister of Foreign Affairs. The choir sang. Everyone rose. Talleyrand now spoke. The speech was quite short, and ended with a passage that was of some significance. Alluding to the reticent Roman general Cincinnatus, he declared: 'Far from fearing what people might like to call [Napoleon's] ambition, I am conscious that it will perhaps be necessary for us one day to drag him from his studious retirement. France as a whole will be free; perhaps he will never be – such is his destiny.'

Barras thought that only Talleyrand could have delivered himself of this improbable prediction while keeping a straight face. But then, all concerned had an interest in the pantomime.[38] The general's own speech in reply was even shorter than Talleyrand's. It included, however, the obscure but ominous line: 'When the happiness of the French people is based on the best organic laws, the whole of Europe will be free.' At this, Talleyrand was heard to mutter: 'There lies the future.'[39]

For the next few weeks, Bonaparte lodged in his modest house in the rue Chantereine, now in his honour renamed rue de La Victoire. He spent his time holding meetings, issuing military instructions, attending dinners and receptions – which he disliked – and successfully impressing his dynamism and intellect on Parisian society.[40] To his annoyance he found that, despite the plaudits, there was no inclination to remove in his favour the age qualification that prevented his becoming one of the Directors. Talleyrand had, apparently, encouraged this ambition.[41]

The Foreign Minister decided to stake a special claim to the general's recognition and to his own superiority over the vulgarians and mediocrities who flourished under the Directory. He therefore arranged a superb *fête*, the first of its kind in Paris since the Revolution, to be held on 3 January 1798 in the Hôtel Gallifet, which for the last four years had been home to the Ministry of Foreign Affairs.[42] In order to provide a refined note of gallantry, the occasion was officially offered in honour of 'Mme Bonaparte'.

The Hôtel Gallifet was splendidly suited for the purpose. Access to it was from the rue du Bac, although the building itself was well set back from the thoroughfare. It had two courtyards; at the bottom of the second of these, framed by a peristyle of thirty-foot columns, stood the façade of the main buildings. On the far side, they looked on to gardens. Columns led to a great staircase, decorated by more columns and reliefs. The ground and first floors were used by the minister to live, work and entertain, while the other services operated from the upper floors. In 1798 Talleyrand had also obtained the adjoining Hôtel Maurepas in the rue de Grenelle in order to house the department's archives.[43]

Extensive and expensive preparations were now undertaken to make the occasion a success worthy of the principal guest. The architect François-Joseph Bélanger, who had previously served the comte d'Artois, was commissioned by Charles-Maurice to take charge of the decoration.[44] The result was a unique combination of luxury and good taste of the sort that Talleyrand himself would come to personify. The rooms were filled with real and artificial flowers and perfumed with amber, the stairway embellished with sweet-smelling shrubs. On the walls were hung copies of paintings seized by Bonaparte from Italy. There were a choir, dancers and an orchestra. The courtyard was laid out in the form of a military encampment. The bust of Brutus which the general had plundered from the Capitol in Rome was displayed in a little Etruscan-style temple. Fashion among the ladies could best be described as lascivious-classical. The only requirement, expressed by the Foreign Minister in his letter of invitation, was that garments of British cloth should be avoided.[45]

Bonaparte arrived, accompanied by Joséphine, her daughter Hortense de Beauharnais, and his aides, including Arnault, at about half past ten. In deference to the civilian nature of the occasion he was out of uniform. A waltz struck up and then a quadrille called, in the general's honour, the 'Bonaparte'. Obviously ill at ease, he took hold of Arnault's arm and made him accompany him around the *salon* as he greeted the other guests. Eventually, he regained sufficient composure to face them alone and Arnault was able to find a seat and relax. But no sooner had he done so than Mme de Staël sat down beside him. She was desperate to make an impression on Bonaparte and badgered Arnault for an introduction. Eventually, he obliged. Hoping to extract a compliment from the general, she asked provocatively which woman he would love the most. He replied that that would be his wife. She insisted: 'But which woman would you esteem the most?' Bonaparte answered more dangerously: 'The one who knows best how to do the housekeeping.' Refusing to be defeated, she continued: 'But which would in your view hold the first rank among women?' He responded with vulgarity: 'The one who produces the most children, Madame.'[46] (Since Napoleon had a particular dislike of pregnant women this was, in fact, a lie as well as an insult.)[47]

Anyone less thick-skinned would have understood the significance of this put-down. But it took some time for it to sink into Germaine de Staël. Not so with Talleyrand, however: Charles-Maurice's abandonment of her sprang from this moment. She would send letters begging to be invited to his receptions for Bonaparte, once doing so 'in the name of our old friendship'. Talleyrand callously asked her, 'in the same name', not to attend.[48] For now, his attention was wholly focused on Bonaparte and his circle. During dinner that evening, while the ladies sat at the table, the men remained standing. The Minister of Foreign Affairs, for whom this cannot have been comfortable with his bad foot, stood behind the chair of Mme Bonaparte.

Only three of the five Directors had attended: Reubell and La Revellière-Lépeaux snubbed the occasion. Charles-Maurice regarded this as a blessing, since he dreaded the discordant vulgarity of the Directors' wives. As it was, Mme Merlin observed: 'That must have cost you plenty, Citizen Minister.' 'Not Peru, Madame,' he replied.[49] It is no surprise that the Directors resented the success of the occasion.[50]

But the Directory needed Talleyrand to help manage Bonaparte. The general's presence in Paris was unsettling. For example, he complained about what he saw as disorders permitted by the Directors, and was stubbornly determined not to be tarred by the brush of the Revolution. Thus he was only with the greatest difficulty persuaded by Charles-Maurice to attend the 'celebration' of the anniversary of Louis XVI's execution, on 21 January at Saint-Sulpice.[51] But the two men were certainly also collaborating at this time in ways that the Directory did not suspect – above all about the projected expedition to Egypt.

Talleyrand, it will be recalled, had addressed the topic in the second of his lectures to the Institut in July the previous year. Napoleon was discussing Egypt at about the same time in Italy, when the Peace of Campo-Formio was in the course of negotiation.[52] As a Corsican, the prospect of expansion across the Mediterranean appealed more naturally to Bonaparte than to the Directory. In any case, he wanted a new and attractive commission now that the end of his work in Italy was in sight. With good reason, he was apprehensive as to what the Directory might have in store for him. His imagination was also fired by an expedition to the Orient. In the evenings at Passariano his conversation was all about the history and heroes of the East.[53] In August the general wrote to Talleyrand asserting that it was 'necessary to seize Egypt'. Charles-Maurice replied: 'As for Egypt, your ideas in this matter are grand and their usefulness should be understood.'[54]

By the beginning of 1798, the enterprise of Egypt had acquired a still greater attraction. On his return to France, via Rastadt, Bonaparte became increasingly worried that the invasion of England, to which the Directory had now committed him, was fraught with risk. The visit he paid to the Channel coast in early February reinforced his conviction that he must find another less dangerous and more glamorous field for his exploits. Talleyrand, too, now had high hopes of an Egyptian expedition. It would redound doubly to his own reputation, both through reflected glory from Bonaparte's expected triumphs, and because he had publicly proposed the idea before he took office.

In fact, Talleyrand had already, on 27 January 1798, sent the Directory his first memorandum on the subject. It argued that the Ottoman Empire could not last more than another twenty-five years and France must act now to seize those parts that most suited its interests, notably Egypt, Crete and Lemnos. Malta must also be taken, which would give France dominance over the Mediterranean. Egypt, though, was the great prize, one that (according to Talleyrand) meant 'nothing to Turkey, which does not have even a shadow of authority there'.[55]

On 14 February Talleyrand provided the Directors with a more detailed analysis. He now stressed the fertility and productivity of Egypt and emphasized its strategic and commercial importance. 'Egypt seems to be, by its geographical position, the natural centre of trade for three-quarters of the world.' Above all, the country would be useful as the platform for a future invasion of British India. The memorandum concluded 'that the conquest of Egypt is no more than a just reprisal against the wrongs and insults that we have endured from the Porte; that it is easy and indeed certain; that it will entail only moderate expenses, for which the Republic will soon be compensated; finally, that it presents innumerable advantages for the Republic.'[56] Omitting, as it did, any serious evaluation of the risks of British naval attack, or of the reaction of other European powers, and completely misrepresenting the Ottoman Sultan's attitude, Talleyrand's memorandum must rank as one of the worst analyses of a major military undertaking ever submitted to a Western government. It is no wonder that he subsequently strove to conceal his role. In the immediate aftermath, Charles-Maurice blamed the policy on his predecessor, Delacroix. In fact, it was clearly Talleyrand not Delacroix who proposed the expedition, as Delacroix was able convincingly to demonstrate in later public exchanges. In his memoirs, Talleyrand holds Napoleon entirely responsible.

At some later stage, Bonaparte annotated Talleyrand's damning second memorandum. Where Talleyrand had written that the local population would welcome the French, Napoleon scribbled 'False'. And where the Foreign Minister had proposed that the expedition be led by two or three commissioners rather than by a single general, he scrawled 'What madness!' But these observations merely demonstrate Napoleon's personal vanity, not a belated access of common sense: indeed, Talleyrand had probably only inserted these points to swing the Directory behind the scheme by downplaying Bonaparte's role.[57]

Eventually, the pressure succeeded. The Directory reluctantly gave its consent. Perhaps it even appeared, by the end of deliberations on the matter, that there were advantages in having the uncontrollable Bonaparte out of Europe.[58] So, when there suddenly seemed a possibility of his postponing the expedition in order to go back to Rastadt, Barras urged the general to depart at once.[59] Accordingly, on 4 May Bonaparte left Paris for Toulon, and on 18 May the French fleet left for Malta en route to Egypt.

This was not, however, intended to be the end of Talleyrand's involvement. Bonaparte had insisted that Charles-Maurice be sent as ambassador to Constantinople in order to soothe the Sublime Porte's concerns – which both men minimized – at the French invasion of Egypt. Talleyrand was tired of being humiliated and overruled by the Directory and had already contemplated resignation.[60] But it is hard to imagine that he would ever have exchanged Paris for Constantinople.

With Bonaparte now on his way to Malta, it was clearly time for Talleyrand to leave. The French ambassador to the Ottoman Empire had just died, and France's agent at Pera was appointed to fill his place until another permanent envoy (that is, Talleyrand) arrived. But Talleyrand did not go to Constantinople. On 23 May 1798, on board the *Orient*, Bonaparte wrote that a French frigate and two Venetian war galleys would soon be at Toulon, where Talleyrand should go 'as soon as possible'.[61] On 18 June he wrote from Malta, which had been successfully conquered, to say that a further frigate had been sent to collect Talleyrand.[62] On 24 July Bonaparte complained from Cairo, now in French hands: 'I hear nothing spoken of Talleyrand. It is, however, extremely important that he does not delay his arrival in Constantinople.'[63]

On 30 August, a little wistfully now, he wrote to the Directory: 'I imagine Talleyrand is in Constantinople.'[64] But all the while Charles-Maurice was still comfortably installed in Paris. At the same time, the acting French plenipotentiary to the Ottoman Empire, whose security Talleyrand had personally guaranteed in a reassuring letter, was incarcerated by the Porte. He would remain in prison under miserable conditions for three years.

The reason why Charles-Maurice stayed behind is not hard to fathom: he thought the risks of going were too great; and, of course, he was right. The Sultan was by no means as nonchalant about the loss of his Egyptian dominions to France as Talleyrand had predicted. In any case, once the French fleet was destroyed by the British on 1 August at the Battle of Aboukir Bay, the Egyptian venture was militarily doomed. The priority for Charles-Maurice was henceforth to extricate himself from blame. A more complicated question is why the Directory, which had approved Talleyrand's mission to Constantinople, was so compliant. The conundrum is resolved, however, by other difficulties in which Talleyrand had helped embroil the Directors.

Since 1796, French corsairs had been attacking American shipping, in retaliation against the Jay Treaty between the US and Britain, which was deemed by Paris to have breached the terms of American neutrality. A delegation was sent to Paris in the autumn of 1797 to recover damages for US losses and to bring an end to the dispute. But the three American negotiators, John Marshall, Charles Pinckney and Elbridge Gerry, were shocked by the treatment they received. They were approached by a series of agents, whose precise status was obscure, but who were clearly working for Talleyrand and who figured in President Adams's later report to Congress on the matter as 'X', 'Y' and 'Z'. The American envoys were told that the precondition for success was the payment of what amounted to substantial bribes. Specifically, they were asked to underwrite a loan of 32 million Dutch florins, to make a gift of 50,000 gold louis to the Directory, and to provide 'sweeteners' for the Foreign Minister and his intermediaries. The Americans sent back a long indignant report about these outrageous proceedings, which President Adams duly conveyed to Congress.

The scandal in the United States was immense. It then reached the French public through British press reports. Talleyrand indignantly defended his reputation. He even managed to persuade Gerry, the most francophile of the US negotiators, to lend some support to his protestations of innocence. To the Directory, he simply denied any knowledge. His protestations can hardly have been credible, but for a time he survived in office. This was partly because Barras, his protector, was involved as well. But it was also because, despite the scandal, both the French and American governments knew that no one was better equipped to negotiate peace between them than Talleyrand. It was in order to press these complicated negotiations forward that the Directory wanted Talleyrand to stay in Paris, rather than go to Constantinople. And this, of course, very much suited Charles-Maurice.[65]

The Americans clearly did not understand how the practical business of negotiation was done in Europe. By contrast, the Prussian minister Sandoz-Rollin, who enjoyed good personal relations with Talleyrand, was realistic. For example, in January 1798 he reported to his government: 'All manner of business is for sale here, not with the Directory but at the level of the ministers, who are its subordinates. The Minister of Foreign Affairs loves money and says loudly that when he leaves his position he does not intend to ask alms from the Republic. His friends confirm him in this idea.'[66]

Yet, far from alienating foreign powers, Talleyrand's venality pleased them. It seemed to guarantee his flexibility. They also admired his ability to manage the Directors. Moreover, he consistently portrayed himself as a man of peace.[67] No wonder, then, that the foreign powers desperately hoped to see Talleyrand become a member of the Directory, where he might have greater impact on policy. His 'system would be perfectly favourable for Prussia and for the peace of Europe', Sandoz-Rollin reported. Others thought so too. The courts of Spain and Portugal even offered 1.5 million francs to support Charles-Maurice's campaign for nomination to the Directory, if he should need it.[68]

During Talleyrand's term as Foreign Minister under the Directory, French expansion continued. France gained Mulhouse and Geneva. Puppet states were established by force in Switzerland (the Helvetian Republic), the Papal States (the Roman Republic) and Naples (the

Parthenopean Republic). But this was mainly despite, not because of, Charles-Maurice's efforts, which were principally concerned with creating stability, albeit on the most favourable terms, along France's borders. In Italy the ambitions of Bonaparte, and in Switzerland the enthusiasm of its home-grown revolutionaries, were the driving force of events. Meanwhile, in the larger questions of relations with Austria and with Britain, Talleyrand's options for influencing events were very limited indeed.

Moreover, in the courts of Europe, France was often represented by undiplomatic diplomats, who swaggered, specialized in *faux pas*, and insulted their hosts at random. The Foreign Ministry had to spend its time repairing the errors; and the Foreign Minister himself lamented the quality of ambassadors, appointed for their political not diplomatic credentials, whom the Directory forced upon him.[69]

When he could, however, Talleyrand sought to educate the Directors in the broader principles according to which French foreign policy should be conducted. The emphasis was, as before, on the need for limits and restraint. In December 1797 he boldly asserted that all the peace treaties that the Republic had signed, including the recent Treaty of Campo-Formio, were essentially just military capitulations. Such agreements were well and good, but having been imposed by force, they could not lead to an enduring peace.[70] In July 1798 he submitted a more comprehensive assessment to the Directory. It contains a bellicose set of proposals for the struggle against Britain: threatening India through Egypt, fomenting revolt in Ireland, and stimulating civil discord in England itself. But neither does Talleyrand lose sight of his fundamental concern for stability. The aim is still to convince France's enemies that they will not change its régime, while reassuring France's neighbours that the French Revolution itself need pose no threat to them.[71]

Shortly before he left office, he took the opportunity to reinforce this message in an analysis of 2 July 1799, delivered in a 'private' capacity as a member of the Institut:

> Lay hold, then, of these two points. Tell France, tell Europe, that regarding our internal and constitutional affairs no negotiation is possible, and that the last drop of French blood will be spilled to maintain the Republic. Then tell them, repeat to them (and let not any of your

actions give the lie to your declarations), that the Republic does not seek to involve itself in the affairs of any other nation, that it respects the independence of all, and that as long as it is not attacked it will show itself religiously faithful both to the general law of nations and to individual treaties.[72]

Talleyrand's last few months as Foreign Minister were a difficult and humiliating period. News of the destruction of the French fleet at Aboukir Bay and a growing realization that French forces were effectively marooned cast serious doubt on Talleyrand's judgement. One by one – Reubell most loudly – the Directors dissociated themselves from the venture. A Second Coalition of powers was now in preparation against France and hostilities began in earnest when French troops crossed the Rhine in March 1799. The following month, the Republic's negotiators were assassinated at Rastadt. French armies in Germany and Italy now suffered a series of defeats. The Directory was ferociously criticized, as was Talleyrand, who looked more and more like a convenient scapegoat.

He had also been forced to defend himself against damaging allegations made by a certain Lieutenant Sébastien Jorry. Jorry was one of several dubious characters whom the Foreign Minister, at the Directors' bidding, had provided with money to go and apply their talents for causing trouble as French agents in Italy. But, for whatever reason, Jorry stayed instead in Paris, spending the money he had been given, until he was arrested in April 1798. This marked the beginning of his long campaign against Talleyrand, which took the form of slanderous posters displayed around the streets. The Foreign Minister responded through the newspapers and in the courts. He told the Prussian minister that he suspected that Jorry was the instrument of some higher intrigue aimed at undermining him.[73]

By January 1799 he was expecting to be out of his job within two months.[74] But he lingered on. In May a deputation of Jacobins approached the Directory and explicitly blamed Talleyrand for the military reverses, demanding his dismissal.[75] The pressure on the Directory grew. Talk of another coup based on the Corps législatif and the left faction was in the air. The outcome, however, was the return to power of a rejuvenated abbé Sieyès. Elected as a Director in

June, replacing Reubell, he immediately set about preparing the way for constitutional reform.

Sieyès and Talleyrand knew each other well and had much in common. Both were renegade clergy; both had with difficulty survived the Revolution, and neither wished to repeat the experience. But whereas Sieyès retained a belief in systems, Talleyrand did not. There were even more important differences of temperament. Sieyès was chaste and honest, Talleyrand was neither. But he had a capacity for human engagement that Sieyès lacked. Talleyrand includes a character sketch of the abbé Sieyès in his memoirs: 'Sieyès has a mind that is vigorous to the highest degree; his heart is cold and his soul is pusillanimous: his inflexibility is only in his head. . .It is not by philosophy that he professes equality, it is by a violent hatred of the power of other people.'[76] More pithy but hardly more charitable is Charles-Maurice's reply to someone who suggested to him that Sieyès was 'deep': 'Deep? No. Hollow, very hollow – that's what you mean.'[77]

For a time it seemed as if Sieyès's arrival might save Talleyrand. The new Director even spent his first day back in Paris closeted with Charles-Maurice.[78] The coup of 30 Prairial (18 June) resulted in the removal and replacement of two Directors, consolidating power in the hands of Sieyès and Barras, which should have helped. But it did not.

Talleyrand wished, at least, to clear his name, and to this end on 13 July he published a long, self-justificatory statement. It proclaimed his Revolutionary credentials, restated that he had never been an émigré, rehearsed the terms on which he had left France, and then proceeded to defend his conduct as Foreign Minister. Correctly, he claimed to bear no responsibility for the actions taken in Switzerland and Italy which had stirred up hostility to France. With astonishing mendacity, he also claimed to bear no blame either for the expedition to Egypt which, he asserted, had been devised during the time of his predecessor.[79]

On the same day, he submitted his resignation to the Directory. It was refused, but when he submitted it again a few days later it was accepted – albeit in terms that emphasized the Directors' satisfaction with his performance. That merely inflamed his critics more. The last straw for the Jacobins was when Reinhard, a close collaborator of Talleyrand, and judged as merely an 'interim' (in Barras's expression), was appointed to succeed him as Foreign Minister.[80]

Talleyrand's resignation left him exposed; but it also freed him to choose whatever course offered the best prospect of advancement. Bonaparte's sudden return from Egypt, landing at Fréjus on 9 October and arriving a week later in Paris, provided him with the opening he needed.

After 30 Prairial, it was only a matter of time before the Directory was overthrown. Barras was by now mainly interested in money; Sieyès, for his part, was searching for a reliable 'sword' to wield – that is, a general to suborn – in order to impose his ideal Constitution. Of the other Directors, no one would take much notice of Gohier or General Moulins, and Roger Ducos was an acolyte of Sieyès. Talleyrand's obvious opportunity, therefore, lay in bringing together Bonaparte and Sieyès, while neutralizing Barras: and this was the strategy he now adopted.

Unfortunately, the egos of the two architects of the coup were equally large and their characters were not easily compatible. Moreover, they wanted different things: Bonaparte wanted absolute power; Sieyès wanted an 'umpire' to protect the Republic. It was only with the greatest difficulty that Charles-Maurice persuaded each of the need to cooperate with the other. The two principals eventually agreed to meet and act together. Strategy was then planned by a wider committee, in which Talleyrand and Roederer played the most important roles.[81]

There were unpleasant moments. One of these, recalled by Talleyrand in his memoirs, occurred a few days before the coup. Bonaparte had come to see him one evening at his house in the rue Taitbout. At one o'clock in the morning they were still talking by candlelight, when the sound of carriage wheels and cavalry was heard. They imagined that the plot had been discovered and that they were about to be arrested. Charles-Maurice extinguished the candles and went to a room overlooking the road. It turned out to be the banker of a gaming house, escorted by mounted guards, whose carriage had had an accident outside. Charles-Maurice and his co-plotter laughed loudly in relief.[82]

Talleyrand was equally important in securing the support, or at least the neutrality, of Barras. The plan required that a majority of the Directors should voluntarily resign so as to make way for three

Consuls, who, assisted by two commissions, would prepare a new Constitution. Since Gohier and Moulins were likely to prove troublesome, Barras would have to join Sieyès and Roger Ducos in the manoeuvre. Skilfully, Talleyrand, accompanied on different occasions by Réal and Fouché, worked on Barras's expectations. Initially, the Director was led to understand that he was to be a major beneficiary of the constitutional changes. Later, it seems, the lure of money and the implicit risk of trying to resist were more important.[83]

The different parts of the plan had to work together for it to succeed, and so the exact timing was vital. This was in the hands of Bonaparte and the military. At last, the coup was set for 18 Brumaire (9 November 1799). Early that morning Roederer went to see Talleyrand. Charles-Maurice was getting dressed, which was a long and elaborate business. He had Roederer draw up an 'honourable plan of resignation' in the form of a letter to be taken to Barras for his signature. While Roederer then busied himself with the preparation of propaganda, Talleyrand, joined by Admiral Bruix, set off to see Barras.[84]

Talleyrand now argued that the Republic was in the greatest danger and that only urgent action could avert it. Sieyès and Roger Ducos had, he claimed, already resigned as Directors, and Gohier and Moulins were on their way to the Conseil des Anciens to do the same. (This, as Barras knew, was quite false.) More ominously, Talleyrand added that the army was under Bonaparte's complete control. Barras opened the windows of his office and looked out. Sure enough, a troop of soldiers was marching towards the Tuileries, cheered on by the crowd. So he sat down and signed the letter of resignation that had been prepared for him. Did he receive a large bribe to do so? It seems probable. Barras, though, later claimed that the money given earlier to Talleyrand to hand over was never, in fact, offered and that Charles-Maurice took it for himself.[85]

The politicians had so far played their part with finesse. It was now left to Bonaparte to perform the coup itself, and here the trouble began. The two legislative councils had been summoned away from Paris to meet in Saint-Cloud the following morning (19 Brumaire). But they proved less easy to intimidate than the Directors, and less gullible than the plotters had hoped. Talleyrand had arranged to take a house nearby, owned by the financier and government victualler

Jean-Pierre Collot, who also helped bankroll the coup.[86] He was accompanied there by Roederer, Desrenaudes, Adrien Duquesnoy and Casimir de Montrond, whom he instructed to keep him constantly informed of what was happening. So he quickly learned of the opposition Bonaparte faced from the increasingly fractious politicians. When the Conseil des Cinq-Cents threatened to declare the general an outlaw and it looked as if all was lost, Talleyrand was now standing just outside the hall with Arnault. Other civilians fled but these two remained. Lavalette later claimed that Charles-Maurice had turned pale. But Arnault denied it: even in such extremities Talleyrand's expression was constitutionally incapable of change. Napoleon's brother Lucien, Murat and the soldiers then saved the day, and with it the general's skin and probably Talleyrand's too. The coup, which had begun with such delicacy, was concluded with clumsy brutality.[87]

Talleyrand must, though, have been well satisfied. A new régime was born, one that owed him a huge debt. He had encouraged Bonaparte during that difficult evening, when everything appeared to be going awry. And he stayed until midnight to see the final embers of democracy extinguished, as the remaining deputies voted themselves out of existence.[88] Then he could relax. 'We must have dinner,' he said, and took his colleagues – the Roederers, father and son, Montrond, Arnault and Radix de Sainte-Foy – off to dine at the nearby country house of another friend, the banker Michel Simons, in Meudon, where they were expected. Simons's wife, otherwise known as Mlle Lange, was a great beauty. She had at one time been the mistress of Barras, who was now on his way into internal exile. As for the house at Meudon, Charles-Maurice liked it so much that in future years he lived there himself.[89]

7

Bonaparte's Foreign Minister

⌐⌐⌐

THE RELATIONSHIP BETWEEN Talleyrand and Napoleon was complex. Moreover, it evolved over time. It sometimes resembled a love affair, or perhaps a marriage, even if it never amounted to a friendship. It left its marks, and in some respects scars, on both men, but particularly upon Napoleon, who was more sensitive and more vain. Before 18 Brumaire, Talleyrand's age, experience, sophistication and connections had given him a social edge over the young general. He even exhibited a quasi-paternal affection. Bonaparte, for his part, seems on occasion to have played on it. Sick in bed and learning from Napoleon that he was departing for Egypt without any money, Charles-Maurice told him to go and take 100,000 francs from his desk drawer. Some years later, Napoleon asked him what he had hoped to gain from this generosity and his Foreign Minister answered, perhaps even truthfully, that it was just an impulse. The (now) Emperor replied brutally that, in that case, it had been the action of a dupe.[1] But Napoleon in the years that followed would be more frequently duped by Charles-Maurice.

In his memoirs, Talleyrand speaks simply and persuasively of his early attitude to Napoleon: 'I loved Napoleon. I was even attached to him as a person, despite his faults. At the start, I felt myself drawn towards him by that irresistible attraction that a great genius brings with him. His generosity had provoked within me a sincere gratitude. Why should I be afraid to say so?. . .I had enjoyed his glory and the reflections of it that fell on to those who assisted him in his noble task.'[2] The gratitude would turn to hatred. But, still, at the end of the 'Manifesto' or 'Declaration', written in 1836 to justify his conduct, Talleyrand would recognize how much he owed Napoleon. He, therefore, imposed upon his family a solemn obligation: 'If ever a man bearing the name of Bonaparte should find himself in need of help or succour, may he obtain from my immediate heirs or their descendants every kind of assistance that it is in their power to give him.'[3] More important than affection, and more enduring, was Talleyrand's admiration for Napoleon's qualities. In old age, the Emperor's former Foreign Minister summed up his feelings in conversation with an English friend: 'Napoleon's genius was inconceivable. Nothing equalled his energy, his imagination, his intellect, his capacity for work, his ability to produce. He had wisdom too. His judgement was not so good. But still, when he wanted to give himself the time and he chose to profit from other people's judgement, it was only rarely that his own bad judgement led him astray.'[4]

Napoleon's own reflections upon Talleyrand were variable and also at times obsessive. Towards the end of his rule, as disasters bore down on him, and in exile, as bitterness at what he had lost ate into his soul, the former Emperor could not get Talleyrand out of his mind.[5] Charles-Maurice, for his part, certainly found it much easier to get over Napoleon. The Duke of Wellington was present at Mrs Crawford's house in Paris in July 1821 when it was finally learned that Napoleon had died two months earlier. Mrs Crawford exclaimed: 'What an event!' Talleyrand quietly corrected her: 'No longer an event, merely news.'[6]

But all this lay far in the future. The delay – ten days after the coup – in reappointing Talleyrand as Foreign Minister may, as Napoleon later suggested, have reflected Charles-Maurice's unpopularity and the need to allow public opinion to become accustomed to the new order of things. Possibly Charles-Maurice had tried to obtain the portfolio of Finance, which would have yielded richer pickings with less risk.[7] But most likely, Bonaparte had simply decided to make him wait a little for his promised reward, so as to prove from the start who was master. But there was no question of the First Consul keeping the German-born Reinhard in post. Bonaparte thought it ridiculous that when foreign diplomats spoke French, France's own Foreign Minister should converse with them in another language.[8] In any case, he required his Foreign Minister to have style, which Reinhard lacked and Talleyrand personified. So, on 22 November, Charles-Maurice duly returned to the Foreign Ministry in the rue du Bac, just four months after leaving it under the Directory. He would remain at the Hôtel Gallifet for the next seven and a half years.

The first step in securing his position was to attach himself closely to Bonaparte, the real source of authority in the régime. So at their first official meeting, he proposed that the First Consul alone should have charge of France's internal and external affairs. The secondary portfolios could be delegated to the other Consuls, Justice to Cambacérès, and Finance to Lebrun.[9] Bonaparte agreed enthusiastically. Indeed, as he confided to his secretary Bourrienne, it was precisely what he had secretly wanted. Gaining direct control of internal and external security was the way to absolute power.[10] Talleyrand had, of course, seen this and turned it to his own advantage.

Reading, rather than changing, the mind of Napoleon was, indeed, the key to Talleyrand's success. Others mocked his lack of real influence over events. Narbonne, for example, suggested that Charles-Maurice's pointed remarks to Napoleon were always delivered with a view to style, rather than to the substance of public affairs.[11] And that may well be true. Chateaubriand, for his part, diminished Talleyrand's role by saying that he 'signed events, not made them'.[12] In fact, he did not even do that, because Napoleon preferred to have his brother, Joseph, sign such treaties as those of Lunéville (with Austria), Amiens (with Britain) and Paris (with the United States).[13]

What Charles-Maurice could do, however, was manage Napoleon's moods. He knew how to deflect the imperious and impatient leader's wrath with an anecdote, a *bon mot*, or an amusing impertinence. For example, in 1802 while Bonaparte was fretting about whether the crucial Peace of Amiens with Britain had at last been signed, Talleyrand had it all the while in his capacious pocket as he obtained the First Consul's approval for various pieces of business. Finally, he said that he had good news and pulled out the treaty. When Bonaparte demanded to know why he had not done so earlier, he smiled and replied: 'When you are happy, you can't be approached.'[14] The technique of turning aside awkward criticism with subtle flattery was another of Talleyrand's favourites. The following year in Brussels, when the First Consul was angry about stories that circulated of Talleyrand's corruption, he bluntly asked him how he had made his fortune. 'Nothing simpler,' replied Talleyrand. 'I bought *rentes* on 17th Brumaire and sold them on the 19th.'[15]

In Talleyrand's own estimation it was by his restraint of Napoleon's impulsiveness that he most consistently served his master's and France's interests. His belief in a slow, orderly, timely approach to the most important, as to the most trivial, affairs in life was the result of several influences. As an aristocrat of the *ancien régime*, perhaps even as an ecclesiastic, he had absorbed an appreciation of rules and rites. He also delighted in enjoying life's slower moments, whether in elaborate flirtation, conversation at the dinner table, or long evenings playing whist. An expression attributed to him was: 'I have never hurried, but I am always on time' – and that had a political significance as well. As minister, he brought this philosophy to bear on the internal working of the Department of Foreign Affairs. But he applied it in particular to his dealings with Napoleon, notably by delaying the execution of the First Consul's (or Emperor's) orders until sufficient time had passed for proper reflection.

On presenting the *chefs de service* of the ministry to his successor, Champagny, in 1807, Talleyrand told him: 'You will find them loyal, clever, exact, but, thanks to my efforts, not at all zealous.' And when Champagny expressed surprise, he continued: 'Yes, Monsieur. Apart from some minor duty clerks, who, I think, close their envelopes a little hurriedly, all here maintain the greatest calm, and have grown out of the habit of rushing. When you have had to deal for a while with the interests of Europe and of the Emperor, you will see how important it is not to hasten to seal and despatch his wishes too quickly.'

Talleyrand later repeated what he had said to Napoleon, who found Champagny's reaction most amusing. But he also endorsed the advice.[16]

Talleyrand had no illusions about the limits of his ability to determine events. As the accounts he gave of his dealings with Napoleon implicitly recognize, he was even prepared to joke about it. In fact, when it suited his purpose, he deliberately understated his influence and, as difficulties grew, that became increasingly convenient.

Napoleon, for his part, was foolish enough to think that he had fully penetrated the psychology of Talleyrand and had thus finally gained control of him. So, when Charles-Maurice was appointed as Foreign Minister, the First Consul assured Cambacérès:

> Talleyrand has a lot of what is necessary to engage in and follow diplomatic negotiations: *esprit du monde*; knowledge of the courts of Europe; subtlety, not to mention something else – an immobility of the features that nothing can change; and finally a great name. By these means, he will be a good Minister of Foreign Affairs. I know that he only belongs to the Revolution by his misconduct, but the commitments that he has made are such that it would be impossible for him to gain pardon for his crimes. Bishop and *grand seigneur* under the *ancien régime*, Jacobin and deserter of his order under the Constituent Assembly, he would be lost if a prince of the royal house should regain the throne. We can, therefore, use Talleyrand without fear: his interest answers for him.[17]

Charles-Maurice was able to benefit from the – ultimately false – confidence which this smug analysis inspired in Napoleon. In doing so, he strove incessantly to flatter his master's ego. It must have been easier in the first three years or so, when Bonaparte's ambitions appeared containable, than later, when they increasingly broke free of reality. Although some of the language now seems extravagant, it was clearly well enough judged in the circumstances.

No detail was too small to overlook. For example, Bonaparte as a young man had won a prize for an essay submitted to the Académie de Lyon. Knowing this, Talleyrand unearthed the piece from the archives of that institution and presented it to the author, who, however, reading a few pages and regretting the immature radicalism it displayed, promptly threw it into the fire.[18] But it was only a minor setback. Charles-Maurice remained sensitive to all Napoleon's vulnerabilities and exploited them. He had offered his first splendid banquet and ball in honour of Bonaparte's beloved Joséphine, and he continued to remember the Corsican's sense of family. When Napoleon's brother-in-law, General Leclerc, husband of Pauline Bonaparte, was killed in Santo Domingo in 1803, Talleyrand privately suggested to foreign ambassadors that they should appear at the next imperial audience in mourning. The First Consul was so moved that he took Charles-Maurice aside and hugged him.[19]

The greater part of Talleyrand's correspondence with Napoleon is disappointingly unrevealing of the direction of foreign policy. But then his role was more secretary than policy adviser, let alone policy maker. That is not surprising, considering that policy itself in these years reflected the reality or potential of war, in which Bonaparte, not Talleyrand, was the expert. Indeed, Napoleon's instructions have the feel of the parade ground not the office. Addressed frequently to 'Monsieur Talleyrand' (omitting the 'de'), they contain rebukes for idleness: 'A large number of letters which have been written to me by different princes have been sent to you to draw up replies. However, I have not yet signed a single one.'[20] The tone is brisk, the tense imperative: 'You will leave for Berlin.'[21] 'You will send a messenger to Cassel before you go to bed.'[22]

As his self-confidence increased with the years, Napoleon exercised even closer control over Talleyrand's portfolio, concerning himself with points of drafting. Talleyrand is instructed on whether letters to foreign powers are to be short or long. He is sent Napoleon's 'ideas' about what is to go in them. The final draft must be approved word for word by the Emperor before it is despatched.[23]

Charles-Maurice's own letters, by contrast, reveal much of how he kept his grip on power: by the graceful insinuation with which he cultivated the great man's favour. Thus, departing for his annual cure to Bourbon-l'Archambault in June 1801, and conscious, it must be added, of the First Consul's own fragile health, he wrote:

> I leave with the sole but lively regret of going far away from you. The feelings that attach me to you and my conviction that the devotion of my life to your destiny, to the large vision that inspires you, is not useless to its fulfilment, have brought an interest to the care of my health that I never previously felt. . .Permit me to repeat that I love you, that I am afflicted at leaving, that I have the most lively impatience to come near you again, and that my devotion will only end with my life.[24]

The following month, having heard that a parade had been cancelled, and surmising that the First Consul was seriously ill, Talleyrand wrote:

> I cannot entertain the idea of seeing pain approach you, first because I love you, and after that because, being the person best equipped for all happiness, you would be the most pitiable of all if you saw before you a prospect of suffering against which force of character could do nothing, and philosophy still less. . .

I do not like your library, you spend too long there. I believe it to be damp; ground floors do not suit you; you are made for the heights.[25]

News that the First Consul's health had improved prompted a further letter on 19 July: 'I very much needed to know it, for at a distance one is horribly tormented.'[26] Later that year Bonaparte, as a favour to Talleyrand, removed his family from the list of *émigrés*, thus allowing them to return to take up their property and position in France. Charles-Maurice wrote to express his thanks: 'Allow me to borrow from a very famous friendship in history what a minister of Henri IV said to his master. "Since I attached myself to your destiny, I am yours – come life, come death." '[27] In fact, the comparison here between Talleyrand and Henri IV's great minister, Sully, was not unflattering to Charles-Maurice either.

As Napoleon recognized, Talleyrand brought an unmatched flair and finesse to his role as Foreign Minister, already evident under the Directory. Mme de La Tour du Pin, now back from America, was present at a magnificent lunch hosted by Charles-Maurice in honour of the new Ottoman ambassador. The guests were not served at a central dinner table, but instead from a *buffet*, constructed in tiers and reaching halfway up the wall. It was covered with various dishes, arranged among vases of rare and beautiful flowers. At the other side of the *salon* were couches and beside them little round tables on which the delicacies were placed. The Foreign Minister himself led the ambassador to a Turkish-style divan, where they squatted 'in oriental mode', while conversing through an interpreter.[28]

But what of the regular business of Foreign Affairs? Did Talleyrand truly run his department, or was it – and, indeed, was he – run by others? It has, after all, often been maintained that he simply left other people to do the work and then took the credit. Chateaubriand, for example, declared that he could not 'write a single sentence', that he was 'lazy and uneducated', and that he entirely relied on his underlings.[29]

An apocryphal anecdote sums up the perception. It has Hauterive approach the minister, holding a letter from a German Elector.

'Well?' says Talleyrand.

'A reply is needed,' explains his *chef de service*.

'What! In my own hand?'

'But certainly, *mon prince*, an Elector. . .'

'It is tyranny! What, to compose and write at the same time?. . .Oh well, Hauterive, I shall write, you dictate.'[30]

But, though constitutionally somewhat idle, and very appreciative of all the arts of leisure, Talleyrand was for most of his professional life an extremely productive worker. He followed, in fact, Choiseul's advice, delegating to others all that could be delegated, so that he could apply his time effectively – whether for state business, for personal pleasure, or for financial gain. Having a rare degree of self-possession, he was able to do all this with a nonchalance that observers often confused with indolence.

Napoleon's secretary, Méneval, was, for example, very unimpressed by Talleyrand's failure to contribute substantially to foreign policy:

> Napoleon would read the despatches that his minister submitted and speak in detail about the subjects they contained. M. de Talleyrand appeared to listen to him attentively. I rarely heard him reveal his own ideas. He barely responded except in monosyllables. Was it circumspection or a desire to know what the Emperor felt before explaining himself? When the discussion was approaching its end, it sometimes happened that Napoleon was called elsewhere to give an audience. He would leave M. de Talleyrand, saying to him: 'You understand: summarize it for me on paper. I shall return.' He would come back an hour or two hours later. M. de Talleyrand had written nothing. Then Napoleon, without showing any surprise, without complaint, would gather together the papers, and dictate at length whatever reply was required. He would then tell his minister to take away his dictation and bring back a clean copy. . .M. de Talleyrand, having gone back to his office, called in his *chefs de division*, who set about the task. It sometimes happened – rarely it is true – that I found him in the morning in bed, in a little room in which one or sometimes two of his draughtsmen were standing before an upright desk, giving the final touches to a report that he had to take to the Emperor, and that he would subsequently copy in his own hand. He was incorrigibly lazy, but he would do anything not to diminish his reputation for cleverness.[31]

Méneval was probably not equipped to judge which parts of Napoleon's dictation needed to be retained, remodelled or jettisoned, so in that respect his judgement is questionable.[32] But in any case, those who work for personalities like Bonaparte, and who survive the experience, understand that trying to second-guess them is a waste of time. Talleyrand used his access wisely, and conserved what influence he had, by relegating his role to that of secretary.

Vitrolles made a similar mistake in underrating Talleyrand's skill. But, for all that, his account of how Talleyrand dealt with his subordinates is revealing of a kind of professional mastery:

> He wrote little, and only very important personal letters. But he chose well those who acted for him. When he ordered the preparation of despatches or diplomatic notes, he explained in a few words and in broken sentences what they should contain; and when somebody brought him the piece he had ordered he read it with attention. If he was not fully satisfied, he folded the paper and gave it back, saying: 'That's not it', or 'That's still not it', or indeed 'That's not quite it', without any other explanation. One had to guess, until one attained the final triumph: 'That's it!'[33]

The Foreign Minister was only able to work in this manner because he encouraged his officials to understand his thinking, in the same way that he himself tried to immerse himself in Napoleon's. His staff knew, for example, what to make of the little notes and odd sentences that Talleyrand would carry around in his briefcase.[34] Moreover, at some stage in the work he would usually make his own substantial and distinctive changes. That has been proved by comparison between the draft and the final versions of documents sent on to the Emperor.[35] The system worked because at its head was a minister who, though hardly the kind of figure that a modern bureaucracy would appreciate, knew exactly how to get the best out of his department's modest, forty-four-strong complement of staff. (There was also a monkey, brought back by Denon from his travels, which proved very adept at sealing letters: it was later retired to the menagerie at Malmaison.)[36]

Maxime de Villemarest came to the ministry as one of three 'pupils' (élèves) recruited directly by Napoleon. In later life he went on to act as Talleyrand's secretary and then to write his colourful if well-informed volume, *Monsieur de Talleyrand*. Villemarest saw, as outsiders could not, what made Talleyrand's direction of his department so unique:

[His secretaries] adored M. de Talleyrand, because no reproach ever left his lips, because he never overlooked an opportunity to say something pleasant to them, because he invited them to his dinners, his balls, his *soirées*, because independently from their salaries he would say to them from time to time: 'I think that you ought to pay a little visit to M. Bresson.' That meant that the head of the Division des fonds had to pay them a bonus, because perhaps no man has known like M. de Talleyrand how to make himself loved by those who came into regular contact with him.[37]

Talleyrand's own offices – what would today be called the Private Office – were situated on the ground floor of the main building of the Hôtel Gallifet. They consisted of two rooms. The first, the outer office, was quite large and lit by French windows looking out on to the gardens. It was usually occupied by the three or four secretaries. These drafted all the minister's own correspondence. A second, smaller room was where the minister conducted his most private discussions. When he was absent and affairs were sluggish, the secretaries would sit out in the garden. But there were still rules: in particular, Talleyrand did not like anyone coming into his own room while he was away, not least because it was connected by a staircase to his personal apartments on the first floor.

A number of Principal Private Secretaries served Talleyrand over the years. Characteristically, he used them for extraneous purposes as well. Osmond oversaw all his personal and public affairs, while his brother acted as tutor to Charles-Maurice's two nephews, Louis and Edmond de Périgord. Tony Roederer, the son of Talleyrand's collaborator in the plot of 18 Brumaire, cut his teeth working for Talleyrand before his promotion to the ranks of the auditors of the Conseil d'État and to a post in Italy. Another of the minister's secretaries was Roux de Laborie (otherwise known as Roux de Rochelle), a somewhat shadier character. Like others around Talleyrand, he had his own peculiarities – at one level a man of letters, at another a thief who in mysterious circumstances fled with a treaty concluded between Napoleon and Tsar Paul I, which he sold in England. In 1804 he was pardoned and returned to France, where he continued to enjoy Talleyrand's favour, achieving importance as his right-hand man at the Restoration.[38]

From these divisions came the oral advice, the written briefing, and the memoranda which constituted the bulk of the important material emanating from the ministry. The First Division (or Division of the North) was headed by Durant de Mareuil, a stylish figure who modelled himself on Talleyrand and even adopted some of his mannerisms. This division was, as its name suggests, the most politically important section of the department. It covered affairs relating to Britain, the Batavian Republic (Holland), Austria, Prussia, the German Empire, Denmark, Sweden, Russia and the United States. It was situated overlooking the principal courtyard, on the fourth floor of the ministry's main building.

The Second Division (or Division of the South) overlooked the first courtyard on the left. Its business was relations with Spain, Portugal, the Helvetian Republic (Switzerland), Italy and the Ottoman Empire. At its head when Talleyrand arrived as minister under the Consulate was his long-time collaborator, Hauterive, who had been promoted by Reinhard from his previous position as *souschef* in the consular section. Hauterive was a more powerful character than Durant, a thinker about foreign policy in his own right, and a strong critic of Napoleon who had no fear of expressing himself forcefully on this as on other matters to the minister. In 1807 Hauterive was moved sideways to take over the archives, housed in the Hôtel Maurepas, where his memory rather than his opinions was at a premium, and was replaced by Roux de Laborie.

Until then, the archives had been the preserve of one of the ministry's most experienced and eccentric figures, Antoine-Bernard Caillard, who lived a solitary but sybaritic life. He was an aesthete: a bibliophile who had the leather for his priceless books imported from Constantinople and cut and bound in London, a wine buff whose cellar was legendary, and a gourmet whose dinner hours were sacrosanct. This, naturally, was an incentive for the minister to devise malicious schemes to interrupt them. Also in the Hôtel de Maurepas were to be found M. Tessier, the oldest employee of the ministry, whose thankless task it was to instruct the *élèves*, the cartographer and geographer Barbier du Bocage, and several other elderly former diplomats whose role would nowadays be described as that of consultancy. In fact, a characteristic trait of Talleyrand's tenure of the ministry was his appreciation of experience and of the traditions that lent to its personnel a distinctive *esprit de corps*.[39]

There were two offices whose functions were strictly covert: one was the Code Office, where a large collection of seals from other powers was kept for various nefarious uses. Situated nearby, and no less nefarious, was a propaganda office which specialized in the disinformation of British public opinion, one of its works being a journal called *The Argus* produced by a British-born Jew, Lewis Goldsmith. Unfortunately for Charles-Maurice, the propagandist unexpectedly turned traitor (or, depending on one's perspective, he ceased his treachery), fled to Britain, and wrote instead disobliging material about the Emperor's conduct and the minister's peccadilloes.[40]

Apart from his officials, or his valet Courtiade, one other group was allowed into the minister's inner sanctum – his ever-present clique of personal and political cronies. The department's burly Swiss porter, Jorris, had been known to carry an importunate comtesse out of the building; but this group could always gain entry.[41] Talleyrand's *hommes de confiance* were a greedy, unscrupulous, though able and energetic team, who followed their principal's fortunes and expected to share in them. They inspired the contempt of Charles-Maurice's colleagues – Vitrolles described them as 'parasites' – but they served their purpose as spies, agents of influence, deputies, messengers, intermediaries, negotiators, financial advisers, and not least companions to while away a boring evening.[42] The names of some have already appeared, such as Cazenove, Radix de Sainte-Foy, later Emerich von Dalberg, and always Casimir de Montrond. This last, as Vitrolles recognized, had a place apart, despite passing unmentioned by Talleyrand in his memoirs.

Montrond, a cavalry officer under the *ancien régime* and a royalist, had stayed in France at the outbreak of the Revolution. He was imprisoned at Saint-Lazare, where he saved from death Aimée de Coigny – Chénier's heroic *'jeune captive'* - and they were later briefly married. He seems to have met Talleyrand in exile in England, where his perfect English and the protection of Lady Holland assured him an *entrée* into English society. Indeed, it is very likely that Montrond was for many years a British agent. On suspicion of treason, he was imprisoned by Napoleon in the fortress of Ham, but escaped and re-entered, at least nominally, the Emperor's service during the Hundred

Days. Handsome, witty, intelligent, gallant, brave, unscrupulous and corrupt, he was, in the eyes of the outside world, not just an agent but rather a clone of his friend and master. 'Do you know why I like Montrond?' asked Talleyrand one day of the duchesse de Laval. 'It's because he has so few prejudices.' 'And do you know, duchesse, why I like M. de Talleyrand so much?' responded Montrond. 'It's because he has no prejudices at all.' Charles-Maurice was known to remark of Montrond: 'He is certainly the cleverest man in the world. He hasn't a sou to his name, he has no salary, he spends sixty thousand francs a year and he has no debts.'[43] With age Montrond's charm palled somewhat: Charles-Maurice quarrelled with him and the duchesse de Dino could not abide him. But he was never cut off entirely.[44]

Talleyrand had, of course, first come to the department under the Directory. His predecessor, Charles Delacroix, who despite his successor's sneers demonstrated considerable competence, had spent his last days in office conducting a thorough reform. As a result, a number of posts were abolished and tasks rationalized. Talleyrand accepted these changes, while modifying certain details.[45] Prompted perhaps by the planning of the Egyptian expedition, and a good linguist himself, he reorganized the education of the young men who were destined to act as 'dragoman' (interpreter) to the Porte.[46]

As part of the Napoleonic reform of government, Talleyrand (greatly assisted by Hauterive) in January 1800 reorganized the personnel of the department. This can be seen as the first stage of the recreation of a diplomatic corps after the disorders of the Revolution. All the members of the service were divided into seven grades, from 'aspirant' at the bottom to 'ambassador' at the top. No one could be promoted to a grade unless he had passed through the previous one, except by a special decision of the First Consul. Each grade had a set salary, and different posts corresponded to different grades. Employees of the department were supposed to alternate between service within France and overseas. In fact, the reforms proved impossible to put fully into effect. The first three grades were suppressed and replaced by that of the *élèves*. More importantly, it was discovered that the qualities required of diplomats were different from those required of staff at the ministry itself, so the original rule of alternation between internal and external postings was changed. But the fundamentals of the Talleyrand reform remained.

That the reforms were part of an overall philosophy rather than mere bureaucratic fiddling is demonstrated by the long report despatched to the First Consul in March 1800. It was substantially the work of Hauterive, but it reflected Talleyrand's view of the need for an *esprit d'administration* which had to operate through intelligently established rules for promotion. The report enumerated the special qualities, both of character and of intellect, required of an official of the department and argued that these should be valued and rewarded.[47]

Talleyrand was also convinced that the department's personnel had to be offered financial security through a decent pension. This was now fixed as half of the salary appropriate to the grade at which a member of the service retired if he had served twenty years, and the equivalent of full pay if he had served twenty-five years. This provision was even retrospectively offered to those who had served the ministry under the *ancien régime*. The underlying purpose was to ensure that former or even current diplomats were not bribed to sell state secrets – a danger that Talleyrand had more reason to understand than most. Such security also helped provide the degree of continuity and expertise that he so valued in his officials.[48]

Talleyrand had, indeed, a very clear idea of how both the minister and his officials should behave. On 3 March 1838, shortly before his death, he delivered a eulogy of his predecessor, Reinhard, before the Académie des Sciences Morales, asserting that:

> The Minister of Foreign Affairs must. . . have the faculty of appearing open while remaining impenetrable, of being reserved without appearance of constraint, of being shrewd even in his choice of distractions. His conversation should be simple, varied, unexpected, always natural and sometimes ingenuous. In a word, he must never for a moment in twenty-four hours cease to be Minister of Foreign Affairs.[49]

The description is clearly of Talleyrand, not of Reinhard. There is, notably, his inscrutability, which prompted Lannes and Murat to joke that if you were talking to Talleyrand and someone kicked him from behind, you would never know anything of it from his face.[50] The picture is, in truth, that of an old-fashioned view of foreign policy dominated by the techniques of personal diplomacy. Yet it was one to which Napoleon himself subscribed. He told Méneval that Talleyrand was 'without equal in diplomatic conversations' because he revealed nothing and discovered from his interlocutors what Napoleon needed to know.[51] Of course, this simplistic view was self-serving too, because it suggested that his minister was a mere information-gatherer.

By contrast, Talleyrand's description in the Reinhard eulogy of the role of the departmental official is more revealing of the administrative ethos that he had quietly championed during his time as Foreign Minister:

> A delicate tact had led [Reinhard: for whom read 'Talleyrand'] to understand that the behaviour of a *chef de division* must be simple, regular, solitary; that, a stranger to the tumult of the world, he must live uniquely for public affairs and commit to them an impenetrable discretion; that, always ready to respond about facts and about people, he must at all times keep stored in his memory all the treaties, know their dates, judge accurately their strong and weak points, their antecedents and their consequences. [Reinhard knew] that, while making use of this knowledge, [the *chef de division*] must take care to avoid disquieting the eternally alert *amour-propre* of the minister, and that even when winning him over to his opinion, his success must remain in the shade; for [the official] must never shine, except with a reflected brilliance.[52]

In preparing the substantial volume that appeared in October 1800, entitled *L'État de la France à la fin de l'an VIII*, Talleyrand certainly relied upon his *chefs de division*, above all upon Hauterive, who appears as the book's officially acknowledged author. It is an impressive survey of France's global standing. Charles-Maurice's most recent French biographer has even described it as demonstrating a 'true European vision'.[53] This is perhaps an exaggeration. But the work is certainly comprehensive, both in its detailed discussion of the other powers and in its attempt to fit current French preoccupations into a historical framework. It places the blame for the destabilization of Europe not on the French Revolution, but rather on three developments that preceded it: namely the consolidation of Prussian dominance in north Germany, the expansion of Russia into Europe through the partition of Poland, and the near monopoly of maritime power wielded by Britain. Of the three problem powers, Britain receives harshest treatment as prime disturber of the peace. Despite the historical and philosophical references, *L'État de la France* is, in essence, a piece of propaganda, commanded by the First Consul and intended to justify his current policies.[54] As such, it reflected what he expected of his Foreign Minister. Only later, and at the expense of his relations with Napoleon, did Talleyrand seek to advance his own opinions.

More generally, it suited Napoleon, and it served the interests of France, for Talleyrand to adopt a more emollient tone than that of his master. In current parlance, between them they played 'hard cop, soft cop' with representatives of the other powers. This gave Napoleon time to pursue his ends by exploiting the hopes raised by Talleyrand's diplomacy. It also allowed Charles-Maurice to attract the blandishments, and so receive the bribes, that he needed to sustain his expensive lifestyle and his little court. The representatives of Prussia, for example, were constantly deceived by the act. Combined with divided counsels and the interference of a politically witless monarch, this would lead the country to the edge of oblivion.

In truth, Talleyrand had little respect for Prussia, either now or later. Perhaps this reflected the fact that Prussia's recent emergence as the dominant power in north Germany excluded France from exerting serious influence in an area that it had long sought to dominate. Or possibly the Hohenzollerns were just all too evidently *parvenus* compared with the Habsburgs. Charles-Maurice enjoyed good personal relations with a series of Prussian ambassadors: but then they were not usually Prussians. Under the Consulate and Empire, the Prussian minister in Paris was the marquis Girolamo Lucchesini. Talleyrand adeptly worked on his sympathies and distracted his attention. Thus the Foreign Minister would exaggerate French hostility towards Russia (which the Prussians feared) and Austria (which they hated) in a manner calculated to suggest that Prussia itself was not a potential prey.[55]

Talleyrand spent years trying (and eventually failing) to lure Prussia into a coalition against Britain, by offering Berlin the tantalizing prospect of acquisition of the electorate of Hanover.[56] Meanwhile, he conveyed to France's representative at the Prussian court Napoleon's (and doubtless his own) scorn for Prussian shilly-shallying – for Frederick William III hoped desperately to enlarge his state without incurring the risk and expense of war.[57] But at the same time Charles-Maurice dazzled Lucchesini with his extraordinary ideas and conceptions. Thus in December 1801 he told the minister that Prussia was 'of all the powers, the one that it most suits us to see expand'; it was the power that must 'dominate North Germany'. He even apologized, in characteristic vein, about that French 'amour-propre. . . which renders us sometimes difficult with our neighbours'. Referring to the process of secularization of German ecclesiastical principalities, he added in a final intriguing remark that it was necessary to 're-work the whole of Germany'.[58] (This was, indeed, duly achieved by the imperial Recess of Ratisbon of 1802–3.)[59]

Charles-Maurice liked to introduce historical allusions whenever he thought they would prove flattering. Thus, in dealing with Berlin references to Frederick the Great of Prussia kept appearing.[60] Similarly, in May 1803, as war reopened with Britain, it was the Franco-Austrian Treaty of 1756, signed under Choiseul, that was invoked to chill Prussian blood and prompt Prussian compliance.[61] Talleyrand warned that 'some of those' around Napoleon favoured such an opening to Austria, but that the First Consul was determined to resist Austrian blandishments and show favour to Berlin.[62] In truth, Talleyrand himself strongly favoured a strategic accommodation with Austria.

The early period of Talleyrand's collaboration with Napoleon was his most successful. It was also extremely advantageous for France. The close-run Battle of Marengo in 1800 had made the French masters once more of Italy, and Moreau's crushing victory of Hohenlinden in the same year had secured the position in Germany. Austria was forced to make peace by the Treaty of Lunéville the following February. French internal order and prosperity had in large part been restored. Reconciliation both with the Church (through the Concordat) and with the old nobility (many of whom had now lost hope in the Bourbons) had been successfully undertaken.[63] The revolt of the Chouans in Brittany and the Vendée had dwindled. At last, even the old enemy, Britain, exhausted and isolated, finally agreed to the Peace of Amiens in March 1802. In his memoirs, Charles-Maurice sums up the achievement:

> At the time of the Peace of Amiens, France enjoyed externally a power, a glory, an influence such that the most ambitious spirit could desire nothing further for his country. And what rendered the situation still more wonderful was the rapidity with which it had been achieved. In

less than two and a half years. . .France had passed from the debasement into which the Directory had plunged it to the first rank of Europe.[64]

This assessment is over-harsh on the Directory, whose record it was in the interests of Napoleonic propagandists to besmirch.[65] But it had enough substance, and it was widely enough shared among Frenchmen, to provide legitimacy for the new order. On the proposal of his two Consul colleagues, in August Bonaparte was named First Consul for Life, endorsed by a plebiscite.

Yet, if Talleyrand is to be believed, it was now that the seeds of future catastrophe were sown. Marengo had been so nearly a disaster that Bonaparte had been shocked (as the memoirs put it) into 'profiting by the victory without abusing it'. Bonaparte had decided, therefore, to 'consolidate his power before increasing it'. Moreover, he was jealous of Moreau's success and so wanted to establish peace without allowing his sometime rival the glory of a fresh success.[66] In other words, only circumstances rather than settled policy had forced him to pursue peace. Moreover – again following Talleyrand's line of argument – the Peace of Amiens 'was barely concluded when moderation began to abandon Bonaparte; this peace had not yet received its complete execution before he was already casting the seeds of new wars which, after having crushed Europe and France, would lead [Napoleon] himself to his ruin'.[67] Upon the correctness or otherwise of this analysis depends history's judgement of Napoleon and of the subsequent conduct of Talleyrand himself.

The view expressed in Talleyrand's memoirs is not just hindsight. He held it at the time. One day after the peace imposed by the Battle of Marengo, the financier Ouvrard visited Talleyrand to find the latter ill in bed, and in reflective mood. He told his visitor that the First Consul now had to choose between two paths. The first was that of a 'federal [i.e. treaty-based] system' which would leave each ruler in place 'as master of his own domain on conditions favourable to the victor'. The second was the path of incorporation within the extended French state. The latter, Talleyrand predicted, would lead to a war without end.[68]

So Talleyrand was, in this, remarkably consistent. Moreover, his views became accepted wisdom after Napoleon's fall. This does not, though, mean that they were wholly original. As Chateaubriand remarks: 'When Napoleon became inebriated by power he committed mistakes that were enormous and striking to everyone. M. de Talleyrand saw them as did everyone else. But that does not imply a lynx-like vision'.[69]

More important, at least for Talleyrand's own reputation, is whether his fundamental criticism was correct: was there, in truth, an alternative strategy that Napoleon could have been expected to pursue? It is not necessary to suggest that Bonaparte was sincerely wedded to peace in order to see that it was bound to be extremely difficult for him to avoid war. It was politically unthinkable – and Napoleon never seriously thought about it – to relinquish French acquisitions in Belgium and along the left bank of the Rhine. These gains had first been made by the Directory, and owed nothing to Napoleon's personal feats of arms. Moreover, they were seen by the majority of Frenchmen as the most tangible reward for years of bloody fighting. For centuries, the region had been viewed as of vital strategic importance to France.

It would perhaps have been possible to buy off Prussia in Germany, to compensate Austria in the Balkans (as Talleyrand himself wished), to give up (at a pinch) the dream of a Napoleonic Italy, and to keep Russia through fear and flattery out of central Europe. Under these conditions, the various potentially hostile powers might just have been contained, intimidated, or induced to squabble among themselves. But Britain presented a problem of a quite different order. This stemmed from the fact that any British government, conscious of British security and trade interests, would oppose indefinite French control of Antwerp, the River Scheldt and the west bank of the Rhine – let alone in conjunction with French domination of Europe as a whole. This issue, after all, rather than revulsion at French Revolutionary excesses, was what had brought Britain into the war with Revolutionary France in the first place.

The question as to whether Talleyrand's analysis and prescription were correct, therefore, ultimately comes down to whether Britain could have been induced, albeit reluctantly, to subordinate its fundamental strategic interests to those of France. Those who argued, and still argue, that it might have done can point to the fact that in 1802 this is precisely what happened under the terms of the Peace of

Amiens.[70] At the low points of Britain's struggle – when military disasters incurred by continental allies, Irish uprising, domestic discontent and economic crisis convinced much of the political élite that it was necessary to sue for peace on whatever terms could be obtained – such an outcome seemed possible. Talleyrand personally placed high hopes in his friend Charles James Fox, who became Britain's Foreign Secretary in 1806. But the latter's early enthusiasm for peace in the wake of Napoleon's victory at Austerlitz soon diminished, and Fox's death in September marked the end of negotiations and a resumption of war. At no point was Britain forced permanently to renounce its goal of defeating France. Meanwhile, the British government's propaganda programme to diabolize Napoleon made any settlement with France even more unthinkable.[71]

If there was no hope of peace on acceptable terms with Britain, as Napoleon believed, only total and unconditional war made sense. The Continental Blockade, which would itself lead France into new, more exhausting wars in Europe, first in the Iberian Peninsula and then in the depths of Russia, offered a last hope of victory over the British foe. But overstretched interventions provoked waves of Spanish and German nationalism, the hostility of peoples not just princes.[72] For Napoleon this meant defeat and exile. For France it meant occupation, the permanent loss of its 'natural borders', and relegation to the role of second, and later (with German unification) third, power in Europe.

This is not to say that Napoleon's tactics were wise, nor that his judgement was sound, nor that, if he had shown the moderation Talleyrand advised, his régime might not have survived somewhat longer than it did. But the idea that Napoleon could have secured a lasting peace on the terms that Talleyrand wished is unconvincing.

In his memoirs, Talleyrand places responsibility for the breakdown of the Peace of Amiens in 1803 on Napoleon's decision to annex Piedmont rather than to return it, as his Foreign Minister apparently advised, to its ruler, the King of Sardinia. But at the time Talleyrand's main task was simply to ensure that the rupture came at a time that suited France and that the British government emerged as culprit.

In truth, responsibility for the renewal of war was evenly shared. Bonaparte had intervened against the spirit of the treaty in Italy and

Switzerland. He had sent missions to India and the Middle East. He had despatched an expedition to Santo Domingo. He had signed a new treaty with the Porte. He had refused to evacuate Holland. He had dashed British hopes of trade with continental Europe. For their part, and in still more flagrant breach of the treaty, the British had failed to evacuate their troops from Malta – crucial to French ambitions in the Mediterranean. War was thus inevitable. Its consequences for French foreign policy were problematic. But, in war as in peace, the Foreign Minister would display shrewdness bordering on genius in advancing his own personal interests.

8

Political Fortunes

—◦—

WHEN BERTIE GREATHEAD, an English visitor to Paris in January
1803, was presented to the French Foreign Minister, he was not
favourably impressed. 'Talleyrand,' he wrote, 'is a nasty looking dog'.
He added: 'They say he has made two millions sterling since he has
been in office.'[1] Charles-Maurice's reputation for venality was thus
already well established, even among foreign tourists. Chateaubriand
would pithily encapsulate it: 'When M. de Talleyrand is not conspir-
ing, he is trafficking.'[2] And he would repeat, in the course of a scathing
biographical notice, the various notorious incidents surrounding the
Foreign Minister's career in corruption, estimating that he made and
re-made his fortune five or six times, notably:

> [b]y the million that he received from Portugal in the hope of signa-
> ture of a peace with the Directory, a peace that was never signed; by
> the purchase of Belgian bonds at the Peace of Amiens, which he, M.
> de Talleyrand, knew about before it was known by the public; by the
> erection of the temporary kingdom of Etruria; by the secularization of
> ecclesiastical property in Germany; by the trading of his opinions at
> the Congress of Vienna.[3]

Charles-Maurice, who always had Chateaubriand's measure,
replied to such suggestions with the line: 'My problem is not at all that
of buying M. de Chateaubriand, but of paying him what he thinks
he's worth.'[4] But the fact remains that, unlike a number of other
unpleasant accusations from the pen of Chateaubriand, these certainly
contain a large amount of truth. Indeed, they are by no means exhaus-
tive. Barras's list of Talleyrand's malversations, derived from other lists
circulating in England, has already been mentioned. Villemarest, who
admired Talleyrand, albeit without illusions, includes in *Monsieur de*

Talleyrand a still longer list. It enumerates *pourboires* from, alongside those described by Chateaubriand, Austria, Prussia, Naples, the Pope, the King of Sardinia, the Cisalpine Republic, the Batavian Republic and the Ottoman Grand Vizir.[5]

Talleyrand was not, of course, unique in being venal. But the scale of his corruption and the shamelessness he exhibited were unusual. As one of those involved in his lucrative transactions would observe: 'He thought of his high position like a gold mine. His favours had to be paid for not in snuff boxes or diamonds but in cash.'[6] Talleyrand's corruption was common knowledge in the courts of Europe. It was particularly useful to those whose greed rivalled his own. For example, Talleyrand and Godoy, the Spanish Chief Minister, managed to extort between them from the King of Spain's coffers payments that Bonaparte had suppressed. It was a year before the First Consul discovered the truth and had the malversation stopped.[7]

Probably, though, the most financially fruitful diplomatic negotiations undertaken by Talleyrand under the Consulate were those associated with the Recess of Ratisbon, which led to the abolition of the Holy Roman Empire and the re-ordering of Germany. Talleyrand's virtuosity as a diplomat was vital to the whole operation. Napoleon's secretary, Méneval, doubtless reflects his master's view when he describes the Foreign Minister as the First Consul's 'precious instrument' in the affair.[8] These manoeuvres had all the characteristics that Talleyrand, as a 'trafficker' of favours, could desire. They were lengthy, detailed and complicated. Moreover, it was possible to ensure an overall settlement that suited the interests of France and the other main powers – Prussia, Austria and (at a distance) Russia – while forcing the smaller German entities into competitive bidding for advantage from the processes of secularization, consolidation and indemnification.[9] Pasquier claims to have heard from 'well-informed people' that Talleyrand received at least 10 million francs from the process and that his collaborators did well out of it too.[10]

Another indemnification turned out more awkwardly. The Prince of Nassau-Orange, former stadholder of Holland, had been granted a substantial indemnity in compensation for his losses as a result of the creation of the Batavian Republic. Napoleon had decided to deal with the matter himself, in view of the fact that the King of Prussia was the

Prince's brother-in-law. But while at Aix-la-Chapelle, sightseeing and receiving congratulations on his new title of Emperor of the French, he learned that, quite separately, another negotiation was under way. The Foreign Minister was seeking to obtain 12 million francs for the same object from the Batavian government. A large slice was, evidently, due to go into Talleyrand's own pocket. Napoleon initiated an enquiry. It turned out that Talleyrand and his agents, notably Durant de Mareuil and Sémonville, were indeed implicated. Charles-Maurice brazened it out with the Emperor, just as he had brazened out the XYZ Affair with the Directory. Napoleon was entirely unconvinced and considered replacing him, but could not think of anyone else to do the job. As a sign of his disgrace, Talleyrand was not allowed to join the First Consul in Mainz. But he quickly returned to favour.[11]

Nor was Charles-Maurice apparently repentant as a result of that earlier scandal in his dealings with American envoys. When the ambassador of the United States, Robert Livingston, came to see the Foreign Minister with a view to signing the Peace of Paris between the two countries in September 1800, he was asked by Talleyrand: 'Have you any money?' The question was then repeated in the form: 'Have you a lot of money?' The Foreign Minister went on to explain: 'You see, in this country business is very difficult to transact. One needs lots of money. With that, there are no difficulties that cannot be overcome.'[12]

How many millions of francs in total such dealings netted Talleyrand one can only guess. The figures neatly added up and published by his detractors may not be an exaggeration, but neither are they reliable. The best indication of Talleyrand's gains is his wealth, and the best measure of that is his expenditure. He spent huge sums. Talleyrand needed money for a number of reasons, by no means all concerned with his sophisticated tastes. He had, of course, the 'court' that surrounded him all day: its members required rewards for their service.[13] He had to keep a great house, indeed several houses, within which he could entertain. That hospitality was not a luxury, but a necessity, because lacking real power he had to rely on influence. Such influence depended upon the use of guile, charm and wit, but it required that *chez M. de Talleyrand* was where the men of the moment, and the beautiful women they wanted to meet, should habitually assemble.

Charles-Maurice was businesslike but never merely avaricious. He spent freely in order to earn still more. His fundamental conviction was that money breeds money, so that it is always necessary to be rich today – or, in the last resort, to appear rich today – if one wants to avoid poverty tomorrow. One must never, he would tell Vitrolles, be a 'poor devil', adding (mendaciously) that he had always been rich. Vitrolles believed that the two driving forces of the man were 'the love of women and the love of money' and that 'politics was his industry'.[14] This had long been the case. In his youth Talleyrand once sardonically admonished his friend Narbonne, who said that he could not afford a carriage, with the words: 'One pays for a carriage with a carriage.'[15] How, precisely, one might expect to do so was demonstrated in another anecdote that circulated. Approached respectfully by someone soliciting his attention, he discovered that it was his carriage maker, who wanted to be paid. 'You will be paid,' Talleyrand assured him. 'And when, Monseigneur?' 'Well,' replied Talleyrand, getting into his new carriage, 'you are very curious!'[16] Of course, the non-payment or late payment of bills can only be taken so far. But they can be taken further if one's prestige is greater, which was another advantage that Talleyrand gained from living in such style.

Charles-Maurice had, indeed, always lived stylishly. But as Foreign Minister he began to live in considerable grandeur. In early 1800 he purchased for his private use in Paris the Hôtel de Créqui, built in the reign of Louis XV and situated in the rue d'Anjou. (The house no longer exists.) But he also had a succession of country residences. First, there was briefly a small property in Auteuil, and then in 1802 a more substantial house at Neuilly where he entertained in the grand manner. The following year he rented a house on the heights of Passy, near Ranelagh, where the fare was superb.[17] He also had for a time the house at Meudon, where the banker Simons and his wife had entertained him and his friends at the time of the coup of 18/19 Brumaire. From 1803 until 1809 he rented the beautiful château of Bry-sur-Marne just outside Paris. Built originally for Louis XV's contrôleur-général, Silhouette, it had a fine library, whose contents Talleyrand tried unsuccessfully to buy. For most of the period it was the regular home of his wife, and later passed to Charles-Maurice's close collaborator, Baron (formerly abbé) Louis.[18]

Above all, from 7 May 1803, Talleyrand also owned the magnificent château of Valençay, whose name remains so closely associated with his. It was purchased at the suggestion and with the assistance of Bonaparte. The First Consul, anxious to impress foreign dignitaries and to exploit Charles-Maurice's lineage and polish in doing so, wanted his Foreign Minister to acquire a great house for the purpose. One of Napoleon's courtiers, Jean-Baptiste-Charles Legendre de Luçay, was eager to sell Valençay, but Talleyrand did not have sufficient funds to purchase it.[19] Accordingly, the 1.6 million francs required were granted by Napoleon from state funds.

Valençay is one of the great Renaissance châteaux of France. It had been completely rebuilt more than two centuries earlier by Jacques d'Estampes with the benefit of his wife's money, she being the daughter of a rich financier. The tall *pavillon d'entrée* is in the form a square keep (*donjon*), but its massive chimneys, corniche, numerous windows, domed corner towers and false machicolations proclaim it a structure designed for pleasure not defence. Its style resembles that of Chambord, and the central structure dates from about 1540. From this keep, two lengths of unequal dimensions lead off. Each ends in a cylindrical tower surmounted by a dome, the west much larger than the east. In the mid-seventeenth century a new wing was added facing west. In the mid-eighteenth century it was reconstructed and a further large domed tower was added at the south end. Indeed, Valençay's most distinctive features are these towers, with their slate domes. The Prince was proud of their 'Moorish' appearance.[20]

The main approach to the château is by the road from Blois. The visitor turns down along a tree-lined avenue, passes through courtyards and enters through a gateway set in an iron grille fence. Ahead lies the north façade of the château beyond a dry moat and stone bridge. Passing through the gateway of the keep one comes to the *cour d'honneur*. Beyond, the view over the Nahon valley is of hills and forests and, more immediately, of those gardens that the duchesse de Dino would make her own and to which she would descend by a separate staircase from her private apartments: they are still known as *Le Jardin de la duchesse*.

Talleyrand made relatively few changes to the externals of the château itself, though he had to renew the chimneys of the keep when they were blown down in a storm in 1836. He also improved the out-buildings and grounds. He rebuilt the orangery; he added stables; he created a theatre; he built a mock hunting lodge in the Italian style, in which to entertain; he added several follies, including an 'Egyptian temple'. But Valençay was thoroughly rebuilt internally, removing what remained of its traditional aspect of mock-feudal manor and transforming it into a palace capable of accommodating a large personnel. Apartments, state rooms and corridors were thus created, all to be filled with sumptuous furniture. And once the château finally ceased to be a glorified prison for the Spanish princes – under circumstances to be described – it was steadily adorned with the paintings and other memorabilia that testified to its owner's wealth, distinction and political longevity.[21]

Talleyrand took a close interest in working the estate, particularly as he grew older and his public responsibilities diminished. He had inherited from the previous owners a spinning mill and a forge, which was fuelled by wood from the surrounding forests. Talleyrand kept on planting trees and expanding his holdings. He proudly noted in posthumous instructions to his heir, Louis: 'I have administered the lands and forests of Valençay as the father of a family, that is to say that the present has been sacrificed to the future.'[22] Such benevolent paternalism was reflected in the view he took of his duties to his tenants, to his neighbours and to the wider community of this area of Berry. Life in the village of Valençay revolved around that of the château in intimate detail, to the extent that a local hosiery even kept moulds of the legs of the Prince's female guests, in case they laddered their stockings.[23]

Only in later life would Talleyrand have much opportunity to sample the delights of Valençay, when it became a home for him. He would regularly visit at the tail end of his annual cure at Bourbon-l'Archambault. In old age, the Prince, accompanied by his spaniel, Carlos, would be pushed around the grounds of the château by a servant in what had been Louis XVIII's wheelchair. On one occasion it overturned, throwing him out.[24] Inside the château, he used another little wheelchair sent over from England by Lady Holland.[25] In these last years he was joined at Valençay by the last love of his life, Dorothée, duchesse de Dino. For the woman he actually married,

Valençay was on occasion a burden, and once, it seems, a source of disgrace, but never much more.[26]

Talleyrand's marriage mystified his contemporaries even more than did his political intrigues. Opinion was sharply divided about his motives, though unanimous in regarding the union as a grotesque mistake. Mme de Rémusat, a dear friend though a jealous one, thought, like many others, that Napoleon might have forced his hand.[27] She was probably right.

Catherine Verlée (or Worlée) was born in the Danish Indian settlement of Tranquebar in 1762. Her father had been a French port official at Pondicherry in French India. At the age of fifteen in Chandernagor she married a naturalized Englishman (born Swiss) working for the British East India Company, one George Francis Grand. She was then seduced by another Englishman, Sir Philip Francis, in Calcutta the following year. The lovers were discovered *in flagrante* by her outraged husband and there ensued a huge scandal, a court case and permanent separation. After a brief stay in England, she was back in Paris from 1782 and enjoyed the protection of a series of well-placed dignitaries, including Valdec de Lessart, the later Foreign Minister. Her portrait, painted the following year by Mme Vigée-Lebrun, reveals a woman of languorous beauty, flowing blonde hair and milk-white skin set off against a pale blue corsage.

After the upheavals of 10 August 1792, Mme Grand fled to London and remained there, kept by a series of well-connected English lovers until May 1797. Some months later she became Talleyrand's mistress.

The exact circumstances are unclear and different versions of them abounded. But she apparently went, on the recommendation of a friend, to seek the Foreign Minister's help: perhaps in order to safeguard her money invested in England, perhaps because she was suspected of being a British agent. Whether she found him in, or whether (as another account has it) he later found her fast asleep in his study on returning late, the outcome at least is certain: she stayed the night and did not move out.[28] The reason why Talleyrand made her his mistress seems clear. The attraction was sexual. She was by now fourteen years older than the beauty portrayed by Vigée-Lebrun, but she was still beautiful – as even Mme de Rémusat conceded.[29] Only later would she start to develop the large paunch that provoked so much ridicule among people who had long found her ridiculous for other reasons.

Mme Grand undoubtedly had certain things in common with her lover: she had no scruples of any kind; she knew how to employ her charms to advance her interests; and she had a sensitive ear for politically useful gossip – so much so that it has been plausibly suggested that she was an active British spy.[30] She was, indeed, denounced as such, and in March 1798 Talleyrand wrote a letter to Barras seeking her release from arrest: 'She is the person in the world most distant from intrigue and the most incapable of involving herself in one. She is an Indian, very beautiful, very idle, the most disengaged of all the women I have ever met.'[31]

Like Charles-Maurice, Catherine Grand was corrupt. Although Napoleon's allegations about the Talleyrands cannot be taken at face value, he later claimed that he had banned Mme de Talleyrand from his presence because he found that she had been selling influence to the Genoese for 400,000 francs. She may, in fact, have gained a good deal more from such transactions.[32] Barras, admittedly another questionable source, says that she, like her husband, speculated on the exchanges using politically privileged information.[33] At one level, therefore, Charles-Maurice's liaison with Catherine made sense.

But, for all that, she was in the end a profoundly unsuitable spouse. She was dull, gauche and self-important. In the judgement of Talleyrand's secretary Colmache, and it has been argued since, Catherine Grand's reputation for being a fool was unwarranted.[34] Mme de Chastenay affirmed that she 'had never heard proceed from [Catherine Grand's] mouth anything resembling the senseless remarks people delighted to attribute to her'.[35] She could make a good impression on those unbiased against her. But she made dangerous enemies – not least Montrond, who spread her stupider comments, suitably embellished, around the *salons* of Paris. Certainly, one of the most famous anecdotes about her, which caused Napoleon much merriment even in exile, seems a complete fabrication. In it she is depicted at dinner confusing the explorer Denon with Robinson Crusoe, and asking him what happened to Man Friday. In fact, the story is merely recycled from one of Horace Walpole's fifty years earlier.[36] That said, Talleyrand's wife was altogether out of her depth in the company he kept. Her verbal infelicities sounded even sillier when contrasted with her husband's wordplay. Asked where she came from, she replied: '*Je suis d'Inde*' – which, while true enough, if phonetically understood meant that she claimed to be a turkey.[37] The playwright Lemercier, invited to a gathering in the Talleyrand country house at Neuilly, began to read his work and said: '*La scène est à Lyon.*' ('The scene is Lyon.') Catherine interrupted: 'There, M. de Talleyrand, now I know you were wrong: you say that it is the "Saône".'[38]

Charles-Maurice almost always refused to talk about his marriage.[39] All he would say was that 'a witty woman often compromises her husband, a woman of no wit only compromises herself'.[40] Talleyrand doubtless initially enjoyed Catherine Grand's company for the obvious physical reasons. Moreover, she did not trouble him with her opinions. Asked why he preferred the company of Mme Grand to Mme de Staël he replied: 'It relaxes me.'[41] But he could surely only have married such a woman if he felt that he had little choice. Napoleon was lying when he later claimed that he had opposed the marriage.[42] The only question is why Bonaparte exerted pressure upon Charles-Maurice to wed. In all probability, Mme de Rémusat's account comes closest to the truth. Napoleon, who became more of a prude as his opinion of himself increased, had heard that the wives of foreign ambassadors objected to being presented to Talleyrand's mistress at his receptions. He therefore instructed Charles-Maurice to send her away. Catherine wept at the First Consul's feet and begged him to reconsider. Joséphine also intervened on her behalf. So Napoleon gave Talleyrand the option of marrying her instead. Talleyrand took the line of least resistance. First, on 10 September 1802, a civil ceremony and then, the following day, a discreet church marriage – conducted by the *curé* of Épinay-sur-Seine in the valley of Montmorency – quickly took place.[43]

Despite his impassiveness, Talleyrand must have felt humiliated. A telltale sign is that he claimed on his marriage certificate that both his parents were dead. His mother, though, was very much alive and would return from exile the following year to live in the same street as her son until her death in 1809. Charles-Maurice must have known exactly what she would make of such an unsuitable union.[44] Napoleon, for his part, seems quickly to have seen its possibilities. He could now enjoy humiliating Talleyrand by snubbing his wife, and he continued to keep her away from court. Doubtless, he also encouraged the disobliging stories about her and liked to allude to her infidelities in vulgar terms.[45] In 1813, in a final act of self-destructive pettiness, and at the very time when he hoped to bring Talleyrand back into his service, the Emperor imposed the condition that he should never have to receive Mme de Talleyrand. This provided her husband with a convenient, and doubtless delicious, excuse to decline to serve.[46]

Talleyrand's marriage was, it seems, unhappy from the start, but for a long time appearances were maintained. They received their guests together at home, though Charles-Maurice visited other *salons* without her.[47] The couple may also have been held together by Charlotte, ostensibly adopted from a poverty-stricken exile family living in England, but most probably Charles-Maurice's and Catherine's illegitimate daughter.[48] With the arrival of Dorothée de Périgord, the future duchesse de Dino, to take a dominant place in Talleyrand's heart and home, the mere presence of Catherine became intolerable to him, and even more so to Dorothée. Charles-Maurice's absence in Vienna at the time of the Congress provided an opportunity to end the marriage in all but name. From then on Catherine lived separately. Talleyrand's agent, Roux de Laborie, was entrusted with the business of negotiating with this money-grabbing woman the cost of housing her.[49] Many years later, on learning the news of her death, Charles-Maurice expressed no regrets, merely remarking: 'This greatly simplifies my position.'[50] It was a reference to Talleyrand's planned reconciliation with the Catholic Church; but it was also an expression of relief after a lifetime of conjugal embarrassments.

The speed with which Talleyrand had married Catherine Grand after being given his ultimatum by Bonaparte no doubt reflected the latter's habitual impatience. But it was also directly linked to the papal brief pronouncing Charles-Maurice's secularization, dated 29 June and registered by the Conseil d'État on 19 August. In his memoirs, Talleyrand mentions the issue of this brief without discussing its implications.[51] The obvious assumption would be that it permitted the former bishop of Autun to marry. But it did not. The Vatican held firmly to the rule, despite pressure exerted by Napoleon on

Talleyrand's behalf, that laicized bishops could not be dispensed from their obligation of celibacy. At the time of the brief, Charles-Maurice certainly knew this, even if the French population did not, and he was obviously not greatly worried about it. As inconvenient memories faded, he may even have convinced himself that the brief had allowed him to marry after all. In 1836 he wrote in his Declaration that after his secularization he 'was free' to pursue his own course. It was later pointed out to him by the duchesse de Dino that he had had no such liberty as regards his marriage and he accordingly changed the wording to 'I believed myself to be free'. But this, though less theologically offensive, was certainly still untrue.[52]

Talleyrand's brief of laicization was a consequence of the Concordat agreed in 1801 between the First Consul and the Pope. Charles-Maurice's attitude as Foreign Minister during the stormy negotiations that preceded the Concordat was later the subject of careful concealment and distortion. In his memoirs Talleyrand states that he had 'powerfully contributed' to the successful outcome.[53] Cambacérès, it is true, supports this, noting that Talleyrand 'worked with zeal for the reconciliation of state and Church'.[54] But most of those involved thought differently. Cardinal Consalvi, Papal Secretary of State and special envoy appointed to negotiate the Concordat, felt no reason to be grateful to the Foreign Minister. Talleyrand performed his role in introducing Consalvi to the First Consul with propriety. But he left the negotiating to a former Chouan priest, the abbé Bernier, restricting his interventions to generally hostile observations about Rome's proposals.[55] Cobenzl, Austria's envoy, who took a close interest in the proceedings, was convinced of Talleyrand's hostility throughout.[56]

The explanation is probably threefold. First, of course, he cannot have been satisfied with the terms offered by Rome for the laicization of the Constitutional Clergy. In this he had a personal interest and a grievance. Second, as a liberal who held by the principles of 1789, Talleyrand probably genuinely believed in freedom of conscience and disliked the restoration of Catholicism as a state religion.[57] Third, he always took, like most *ancien régime* politicians, a strongly Gallican view of the relations between Church and state. Of the three motives for his uncharacteristically hard line over the negotiations, the last is probably most important. It is significant that appending the so-called 'Organic Articles' to the Concordat, which limited Rome's control over the French Church, was Talleyrand's initiative. Napoleon was more far-sighted in these matters than his Foreign Minister, recognizing that the restoration of Catholicism was essential to French social and political stability. Perhaps the Prince came round later to the same opinion, as his memoirs suggest. The fact remains that the Concordat was only finally agreed after Talleyrand had left Paris for his summer cure.

The Concordat was one aspect of Napoleon's policy of restoring continuity with the pre-Revolutionary era while upholding the legitimacy of the Revolution itself. Another was the recreation of social hierarchy and aristocratic culture. Napoleon came to regard Charles-Maurice as a kind of glorified social secretary, a role that was formalized when he was made Grand Chambellan of his court.[58] Talleyrand provided lists of the ladies who had attended his receptions for his master's later perusal.[59] He also had to tolerate some imperial petulance, for like other *parvenus* Napoleon rapidly became a stickler for etiquette. For example, on one occasion he wrote to complain that an invitation had been issued for 'supper' rather than 'dinner'.[60] Talleyrand was a natural courtier and under normal circumstances would have played his role with aplomb. Unfortunately, Napoleon's behaviour was not normal, his impatience prevailing over dignity. In processions he would insist on walking so fast that Charles-Maurice with his bad foot, like the ladies with their long trains, could not keep up – to the amusement of the military men.[61] Fortunately, Talleyrand was able to rely on Augustin de Rémusat – Mme de Rémusat's husband – acting as Premier Chambellan, to fulfil the more humdrum court duties.[62]

According to Méneval, Napoleon's wish to attract the great noble families of France to his cause was 'one of the reasons for his partiality for M. de Talleyrand, who was one of his principal intermediaries in this work of amalgamation and conciliation'.[63] But the Emperor later felt disappointed by the results.[64] On St Helena, he even blamed Talleyrand for having thwarted his plan to re-establish an aristocracy, claiming that he had prevented the old noble families from gaining his favour.[65] This, though, was far from the truth: it merely reflects the fact that he resented Talleyrand for preventing the comte de Narbonne, member of one of France's greatest families and finally a prized aide-de-camp, from coming to his notice earlier. In practice, Charles-Maurice did favours for many of the old nobility.[66]

Napoleon was always afraid of sarcasm.[67] He was thus obsessed by the opinions of the hereditary aristocracy before whose (real or imagined) mockery he alternately cringed and raged. In exile, he continued to speak angrily of the 'Faubourg Saint-Germain', referring to them collectively by the name of the Paris *quartier* where their great houses clustered.[68] Talleyrand despised this mentality. In his memoirs, he describes the Emperor in December 1805 declaiming against the Faubourg on the basis of tittle-tattle relayed in a letter from Mme de Genlis, just a few hours after winning Austerlitz.[69] Not that Charles-Maurice underrated the poisonous gossip from that quarter: he once remarked that 'the tongues of the Faubourg Saint-Germain have killed more generals than Austrian cannons.'[70]

The return of the old aristocracy was the result of Napoleon's policy rather than any proposed or implemented by Talleyrand. But the latter's public presence was reassuring to them. He was the most prominent civilian in a world dominated by the military; he exuded the culture of the *ancien régime* at a time when regicides and neo-Jacobins held most prominent positions. Above all, he knew how to entertain with good taste, luxury and elegance, and with precisely the right guest list. His houses thus provided the setting for the political reconciliation and social restoration that Bonaparte's victories had made possible.

Napoleon wanted to encourage a return to the old '*divertissements*' that had gone out of fashion with the Revolution. So, for example, masked balls were held once more.[71] Naturally, Talleyrand led the way. On 25 February 1800 he gave a great reception at his country house in Neuilly where the First Consul was guest of honour. It was an evening of cultured entertainment, not merely a sumptuous dinner, at which the internationally known singer Garat and the famous dancer Vestris both performed,[72] and La Harpe recited his translation of Tasso's *Gerusalemme liberata*.[73] But what lent the event political significance was the presence of figures from the *ancien régime*, of those who had been proscribed in the left coup of 18 Fructidor, and even of prominent figures from among the Chouans after the recent pacification of the Vendée. Aristocratic *cachet* was bestowed on the occasion by the attendance of great ladies from the Faubourg Saint-Germain. Again that year, on 2 July, on Napoleon's return to Paris from Milan after the Battle of Marengo, Talleyrand offered a splendid evening's entertainment for the First Consul and his guests. The diva Giuseppina Grassini's performance recalled Napoleon's Italian triumphs.[74] At about the same time, Charles-Maurice's brother, Archambaud, newly returned from exile thanks to Napoleon's clemency, organized his own ball, almost entirely dominated by the old nobility. Hortense de Beauharnais attended with her mother, Joséphine, and was entranced by the exquisite manners of the other guests.[75]

On 19 February 1801 the Foreign Minister organized a magnificent reception for the First Consul in order to celebrate the signing of the Peace of Lunéville, commissioning the poet Esménard to compose suitable verse for the occasion.[76] Not only members of the different elements of the French élite but also numerous foreign dignitaries attended.[77]

Talleyrand hosted his most extravagant and most memorable reception, again at Neuilly, on 8 June, its ostensible purpose to honour the King and Queen of Etruria. Indeed, Florence provided the theme of the evening: a theatre had been constructed in the gardens which portrayed the façade of the Palazzo Vecchio; there was a concert with choirs dressed in picturesque Italian costume and singing in Italian; La Grassini and Crescentini provided solo performances.[78] Wreaths of flowers were thrown down at the royal couple's feet. A ball was then held outside in the illuminated park, while thousands of guests supped within. The dancing ended only with the breaking of dawn. Contemporaries regarded it as marking a distinct change of tone in French society. One described it as 'the finest *fête* that the age had seen. . .a masterpiece of artistic and courtly genius'.[79] But it was also a political event. The King and Queen of Etruria were the first Bourbons to visit France since the Terror. Tuscany had been elevated into the Kingdom of Etruria by Bonaparte and given to Louis of Bourbon-Parma, a cousin of the King of Spain, in exchange for the duchy of Parma annexed by France.[80] Talleyrand's great *fête* was, therefore, a symbolic demonstration that representatives of the *ancien régime*, even members of the Bourbon family, could hope for gracious treatment if they recognized and served the purposes of Napoleonic France.

Not everyone around Bonaparte approved of this direction of policy. The most astute and most influential member of that internal resistance was Joseph Fouché. Napoleon on St Helena described Fouché as the 'Talleyrand of the clubs' and Talleyrand the 'Fouché of the *salons*'.[81] At one level, the two had much in common. Both were renegade clerics (Fouché, admittedly, received only minor orders). Both were cunning and unscrupulous. Both accumulated great fortunes. Both had an eye for securing themselves against changes of régime. Oddly perhaps in the case of the regicide Fouché, both proved adept at wooing the Faubourg Saint-Germain. Not surprisingly, both sometimes collaborated. They were both, for example, involved in the plotting of 18 Brumaire, though Talleyrand was more important. While Talleyrand was rewarded with the Foreign Ministry, Fouché got that of Police. They plotted the succession to Napoleon, first in the run-up to the Battle of Marengo in 1800, then again as French armies sank into the Spanish mire in 1809. They both played prominent parts in Napoleon's replacement by the Bourbons, Talleyrand in 1814 and Fouché the following year. Finally, they were both ultimately unable to escape their reputations.

Yet the differences are even more striking and more historically important. Fouché was much more radically hostile to the Church, the nobility and monarchy than was Talleyrand. Their characters were different too. Fouché was ugly, unhealthy, austere, industrious, talkative but serious, honest and uxorious. Talleyrand was good-looking, physically robust, extravagant, idle, frequently taciturn but witty, venal and promiscuous. Where Fouché had a reputation for cruelty, Talleyrand's generosity of nature was widely acknowledged – too widely, perhaps, because he could be unflinchingly brutal when he deemed it necessary. They were both useful to Napoleon, but while the Emperor was charmed by Talleyrand, even after he had disgraced him, he feared Fouché, and so he did not dare to disgrace him permanently. That also, as he subsequently realized, was a mistake; for Talleyrand was, in the long run, even more dangerous than his rival.[82]

The fortunes of Talleyrand and Fouché were heavily influenced by threats to the régime. The contrast between glorious victories abroad and continued insecurity at home pressed France towards the authoritarian rule that Bonaparte secretly desired. In October 1800 an alleged plot to stab the First Consul was unearthed. It had little substance and may have been the work of *agents provocateurs*; it served, all the same, as an excuse to clamp down on Jacobin opponents.[83] Talleyrand seems to have seen an opportunity. A police report the following month described a meeting at his house called to discuss how to oust Fouché.[84] On Christmas Eve, Bonaparte barely escaped death from a bomb in the rue Saint-Nicaise as he travelled in his carriage from the Tuileries to the Opéra. Talleyrand immediately determined to use this to destroy Fouché. Suspicion again initially fell on the left. Their involvement would have well suited Charles-Maurice, since Fouché was thought to be of that faction himself. But the Police Minister successfully demonstrated that it was, in fact, the work of the right, of royalists and Chouans. Fouché's stock rose in consequence, but he did not forget how near Talleyrand had come to having him dismissed and disgraced.[85]

The assassination attempt had renewed concern among all those dependent on the régime about its fragility. From now on Talleyrand, Roederer and Lucien Bonaparte pressed for a reinforcement of the First Consul's powers with a view to making Napoleon's rule permanent. The same concern for security, and for guarding his own interests against a Bourbon restoration, placed Talleyrand at the head of those wanting to make that monarchical power hereditary. In the ensuing debate Fouché permitted his Jacobin convictions to get the better of him.[86] His opposition became too well known, and this allowed his enemies to have him dismissed. But Napoleon was, as ever, loth to lose his services altogether, so he was sent to the Senate. In May 1802 Napoleon's supporters in the Tribunat pressed for a constitutional measure to acknowledge the First Consul's achievement: a lifetime appointment as First Consul was envisaged. But under Fouché's influence the Senate proposed only a ten-year extension. To circumvent this, and following Talleyrand's advice, a plebiscite was called which overwhelmingly endorsed the proposal to make Bonaparte Consul for Life.

Talleyrand's strategy had thus advanced a huge stride, though it would be wrong to imagine that he ever pursued only one at a time. It is clear, for example, that he kept open channels with the Bourbons and their advisers.[87] In any case, gathering information about Bourbon intentions had its uses. Talleyrand still had a strong interest in resisting a return of the old royal house, despite being by temperament a monarchist. In his memoirs he claims that throughout the Napoleonic years he was consistently working for a return of the old monarchy.[88] This is obviously untrue. Mme de Rémusat, in whom he confided, more accurately describes his attitude. Talleyrand, she confirmed, had always been convinced that only a monarchy suited France: 'In any case, he needed to recover his lifetime habits and to place himself once again on terrain that was known to him. The advantages and the abuses that flow from courts offered him his opportunities of power and influence.'[89] It would, however, clearly be better for Talleyrand to have a Bonaparte court than a Bourbon court.

The various accounts of Talleyrand's plans to eliminate the Bourbons should, therefore, probably be believed – despite the prejudiced sources. Barras tells of Charles-Maurice's proposal as Foreign Minister under the Directory to trick all the Bourbons and their agents into gathering in Wesel, to seize them and bring them back to be dealt with in Paris.[90] Napoleon claimed that everything that 'had been done against the Bourbons had been done when [Talleyrand] was minister and prepared by him'. It was Talleyrand 'who had constantly talked to [him] about the necessity of distancing [the Bourbons] from all political influence'.[91] This last was a reference to driving the Bourbons off the throne of Spain; but it also provides the background to the murky affair of the duc d'Enghien.[92]

The conspiracy for which Louis de Bourbon-Condé, duc d'Enghien, died was real enough, even if the victim's involvement in it was not. The presence in Paris of Georges Cadoudal, the most resolute of the Chouan leaders, acting as an agent of the British government, was known from the autumn of 1803. The first arrests of minor figures were now made. The more that was learned the more serious the plot seemed. The following February Cadoudal and other conspirators, including the former General Pichegru, were also arrested, through information gathered by Fouché. Even General Moreau, the hero of Hohenlinden, was implicated. This triumph of Fouché's informal intelligence network would win him back his old job as Minister of Police. Meanwhile, the conspirators revealed under torture that an unnamed Bourbon prince was shortly to join them. The government initially found it difficult to guess his identity, but by a process of elimination suspicion finally settled on the duc d'Enghien, residing with other *émigrés* across the frontier at Ettenheim in Baden. The young prince was wrongly believed to be in the company of that other renegade Revolutionary general, Dumouriez. Urgent action was clearly needed.

Subsequently, each of the main actors in the tragedy sought to diminish or distort his own role. Napoleon, at least, accepted responsibility, though he maintained that others had pre-empted his final decision to execute d'Enghien. General Caulaincourt explained to anyone who would listen how he had been an unwitting instrument in the prince's death.[93] General Savary, the future duc de Rovigo, tried to shift the blame on to others, especially Talleyrand,[94] who went to great lengths to exculpate himself entirely.

When he came to write the first version of his memoirs, Talleyrand made no mention of his role in the affair, limiting himself to the poisonous observation: 'The murder of the duc d'Enghien, commited solely to assure himself, by placing him among their ranks, of the support of those whom the death of Louis XVI caused to fear any sort of power not coming from them – this murder, I say, could neither be excused nor pardoned, and it has never been so; therefore, Bonaparte has been reduced to boasting about it.'[95]

However, in 1823 Savary published an extract from his memoirs giving his own version. This directly, indeed principally, implicated Talleyrand as the moving force of the whole affair. Charles-Maurice defended himself with cunning and success, in circumstances that will be described. It also forced him to add an explanatory note and correspondence to his own memoirs.

In fact, this material does nothing to resolve the matter one way or the other. There is Talleyrand's letter to Baden of 10 March 1804, demanding that the alleged conspirators be handed over. A second letter of the same date, written on Napoleon's command, adds that General Caulaincourt had been directed to seize d'Enghien and Dumouriez. A further letter of 11 March provides Caulaincourt with his instructions. These three letters, Talleyrand states, 'constitute the only real part' he played.[96] In other words, he was merely following orders. To those of his friends at the time who were soft-hearted enough to express sorrow at the death of the prince he had a similar tale to tell. So Mme de Rémusat wrote: 'The known character of M. de Talleyrand scarcely admits of such an act of violence. He told me more than once that Bonaparte had informed him, as he had the two Consuls, of the arrest of the duc d'Enghien and of his invincible determination. He added that all three had seen that words were useless and they had remained silent.'[97]

The truth, however, is altogether different. Although Napoleon exaggerated when he said that without Talleyrand he would have known nothing of the duc d'Enghien, it is clear that his broader allegations are well founded. Talleyrand (along with Fouché and possibly Murat) did, indeed, insist on d'Enghien's importance. And Napoleon did not blame him for this.[98] Indeed, given the threat, Bonaparte confirmed that he would have taken the same decisions again.[99] In his will on St Helena he repeated this.[100] What he objected to was the way in which Talleyrand later tried to escape all blame.

In reality, at the meeting of the council called to advise the First Consul on the action to take, Talleyrand was the leader of those arguing for the most rigorous measures against the Bourbon prince. Cambacérès, demonstrating an uncharacteristic bravery, argued the opposite case and lost, earning some insults from Bonaparte for his pains. The First Consul was entirely of his Foreign Minister's opinion. But, in any case, this was only Talleyrand's formal advice. In private he apparently went further, convincing Napoleon after d'Enghien's arrest that (in Pasquier's words) it was 'no longer possible to draw back'.[101]

There is damning proof that Talleyrand had urged upon the First Consul the need for the prince's death. On 8 March he wrote a letter to Napoleon on the matter. The original has since disappeared, but it was seen by Méneval, and Chateaubriand had a copy. The letter apparently escaped the operation mounted by Talleyrand at the Restoration to burn all incriminating papers. It may have been kept by Napoleon for future use; though presumably he later mislaid it, or he would have produced it himself on St Helena. In this letter Talleyrand urges the First Consul to take the strongest action against his enemies. There is no reason to contest its authenticity: it has all the marks of Talleyrand's style. It concluded: 'If justice obliges one to punish with rigour, political necessity [*la politique*] demands that one should punish without exception.'[102]

The seizure of the duc d'Enghien was duly effected on 15 March by soldiers under the command of Caulaincourt and General Ordener. The young prince was taken first to Strasbourg and then to Paris. A hasty trial was convened at Vincennes and the accused, having been found guilty by a military commission, was shot by firing squad on the night of 20/21 March.

Two factors should be borne in mind when interpreting what is known of these events. First, because Napoleon notoriously made hasty decisions and often sought to change them, his wishes may well have been communicated differently to different people at different times. So his well-attested order to Réal, acting *préfet de police*, to interview d'Enghien, after the latter had in fact been executed, is not, of itself, proof that the First Consul had never envisaged the prince's death. It may just mean that he had second thoughts about quickly despatching him.

Second, one can also surmise that Napoleon's agents, seeking to win favour or to prove themselves, may well have taken matters into their own hands. Napoleon's later reproach of those 'carried away by criminal zeal' suggests as much. The reference is, presumably, to Savary, who was sent to Vincennes to organize the trial of d'Enghien and who, according to credible evidence and contrary to his own account, intervened to stop any delay in the execution by appeal to the First Consul.

But Talleyrand's own role is not affected by either of these considerations. He was directly party, as Foreign Minister, to the original kidnap of d'Enghien. He clearly urged, both privately and publicly, that the prince be removed permanently from the scene. Napoleon would later recall his exact words, which sound all too characteristic: 'The wine is drawn; now it must be drunk.'[103] And was there perhaps more? Savary, admittedly not an impartial witness, describes how he met Talleyrand leaving the First Consul's office just before he was called in to receive his commission to go to Vincennes. Savary also describes a later nocturnal visit by Talleyrand to see Murat, in the latter's capacity of military governor of Paris. And it was Murat who then gave Savary his final orders. The suspicion must be that, having urged Bonaparte throughout to destroy d'Enghien, Talleyrand was finally entrusted with secret instructions to ensure that the deed was done without delay.[104]

This does not, though, mean that Talleyrand was acting on some personal agenda. His future colleague Molé's judgement has, in this context, been too widely accepted: 'The duc d'Enghien perished as a result of an intrigue by Talleyrand and Fouché, who wanted to draw Napoleon into their power by a crime that would make him their accomplice and after which he could not reproach them for their lives under the Revolution.'[105] The more it is examined, the less likely this is. Fouché had a Revolutionary past to live down in Napoleon's eyes, but not Talleyrand. Fouché was restored as Minister of Police as a result of his unearthing of the main plot, not because of the death of d'Enghien. Talleyrand, for his part, seriously underestimated the impact of the prince's death on the attitude of foreign powers, whose anger made his professional life more difficult. That impact was greater than on domestic opinion; but even in France before the Restoration, let alone after it, all those concerned found their reputations besmirched. The immediate effect was to make for a further consolidation of power by the declaration of a hereditary Empire of the French. That was certainly what Talleyrand wanted, though not, of course, Fouché. But it would have happened sooner or later, with or without the quasi-judicial murder of a minor Bourbon prince.

Talleyrand's real view at the time was almost certainly that of Napoleon, namely that *raison d'état* required that an example be made. A Bourbon must die to show that no one could expect immunity in the case of further treason. That is the meaning of the phrase in his letter of 8 March, that punishment be administered 'without exception'. This may be an unpleasant, even an immoral, doctrine, but it has an established, if not an honourable, role in European statecraft.

It is unclear whether Fouché or Talleyrand coined the memorably cynical observation that the execution of the duc d'Enghien 'was more than a crime, it was a mistake'.[106] Considering that Fouché had promised Bonaparte that a case full of damning material would be found with d'Enghien, and that there was no such case, this was an extraordinarily shameless quip if it came from him.[107] And if it was Talleyrand's it is even more shameless. But then he had no shame. On the evening that a telegram alerted Paris to the arrest of the duc d'Enghien, Talleyrand was attending a ball at the Hôtel de Luynes. Someone asked him what would happen to the prince. He replied coldly: 'He will be shot.'[108] And later, after the deed was done, when he was in the *salon* of the vicomtesse de Laval, he casually mentioned in the early hours: 'At this moment the last Condé has ceased to exist.'[109]

When news of the execution appeared in the French press, Hauterive burst into Talleyrand's office.

The Foreign Minister looked up and asked: 'What's wrong with you, with your eyes standing out of your head?'

Hauterive exclaimed: 'What's wrong with me? The same as should be wrong with you, if you've read *Le Moniteur*! How horrible!'

Talleyrand replied: 'Well, well! Are you mad? Is it worth making such a fuss? A conspirator is seized near the frontier; he is taken to Paris; he is shot. What's so extraordinary about that?'[110]

And then, with finality: '*Ce sont les affaires.*'[111]

9

Re-shaping Europe

~~

THE PROCLAMATION OF Napoleon as hereditary Emperor of the French was widely seen to mark a victory for Talleyrand's policy for the restoration of monarchical institutions to France. He had talked up the advantages of the hereditary principle in the *salons*. He had consistently turned political events to that end. He advised the First Consul on the tactics of how to bring the enterprise to its final fruition.[1] A *sénatus-consulte*, a special decree of the Senate, of 18 May 1804 duly proclaimed the new Imperial Constitution. Long after Charles-Maurice had lost his favour, Napoleon recognized that he was among those who had most contributed to establishing the Bonaparte dynasty.[2]

According to Cambacérès, it was also Talleyrand who proposed the creation of an imperial court.[3] On 11 July Talleyrand was himself appointed to one of the great court offices as Grand Chambellan. He had, it seems, hoped for more. Napoleon had considered appointing him Archichancelier d'État, but his sisters wanted to keep the post open for their disgraced brother Lucien, in the event of his being reconciled with the Emperor.[4] In any case, such games of cat and mouse played with the expectations of those around him were Napoleon's favourite pastime.

Perhaps Talleyrand was less than completely satisfied with his work for other reasons too. He later told Mme de Rémusat that he had been uneasy about the title of Emperor. It had about it a 'combination of the Roman Republic and Charlemagne, which turned [Napoleon's] head'. But Bonaparte was, probably rightly, convinced that it was more acceptable to France than the title 'King'. This had offered Charles-Maurice the opportunity to play a malicious trick on General Berthier by persuading him to suggest that title to Bonaparte and receive a thunderous rebuke for his pains.[5] Certainly, Talleyrand did not allow any misgivings to spoil his flattery. In August, when Napoleon was visiting Aix-la-Chapelle, where Charlemagne is buried, Talleyrand wrote to him that it was only right that the city that had for so long been the first city of the empire and the seat of Charlemagne's government should 'gloriously echo the presence of Your Majesty and demonstrate the similarity of destinies that Europe has already grasped between the restorer of the Roman Empire and the founder of the French Empire'.[6]

Napoleon had decided upon a coronation, modelled in many ways on the coronations of the *ancien régime*. But, as Emperor, he wished to revert to a still more venerable tradition and have the Pope, Pius VII, present. The quasi-religious ceremony duly took place in Notre-Dame on 2 December. The unseemly scoffing by Napoleon's irreligious generals was ignored. But David's famous depiction, *Le Sacre*, does catch the berobed Grand Chambellan with a rather impudent smile on his face, the expression of one who is pleased at the course of events, is even happy for those involved, but does not take it all too seriously.

Talleyrand did, however, take seriously the turn of international events, and with good reason. Since May the previous year, Britain and France had once again been at war. Britain's only hope of dealing a serious blow to France was through bringing together a new coalition of continental powers. The decisions of Vienna, Berlin and St Petersburg would, naturally enough, be based on opportunism and on the quantity of subsidies to be provided by London. But French actions could also contribute. In his memoirs, Talleyrand blames Napoleon for acting provocatively at this juncture because of 'vanity' – notably by having himself proclaimed King of Italy, which frightened Austria with its implicit claim of French dominance throughout the Italian peninsula. Another coronation duly followed, this time in Milan, on 26 May 1805. Talleyrand was again present.

He had also taken the leading role in explaining, first to the Conseil d'État and then to the Senate, what had prompted Napoleon to take the new Italian crown. Yet the words of his speech to the Senate of 18 March suggest, beneath the orotund hyperbole, an anxiety about the course upon which the Emperor had embarked. Whether the intention was to assuage his own doubts or those of others, or even to implant some doubts in the mind of Napoleon, is unclear. Talleyrand drew a distinction between Napoleon on the one hand and Charlemagne and, above all, Alexander the Great on the other, who 'in endlessly driving back the limits to his conquests only prepared for himself bloody funerals'. Bonaparte, by contrast, as a founder and not a conquerer, had from the beginning of his 'noble career. . .wanted to recall France to ideas of order and Europe to ideas of peace'. Stretching the credulity of his audience even further, Talleyrand suggested that the time would come when even England, 'overcome by the ascendancy of [Napoleon's] moderation', would 'abjure its hatreds'.[7] Had the Emperor understood such matters, he might have perceived in Talleyrand's words an undercurrent of what, across the Channel, would be classed as 'loyal opposition'. And the opposition would not, in fact, stay loyal.

The Channel, rather than Italy, was now the principal focus of Napoleon's attention, as a 200,000-strong army assembled at Boulogne for the planned invasion of England. The previous July a violent storm had disrupted preparations. But with the entry of Spain into the war as France's ally, bringing its fleet to reinforce that of the French, the practicality of maritime operations greatly increased. During the summer of 1805, the Emperor impatiently awaited news that the British fleet had been diverted or at least damaged. But it never came. All that arrived were disturbing messages about Austrian preparations for war. Austria's intentions were made still clearer by what amounted to an ultimatum for Napoleon to give up the Kingdom of Italy. Talleyrand departed at once to join the Emperor at Boulogne. At the end of August Napoleon decided to despatch his army to Germany to confront the danger.

This transformed Talleyrand's life. Just as Napoleon expected his Minister of the Interior to accompany him on his travels around France, so he expected his Minister of External Affairs to follow in the wake of his campaigns.[8] From September 1805 it was the unpleasant lot of Charles-Maurice to do this. For the best part of two years he moved in the train of the imperial armies from the Rhine to the Niemen, across Germany and Poland to the borders of Russia; he witnessed the aftermath of the battles of Ulm, Austerlitz and Jena; he negotiated peace at Vienna, Pressburg and Tilsit. In all his travels, he was accompanied by La Besnardière from the ministry,[9] who would become one of Talleyrand's closest collaborators. Having trained as an Oratorian and served as a private tutor, he had joined the department under the Directory. Coming to Talleyrand's notice, he was promoted from the Consular Section and now, and later at the Congress of Vienna, he was the minister's principal aide and chief draughtsman.[10] But Talleyrand also relied on the expertise and advice of Hauterive back in Paris, to whom he gave instructions for the memoranda and treaties he was expected to provide for the endlessly demanding and always impatient Emperor. Indeed, his exchanges with Hauterive are the best guide to the way his opinions evolved about the great enterprise on which he was embarked.

At Strasbourg, on the eve of Napoleon's departure for the front, there occurred an event that must have attached the Emperor to his Foreign Minister at a more intimate level. Moved by the need to bid farewell to Joséphine, and in a state of anxiety about the forthcoming campaign, Napoleon fell to the ground with an epileptic fit. Fortunately, only Talleyrand and Rémusat were present. The one loosened his tie and covered his face with eau de cologne, while the other gave him some water. The fit passed and shortly afterwards Napoleon left for Karlsruhe, swearing them to silence.[11]

Ranged against Napoleon, and financed by a British annual subsidy of £1.25 million, was the Third Coalition consisting of Britain, Austria, Russia and the Bourbons of Naples. The initial French objective was to drive the Austrians back from Bavaria. Begun by Ney at Elchingen, the plan was completed by the Emperor with the capitulation of the Austrian forces under Mack at Ulm on 20 October. From Ulm, Napoleon moved on to Vienna, which he entered, without any resistance, on 15 November. On 2 December he confronted the Austrian and Russian emperors and their armies at Austerlitz, winning what is widely acknowledged as the greatest of his victories. The enemy lost 27,000 men and 180 cannon. The Austrians now entered into negotiations, while the Russians withdrew.

Talleyrand had, for the time being, remained behind at Strasbourg. It was a dreary place, he found, with the streets deserted and everyone going to bed at nine o'clock.[12] But, then, he had much on his mind. The concerns he harboured about a policy based exclusively on conquest, his instinctive and philosophical preference for a balance of European power, and perhaps the absence of the domineering personality of the Emperor himself, had finally allowed a resolution to be formed. He would seek, not by hints, observations and tacit resistance, but rather by offering an alternative strategy, even an alternative vision of Europe, to change the direction of Napoleon's policy. He already knew what to say, and he tried it out in a letter of 11 October to Hauterive:

> Here is what I would like to make of the successes of the Emperor – I presume them to be great. I would like the Emperor, on the day following a great victory, which does not seem to me to be in doubt, to say to Prince Charles [i.e. the Archduke Charles, Austrian supreme commander]: 'You have your back to the wall. I do not wish to abuse my victories. I wanted peace, and what proves it is that I still want it today. The conditions for such an arrangement cannot be the same as I would have proposed two months ago. Venice will be independent and will not be joined to Italy or to Austria. I abandon the crown of Italy, as I promised. Swabia, which is an eternal subject of disagreement between the Elector of Bavaria and you, will be joined to Bavaria or to some other principality. I shall help you take Wallachia and Moldavia. On those conditions, I shall make an offensive and defensive treaty with you – any idea of an alliance with Prussia can go to the devil. Do you want forty-eight hours? I agree. Otherwise, you should fear the good fortune that belongs, almost by right, to a victorious army.'[13]

The result was the long memorandum of 17 October addressed to the Emperor. The proposals it contains are those that Talleyrand outlined to Hauterive but placed in a broader framework. The Foreign Minister emphasizes that they are intended for a 'future peace', one that he wants to see endure. Europe he sees as consisting of four great powers, Prussia being the first of the second-order powers. At the head of the four is France, unique in having the right proportion between manpower (for its armies) and wealth. Two other powers – Austria and Britain – are France's rivals, and are thus forced towards a mutual alliance. This alliance will certainly materialize, unless Austria and Russia also become rivals. But at present Russia's eyes are focused on gains at the expense of the Ottoman Empire – so it is not at logger-heads with the Austrians. While such a system continues, there can be no peace, only a succession of bloody wars.

Looking back to the eighteenth century, to the time of Frederick the Great – continues Talleyrand – France had enjoyed an alliance with Prussia. But that is no longer possible. Prussia today is poorly and weakly led. Moreover, though an alliance with Prussia might have immediate benefits – this was a concession to the fact that French official policy was still seeking such an alliance – in the longer run it could prove a problem not least because of the tensions that would arise with Austria. By contrast, the causes of war will cease if a com-pletely new system of international relations is created. This system would have three features. It would remove the causes of mistrust between France and Austria. It would separate the interests of Austria and Britain. And it would put both those two powers in opposition to Russia, and, incidentally, through that opposition guarantee the integrity of the Ottoman Empire.

The means suggested of achieving this fundamental change are the same as those sketched out in Talleyrand's letter to Hauterive. Austria must cease to have any territorial contact with France or with the states France has founded (i.e. those under French control). Venice must become, once again, an independent, oligarchic repub-lic. Austria must keep out of Switzerland and Swabia. But imposing these sacrifices on Vienna without compensations would lead to enduring resentment and unrest, and push Austria even further towards Britain. It would be a prescription for war. This is where Russia comes into the picture.

Again, Talleyrand takes an example from France's past, and from the only Bourbon monarch whose memory engaged Napoleon's respect. He notes how Louis XIV, despite the long-standing alliance between France and the Porte, when he saw the Turks threatening Europe lent support to Vienna. Russia, for Talleyrand, is the new Ottoman Empire, an alien, aggressive, barbarian force. Austria is still the main bulwark in Europe's defence, and it must be strengthened. This dic-tates the recompense Austria should receive for its losses in Italy, namely Wallachia, Moldavia, Bessarabia and northern Bulgaria. The Sultan, their nominal sovereign, would not miss them. Indeed, the

Porte would be pleased that its Russian enemies, who were now in effective control there, should be forced out.

Austria's expansion eastwards into the northern Balkans to the Black Sea would result in it adopting a new policy. The Russians would immediately become Austria's natural enemies. Moreover, the fact that the Orthodox population in these areas would prefer rule from Orthodox Russia to that of Catholic Austria would keep Vienna constantly tied down. Austria would have to seek out France as its new natural ally. Other wider advantages would also ensue. The Germans would finally be excluded from Italy, where their claims over the centuries had created numerous wars. Britain would find no powerful allies on the Continent. The Russians, frustrated in their expansion into the Balkans, would turn towards Asia and India, which would set them at odds with the British, their current allies.

Obtaining the benefits of such a strategy would also require sacrifices by France, notably abandonment of the Kingdom of Italy and of French pretensions there. It would also require French intervention to force the Porte to cede its provinces and to assist Austria in defending them from the Russians. Implicit in the scheme is, of course, something else for which Talleyrand had long argued: a policy of restraint and consolidation by Napoleon.[14]

But how viable was such a plan? There is no doubt about its sophistication or its comprehensiveness. It also has the merit of offering a way to break up the combination of Britain, Austria and Russia, which was at the heart of the coalitions. And it did so without either war *à l'outrance* across Europe or the imposition of a European-wide blockade of Britain – two strategies that were doomed, in the long run, to certain failure. It can be objected that at the stage when Talleyrand wrote Austria had as yet no sense of an 'Eastern vocation'. This would emerge only after its exclusion from Germany at the hands of Prussia through defeat at Königgrätz (Sadowa) in 1866.[15] Yet Austria's exclusion from Italy, which Talleyrand was proposing to make permanent, was not much less of a shock. And, unlike Bismarck, who would follow exactly the same strategy of concentrating Austria's attentions on the Balkans, Talleyrand was at least clear from the start about the trouble that controlling the Balkan populations and containing Russia would cause. A further objection that can be made is that it was impossible for someone of Napoleon's background and temperament to give up his ambitions in Italy. But that marks, at most, a fault of character assessment rather than of policy analysis.

The most serious objection, though, to Talleyrand's plan is that it underrated the power of Britain and Russia to act against France, even without Austrian involvement. Moreover, it assumed that Prussia was destined to remain a 'second-order' power and could thus be left out of the equation. One can only say that these were easy errors to make and that the strategy suggested by Talleyrand at least offered better prospects for French peace and prosperity than those preferred by Napoleon at this point.

In any case, whatever the scheme's weaknesses, the timing was unfortunate. Unbeknown to Talleyrand, just three days after his memorandum was sent Napoleon took Ulm. The Emperor's thoughts were already on seizing Vienna and destroying the rest of the Austro-Russian forces. Talleyrand was now summoned to join him in Munich. Napoleon discussed the memorandum and at one moment expressed his agreement. But at the next he learned of new successes by his advance guard against the Austrians and his mind turned again to military matters.[16] He was more interested in having from his Foreign Minister a draft treaty to extract the gains he wanted than to debate the future shape of Europe.

Talleyrand wrote on 27 October to Hauterive, giving in telegraphic style the main features of such a treaty: 'No more German Emperor! Three Emperors in Germany. France, Austria and Prussia. No more Ratisbon. . .All the Italian Tyrol would be added to the Kingdom of Italy, as well as Venice and all the Adriatic coast. The acquisitions [*réunions*] are all decided *against my advice* [emphasis in the original].' Talleyrand added, with some bitterness: 'A treaty of alliance with Austria, giving it Wallachia and Moldavia, as well as Bessarabia and Bulgaria, has been rejected despite ten thousand good reasons. The preference is for a treaty with Russia, after having weakened its tutelage [of Austria]. *That is not my opinion* [emphasis in the original], but my view in this matter is rejected.'[17]

Belatedly, news also arrived of the destruction of the French and Spanish fleets by Nelson at the Battle of Trafalgar on 21 October. In his despatch to Napoleon of 12 November informing him of the defeat, Talleyrand affected a cool tone and added, with a note of flattery, and referring to Napoleon's successes, that 'genius and fortune were in Germany'.[18] But on the same day, in a letter to Hauterive, he revealed his real reaction: 'What horrible news from Cadiz! May it not hinder any of the political transactions that seem to me appropriate now.'[19]

On the evening of 16 November, Talleyrand arrived in Vienna. His spirits quickly rose. He thought the Viennese air even better than that of Paris. And he advised Hauterive that rumours of his death, which had apparently been doing the rounds, were greatly exaggerated.[20] But his visit to the battlefield of Austerlitz where the dead still lay strewn was a frightful experience.[21]

While at Vienna he addressed a further, shorter memorandum to the Emperor, written two days after the victory. It reveals more of his underlying thinking about Europe, and in particular about Austria and Russia, casting the former in the role of a conservative, civilized power and the latter as a violent, primeval force:

> I rejoice in the idea that this last victory of Your Majesty enables him to ensure the peace of Europe and to guarantee the civilized world against the barbarian invasions. Your Majesty can now break the Austrian monarchy or raise it up again. Once broken, it would not be within the power of even Your Majesty to reconstitute it in a single mass. But the existence of this mass is necessary. It is indispensable to the future well-being of civilized nations.
>
> From the past greatness and power of the house of Austria it is all too often concluded that it is great and powerful today. . .[But, unlike France], the Austrian monarchy is an ill-assorted construct of different states, nearly all of them differing in language, customs, religion, political and civil systems, which have no common bond other than the identity of their head. Such a power is necessarily weak. . .But it is a bulwark, both sufficient and necessary, against the barbarians.[22]

The language prefigures Cold War rhetoric. But Napoleon's conclusions from Austerlitz could not have been more different:

> M. de Talleyrand,
>
> I can only write you a few words. An army of 100,000 men commanded by the two Emperors [of Austria and Russia] is completely destroyed. All protocols are void. The negotiations are nullified

because it is clear that they were a ruse to put me to sleep. . .Since the battle is lost, the conditions cannot be the same.[23]

The Emperor duly pressed on into Moravia, inflicting a further defeat on the enemy at Brün (Brno). Talleyrand followed and engaged in the first serious contacts with the Austrians. Brün itself he found detestable. It was full of dead and wounded, and the stench was abominable. Happily, everything later froze, which was a mercy. Charles-Maurice asked Hauterive to send out some of his favourite dry Málaga wine. The circumstances surely required it.

The business of negotiation now continued in Pressburg (Bratislava). On 23 December Talleyrand reported to the Emperor in Vienna, before returning to his lodgings. Crossing the Danube was a nightmare: on the way back, the boat had to navigate between great blocks of ice, to the boatman's alarm and Charles-Maurice's discomfort. At Pressburg, at least, he had a relatively free hand in what he described as his 'campaign'. His view was that 'moderation must go hand in hand with power', and, at this stage, he seems to have thought that Napoleon agreed with him.[24]

The Treaty of Pressburg was finally signed by Napoleon and Francis II of Austria on 26 December 1805. Its moderation is not obvious. Austria lost Venice, Istria and Dalmatia to the Kingdom of Italy, and Swabia and the Tyrol to the former electors – now kings – of Württemberg and Bavaria. It received no compensation. An indemnity of 40,000 francs was also to be paid to France. Napoleon subsequently complained that Talleyrand had been too soft on the Austrians, apparently because he had reduced the level of reparations from the figure the Emperor had wanted.[25] But, in truth, Pressburg marked a signal defeat for Talleyrand's strategy.

Nor was moderation apparent elsewhere. In a move that Talleyrand strongly condemns in his memoirs, on 27 September Napoleon unilaterally declared the transfer of the Kingdom of Naples from the reigning Bourbons to his brother Joseph,[26] forcing Ferdinand IV and his wife to flee to their domains in Sicily.

In Germany, the following year, the changes were still more far-reaching. On 12 July 1806 a new Confederation of the Rhine was created from the southern and western German states, under the formal protection of France. As a result of pressure from Talleyrand and his successor, Champagny, the number of German participants rose in due course from the initial fifteen to eighteen states. The Confederation hammered the last of many nails into the coffin of the German (Holy Roman) Empire. On 7 August Francis II 'abdicated' and henceforth styled himself Emperor of Austria.

Talleyrand negotiated the details of the Confederation of the Rhine while briefly back in Paris. It was very profitable to him. If Barras's enumeration of the benefits is to be believed, he scooped the enormous total of 2.7 million francs in bribes.[27] On St Helena, Napoleon would claim that it was as a result of the protests of the kings of Bavaria and Württemberg at this extortion that he subsequently dismissed Talleyrand as Foreign Minister.[28] As it stands, this is untrue; but, like many of Napoleon's later assertions, it contains an element of truth.

One other benefit that Talleyrand derived at this time was entirely above board. On 5 June 1806 he was appointed by the Emperor 'Prince and Duke of Benevento', a previously papal enclave within the Kingdom of Naples. From now until the end of Napoleon's rule, Talleyrand would be known as prince de Bénévent. He probably took some secret pleasure in the title – even Napoleonic honours mattered to him, though he only really respected those of the *ancien régime*. His wife's delight, however, was boundless and unabashed. Charles-Maurice ironically observed to someone who congratulated him on the title: 'Go and see Mme de Talleyrand. Women are always charmed to be princesses.'[29] Others, like Countess Potocka, found her pretensions less amusing.[30]

In his memoirs, Talleyrand merely observes of his appointment as ruler of Benevento that it allowed him to protect the people of the principality from the worst exactions of war.[31] It also brought in a useful profit each year, receipts well exceeding expenses.[32] Talleyrand was always conscientious about those in his charge; and in Benevento, which he never personally visited, he appointed an able administrator in the shape of Louis de Beer. Reforms, mirroring those associated with Napoleonic rule elsewhere, led to material improvements in the lives of the inhabitants. Schools, a library and a museum were among the more obvious results.[33]

The immediate loser from developments in Germany was, naturally enough, Austria. But Prussia was not far behind. The French had been monitoring Prussian movements closely for some time. From September 1805, Talleyrand was receiving reports of the Prussian army's partial and arthritic mobilization. The arrival in Berlin of the Tsar in October had further stirred the Prussian King's bellicosity. But news of Austrian and Russian defeats induced a temporary change of mood: Prussia now hastened to proclaim its peaceful intentions.[34]

Talleyrand had earlier tempted the Prussians with the prospect of a North German Confederation, of which Prussia would be the effective head. Napoleon had offered Hanover in exchange for an explicit alliance. But by refusing to commit himself, Frederick-William III lost whatever opportunities there might have been, and earned only the French Emperor's distrust and his Foreign Minister's contempt. Hauterive wrote to tell Talleyrand about a joke of Fouché's, which circulated in the *salons*, to the effect that the two most embarrassed people in Paris were Lucchesini, because of the decline of Prussia, and Cambacérès, because of the decline of the Black Eagle (the decoration that the Prussians had awarded him).[35]

French scorn was more than matched by Prussian anger. Grasping after Austerlitz that his timidity had reduced Prussia's importance still further, and learning that Napoleon was trying to secure peace with Britain by handing back Hanover, Frederick William sought revenge. But, as Metternich observed, because of this fit of royal anger, Prussia had chosen the worst possible time to act.[36] Without waiting for support from Russia, in August 1806 the Prussian mobilization went ahead and an ultimatum was duly issued by Berlin to Paris, demanding the withdrawal of French forces from beyond the Rhine. The ensuing campaign was short, though bloody. On 14 October the Prussians were surprised and crushed by Napoleon at Jena and by Davout at Auerstadt. Twenty-seven thousand Prussian troops were left dead or wounded and all the artillery was lost. Prussian fortresses fell swiftly one by one. A fortnight later Napoleon was in Berlin.

Talleyrand joined him there. It was in Berlin that Napoleon learned of the imprudent – and quickly reversed – decision by Godoy to mobilize Spain against him, taken when he thought that the coalition would prove victorious. According to Talleyrand, Napoleon now resolved to crush the Spanish Bourbons, a decision that was to lead to the later disastrous intervention. Also according to Talleyrand, it was now that he himself 'swore that, at whatever price, he would cease to be [Napoleon's] minister when [they] returned to France'.[37] The implication is that the two decisions were linked. But, for reasons to be examined later, this is extremely unlikely. Napoleon may, in his anger, have decided to punish Spain. And Talleyrand, in his frustration at seeing his preferred policy ignored, may have meditated resignation. But the Emperor and his Foreign Minister do not seem to have been at odds over an even more important decision, that of imposing a Continental Blockade against Britain by the Berlin Decrees of 21 November 1806. And it was in order to enforce this blockade, which necessitated closing every European port against British vessels, that both the disastrous intervention against Spain and Portugal and the catastrophic final intervention against Russia would be undertaken. Talleyrand's memoirs convey no impression of this.

Negotiations began with Prussia. But Russia remained obdurate. The Tsar had refused to ratify the earlier peace agreement initialled in Paris, and he now refused to accept either Austerlitz or Jena as decisive. In mid-December Napoleon gave orders for a new levy of conscripts in France, and then he set out into eastern Prussia after the elusive enemy.

Talleyrand had, meanwhile, busied himself in Berlin with bringing Saxony and its Elector, Frederick Augustus, previously allied to Prussia, into the Confederation of the Rhine as the protégé of France. Saxony's accession, along with five other lesser principalities, tightened Napoleon's grip on Germany as a whole. Now and later, Talleyrand favoured Saxony, doubtless with some financial recompense but for personal reasons too. He liked the Elector, whom he described to Napoleon as 'a simple man with noble manners'.[38] Simplicity and nobility being among Charles-Maurice's favourite qualities, that was the highest praise. He even intervened to prevent the family paintings from disappearing from Dresden back to France.[39] Later, in gratitude, Frederick Augustus provided him with a portrait of himself by Gérard, which was hung in the Prince's billiards room at Valençay.[40]

The Foreign Minister's next stop was Poznan, the western outpost of historic Poland, and then on to Warsaw. It was an unpleasant journey as the central European winter closed in. On one occasion, Talleyrand's carriage was stuck in the mud for twelve hours, and the soldiers grumbled about having to dig it out.[41] The Emperor's forays against his Russian foe failed because of the conditions, so he took up winter quarters in the Polish capital. This, of course, meant that Talleyrand did so too. Napoleon still relied on him as a sounding board, if not a source of advice. One night the Emperor fell asleep on his bed in the course of a discussion about how to deal with the Ottoman Empire, whose Sultan had just been murdered. Talleyrand slept on a nearby sofa. At four o'clock the following morning Méneval's entry woke Napoleon, who, on seeing his Foreign Minister asleep, cried: 'Hey! I think he's gone to sleep. So you're sleeping in my room, you rogue!' The discussion resumed and only finished an hour later.[42]

Both Napoleon and Talleyrand shared, for once, a common view of Poland and of the Poles. They agreed that the partitions of Poland, between Russia, Prussia and Austria, under the *ancien régime*, had worked against the interests of France. There was, it is true, a certain difference of emphasis. Talleyrand also felt that Poland's disappearance had worked against the balance of Europe. In a long report of 28 January 1807 Talleyrand went so far as to assert that if the integrity of Poland had been respected, 'Europe would have avoided the shocks and upheavals that have tormented it without remit for the last ten years'.[43] This consideration had little interest to Napoleon. Rather, a combination of romantic liberalism and political egotism attracted him towards the recreation of a Polish state, naturally under his own protection.

The Emperor and his Foreign Minister also increasingly agreed, however, about something else: namely that the Poles as a nation were impossible. Despite his early enthusiasm and his promises to Polish dignitaries, Napoleon quickly gave up any idea of re-establishing an independent Poland in its old borders, settling for its shadow in the form of the Grand Duchy of Warsaw. For his part, Talleyrand expressed his exasperation with the Poles to Savary on the eve of Tilsit: 'The Emperor must abandon this idea of Poland. You can do nothing with those people. With the Poles you only organize disorder.'[44] This insight, or perhaps prejudice, was not new to him. Even before setting out with the Emperor he had expressed the view that '[the Poles] could not be directed according to any system'.[45]

Talleyrand's wider role in Warsaw that winter was not simply diplomatic but social, or, more precisely, a blend of the two aimed at securing political support for France among the Polish élite. He did Napoleon's bidding by organizing splendid balls and receptions and by gracing those arranged by others. At one of these, he helped the Emperor settle on the beautiful Marie Walewska as a lover. Napoleon, who disliked the indignity of dancing, was even persuaded to take part in a quadrille as a device to make her acquaintance.[46]

As the worst of the winter passed, the Emperor sought once again to try to bring the Russians to a decisive engagement. The bloody Battle of Eylau on 8 February 1807, fought in the middle of a snowstorm, was indecisive. Only at Friedland, on 14 June, did the French emerge the victors. The Russians lost 25,000 men and 80 cannon and withdrew beyond the Niemen. After Friedland, Talleyrand wrote congratulating Napoleon, while urging an early conclusion of hostilities: 'I like to consider [the victory] as a forerunner, as a guarantee of peace, which must obtain for Your Majesty the repose that, at the price of so much fatigue, so many privations and dangers, he secures for his peoples. I like to consider it the last that he will be forced to win. That is why it is dear to me.'[47]

Meanwhile, Talleyrand had remained in Warsaw. His activity there belies the reputation he had acquired – and which on occasion he liked to cultivate – for congenital idleness. His role was that of effective governor of Poland, principal link with Paris, provider of intelligence and, above all, quartermaster-in-chief. This last demanded the highest degree of administrative capacity, and Talleyrand showed that he had lost none of the talent he had demonstrated so many years earlier as agent general of the French clergy under the *ancien régime*. He found clothing for the troops, purchased supplies, visited hospitals, supervised treatment, consoled and rewarded the wounded. In his tasks, he was closely assisted by the Franco-Polish general, Prince Poniatowski, and by the latter's sister, and his own adoring friend, Countess Tyszkiewicz. He wrote almost daily to Napoleon, reporting on his own activity, conveying news, and giving intelligence about enemy troop movements and intentions.[48]

Yet, despite all this activity to advance the Emperor's cause, Talleyrand's ideas were evolving in a very different direction. News of the hard-fought Battle of Eylau set him thinking, as he had thought before Marengo, about what would happen if Napoleon were killed. But on this occasion he was discontented with the direction of affairs, and he found a confidant who was still more so in the form of Emmerich von Dalberg. Dalberg, nephew of the Prince Primate of the Confederation of the Rhine, was a brilliant, bizarre, alternately devious and indiscreet character, who appealed to Talleyrand but whom Napoleon would have been better advised to shun or destroy. While posing as a supporter of Bonaparte – who would take him into his service in 1810 – he was, in fact, a liberal and a passionate German patriot, who was almost as committed to the French Emperor's over-throw as to his own and his family's interests. He and Talleyrand allowed their discussions to range beyond the immediate successor to Napoleon, for which they nominated Joseph Bonaparte. They agreed that Joseph should be persuaded to announce France's unconditional withdrawal to the Rhine. Pasquier asserts and Countess Potocka implies that it was at this juncture, after Eylau, that Talleyrand's thoughts first turned to nothing less than treason.[49]

If Eylau had a catalytic impact on Talleyrand's attitudes, Friedland effected a still more sudden change in those of the Tsar. It would have been possible to continue the struggle, but Alexander quixotically now decided to reach a personal accommodation with Napoleon, who, of course, hoped for nothing better. The result was the meeting of the two emperors at Tilsit on 25 June on a raft moored in the middle of the River Niemen. The King of Prussia also came to Tilsit, but only as the humiliated head of a defeated power. Talleyrand joined the party a few days after the initial meeting, his role a subordinate one throughout. Napoleon apparently still resented his Foreign Minister's leniency towards Austria at Pressburg and so left the hardest business – dealing with defeated Prussia – to Marshal Berthier.[50] If Talleyrand's account in his memoirs is to be believed, the Foreign Minister was appalled at the treatment of Prussia and even wept a tear at the noble bearing of its Queen.[51] But other sources suggest differently. He had no love of Prussia, and he may even have been uneasy at Napoleon's concessions.[52] He need not have been. Prussia survived but with the loss of all it possessed between the Elbe and the Rhine, including Magdeburg, and almost all of its Polish provinces. Its population was reduced from 9 to 4 million. It was not even party to the main Treaty of Tilsit, owing its survival at all (as the document has it) to 'consideration' for Tsar Alexander.

From Napoleon's viewpoint, the main objective at Tilsit was to induce Russia to enforce the Continental Blockade against Britain and to compel other states to do so too. To that end, he was prepared to allow – or more accurately to appear to allow – Russia a free hand in its dealings with the decrepit Ottoman Empire. While Russia offered to 'mediate' between France and Britain as a prelude to siding with the former against the latter, France undertook a similar role as regards the Russian and Ottoman empires. Russia also recognized the King of Saxony as Grand Duke of Warsaw and Napoleon's brother Jérôme as King of the (newly created) Kingdom of Westphalia. The settlement was clearly a further setback to Talleyrand's preferred strategy advanced before Ulm and after Austerlitz.

By now Talleyrand therefore had three fundamental quarrels with Napoleon over the direction of policy. First, the Emperor had chosen as his principal strategic ally Russia, which Talleyrand feared and detested, rather than Austria, which he regarded as quintessentially European and the pivot of European peace. Second, Napoleon had started placing members of his own family on the thrones of Europe – Louis in Holland, Joseph in Naples, Jérôme in Westphalia – rather than adopting that 'federal' system with friendly powers that Talleyrand advocated. Third, and most important, despite Talleyrand's urgings, despite unrest among the French middle class, despite a financial crisis that victory subdued but which exposed the French economy's fragility, Napoleon showed no serious desire for peace.[53] Perhaps, as has been suggested earlier, such a peace, above all peace with Britain, was simply incompatible with his own long-term survival. But for that very reason, Talleyrand and others had now begun to distinguish between the interests of France and the interests of Napoleon. As he puts it in the memoirs: 'I served Bonaparte as Emperor, as I had served him as Consul: I served him with devotion, in so far as I believed that he was himself exclusively devoted to France. But as soon as I saw him begin to undertake the

Revolutionary enterprises that destroyed him, I left the government – which he never forgave.'[54]

In this, from Talleyrand's Declaration, there is, alongside a slippery manipulation of dates and motives, an important kernel of truth. Despite the high favour that he still enjoyed personally with Napoleon, despite his enormous financial benefits, and despite experiencing some modest satisfaction at the advancement of the interests of the King of Saxony – with whom he stayed in Dresden on his way back to Paris – Charles-Maurice had little in terms of foreign policy to show for his pains. That was one, though only one, of the reasons why, on 9 August, he relinquished his post as Minister of Foreign Affairs.[55]

IO

The Business of Pleasure

⁓

TALLEYRAND NEVER LOST his appreciation of life's pleasures, even amid the stresses of his time as Napoleon's Foreign Minister. In Warsaw, with Russian troops marauding outside the city, and a terrified population to administer within, Charles-Maurice solicited some of the Emperor's Madeira from his quartermaster, observing that when Horace famously urged '*Nunc est bibendum*', the poet certainly did not have water in mind.[1] Talleyrand maintained his priorities. With the end of his term in office, he could further indulge them.

The summer heat was now upon Paris: it was the time when Talleyrand regularly left the city. Every year, between 1801 and 1832, he spent three or four weeks in August at the spa of Bourbon-l'Archambault, near Moulins in Auvergne, and 1807 was to be no exception. The spa provided precisely the ambience that Charles-Maurice most appreciated. The waters of this rural hamlet, its name recording the historic origin of the Bourbon family, had for generations been royalty's favourite cure. The traditions remained those of the *grand siècle*, and fashionable society flowed in from the capital each season.

As the spa's most celebrated visitor, Charles-Maurice had a large pool set aside for his private use. He lodged in different houses over the years, their nomenclature recalling the great figures who had used them in the past, such as the Hôtel Montespan.[2] He was guaranteed against boredom because he took his own private court with him, though on occasions this had to include his wife. The princesse de Talleyrand's presence was more than compensated, however, by the presence of the couple's allegedly adopted but probably natural daughter, Charlotte.

While Talleyrand was minister, he was often accompanied by Hauterive. There would also be two or three young secretaries from his office, for under Napoleon business continued whatever the season. He would frequently write to his master from Bourbon-l'Archambault, rarely without some allusion, by way of an excuse, to his absence from the seat of affairs. Thus in 1801, proffering views on Spain, he ends his letter: 'I am very afraid, General, that you will find that my opinion smells somewhat of the showers and baths.'[3] In 1803 he regrets that his absence in Bourbon-l'Archambault prevents his witnessing Napoleon's return to Paris.[4] In 1804 he testifies from the spa that 'every voice [here] is raised to bless you and everyone's good wishes are with you'.[5]

But there was also time for more serious reflection about politics. It was at Bourbon-l'Archambault that Talleyrand formulated his views about the need for Napoleon to divorce Joséphine, to marry an Austrian princess and to achieve the final elimination of the Bourbons.[6]

Generally speaking, though, Charles-Maurice's stays at the spa were a time for repose. This meant that he did more or less what he did in Paris, but he did it in a more relaxed environment. Thus, apart from his showers, baths and consumption of mineral water, he played whist, he gave dinners and, above all, he talked as, by common consent, he alone could talk.

Lord Holland observed of Charles-Maurice, who was then ambassador in London, that, 'for thirty or forty years, the *bons mots* of M. de Talleyrand were more frequently repeated and more generally admired than those of any living man'.[7] But while the reputation was real it only imperfectly reflects the reality. Charles-Maurice was not a specialist in jokes or even epigrams though he was capable of both. His wit (*esprit*) was more often a matter of wordplay and punning, apt for the circumstances, and necessarily for the language, rather than for retrospective quotation let alone translation.[8] He was certainly not comic, in that he was interested not primarily in amusing others but in amusing himself. He believed that the 'art of conversation' had been lost with the Revolution. In later years, he would urge his *protégé*, the journalist, historian and future statesman, Adolphe Thiers, to make a study of this lost art.[9]

Near the end of his life, Talleyrand's conversation, as is the way of old men, had become heavily dominated by anecdotes. But he still managed to impart a special quality to his story-telling. Charles Greville, who came to know Talleyrand in London, was impressed: 'Still retaining his faculties unimpaired, and his memory stored with recollections of his extraordinary and eventful career, and an inexhaustible mine of anecdotes, his delight was to narrate, which he used to do with an abundance, a vivacity, and a *finesse* peculiar to himself, and to the highest degree interesting and attractive.'[10]

In his earlier years, Charles-Maurice had, as he admits, deliberately cultivated a certain coldness and distance.[11] It took some time for this mannerism to wear off, and it never did completely. Anyway, reserve continued to have its uses, not only (and obviously) as a diplomat, but socially too. The case of Hortense de Beauharnais is one illustration, and is worth quoting:

> I am convinced that [Talleyrand's] great reputation for wit stems more from the little he says, and says well, than from anything remarkable, though I certainly do not deny him capable of that. He is, above all, remarkable by reason of his well-chosen words, a faultless tone, lots of *finesse* in judging people and in concealing himself from them, the assurance of a *grand seigneur*, and an idleness that makes dealing with him so easy and so pleasant that it can seem very like good nature. . .The attraction he possesses, and which is great, comes largely from the vanity of others. I was, myself, an example of it. The day that he deigns to speak to you, he is already lovable; and you are completely ready to fall for him if he only asks after your health.[12]

Hortense did not like Charles-Maurice very much. But she bears witness, despite herself, to his seductive conversational technique, one based on calculation as much as charm. As for the famous *bons mots*, Pasquier, who knew Talleyrand better than Hortense and did not like him greatly either, suggests that they were prepared in advance. He was probably right. He also observes, equally correctly, and indeed from his own experience, that when Talleyrand was angry he could use language of extreme vulgarity.[13]

But this, it must be added, was towards men. The nearest he came to downright rudeness to women was with Mme de Staël, whose masculinity of features and assertive temperament brought out the worst in him. In her novel, *Delphine*, she had portrayed herself as the heroine and Charles-Maurice as the cynical, selfish Mme de Vernon. He observed (in one version to Germaine's face, but more probably in the *salons*, behind her back): 'I am told that both you and I appear [in the book], disguised as women.'[14] But, that said, his women friends, like Mme de La Tour du Pin, appreciated a 'charm of conversation that no one has ever possessed like him'.[15]

Hortense de Beauharnais's judgement, derived from social contact, can be complemented by that of the baron de Vitrolles, who worked closely with Charles-Maurice during the Restoration:

> I have hardly ever heard from him those shafts, those apt phrases that have been attributed to him, and from which one could assemble a collection of apocryphal *Talleyrandiana*. He adopted in public a deep reserve, never hurrying to speak, and not speaking merely in order to say something. He carefully avoided ready-made expressions, vulgar comparisons, trivial remarks, and to the end of his life he detested: 'How are you?' He never said it and he never replied to it, probably not even to his doctor.
>
> The character of his conversation was that of grace and *finesse*. Its construction was simple, often ingenious and always individual. He knew the art of concealing his thought or his malice under a transparent veil of *sous-entendus*, those words that permit you to guess what is meant beyond what is said. It was the finest spice of the conversation of the past, from the days when conversation was entirely a way of employing the intellect.
>
> The choice of his anecdotes was apt. He only had himself appear in them as much as was necessary, and they usually had a subtle application which he allowed you to guess. Apart from these stories, he rarely went beyond two or three sentences, above all when it concerned serious matters.[16]

Molé, who also had close professional dealings with Talleyrand, similarly emphasized his economy of words and provides a further insight into it: 'He maintains an obstinate silence whenever he is not sure of creating the effect he would like to produce, but as soon as he is sure of pleasing or of succeeding, his manner becomes gracious and lively, without ceasing to be noble and in good taste.' Molé echoes Pasquier in noting the extreme contrast between Talleyrand's moods, as expressed in his speech: 'His intimacy is full of charm, although you never feel at ease with him; he tells stories and he teases with inimitable grace, he denigrates and criticizes with great guile; his bantering is ingenious, his humour refined and sharp, but if he wants to make it strong or bitter, he is brutal and vulgar. He scarcely ever argues, unless he is excited by interest or anger.'[17]

The poet Lamartine got to know Talleyrand as ambassador in London. The Prince took him aside and explained: 'People make out that I am a man of *bons mots*. . . I have never said a *bon mot* in my life. But I try to say, after a lot of thought, on many matters, the *mot juste!*' Lamartine agreed.[18]

Talleyrand was flattered by the attentions of such literary figures, as long as he managed to work his magic upon them. Only once was he seriously let down. This was by the writer George Sand, who appeared unannounced with her lover, the playwright Alfred de Musset, at Valençay in 1834 and wrote a cruel and scandalous account of Talleyrand which caused the duchesse de Dino great offence.[19]

The Prince liked to collect celebrities, particularly those he hoped would enhance his historical reputation. He also never made any bones about wanting to know a man's background in cases of political preferment. 'Is he somebody?' was the first question he would ask when a post was solicited.[20] But being entirely confident of his own standing, he took people as he found them. He did not mind their peculiarities if they amused him or were attached to him.

On holiday at Bourbon-l'Archambault, he was surrounded by an even great variety of characters than in Paris. Apart from his family and his staff, there would always be Countess Tyszkiewicz, his devoted friend. She had fallen in love with him, lavished her fortune on him, and sent him *billets doux* that he received in bed each morning. Disfigured by a glass eye, distinctly eccentric, affecting a certain haughtiness with inferiors that Charles-Maurice himself never showed, she irritated him and provoked him to play tricks at her expense.[21] But he put up with her, accepted her company and accommodated her in a wing of Valençay. She is buried in the chapel there. Also present at Bourbon-l'Archambault were other ladies to whom he was intimately linked, such as, for example, the comtesse de Bonneuil, mother-in-law of his long-time collaborator, Regnault de Saint-Angély.[22] Mme de Bonneuil, now sixty, was at this stage still an active spy with excellent connections in the courts of northern Europe.

Nor were the regular staff of the spa left out of the Prince's circle. Its physician, Dr Faye, was a favourite with him, not so much for his skills as for his pedantry, which Talleyrand found very amusing. Faye's speciality was to lard his conversation over dinner with superfluous Latin tags, about which Charles-Maurice teased the ladies, who had no idea what the doctor meant, by pretending that these were highly improper expressions.[23]

The Prince had long managed to integrate the demands of business into the rhythms and routine of his private life. This was so from the first moment of his waking day, for he continued to practise the full, semi-public *lever* of the *ancien régime*. Charles de Rémusat witnessed it and recorded his impressions, and so, less diplomatically, did Molé.[24]

Rémusat used to come to the Hôtel Talleyrand to see the master of the house several times a month. Apart from the Prince's family, there were other guests with whom to pass the time until Charles-Maurice was ready. These included the latter's old tutor, M. Bertrand, who talked in both Greek and English and discoursed on economics until the hour arrived to descend to the Prince's apartments. There a group would gather, whose membership extended well beyond family and close friends. His secretary and his private doctor were present. Statesmen and ambassadors and political colleagues might arrive at any time. Even the Tsar had been known to attend. There were always several of Talleyrand's *hommes de confiance*, Dalberg, Durant de Mareuil and above all Montrond; bankers and financial agents. Anyone who was amusing and had gossip to impart might gain leave to enter. The gathering was of both sexes, since neither the Prince nor his women guests suffered from inhibitions.

At about eleven o'clock, the door from the bedroom opened and Talleyrand appeared in the *grand cabinet de toilette*, vaguely acknowledging those in the room as he limped over to a chair by the fireplace. It was, for the uninitiated, an unnerving sight. Before retiring he had his valets wrap him in layers of flannel and several nightcaps, before helping him into his specially designed bed – it had a deep hollow, shaped like a hammock, because he was terrified of falling out during the night.[25] These extensive coverings now made him appear, as he emerged into public view, like a huge mass of white cloth. Three valets were already waiting to perform their morning duties. The senior valet, none other than the famous Courtiade, was too old by this time to do more than supervise. The other two, however, immediately set about combing, pomading and powdering Talleyrand's long grey hair. (He wore so much powder that Hortense de Beauharnais had felt sick at the smell when the then Grand Chambellan leaned over her in bed to congratulate her on giving birth to her son, the future Napoleon III.)[26] Someone would bring Charles-Maurice a cup of camomile tea, which he nowadays drank in the morning in place of coffee. That was his breakfast. A silver bowl next appeared and with it a sponge, with which he wiped his face. He then bent forward and noisily inhaled the equivalent of two glasses of warm water through his nose and exhaled it through his mouth. It was something he swore by, and which he had no compunction about doing in public on even the smartest occasions. Thus when he was ambassador in London, he was seen by the writer Mérimée performing his nasal gargle after dinner, while the diplomatic corps looked on, and as the rich and fashionable Lady Jersey held his towel.[27]

Once his hair was arranged, a valet brought him his hat, because this was supposed to be worn as soon as the pomade had been applied. Still more water was fetched. The bands of flannel around his legs were unfurled and without any embarrassment his misshapen feet – the right wide, foreshortened and claw-like, the left narrow and extended – were washed in full of view of the company. Then, with equal nonchalance, he stood up and walked slowly around the room, while his valets removed one set of garments and struggled to replace them with another, almost equally voluminous; for Talleyrand wore several layers of cravats, waistcoats and stockings. They then helped him put on his breeches, which he did without regard to modesty. And all the while he talked, joked, recited stories, gave his opinions about people and events, stopping from time to time to sign letters or to give instructions, or listen as people read newspaper articles out to him. The whole process took about two hours. It was often the busiest part of his day.

Apart from camomile tea or a biscuit with his Madeira, Talleyrand ate nothing until dinner, which he took at about six o'clock. His table was famous, and his invitations precious, whether he dined as Foreign Minister, President of the Council, ambassador, or as a private citizen.[28] Paris under the Consulate, the Empire and the Restoration saw extraordinary gastronomic achievements: in its scale and its artifice French cuisine dazzled. Napoleon, with his simple tastes, his preference for fried chicken, and his refusal to spend more than a quarter of an hour at the table unless compelled to do so, provided no example. Nor, indeed, did his successor, Louis XVIII, for different reasons. Whereas Napoleon talked throughout the meal, ignoring the food, the King was so obsessed with it that meals were eaten in complete silence.[29] Neither style was satisfactory.

The most celebrated table of the Napoleonic era was probably that of Cambacérès.[30] Napoleon was amused at his *gourmandise*, particularly when on one occasion Cambacérès sought exemption from a ban on certain rare delicacies by advancing the principle that 'it is largely through the table that one governs'.[31]

Antonin Carême, the pastry cook who became one of France's greatest culinary authorities, knew all about Cambacérès's fare and could compare it to Talleyrand's.[32] He had no doubt that Charles-Maurice's table was superior. Cambacérès sought his specialities from all over France, but he allowed himself to become obsessed with them. He was also not just personally greedy but stingy, and committed the unforgivable sin of serving up again what was left over from the previous day. By contrast, Talleyrand, for whom Carême worked on and off for twelve years, was simply the greatest gourmet of them all, his house the perfect place for a chef to practise his art. As Carême recalled: 'It was all cleverness, order, splendour. Talent was regarded and promoted. . .Dinners of forty-eight *entrées* were given in the galleries of the [house in the] rue de Varenne. I have seen them served and I have designed them myself. . .What a picture those gatherings presented! Everything proclaimed that this was the greatest of the nations. The man who has not seen that has seen nothing!'[33]

Carême made his first public impact as *pâtissier* with his '*extraordinaires*', elaborate, sculptural creations, in the Hôtel Gallifet under Talleyrand. But he was only one of a much larger team of cooks whom the Foreign Minister engaged, all working to M. Boucher, the *chef de services*.[34]

Napoleon expected Talleyrand to entertain on his behalf. Nor did the duty lapse with Charles-Maurice's departure from the ministry. In

October 1808 he was instructed by the Emperor to hold 'at least' four dinners a week, each of 'thirty-six *couverts*', for ministers, *conseillers d'état* and parliamentarians, so that they could get together – and doubtless so that Napoleon could find out what they were thinking.[35] Nor did the entertaining end with Napoleon. At Valençay, once it reverted to Talleyrand's private use, he might entertain as many as thirty around his dinner table, though usually there would be a dozen. Service in the Talleyrand household remained *à la française* rather than the increasingly fashionable *service à la russe* – that is, all the dishes (except soup) were served at once, which had the advantage of eye-pleasing symmetry though, as Carême would come to recognize, the disadvantage that they went cold. On a typical evening, Talleyrand's guests might expect to eat from among two *potages*, two *relevés* (one of fish), four *entrées*, two *rôtis*, four *entremets*, and dessert.[36]

Wherever Talleyrand went, he would take his four principal chefs, one each responsible for the roasts, the sauces, the *pâtisserie*, and the ices/desserts (of which Charles-Maurice did not himself partake). Ten men would regularly be employed to produce dinner for the Prince and his guests. At both his Paris home and Valençay the menu was never the same two days of the year. Each morning, Talleyrand's *maître-d'hôtel* would agree with the Prince exactly what was to be served, and Charles-Maurice took a close interest in every course. English guests were taken aback to find how Charles-Maurice delivered eloquent dissertations on every dish and bottle served from his superb wine cellar (between 1801 and 1804 he owned the château of Haut-Brion, greatest of all the Graves). He himself always drank a good claret at dinner, with a little water added. But this gourmet was no *gourmand*. He ate sparingly of each course, usually a mouthful followed by a glass of wine. He claimed never to have had indigestion, and strongly believed that a healthy diet was the key to a healthy life, as those who saw him in old age were inclined to agree. Even when very old, he ate well, while he and his chefs carefully adjusted the fare to his needs and capacity. He continued to keep what one British observer described as a 'regular table of the old school', which the French nobility in general were too poor any longer to maintain. Indeed, Talleyrand's most frequent complaint about his chef was: 'Why does he not spend more?'[37]

He had decided views about how to drink Cognac, and they quickly constituted a rule for general application: the glass must be warmed in the palm of the hand, the contents gently swirling to release the bouquet, you smell it, you put it down, and then you talk. He was equally firm about how to make the best coffee: it should be four-fifths mocha, one-fifth Martinique, slightly burned, 'as black as the devil, as hot as hell, as pure as an angel, as sweet as love'. After leaving the table, he would take a large cup, fill it with pieces of sugar and then have the coffee poured over them. He enjoyed tastes that stimulated his palate and excited his rather sluggish metabolism – his doctors noted that he had a markedly slow pulse rate – such as dishes made with peppers. Talleyrand achieved a distinctive gastronomic legacy, introducing, for example, the custom of serving Parmesan with soup and Madeira afterwards. Several classic dishes were made in his honour and bear his name, such as turkey fillet powdered with truffles, *timbales* of truffles, *blanquettes* of chicken with chicory, all '*à la Talleyrand*'. Among cheeses, he extolled the virtues of Brie, 'the king of cheeses' – the only monarch he had not betrayed, one wag remarked. His favourite fruit was the peach, and he grew many different varieties at Valençay. Looking back on his years in his employment, Carême judged that, along with the famous chef/restaurateur Robert, Talleyrand had contributed more to the growth of what he called '*la cuisine moderne*' than anyone else.[38]

After dinner, Talleyrand would either attend a reception or give his own. In the latter case, guests would arrive and take their seats. He would go from room to room, greeting and talking to them. Until the Congress of Vienna, the princesse de Talleyrand presided along with the Prince at these occasions; later the duchesse de Dino took her place. The comtesse de Boigne attended the Talleyrand *salon* in 1814 and found it most amusing: it only opened at midnight, and all of Europe crowded in.[39] During Talleyrand's years of disgrace at the end of the Empire the *salon* had made up for whatever it lost through official disfavour, in part at least, by its seditious attraction. Not only did Parisians arrive to exchange gossip, so also did foreigners. Charles-Maurice, whose manner people found quite unchanged, proclaimed to his visitors that he still served as the 'centre of European equilibrium'.[40]

But, above all, Talleyrand's *soirées*, particularly in politically troubled times, allowed him to unwind in the way that he preferred, that is in the company of women who loved, liked, or at least enormously admired him. People laughed at the 'old seraglio' of doting ladies who hung on his every word. Some, like Countess Potocka, found the whole business unbearably irritating, as the Prince, surrounded by his former mistresses, 'yawned at some [and] rebuffed others. . .maliciously reciting reminiscences and dates'.[41] The seraglio was most in evidence not so much at Talleyrand's house, overshadowed as it was by the unwelcome presence of his wife, but at the houses of his friends. The princesse de Vaudémont, for example, held a *salon* frequented by Talleyrand and other politicians which, like other *salons*, was a centre of political power, particularly after the overthrow of Napoleon.[42] Ministers and ambassadors clustered there, willing to suffer the indignity of being bitten by her lapdogs, so long as they could be at what one participant described as the 'sweetest haven of friendship and the most dangerous place for unstable governments'.[43]

Other *salons* provided Talleyrand with greater intimacy. One such was that held by the Mlles de Bellegarde, Adélaïde-Victoire and Aurore, friends of Aimée de Coigny, two elderly eccentric ladies who were of no importance except that they knew how to entertain, to cultivate uninhibited conversation, and thus to provide an atmosphere conducive to Talleyrand and his circle. Artists, men of letters, members of the old aristocracy recreated there the atmosphere of pre-Revolutionary sophistication and courtesy that Charles-Maurice craved.[44] An even more important place of refuge was the *salon* of another old friend and former mistress, the vicomtesse de Laval in the rue Roquépine. Aimée describes her, 'now old, but her wit and her eyes still [retaining] a youthful charm'.[45] Mme de Laval lived with another of Charles-Maurice's old acquaintances, Narbonne. While Narbonne played the husband, Talleyrand acted the role of the lover. The house passed for modest, the *salon* was small, but the company was select. A number of those present were among Charles-Maurice's oldest friends, such as his former mistress Adélaïde de Souza (formerly de Flahaut), Mme de La Tour du Pin, the explorer Choiseul-Gouffier and his future ministerial colleague François de Jaucourt. One visitor summed it all up as a school of '*grandes manières*, traditions and memories'. It was, in short, all perfectly suited to the needs of an aristocratic statesman fallen on politically hard times.[46] And when he felt like demonstrating the assurance that only those of the highest birth and the greatest cultivation can afford, Charles-Maurice would amuse himself and others by indulging in buffoonery with Mme de Laval's black servant, Zoé.[47]

With the arrival of the duchesse de Courlande in Paris, however, the life of the seraglio, and indeed that of Mme de Laval's *salon*, suffered a sharp alteration. Dorothea von Medem, Herzogin von Kurland – or Dorothée, duchesse de Courlande as she is known in French historiography – was immensely wealthy, owning huge tracts of land in Saxony, Silesia and Bohemia, and enjoyed close relations with the princes of northern Europe, especially with the Prussian royal family. She met Charles-Maurice after the marriage of her daughter Dorothée, the future duchesse de Dino, to the Prince's nephew Edmond, under circumstances shortly to be described. But she then followed Talleyrand back to Paris, initiating one of the greatest love affairs and most important friendships of his life. The sight of this pair, neither of whom was in the first flush of youth, he fifty-five, she forty-eight, at the most fashionable *salons* provoked sarcasm and envy. Countess Potocka complained that at Mme de Laval's *salon* it was now required that everyone admire the duchesse de Courlande's dress and jewels, while Talleyrand 'contemplated her with such admiration as to make all his old seraglio die of jealousy'.[48] Charles-Maurice valued his friend's shrewdness as much as her beauty and affection. She was his regular correspondent during the Congress of Vienna. When she died in 1821 in her castle of Löbikau at the age of sixty-one, he wrote to the duchesse de Dino: 'My heart is broken. I thought, and I took pleasure in thinking, that your sweet mother would close my eyes.'[49]

Apart from a love of conversation, and of flirtation, what Charles-Maurice and his friends had most in common was a love of whist. (Sometimes they opted for the newer import of craps instead.) Once the news had been exchanged and casual callers had left, the party would sit down to this, the serious business of the evening. Supper would be served at some point. Play would go on into the early hours, sometimes until four o'clock in the morning.[50] Talleyrand's explanation of why he found the game so satisfactory was that it 'engages but does not engross, and it dispenses with connected conversation'. To a young diplomat who prided himself on not knowing how to play he remarked: 'What a sad old age you are preparing for yourself!'[51]

On leaving the Foreign Ministry to become, at his own request, a great official at the imperial court, Talleyrand had a double incentive to buy a new, still grander house. On the one hand, he could no longer entertain on official occasions in the state rooms of the Hôtel Gallifet; on the other, his social obligations and his need to maintain a wide circle of support both increased. The result was his purchase in March 1808 of the magnificent Hôtel Monaco in the rue de Varenne. It was acquired in an obscure transaction with Mrs Crawford, mistress and later wife of Quintin Crawford, Scottish financier and spy. This took the form of an exchange of Talleyrand's old house in the rue d'Anjou, with the deficit of 300,000 francs – his new house was worth double the old – paid partly in cash but principally through a mortgage. Begun for the Montmorency family, construction of the house in the rue de Varenne had been completed for the comte de Matignon in 1725: hence the name, Hôtel Matignon, by which the official residence of today's French Prime Ministers is known. After the Matignons, it had then passed to the Grimaldi family before its acquisition by Crawford. The Hôtel Monaco was rightly described by Fouché's secret police, who followed the purchase closely, as 'one of the largest and finest of Paris'.[52] It was evidently not, though, large enough for its new owner, who also bought an adjoining house in which to expand his domain. The Hôtel Monaco was already sumptuously furnished and full of fine paintings. Talleyrand purchased the contents and added to them, also acquiring a fine library. He engaged in important building work, comprising an extra dining room and a music room.[53] The latter is something of a surprise as Charles-Maurice himself was not musical.[54] But now his guests could hope to hear in the Hôtel Monaco the Prince's director of music, Dussek, at the piano, Libon at the violin and Naderman at the harp.[55]

When he purchased the Hôtel Monaco, Talleyrand does not seem to have allowed for the risk of any drop in his income. In particular, he did not foresee his disgrace, or else if he did he paid insufficient regard to its financial consequences. So, far from reducing his outgoings, he increased them. Of course, he still had influence at home and a plethora of connections abroad. But, as far as Napoleon could ensure, which was not as far as the Emperor would have liked, Talleyrand was excluded from sensitive information. He was no longer in the forefront of diplomacy. He was still able to trade his influence for bribes, but not so easily or so regularly as in the past. All this had serious financial consequences for him and, because it helped edge him across the fine line between opposition and treason, it also had far-reaching political consequences for Napoleon and for France.

I I

Treason and Disgrace

CONTEMPORARIES SPECULATED, AND so have historians, about what exactly drove Talleyrand to resign as Foreign Minister in 1807. Had he, perhaps, sensed that it was time to withdraw from a position that connected him too closely to a doomed régime? That idea took root even in his own lifetime. Thus Vitrolles asserts that, after Tilsit, Talleyrand foresaw Napoleon's military reverses and chose to go into semi-disgrace as the route to a better life beyond the Empire.[1] Yet this seems unlikely. True, Charles-Maurice had excellent political antennae, but there is no evidence that they were already twitching. What is clear is that Talleyrand was by now dispirited and frustrated. He had, after all, seen his advice on foreign policy comprehensively rejected, as Napoleon chose a Russian rather than an Austrian alliance. Nor had his discreet but insistent attempts at finding the way to a negotiated peace achieved any greater success. He had just spent an exhausting two years acting as Napoleon's secretary, quartermaster, propagandist, negotiator and intermittent travelling companion. It had become too much. A quieter life beckoned. And so, apparently, did the prospect of a courtly sinecure and a still higher salary.

According to Méneval, who doubtless echoes Napoleon's own view, money was at the root of Talleyrand's decision. Specifically, Charles-Maurice wanted a salary equal to that of the two ex-Consuls, Cambacérès and Lebrun. But Méneval also reveals that the Emperor had doubts about his Foreign Minister's reliability. He had begun, for example, to make unpleasant remarks about Talleyrand's ill-gotten fortune. And he blamed him, or at least his entourage, for damaging leaks of information.[2]

Napoleon did not want to dispense with Talleyrand's services altogether. To use him when and how he saw fit remained his aim.

There was, however, already a kernel of suspicion in the Emperor's mind when Talleyrand asked to relinquish his post in order to take up the vacant office of Vice-Grand Elector. (Fouché apparently observed in the *salons* that this was the only 'vice' that Talleyrand did not so far possess, but that amid the others it would not be noticed.)[3] There was a rule that the great offices of the court were incompatible with ministerial portfolios. Could this have been overridden? Obviously, it could. But Napoleon was extremely stubborn about such things. And, just as important, Talleyrand knew that he was. As luck would have it, Charles-Maurice was discussing the matter with Cambacérès when Napoleon happened to enter the room. The Emperor asked him why he wanted to give up his position. Charles-Maurice replied: 'I am tired, Sire, and not capable of continuing the life of a minister, which is a great deal too active for me.' Napoleon grumpily accepted the decision.[4]

The future tension between the two cannot, therefore, be attributed to either side's resentment at the change. The fact remains, however, that Talleyrand was soon disappointed with the reality of his new position.

Both the offices of Vice-Grand Elector and that of Archichancelier d'état had become vacant, the former because it had been held by Joseph Bonaparte, now King of Naples, and the latter because it was in abeyance while Eugène de Beauharnais was viceroy of Italy.[5] Talleyrand received the first office in his own right and was allowed to act as substitute for Prince Eugène in the second. His new salary of 330,000 francs was more than three times that which he had received as Foreign Minister. Taking into account his salary as Grand Chambellan, his revenues as prince de Bénévent, and the pension accorded to him as titular of the *grand cordon* of the Légion d'honneur, he was now receiving an annual state income of 495,000 francs.[6] Moreover, combined with his existing role at court, his new position as Vice-Grand Elector also, in theory, gave him the best possible access to the Emperor and to affairs of state. But this is not how it worked out; for Napoleon had decided otherwise.

Perhaps Talleyrand had come to believe that he was indispensable. Certainly, the Emperor was determined to prove that he was not.[7] This helps explain his choice of Champagny as Talleyrand's successor.[8]

Champagny was a competent administrator, but nothing more. In his memoirs, he describes himself as 'fearing blame more than desiring glory'.[9] Pasquier thought him capable, but weak of character, and notes that this was precisely what recommended him to Napoleon, who was exasperated at having a Foreign Minister who took the credit for the Emperor's own successes. From the moment of the appointment, Napoleon made a great show of working only with Champagny, studiously avoiding any occasion for one-to-one conversation with Talleyrand.[10] Naturally, this was publicly noticed; Talleyrand's prestige suffered; his public influence declined; and his resentment grew. He tried to reassert himself, asking to take on permanently the role of Archichancelier d'état and turning it into an office with real power.[11] Cambacérès, who always offered sensible advice which was all too rarely taken, approached Napoleon. He suggested that Talleyrand's wish should be granted and that the latter be given responsibility for some aspects of foreign affairs. But Napoleon sharply refused and changed the subject.[12] The Emperor would later claim that Talleyrand had been mad to give up the Ministry of Foreign Affairs.[13] But it is clear that Napoleon never tried to palliate the consequences of that decision, rather the reverse.

Talleyrand, for his part, now began a campaign of sarcastic remarks against Champagny. The latter was known for his energy and honesty, in sharp contrast to his predecessor. But he was unimpressive and incapable of initiative. Charles-Maurice turned these virtues and vices against him. The Bavarian minister echoed the line that Charles-Maurice had spun, when he reported back to Munich how Champagny, though moral, well-informed and hard-working, was timid and could not stand up to Napoleon.[14] In his memoirs, Talleyrand says that the Emperor complained how Champagny 'appeared each morning, with his zeal, to excuse his clumsiness of the previous day'.[15] And perhaps on occasion Napoleon did regret his choice of minister. At Schönbrunn in 1809 he apparently lost patience with Champagny's pedestrian style of negotiation: 'You have stipulated [in the Treaty] a hundred million in indemnities for France. It will all go the Trésor, I know that. In Talleyrand's time, we probably would not have had sixty. He would have had ten. But it would have been done a fortnight ago. Bring it to an end!'[16]

Attacks on Champagny's competence were not, however, a satisfactory means of returning to influence. It was necessary for Talleyrand to prove his value in some matter of high policy. Events in Spain, and the Emperor's indecision about how to deal with them, now provided an opportunity.

Godoy's imprudent mobilization of Spanish forces against France before Jena has already been mentioned. He quickly reversed his decision. But the harm was done. Napoleon's resentment festered. Back in France – according to the memoirs – Talleyrand 'combated with all [his] force' the Emperor's notion of seizing Spain, 'exposing the immorality and the dangers of such an enterprise'. Unable to dissuade Napoleon entirely, he proposed instead the occupation of Catalonia, 'until [France] managed to obtain a maritime peace agreement with England'.[17] The truth about Talleyrand's conduct at this juncture is very different. And it is particularly important to establish, because it both helps explain Talleyrand's subsequent disgrace and also bears on his wider reputation as a statesman.

Napoleon had good reason to be worried about events in the Iberian Peninsula. The closure of Portuguese ports against Britain was fundamental to his strategy of Continental Blockade, but it was very difficult to enforce. The most obvious way was through Spain. Godoy, anxious to restore good relations and spotting an opportunity for his private aggrandizement, was now a model of cooperation. The Treaty of Fontainebleau in October 1807 accordingly divided up Portugal, attributing the south as a principality for Godoy, the north to the Queen of Etruria, and reserving the centre for future decision. A month later, Lisbon fell to French troops, and the Braganzas fled to Brazil.

The ease with which this was accomplished, and the equal facility with which the Bourbons of Naples had been dethroned, encouraged Napoleon's ambitions. While French troops remained in Spain, divisions in the Spanish court, largely prompted by hatred of Godoy, played into French hands. The tutor of the young Ferdinand, Prince of Las Esturias, secretly proposed, at the French ambassador's suggestion, a marriage for Ferdinand with a member of Napoleon's family, in exchange for action against the Spanish royal favourite. The plot was quickly discovered. Godoy had the King arrest his son and then seek 'advice' from Napoleon. In March 1808, however, a riot forced the dismissal of Godoy and the abdication of Charles IV in favour of Ferdinand. These events put into Napoleon's head the plan of summoning the Spanish royal family to Bayonne in order to 'arbitrate' between father and son.[18] It was a trap. Under pressure from the Emperor, Ferdinand was induced to cede the crown to his father, and Charles IV then ceded it to Napoleon. Finally, the latter forced it upon his reluctant elder brother, Joseph. Only now, though, did the main challenge have to be faced: that of imposing their new monarch upon a bemused and soon ferociously hostile Spanish population.[19]

Talleyrand subsequently claimed to have known nothing of the Treaty of Fontainebleau, let alone advised upon later developments. This, though, is a lie. Even he admits that he was at Fontainebleau at the relevant time, in his court capacities. How could he, with his many Spanish contacts, not have known what was in the air? Indeed, Cambacérès states that every evening at Fontainebleau the Emperor and Talleyrand were closeted together discussing Spain.[20] Napoleon definitely and repeatedly told Caulaincourt that it was Talleyrand himself who secretly negotiated the treaty with Don Isidor Izquierdo, Godoy's envoy, though General Duroc actually signed it.[21] This has the ring of truth.

The evidence pointing to Talleyrand's later involvement is also persuasive. Charles-Maurice was much less interested in the Continental Blockade than was Napoleon, and thus less convinced of the need for domination of the Iberian Peninsula so as to seal its ports. But he had a different reason for wanting to see a French puppet rule in Madrid – one that he dared not acknowledge in his memoirs or in any public statement after the Restoration. This was his conviction, spurred on by a strong sense of his own interest, of the need to drive the Bourbons off the thrones of Europe. His hostility to them is repeatedly witnessed by accounts of his private conversation.[22] Moreover, the traditionalism that marked his foreign policy, evident in his attitude to Austria, was no less so in his view of Spain. Just as he favoured the policy practised by the old monarchy between 1756 and 1789 in central Europe, so he hankered after a new version of the 'Family Pact' that had united France and Spain through rule by different branches of the Bourbons since 1713 – though now with Bonapartes in place of Bourbons.[23]

Pasquier heard him talk openly in these terms in the *salons*. He even used to refer to the Franco-Spanish link as 'one of the finest parts of the legacy of the Great King [Louis XIV]'.

But what had he been saying privately to the Emperor? Pasquier was convinced that Talleyrand had placed the idea in Napoleon's mind, a conviction that was reinforced when he heard the Emperor using exactly the same language as his former Foreign Minister.[24] Méneval probably knew the facts of the matter best. He thought that in the wake of the arrival of the different proposals from Spain, and knowing how Napoleon liked to talk over the options, Talleyrand had initially used the occasion to insinuate himself. Charles-Maurice offered himself, in short, as a sounding board, which was exactly the role in which Napoleon valued him. As the Emperor used to say: 'Only Talleyrand understands me. I can talk only to Talleyrand.'[25] But Charles-Maurice did not just listen, for, as Méneval reveals:

> He threw in, with the appearance of a studied response, the advice to the Emperor to profit from the disputes that had divided the court of Spain in order to change the dynasty, which would never be a useful ally against England, and which, in circumstances that could not fail to occur, would favour that power to France's disadvantage. As a variant of this extreme measure, he proposed to obtain from Spain some cessions of territory which would make it dependent on us.[26]

Yet, at about the same time, Talleyrand was expressing elsewhere his doubts about the outcome of the Spanish enterprise. Sometimes this just consisted of disobliging remarks about the inadequacies of Champagny and of his former friend, but now enemy, Maret, who were his rivals in advising the Emperor on Spanish policy.[27] But on other occasions the doubts he expressed went deeper. At the end of March 1808, Mollien, running into Talleyrand at the Tuileries, asked him his view about what was being planned for Spain. 'Whatever is done, they are only preparing future regrets,' was the gloomy reply.[28] To express such doubts so early suggests, at the least, that Talleyrand envisaged the possibility of disaster at the same time as he was urging the intervention.

These initial doubts, which he concealed from the Emperor, probably hardened when he learned what happened at Bayonne. The memoirs state that he upbraided Napoleon with having behaved like a card-sharp and that he was never forgiven.[29] This is obviously a later invention, though he may well have expressed semi-public disapproval. Or, again, perhaps Napoleon just wanted finally and brutally to disillusion him about the prospect of his return to influence. In any case, the Spanish captives – Ferdinand, Prince of Las Esturias, his brother Don Carlos and their uncle Don Antonio – were despatched to Valençay, Talleyrand's great château, as a suitable jail. It was a deliberate insult. The Emperor even sent insolently detailed instructions as to how the princes were to be entertained during their stay. Talleyrand, who must have been inwardly seething, replied in inimitable style. The château, he reassured the Emperor, was well supplied with cooks, crockery and bed-clothes. The princes would have all the pleasures that the weather allowed. They would be provided with mass every day, a park to walk in, and a forest with plenty of clearings though poorly stocked with game. There was no theatre, but young people could be invited to dance with the princes if they liked. Whether Napoleon was aware of the mockery in all this is unclear.[30]

In fact, Talleyrand treated his captive guests well. What he calls the 'horrible stews' of Spain were served. He protected the princes' privacy as far as he could from prying eyes and from the heavy-handed attentions of Napoleon's agent, a certain Colonel Henri. Talleyrand found guitars and players to remind the princes of their homeland. Every member of the château staff, and the guards too, had to attend evening prayers: atheism was no excuse. The princes had, in fact, more freedom than they would ever have enjoyed at the Spanish court. This did not, it seems, have a great effect on Ferdinand, who as Ferdinand VII proved a bigoted and ruthless tyrant. Nor did it do much to broaden their minds. When the Spanish left, Talleyrand found that their uncle, Don Antonio, had torn the illustrations from his library books so as to remove any source of moral temptation to his young nephews.[31] Other damage was the result of firework displays organized by the Spaniards in honour of Napoleon's victories.[32] But, at least, the two royal princes left with fond memories of the place; weeping tears of gratitude, and unconscious of the irony, they presented Talleyrand with their prayer-books on their departure six years later.[33]

The despatch of the princes to Valençay in May might have seemed to signal the beginnings of a permanent disgrace. But Napoleon thought that he could use Talleyrand while still humiliating him, and so Charles-Maurice found himself summoned to Nantes to be briefed for a special mission. He was in noticeably good spirits on receiving the news.[34] But it is clear from subsequent events that this mood reflected something more than delight at having regained Napoleon's favour.

At Nantes, the Emperor revealed his plans for a new meeting and treaty with the Tsar, to take place at Erfurt. He had by now realized that he himself would have to supervise a large-scale military intervention in Spain, and he wished to ensure a free hand in central Europe while doing so. Above all, he expected the Tsar to keep a restive and re-arming Austria in check. In exchange, he would offer the prospect of Russian gains at the expense of the Ottoman Empire, though he wanted to make these promises as vague as possible. Such subtle manoeuvring was much more Talleyrand's forte than Champagny's. Moreover, although the substance of the agreements at Tilsit had been drawn up without the then Foreign Minister's involvement, Charles-Maurice had struck up a good personal relationship with the Tsar.

Still more important, though a distinctly mixed blessing from Napoleon's viewpoint, Talleyrand had achieved a powerful ascendancy over Caulaincourt, who since the previous year had been French ambassador in St Petersburg. This relationship would be of great importance between now and the fall of the Empire. Caulaincourt was a simple, emotional man, prone to burst into tears in public. He had been grieved at the consequences of his own actions in the affair of the duc d'Enghien, and even more so by the way he was shunned in its aftermath.[35] He was easily impressed by great men and by now had fallen under the spell of both Napoleon and Tsar Alexander, without apparently grasping the contradiction. He was particularly badly treated by Napoleon, who, while relying on his loyalty, petulantly prevented his marrying his beloved Mme de Canisy. Seeing this, Talleyrand acted the part of romantic go-between, passing on news of her to her anxious lover in Russia. It was to prove a shrewd investment.[36]

At Nantes, Napoleon had Charles-Maurice read through all the relevant correspondence. The Emperor then dictated the main articles of the agreement he wanted and Talleyrand went away to prepare a draft. On his return, Charles-Maurice read out the text. Napoleon interrupted, approving of the way in which Talleyrand (echoing Tilsit) proposed French 'mediation' between Russia and Turkey over Moldavia and Wallachia. This, he said, would worry Austria, which was his 'true enemy'.

Talleyrand corrected him: 'Your enemy for the moment perhaps, Sire. But fundamentally its policy is not in opposition with that of France. It is not aggressive, it is conservative.'

'My dear Talleyrand,' answered Napoleon, 'I know that is your opinion. We shall talk about it when the Spanish business is finished.'

The Emperor now remembered the stipulation he had made of an article requiring Russia to side with France in case of a war with Austria: 'It's the essential article. How could you forget it? Are you still an Austrian?'

Talleyrand replied: 'A bit, Sire. But I think that it would be more accurate to say that I am never Russian, and always French.'[37]

Perhaps Napoleon, who had discarded Talleyrand's advice on these matters before, thought that he could do the same now. But he had not reckoned with his former Foreign Minister's ability to pursue a secret policy which entirely contradicted that to which he was officially bound. Part of Napoleon's problem was that he, too, was in the business of deceit. He was not prepared to act on Talleyrand's analysis, according to which Russia was a greater danger than Austria, because he needed Russia to threaten Britain and to keep Austria from attacking while he was in Spain. But he did not want Russia to advance too far towards Constantinople, a prize that must fall, in due course, to French not Russian control. Hence he wanted to avoid specific commitments. This, though, allowed Talleyrand a dangerous amount of room for mischief.

The Prince arrived at Erfurt on 24 September, three days before the Emperor. On 18 September Napoleon and the Tsar met, with Talleyrand present, whom Alexander welcomed as an old friend. The discussion was all generalities. Napoleon was pleased by the way it went. What he did not know was that the same evening the Tsar, doubtless by design, met Talleyrand over tea with the latter's friend the Princess of Thurn und Taxis, who was also staying at Erfurt. This became a regular fixture throughout the negotiations. Each evening, Talleyrand would reveal the Emperor's secret thinking to the Tsar and suggest responses designed to frustrate Napoleon's plans the following day. On occasion, Alexander took notes.

Charles-Maurice was most concerned to stop Russia signing up to any agreement to threaten war against Austria. He was also strongly opposed, for quite different reasons, to the marriage alliance that Napoleon wanted to secure by divorcing Joséphine and marrying the Tsar's sister. He managed to frustrate both objectives of French policy. Thus Napoleon finished by signing alone a formal warning to Austria. The treaty itself left the circumstances in which Russia would move extremely vague. The marriage negotiation was left in abeyance: indeed, shortly after leaving Erfurt, Alexander would have his sister, the Grand-Duchess Catherine, betrothed to a minor German prince. And, on top of all that, Talleyrand also managed to half convince Napoleon that he had every reason to be satisfied.[38]

Talleyrand exerted his flattery to great effect on the Tsar at Erfurt. Given Alexander's anger at the fate of the duc d'Enghien, in which Talleyrand had played such a large part, this was an extraordinary achievement. Caulaincourt – also heavily implicated – had done the preliminary work to remove the Tsar's suspicions.[39] Talleyrand played for very high stakes. His remarks to the Tsar about Napoleon were extraordinarily disloyal, not to say treasonable. Talleyrand reported a little later to Metternich that he had boldly asked Alexander on the first day: 'Sire, what are you here for? It is for you to save Europe, and you will not succeed unless you stand up to Napoleon. The French people is civilized, its sovereign is not. The sovereign of Russia is civilized, and his people is not. So it is for the sovereign of Russia to be the ally of the French people.'[40]

Nor will Talleyrand's quip when Alexander was about to depart have missed its mark. Seeing the two emperors' carriages side by side, Charles-Maurice whispered to the Tsar: 'Ah! If only Your Majesty could take the wrong coach!'[41]

The political effects of such flattery would take time to mature. But Talleyrand's intrigue with Alexander yielded an immediate personal benefit. He secured the Tsar's intervention to facilitate the advantageous marriage of his nephew, Edmond, which has already been mentioned. Dorothea (Dorothée), fourth daughter of the Duke of Kurland (Courlande), was just fifteen when the Tsar descended that October upon the castle of Löbikau to arrange the match. His arguments prevailed; Talleyrand wrote a warm letter of thanks; and the marriage duly took place at Frankfurt the following April.[42]

In later years, after the Restoration, Talleyrand liked to boast about what he had done at Erfurt. On one occasion, Vitrolles and he were standing at the window of the Hôtel Talleyrand, looking down at a brawl between monarchists and Constitutionalists. The conversation turned somehow to Erfurt, and Talleyrand fetched the manuscript of his memoirs and read out that section to his guest. Afterwards, he gave his malicious smile and said: 'You know how everyone has saved France, since it is saved three or four times a year. But note that at Erfurt I saved Europe from complete upheaval.'[43]

The question remains, and very much in the terms he used with Tsar Alexander: what did Talleyrand think he was doing at Erfurt? He was no longer pressing French policy in one direction rather than another. He was seeking to remove an essential guarantee for France against Austria, while Napoleon focused on Spain – a project that he himself, despite his later protestations, had encouraged. He was, therefore, seeking to engineer France's defeat, one that must inevitably bring with it Napoleon's downfall. A remark he made about this time to Mme de Rémusat suggests how far his hostility to the Napoleonic régime had developed. In a moment of anger, provoked by some patriotic banality, he turned on her and exclaimed: 'Tremble at the Emperor's victories over the English! For if the English [sic] Constitution is destroyed, get it into your head that the civilization of the world will be shaken to its very foundations.'[44]

But closer to his heart, and more important to his pocket, than Britain was Austria. Pasquier believed that Talleyrand's penchant towards Vienna, at Erfurt and elsewhere, was explicable by the fact that it provided the largest and most reliable bribes.[45] This is a partial and ultimately insufficient explanation. After all, Talleyrand sought and received bribes from all parties, with little discrimination. For example, the Bavarians were sufficiently impressed by his influence at Erfurt that they now decided to pay him the sum of 200,000 francs, originally agreed when he was Foreign Minister but suspended after his resignation.[46] That said, the link with Austria was particularly close, and its closeness was both facilitated and encouraged by *pourboires*.

It was, in fact, at the Peace of Pressburg in 1805 that Talleyrand began to work directly in Austrian interests. Metternich confirms this – also, incidentally, confirming Napoleon's suspicions about his Foreign Minister's conduct of those negotiations.[47] But contacts had become still more fruitful since Metternich's arrival as Austrian ambassador to Paris in 1806. It was a difficult time, and Metternich regretted the posting. But Talleyrand, at least, was welcoming. Metternich found in him an 'extraordinary intelligence'.[48] This appreciation was useful, because back in Vienna Talleyrand was viewed with great mistrust by unimaginative courtiers, who could not forget his dubious past. In September 1808 Metternich tried to explain to them why Charles-Maurice was to be cultivated:

> One cannot separate in M. de Talleyrand the moral from the political man. He would not have been, he would not be now, what he is, if he were moral. On the other hand, he is eminently political, and, in so far as he is political, a man with political ideas ['*homme à systèmes*']. As such, he can be useful or dangerous; at this moment he is useful. . .Men like M. de Talleyrand are like sharp instruments with which it is dangerous to play; but serious wounds require serious remedies, and the man responsible for treating them should not be afraid of using the instrument that cuts the best.[49]

This despatch was sent after Erfurt, where Talleyrand had been in regular contact with the baron de Vincent, Austria's envoy and already a close collaborator. Prior to that, Talleyrand had also had long interviews with Metternich about the best policy for Austria to follow; and afterwards, he gave him a full account of all that had occurred. Above all, through Talleyrand's conversation Metternich had gained a grasp of the sharpening political divisions within the Napoleonic régime. The Prince had thus begun the process of educating the coalition against France in the realities of French politics, without which no successor régime could be safely installed.

Metternich's despatches thus portray two parties. One party with the Emperor at its head consists of the whole military apparatus. In opposition to it a second party is composed of 'the great mass of the nation, but inert and sluggish like the detritus of an extinct volcano', at the head of which were the civilians with positions and fortunes to maintain, who longed for stability and feared for the future. The principal figures were Talleyrand and Fouché. The strength of this second party had increased as a result of the military setbacks experienced in Spain in 1808. By early December that year, Metternich was reporting on a further significant development: the rapprochement between Fouché and Talleyrand, despite their 'radical antagonism'.

On 16 January 1809 Metternich had another long conversation with Charles-Maurice. Afterwards he noted: '[Talleyrand and Fouché] are in the position of passengers that see the tiller in the hands of a crazed pilot, who is happy to see the ship wrecked on reefs that he has sought out to satisfy his pleasure. They are prepared to seize the helm at a moment when their personal security may be yet more threatened than it is – indeed, at the moment when the first collision knocks over the pilot himself.'[50]

The reconciliation between Fouché and Talleyrand was real and it had been arranged by Hauterive, who had been an Oratorian with the first and, of course, the most important foreign policy collaborator of the second. It took place in Hauterive's country house. Characteristically, it was Charles-Maurice who first offered his hand.[51] It was, though, the public manifestation of this new friendship, as Talleyrand walked arm-in-arm with Fouché around the *salon* in the Hôtel Monaco, that prompted public comment and the alarm of the authorities. The two seemed determined to draw maximum attention, as if to encourage other such demonstrations. Talleyrand declaimed ever more openly against the Emperor's Spanish policy. Fouché wrote incriminating letters to Murat, whom the two plotters had designated to succeed Napoleon in the event of the latter's – possible, or planned? – death in Spain. Lavalette, Director General of the Post, informed Napoleon of what was happening. A letter to Murat was intercepted by Prince Eugène.[52]

Public opposition of this kind had not been seen since 18 Brumaire. That two such wily politicians as Talleyrand and Fouché thought that it would go unpunished is a reminder of how much milder Bonaparte's authoritarianism was than the totalitarianisms of the following century.

Talleyrand had the greater sense of grievance and he had clearer ideas about what changes needed to be made. But it was Fouché who, as Police Minister, wielded more power. Charles-Maurice was, therefore, the more vulnerable when the Emperor returned to Paris from Spain on the morning of Monday, 23 January.[53]

What seems to have driven Napoleon into a frenzy of anger at the various reports he had received was not the danger from plots – which he felt strong enough to discount – but rather the impudence and, in his eyes, the injustice of the criticisms made about his policy towards Spain. This too made Talleyrand, as propagandist-in-chief in the *salons*, the main target of his wrath. Napoleon was unused to having his military campaigns criticized, and more hurtful still was the knowledge that Charles-Maurice's remarks echoed French public opinion.[54]

Talleyrand had some warning of what was to come. On Friday (27 January) he received a letter from Napoleon ordering him to hand over to Duroc his ceremonial key as Grand Chambellan for transmission to his successor, the comte de Montesquiou. The following day he replied with a letter of regret, written in his accustomed style of flowery flattery, that cannot have failed to irritate the Emperor further.[55] On Sunday, after the general audience at the Tuileries, Napoleon held a meeting of his council. Present were Cambacérès, Lebrun, Talleyrand, Ministers Gaudin (finance), Decrès (navy) and Fouché (police).[56] Montesquiou arrived part of the way through on other business. The purpose of the gathering was soon clear.

Napoleon enjoyed making violent scenes, but he also prepared them carefully beforehand.[57] On this occasion, he had decided to humiliate Talleyrand and, in doing so, to frighten Fouché and anyone else tempted to consider opposition.[58] The Emperor's attack was initially launched at both Talleyrand and Fouché. He shouted that he had returned with evidence of a plot they had hatched in order to turn public opinion against him. He declared that those who held great offices of state no longer had the right to express their own thoughts, but rather his. Treason had already begun once they allowed themselves to doubt and was complete when these doubts resulted in dissent. Again addressing both men, he told them that they owed all they had to him. If a revolution against his régime should occur they would be the first to be crushed. (As Mollien observes, this prediction would prove very wide of the mark.)[59]

So far, Napoleon had remained within the limits of a kind of savage decorum. But when he turned on Talleyrand personally he began to lose control. He bawled:

> You are a thief, a coward, a man without faith. You don't believe in God. Throughout your life, you have failed in your duties. You've deceived and betrayed everyone. You hold nothing sacred. You would sell your own father. I have showered you with favours. You can do nothing against me. Yet for ten months, because you wrongly thought that my affairs in Spain were going awry, you've told anyone who would listen that you'd always condemned my undertaking against that kingdom. Yet it is you who kept pushing me into it.
>
> And that man, that poor fellow [the duc d'Enghien] – who told me where he was living? Who encouraged me to act against him?

Then, beside himself with fury, provoked even further by Talleyrand's impassivity, Napoleon raged: 'What are your plans? What do you want? What do you hope for? Dare to say! I should break you like a glass. I could. But I despise you too much.'[60]

The scene lasted for at least half an hour. Some details are unclear. Napoleon did not, in all probability, describe Talleyrand to his face as 'shit in a silk stocking' ('*de la merde dans un bas de soie*'), despite the legend.[61] But what he said and his manner of saying it were shocking enough. If Talleyrand was shocked, however, he did not show it. He remained (as one of those present observed) as 'pale as death', yet also entirely expressionless throughout. But then, as contemporaries remarked, 'no face was ever less of a barometer' than his.[62] He just stood there, leaning on a table to rest his bad foot, waiting for the storm to pass. The Emperor finally marched out and slammed the door. Talleyrand, too, left a little later, without immediate comment. But outside he ran into an acquaintance, the comte de Ségur, who expressed surprise that the session had taken so long. Talleyrand took his hand and said: 'There are some things that one never forgives.'[63] Later still he remarked: 'What a pity that such a great man should be so badly brought up.' Napoleon had intended that Talleyrand's humiliation should be publicly known.[64] But so was Talleyrand's subsequent riposte.[65] And Talleyrand would never forgive, even though Napoleon at least half forgot.

Charles-Maurice had great reserves of self-control, but his nonchalance on this occasion was certainly assumed. He was obviously in immediate danger. So, swallowing his pride, he took action to minimize the risks to his person. True to his own dictum, he mobilized Mme de Rémusat. She, in turn, sought out Hortense de Beauharnais and tearfully protested that Napoleon had blamed Charles-Maurice because of false gossip, begging Hortense to intervene with her brother-in-law on his behalf. A little later who should arrive at her house but Talleyrand. Hortense duly interceded with Napoleon, who laughed loudly at Charles-Maurice's tactics. He assured her that he would do him no harm.[66]

Talleyrand also knew that he must prevent, if at all possible, Napoleon's terrible rebuke from resulting in a total break. So, to general astonishment, he turned up on Monday, the day after the great scene, at the Emperor's regular political reception ('*cercle*') in the Tuileries, arriving early and taking up his usual position by the fireplace. Napoleon entered and went round the room. He spoke to someone on Charles-Maurice's left and then on his right, but not to his former Grand Chambellan. The following Sunday there was another *cercle*. Again, Napoleon made his way around the room. Again, he asked a question of Talleyrand's neighbour, who for some reason hesitated to reply. Charles-Maurice quickly cut in. He and Napoleon exchanged observations on the subject. The ice was broken.[67]

People had initially thought that Talleyrand would be exiled and that Fouché would lose his position as Minister of Police. Neither, in fact, occurred. The Emperor feared Fouché and considered it dangerous to create two deadly enemies of such stature. As for Talleyrand, it was soon clear that Napoleon's treatment of him had incurred public disapproval, particularly among those who, like Charles-Maurice but enjoying much less distinguished positions, had believed that their position in the régime was secure.[68] In any case, once his anger abated, Napoleon started to wonder whether he might not have further use for Talleyrand.

Napoleon's rages always left him with mixed emotions. Part of him regretted his outbursts, even when he had carefully planned them.[69]

Moreover, being a sentimentalist as well as a bully, he never liked to cut off entirely those who had shared his fortunes over the years, however profound his sense of grievance.[70] In Talleyrand's case, a mixture of hurt, anger, outraged pride and perhaps an unacknowledged element of regret contributed towards nurturing what became an obsession with him. Charles-Maurice's misconduct – even, as the years went by, his rare merits – cropped up time and again in Napoleon's tirades. For example, some weeks after the scene, as the Emperor raged to Roederer – this time about Joseph Bonaparte's ingratitude – he posed the question: 'Does [Joseph] wish to do a Talleyrand? I've covered him with riches and diamonds. He's used it all against me. He has betrayed me.'[71]

But the Emperor did not fully understand what he had done that Sunday morning at the Tuileries, because, in the end, he did not understand Talleyrand. Charles-Maurice would surely have his revenge, but at the appropriate time. The scene of 29 January turned Talleyrand from a slippery opponent into a determined enemy. He had always, despite his protestations, despite the estimates Napoleon confidently made of where his interests led him, been a potential traitor. He was prepared for betrayal in the sense that his allegiance to Napoleon, as to any régime, was conditional. That was, indeed, an essential part of his politics, as he explained to Mme de Chastenay: to put himself 'in a position to be able to choose between two parties'.[72] It was why he had kept up indirect contact with the Bourbons, surprising their representatives by his apparent openness.[73] It was also why he allowed some of his closest associates to feed information to Britain and Russia.[74]

From 1805, Talleyrand's opposition had become more consistent, more pronounced and more squarely based on a programme. And as discontent with the Spanish venture grew, so had the programme's breadth. Charles-Maurice articulated it, in distinctive style, during a conversation with Mme de Rémusat on the eve of his disgrace:

> The Emperor will not see that he was summoned by his destiny to be always and everywhere the Man of the Nations, the founder of useful and possible reforms. Restore religion, morality, order to France, extol the civilization of Britain while containing its policy, strengthen the frontiers by the Confederation of the Rhine, make Italy a kingdom

independent both of Austria and of himself, keep the Tsar closed in at home by creating the barrier offered by Poland – those are what should be the timeless objectives of the Emperor, to which each of my treaties led. But ambition, anger, pride and the imbeciles to whom he listens often blind him. He suspects me as soon as I speak to him of *moderation*, and if he stops believing me, you will see one day by what stupid acts of imprudence he compromises himself, him and the rest of us. However, I shall keep watch until the end. I attached myself to the creation of his empire. I would like it to be my last work, and for as long as I see any success for my plan I shall not give up.[75]

The end of this passage, for all its nobility of expression, must have been less than sincere: his behaviour at Erfurt was already treasonable. But after the scene in the Tuileries Talleyrand was determined to destroy Napoleon, and he worked to do so without remission. The most convenient means at hand was Austria.

Talleyrand, therefore, approached Metternich and told him that he had now decided to enter into direct relations with Vienna. But he needed money; in fact, he needed several hundred thousand francs. Vienna was cautious. But, on the back of Metternich's assurances, on 10 February an initial payment of 100,000 francs was duly provided. And Metternich kept up pressure on Talleyrand's behalf for the rest. In exchange, the Prince provided advice on French troop movements, as Napoleon prepared for what was now seen as an inevitable renewal of war. He even provided copies of two memoranda that had been seen by the Emperor. It seems that Caulaincourt was the main source, which demonstrates the French ambassador in St Petersburg's naïve confidence in Charles-Maurice. A special system was established via Frankfurt, at Talleyrand's suggestion, for the communication of information to Vienna once war actually broke out.[76]

Whether the Austrians were really beneficiaries from these exchanges is more doubtful. Talleyrand was never a good judge of military matters. That had been clear as early as Napoleon's expedition to Egypt. It was a factor, too, in Talleyrand's wavering advice about Spain. In now encouraging Austria to act against Napoleon, he did his patrons no good, and there was little, anyway, that he could provide in the way of intelligence useful in the battlefield.

In fact, the Austrians were defeated at a series of battles in April. Napoleon entered Vienna in May. In July, after the victory of Wagram, the Austrians sued for peace. By the treaty then agreed at Schönbrunn, Austria had to yield Carinthia, Carniola and most of Croatia to France, and other territories to Bavaria, the Grand Duchy of Warsaw and Russia. A crushing war indemnity was imposed. Not that the longer term future for France was particularly encouraging. The Grand Empire, which had expanded in part through movements of national liberation, was itself viewed, already in Spain, increasingly in Germany, incipiently in Russia, as the main obstacle to national self-expression. Russia was, of the three, destined to be most important, because its mercurial Tsar now felt ill-rewarded for his friendship. But, that said, Napoleon was, for the moment, again triumphant, his enemies crushed. Not surprisingly, when Metternich returned to Vienna to become Foreign Minister, Charles-Maurice's Austrian subsidy seems to have been discontinued, though the correspondence still flowed – now via Vienna's representative, the chevalier de Floret, and with Talleyrand figuring mysteriously as 'X'.[77]

Fortunately, Charles-Maurice had hopes of other sponsors. Among the Tsar's representatives in Paris was Count Karl von Nesselrode. Nesselrode's first port of call on his arrival in the capital in 1810 was the Hôtel Monaco, where he informed Talleyrand: 'I have arrived from St Petersburg. I am officially connected to Prince Kouryakin, but I am accredited to you. I am in personal contact with the Tsar, and I bring a letter from him.'[78]

Nesselrode did not start with much sympathy for his high-placed informant. Two years earlier, he had privately described Charles-Maurice as 'that infamous Talleyrand, that defrocked monk, as deformed physically as he is morally'.[79] But, as a good diplomat, Nesselrode swallowed his feelings and initiated what both sides hoped would be a fruitful correspondence. It was also secret, concealed successfully not just from Napoleon's spies but from Russia's own embassy. Talleyrand figured in Nesselrode's despatches as, among other things, 'Cousin Henry', 'Dad', or 'the Jurist'.[80] He advised the Russian government about Napoleon's thoughts on Poland, Sweden and Turkey. He even counselled the Russians about financial reform, a subject on which he was, of course, an expert. The worry that now preoccupied both Russia and Austria was what Napoleon would do, once he had successfully subdued Spain. It was a concern that Charles-Maurice encouraged. Above all, reflecting his consistent strategy, he strongly urged upon St Petersburg a rapprochement with Vienna.[81]

Talleyrand's position was, all this time, both complicated and precarious. He was trying as best he could to undermine Napoleon. Yet, at the same time, he needed to dissimulate his feelings, to ignore rebuffs, and to insinuate his presence, because he also had to retain regular access to the Emperor and his plans. This became more difficult and more dangerous after the dismissal of Fouché, Talleyrand's most important source and, indeed, his protector.[82]

Both men were lucky to escape with their freedom, even their lives, as a result of Napoleon's discovery of unauthorized negotiations with Britain in May 1810. Fouché was the originator of the plot. But Napoleon was also deeply suspicious of Talleyrand – and doubtless correctly so, since the intermediary with the British was Talleyrand's long-standing collaborator, the financier Ouvrard. Oddly enough, Napoleon appointed Talleyrand's other friend and collaborator, Hauterive, to conduct an investigation. And, not at all oddly, Hauterive concluded that Talleyrand was entirely innocent. Napoleon expressed disbelief but allowed the matter to drop.[83] Charles-Maurice visited Fouché to offer his condolences. He also expressed his support in the *salons*: 'Undoubtedly, M. Fouché was very wrong. For my part, I would find a replacement for him, but only one – M. Fouché himself.'[84]

At this time, Talleyrand's position was difficult for other reasons: he was in severe financial straits. His income had dropped but his expenditure was undiminished. He sought and probably received money from Russia, but not as much as he hoped. On 15 September 1810 he had the effrontery, or desperation, to write directly to the Tsar explaining his predicament, asking for 1.5 million francs, and suggesting the precise means of getting it to him without arousing suspicion. The request was politely refused.[85] In March 1811 he suggested to Nesselrode that the Russian government should grant him a licence to import prohibited commodities into Russian ports, a privilege that when granted in France was extremely lucrative. But there was no response.[86]

Talleyrand's treachery was sustained and remorseless, occupying all his waking moments. The Countess of Kielmannsegge, a devotee of Napoleon, stayed in the summer of 1811 with her friend the duchesse de Courlande in Saint-Germain at Châteauneuf, a pleasant little château that had once belonged to Henri IV. Here she found Talleyrand, Nesselrode, General Chernyshev (of the Russian embassy), Mme de Laval and her hostess, all carefully preparing letters for despatch to the Tsar. On one occasion, she overheard Charles-Maurice conclude some plan to remove Napoleon by exclaiming: 'And that's how we will get rid of him!' The seraglio applauded.[87] Talleyrand was now, through Nesselrode, advising St Petersburg to adopt a strategy wholly at odds with that of France. Thus he urged an early end to Russian military entanglements in the Ottoman Empire, an offer to Austria of a defensive alliance in exchange for a free hand in Moldavia and Wallachia, and the formation of a Russian Kingdom of Poland opposed to the French Grand Duchy.[88] For such far-sighted counsel he must have seemed worth his subsidy.

In the end, however, Talleyrand's financial position depended on his political standing within France. Here events were on his side. During the last years of the Empire, his fortunes rose and fell according to Napoleon's moods and requirements. Despite his removal as Grand Chambellan, he continued to take a close interest in the question of the Emperor's divorce and remarriage. He had been convinced of the necessity of divorce since the time of the Consulate, although he put on a good show of sympathizing with Joséphine, and he later commiserated with her son, Prince Eugène.[89]

As for the new marriage, he had a strong personal as well as political motive in advocating that it be with an Austrian, rather than a Russian (or, as was also suggested, Saxon) princess. At the meeting of Napoleon's council held to debate the matter, Talleyrand was one of the first to give his opinion on the three possibilities. He probably knew where the Emperor's preference lay, and he was anyway a long-standing advocate of close relations with Austria; but his reasoning is still of interest. He argued that an Austrian marriage would create a lasting union, because of the stability of its court, whereas a Russian marriage could overnight cease to have value when a new Tsar succeeded. He added that an Austrian marriage would, in some sense, make reparation for the fate of Marie-Antoinette.[90] This apparently whimsical point was, in fact, a true reflection of French public opinion.[91] It was also undoubtedly one that would, when relayed to Vienna, touch the hearts of his collaborators there. Talleyrand's view – supported by Mollien, opposed by Lebrun (for Saxony) and Cambacérès, Murat and Fouché (for Russia) – prevailed.[92] He duly attended the magnificent marriage of Napoleon and Marie-Louise of Habsburg on 2 April.

He might, perhaps, have hoped that all this would have prepared the way back to favour. But there intervened the discovery of Fouché's plans, described earlier. Undaunted, Charles-Maurice wrote later that summer asking for a full return to grace – and perhaps for some new role – only to receive from Napoleon a terse refusal that brooked no discussion.[93] This was still more of a blow because it coincided with a financial and economic crisis that struck France and the rest of Europe,[94] and from which Talleyrand, with his numerous investments, could not emerge unscathed. In fact, the collapse of the bank of his friend Michel Simons in Brussels brought him near to ruin. He may have lost some 1.5 million francs – the same sum that he unsuccessfully sought from Tsar Alexander. He could barely pay his staff or the interest he owed on the mortgage incurred on the Hôtel Monaco.[95] This placed him more than ever at Napoleon's mercy.

Napoleon enjoyed inflicting humiliations, particularly on Talleyrand. Alone of the great officers of state, Charles-Maurice was refused all regular personal access to the Emperor, both the *grandes* and *petites entrées*.[96] The most promising opportunities for minor persecution were those that wounded Charles-Maurice's family pride: each was enthusiastically grasped by Napoleon. At the height of his financial difficulties, the Prince had passed to a third party a bill of 300,000 francs, covering the debt that his cousin Auguste de Talleyrand, French ambassador in Switzerland, had incurred for a valuable marriage. Unbeknown to Charles-Maurice, it was presented for payment and a huge family dispute occurred, into which Napoleon was happy to be drawn. He ordered that the Prince withdraw the bill.[97] On another occasion, the Emperor reproached Dorothée, wife of Talleyrand's nephew Edmond, for the (real) extravagance of her husband and made derogatory remarks about the 'Périgords'. She tearfully defended the family, and Napoleon invited her to lunch to make amends. 'It is a sad way to show his power,' commented Talleyrand when told.[98] Most galling of all must have been when Talleyrand was informed of an order exiling his wife to Belgium because, against the Emperor's orders, she had paid a secret visit to her lover, the Duke of San Carlos.[99] Charles-Maurice had to hurry back from Valençay to Paris to have Napoleon retract the order. It was probably on this or a connected occasion that the Emperor vulgarly observed: 'You did not tell me that the Duke of San Carlos was your wife's lover.' Talleyrand replied: 'I had not thought that the tale could relate to Your Majesty's glory or to mine.'[100]

Yet Napoleon was also, during this same period, engaged in delivering Talleyrand from his crippling indebtedness. Between February 1811 and April 1812 he ordered that Charles-Maurice be paid a total of 2,697,000 francs from state funds. Admittedly, 150,000 of this was owed for the cost of accommodating the Spanish princes at Valençay. But the state also purchased the Hôtel Monaco for 2,180,000 francs, its furnishings for 307,000 francs, and Talleyrand's country house at La Muette for 60,000 francs. This generosity is all the more striking the more closely it is examined. Napoleon had been given the opportunity, separately, to demand repayment of a huge bribe paid by Hamburg to Talleyrand that had recently come to light; but, in practice, and after expressing suitable indignation, he renounced it.[101] He allowed Talleyrand to make a substantial profit on the Hôtel Monaco, when the state could have obtained it for a song. As a result, far from simply paying his debts, Talleyrand was able to make new purchases. In March 1812 he bought the splendid Hôtel de l'Infantado, the name reflecting its ownership by the Spanish dukes of that name before the Revolution. It was situated in the rue Saint-Florentin, off the newly constructed rue de Rivoli, close to the Tuileries. Commonly known as the Hôtel Saint-Florentin, but in due course the Hôtel Talleyrand, it would be Charles-Maurice's home for the rest of his life. He also purchased a delightful country house at Saint-Brice, near Écouen, on the slopes of the forest of Montmorency. In each case, he struck an extraordinarily good bargain.[102]

Napoleon's generosity, accompanied by the inevitable pettiness, can be explained not just by his personality, but by his political requirements. He was beginning to feel vulnerable. Talleyrand represented unused talent, and all the talent of former years was once again needed if the Empire was to withstand the approaching crisis. Had Napoleon known how far Talleyrand's contacts with Vienna and St Petersburg had gone, he would not have dared to use him. But he did not know.

Consequently, in March 1812, as the Emperor prepared for a campaign against Russia, he summoned Talleyrand, and engaged him in long conversations far into the night. Napoleon's plan was to use his former Foreign Minister as he had in 1807. Talleyrand was to go to Warsaw, to direct affairs in Poland, and to keep a close eye on developments in Austria and Prussia, while Napoleon dealt with the Russians. It was all agreed. There is no reason to believe that Talleyrand wished to decline the task, given the influence, let alone the rewards, he could expect. What he might actually have transacted in Warsaw is, of course, another matter. But once again Napoleon's lack of self-control aborted his schemes. Perfectly innocently, it seems, Talleyrand opened an account in Vienna for the money he would need in Poland. He also let Mme de Laval into the secret. But it was, in the end, Maret's wife, the duchesse de Bassano, who deliberately caused news of the appointment to leak out. Desperate to prevent Talleyrand pushing aside her husband, she spread word of the mission around Paris. As intended, the gossip got back to Napoleon and renewed all his old suspicions; as a result, he rescinded the decision. He was, indeed, so angry with Talleyrand that he considered sending him into exile. He took in his place the archbishop of Malines, known as the abbé de Pradt.[103]

The Emperor later greatly regretted it. Pradt's high opinion of himself was unmerited, and it was soon shared by no one else. Napoleon blamed him for all his problems. He complained in Moscow that if Talleyrand, not Pradt, had been back in Warsaw, he would now have 6,000 Polish cossacks in support. He wished he had not allowed the intrigues of the duchesse de Bassano to alter his original choice.[104] But there was worse: he had left Talleyrand in Paris, more embittered than ever, with no expectations of the present régime, and time on his hands to plan for a different one.

12

Régime Change

~

BECAUSE OF THE duchesse de Bassano's manoeuvring and his own intemperance, Napoleon left without Talleyrand for the Russian campaign that June. For his part, Charles-Maurice spent the summer at Bourbon-l'Archambault and later at Saint-Brice, in the company of his brother Boson and the latter's family. The Prince followed on his maps, as best he could, the French army's movements. On 4 October, he briefly returned to Paris for the Te Deum staged to celebrate Napoleon's victory on the Moskva. The following month, bad weather forced him back to the capital for the winter.[1]

He now began, as usual, to entertain, and also to plot. In that he was far from alone. No one knew for certain what was happening in Russia, but increasing numbers feared the worst, and not a few began to hope it. All pretence of normality had been shattered by the attempted coup by General Malet. Though quickly reversed, it demonstrated the degree to which leading figures had already lost confidence in Napoleon's success, and thus exposed the fragility of the régime.[2] Many years later, Talleyrand still thought that it might have succeeded.[3] Fortunately, he had been out of Paris at the time, and so could not be implicated. But he began, increasingly openly, to sound out opinion.

One of his friends, Aimée de Coigny, played an important role in this. She was now the lover of the marquis de Boisgelin, a leading Bourbon agent, and her sympathies and connections were well known to Talleyrand. He wanted to set down a marker and initiated a discussion by declaring abruptly: 'He must be destroyed, by whatever means.' (There was no need to ask who.)

'That is certainly my opinion,' she replied.

'That man,' he continued, 'is worth nothing for the kind of benefit that he once could bring. . .He has destroyed equality, and that is good. But liberty must remain. We need laws. With him, it is impossible.'[4]

On the morning of 19 December the Prince was woken by a note from Dorothée telling him that Napoleon had returned to the Tuileries the previous day, leaving his shattered army behind in Russia.[5] A new horizon of opportunity suddenly opened before the Emperor's enemies at home.

On Boisgelin's suggestion, Mme de Coigny again approached Talleyrand. But Charles-Maurice was not ready to contemplate a Bourbon on the throne. He insisted, rather, on a regency for Napoleon's son, the King of Rome. The regent would evidently be the boy's mother, the Austrian Marie-Louise. The unspoken but obvious implication was that Talleyrand's influence in such circum-stances would be immense. Aimée, though, hotly disputed the notion of a regency. Charles-Maurice obfuscated. Eventually, he suggested as an alternative that the duc d'Orléans, accompanied by some 'patriotic ideas' and a 'national throne', could be the best answer. She, however, denounced d'Orléans as a 'usurper': why not, instead, support the brother of Louis XVI?

There, for the moment, the conversation ended. A few days later, though, it recommenced, initiated this time by Charles-Maurice, and not without a touch of theatre. He invited her into his picture gallery, checked to see no one was near, closed the door, and began: 'Mme de Coigny, I do want the King, but. . .'

She ran forward and hugged him, and he laughed.

He then explained: 'Yes: I do want him. But they must tell you how I stand with that family [the Bourbons]. I could get along with M. le comte d'Artois, because there is something between us that makes him understand my conduct. But his brother does not know me at all. I do not want, I admit, in place of being thanked, to rely on a pardon or have to justify myself. I cannot get through to him and. . .'

The point of the conversation had now been reached: he needed a go-between. Aimée de Coigny promised to help. She and Boisgelin duly prepared a letter to Louis, stressing Talleyrand's vital role if any Restoration was to be effected. She showed him a copy and he expressed the greatest satisfaction: 'That's it! Marvellous! Perfect! It is explained marvellously!' Then, having destroyed the incriminating paper, he assured her: 'Well! I am entirely in favour of this business. Consider me part of it. Let M. de Boisgelin send the letter, and let us work to deliver the country from this madman.' He informed her that he himself was in regular contact with Caulaincourt by coded correspondence. He would thus be alerted to all the Emperor's decisions. He was also in touch with a party in the Senate that could have a crucial role in dethroning Napoleon.[6]

Although this account accurately reveals Talleyrand's moods and worries, the suggestion that he had irrevocably decided for a return of the Bourbons is misleading. His aim, at this stage, was still to restore, as far and as fast as he could, his contacts with the Bourbon court at Hartwell in England. To this end, he had also written to his uncle, Alexandre-Angélique, now Grand aumônier to the court in exile, for the same purpose. When the former archbishop of Reims reported his nephew's expression of devotion to Louis, the latter replied that this was a good omen, since Charles-Maurice had written in similar terms to Napoleon when the Directory was about to fall.[7] Talleyrand was also, one can assume, in close touch with other Bourbon agents in Paris, such as the abbé de Montesquiou. In December 1813 he even received a commission from Louis's favourite, the comte de Blacas, empowering him to act in the King's name, though he never used it.[8]

All the while, Talleyrand's relations with Napoleon were dangerously tense. In January 1813 his correspondence was intercepted and deemed to offer proof of treason. So when the Prince next presented himself at the Emperor's *lever*, he was met with a torrent of abuse and renewed threats. He protested his loyalty. But Napoleon later decided on his arrest. Fortunately, Cambacérès and Savary intervened, claiming that the evidence was insufficient, which was clearly true. Talleyrand then demanded the right to explain himself personally to Napoleon. The interview was successful: the order was rescinded.[9]

The Emperor could not, in any case, concentrate for long on Talleyrand. Campaigning in Germany demanded his absence from Paris. Early successes there were followed by the crucial defeat at Leipzig, on 16–19 October. French Germany was now definitively lost and France itself was threatened on both flanks. It was probably at about this time that Charles-Maurice uttered his famous remark: 'It is the beginning of the end.'[10]

On Napoleon's return from Mainz on 9 November, there was another scene with Talleyrand, again at the *lever*. 'You think that if I were out of the way you would be head of a Council of Regency?. . .I promise you, if I were dangerously ill, you would be dead before me.'

The Prince replied sweetly: 'Sire, I had no need of such a warning in order to address heaven with the most ardent wishes for the conservation of Your Majesty's life.'[11]

Yet, despite his tantrums, the Emperor sensed that he needed Talleyrand's presence, and his increasingly panicky ministers felt that too – hence their several interventions to protect the Prince. After Napoleon's return from Moscow, when he first offered Talleyrand the Ministry of Foreign Affairs, Charles-Maurice had simply replied: 'I know nothing of your affairs.'

'You know them!' replied Napoleon angrily. 'But you want to betray me.'

'No,' said Talleyrand, 'but I do not wish to become involved in them because I think they are in contradiction with the glory and happiness of France.'[12]

With the situation now graver, and Napoleon more desperate, Talleyrand deemed it prudent to appear more open to persuasion. He will certainly have taken due note of the Emperor's warning: 'The man who refuses me his service today is necessarily my enemy.'[13] So he prevaricated. And Napoleon still raged. On one occasion, Talleyrand only escaped arrest because Maret, who was to effect the order, was absent.[14]

Napoleon also tried a less formal approach to picking his former Foreign Minister's brains, asking him directly what needed to be done. Talleyrand exclaimed: 'You are consulting me on this matter as if we'd never quarrelled!' Napoleon replied that it was all a matter of circumstances, and circumstances change. They should put the past behind them. What he wanted was Talleyrand's opinion now. He even seems to have listened, for he accepted the advice to cut his losses and send the Bourbon princes back to Spain – which, of course, from Talleyrand's viewpoint had the added advantage that he would get back the use of Valençay.[15] Other advice he offered cannot, though, have been meant seriously, such as the suggestion that Napoleon try to bribe the Duke of Wellington in order to obtain more favourable terms.[16] Such counsel was, in truth, a subtle form of insolence.

Talleyrand in his official dress of imperial Grand Chambellan, painting by Pierre-Paul Prud'hon (1807). His (right) club foot is, as usual, concealed by the artist. The Prince leans against a bust of Napoleon

Madame Grand, the future princesse de Bénévent, painting by Élisabeth Vigée-Lebrun (1783). Catherine, still a great beauty, would marry Talleyrand some twenty years later. Her charms decreased, her girth grew, and her (probably exaggerated) stupidity embarrassed her husband

Boney and Tally (Bonaparte and Talleyrand), cartoon by James Gillray (1803). Charles-Maurice, already internationally known as an advocate of peace, struggles to prevent the First Consul taking his axe to the British bull, while the Russian bear looks on

Le Sacre (Napoleon's coronation), detail, painting by David (1804). Talleyrand, dressed as Grand Chambellan, does not seem to take the proceedings too seriously

Joseph Fouché, duc d'Otrante. This lithograph captures something of the cold cunning of Napoleon's Minister of Police, Talleyrand's sometime collaborator but also rival and enemy

Tsar Alexander I of Russia, painting by François Gérard (1814). Talleyrand's good personal relations with the Tsar were of use to him under Napoleon, but their clashes at the Congress of Vienna turned Alexander into a dangerous opponent

Above: Louis XVIII, painting by Antoine-Jean Gros (*c*.1814). Louis appears in his coronation robes, though he was never solemnly crowned, and standing, though he was so fat and afflicted by gout that he was rarely on his feet. He owed his throne, in part at least, to Talleyrand, but it never induced any obvious gratitude

Left: L'Homme aux six têtes (The Man with Six Heads), anonymous cartoon (1815). Talleyrand is shown holding a bishop's crozier in one hand and a weather-vane in the other and proclaiming his loyalty to the different régimes he supported and then, really or supposedly, betrayed

Le Congrès de Vienne (The Congress of Vienna), lithograph after the painting by Jean-Baptiste Isabey (1819). It was at Talleyrand's suggestion that Isabey came to the Congress and recorded its proceedings in this famous scene. The Prince, seated on the right, stares out towards the artist with an air of cool authority

Dorothée, duchesse de Dino, engraving by Jean-Baptiste Isabey after the painting by François Gérard (1824), from the collection of André Beau. Dorothée had long since displaced the princesse de Talleyrand as Charles-Maurice's consort. Not just political hostess but political adviser, she would also play a key role in his final reconciliation with the Church

Talleyrand, lithograph by François-Séraphin Delpech from a drawing by Zèphirin Belliard (1824). The Prince's character at the age of seventy, during his years in opposition, is caught with striking accuracy – calm, sardonic, wily, deep

The Lame Leading the Blind (Talleyrand and Palmerston), cartoon by John Doyle (1832). The impression conveyed, namely that Talleyrand, as French ambassador in London, was directing British foreign policy during the Belgian crisis, was profoundly irritating to Palmerston. It was also false, despite the Prince's stylish diplomacy

Talleyrand, painting by Ary Scheffer (1828). The Prince, at seventy-four, is portrayed in realistic fashion as old, tired and sombre, but alert and dignified. He had given up all expectation of a return to office or even influence. Two years later, the July Revolution dramatically revived his career

Talleyrand, lithograph by 'Alfred Croquis', i.e. Daniel Maclise (c.1833).
The elderly ambassador sleeps by the fire after a hard day's diplomacy: arrayed
along the chimney piece are busts of the sovereigns he has served

Left: Château of Valençay: a view of the keep (*donjon*). This central pavilion, like the rest of the château, was already designed in the sixteenth century not for defence but for aesthetic effect. Talleyrand's guests would enter the main courtyard (*cour d'honneur*) through this archway

Below: Château of Valençay: a view, up from the Nahon Valley and the road to Châteauroux, of the two right-angled wings of the château. The main residential wing is on the left, with at each end its distinctively domed 'Moorish' towers, of which the Prince was particularly proud

It delighted the Prince to be called to give advice and, even more, to be asked to return as Foreign Minister, not least because it implied that his arch-enemy Maret had been deemed inadequate. The rudeness with which Charles-Maurice had assailed the duc de Bassano's reputation, since the latter took over the post of Foreign Minister from the duc de Cadore (Champagny) in 1811, was notable even by Talleyrand's standards.

On one occasion he observed: 'I know only one person in the world stupider than M. Maret.'

'Oh? And who is that, Monseigneur?'

'His Excellency, the duc de Bassano.'

When it was stated, at a council summoned by the Empress, that Napoleon had lost all his baggage and equipment in Russia, and someone then announced the arrival of Bassano, the Prince remarked: 'You see how people exaggerate. Did not they say that all the *matériel* was lost? But here is Maret who has returned!'[17]

Exposing Maret's shortcomings was, however, more attractive than trying to rectify them as Foreign Minister. Caulaincourt recalls how on three separate occasions, in the course of October and November 1813, Napoleon asked Talleyrand to take on the thankless task, before Caulaincourt, with the greatest reluctance, accepted it himself. In this fencing between the two enemies it is difficult to know what either party's intentions truly were. Thus when Napoleon asked Talleyrand to become Foreign Minister, he on one occasion also insisted that the Prince renounce his position of Vice-Grand Elector, and on another, still more absurdly, required that he never bring the princesse de Talleyrand into his presence. Such conditions, naturally, provided Charles-Maurice with excellent excuses to refuse, and further motives for hatred – if more were needed.[18]

The Emperor's attitude towards Talleyrand in the final period of their acquaintanceship – they would never see each other again after the Council of War held on 25 January – ultimately lacks any logic. Napoleon distrusted Charles-Maurice, resented his refusal to serve, understood the harm which such a man could do to his interests. He erupted with fury at the sight of the Prince chatting unconcernedly with Joseph Bonaparte in the margins of the meeting.[19] Yet even in exile on St Helena, he could not bring himself to believe that Talleyrand had been engaged in treason before the last weeks of his reign.[20] His contempt for Talleyrand's character led him to underrate both his enmity and his capacity. Thus he appointed the Prince a member of the Council of Regency, set up to advise the Empress in his absence. Yet, on 8 February, Napoleon wrote from Nogent to his brother Joseph about him: 'I repeat, beware of this man. I have dealt with him for sixteen years. I even favoured him. He is certainly the greatest enemy of our house, since Fortune has recently abandoned us.'[21]

For once, he was at least half right. In private, Talleyrand's personal hatred for Napoleon shocked even his closest friends. When Mme de La Tour du Pin visited him and began to bewail the Emperor's plight, her host suddenly turned on her: 'Oh! Don't bother me with your Emperor. The man is finished.'

'How "finished"? What do you mean?'

'I mean,' he replied, 'that he is a man who will hide under his bed.'

Charles-Maurice then handed her an article from the British press which described a dinner given by the Prince Regent for the duchesse d'Angoulême, Louis XVI's daughter. The clear implication was that her uncle, Louis XVIII, would be installed on the throne by Napoleon's enemies. Putting the paper back in his pocket, and smiling maliciously, he added: 'Oh! How silly you are! Now leave, and don't catch cold.'[22]

With the Emperor finally out of Paris, Talleyrand felt freer to make his plans. Savary's surveillance of the Prince now descended into something like farce. The Police Minister on one occasion burst into a suspect discussion between Talleyrand, Pradt and their friends, only to be amiably chastised as an eavesdropper.[23] To keep up the charade, Charles-Maurice provided titbits of information to Savary, which both must have known were entirely valueless.[24]

No one, with the intermittent exception of the Emperor himself, seriously doubted Talleyrand's disloyalty to the existing régime. It was where his loyalties actually did lie that excited speculation. And, despite the hopes he now had that the difficulties of a Bourbon Restoration might be overcome, it is probable that even at this point he would have favoured a regency for the King of Rome. So, in quali-fying him to Joseph Bonaparte as an enemy of 'his house', Napoleon may have maligned him.

During February, Caulaincourt negotiated at Châtillon, and Napoleon stubbornly undermined him after each fleeting military success. Talleyrand was not surprised. He had never believed that Napoleon would keep his word, and he hoped the allies would impose the most rigorous terms.[25] Finally, on 22 February, Lord Castlereagh, the British Foreign Secretary, left Châtillon.[26] The allies were henceforth no longer willing to negotiate, even in appearance, on the basis of France's natural frontiers. And Napoleon, for his part, could settle for nothing less. The negotiations at Châtillon were finally ended on 19 March.

Through his relations with Lavalette at the Post on the one hand, and his coded communications with Caulaincourt on the the other, Talleyrand was aware of all that was happening from the French side.[27] But he was frustrated by his inability to penetrate, let alone influence, the thinking of the allies. Would they support, or impose, a Bourbon Restoration? No formal statement had been made, and, in any case, the opinions of the allied leaders differed. Castlereagh and the British government – still more the Prince Regent – wanted Louis XVIII. The mercurial Tsar, whose liberalism in western Europe was as pronounced as his authoritarianism in Russia, had no time for the Bourbons. But what he actually wanted was unclear. Austria, in particular Metternich, was more sympathetic to a regency for the King of Rome, for much the same reasons as Talleyrand – a desire to maximize the influence of Vienna and limit that of St Petersburg. It would take time and events – and Talleyrand's own influence – to iron out these contradictions. But what at this juncture seemed least explicable, and most hazardous, from Charles-Maurice's viewpoint, were the allies' continued negotiations with Napoleon and their slow pace of advance. He urgently needed the enemy to know how easy it would be to move on Paris. Fortunately, the baron de Vitrolles, a reactionary royalist friend of Charles-Maurice's crony Dalberg, appeared at exactly the right moment to undertake the required mission.

Vitrolles and Dalberg, though their philosophical and religious convictions differed sharply, were both partisans of a Bourbon Restoration. Since the previous October, Dalberg had been trying to persuade Talleyrand to share their point of view, though with limited success. Vitrolles's main purpose was to join the comte d'Artois at Vesoul. But he also carried secret accreditation to the allies, namely

Dalberg's seal, known to the Austrian representative Prince Stadion, and a note on which were written in invisible ink the names of two of Stadion's lovers. There were also two other notes in invisible ink, one for Nesselrode and the other for delivery later to the comte d'Artois. That to Nesselrode read, cryptically but to the point: 'The person that I send you is to be trusted completely. Listen to him and recognize me. It is time to be clearer. You are walking on stilts. Use your legs. Decide to do what you can.'[28]

Vitrolles had also hoped for a personal note from Talleyrand, whose name could most easily sway the allies. But he was unlucky. As Dalberg explained: 'You don't know this monkey; he wouldn't risk burning the tip of his paw, even though all the chestnuts were for him.'

Adopting the name of 'M. de Saint-Vincent', Vitrolles set off on 6 March for Châtillon, the allied headquarters. He first met Stadion, who recognized Dalberg's writing, and was then introduced to Nesselrode, Metternich, Castlereagh and Hardenberg (of Prussia).[29] Vitrolles argued vigorously for breaking off the negotiations. But when he also urged a declaration in favour of the Bourbons, Metternich, who was still hostile to a Restoration, stalled. 'Who could organize such a transfer?' he asked. After alluding to those around the comte d'Artois, which cannot have inspired much confidence, Vitrolles reluctantly mentioned Talleyrand: 'You must consider him completely committed to [the Bourbon] cause, at least in his heart.' Everyone laughed at the phrase, 'in his heart'. But they were impressed. They also asked what Fouché would do, which Vitrolles found still more distasteful. It was an early indication of the way things would go once the allied forces eventually controlled Paris.[30]

Vitrolles's visit had a real if not, in itself, decisive effect. By informing the allies that Talleyrand and his friends were at the head of a faction ready to welcome them he had reduced their willingness to make concessions to Napoleon. The news he brought also made it harder for Metternich to argue for a Bonaparte regency as the only means of winning over French opinion. More important, though, was the royalist coup on 12 March at Bordeaux which resulted in the entry of the duc d'Angoulême into the city amid wild acclamation.[31] The allies were interested in political facts, not sentiment or doctrine. This, at last, was a fact. It even convinced Metternich, when he finally heard of it a fortnight later, that a Bourbon Restoration was probably inevitable.[32] That left only the Tsar to be persuaded.

Meanwhile, the agony of the French Empire continued. On 23 March Napoleon tried to force his enemies to retreat by wheeling his remaining forces round to attack their communications. But this last throw failed, and catastrophically so. Through Tsar Alexander's resolution, the decision was made, on the 25th, to continue to advance on Paris, now just a hundred miles away.[33] Within three days, the road to the capital was open. Charles-Maurice was, of course, informed by his spies of what was afoot. But what remained of the Emperor's court was still in blissful ignorance. On the evening of 27 March, Talleyrand was playing whist with the Empress, Queen Hortense, Molé and others. No allusion was made to the impending disaster. The following morning, the allies were on the banks of the Marne, within reach of Paris.[34]

An urgent meeting of the Council of Regency was summoned by Joseph Bonaparte to decide whether the court should stay or abandon the capital. Talleyrand, Cambacérès, Lebrun, Molé and other ministers and military men were present. According to Pasquier, Talleyrand remained silent, merely nodding.[35] But Savary, who was actually there, affirms that Talleyrand spoke with the majority, urging Marie-Louise to remain.[36] Finally, however, Joseph produced a letter dated 6 March from Napoleon instructing him to ensure that under no circumstances must the Empress and the King of Rome fall into enemy hands. The decision was thus already taken. The council broke up and the court made preparations to depart.

Whether he spoke or not, it is clear that Talleyrand had indicated that in his opinion the Empress should remain. His motives cannot now be divined with certainty. The position he adopted was certainly useful later, when it came to defending himself to Caulaincourt after Paris was lost.[37] He could thus afford to blame Napoleon's decision for the collapse. And it fitted in nicely, too, with the assertion in his memoirs that Napoleon 'never had a dangerous conspirator against him apart from himself'.[38] Yet he had earlier warned Pasquier about urging such a course, because it would harm the Bourbons' interests, and done so with such emphasis that Mme de Rémusat had run off to warn her cousin of the Prince's words.[39] The most likely explanation of Talleyrand's stance is that he would, even at this late stage, have preferred the King of Rome and his mother to remain, so as to leave open the possibility of a regency. Such a regency might or might not endure. It must, though, be one in which the former Emperor was absent, and preferably dead. (He had expressed that thought in a letter to the duchesse de Courlande a few days earlier.)[40] Otherwise, as he would later explain, Napoleon would always have been 'listening at the door'.[41] In truth, he had played the game as he always did, ensuring that he was well placed to exploit whatever events would bring.

With the imperial court's departure, the course that Talleyrand had to pursue was simpler. He had to make contact with the allies and make himself indispensable to whomever would finish up ruling France. In the meantime, he must survive the final days of the dying régime. Playing for time, he sent word to the Empress, who wanted to know when he would be ready to leave, that since the roads were so difficult he would need to travel separately.[42] Then he began to make alternative plans.

His intention was to stay in Paris, so that he could act as the main negotiator with the allies. But he also wanted to guard against committing too overt an act of treason, for which some hot-head might make him pay the consequences. Fortunately, the Emperor had only belatedly realized that his ploy had failed: he would be just too late to prevent his enemies entering the capital. There, authority was in the hands of Savary and Pasquier. Both were already anxious about their own preservation, and both had been the objects of Talleyrand's subversive conversation – particularly Pasquier, who, through his presence at the Rémusat *salon*, had heard the Prince eloquently explaining why Napoleon was doomed.[43] So when Mme de Rémusat now turned up at Pasquier's office with Charles-Maurice in tow, it cannot have been a great surprise. She explained how important it was for the security of Paris and its inhabitants that Talleyrand be present to deal with the allied forces. But he needed an excuse to remain. Could Pasquier not arrange a small riot at one of the *barrières* to prevent the Prince's departure? He tactfully explained that as Préfet de police his job was to stop riots not start them. But since her husband, M. de Rémusat, was himself commanding a unit of national guards at one of the city gates, could not the Rémusats arrange it between them?

Pasquier's advice was followed. Moreover, his complicity had given the manoeuvre official blessing. When Talleyrand's carriage turned up at the Barrière des Bonshommes, near Passy, he was duly stopped by Rémusat and asked politely to return home, because of the dangers of travel. This the Prince quickly did, being careful to avoid the Faubourg Saint-Honoré, whose proletarian population were rumoured to want to throw him in the river, and arrived back safely at his house in the rue Saint-Florentin, where his friends and co-plotters were already assembled.[44] Later that night, Talleyrand went to see General Marmont, commanding the troops in charge of the defence of Paris. Although the content of their conversation is unknown, it certainly helped undermine Marmont's already wavering loyalty to the Emperor, who that same night had reached Fontainebleau. At three o'clock the following morning, the instrument for the capitulation of Paris was signed and French troops left the city.

The Prince was now free to make his move with the allies. In practice, this meant with Tsar Alexander, and that was to Talleyrand's advantage. Both Metternich and Castlereagh were still back in Dijon. Had they been present, the Prince's early manoeuvring would have been less swift, and probably less successful. The Tsar sent Nesselrode from Bondy, where representatives of Paris had arrived to offer the city's submission, on a personal mission to Talleyrand. Nesselrode entered the Hôtel Saint-Florentin when the Prince was (as usual) engaged in dressing. Charles-Maurice embraced him, uttering exclamations of joy and covering him with powder. Then Talleyrand summoned Dalberg, Pradt and Baron Louis into the room. Nesselrode told them that the Tsar was already on his way into the city. The only decision yet made was that Napoleon must not remain Emperor. Otherwise, the Tsar would take advice on what to do.[45]

The allied forces entered Paris at eleven o'clock that morning, to mighty cheers. At the head of the dignitaries was the Tsar, with King Frederick-William of Prussia beside him. The parade lasted all day.[46] But at one point a message was passed to the Russians to say that the Élysée Palace, where Alexander was proposing to stay the night, had been mined. (This turned out to be false.) As a result, the Tsar accepted Talleyrand's invitation to stay at his house. This was so politically advantageous to his host that perhaps the note had its origin with Charles-Maurice himself.

In fact, within an hour of Nesselrode, Alexander himself arrived at the Hôtel Saint-Florentin, accompanied by the King of Prussia and the Austrian commander-in-chief, Prince Schwarzenberg. Talleyrand invited them, along with Prince von Liechtenstein, Nesselrode and Pozzo di Borgo – another adviser to the Tsar, who as a Corsican had the merit of viscerally disliking the Bonapartes – into an impromptu council in his *salon*. He then introduced Dalberg, Pradt and Louis. Dalberg, under Talleyrand's supervision, had already been working on a draft declaration, intended to cut the ground, once and for all, from under Napoleon. But before that matter was addressed it was neces-sary to divert the Tsar away from his lingering sympathy for Napoleon and his family – or, indeed, for the house of Orléans, or for Bernadotte, whose claims he also occasionally favoured – and rein-force the case for the Bourbons. Talleyrand allowed Louis to make the case, which he did with some force, supported by Pradt. The Prince, finally and successfully, took up the argument himself. Dalberg and Nesselrode were then sent into another room to draft (or, in fact, copy) the text already prepared. This, with the Tsar's agreement, now contained the vital phrase that the allies would not negotiate any longer with Napoleon, 'nor with any member of his family'.[47] As soon as Alexander appended his signature, Roux de Laborie rushed out of the room with the text and took it off to the printers. Within the hour, copies were appearing on walls around Paris.[48]

The next step was to give institutional legitimacy to a Bourbon restoration. Of course, to the royalists such attempts had no value what-ever; indeed, they were somewhat offensive. For them, history had been suspended at the Revolution and it was essential to proceed as if the awkward Revolutionary and Napoleonic interludes had simply not occurred – except in the matter of punishment. But for Talleyrand and his friends institutional legitimization was vital as a guarantee of their interests; and for the allied powers it was equally so, as a guarantee of stability for France and of peace for Europe.

In these circumstances, Talleyrand knew exactly how to proceed. When the Tsar asked him, in the course of their discussions, how the powers could know that France would accept the Bourbons, the

Prince replied that the means must be through the deliberation of the Senate. The Tsar was still doubtful. But Talleyrand insisted. He could be so confident because he had long cultivated contacts in that body, and because he could rely upon the fact that troublesome Bonapartists would be afraid to attend. So, blatantly ignoring all constitutional propriety, Talleyrand duly summoned the Senate to meet on 2 April.[49]

The discussion at the Hôtel Saint-Florentin thus ended very satisfactorily. But Talleyrand knew how changeable the Tsar could be. And he knew too that, despite the presence of Schwarzenberg, he could not completely rely on the Austrians endorsing his brutal abandonment of a regency for the King of Rome if Alexander were permitted second thoughts. Consequently, he had not been at all pleased to see his long-time collaborator, and now Napoleonic plenipotentiary, Caulaincourt arrive, demanding to see the Tsar. Talleyrand initially stalled, blamed Bonaparte for France's woes, excused his own conduct, and managed to avoid what might have been an awkward encounter. When Caulaincourt returned at ten o'clock that evening to see Alexander, he found that the latter, having just put his signature to the declaration, was adamant. The moment had been lost. Napoleon's offer to abdicate in favour of his son was now unacceptable. Indeed, Caulaincourt himself was only received on sufferance; Talleyrand, he later learned, had urged that he be expelled from Paris.[50]

The Tsar and the King of Prussia enjoyed the cuisine of Carême over dinner and then went off to the opera. Talleyrand, who joined the party, had tactfully had the production changed at the last moment. The proposed *Victory of Trajan* had struck him as provocative. But he need not have worried. The conquering monarchs, as they took their seats, were cheered loudly.[51]

In order to increase the mutual understanding between the Senate and the Tsar, on which the fulfilment of his plans depended, Talleyrand organized a reception. The Senators accepting the invitation were fewer than the Prince had hoped: many were still, understandably, uneasy about committing themselves while Napoleon was nearby. Nothing daunted, the Prince reinforced their numbers by hiring actors, dressed in Senatorial uniform, in order to impress the Tsar. He also cleverly pressed Alexander and the Senate further down his chosen route by having the former propose a toast to Louis

XVIII, which – if only through politeness – the Senators felt bound to applaud.[52]

The need for him to seize the initiative during this period was all the greater because Talleyrand and his friends were not alone in claiming the right to act. Committed royalists, such as the members of the shadowy but powerful organization the Chevaliers de la Foi ('Knights of the Faith'), had been arriving in Paris in advance of the Bourbons. Such people wanted a clean break with the Revolutionary past and all the people associated with it, including Talleyrand. They were determined to take the intiative, and indeed they were wise to try to seize it, as events would show. But the Prince outwitted them. When the royalist comte de Semallé arrived at the Hôtel Saint-Florentin and presented a letter from the comte d'Artois, Talleyrand cried out with what passed for joy at the sight of Monsieur's writing. But he proceeded to warn his guest that the Bourbon Restoration was not yet secure. It was too dangerous to take risks. He would contact him, but now he must leave. It was the last that Semallé ever heard.[53]

Somewhat less than half of the Senators arrived to hear Talleyrand on the afternoon of 2 April, acting as President of that body, deliver a short explanatory speech. The Senate then endorsed a five-man provisional government consisting of Talleyrand (acting President of the Council), the comte de Beurnonville (from the military), Jaucourt, Dalberg and the abbé de Montesquiou. The latter was the only member not personally committed to the Prince. Dupont de Nemours, a former collaborator of Mirabeau and Talleyrand, was appointed secretary general, but all the administrative work was done by Roux de Laborie as his assistant secretary. Roux was a practised intriguer, well qualified for the purpose at hand. He flitted around Paris from *salon* to *salon*, delivering and receiving snippets of information, adopting a kind of code for his communications, not always easy for even the initiated to grasp.[54]

Roux was also Talleyrand's right-hand man at the Hôtel Saint-Florentin, where the provisional government met on the mezzanine floor. There were just six rooms: three overlooking the Tuileries (these had been Talleyrand's sleeping quarters), and three facing the courtyard. The latter served as outer offices and were presided over by Roux, who strove to bring some order to the crowds of plotters and petitioners who crammed into them. The rooms facing the Tuileries consisted of, at one end, the Prince's bedroom, now commandeered by the provisional government for its deliberations; then a room occupied by secretaries and functionaries, and frequently invaded by others from the adjoining anterooms; and, finally, a library to which Talleyrand retired to snatch private conversations with special visitors.[55]

On 3 April a full array of ministers was appointed. Baron Henrion de Pansey, the distinguished jurist, took Justice. La Forest (acting for Talleyrand, as in the past) had Foreign Affairs, and Beugnot the Interior. General Dupont (disgraced and imprisoned by Napoleon after the defeat at Beylén, and thus now politically reliable) was at the War Ministry, and Malouet (an elderly admiral) at the Navy Department. Baron Louis was appointed to Finance (where his formidable skills all lay). Comte Anglès (after Pasquier refused) took Police. Finally, the wily Bourrienne, former friend and now sworn enemy of Napoleon, was put in charge of the postal service, that source of invaluable intercepted information.[56]

The provisional government now faced three tasks, each of which was full of risk. First, and most pressing, it was necessary to remove the potential threat posed by Napoleon, still holed up at Fontainebleau. Second, the best possible settlement had to be reached with the victorious allies, who in practice could do much as they pleased. Third, political and institutional provision had to be made for the Restoration of the Bourbons to the French throne and for the return of Louis XVIII to Paris. The weight of each of these undertakings fell principally on Talleyrand's own shoulders. If he failed, so would the provisional government, and so, despite the suspicions he aroused among die-hard royalists, might the Restoration itself.

The first act of the provisional government was a declaration addressed to the French army, urging the soldiers to abandon the man who had left France 'without arms, without defence, its name rendered odious in the eyes of every nation' – a man who was 'not even French'. Charles-Maurice's venom is unmistakable in that phrase.

Talleyrand had, meanwhile, concentrated his efforts on persuading Marmont to withdraw his troops stationed at Essonnes, from where they could still have attacked Paris, to Normandy. In circumstances that remain obscure, the plan worked, and even better than expected.

Marmont arrived at the Hôtel Saint-Florentin, where Talleyrand immediately sat him down at a small table and provided him with dinner. Meanwhile, his army, under the command of his chief-of-staff General Souham, marched to Versailles. Marmont, well fed, tacitly subscribed to the new order of things and waited for his reward. At Fontainebleau, Napoleon still retained the remains of the New and the Old Guard; he could perhaps have yet withdrawn and regrouped. But, impulsive and imprudent to the end, he prepared to attack Paris. His marshals were unwilling to accept this and decided that it was time to impose their own terms. They forced the Emperor's abdication, undertaking in exchange to demand the succession of the King of Rome and a regency. This initiative, too, now had to be blocked by the provisional government.

The Tsar gave several hearings to Napoleon's representatives: Caulaincourt, Ney and Macdonald, who were later joined by a shame-faced Marmont. Alexander was sympathetic to their arguments. But Talleyrand fought a remorseless, and ultimately successful, struggle to prevent such back-sliding. Indeed, the Prince was, at every stage, as Caulaincourt bitterly complained, the principal obstacle to any concessions. He also resisted every proposed provision to make Napoleon's and his family's lives easier in exile. All that the Tsar managed to achieve – and this to Talleyrand's great dismay – was to give Napoleon the island of Elba to rule as a toy-town empire. The Prince thought that this was too near France or indeed Naples, where the unreliable Murat was in control; and, of course, he was right. He, better than anyone, knew what Bonaparte was like.[57]

It is within the context of what to do with Napoleon that the shady, scandalous affair of Maubreuil must be placed. Marie-Armand, comte de Guerry-Maubreuil, marquis d'Orvault, formerly *écuyer* to Jérôme Bonaparte, King of Westphalia, was slightly mad. He had chosen to demonstrate his royalism, on 31 March, by parading around Paris with his cross of the Légion d'honneur tied to his horse's tail.[58] He was, though, commissioned in these odd times by the government to effect the return of diamonds, which the Empress and her entourage had taken away on their departure, and which were deemed to be state property. On the basis of this authority, Maubreuil and a party of soldiers proceeded to attack the carriage of the Queen of Westphalia, wife of his old master, and retrieved from it a large quantity of jewels. The Tsar was furious when he heard about this shameful incident. Maubreuil was promptly arrested. In order to exculpate himself, he told his interrogators that he had, in fact, been commissioned by Roux at the Hôtel Saint-Florentin to undertake a far more sensitive and scandalous assignment – namely the assassination of Napoleon. Talleyrand had even, he claimed, been visible, listening in the wings, as Roux gave his orders. The Prince denied it all, of course, and because of Maubreuil's renewed attack upon him thirteen years later he also included a detailed refutation in his memoirs.[59]

There were certainly discussions at this time of the benefits that would follow Napoleon's death. Perhaps Maubreuil was involved in a scheme to bring this about. Perhaps he even discussed the possibilities with Roux. But the allegation against Talleyrand personally is unproven.[60] Not that the Prince was much shocked by such suggestions. When someone expressed surprise that French kings had proved so vulnerable to assassins, but that there was no attempt to kill Napoleon, Talleyrand replied mischievously: '*Que voulez-vous*? There is no longer any religion left in France.'[61]

If the Prince's reputation has generally withstood the allegations of Maubreuil, it has been effectively assailed by much more respectable critics. In particular, Talleyrand has been strongly condemned, both by contemporaries such as Chateaubriand and Thiers, and by his biographers, including Lacour-Gayet, for the terms of the peace that he now negotiated with the allies.[62] The Prince himself considered it an achievement of which he could be proud. The 'armistice' – an exact description in the circumstances – was, he told the duchesse de Courlande on 23 April, the day of its signature, 'already a fine thing'.[63] It was the basis of the formal Peace Treaty of Paris of 30 May, which he also considered 'very good'.[64]

The terms were, in the circumstances, extremely generous. The Austrians and Prussians had talked earlier of returning France to its borders of 1789, thus wiping out all the gains made under the Revolution, the Directory, and Napoleon. But Talleyrand secured for France the borders of 1792. Indeed, there were some modest but useful territorial gains – several communes on the Belgian border, the canton of Sarrebruck, the fortress of Landau, the county of Monbéliard, part of Savoy including Chambéry and Annecy, Avignon and the Comtat Venaissin – amounting to a population increase of some 640,000 souls. Against that – and this was to become the core of the criticism – France unconditionally abandoned some fifty fortresses and demobilized its army. Could this sacrifice have been avoided?

Almost certainly not. Talleyrand rightly emphasizes in his memoirs that these fortresses were scattered from the Vistula to the Seine. They were besieged. They were destined to fall. It was, above all, important to bring the soldiers home quickly. The reality was that the French nation was defeated and exhausted. It desired peace above all else. Talleyrand's actions made complete sense in this context.

Moreover, there were other bonuses. There was no war indemnity to pay and none of the traditional demands for payment of the costs of prisoners-of-war. France even retained (for now) the works of art that its troops had looted from around Europe. In any case, beyond the specific terms, Talleyrand had a strategy – one to which he had held for many years. He strongly believed that without the benefits of peace no political stability was possible within France, and he was prepared to make sacrifices for that end. So when Louis XVIII foolishly demanded incorporation of a substantial part of Belgium, which Talleyrand knew that the British would not tolerate, he ensured that French negotiators backed down.[65] In exchange for such cooperation, Talleyrand won the withdrawal of foreign troops from Paris on 3 June, though the allies, at the Prince's request, undertook to leave 70,000 soldiers in the vicinity, in order to support the new government's authority.[66]

The thorniest problems in the negotiations had turned out to be those relating to the colonies and to the slave trade, on both of which the British government, under strong parliamentary pressure, took a hard line. The former was resolved on the basis that Tobago, St Lucia, and Île de France and its dependencies were abandoned to Britain. The abolition of the slave trade, much to the disgust of the abolitionist House of Commons, would only be phased in over five years. Talleyrand himself had no liking for slavery, but so strong were the slaving interests within France that this was the best he could offer.[67]

The first and second tasks – that is, the removal of Napoleon and the negotiation of peace – were essential components of the third: the return of the Bourbons. On the night of 2/3 April the Senate had voted for the dethronement of Napoleon. The Lower House – the Corps législatif – followed suit. On 6 April Napoleon, recognizing reality, signed his unconditional abdication. It was now necessary to summon Louis XVIII to the throne and, equally important from Talleyrand's point of view, to establish a secure constitutional framework.

The Prince had initially asked Lebrun to prepare a draft constitution. But the ex-Consul produced merely a plan to return to the Constitution of 1791. Talleyrand politely rejected the effort. The role of the King would have to be greater and there must be an Upper House: Lebrun's effort failed on both counts. The work was now left, instead, to a commission of Senators, and was completed in haste, which accounts for some of its incoherence. Talleyrand christened the resulting document the 'Charte constitutionelle' (or just 'la Charte'). The term had welcome overtones of the English Magna Carta. It also emphasized the fact that it represented a royal grant rather than an imposition upon the King by his subjects. Unfortunately, that principle was not properly grasped by the Senators themselves. The second article thus read: 'The French people freely call to the throne Louis-Stanislas-Xavier of France, brother of the last King, and after him the other members of the house of Bourbon, in the old order.' And article 29 stated that Louis would be proclaimed 'King of the French' (a title objectionable in itself) only after he had sworn to uphold the Constitution. Talleyrand seems to have been uneasy about this insistence: he must have known how it would offend high royalist doctrine.[68] But, given that it had the support of the regicides, not just royalists, and given the pressure of time and events, it would have to do: it would certainly smooth the way for the King's return.

Louis himself had been held back all this time in England by an attack of gout, and landed at Calais only on 24 April. He had foolishly proclaimed that he owed his crown, above all, to the British and to the Prince Regent. These words would not be forgotten by the dynasty's enemies.[69] Nor did the King-in-waiting have much idea about how to deal with Talleyrand. Presumably, he hoped simply to have as little to do with him, and that for as short a time, as was politically possible. Talleyrand, for his part, knew so little of Louis's affairs that it was only late in the day that he discovered that the comte de Blacas wielded enormous influence over him.[70] That was a large oversight, since Louis's tendency to favouritism was a determining vice of his character.

At a personal level at least, Talleyrand could hope for a better reception from Monsieur (the comte d'Artois).[71] As he emphasized to Vitrolles, the two men had had friendly if unfruitful conversations at Marly on the eve of the emigration.[72] For his part, d'Artois, who in private still referred to Talleyrand as 'the bishop of Autun', retained a certain sympathy for Charles-Maurice. As he was wont to observe: 'Whatever [Talleyrand] has done, there is still something of the *gentilhomme* about him.'[73] But whether such a combination of nostalgia and snobbery could yield political results was another matter.

Monsieur was now approaching Paris. The Prince decided to despatch Vitrolles with a letter. It was an understandable but unfortunate choice, since while the messenger would find a sympathetic reception he was also a hard-line monarchist with pronounced views on the disadvantages of constitutions. Talleyrand's message to Monsieur was characteristic: 'We have had enough of glory, Monseigneur. But come – come and give us back our honour.'

There later followed a more substantial letter from the provisional government, which informed d'Artois of the Senate's decisions on the Constitution and which urged him to don both the tricolour rosette and the uniform of the National Guard for the occasion of his entry into Paris. Rejecting Vitrolles's advice, d'Artois settled on a compromise. He would continue to wear the white rosette of the Bourbons, but also agree to don the uniform.[74] Talleyrand was displeased, but accepted the decision. In any case, he had already in practice accepted the return of the Bourbon colours when he tricked Generals Marmont and Jourdan into having their troops wear white rosettes, by pretending to each that the other had already given the order to do so.[75]

The management of Monsieur's arrival was now clearly of the highest importance. On 12 April the five members of the provisional government were at the Barrière de Bondy to meet him. Talleyrand spoke briefly and graciously, Monsieur replied politely and unmemorably. Afterwards, Talleyrand decided that d'Artois's speech needed to be rewritten for publication in *Le Moniteur* and he entrusted comte

Beugnot, at the Interior Ministry, with the task. Beugnot's first attempt was rejected in words that reveal the scriptwriter at work: 'That's not it: Monsieur does not use antithesis, nor even the lightest touch of rhetoric. Be simple, be short. Say what most suits both the speaker and the audience. That is all.'

Finally, they placed on Monsieur's lips the memorably patriotic sentiment: 'I see France once more! And nothing has changed, except that there is one more Frenchman.'[76]

Whatever his hopes that his earlier good relations with d'Artois might smooth the way for better relations with the returning *émigrés*, Talleyrand left nothing to chance. On 4 and 7 April he had sent an agent, Villers, accompanied by his secretary Gabriel Perrey, to the archives contained in the Louvre. They were charged to take away with them all compromising papers and bring them back to the Hôtel Saint-Florentin. Here Talleyrand and his staff went through them, burning anything relevant to embarrassing episodes, not least the execution of the duc d'Enghien.[77] On that matter, where if the truth were known Talleyrand's political prospects would have been destroyed and even his safety compromised, he showed astonishing bravado, and it worked. In a host of other respects, however, Monsieur and the royalist clique that gathered around him proved less amenable. There was, for example, a dispute about whether the crown jewels retrieved from Marie-Louise should be in the safe-keeping of the government or of Monsieur. D'Artois prevailed.

But the most serious matter, which Talleyrand needed all his guile to resolve, concerned the post of lieutenant-general of the kingdom with which Monsieur had been invested by the still absent King. The Senate, for their part, insisted that they alone had the authority to make this appointment. In their annoyance, the Senators even refused to attend the solemn Te Deum in Notre-Dame to mark Monsieur's return. And both Fouché and Tsar Alexander intervened to support the Senate's pretensions. Eventually, Talleyrand himself brought d'Artois the confirmation which the lieutenant-general insisted he did not need from the Senate. Talleyrand was already finding out how prickly and irresponsible the ultra-royalists could be.

Nor did Monsieur's speech in the Tuileries to the assembled Senators help matters. Originally drafted by Fouché, it was then significantly modified by Vitrolles. In it, d'Artois promised, within the limits of his authority, to accept on Louis's behalf the 'basis' of the Senatorial Constitution.[78] Talleyrand's subsequent criticism of Monsieur's speech was the first serious break in their previously good relations.[79]

The lieutenant-general, as Talleyrand had proposed, now took upon himself the role of the provisional government. In that capacity, he appointed a new ministry, in the form of a Conseil d'État, which remained in place for the next fortnight (from 16 April to 2 May). Within this, Talleyrand lost his earlier pre-eminence, becoming Foreign Minister. The other four members of the old provisional government also remained. They were joined by Martials Moncey and Oudinot, General Dessolle, commander of the Paris National Guard, and most significantly by Vitrolles as minister-secretary of state, i.e. secretary to the Conseil. Vitrolles was essentially d'Artois's spy, and his presence now and later at the end of the Cabinet table was a source of resentment, not just for Talleyrand but for his colleagues. It was, indeed, one of the only things on which Talleyrand and his enemy Montesquiou agreed. The Prince's view was: 'They owed [Vitrolles] a lot – court offices, even the highest ones, titles, a fortune. But ministries are not bestowed as rewards.'[80] Given the trouble that Vitrolles caused, Talleyrand's apprehensions were entirely justified.

The next and concluding stage of the Restoration was about to be reached. On 24 April Louis XVIII finally reached Calais. Five days later, at Compiègne, he graciously received the marshals and the members of the Corps législatif. But his intentions towards Talleyrand and his colleagues, and towards the Senatorial Charte, were still unclear. The Prince had sent ahead a letter of political advice, asking (modestly enough) to be retained as Foreign Minister and seeking various preferments for his family.[81] But he certainly expected to be treated better than he eventually was. In the event, he was kept waiting for several hours and only managed to obtain an interview through Blacas. The conversation that ensued was relaxed enough, the King affecting to treat Talleyrand as almost an equal. Louis's conversational tone was a little like Charles-Maurice's own, opaque with an undefinable trace of sarcasm. Now he said: 'I am very happy to see you. Our houses date from the same period. My ancestors were cleverer. If yours had been more, you would say to me today: Take a chair, come forward, let us speak of our affairs. Today it is I who say: Sit down and let us talk.'[82]

But on matters of substance, the Prince made no headway. While determined to save face, Charles-Maurice came away disappointed and resentful. Still more serious, Louis's manner, which owed everything to Bourbon self-importance and nothing to current realities, seriously damaged the King's relations with Tsar Alexander. Louis XVIII insisted on walking ahead of his guest and on sitting in an armchair at dinner, while the Tsar was relegated to a simple chair without arms. Clinging to the ancient habits had perhaps made sense in exile, when morale was everything. Trying to impose them from a position of weakness now was to invite not just offence, but contempt.[83]

The scant respect that Louis had for Talleyrand's advice was demonstrated by the royal Declaration of Saint-Ouen of 2 May. This was drafted by Vitrolles and others with virtually no reference to the Prince. It implicitly rejected the theory behind the Senatorial Constitution – that of a contractual monarchy based upon a pact between ruler and ruled – and re-stated, instead, that of pure Bourbon sovereignty. It accepted the Constitution as a 'good basis', but noted that many of its articles had been drawn up with haste. It accepted, too, the key principles demanded by Constitutionalists since the Revolution: two Chambers, responsible ministers, independent judges, inviolable property rights, the voting of taxes and so on. But it did so in general terms and within a framework in which all initiative and ultimate authority lay with the King. Talleyrand managed to secure that the Declaration at least omitted mention of the desirability of exchanges between present and former owners of confiscated property ('*biens nationaux*') – the source of future problems throughout the Restoration.[84] He also ensured that the Declaration was dated without the inclusion of the phrase 'in the nineteenth year of our reign', a red rag to Revolutionary bulls.[85]

In presenting the Senate to the King, on the eve of Louis's entry into the capital, Talleyrand clearly expressed his own preferred alternative – one requiring a constitutional settlement to mirror that of Britain: 'The more difficult the circumstances, the more royal authority must be powerful and revered. . .A Constitutional Charter will unite every interest to the interests of the throne. . .You know better than us, Sire, that such institutions, so well tested by a neighbouring people, provide support not obstacles to monarchs who are friends of the law and fathers of the people.'[86]

Louis XVIII's journey through the streets of Paris to the Tuileries of 3 May was marked by widespread celebration. Even those who were curious rather than devoted turned out to cheer the return of a régime which, more than anything else, represented the prospect of peace. Only the army was sullen, and for much the same reason. A new government was formed. There was no President of the Council, though Talleyrand, as Foreign Minister, was the most prestigious, if not, as it turned out, the most influential member.

Louis XVIII had a certain admiration for the British way of conducting their affairs. He accepted the advantage of a constitution. But he had no intention of installing a parliamentary monarchy in which the king reigned and politicians ruled. The council was thus only called sporadically. The Bourbon princes sat there as of right. The King summoned to advise him individual ministers and *conseillers d'état* as and when he wished. There was no collective responsibility. Within this haphazard system, the influence of apparently unimportant figures loomed large, excessively so for the conduct of orderly government. Above all, Blacas, at the head of the re-established Maison du Roi, held sway over the King's private opinions.

The allies, particularly the Tsar, were uneasy at what they saw of the Bourbon style of government. Alexander was by now heartily sick of Louis XVIII. The way that the King had received him at the Tuileries made him feel as if 'a bucket of water had been thrown over his head'.[87] All the powers wanted to end their expensive post-conflict commitments, but they worried about stability. Louis was, therefore, pressed hard to devise the new Constitution which, also to Alexander's annoyance, he had stated was needed in the Declaration of Saint-Ouen. The King ensured, once more, that Talleyrand's influence was kept to a minimum: the members of the drafting commission were explicitly told not to communicate with him.[88]

In many respects, the Charte was a considerable achievement, and would remain the basis of the political settlement until the end of the Restoration period. Its ambiguities, of which both ultra-royalists and liberals were aware, were perhaps inevitable, given the still unresolved question of the ultimate source of authority in the state. The Prince, though, was unhappy: he retained his belief in many of the ideas of 1789 and in the adoption of a constitutional system based as closely as possible upon that of Britain.

Talleyrand, supported by Jaucourt and Dalberg, argued strongly in the council against the provisions for censorship of the press proposed by Montesquiou. Indeed, he felt so strongly about it that he contemplated resignation.[89] Eventually, he won a small concession. But when he opposed the declaration that Catholicism be declared the state religion, he was overruled by the King.[90] It was, therefore, very clear by the end of the summer of 1814 that the Prince was to be accorded no precedence and only restricted influence by the Bourbons. He could not even have friends, like Rémusat, appointed as *préfets*.[91] His political future seemed bleak. Only his standing with the allied powers and the tasks that he alone was equipped to fulfil at the forthcoming Congress in Vienna made him, as yet, indispensable.

Both the King and Monsieur preferred to listen to their own men, and they thought they could afford to do so. The welcome that the Bourbons had received induced complacency. The former *émigrés* thought that they had no need for compromise, nor for Talleyrand. Despite the exertion of all his charm – he walked arm-in-arm with Blacas at the *fête* given by the National Guard, and the two shared ice cream in a café off the rue Taitbout – Charles-Maurice could make no impression. In Talleyrand's words: 'These people have learned nothing and forgotten nothing.'[92] More specifically, they failed to understand that opinion in Paris and the army was more important than that of the provinces in determining who ruled France. Oddly enough, Talleyrand, who should have known – and probably did know – better, gave elegant expression to that misreading in a letter he wrote on 13 June to the Tsar. Alexander had flounced away from Paris without bidding farewell. The Prince gently chided him, acknowledged that some malcontents had been complaining, but then observed: 'What is Paris, after all?. . .The provinces – they are the true France. It is there that people really bless the return of the house of Bourbon and that they extol your great victory.'[93]

Unfortunately, the support of provincial France was not enough.

13

The Congress of Vienna

⁓

SHORTLY BEFORE TALLEYRAND left Paris for the Congress of Vienna, he gave Pasquier a gloomy assessment of his prospects. He doubted whether anyone there would even listen to him. And yet, on the other hand, if he failed to match the hopes raised in France, he would surely be blamed. Pasquier thought, perhaps rightly, that this was a performance, designed to lower expectations and so ensure for the Prince greater plaudits for any success he actually achieved. Yet Talleyrand's reasoning was sound when he noted just how restricted his powers would be as a result of the secret terms appended to the Treaty of Paris, which he had earlier signed.[1] The operative clause stated: 'The disposition to be made of the territories which His Most Christian Majesty [Louis XVIII] renounces in the treaty patent of this day, and whose relationships must result in a system of real and durable equilibrium in Europe, will be organized at the Congress *on the bases decided by the Allied Powers between themselves*' (emphasis added).[2]

Taken at face value, that limited the role of France, or indeed of any power at Vienna other than Russia, Britain, Austria and Prussia, to that of observation and ratification. The treaty thus looked back to the Treaty of Chaumont of 1 March 1814, at which the allied powers undertook to maintain a common front against the common enemy, Napoleon's France, and to pursue the war until their objectives were attained. If that alliance was to remain the basis for diplomacy in the reconstructed Europe which the Congress was expected to establish, France would automatically be isolated and sidelined, rendered incapable of playing the role of a great power, or even of defending its interests through effective alliances. This was unacceptable. But what was to be done about it?

Part of the answer must be to turn France's weaknesses into strengths. A decade earlier, Talleyrand had been in Vienna, acting as the principal agent of the dominant power in Europe. Now he would be there as the representative of a humiliated, defeated country. He was, therefore, clearly no threat to anyone. Moreover, he represented a power that had made large territorial concessions – at least of territories acquired by recent conquest – without demur. He expected to receive the credit. As he would repeatedly assert, he alone had nothing to demand at the Congress.

The next step would be to use the moral advantage gained in this fashion in order to impose a distinctive philosophy of international relations. This must both encapsulate the principles for which the allies had publicly fought and, at the same time, allow France to emerge as a great European power. The central concepts of this philosophy were to be 'legitimacy' and 'public law'. At Vienna the Prince would have much to say that was irritating, but also unanswerable, about both.

Talleyrand knew as well that, beyond these generalities, he had certain very specific aims to fulfil. First, he must represent Louis XVIII's commitment to the wider interests of the house of Bourbon. These fitted in nicely, of course, with the concern for legitimacy. The main focus would be on Saxony – Louis was related to King Frederick Augustus through his mother – and on Naples (the 'Kingdom of the Two Sicilies') where Murat was still ensconced, to the continuing discomfiture of Ferdinand IV.[3] Second, Talleyrand must, once enabled procedurally to do so, fully engage in the collective approach of the powers intended to provide a lasting 'equilibrium' (or in modern terms 'balance') which would ensure peace and stability. This would govern his approach to Poland, and also to some extent Saxony. Finally, Talleyrand had to be concerned about any emerging future threats to France. It is in this last respect that his conduct at the Congress has been most harshly judged.

In all these tasks, the Prince wanted, like any diplomat, to have as free a hand as possible. Yet he needed to ensure that the King and his advisers, notably Blacas, were fully signed up to the approach he chose to pursue.[4] The means he adopted to square this circle were the remarkable 'Instructions for The King's Ambassadors at the Congress', the brief drawn up by himself for himself, but with Louis XVIII's authority.[5]

The first section of this document methodically, indeed pedantic-ally, fits all the states and regions whose future was still unresolved into a sophisticated framework of law and precedent. It takes as its starting point the assertion that sovereignty cannot be acquired merely by con-quest. A change of sovereignty requires cession by the legal sovereign. Thus right not might must govern international relations, providing the ultimate antidote to the Napoleonic ideology of conquest and chaos. The document then examines how an equilibrium at once favourable to France and beneficial to Europe can be established. Talleyrand rejects the notion of a perfect equilibrium between states. Such a thing can never be found. And it can never be statistically com-puted; the assumption that it could was one of his more theoretical quarrels with the British representative at Vienna, Lord Castlereagh. Moreover, such a balance is not automatic. It requires that a small number of great powers should deliberately pursue it, while animated by 'a spirit of moderation and justice'. This, Talleyrand asserts, was the policy of pre-Revolutionary France, and it must become so again.

Equilibrium, once created, has a momentum of its own. But there are two regions, each overshadowed by the ambitions of a single power, where a more direct strategy is required: 'In Italy it is Austria that it is important to stop becoming dominant, by opposing it through contrary influences; in Germany, it is Prussia.' In the case of Italy, restoring Naples to the Bourbons (and displacing Austria's ally Murat), returning Tuscany to the (Bourbon) Queen of Etruria, enlarging the territories of the Holy See, and expanding the Kingdom of Sardinia, would greatly help.[6] But the case of Germany and Prussia, as Talleyrand was right to recognize, was more difficult. His dislike and distrust of Prussia were undiminished: 'The physical constitution of [the Prussian] monarchy creates out of ambition a sort of necessity. Every pretext suits it. No scruple inhibits it. Expediency is its law.'

The allies had promised to return Prussia to its size on the eve of its mutilation by Napoleon. In fulfilment of that, the Prussians now demanded Saxony, Belgium, Luxembourg and the fortified city of Mainz. Such concessions, Talleyrand asserts, would be disastrous and must be resisted. Within Germany, the small states must be preserved against Prussia, and the medium-sized states must be enlarged to resist it. In this, the fate of Saxony is crucial. If Saxony should fall to Prussia, the latter 'would take by this acquisition a huge and decisive step towards absolute dominance in Germany'.[7]

The final, indeed in many respects central, issue before the Congress was the fate of Poland. Talleyrand argues that the restoration of the Kingdom of Poland would be a great benefit, but only if it were genuinely independent, if it had a strong constitution, and if it were not necessary to compensate Prussia and Austria for the loss of undoing the earlier Polish partitions. These conditions are, in fact, impossible to meet. So, reversing his views of earlier years, Talleyrand now accepts Polish partition as the least bad option, above all because anything else will enhance Russian power. Allowing Poland to pass entirely into the hands of the Tsar, 'expanding [Russia's] European population to 44 million subjects and its frontiers to the [River] Oder would be to create for Europe a danger, so great, so immediate, that although everything must be done to preserve the peace, if the execution of such a plan could not be stopped except by force of arms, one must not hesitate to consider for even a moment that option'.[8] War against Russia, or at least the threat of it, was thus envisaged by Talleyrand, even before the Congress opened – and only weeks after he had entertained Tsar Alexander at the Hôtel Saint-Florentin.

The immediate ally to which Talleyrand looked in order to help secure France's reintegration into the company of the great powers was Britain. Britain, as he observes in the Instructions, shares France's 'conservative' views, in that it has nothing to gain from overturning the existing international order in Europe.[9] Britain had already made its colonial gains, and these it would keep. It was still agitated by the desire to achieve a worldwide end to the slave trade, and on this too it must be given its way. Similarly, its interest in ensuring that the mouth of the Scheldt should not fall into hostile – traditionally French – hands must be respected. On this basis, Talleyrand saw a *rapprochement* with Britain as the starting point for his wider objectives.

Fortunately for France, the political atmosphere in London, where the leaders of the allied powers had repaired after Paris, had been terrible. Far from resolving the outstanding issues, personal bad feeling – notably between the Tsar and the Prince Regent – had set back negotiations. Talleyrand, who had pointedly been excluded from London, was thus able to make successful overtures in Paris through Lord

Stewart to his half brother, Castlereagh.[10] The Foreign Secretary himself duly visited Paris and had friendly discussions with both Louis XVIII and Talleyrand.

Castlereagh's views were not yet the same as those of his French hosts. But he already shared Talleyrand's distrust of Russia and wanted to check its European ambitions. He was, therefore, open to admitting France to a wider role than the strict letter of the secret provisions of the Treaty of Paris would warrant.[11] Metternich too, despite his differences with the French about Murat in Naples, could see benefits in Talleyrand's admission to some of the more important conferences at the Congress. Such was the diplomatic background to the Prince's arrival in Vienna on 23 September 1814.

Back in Paris, he had entrusted the Foreign Ministry to his old friend Jaucourt. In Vienna, the Prince's main political agent was the well-connected, shady, indiscreet Dalberg. Talleyrand would joke that he had brought him along to 'propagate the secrets that I wanted the world to know'. Noailles was part of the mission because Talleyrand believed that an agent of the comte d'Artois would be appointed come what may, and so it was better to choose one's own. As for his friend La Tour du Pin, he could sign passports. Talleyrand's long-time collaborator at the Foreign Ministry, La Besnardière, would actually 'do the work'.[12] He was joined by three secretaries, including one Achille Rouen, who sang Talleyrand's praises in Vienna to anyone who would listen.[13]

Nor was the cultural dimension neglected in this embassy, which was, after all, intended to impress the crowned heads of Europe. Talleyrand's own resident musician, Neukomm, a pupil of Haydn, accompanied the Prince. The imperial spies were convinced that Neukomm was a spy himself and followed him about everywhere, until they discovered that he was just what he seemed. Neukomm would play the piano for hours on end as Talleyrand worked at his desk, but never knew whether the Prince was really listening.[14] The painter Jean-Baptiste Isabey also joined the mission. Isabey had temporarily fallen out of favour on the fall of Napoleon. One day he and Talleyrand were admiring an engraving that depicted the signing of the Peace of Münster (which ended the Thirty Years War in 1648). Talleyrand pointed at the work and said: 'A Congress is going to open

in Vienna: go there.' Isabey complied. His famous picture of the negotiations is the result.[15]

The Prince needed an escort to help him entertain. He accordingly
took, not his wife, whose effective banishment now began, but rather
his niece by marriage, Dorothée de Périgord. She was twenty-one,
and had matured from a mousy girl into an extraordinarily attractive
young woman, with slender neck, pale complexion and large, very
dark blue eyes.

The question of whether – and if so when – Dorothée, the future
duchesse de Dino, became the Prince's mistress is now unresolvable.
But the relationship was almost certainly not sexual while the two
were together in Vienna. Not even the smutty-minded imperial spies
suggested so. Her presence is easy enough to understand: Talleyrand
believed that the services of a pretty hostess would be invaluable.
His own wife was manifestly unsuitable. His beloved duchesse de
Courlande was politically problematic and anyway unavailable. Her
daughter, therefore, was the obvious choice. The duchesse de
Courlande, who was nobody's dupe, clearly trusting Talleyrand to
behave, evinced no jealousy, even rebuking Dorothée for a lack of
appreciation of the older man's solicitude.[16]

But prolonged proximity had its effect. By the time he left Vienna,
the Prince was clearly smitten, as his contemporaries noted. Dorothée
was not in love with him, however. She was, instead, passionately
involved with an Austrian soldier, Count von Clam-Martinitz, with
whom her husband, Edmond, eventually fought a duel. Perhaps the
relationship between the Prince and his niece was later sexually con-
summated. Contemporaries often assumed so. Talleyrand is said to
have fathered a child by Dorothée, when he was sixty-one. But
Pauline, on whom he doted, was probably in fact, and not just in
polite fiction, the legitimate daughter of his nephew Edmond.[17]
Whatever the truth, Talleyrand's relationship with Dorothée evolved
into a loving friendship, which in his extreme old age became almost
complete dependence. She was the final, and perhaps the greatest, love
of his life. Nor did she forget after his death what he had done and
been for her.[18]

Talleyrand was delighted that he had been able to hire the Kaunitz
Palace in Vienna as headquarters of the French mission. He had long

admired Kaunitz, the Austrian Chancellor and Foreign Minister who had steered the eighteenth-century Franco-Austrian alliance.[19] The magnificent baroque Kaunitz Palace was, however, in a somewhat dilapidated state. Austrian spies reported how a team of servants busied themselves throwing out bug-ridden mattresses and making other preparations before the Prince himself arrived.[20] But the palace now took on the character of the greatest of the great embassies, which entranced the swelling diplomatic population of the city.

Talleyrand lost no time in making diplomatic contacts, and his urgency was justified. Just before his arrival, the representatives of the four victorious powers had renewed their mutual commitment to decide between themselves on the disposition of the states and territories whose future was unresolved. His efforts bore fruit in the invitation extended to him (and to the Spanish envoy, Don Pedro Labrador) to attend a conference of the powers at Metternich's villa on the Rennweg on 30 September. Whose idea it was to include Talleyrand is unclear, but all four major powers quickly repented of it. The Prince behaved extremely badly, albeit in a masterpiece of histrionics. Indeed, as Gentz, the meeting's secretary, complained, Talleyrand and Labrador entirely disrupted everything that had been planned. The stormy discussion lasted for more than two hours.[21] Talleyrand was troublesome right from the beginning. He complained that the other delegations present were larger than his. Why? He complained that the Portuguese and the Swedes (signatories of the Treaty of Paris, for whom, naturally, he cared nothing except for tactical purposes) were absent. Why was that? He received no answer. Then the temperature rose further. On reading a protocol of 22 September, signed by the Big Four, which mentioned the phrase 'allied powers', Talleyrand at once demanded to know which 'allies' were meant. Allies against whom? Against Napoleon? But Bonaparte was in exile on Elba. Against Louis XVIII and France? If so, then they were still at war. In that case, his own presence at Vienna was pointless. And yet (Talleyrand proceeded):

> If I were not here, you would truly miss me. Messieurs, I am perhaps
> the only one who asks nothing. . .I repeat: I want nothing. And I bring
> a great deal. The presence here of a minister of Louis XVIII conse-
> crates the principle on which the whole social order rests. The first
> need of Europe is to banish for ever the view that one can acquire

rights by conquest alone, and so to revive the sacred principle of legitimacy, from which flow order and stability.[22]

The Prince then demanded the swift opening of the Congress, quoting the passage of the Treaty of Paris that promised it. But the four powers had, of course, no such intention. Complicating their decisions by throwing them open to wider participation was the last thing they wanted. The conversation, therefore, turned to other matters, both administrative and substantial, including whether Naples (in the form of Murat's representatives) should be admitted. Talleyrand now clashed with the near deaf, cantankerous Prussian representative, Hardenberg, who declared that the possessions of Murat had already been guaranteed.[23] Drawing on his doctrine of legitimacy, Talleyrand crisply replied: 'Those who made such a guarantee should not have done, and consequently could not have done.' The meeting adjourned in some disarray. Talleyrand had won his immediate point: the protocol established by the previous meeting was torn up by Gentz, and there was no more mention of 'allied powers'.

Had France thus shouldered its way back to the top table of the powers? Not yet, although a start had certainly been made. But the real decisions continued to be taken informally between the Big Four. Talleyrand nourished no illusions. As he observed in his report to Louis XVIII: 'Your Majesty sees that our position here is difficult.'[24]

In fact, he now proceeded to make it a good deal more difficult by circulating an official note about the meeting, which it had been understood was to remain private. The note formally demanded that a commission of eight powers – those that had signed the Treaty of Paris – be appointed to have charge of drawing up the questions to be put before the Congress. This infuriated the Big Four.

Yet the confusion was, in part, their own fault. They had not resolved which committees would be entrusted with which tasks, and which powers would be represented at them, in good time before arriving at Vienna. Only at the last moment did they settle upon the compromise that had so signally failed, namely to reserve to themselves the decisions about who got which states, but to 'communicate' these in an enlarged conference to France and Spain. The six would also discuss arrangements for the opening of the Congress, which the four, of course, wanted to postpone *sine die*. A further special committee of the five German powers (Austria, Prussia, Bavaria, Württemberg and Hanover) would be entrusted with drafting a scheme for a Germanic federation.[25] Talleyrand's assertiveness, his raising questions of substance and basic procedure at what was meant to be a meeting called for his information, and finally his broadcasting the matter in the version of a formal note threw these plans into disorder.

Talleyrand was bitterly criticized to his face for the note by both Humboldt (assisting Hardenberg) and Nesselrode. More serious, though, was Castlereagh's anger, since without British support no serious improvement in French standing was possible. In revenge, Castlereagh now drew up a draft declaration making explicit mention of the secret terms of the Treaty of Paris, which had reserved the key decisions to the allies and excluded France. This was intended as a public humiliation, since the weakness of France's position was something that Talleyrand had taken pains to conceal from Viennese opinion. The four powers did, however, now accept that the eight countries that had signed the Treaty of Paris should constitute the main steering committee. Talleyrand had wanted this expansion, because he was worried that in a group of the four + two (i.e. with just France and Spain added) he would constantly be outvoted. But it was a hollow victory if the four powers themselves were even more firmly united against him. Talleyrand now, therefore, toned down his language and moderated his positions.[26] This did not, however, prevent another sharp exchange with the Prussians. At a conference held on 8 October, Talleyrand insisted – thinking specifically about Saxony and Naples – on the inclusion of the concept of 'public law' as a governing principle to be applied to the decisions of the Congress. Humboldt sneered: 'What has public law got to do with it?' Talleyrand acidly replied: 'It is what sends you here.'

The Prince's personal exchanges with the Tsar had been equally unpleasant. Alexander was furious at the obstruction of his deal with Prussia, by which the Prussians should gain Saxony while Russia acquired Poland. Again, the argument centred on the concepts of law and power. The Tsar bluntly asserted that expediency was the same as law. Talleyrand turned to the wall, and beat his head on the panelling in simulated despair, crying: 'Europe, Europe, poor Europe!'

But the Tsar was adamant: 'Better war, than renounce what I have [i.e. Poland]!'

And when Alexander attacked 'those who have betrayed the cause of Europe' – alluding to Saxony, which had remained true to its alliance with Napoleon – Talleyrand sarcastically observed: 'Sire, that is a matter of dates.' This reference to Alexander's own alliance with Napoleon will not have improved the Tsar's disposition.[27]

In these early days, Talleyrand had created a great deal of ill-will, and he knew it. He confided to the duchesse de Courlande: 'My firmness annoys everyone. But I shall not bend. The house of Bourbon was lost through its weakness. I shall not contribute to that.'[28]

In his reports Talleyrand blamed Metternich for sloth and Castlereagh for feebleness in failing to confront Russia and Prussia. But neither statesman intended lightly to abandon the four-power framework simply to satisfy France. The French at least made the running in the cultivation of public opinion, through orchestrated leaks and disinformation. Thus Talleyrand's jibes and barbs at the expense of the Tsar and others rapidly circulated through the *salons* and reached the Viennese Chancellery.[29] Talleyrand's insistence on a formal date for the opening of the Congress proper appealed strongly to the lesser powers which regarded the French as a champion. His ferocious defence of the rights of the King of Saxony against Prussia was most popular with the Germans, who disliked the hegemony of what French propaganda termed 'the barbarians of the north'.[30] Others appreciated it too. The prince de Ligne, whose house was frequented by Talleyrand and whose sophisticated gossip and epigrammatic observations rivalled those of his guest, was heard to remark: 'What is being done to the King of Saxony is atrocious. I do not like Talleyrand, but I like to see him taking the side of that monarch.'[31]

The problem was that power at Vienna was not going to be allocated, and decisions were not going to be made, as a result of mere diplomatic bravura. The Prince will not have been displeased to hear that the Tsar grumbled how Talleyrand was behaving 'like the minister of Louis XIV'.[32] But now he must watch and wait for an opportunity to split the allied coalition, rather than attacking its members frontally.

That meant finding common ground with Metternich and Castlereagh. Each was problematical. Castlereagh blamed Talleyrand for his early obstructionism. He also criticized him for concentrating on Saxony and Naples instead of Poland. But this was unfair: British and French priorities were just somewhat different. As Talleyrand recognized, Castlereagh was well disposed to Prussia, which Britain regarded as a useful bulwark against France in the Rhineland. Castlereagh's larger aim was to draw Prussia and Austria together against Russia, which the British regarded as the only serious threat to European equilibrium.[33] Consequently, he was prepared to be accommodating over Saxony, as long as Metternich raised no strong objections. Whereas Saxony's fate affected the balance of power in Germany, Poland's was important to that of Europe as a whole. The latter, not the former, was Britain's business.[34]

But, even allowing for this difference in great power interests, there was a further problem: Britain's policy towards Poland, unlike that of France, was somewhat muddled. Whereas Talleyrand had already decided (as his Instructions show) that Polish independence was a lost cause and that the least bad option was the return to a partitioned Poland under the control of the neighbouring powers, British opinion, and occasionally policy, still hankered after Polish independence. Castlereagh was less moved by that ideal than his liberal critics at home, but he still hoped to persuade, rather than compel, Russia to restrain its ambitions. This, though, was a hopeless cause, since Alexander had now, in Talleyrand's words, adopted an 'aggressive philanthropy', in which domination not liberation was uppermost.[35] On top of that, any attempt to have Prussia and Austria give up the Polish territory they had acquired in order to help regenerate a viable Polish state would require compensations elsewhere – and already Prussian desire for compensation threatened to wipe Saxony off the map. The implications of all this took several months – and several bruising encounters between Castlereagh and the Tsar – to become apparent to the British. When they did, Castlereagh abruptly ended his 'mediation' and handed the business over to Metternich.[36]

Metternich, for his part, again saw matters rather differently. He had no illusions about managing Tsar Alexander, whom he considered impossible, and who also hated him personally. The Austrian

Foreign Minister was, in any case, playing a waiting game, delaying all concrete decisions, engrossing himself in procedural questions, and partaking of the glittering social life of Vienna. This seemed reprehensible to Talleyrand, no slouch in these respects, and it appalled Metternich's own colleagues.[37] But in the end it made sense, because it reflected the overwhelming desire of the Austrians to avoid a war whose consequences might prove terminal to the Habsburg dominions. Austria was, above all, terrified of Russia. Metternich needed none of the lectures he received from Talleyrand about the danger of allowing Russian power to become 'a belt around [Austria's] principal and most important possessions, Hungary and Bohemia'.[38] He was equally conscious of Prussian ambitions. But he thought that Alexander might be worn down. And he believed that any durable settlement within Germany as a whole depended upon securing Prussian cooperation. So he delayed.

In these circumstances, France, recently defeated and with little credibility in any military intervention, paradoxically became the most aggressive proponent of a policy to resist the Russian–Prussian axis. Fortunately for Talleyrand's strategy, first the Russians and then the Prussians proceeded to overplay their hand.

Meanwhile, the French mission continued to make up in style for what it lacked in influence. A visiting Frenchman, the comte de La Garde-Chambonas, understood precisely what was happening. Talleyrand, 'the first diplomat of all time', made up by his own demeanour for the strength that was lacking in the French government. The Prince would preside at receptions, seated on a sofa, surrounded by standing diplomats 'like schoolboys listening to the lessons of a master', while Dorothée 'did the honours of the *salon* with ravishing grace'.[39]

Behind the façade of festivity at the Congress there was a good deal of tension, most of it surrounding the Tsar. Having been applauded in Paris and in St Petersburg as a triumphant liberator, he had been bruised in London and now he faced growing unpopularity in Vienna. Talleyrand was pleased to note that the police presence around Alexander had to be increased threefold just to prevent him being insulted in the streets.[40] The prince de Ligne's much quoted remark that 'the Congress dances but does not advance' was aimed at the Tsar, who was proud of his waltz and whom it greatly irritated.[41] Alexander had soon discovered obstacles to the achievement of his objectives in Poland that he had not foreseen. Some of these came from his own advisers, who had grave doubts about the wisdom of the course he was pursuing. He had also expected cooperation from Austria, and he did not receive it. Under Metternich's pressure, even Prussia started to waver.[42] The Tsar's language and behaviour became increasingly intolerable. When Metternich tried to negotiate with him on Poland, Alexander exploded and addressed him (as Talleyrand reported to Louis XVIII) 'with a haughtiness and violence of language that would appear extraordinary, even towards one of his servants'.[43] The Tsar tried to have Metternich dismissed, though without success. Their relations were complicated by the fact that they both visited mistresses residing in the Palais Palm, respectively the Princess Katharina Bagration and Duchess Wilhelmina von Sagan. Talleyrand had hoped that the latter, Dorothée's elder sister, might captivate the Tsar's affections and so provide the French with useful information. But Alexander seems to have preferred Princess Bagration.[44]

By contrast, there was now a brief period of *rapprochement* between Alexander and Talleyrand. After more than a month of angry discussion, Talleyrand came under pressure from Louis XVIII – who had been visited by the Duke of Wellington – to support Castlereagh's initial preference for a fully independent Poland.[45] The Prince knew, of course, that this was a diplomatic cul-de-sac. But even the mirage of a deal with the Tsar offered the opportunity of humiliating Metternich, whom Talleyrand longed to jolt into action. For his part, Alexander, too, was inclined to be more amenable. He was both angry with Austria and uncertain of Prussia. So the Tsar invited Talleyrand to come and have a private discussion with him. At their meeting, the Prince duly offered to support a fully independent Poland. As expected, the Tsar said that as a devotee of liberal principles he would have favoured such an outcome, but it was just not practical. The discussion moved on to Saxony. Talleyrand said that France would consent, in order to secure peace, to Prussia receiving in compensation 300,000–400,000 Saxons. But the mention of 'peace' aroused the Tsar's suspicions. Standing with his face just inches from Talleyrand's, he asked whether it was true that France was arming. Talleyrand confirmed the fact, but claimed that this threatened no one. Alexander now offered to support France on Naples if Talleyrand would support Russia on Poland and Saxony. But the Prince refused to negotiate on that basis.[46]

As the tenor of this discussion shows, a crisis was rapidly approaching. For some time, Talleyrand had been urging Louis XVIII to give military support to the diplomatic position he had adopted. The King now agreed. On 25 October Talleyrand was formally authorized to tell the Austrians that they could count on active French military cooperation to oppose Russia and Prussia.[47] This, of course, was a dangerous game. Talleyrand was assuring Louis XVIII in Paris that there would, in fact, be no war, while he was letting it be known in Vienna that war was a real possibility. In fact, it was a bluff. He must have known that such a war was unthinkable for France. He certainly had no excuse for thinking otherwise. The French press, which he read closely and tried in vain to influence, was unhelpful. In a letter to Talleyrand of 9 November, Jaucourt summarized national sentiment: 'The line of the Rhine, Belgium, even the fortress of Luxembourg, would make recruits leap forward to enlist. But, believe me, people are not in the slightest bit moved by a disinterested policy, which would mobilize for the integrity of Saxony and the balance of power in Europe as it was in 1792.'[48]

The main problem was that Talleyrand still did not know whether he could trust Austria. True, Prince Schwarzenberg bluntly threatened the Tsar with war if Russia continued to fail to see reason. Stadion and Francis I were also robust. But Metternich appalled Talleyrand by offering to abandon Saxony entirely to Prussia if the latter would only break with the Tsar over Poland. And the Austrian Foreign Minister had been heard to boast at one of Vienna's balls ('where,' added Talleyrand cattily in his despatch, 'he spends three-quarters of his day') that he would never abandon Murat in Naples.[49] In such circumstances, were Austrian and French fundamental interests compatible?

As for Castlereagh, Talleyrand was once again full of contempt for his approach to both Poland and Saxony: it was 'a policy of schoolboys and coalitionists'.[50] Castlereagh was in an invidious position. As Talleyrand noted with pleasure, British sentiment was increasingly hostile to the extinction of Saxony simply in order to assuage Prussia. Castlereagh knew that he would soon have to return and explain his actions to the House of Commons. Above all, he was not allowed to forget that the British Cabinet was resolutely opposed to war for any of the objectives that preoccupied the parties at Vienna.[51]

The crisis now came to a head. In November Russian and Prussian forces started to act as if the diplomatic option had closed. The Russian general whose forces were occupying Saxony handed over administration of the territory to the Prussians. Shortly afterwards, the Russian authorities in Poland issued a proclamation calling for all Poles to unite and fight for their independence. Both Austria and, more reluctantly, Britain finally now accepted that the confrontation favoured by Talleyrand was the only way forward. In early December Castlereagh received new instructions to support Saxony, whose abandonment in the face of Russian intransigence over Poland was anyway now pointless. Austrian attempts to do a separate deal with Prussia also finally failed. The imperial court ruled out any further concessions as imperilling Austrian security. Austrian troops were mobilized. Metternich insisted that Austria must retain Cracow in Poland and that Prussia could only acquire some, not all, of Saxony. But Hardenberg for the Prussians renewed the demand for the whole of Saxony, proposing that King Frederick Augustus be installed, as compensation, in a modest new realm in Westphalia or the Rhineland. (This last proposal would surface again later; but, in any case, it did not affect the way in which Vienna now looked at the planned Prussian expansion on its doorstep.)

Metternich's note to Hardenberg of 10 December, rejecting Prussia's designs on Saxony, was copied to Talleyrand, at the latter's specific request. This formally registered France's entry into the counsels of the Big Four. As such it had, for Talleyrand, a value far above the details of the current crisis. The Prince announced the news to Louis XVIII as a major step towards the definitive 'rupture of the [Allied] coalition'.[52] Nor did he allow the momentum to be lost.

On 19 December Talleyrand sent a note in answer to Metternich's. It took the form of a grandiloquent manifesto which elevated opposition to the proposed carve-up of Saxony to a matter of the highest principle. It asserted that the aim, set out in the Treaty of Paris, of establishing 'a real and durable equilibrium' in Europe must not be understood as justifying the division on proportionate grounds of territories and populations. Rather, 'legitimate right' (*droit légitime*) must be respected in conformity with 'principles that conserve the rights of each and the repose of all'. Precisely because such a solution was not available for Poland, the future of that fatally compromised state could not have the same importance, either for France or for Europe, as the future of Saxony. In Saxony, both the principles of legitimacy and of balance were uniquely endangered by its proposed extinction. Permitting such an outcome would be to accept the notion that 'everything is legitimate for the one who is strongest'. Moreover, it would upset the balance of Europe in two respects. First, a Saxony swallowed up by Prussia would also threaten the security of the Habsburg state. And second, by creating in Prussia 'an aggressive force disproportionate to the forces of resistance of all the other [German] states', it would make the latter look outside Germany for assistance. This would destabilize the planned German Federation.[53]

Prussian anger erupted at Talleyrand's intervention. The Prussians, clumsily encouraged by the British, insisted that France be excluded from a proposed 'Statistics' Commission, intended to compute the territorial extent and populations involved in the various proposals to carve up states. Talleyrand used the occasion to explode at Lord Stewart, who brought the news. In his contrived tantrum, the Prince even threatened to leave Vienna and return to France unless the decision were immediately rescinded. It was. Talleyrand could afford such tactics, because by now Britain and Austria were so engaged against Russia and Prussia that they needed France beside them.[54]

Talleyrand and Metternich were, in fact, already working closely together. It was now necessary to wind Castlereagh all the way in. Talleyrand, therefore, casually approached him to suggest 'a little convention' that France, Austria and Britain might make. Castlereagh was startled. Did not this amount to an alliance? He did not want war. He finally replied: 'Not yet.'[55] But Prussia now over-played its hand. On 29 December Hardenberg announced that if Prussia were any longer frustrated in its claim to Saxony it would regard this as a declaration of war. The reaction was swift. Castlereagh sharply warned that, in that case, it were better that the Congress be dissolved at once. Suddenly, the 'little convention' or even an alliance seemed not only possible but prudent; and, to Talleyrand's delight, Castlereagh himself took up the plan and insisted on drafting the document. Castlereagh brought it over to the Kaunitz Palace, where Metternich and Talleyrand read it through, made a few minor changes, and signed it on behalf of their governments.

The Triple Alliance of Tuesday, 3 January 1815 was a defensive agreement. It was not intended to last beyond the Congress, which Talleyrand would have preferred, although Castlereagh said that, at least, its 'spirit' would do so.[56] The Netherlands and Hanover – perhaps Bavaria – were also expected to become parties. But the true significance was that France was now on an equal diplomatic and military footing with two of the Big Four, which must henceforth, indeed, be considered a 'Big Five'. Talleyrand in his despatch to the King in Paris did not understate his achievement:

> Now, Sire, the coalition is dissolved, and it is dissolved for ever. Not only is France no longer isolated in Europe, but Your Majesty already has a treaty-based system such as fifty years of negotiation seemed incapable of giving him. He goes forward in concert with two of the great powers, three states of the second order, and soon all the states that serve other maxims than those of revolution. He will in truth be the head and the soul of this union, formed for the defence of principles that he has been the first to proclaim.[57]

The Triple Alliance itself looks, in the light of events, of much less significance than Talleyrand suggested. It was serious enough, and war was imminent enough, for discussions about what each power would contribute by way of men and (in Britain's case) money. But the agreement rested on shaky foundations. In France, where discontent was brewing, the régime could have been destabilized by mobilization. Austria was uneasy and its military sclerotic. Castlereagh had as yet no authority from the Cabinet for the commitments he had given.[58] Fortunately, however, the northern powers were equally embarrassed. Prussia would have been prepared to fight, but only in alliance with Russia. And suddenly that looked unlikely, not principally as a result of the Triple Alliance, which was intended to be secret though some knowledge of it dribbled out, but rather because of the Tsar's mercurial personality.

A subtle change of political atmosphere at Vienna may have helped. On 21 January Talleyrand excelled himself as a political impresario by staging a magnificent requiem mass in memory of Louis XVI. It was celebrated by the aged archbishop in Vienna's great cathedral, the Stephansdom. It had, as Talleyrand emphasized to the King, 'a moral and political purpose', namely to recall to the assembled monarchs the dreadful consequences of departing from the sacred principle of legitimacy.[59] The mass had been composed by Neukomm, who with Antonio Salieri, the imperial Kapellmeister, alternately conducted the choir of 250 voices. Amid the vast crowd that filled the church was erected a tribune covered in black velvet: here sat the reigning monarchs, resplendent in their uniforms and decorations. They had to listen to a sermon, delivered by a local cleric of Alsatian origin, that had been largely crafted by Talleyrand. The cost was entirely met by Francis I of Austria. But the political benefit accrued to Louis XVIII of France, and to his envoy.[60]

The mood was, therefore, ripe for Alexander to have a change of heart. The Austrian Emperor had informed him to his face that the King of Saxony should not be forced to abdicate. This admonition from a fellow monarch had a strong impact, as did the continued urging of his own sceptical advisers. Quickly, his obduracy turned to something like cooperation. He lost his enthusiasm for Prussia's demands for Saxony and modified his demands for Poland. In the third week of February the Tsar accepted a new partition of Polish territory to the benefit of Austria and Prussia. Cracow became a Free City. The Napoleonic Grand Duchy of Warsaw became a kingdom to be ruled in perpetuity by the ruler of Russia. Saxony, which most preoccupied Talleyrand, took longer to resolve; but now the argument was about the details of the carve-up, not about the state's very existence – or at least once Talleyrand had ensured the failure of attempts to give Frederick Augustus a new kingdom in the Rhineland. The Prussians, finally, in February, accepted a deal that gave them 40 per cent of Saxony but denied them Luxembourg and Mainz. Not until April did the King of Saxony bow to this, but his stubbornness gained him nothing. Talleyrand's now somewhat shop-soiled principle of legitimacy was thus upheld. The balance between Prussia and Austria and the other smaller German states, to which he had attached such great importance, was in some measure preserved. And Russia, though the master of most of Poland, had been prevented from advancing as far as the Oder.

Yet two serious drawbacks ensued for France from Talleyrand's diplomatic strategy. First, Prussia was compensated for its disappointment in Saxony by being granted the fortresses of the Elbe, Swedish Pomerania and much of the left bank of the Rhine. The Prussians thus acquired unchallenged dominance in northern Germany. This was perhaps ultimately inevitable. But, as Talleyrand himself was well aware, Prussia was bound to continue its pressure to expand beyond that. In 1816, after he had left government and had had time to reflect on what he had done at Vienna, he wrote presciently of Prussia's destiny: 'A state whose configuration is such that the result of a single battle can be to cut it up in several pieces, so as to intercept all communication between them, is in a situation at once too perilous and too precarious not constantly to be trying to alter it. It seems inevitable either that Prussian power will soon perish, or that it will unite under its domination a considerable part of Germany.'[61]

Prussia's acquisition of all of the Rhineland was bound to encourage that tendency towards expansionism, and in doing so cause Prussia's rulers to regard with wary resentment the influence of France in the region. It can be argued in Talleyrand's defence that the Rhineland was more difficult to assimilate, for religious and cultural reasons, than would have been Saxony: that should present a useful obstacle to Prussian great power aspirations. It must also be emphasized that the major strategic error in dealings with Prussia was made not by Talleyrand but by Napoleon III, who smiled on Prussian action against Austria in 1866, which established Prussia overnight as the dominant power in Germany. That, rather than the settlement negotiated at Vienna, was the condition for France's later defeat in the Franco-Prussian War, and, indeed, for the disaster of the First World War, of which it can be seen, in French terms at least, as a continuum. All that said, the nonchalance with which Talleyrand approached Prussia's appearance as a near, if not direct, neighbour of France betokens an excessive concern for grand principles of European order at the expense of French national interest. In this, he looked backward to the late eighteenth, not forward to the late nineteenth, century.

Not, however, that the Prince was unaware of the power of nationalism, particularly German nationalism, which he feared and disliked. Early in the Congress he warned Louis XVIII about its partisans:

> The unity of the German fatherland is their cry, their dogma, their exalted religion, which reaches as far as fanaticism; and this fanaticism has even won over reigning princes. That unity, from which France had nothing to fear when it possessed the left bank of the Rhine and Belgium, would now be of great consequence for it. Who can, in any case, foresee the results of the upheaval of a mass such as Germany, when its divided elements come to be shaken and mixed up together?[62]

What Talleyrand does not seem to have done is to link this ideological ferment to Prussian power, nor to foresee how Prussian interests must dangerously intrude on those of France. But then, a contempt for Prussia's rulers and statesmen had often penetrated his observations. So, too, had fear and hatred of Russia. And here lay the second problem resulting from his diplomatic successes.

The Tsar's new-found cooperativeness did not, as events would prove, extend to forgiving the way in which the Prince had made him look a fool at Vienna. Talleyrand had also successfully turned Louis XVIII against a marriage alliance between his nephew, the duc de Berry, and the Tsar's sister. But Alexander's resentment reached a new pitch when he finally read, in March, a copy of the 'secret' Triple Alliance, after it was sent to him by Napoleon, who had discovered a copy left behind by Jaucourt. Of course, if there had been no Hundred Days and no allied re-conquest of France, Talleyrand's diplomatic triumphs might well have more than compensated for both Russian hostility and a Prussian presence on the left bank of the Rhine. But that was not to be.

Talleyrand's policy at Vienna was, as a result, severely criticized by his contemporaries as well as by subsequent generations of Frenchmen. The most reasonable formulation is perhaps that of Pasquier, who while recognizing Talleyrand's brilliance considered that his priorities had been faulty. Talleyrand should, he believed, have allowed Prussia to receive its compensation in Saxony, not the Rhineland; he should have realized that Russia could not be forced to relinquish control over Poland and so not demanded it; and in his dealings, generally, he should have favoured alliance with the Tsar rather than with Britain.[63] These criticisms carry some weight. But, then, as Pasquier himself acknowledged, Talleyrand was not a free agent. He was the envoy of Louis XVIII and thus of a dynasty, not just a country. He was bound to be especially interested in the fate of Saxony because of Louis's blood ties with that country's ruler.

Talleyrand was, on these same dynastic grounds, even more interested in the restoration of the Bourbons to Naples where, even when Poland and Saxony were settled, he made little progress. The root of the problem was Austria. Talleyrand could, at least, stop Murat's rule in Naples being formally recognized. When 'King Joachim's' delegation visited him in October, he had treated them with undisguised scorn. They left threatening to raise the whole of Italy for Murat, which was precisely what Metternich feared.[64] Talleyrand wanted to persuade the Austrians that to leave Naples in such hands was a risk which they could and should take action to eliminate. Fortunately, Murat's blundering made the task easier. Evidence of his plotting was assembled at Talleyrand's instructions to present to Wellington, who in February replaced Castlereagh as Britain's representative at the Congress. Murat then obligingly sent a note to Vienna demanding an explanation of France's moves against him. It was not, in fact, delivered, because by then the prospect of war over Saxony, on which Murat was bargaining, had receded. But its contents were known by the British, who told the French. Unluckily for Murat, his manoeuvrings, which had by now thoroughly alarmed Austria, coincided with Napoleon's escape from Elba. Talleyrand immediately – though inaccurately – declared a link between the two, and persuaded the other powers of it. Austria duly mobilized its troops. On 18 April Metternich declared that Austria was at war with Murat's Naples. Napoleon's return also simplified another Italian problem, as Austria took control over Marie-Louise's possessions of Parma, Piacenza and Guastalla.[65]

Talleyrand's reaction to news of Napoleon's escape – which was brought to him in bed by the duchesse de Dino on the morning of 7 March – was characteristic. He wrote to Louis XVIII: 'The consequences of this event cannot yet be foreseen. But they could be beneficial, if one knows how to take advantage of them'.[66] The principal benefits he had in mind were getting rid of Murat and also, once and for all, getting rid of Napoleon. The latter had, indeed, been a French preoccupation throughout the Congress. Talleyrand believed that Bonaparte should never have been given Elba. He had in October proposed that Napoleon be sent to the Azores: Castlereagh thought this a possibility; and Louis XVIII was enthusiastic.[67] Unfortunately such rumours, which filtered back to Napoleon, combined with the failure of the French government to pay the pension that was due him, made attempting a return to power all the more attractive.

Talleyrand had never imagined that Bonaparte would dare land in France. He would surely opt for Italy, where Murat could provide an army. This misconception perhaps explains the calm with which he had greeted the initial news. But he was wrong. Napoleon was now making his way through the Midi. Within days, Austrian spies were reporting that Talleyrand's sangfroid was just an act. In truth, he was now extremely worried.[68] He was also furious, knowing that if Napoleon's adventure prospered, the Herculean efforts he had made at Vienna to break the anti-Napoleonic alliance and to reassert French interests would be rendered void. His anger was reflected in the zeal with which he roused the powers to denounce his former master, described in his despatches to Louis XVIII as 'a bandit'.[69] It was the Prince who drew up the joint declaration of the allied powers, which stated that: 'Napoleon Bonaparte has placed himself beyond civil and social relations and that, as an enemy and disturber of the peace of the world, he has abandoned himself to public retribution.'

Apart from relieving his feelings, and asserting some dignity in an assembly where his position was becoming less credible by the day, Talleyrand viewed the declaration as important because it bound Austria into the coalition against Bonaparte.[70] Not that there should have been any doubt about Austrian intentions; but Napoleon had bruited it about that his Austrian father-in-law supported his return. Despite this activity, on 20 March Napoleon was back in the Tuileries.

The remainder of Talleyrand's stay in Vienna was a sad affair. The news from France was sparse, tardy and unremittingly bad. Wellington left for his army at the end of March. Tsar Alexander and King Frederick William departed on 26 May, and Francis I the next day. Talleyrand himself stayed on until 9 June, in order to append his signature to the Final Act of the Congress. The next morning he left for

Frankfurt. There had been good diplomatic reasons for him to stay until the end, despite the pressure on him to join Louis XVIII, who had now withdrawn to Ghent.[71] But perhaps he had other reasons not to hurry.

There is no truth in Napoleon's allegation that Talleyrand had treasonably offered his services to the Emperor on the latter's return.[72] His property had been confiscated and he was one of the few exempted from the general pardon granted to Bonaparte's enemies. Charles-Maurice was thought by the Austrians to have been approached by Montrond, who had suddenly turned up at Vienna, to induce him to support the new régime. But even this is doubtful.[73] On the other hand, it was his instinct to wait on events. Even if there was no possibility of accommodation with Napoleon, it was not yet clear that the great powers would reinstall Louis XVIII. The Tsar was particularly exasperated with the Bourbons. Perhaps the duc d'Orléans might emerge as a credible candidate?

It was not just political uncertainty that weighed on Talleyrand's shoulders. There was no money to pay for the French mission, which had to look to the British for charity – a sad affront to French dignity, after all the Prince's lecturing of Castlereagh. On an emotional level, life was also difficult. In March he had visited his old friend the comtesse de Brionne at Pressburg. Ten years earlier, in Linz, she had refused to see him, in disapproval of his politics. Now they were reconciled, but she was already dying. In tears, as the end approached, she told him: 'Ah, Monsieur de Périgord! You alone can tell how much I have loved you!'[74] Still more upsetting was the fact that Dorothée was now completely and indiscreetly infatuated with Count Clam-Martinitz, aide-de-camp of Prince Schwarzenberg. Talleyrand himself was almost certainly by now secretly in love with her. And to complicate matters, at the end of March 1815 Dorothée's mother, the duchesse de Courlande, also arrived in Vienna. It must have been a tense *ménage*. The Prince, now sixty, was feeling his age. He complained: 'Having to face so many dangers at my time of life is a bit hard.'[75] But somehow he would manage.

14

President of the Council

▬ ～ ▬

TALLEYRAND WAS SLOW to join Louis XVIII at Ghent. But he had not been slow to give the King the benefit of his advice on what must be done if a second Restoration was to prove more enduring than the first. On 23 April he sent a long memorandum purporting to inform Louis of the views of the Tsar and the other monarchs, but clearly containing his own. It was couched in the language of frankness, bordering on impertinence. It listed the Tsar's grudges against Louis, though not the main source of complaint, which was, of course, Talleyrand's own behaviour at the Congress. It then described a discussion between Alexander and the British ambassador, Lord Clancarty, in which the Tsar cast doubt on whether a Bourbon monarchy would ever be stable and suggested support for the duc d'Orléans as an alternative. Since d'Orléans was, with good reason, regarded by Louis as fundamentally disloyal, this news was, naturally, bound to be disconcerting. Talleyrand carefully added that Alexander was at present alone in that view. But the allies were united in calling for a swift summons of the Corps législatif and a declaration from Louis of his commitment to constitutional government.

Still more provocatively, Talleyrand added that the allies wanted the King to cast blame on his ministers (that is, on Blacas and other former *émigrés*) for 'faults that may have been committed, and to form a new government in which each party [that is, ex-Revolutionaries as well as ultra-royalists] may find the guarantees it wants'. Then, placing in Alexander's mouth his own opinions, Talleyrand condemned the King's choice of inexperienced ministers and his permitting the royal princes (that is, d'Artois) to wield excessive influence. The despatch was, in effect, a claim to form a constitutionalist government that would impose on the King the liberal programme whose absence had (allegedly) caused the country to rally to Napoleon.[1]

Talleyrand was convinced that he and other critics of the first Restoration government had been proved correct. Yet he and his fellow liberals were not entirely blameless either. Louis XVIII's reactionary ministers had certainly annoyed the former Revolutionaries and worried those who had acquired confiscated lands. But their most important errors were those that alienated the army and its commanders: these had directly paved the way for Napoleon's successful return. Alongside symbolic snubs, money was at the root of military discontent. And the sharp cuts in the military budget effected by Baron Louis had been strongly supported by Talleyrand.[2] Liberal economics, not just royalist politics, were, therefore, part of the explanation of the Hundred Days. Nor is it clear that, outside Paris at least, French opinion was particularly interested in constitutional guarantees. Talleyrand's short-lived administration would lead, not follow, political pressures in its reforms.[3]

The political programme he now favoured was, indeed, bold, progressive and much less cynical than his reputation would suggest. He had encapsulated its rationale in a report he drew up for the King:

> People want guarantees. They want them for the sovereign. They want them for subjects. People do not think they have these: if individual liberty is not protected by laws against every assault; if the judicial order is not independent, and so composed of judges who cannot be removed; if the power to judge is reserved in certain cases to the administration, or to any other bodies than tribunals; if ministers are not collectively responsible for the exercise of the power with which they are entrusted; if there could enter the councils of the sovereign any one other than such responsible persons; finally, if the law is not the expression of a will formed by three distinct wills.[4]

The author of this document still sounds like the reformer who in his youth had helped draft the Declaration of the Rights of Man and of the Citizen. But the model is very clearly the British Constitution. Unfortunately, to try to persuade the Bourbons of the merits of such a system would prove a task beyond Talleyrand's (or any one else's) capacity.

The Prince was in Brussels when he learned of the defeat of Napoleon at Waterloo. The King had already left Ghent and was heading towards the French border, and Talleyrand caught up with him at Mons late in the afternoon of 23 June. What subsequently transpired has been brilliantly distorted by the pen of Chateaubriand, according to whom Talleyrand, out of self-importance, refused to go and see the King and stayed basking in the admiration of his cronies. But Talleyrand did, in fact, see Louis. He saw him first at dinner, where the King, as usual, refused to discuss business. The duc de Duras broke the silence at one point to pronounce that the butter was rancid; but otherwise Louis XVIII simply ate.[5] At eleven o'clock that night Talleyrand managed to obtain an audience. The King planned to leave early in the morning, was making preparations and was in no mood to listen to what his minister had to say. But Talleyrand argued his case for an hour. He urged the removal of Blacas. This, at least, presented no problem, because Louis was already resigned to the loss of his favourite.[6] More importantly, Talleyrand spoke in support of the constitutional ideas contained in his report, which he now handed to the King. Finally, he argued against the King continuing his journey into France in the train of Wellington's army. Talleyrand believed it vital that Louis should not seem to have been placed on the throne by foreign troops, returning, as the quip later had it, 'in a Prussian wagon'. He would have had him go, rather, to Lyon, leaving the provisional government in Paris to incur the odium of managing the occupation. The King would have none of it.[7] Perhaps Talleyrand also offered his resignation. If so, it was not explicitly accepted.

In Chateaubriand's account, the Prince was furious to be woken early the next morning to be told that the King was leaving. The royal coach was, apparently, held back, while a breathless Talleyrand limped alongside, only to be greeted by Louis with the words of dismissal: 'Prince de Bénévent, you are leaving us? The waters will do you good. You will send us your news.'[8]

Perhaps this even happened. But the events were of far greater political moment than Chateaubriand suggests. The King had effectively abandoned his ministers, including the one minister in whom the British and the Austrians had any confidence, in order to place himself under the authority of Monsieur and the ultraroyalists. What sort of Restoration would be possible under these circumstances was debatable. Would, indeed, the allies regard such a Restoration as worth supporting at all?

For his part, Talleyrand deliberately raised the stakes. He was determined to hold to the theory that he had enunciated in his report, and so to assert the rights of the King's ministers. He, therefore, refused all the arguments put to him by the Tsar's representative, Pozzo di Borgo, and others to swallow his pride and follow the King. He spoke, instead, of going to Germany in order to begin the 'new emigration'. Then he changed his tone and entertained his partisans over dinner with amusing stories and anecdotes.[9]

The government itself was split. The majority – including Baron Louis, Jaucourt, Beugnot, Lally-Tolendal, Chateaubriand and Guizot – stayed with Talleyrand in Mons. A minority – notably the War Minister, Clarke (the Duke of Feltre), and the senile Chancellor, Dambray – went to join Louis XVIII at Cambrai.

The allies were aghast. They knew that Talleyrand was indispensable, at least at this stage; and he knew that they knew. Pozzo departed to speak to the King and Wellington, in order to have Talleyrand formally summoned, thus ending his disgrace. The Prince agreed to defer his decision to leave Mons until the outcome of the mission was known.[10] In fact, by the time Pozzo arrived, Wellington had already acted. The duke strongly disagreed with Talleyrand's view that Louis should avoid the capital for some provincial destination. He was determined to keep the King under his own control; and he was probably wise. But Wellington was equally determined that the King should be advised by Talleyrand, whom he respected, rather than by the creatures of Monsieur, whom he did not respect at all. The duke, therefore, made it clear to Louis what had to be done, and then himself sent a letter urging Talleyrand to come to Cambrai.[11] This time, the Prince did not delay. With Wellington's backing, he now had the opportunity to assert himself.

That Wellington's and Pozzo's fears were far from groundless had already been demonstrated by the inept terms of the proclamation issued by Louis at Le Cateau-Cambrécis on 24 June. The document appeared to threaten revenge against those who had joined Napoleon during the Hundred Days; nor did its language offer reassurance to those expecting a restored Bourbon régime to have learned from its past errors. Talleyrand's first task, therefore, was to impose on the King a new document, which would at once please the allies, reassure Paris, and establish his own control of the government. The drafting was, again, entrusted by the Prince to Beugnot.

When the document was read out to the King in the council – in the presence of Talleyrand, the other ministers and the royal princes – Louis was shaken. Never had a Bourbon been expected to use such language. A Bourbon did not apologize. Yet the declaration stated: 'My government was bound to make mistakes; and perhaps it has made some.' It promised, in future, a 'wise and well-ordered liberty'. Of great moment to Talleyrand, it also promised 'the unity of the government' and the 'open and assured functioning' of the Royal Council. It excepted from a general pardon only 'the instigators and actors' of the treason that had occurred; the fate of these people would lie with the two Chambers, which the King promised speedily to summon.[12]

This promise of a collectively responsible government at a stroke removed Monsieur and the duc de Berry from membership of the council. This was bad enough. But the anger of the royal princes was most provoked by the admission of past errors. D'Artois complained at length about the document's wording.

Talleyrand, who was in no mood to mince words, replied: 'The King has made mistakes; his affections have led him astray; there is nothing excessive there.'

Foolishly, Monsieur asked: 'Am I the person to whom it indirectly refers?'

Talleyrand answered: 'Yes, since Monsieur had taken the discussion on to this ground. Monsieur has done a great deal of harm.'

D'Artois: 'The prince de Talleyrand forgets himself!'

Talleyrand: 'I fear so, but the truth overcomes me.'

The duc de Berry now lost his temper and spoke darkly of exacting revenge for such impertinence. But the King intervened. A few face-saving alterations were made.[13] The declaration, dated 28 June at Cambrai, was duly signed by Louis XVIII and by Talleyrand, who thus effectively took full control of the government – one from which the royal princes were henceforth excluded.

Later, when tempers had cooled a little, d'Artois complained to Talleyrand: 'We have no reason to thank you. You have had us put out of the council.'

Talleyrand replied: 'Monsieur will thank me when he is King.'[14]

Someone else who now felt he had little reason to thank Talleyrand was Chateaubriand; and because the latter's animosity, combined with his literary virtuosity, has had a large impact on the Prince's reputation, it is apposite briefly to examine their relationship. By the time he came to write his memoirs, Chateaubriand considered that Talleyrand was responsible for communicating to the Restoration 'a germ of decay and death'.[15] He would, indeed, pursue his enemy to the grave and beyond, though the enemy had notable occasions of revenge. Among Talleyrand's more choice observations were: 'M. de Chateaubriand imagines he is deaf, since he no longer hears any one talking about him.'[16] Somebody remarked on the dramatic description, in Chateaubriand's book, of Christian martyrs 'devoured by beasts' ('*dévorés par les bêtes*': *bête* = either 'beast' or 'stupid'). 'Just like the Work,' Talleyrand observed.[17]

Chateaubriand owed Talleyrand a great deal, though he never acknowledged the fact. When Chateaubriand had resigned his posting as minister to the Swiss canton of the Valais, in disgust at the duc d'Enghien's execution, Talleyrand held back notification of the decision to Napoleon until he deemed that Chateaubriand was not likely to be in danger.[18] The two men's paths then diverged. But Chateaubriand was eager to demonstrate his commitment to Talleyrand, as he waited in Ghent with the King for the Prince's return from Vienna. On 28 April he wrote: 'Your presence here is absolutely necessary. Come and prevent our stupidities. You must place yourself at our head and form a government of which you will be the guide and the support. You know, Prince, how devoted I am to you. . .'[19]

Chateaubriand, though, possessed no political judgement. He imagined that it would be possible not only to place Talleyrand, whom the King disliked, at the head of the administration, but also the duc d'Orléans, whom Louis feared, at the head of the army.[20] Moreover, his political influence could only be temporary, the result of his skills as a propagandist and the absence of other contenders. Yet he convinced himself that he would have succeeded Blacas as Minister of the Maison du Roi, if he had but followed the King to Cambrai rather than stayed with Talleyrand at Mons.[21] He also clearly believed that he should have received a ministerial post from the Prince, once the latter formed his short-lived government. Fortunately, politics did not lose, and literature splendidly gained, from his disappointment.

The choice of ministers to form the new government was, indeed, a very sensitive matter. The most important question, from the start, was whether to include Fouché. Left to his own devices, Talleyrand would probably not have done so.[22] But, as it turned out, he had no choice. Not just Wellington but also Monsieur were both convinced of the need for the appointment. The reasons were obvious. Just as Talleyrand had held Paris in his hand at the first Restoration, Fouché, by equally devious behaviour, had gained a decisive role in determining the capital's fate now.

Once the outcome of Waterloo was known, Fouché had sent an agent to Wellington. Talleyrand, Pozzo and the British ambassador, Stuart, were present at this meeting, where Talleyrand gave reassurances about the future constitutional position and the treatment of those in need of amnesty. Another of Fouché's agents also approached the court directly. Talleyrand, bowing to necessity, now pressed the case with the King for Fouché's return as Minister of Police. So did Vitrolles. At first Louis recoiled, exclaiming, 'Never!' But, in Chateaubriand's words, it was a 'never for twenty-four hours'. The King wept, exclaiming: 'Oh my unfortunate brother, if you see me now, you have already forgiven me!' But he signed the decree that Beugnot had drawn up, and it was duly given to Talleyrand.[23]

Meanwhile, Fouché had asked for a meeting with Wellington and his colleagues. When he arrived in Neuilly, he was accompanied by other plenipotentiaries from Paris, which limited his ability to speak freely. So it was agreed that he should return on his own that evening to dine with the duke, Talleyrand and Pozzo. Talleyrand now handed over the decree of appointment. Fouché's attitude immediately changed. From now on, his concern was not to impose conditions, but rather to smooth the way for the King's return to Paris. It only remained for him to take his oath of office.[24]

At nine o'clock that night, Fouché and Talleyrand left for Arnouville. The scene has been memorably recorded by Chateaubriand, who was brooding in an anteroom:

> Suddenly a door opens. In silence enters Vice, leaning on the arm of Crime, M. de Talleyrand supported, as he walks, by M. Fouché. The

infernal vision passes slowly before me, penetrates the office of the King, and disappears. Fouché came to swear fealty and homage to his lord; the loyal regicide, kneeling, placed those hands, which had caused the head of Louis XVI to fall, between the hands of the royal martyr's brother; the apostate bishop stood surety for the oath.[25]

It is difficult to judge whether Fouché was as indispensable as he seemed. But, in any case, on 8 July Louis XVIII entered Paris to general acclaim, albeit as part of a conquering army. Talleyrand also returned, but separately and inconspicuously in a Prussian army carriage. At least he no longer needed to bother about Napoleon. The allies would show none of that mercy on which the Tsar had misguidedly insisted after the first Restoration. On 3 July Talleyrand had expressed his hatred for his former master in a letter to the duchesse de Courlande: 'Bonaparte is at Cherbourg [*sic*: in fact at Rochefort-sur-Mer], from where he is going to embark. I hope that the British catch him. He is carrying a lot of money. It is said he is going to America. He finishes his career as it deserved. . . in a mire of blood.'[26] Talleyrand was not disappointed. Bonaparte found his plans of escape foiled by the British fleet. After several days of agonized indecision, he left for Plymouth on the British warship *Bellerophon*. He would later depart on the *Northumberland* for exile and death on St Helena.

On 9 July, Louis XVIII had announced the names of his new government. Naturally, Talleyrand was President of the Council and Minister of Foreign Affairs. Baron Louis was again at Finance, and Fouché at the Police. Jaucourt had the Navy, in place of Beugnot. Marshal Gouvion Saint-Cyr was Minister of War, in place of Clarke. Dambray was dismissed as Chancellor, in favour of Pasquier, who was also interim Interior Minister. Yet Talleyrand's success in removing those who had sided with the King, or who, like Beugnot, were sympathetic to him, was more than outweighed by other setbacks. The Prince had hoped that Pozzo would take the Interior, but the latter decided, after consulting the Tsar, to stay in Russia's service. Still more embarrassing, the duc de Richelieu, also in Russian service as governor of Odessa but equally a member of the royal court by right of his birth, was actually announced as Minister for the Maison du Roi. But Richelieu had not even been consulted. On the basis of earlier conversations in Frankfurt, Talleyrand had simply assumed that he would accept. He misjudged his man. Contrary to what the Prince would later suggest, Richelieu was not playing a devious game, waiting to step into Talleyrand's own shoes. But he did not want a post that required intimacy with a King for whose character he always felt a certain antipathy, nor was he prepared to be part of a government that included Fouché, for whom he felt nothing but repulsion. The rift between Talleyrand and Richelieu was widened by the former's insulting letter of reply to Richelieu's refusal, where Talleyrand accused him of betraying his great name and failing in his patriotic duty.[27]

Talleyrand had been desperate to include Pozzo and Richelieu in his government because he was aware, though few others yet were, that the Tsar was intent on having his revenge for the humiliations of Vienna. Neither Pozzo nor Richelieu might, in practice, have been able to assuage Alexander, but their refusal to serve made the task of repairing relations even more difficult.

Then there remained the problem of Fouché. No one was keen to serve as his *préfet de police*, for understandable reasons. Eventually, on Baron Louis's recommendation, Talleyrand decided on the young Élie Decazes, a relation of Louis's by marriage. When Talleyrand actually met him, he thought that he resembled a hairdresser, though 'a good-looking lad'.[28] Decazes's boyish charm soon won him the King's favour. In the short run, this was useful to Talleyrand. In the longer term, however, it was a curse. From the start, the prospects for Talleyrand's ministry looked bleak.

His colleagues would place a large share of the responsibility for its failure on the Prince himself. Pasquier was convinced that Talleyrand's obsession with Dorothée was to blame. As a result, during the two months and seventeen days of his government, Talleyrand 'constantly showed himself not up to his situation and did not even appear to understand it'.[29] Molé echoes the criticism.[30] Talleyrand was undoubtedly tired, emotionally distracted, uncertain of how to proceed in the face of enormous obstacles. But it is Guizot, who, unlike either Pasquier or Molé, actually knew what it is to lead a recognizably modern government competently, whose criticism carries most weight:

> In anything other than a crisis or a Congress, [Talleyrand] was neither shrewd nor effective. Courtier and diplomat, not a man of government,

and least of all of a free government, he excelled in operating through conversation, through charm, through the clever use of social relations, on isolated individuals. But authority of character, fecundity of intellect, urgency of resolution, power of speech, intelligent sympathy for general ideas and public passions, all these great means of acting on men collectively, he completely lacked. Nor did he have the taste for, or the habit of, regular and sustained work, another condition for government in domestic affairs. . .A politician without scruples, indifferent to the means and almost to the ends, provided that they involved a degree of personal success, bolder in his views than he was deep, coldly courageous in danger, suitable for great affairs under an absolute government, but whom the open air and the daylight of liberty did not suit at all, he found himself out of his element and incapable of action.[31]

Talleyrand was better than that, even in 1815. Yet Guizot's analysis contains enough truth to explain, in part at least, why the Prince's only ministry was such a disappointment.

Talleyrand was old-fashioned in his political methods. As in earlier years, he rose late, he did business late, he opened his house late to high society and the diplomatic corps. People like Molé would come and visit him to discuss business at midnight. Then the company sat down to cards, not to break up until four or five o'clock in the morning.[32] The round of receptions and dinners, the *salons* and the banter, had, as they had always had, a serious purpose. But nowadays, as Pasquier noted, the foreign ambassadors spoke more among themselves than with their host or with his French guests. The British and Austrians were friendly; the Prussians and the Russians, with the partial exception of Pozzo, were hostile.[33] The truth was that France was now totally isolated and had no bargaining power. It was an unenviable position for someone like the Prince, who had savoured so recently the taste of diplomatic triumphs.

Talleyrand's political ideas and programme were, by contrast, far from old-fashioned. Indeed, if anything, they were too progressive for his own and for his colleagues' good. He had got his way in the actual ordering of government: all serious business was done in a 'Council of Ministers' – 'Council Number One', as he called it – while a 'Private Council' was established to salvage, in part at least, the vanities of the Bourbon princes.[34] Talleyrand's attention was presently focused on amendments to the Charte, in order to create a constitutional monarchy more on the lines obtaining in Britain. So he fought and won a fierce battle with the King to extend the freedom of the press. He tried to alter the provision whereby the proposal of legislation was reserved to the monarch. He also overcame Louis XVIII's tenacious resistance to making the Upper Chamber hereditary, the lines of argument in this matter very much recalling those of the early days of the Revolution, when Talleyrand had regarded having the French equivalent of the House of Lords as a solid guarantee against both royal autocracy and the demagogues. (The allies now insisted on this, too, as a guarantee of political stability.[35]) The Chamber was, in practice, packed by Talleyrand and his ministers with their nominees, who were approved by the King. At the last moment, it was pointed out to the Prince at a reception he attended that they had omitted to add the King's former favourite, the comte de Blacas, and another of his friends, the duc de La Châtre. Rather than wake Louis, it was decided simply to publish the names in *Le Moniteur* and inform the King later.[36]

One reason why Talleyrand was so keen to have a pliant House of Peers was because he did not yet know the outcome of the forthcoming elections for the body that would succeed the dissolved imperial Corps législatif. This raised the question of the electoral rules to be applied. Here Talleyrand showed his lack of grasp of the kind of managed democracy with which the politicians under the Restoration, and in later years, had to cope. He came up with an unsatisfactory compromise. He kept the system of electoral colleges and then added to their members by government nomination. But at the same time he lowered the age thresholds and property requirements for electors and deputies, and increased the number of deputies by around a third. The ultimate aim, as Talleyrand made clear to one of the electoral college presidents, was 'to avoid the election of pure royalists as much as, or more than, Jacobins', and to promote instead 'Constitutionalists'.[37]

But this was to prove a vain hope. First of all, the government's authority was simply too weak. The new *préfets*, upon whom the exertion of influence rested, found themselves humiliated by the occupying forces: for instance, Talleyrand's cousin, Alexandre de Talleyrand, was arrested initially by the Prussians and then by the Bavarians. On top of this, in the Midi, where a Bourbon-sponsored counter-revolution expressed itself in pogroms of Protestants and the murder of Bonapartists, the central government's agents had little or no control.[38] But, second – and this was something that Talleyrand and his fellow liberals in Paris simply could not grasp – there was a wave of royalist sentiment in the provinces which found powerful expression in the results. Enthusiasm was at a premium because, contrary to Talleyrand's advice, the King had earlier insisted that deputies should serve without a salary; as a matter of honour, their service should be freely given. Talleyrand's reply – 'Free. . . free. . . Yes, Sire; but it will be very expensive' – now proved all too perceptive.[39] Even Louis XVIII would christen it '*la Chambre introuvable*' ('the impossible Chamber'); and if it seemed impossible to the King, it must certainly be unmanageable by Talleyrand.[40]

Once the political complexion of the new Chamber was known, it became evident that the days of the Talleyrand ministry were numbered. Talleyrand himself made little or no effort to woo the deputies. The Prince was finally persuaded to invite one of their leaders, Lainé, to dinner, but only as part of a large diplomatic gathering in which he was dwarfed by the formality of sashes and decorations.[41] Talleyrand still believed, however, that it might be possible to remain in power if he sacrificed Fouché, a figure even more odious to the royalists than himself. In any case, it was worth trying; and removing Fouché, whom he had always detested, would be a pleasure in itself.

Fouché's behaviour had confirmed the fears of all those who had resisted his inclusion. Having obtained his appointment as the representative of a provisional government committed to an amnesty and a Constitution, he now sought to secure his position by sacrificing his associates and by buying favour with reactionary royalists. In accordance with the Declaration of Cambrai, Talleyrand had wanted to postpone drawing up a list of those against whom criminal proceedings for treason would be undertaken until the two Chambers had met. But Fouché unexpectedly produced a list of more than a hundred names, far more than envisaged. Talleyrand fought the proposal in the council, and the list was reduced to fifty-seven, nineteen of whom would go before military tribunals or assizes, the rest to be tried in localities outside Paris. The names of Marshal Ney and General de La

Bédoyère were at the top of the list of those in the first category: both would be executed.[42] Fouché also drew up a long report for the King, suggesting that the country was in the grip of Jacobin plotting against the monarchy. He insisted on reading it out in the council, while his fellow ministers remained in embarrassed silence and Talleyrand from time to time shrugged. At the Prince's orders, it was not published in *Le Moniteur*, but Fouché himself leaked it to the press, to the King's and the government's annoyance.[43]

An early attempt by Talleyrand to secure the Police Minister's dismissal was foiled by Wellington.[44] But Talleyrand was by now determined not only that Fouché should leave the government, but that he should also leave the country. The Prince returned to the charge in his best theatrical manner.

One day, in his office, where several ministers, including Fouché, had assembled prior to a meeting of the council, Talleyrand addressed Pasquier: 'You know, M. Pasquier, that we have in our gift – and the appointment must be made urgently – one of the finest posts possible.'

Pasquier: 'And which is that?'

Talleyrand: 'That of the King's Minister to the United States, of course. In the present state of Europe, in this general upheaval, I do not know of any that is more desirable. Generous conditions, lots of respect, complete peace and quiet, an opportunity to observe and study that great country, so completely new, yet one that already occupies an important place in the world. What could be better than that?'

Then, turning to Vitrolles and warming to his theme: 'It is such a fine country. . .I have known it. I have lived there. There are rivers such as we do not know – the Potomac, for example. Nothing is more beautiful than the Potomac! And then those magnificent forests, full of trees of the sort that we here have only a few examples on display. . . What are they called?'

'Daturas,' interjected Vitrolles.

'That's right! Forests of daturas!'

Fouché appeared to take no notice. But he grasped the significance of the daturas. After all, had he himself not once urged Napoleon to do what was best for France and the Bourbons by going into exile in America?[45] In fact, Fouché was merely sent as ambassador to Saxony, the first step to exile and disgrace.

Talleyrand tried to take maximum credit for getting rid of Fouché, both with the Bourbon princes and with the royalist majority assembling in the Chamber – to no avail. When the latter were told of the decision, they replied: 'Ah! Excellent, the King has dismissed Fouché; but when will he dismiss the other one?' No one needed to ask who 'the other one' was. In these circumstances, the government as a whole understood that it needed the public support of the King in order to maintain any credibility.[46] The occasion for seeking that support was the crisis in which negotiations with the allies were now plunged.

The occupying powers all wanted to exact punishment, although in different degrees. In Austria, Stadion, though not Metternich, was keen to see a dismemberment of France. So, in Britain, was the Prince Regent, if not Castlereagh and Wellington – though they too thought that France should pay a steep price. The Netherlands wanted territory. The most outspoken advocates of a harsh policy, however, were the Prussians, who wanted the maximum possible territorial loss and full payment by France of the cost of the war and of Napoleon's earlier plundering.[47] The Prussian soldiers' depredations reinforced their government's claims. Some of Talleyrand's own property was among the assets they seized.[48] Blücher even planned to dynamite the Pont d'Iéna, whose name recalled the earlier Prussian defeat. Talleyrand had the King quickly rename it the Pont des Invalides; but even then the catastrophe was barely avoided. Subsequently, Talleyrand circulated the story that Louis XVIII had threatened to go and be blown up with it, which no one who knew the King believed.[49]

French emotions were particularly outraged by the demand that the works of art pillaged by Napoleon should all be restored to the countries he had looted. Talleyrand – who had boasted how he had saved these works in 1814 – shared the national outrage. There ensued a furious row between him and Wellington over dinner on the matter. But the duke was brutally dismissive of all his objections.[50]

Despite this setback, Talleyrand still looked to Wellington for some amelioration of the harsh terms demanded. But he could get nowhere with Russia. His colleagues now understood that the cost of having Talleyrand at the head of the government was the Tsar's unremitting hostility to French approaches.[51] Yet who was there to replace the

Prince? None of his colleagues had the standing to do so. The theory of a collectively responsible ministry, upon which Talleyrand had insisted, must in these circumstances be followed in practice. If Talleyrand went, all the ministers would go too.

In truth, the government looked in poor shape, even after the belated dismissal of Fouché. Vitrolles, whose presence was tolerated by Talleyrand, acted as a spy and propagandist for Monsieur. Talleyrand and Baron Louis had fallen out as a result of an angry dispute about finance, in which it seems the Prince's personal involvement with the financier Ouvrard was at least as important as the merits of the measures.[52] Decazes was surreptitiously pursuing his own interests with the King, irrespective of those of the government, and would emerge the long-term victor in the crisis. As Talleyrand confessed to the other ministers over dinner at Jaucourt's house, it was only a matter of time before they were dismissed. And he wrote much the same on the eve of the government's fall to the duchesse de Courlande.[53]

It was the external crisis that most preoccupied the Prince himself. He had been excluded from substantive discussion with the occupying powers. The justification for leaving France to sort out its own problems, which he had put into the mouth of Louis XVIII at the end of July, had fallen on deaf ears. Then had come the non-negotiable demands for return of the works of art. He deployed the argument, in a note of 19 September, that since the recent war had been fought against Bonaparte and for Bourbon France it was unjust to demand changes in the terms of the Treaty of Paris of 1814. His logic was rejected. The allies were not going to be lectured by him about international law – in this case the limits of the 'rights of conquest' – as they had at Vienna on the claims of 'legitimacy' and 'public law'.

Then, on 20 September, they sent a draft treaty containing the precise terms that they intended to impose. Talleyrand, in fact, seems to have learned the contents several days earlier. If the Prussians had had their way, the terms would have been worse, but they were deeply humiliating, all the same, and were based on a system of 'guarantees' against any further trouble from France. In the previous year, Talleyrand had secured for France the territories it held in 1792, with some additions. Now France was restricted to its extent of 1790, and with some losses. The Netherlands received areas that had previously belonged to Austrian Belgium. The King of Sardinia was to have the whole of Savoy. Other fortresses and areas on the German border – France's part of the coal-rich Saar, the fortress of Landau – were lost. The fortress of Huningue was to be permanently demolished. Six hundred million francs of war indemnities were to be paid. On top of that, 200 million francs would go towards building fortresses along the borders of France, to hem it in. Worst of all, northern and eastern France would be occupied by an army of 150,000 troops, at French expense, for a period of seven years.

One can see why Talleyrand, over dinner with the other ministers on the eve of the government's fall, described these conditions as 'mad'. But, true to form, he also saw their very harshness as a political opportunity. He would draw up a protest, refusing such an agreement, and demand that the King issue it in the form of a public statement of confidence in Talleyrand's negotiating stance. If the King agreed, the government was reinforced. If he refused, Talleyrand believed that outraged public opinion would soon sweep the outgoing ministry back into office.[54]

Talleyrand's name – along with those of Dalberg and Louis – appears on a note of 21 September responding to the ultimatum. It re-states the French case for no change from the terms of the Treaty of Paris, but agrees in principle the cession of territories not part of 'old France', an indemnity and the occupation. The allies then responded on 22 September, rejecting the French protest.[55]

But by then the Prince had ceased be President of the Council. The accounts of how, and even precisely when, he resigned are contradictory.[56] Louis XVIII thought that Talleyrand had not been expecting his resignation to be accepted, and rejoiced in the thought that he had played a trick on his minister. Talleyrand also later considered that he had fallen into a trap, once Richelieu quickly emerged to take over his functions. But when he went to see the King he was already expecting that he would lose his post. What he was also expecting, however, was that he would be quickly recalled. Yet Napoleon's prediction of Talleyrand's fate turned out to be right: '[The Bourbons] will drive him out when they no longer have need of him.'[57] And they did not intend to have him back.

15

Opposition and Vindication

⌐⌐

TALLEYRAND MAY HAVE been surprised at the way in which Louis XVIII had accepted his government's resignation. But he was not, in the immediate aftermath at least, very disturbed. He asked the ultra-royalist Vitrolles, in a spirit of curiosity, how he would have been received by the new Chamber – the '*Chambre introuvable*' – if he had ever had to face it.

Vitrolles answered: 'It is difficult to guess, but I do not think it would have been impossible for our deputies, if you had sacrificed to their idols.'

Charles-Maurice, in mock indignation, exclaimed: 'Do you take me for a pagan?'

'Certainly not, *Monseigneur*,' said Vitrolles with emphasis, alluding to the Prince's former episcopal status, 'but it would require you to be Catholic, Apostolic and Roman.'

Talleyrand enjoyed the allusions, and the conversation moved on to other matters.[1] He could afford to be relaxed for several reasons. First, and not least important, he was generously compensated by being appointed Grand Chambellan, the most senior officer of the royal court and a position that he had once held under Napoleon. The symbolic significance was dwarfed by the position's financial importance, because it came with a salary of 100,000 francs: on top of that, the Prince would receive 20,000 francs as a Minister of State.

Second, Talleyrand expected very soon to be recalled. As his question to Vitrolles betrays, he had not given up on reaching an accommodation with the ultras; his subsequent conduct confirms this. He had successfully persuaded his colleagues that the collective responsibility of the outgoing ministry should continue to apply. As in the British party system, which he explicitly sought to follow, those who had supported certain principles in government would also remain together in opposition. This, of course, usefully reduced the pool of talent on which the new ministry could draw. Talleyrand was, above all, convinced that he was indispensable. In this assumption he was not obviously mistaken. The British and Austrians certainly wanted him back. Wellington, in particular, spoke publicly of Talleyrand's indispensability and made a show of dining at the rue Saint-Florentin twice a week. But his and Metternich's influence was more than countered by the Tsar's obsessive hostility, now skilfully propagated by his agent Pozzo di Borgo.

In any case, Talleyrand had seriously misjudged Louis XVIII. The King was resolved to make his former Chief Minister suffer for the indignities of constitutionalism that he had earlier inflicted on him. Louis's pride and pettiness would henceforth constitute an insuperable barrier to Talleyrand's return. It was years before the Prince would finally accept the fact. But as the months passed, it did become clear to him that Richelieu would remain in place, unless something serious was done to dislodge him. Talleyrand's mood and tactics changed accordingly.[2]

He began a sustained verbal assault on his successor, who was in some respects an easy target. Richelieu did not entertain; he had odd and unbecoming mannerisms; he no longer knew Paris society; he had none of Talleyrand's ability to direct the gossip of the *salons*. But it was Richelieu's closeness to Russia that was the most frequent subject of the Prince's attacks. Richelieu, he sarcastically observed, was a good choice to lead the government, as being the Frenchman 'who best knows the Crimea'.[3] The government of France, he claimed, was now altogether in the hands of the Tsar. Charles de Rémusat was present when Talleyrand delivered himself of a tirade on these lines before Mme de Rémusat's guests. The Prince concluded by announcing starkly: 'The country no longer exists.' Charles de Rémusat wept to hear it.[4] Talleyrand's criticisms certainly undermined the government.[5] But they could not in the end destroy it, because Louis XVIII held firm.

Moreover, the Prince was only half right. Although the new ministry was heavily influenced by Russia, Richelieu proved an effective defender of French interests in the painful diplomatic negotiations that ensued. As on other occasions, Talleyrand was thus forced to rewrite history. The response he had given to the allies before his departure, though rhetorically strong, had, in truth, already conceded that the terms of the previous Treaty of Paris would have to be substantially revised to France's loss. Whether Richelieu, with his Russian connections, secured a better final settlement than Talleyrand, with his British and Austrian ones, would have done is debatable. But Richelieu's negotiation was skilful and resolute; and, in the dire circumstances that prevailed, he was reasonably successful. The terms of the Second Treaty of Paris of 20 November 1815 could have been worse. Moreover, three years later at the Congress of Aix-la-Chapelle he achieved an end to the allied occupation of France, two years earlier than envisaged. It was, in its way, a diplomatic triumph.[6] But the Prince never allowed any doubts to creep into his polemic. He maintained that he would never have signed such a peace in the first place. He was still making the point as ambassador in London more than a decade later.[7]

Talleyrand's verbal assaults on Richelieu became ever more embarrassing for the government. But his lack of self-restraint also worried his friends. Having heard one of these outbursts over dinner, Wellington wondered whether the Prince had taken leave of his senses.[8] Nor did events assist his campaign. The dissolution of the old Chamber of Deputies and the election of a more malleable one greatly consolidated the ministry.

Behind this manoeuvre, and increasingly behind the government itself, was Decazes, the Police Minister, who had now fully established himself as the King's favourite. He thus also became Talleyrand's *bête noire*, for whom Charles-Maurice's venom was even greater than that which he directed at Richelieu. Richelieu he could at least respect as a man of substance. For Decazes he felt nothing but contempt; he judged the favourite to be both 'self-satisfied and inadequate', as he hurtfully described him on one occasion to Louis XVIII.[9]

On 17 November 1816 the Prince made a scandalous scene after a dinner hosted by his friend, the British ambassador, Sir Charles Stuart. He appears to have been slightly drunk; but there was also calculation involved.[10] Talleyrand cornered Pasquier, who had been nominated as President of the new Chamber, and had thus to his former colleague's fury effectively thrown in his lot with the new ministry. Charles-Maurice sharply attacked the government's conduct. Pasquier tried to leave, but Talleyrand pursued him. He loudly vented his contempt for the Minister of Police, whom he denounced as a crook, and he expressed his disgust at anyone prepared to have dealings with him. Pasquier gave a short defensive reply and quickly left. But this could not be the end of the matter.

The Prince showed no remorse. His friends, indeed, circulated the scandal around the *salons*. It was immediately and correctly seen as a direct challenge to the authorities. The ultras thought that the Prince would either emerge as head of the government or be completely disgraced.[11] Richelieu, when he heard what had happened, was angry. Decazes was completely beside himself. The council met to discuss how to respond and various ways to signal the Prince's disgrace were debated. It was Molé who persuaded Richelieu that the appropriate course was for the King to suspend Talleyrand from his position as Grand Chambellan and ban him from the Tuileries. The Prince pretended to be astonished and sought to put the blame on Pasquier for distorting his remarks. But he must have known there were plenty of other witnesses to his behaviour.[12] He remained, in fact, quite brazen about the affair. He wrote to the King, again claiming that he had been misrepresented. The letter ended with a characteristic reminder of their previous close relations, observing that he was sure that Louis could read his 'bad writing' after so many years' experience. He adopted the same line of injured innocence to the Duke of Wellington.[13]

And disgrace was no novelty. He had worked his way back before. At the annual memorial mass for Louis XVI on 21 January 1817 at Saint-Denis, the Prince tried an old trick. He advanced to take his place in the choir of the cathedral as Grand Chambellan, as if he had not been suspended. But the master of ceremonies intervened and required him to withdraw. It was a public humiliation. But it was also a reminder to the court that he had no intention of leaving public life. On 28 February Talleyrand's return was authorized by the King. The following Sunday, he presented himself at the Tuileries and Louis conversed with him as if nothing had occurred.[14]

Despite his political setbacks, Talleyrand had much else for which to be thankful. The second Restoration enabled him to take advantage of many of the benefits he had briefly enjoyed under the first. He had skilfully repaired his finances by exploiting his influence. He had, for example, forced the *entrepreneur général* of the gambling houses of Paris to buy his country house at Saint-Brice for the inflated sum of 250,000 francs on pain of losing his position.[15] Talleyrand also liquidated some assets. In 1816 he sold the library that he had sent for that purpose to London in September 1814; it constituted 3,465 items, including manuscripts, incunables and Elzevirs, and it fetched more than £8,400. The following year he sold a fine collection of Dutch and Flemish masters for 320,000 francs.[16]

At Vienna, Charles-Maurice had managed to strike a deal with the Bourbon rulers of Naples, which was greatly to his advantage. He was financially rewarded for his efforts to have them restored to their kingdom, to the tune of 3.7 million francs if Barras is to be believed.[17] A more complicated matter was the negotiation of his relinquishment of the principality of Benevento. In the end, by a deal in which Ferdinand IV and the Pope were the other parties, Charles-Maurice was compensated with revenues equivalent to those he had surrendered. He also received from Ferdinand a dukedom of the Kingdom of the Two Sicilies. It was agreed, in December 1817, that the Prince's title should be 'duca de Dino', the title referring to a tiny and obscure island off the coast of Calabria. Talleyrand was able to pass on the duchy to whomsoever he chose, and he immediately did so to the benefit of his nephew Edmond. Thus Dorothée acquired the title by which she is historically known, duchesse de Dino.[18]

As for the Prince himself, he had been appointed by edict of Louis XVIII, on 6 December 1814, 'prince de Talleyrand' in place of the already politically embarrassing 'prince de Bénévent'. In 1817 he also received a dukedom from the king, but it was as 'prince de Talleyrand' that he would be known for the rest of his life. The previous year, he had ordered the inscription in big gold letters, 'Hôtel Talleyrand', to be placed at the front of his house in the rue Saint-Florentin.[19] Under Charles X, the advance of Talleyrand's dynasty continued. In February 1829 the Prince's great-nephew, Louis, married the immensely rich aristocratic heiress Alix de Montmorency. The following month Louis was made duc de Valençay, a title that Charles-Maurice had sought in vain from Louis XVIII.

Even the Prince's disfavour with the government after the scene at the British residence had some compensations. For example, it greatly increased his attractions in the eyes of the ultras. The comtesse de Boigne was surprised, in the spring of 1818, to witness Talleyrand being greeted with acclaim by hard-line royalists at a ball organized by Wellington. The crowd parted in front of him as he was led to meet the comte d'Artois and the duc de Berry, who both warmly shook his hand.[20] Talleyrand could not bring with him a large political following: it was estimated that he had, perhaps, twelve supporters in the Upper and just four or five in the Lower House.[21] But he contributed a great name and both real and imagined international connections.

Meanwhile, the Russians, refusing to forget his role at Vienna and distrustful of his links with Britain, regarded the Prince as the source of all political intrigues. Thus in April 1817 Pozzo, who worked against his old collaborator with greater effectiveness than did Talleyrand's internal enemies, worried that the ultras would 'gain control of the King [and] recall Talleyrand to assist them', from which would emerge 'the most monstrous coalition'.[22] The following month, Pozzo reproached Monsieur to his face with aiming to bring in a government led by Talleyrand. D'Artois uneasily rejected the suggestion.[23] In October Pozzo concentrated on separating the Prince from his old allies, such as Molé and Pasquier. But in December he was still fretting about Talleyrand, Vitrolles and those around Monsieur, who were intriguing 'in a most criminal and shameful fashion'.[24]

Monsieur even sought to involve Talleyrand as his representative to the allies in the matter of the 'Secret Note'. Drafted by Vitrolles, it was intended to secure a continuation of the occupation by elaborating upon threats to the Bourbon régime. But the Prince craftily kept his distance from this mad scheme, which lost Vitrolles his government post.[25] At the same time, he continued to trade on his British links as a means of embarrassing the government. The British ambassador served as a useful fool in this strategy; on one occasion at a dinner in Talleyrand's house he impertinently called for a reconciliation between the government and the ultras in the interests of European stability.[26]

There is no need to search for any consistency, let alone any idealism, in Talleyrand's alliance with the ultra opposition during these years. It was a response to his exclusion from influence, which required joining forces with the alternative power source that was Monsieur. The tactic was transparent – too transparent for some like Charles de Rémusat, who incurred the Prince's displeasure for criticizing it.[27]

Talleyrand's reconciliation with his old royalist enemies was pursued on a social as well as a political level. This involved confronting some delicate issues. The family of the duc d'Enghien had more reason than most to dislike Napoleon's former Foreign Minister. D'Enghien's uncle, the prince de Condé, probably never received Talleyrand; but, then, he was completely senile, and so the snub could be ignored. On Condé's death, the elderly duc de Bourbon, d'Enghien's father, returned to France. Bad relations with him were potentially more embarrassing.

It was the wife of Caulaincourt, the duchesse de Vicence, anxious to restore her husband's reputation, who gave Charles-Maurice the idea of how to achieve his own reconciliation with the family. She asked Talleyrand's advice about whether she should seek the intercession on Caulaincourt's behalf of the duc de Bourbon's mistress. This last, a former British prostitute born plain Sophie Dawes, now enjoyed the title of baronne de Feuchères through a marriage of convenience. Talleyrand counselled the duchesse de Vicence against any such approach; but he then made it himself, though in a more complex manner.[28]

To her elderly lover's dismay, Mme de Feuchères had been banned from court after the baron de Feuchères tired of the arrangement and denounced her infidelities. Talleyrand now put his plan into effect. He would approach the duc d'Orléans to have Sophie recalled to the Tuileries. She, in exchange, would persuade the duc de Bourbon, who had no heirs, to leave his enormous inheritance to the duc d'Aumale, d'Orléans's fourth son. She would also ensure a formal reconciliation between Talleyrand and Bourbon. The scheme was entirely successful. The baronne returned to court. The Prince was invited to dine with the duc. And when the latter died, under mysterious circumstances in August 1830, his inheritance served to fill the coffers of the newly installed royal family of France. The gratitude that Louis-Philippe showed towards Charles-Maurice at the start of his reign is thus all the more understandable. The business demonstrates, if proof were needed, that Talleyrand had lost none of his manipulative skill.[29]

During these years the Prince remained under surveillance by the authorities. His private letters were opened and shown to Louis XVIII, who commented maliciously on what they showed of Talleyrand's 'wounded vanity' and 'embittered ambition'.[30] The Prince was also spied upon by police agents, who reported back to Decazes. But they were no match for him, repeating almost verbatim the messages he wanted to have conveyed – such as his improbable desire to live a secluded life away from Paris. On occasion, he had to endure some awkwardness. At Bourbon-l'Archambault, the local mayor was rude to him; but it was the mayor who then suffered a rebuke from Decazes. Moreover, Charles-Maurice had an unnerving habit of winning over those appointed to watch him, by flattering them and inviting them to dinner. The head of the local *gendarmerie* at Valençay had to be removed altogether, because he became a devotee and thus, in the government's eyes, a liability.[31]

The opportunity for a political comeback seemed to present itself in 1819. Richelieu's success at Aix-la-Chapelle had, paradoxically, made it easier to attack his ministry now that external issues had been resolved.[32] Richelieu himself was tired of government, and tired too of Decazes, who had surpassed him in influence with the King. Talleyrand, in these circumstances, suddenly found pleasant words to utter about the Minister of Police. At the end of December 1818 there was even talk of a Talleyrand–Decazes ministry.[33] The main obstacle remained Louis XVIII. The King protested to Richelieu, who wanted to resign: 'Consider how you are reducing me to the deplorable extremity of having recourse to M. de Talleyrand, whom I neither like nor respect.'[34]

The Prince drew up lists of potential ministers to serve in the government he hoped to head. It would be a ministry of all the talents, or at least of all the factions and political colours – '*en macédoine*' as he put it.[35] Instead, however, on Richelieu's departure, after a brief period when General Dessole was formally President of the Council, Louis chose his favourite Decazes to head the new government. And Decazes had no intention – now or at any other time – of saddling himself with Talleyrand.[36]

Power would remain beyond Talleyrand's reach. But the political circumstances of France, and the nature of the Prince's opposition to the government, were about to change. The assassination of the duc de Berry on 13 February 1820 marked the beginning of a fierce ultra reaction. It swept Decazes out of office, to be succeeded as President of the Council by Richelieu. He, in turn, made way for Villèle in December 1821.[37] By then, Talleyrand had moved firmly away from alliance with the ultras into the liberal camp. He also re-established his ties with the house of Orléans and those who served its cause.

On 24 July 1821 Talleyrand spoke in the Chamber of Peers against the continued censorship of the press, on which the right had insisted the previous year, the duc de Berry's assassination being connected by the ultras with left-wing press attacks. Boldly, at this time of reaction, Talleyrand looked back to the Revolution to illustrate his contention that censorship was at odds with the spirit of the age:

> The Constituent Assembly was the interpreter [of the times] when it proclaimed freedom of religion, equality before the law, individual liberty, the law of jurisdiction (no one can be withdrawn from his natural judges), the liberty of the press. It was not in agreement with the times when it instituted a single chamber, when it abolished the royal assent, when it persecuted conscience. . .Let us take as certain that what is wanted, what is proclaimed as good and useful by all the enlightened men of a country, without variation during a succession of years, is a necessity of the times. Such, Messieurs, is the freedom of the press.[38]

The following February, Talleyrand again addressed his fellow peers on the same theme in response to a fresh initiative of the government to muffle press criticism. His contribution was brief, but once more it created a public stir. This time he looked back to pre-Revolutionary liberalism and quoted Malesherbes, who had challenged writers to tell him if his administration was failing in any respect. The Prince concluded that today he was voting with Malesherbes against the proposed law.[39]

The effectiveness of Talleyrand's opposition to the government increasingly endeared him to the younger generation of moderate liberals, known because of the purity of their principles, their intelligence and a certain unworldliness – which the Prince himself was not above mocking – as the 'Doctrinaires'. Talleyrand used to say that the Doctrinaires were 'people who live between the courtyard and the garden: they never see what is happening in the street'.[40] He would continue to consider them somewhat emotionally inadequate. Thus under the July Monarchy when the Doctrinaires formed the core of the political élite, he wrote to Victor de Broglie, then President of the Council, seeking a favour for the friend of a friend. He joked: 'You see that I have still some way to go before introducing all the coldness of *la Doctrine* into my social relations.'[41] The group's most notable members, apart from Broglie, were Guizot, Beugnot, Prosper de Barante and Pierre Royer-Collard.[42] The last of these became Talleyrand's neighbour at Valençay in 1822, having inherited the estate of Châteauvieux. Royer-Collard had been an agent for Louis XVIII during the latter's exile, and though politically liberal was a devout Catholic of rigorous Jansenist tendencies. He was a philosopher, austere and somewhat priggish, and he had no wish at all to become friendly with Talleyrand. When the Prince suggested that he and the duchesse de Dino pay a visit, Royer-Collard tried to avoid the meeting, claiming that his wife was indisposed. But Talleyrand and Dorothée came all the same. The journey, though short, was unpleasant and the roads bad. Talleyrand disarmed his unwelcoming host by noting, with obvious ambiguity: 'Monsieur, the approaches here are difficult.'[43] To Royer-Collard's surprise, he found himself becoming firm friends with Charles-Maurice and a devotee of Dorothée, both of whom reciprocated his affection.

The liberal opposition's hopes of inflicting a fatal blow against the government rose once more, as events in Spain, where Ferdinand VII was locked in conflict with his enemies, resulted in ultra demands for military intervention. The project was announced in the speech from the throne at the start of 1823. The French liberals looked forward eagerly to military disaster. Marshal Soult and Talleyrand – now once again close to the house of Orléans – emerged as the main political opponents of the campaign.[44]

The Prince prepared a speech against the Spanish War to deliver in the debate held in the Chamber on 3 February 1823. In this, he posed as a man of principle and statesman of experience, recalling how he had (allegedly) sought to dissuade Napoleon from invading Spain. 'Disgrace was the price of my sincerity,' he added.[45] It was all too much for Chateaubriand, now Foreign Minister: 'When the peddler of these calm assertions gets down from the tribune and goes and sits impassively in his place, you follow him with your eyes, suspended between a sort of horror and a sort of admiration. You wonder if this man has not received an authority from nature to refashion or to obliterate the truth.'[46]

Like other observations from Chateaubriand, this is as unreliable as it is memorable. Talleyrand's speech was not in fact delivered at all, for lack of time; so Chateaubriand could not have heard it; it was printed and circulated later. But in any case, the government's policy was vindicated in the only way that mattered, by victory for the French army. The liberal opposition's hopes were crushed, and at the succeeding elections its candidates were trounced. Talleyrand's prospects disappeared in the defeat.

On top of that, the Prince soon found himself facing other problems with echoes from his past. In October that year, Savary published extracts from his memoirs relating to the death of the duc d'Enghien. Written in answer to attacks from the royalist press, the result was to place Talleyrand in the historical and political dock.

The Prince's general rule in dealing with slanderous accusations was to ignore them. He used to liken himself to 'an old umbrella on which it has rained for forty years', adding: 'What do a few more drops matter to me?'[47] But the question of his role in the death of the duc d'Enghien went to the heart of his standing in French society. Urged on by Royer-Collard, who, of course, knew nothing of the truth, Talleyrand returned precipitately from Valençay to Paris to answer the charges. In a long letter to Louis XVIII he demanded that these be heard before the Chamber of Peers. The gamble paid off. The King had no wish to destabilize France by opening up old wounds. He replied through Villèle, reassuring Talleyrand and imposing silence in the matter. Savary was banned from the Tuileries as a sign of royal displeasure.[48]

The comtesse de Boigne remarked on Talleyrand's adroitness in defeating Savary, adding: 'M. de Talleyrand has come out of this crucible absolutely purified in the eyes of contemporaries.'[49] As for the Prince himself, he took a realistic, not to say cynical, view of public opinion. He explained to Dalberg: 'The frivolity of the French means that the duc de Rovigo could publish ten works without being read in any of Paris's reading rooms. People want to hear nothing more of the business.'[50]

Talleyrand owed Louis XVIII a considerable debt for the King's attitude in this difficult matter, but there is no evidence that he felt it. The two men had long been completely estranged. When public events brought Louis and his Grand Chambellan together, they rarely spoke, and when they did so, there was as likely as not to be an exchange of barbs. It is difficult to believe that even Talleyrand was as insolent as the anecdotes suggest; but, then, he never had any objection to subsequent elaboration of his *bons mots*. On one occasion, the King is said to have commented upon the princesse de Talleyrand's unwelcome return from London to Paris. Talleyrand replied: 'That is quite true, Sire: I too had to have my 20th of March.' Similarly, after publication of Talleyrand's speech attacking the war in Spain, the King dropped the heaviest of hints that he should go into semi-disgrace away from Paris. Louis pointedly asked him how far exactly Valençay was from the capital. The Prince apparently replied: 'Sire, I do not know exactly; but it must be about the same distance as from Paris to Ghent.'[51]

Towards the end of his life, Talleyrand enjoyed telling anecdotes about Louis XVIII, particularly ones relating to the King's absurd concern for formality. The Prince recalled how Louis had once remarked to him that of 30 million Frenchmen he, the King, alone knew the correct way to don and doff his hat.[52]

Talleyrand, too, shared, albeit with more grace and self-awareness, the same attachment to form. He took pride in fulfilling his official duty. During the late summer of 1824, as Louis lay being eaten up by gangrene, he was attended without remit by his Grand Chambellan. The Prince was now seventy years old and the long, sleepless vigils exhausted him. Then, after the old King finally expired, there were the festivities attached to the accession of the former comte d'Artois as Charles X. These culminated in the magnificent ceremony of coronation at Saint-Denis the following May. Dorothée was alarmed about the strain of it all upon his health.[53]

Yet the death of Louis XVIII was also a relief. Talleyrand preferred the new monarch as a man, despite having no illusions about Charles's suitability to be King of France.[54] He knew, at least, that he was unlikely to fall victim to that petty vengefulness that was Louis XVIII's characteristic vice, and which prompted the Prince to refer to him as 'Le Roi nichard' ('The King who plays jokes'). Moreover, with Charles X on the throne life was simpler in another way: there was now no chance of Talleyrand playing a leading political role. With an ultra monarch, the ultra programme would be fulfilled by ultra politicians, not by liberals or renegade bishops. It seemed, indeed, as if the curtain had finally fallen on the Prince's long career; and, to judge by his behaviour, this made retirement easier to accept.

At the end of June 1825 Talleyrand departed for Bourbon-l'Archambault for his regular annual cure. But at the end of September he broke with tradition by embarking on a visit, via Geneva and Grenoble, to the Midi, accompanied by the duchesse de Dino, Countess Tyszkiewicz and others. On 28 October the party, which Talleyrand described as his 'little colony', arrived at Marseilles.[55] Dorothée was delighted by the effect on her uncle's health. He seemed ten years younger. He took exercise, enjoyed the sea air and even developed an appetite for breakfast. There were good libraries in the city and people read to him, which he much enjoyed. He also quickly became the focus of social attention. The *préfet* lent him his box at the theatre. The mayor arranged balls. The local *commandant* played cards. The *receveur général* turned out to be a great wit, whose malicious remarks about their mutual enemy Baron Louis caused Charles-Maurice particular delight. The 'colony' spent Christmas there and in mid-January went on to the resort of Hyères. This was pleasant enough, until Talleyrand found the mortality rate of the sick people who wintered there oppressive. He was back in Paris towards the end of March.[56]

The Prince had recently acquired from his wife the château of Pont-de-Sains, near today's Belgian frontier, having earlier made it over to her on their separation. It was now returned in exchange for a larger allowance. He decided to go there in June, accompanied by Dorothée and Montrond. Talleyrand used to divide his properties between those, like the house in the rue Saint-Florentin or the summer house called Le Petit-Andilly near Montmorency, that served for pleasure, and those that were expected to pay their way. Pont-de-Sains, like Valençay albeit on a much smaller scale, was definitely in the second category. Talleyrand had originally bought it from the banker Simons many years earlier as an investment. There was a busy iron forge there, its hammering a constant background that summer as Dorothée dreamed of nothing in particular, and Charles-Maurice concentrated on business. Pike could be caught in the pond,[57] one prize specimen being despatched years later by Charles-Maurice as a gift to Lord and Lady Holland.[58]

In August he was back at Valençay. The following month he received his friend Barante, who was greatly impressed: 'Here I am in this great château where everything is so magnificently hospitable, where wealth is spent in an aristocratic fashion – a château of which there is no longer (or not yet) another example in France. . .There are very rich furnishings, sculptures, paintings, engravings, a library of ten thousand volumes. . .everything one is told of the great houses of England.'[59]

Talleyrand was a *grand seigneur* by more than mere title. In the same spirit, he sought to improve the life of the inhabitants of Valençay. Every year on the feast of St Charles (4 November) each family received a new set of clothes for the winter.[60] It was a source of great delight when, in January 1826, he was appointed mayor of the town of Valençay. He immediately sought books about local government, so as to be sure that he was fulfilling his duties. He provided a new house for the *mairie*. He founded a girls' school to be run by nuns. He opened a free pharmacy. He paid for a new bell-tower for the church. He founded an alms house for the poor, also administered by the sisters, with a chapel attached dedicated to his spiritual patron, St Maurice. In the last year of his life the Prince had a family crypt built beneath it, where he is now buried.[61]

During the twenty years in which she came to know Valençay, the duchesse de Dino saw the life of the inhabitants transformed by the improvements her uncle effected.[62] Nor did he forget them in his extreme old age. When he was in London as ambassador, he took a close interest in developments in vaccination against smallpox, and he sent back samples of the latest vaccines to his long-time physician, Bourdois, insisting that some be used for the people of Valençay.[63] Two years before his death, the Prince was reluctantly prepared to forgo the celebration of his other patronal feast, that of St Maurice (22 September), in order to attend a meeting of the Conseil général of the *département* so as to obtain some new roads for his area of Berry. In this case, he hoped also to win for Louis, his great-nephew and the heir to Valençay, the gratitude and respect of the *pays* of which he would soon be the leading figure.[64]

By now, Louis's mother, the duchesse de Dino, had long been the effective mistress of Valençay. Yet she sometimes felt depressed by the gloomy vastness and formality of the château, and perhaps also by the constant presence of a man so much older than herself. In April 1828 she purchased in her own right the elegant château of Rochecotte, set in a beautiful nineteen-acre park, near Langeais. Writing to Barante, she admitted to 'a real passion for Rochecotte', because it was her own, because it was set in the most beautiful countryside, because it was so light, and because she 'could embellish it'.[65] In other words, because it was not Valençay.

Talleyrand seems to have felt no resentment at her decision. Indeed, he came to love Rochecotte almost as much as did its owner, praising its 'pure air. . .[and] superb view' in a letter to the Hollands.[66] In 1835 he described Rochecotte to another friend:

> Imagine that at this moment I have before my eyes a real garden of two leagues in width and four in length, watered by a great river, and surrounded by wooded hillsides, where, thanks to shelter from the north, spring appears three weeks earlier than in Paris, and where now all is greenery and blossom. There is, besides, one thing that makes me prefer Rochecotte to any other spot: it is that there I am not only with Mme de Dino, but *chez elle*, which is for me the greatest pleasure of all.[67]

Talleyrand was not, however, destined to spend the rest of his life in untroubled bucolic retirement. Yet again, his past caught up with him. In 1827 the traditional expiatory memorial mass for Louis XVI was celebrated a day early, on 20 January.[68] Talleyrand was there as always, in his capacity of Grand Chambellan. Leaving the basilica of Saint-Denis, the Prince walked ahead of the duc and duchesse d'Angoulême in order to show them to their carriage. Suddenly a man sprang out of the crowd and attacked him, slapping him so hard in the face that the Prince fell to the ground. It was Talleyrand's old enemy, Maubreuil. He then kicked him several times for good measure, before he was seized.[69] Talleyrand, badly shaken, was carried away to his house, where he suffered a double application of leeches. He survived both the attack and the remedy and was consoled by a stream of distinguished visitors. When asked about the episode later by Charles X, Talleyrand emphasized that it was 'a punch'.[70] Even at the age of seventy-two, it would not have been consonant with the Prince's honour to accept that he had been slapped.

He did all he could to avoid bringing Maubreuil to judicial retribution. Writing to Lord Holland shortly after the attack, he observed: 'This is not a medical bulletin. I am well, and I want to be well. The affair of my little assassination ['*mon petit assassinat*'] is over for me, and – if I can ensure it – for every one else too.'[71] To that end he testified, in manifest contradiction of the facts, that he had been at Saint-Denis in a private not an official capacity, so as to reduce the severity of the sentence. Maubreuil's own continued irrational behaviour was the main obstacle to leniency. In 1827, after an appeal and much legal wrangling, he was sentenced to two years' imprisonment and a fine of 200 francs.[72]

The Prince probably felt the financial blow that struck him soon afterwards far more sharply than Maubreuil's 'punch'. An economic crisis had affected Europe since 1825, and Talleyrand had been following its progress while on holiday in the Midi. By January 1826 he was predicting that the financial reverberations would shortly be at an end.[73] But his optimism proved premature. In 1828 he learned of the collapse of the banking house of Pierre-François Paravey, of which Dalberg was co-founder and in which Talleyrand had invested a sum that rumour put at 4 million francs.[74] At more or less the same time, he was struggling to cope with the debts accumulated by his spend-thrift nephew Edmond, who saw the inside of an English prison as a result. The Prince now faced a major crisis in his affairs.[75]

Initially, he hoped that there would be sufficient assets to meet the Paravey creditors' demands. But nothing went right.[76] The fact that on the eve of a new Revolution Talleyrand was in financial straits has a broader political significance. While it would be wrong to suggest that the Prince conceived a change of régime to repair his finances, it is also true that he needed a revival of his political fortunes in order to restore his financial position. He could not afford an idle retirement, despite his age and the fact that in 1829 he was seriously ill.[77] All this was bad news for the house of Bourbon.

In fact, the last of the French Bourbons was by now heading ever faster towards the brink. Arguably, the contradictions inherent in the Restoration settlement could never have been successfully overcome. The Charte was ambiguous as to the balance between the authority of the King and that of the two Chambers. The rights of the previous and current owners of confiscated lands were extraordinarily difficult to reconcile. Above all, the standing of the Catholic Church divided left from right and, to a large extent, Paris from the provinces. Catholicism's advance offered the best hope of extinguishing the doctrines of the Revolution. But the real and alleged influence of the Church, particularly of the Jesuits and of the lay Catholic organizations the Chevaliers de la Foi and the Congrégation, served as a rallying point for all those who feared a return to absolutism.

Charles X was the worst possible monarch to preside over such a confrontation. He had an inflexibly high view of royal authority, but he had no clear idea of how to use it. He was obsessed with the idea that his brother Louis had lost his throne and his head in the Revolution because he had not faced down his enemies. So he was in the habit of declaring that 'a King who is threatened has to choose between the throne and the scaffold'. Talleyrand, who had easy relations with the former comte d'Artois and sometimes played whist at the Tuileries, is said to have replied: 'Your Majesty forgets the post-chaise.'[78] If he did say that, it can hardly have endeared him to the King's ministers. Nor will another of his little witticisms. When someone spoke about the dangers facing the country, he replied, alluding to Villèle and his colleagues: 'Why should not these people save France? After all, geese saved the Capitol.'[79]

Talleyrand publicly opposed the Villèle government's more illiberal policies. In 1827 Royer-Collard and Chateaubriand joined forces to condemn a projected law to muzzle the press. But the Prince's response was no less memorable. Asked what he thought of the measure, he replied: 'I think that it is not French, because it is stupid.'[80] Nor, as a Gallican and a liberal, did Talleyrand have any sympathy with the Jesuits, whose return to France and involvement in education aroused great controversy. Alluding to the tradition

that the Society of Jesus introduced turkeys to France, he observed
that the latter were clearly the most grateful of animals: 'The Jesuits
once brought them to France, and now the turkeys are bringing
back the Jesuits.'[81]

From the time of the elections of November 1827, the government's parliamentary support was shattered, never to be restored.
Liberals, Doctrinaires and anti-government ultras dominated the
Chambers. Villèle resigned and the vicomte de Martignac emerged at
the head of a mildly left-of-centre government.[82] It never enjoyed the
confidence of the King, any internal coherence, or the support of a
solid parliamentary majority. Talleyrand, though, was anxious to come
in from the cold and made a determined effort to cooperate with
Martignac. He even entertained the ministers in his house and visited
their favoured *salons*.[83]

The Martignac compromise could not last long and the summer of
1829 saw its collapse. In August, the King appointed a reactionary
government in which his old friend, the prince de Polignac, emerged
as the dominant force.[84] In his memoirs, Talleyrand describes the
King's 'insane resolution' to appoint this new government as the
moment at which the country headed 'towards the precipice'. He adds
that he still wanted to preserve the régime. But in the new circumstances, it now became necessary to separate the principle of legitimacy from that of monarchy, and to preserve the second by
abandoning the first – that is, by substituting the house of Orléans.[85]
Although this summary skirts some awkward ambiguities about
Talleyrand's position, it is a fair account of the political situation.

Any hopes that the new ministry might be prepared to compromise
were soon dispelled. Even more disastrous election results for the government confirmed that the King would either have to bow to liberal
opinion or suppress it. He chose the second option. On 25 July 1830
Charles X signed four ordinances which amounted to a royal coup.
These measures imposed press censorship, dissolved the Chamber of
Deputies, restricted the franchise, and convoked new electoral colleges. Initially, there was an explosion of opposition from the press.
Then, on 27 July – the first of three 'Glorious Days' – the popular
explosion in the streets of Paris began which would bring down the
Bourbon monarchy.

Like the rest of the respectable political class, Talleyrand was a spectator at these events. He certainly did not manipulate them. Yet nor was he entirely passive. Some years earlier, he had encountered the journalist and historian Alphonse Thiers in the company of Dorothée. Opposites in many respects – age, height (Marx called Thiers a 'monstrous gnome') and class – the two men became close. Talleyrand was flattered to offer his patronage and Thiers was glad to receive it.[86] It was almost certainly at Rochecotte in 1829 that the project was conceived of founding a newspaper, *Le National*, which Thiers and his friends would control. It was supported by Talleyrand's banker Laffitte, the Prince having at this stage no spare capital. But he lent the venture his prestige. *Le National* was an Orléanist paper, and it would be at the core of opposition to the Polignac ministry the following year.[87]

Talleyrand wrote to Lord Holland in the spring of 1830 that he had gone to Valençay 'to wait'.[88] It was clear that a crisis was approaching – the 'moment of decision', as he described it in another letter, to the princesse de Vaudémont. There was now 'no compass, no pilot, and nothing [could] stop the shipwreck'.[89] He left, as usual, for his cure at Bourbon-l'Archambault. But, having perhaps got wind of the government's measures, he hurried back to Paris on 24 July. He at once ordered that the gold letters along the front of his house proclaiming it the 'Hôtel Talleyrand' be taken down.[90] Charles-Maurice knew what revolutionary mobs were like. He also knew how to dabble advantageously in revolutions.

During the three days of disorder, the Prince seems to have kept an almost continuous vigil at his *entresol* window. It was here, on the second day (28 July), that he was seen by Broglie, as the latter walked along the rue de Rivoli in the early evening. Broglie went in and told him the latest news over dinner. As dessert was served, the British ambassador Stuart arrived to have a lengthy, private discussion with his host.[91] The next day, the Prince was again at his window as Pasquier, this time, was passing by. The Prince tapped on the window and beckoned him to come up. Talleyrand said he was worried that the duc d'Orléans might over-reach himself by accepting the post of lieutenant-general of the kingdom. He would prefer him at this stage to be simply military governor of Paris. Above all, he must be patient and be prepared to negotiate. Pasquier agreed.[92]

To this end, Talleyrand sent his secretary Colmache with a message to Neuilly. In it, as well as offering advice on the exact title to accept – which was not, in fact, taken – he urged that d'Orléans should return at once to Paris. In fact, the duc was even more timid than Talleyrand had assumed. He was not at Neuilly at all, having gone into hiding at his château of Le Raincy. Colmache was, therefore, received by Mme Adélaide, Louis-Philippe's sister, and a close friend and long-time collaborator of Charles-Maurice. She promised to pass on the advice.

Perhaps the intervention had an effect, because later that night d'Orléans duly arrived back in Paris, passing via the rue Saint-Florentin for a brief word with the Prince.[93] When he reached the Hôtel de Ville, the new lieutenant-general was received with acclaim. Meanwhile, the old King, demoralized and confused, withdrew first to Trianon and then to Rambouillet, thus removing the remaining inhibitions created by fear of military reprisals. On 3 August, the duc d'Orléans announced the abdication of Charles X and the Dauphin. On 9 August he swore the oath before the assembled Chambers, by which he became Louis-Philippe I, King of the French. Naturally, Talleyrand was present.

As his conversation with Pasquier suggests, the Prince had shifted his ground more than once during the crisis. He may well have favoured, as he did initially in 1814, a regency, this time for Charles X's grandson, the infant duc de Bordeaux, as Henri V, with the duc d'Orléans acting as regent.[94] But the régime crumbled more quickly than he had foreseen. He always maintained that if Charles X had, even on 26 July, dismissed his ministers and withdrawn the ordinances he would have kept his throne.[95] But when Talleyrand heard that the Hôtel de Ville had fallen to the rebels, he lost confidence in the King's ability to survive. Looking at the time – it was five o'clock in the afternoon – he declared: 'A few minutes more and Charles X is no longer King of France.'

Apocryphal, no doubt, but none the less significant is another account:

Talleyrand: 'Hark! The tocsin ceases – we triumph!'

A servant interjects: 'We! Who, *mon prince*?'

Talleyrand: '*Chut*, not a word! I will tell you that tomorrow.'[96]

The Prince's opportunism was self-interested, but it also made political sense. He knew what he wanted: a liberal monarchy as close as possible to the model prevailing in Britain. He also knew what he feared: the demagogy and disorder that the Republican left would introduce unless checked. To promote the former and avoid the latter it was necessary that the duc d'Orléans should assume control of events, whatever his exact title.

Talleyrand never regretted the creation of the July Monarchy, although he privately lamented the necessity that had led to it. On an aesthetic level, he thought its bourgeois, democratic trappings lacked style – not enough 'conquest', as he put it.[97] But he came to admire Louis-Philippe's qualities. He also put up a strong public defence of the régime. Challenged in London by the Russian envoy's wife, Princess von Lieven, who described the change in France as a 'Revolution', he replied: 'Revolution is not the word, Madame. It is a Restoration, and such a one as the Emperor Alexander desired in 1815.'[98] Somehow, the exchange appeared in the columns of *The Times*.[99]

Although Talleyrand had undoubtedly nurtured hopes of a return to political influence, if only to ameliorate his financial problems, he cannot have expected that he would suddenly find himself at the forefront of French public life. He had written in the spring of 1830 to Lord Holland from Valençay, in elegiac style, of how he envisaged passing his remaining years:

> Although the season is not far advanced, I feel better here than in Paris. I am preparing to end my days with a stay-at-home existence. I do not struggle against necessity, I adapt to it. I hardly work. I do not write at all, reading is much more pleasurable than writing. There is more freedom and more relaxation in allowing one's thoughts to flow in the form of rather vague musings than to reduce them to conclusions, with pen in hand.[100]

On 6 September he wrote again, but in a very different manner. He acknowledged Holland's reply, and noted that he had decided to come and thank him for it in person. He planned to be in London at the end of the month.[101] He had, in fact, that day been appointed French ambassador to the court of St James.

16

Ambassador in London

～

ON 24 SEPTEMBER, after an unpleasant Channel crossing, Talleyrand landed at Dover, accompanied by the duchesse de Dino. Thirty-six years earlier, he had left Britain as an undesirable alien: how different was the reception he now received.[1] Cannon-fire boomed out to welcome his arrival as ambassador. They were met by Arthur Wellesley, the son of his old friend Wellington, and escorted to London and to dinner with the duke at Apsley House. In the days that followed, Talleyrand's popularity was evident wherever he went. Recognizing the French colours, people cheered his carriage as it passed.[2] The Prince was no less pleasantly impressed by London. As he told Mme Adélaïde, the capital struck him as more beautiful and much larger than he remembered it; some suburbs were entirely new.[3] *The Times* reported with satisfaction how the Prince and the duchesse de Dino were to be seen in their distinctive yellow carriage, viewing all the improvements made in the Strand.[4]

Talleyrand was not so pleased, however, with what he found at the embassy at 50 Portland Place. For a start, the building itself was a problem because of the staircase, which he found it difficult to climb. In October 1831 he would move into a house at 21 Hanover Square, previously rented to Lord Grey. There was said to be a ghost in residence, but, more importantly, there was also a ground-floor apartment he could use. The staff he inherited at Portland Place were also unsatisfactory. Too few, too inexperienced and too radical in their views, they were quickly replaced. The arrival of Bacourt, who fulfilled the roles of Talleyrand's devoted secretary and Dorothée's devoted lover, was of great assistance.[5]

In all that he wrote about his mission, now and later, Talleyrand emphasized that his role in London was to avoid the catastrophe of

war. To Dalberg he stressed: 'My constant idea is that we must maintain peace: all my initiatives, all my words are to that end.'[6] In practice, the risk of war was always remote, as long as the government in
Paris did not provoke it. Russia, Prussia and Austria were, of course,
bound to view with suspicion the overthrow of Charles X. The July
Revolution was exactly the kind of event that the Holy Alliance had
been founded fifteen years earlier to prevent. Tsar Nicholas I apparently only decided to recognize the new régime once he learned that
Talleyrand, with his legendary political foresight, had joined Louis-
Philippe's service.[7] In practice, however, as long as Britain accepted
the July Monarchy, the other powers would have little option but to
accept it too.

This was why Louis-Philippe, and even those of his ministers who
had long been Talleyrand's critics, thought that the Prince should go to
London. He was ideally qualified, by his prestige and his contacts, to
secure Britain's early support for the new régime. Despite having a Tory
government, whose members were ideologically suspicious of France
and of revolution, Britain had some solid reasons to welcome the
change. Under Charles X, France's seizure of Algiers and its closeness
to Russia had threatened British foreign interests. A liberal constitutional monarchy, with an anglophile monarch and ministers, therefore,
had obvious attractions.

But on 25 August, six days before Stuart, the British ambassador in
Paris, renewed his credentials, a revolt broke out in Belgium against
William I of the Netherlands. This added a new and unwelcome
dimension to Anglo-French relations. The enlarged Kingdom of the
Netherlands was the work of the Congress of Vienna and had been
created as an instrument against French expansion. Of the three allied
powers that imposed this solution, the two most directly affected by
the Belgian revolt were Britain and Prussia. Neither state was prepared
to see its fundamental interests jeopardized. In the case of Britain, that
meant ensuring that Antwerp did not pass under French control and
that free navigation was maintained on the Scheldt. In the case of
Prussia, its acquisitions in the Rhineland must not be threatened by
the immediate proximity of French territory and troops. On top of
that, neither the British, nor the Prussians, nor, for that matter, the
Russians, would accept the thirteen great fortresses that secured the

Low Countries against possible French aggression now falling into French hands. Therefore, the crucial condition for peace, as Talley-rand and Louis–Philippe recognized, was that France should not use the Belgian revolt as an excuse to annexe, or exert control over, the Belgian provinces.

Talleyrand had only indirect influence over the decisions made in Paris. But in London he could and did try to impress his hosts with the moderation of the government he represented. Fortunately, he had good contacts with both Tories and Whigs at a time when British governments were buffeted in and out of power by the burning issue of electoral reform. Moreover, by his side he had the duchesse de Dino, now even more beautiful and more self-assured than in Vienna, who presided at his dinners, charmed his guests, and even drafted his diplomatic notes and speeches. Above all, he possessed the antique grace that the British, from the high aristocracy down to the London working class, expected of a French diplomat. He liked to play up to his image as an experienced and sagacious statesman to whom nothing was new. He spoke before William IV at the palace of how he rejoiced at the happy change he now witnessed in Anglo-French relations, his speech receiving favourable judgements in London's clubs.[8]

Charles de Rémusat visited London two years later and observed the impact made by Talleyrand. The Prince's fellow diplomats were evidently flattered to be working with one of the celebrities of the Congress of Vienna, whose calm and benevolent manner of speech fitted in with the style of the English. Above all, his hosts were intensely curious. Many had expected, on learning of his appointment, to find him too decrepit for the tasks he had assumed. Certainly age had taken its toll. He was slightly deaf. His voice, though strong, had descended so far, it seemed, into his stomach that he was sometimes difficult to understand. His appearance, whose peculiarity made him the rage of the *salons*, was that shown in the striking portrait by Ary Scheffer: long, carefully pomaded hair, a face deathly pale, wrinkled, flaccid skin, the ends of his mouth drooping with what Chateaubriand described as the 'contempt' he had received, all set upon and partly buried within an enormous white cravat. His limp was nowadays still more pronounced, and he had to wriggle around with great ingenuity to climb a narrow staircase. At the Travellers Club, founded by

Castlereagh for politicians and diplomats, they helpfully installed a special handrail on the stairs for him. Yet, despite his infirmities, all who encountered the Prince discovered that his mind was undimmed, his character unaltered.[9]

'His *esprit*,' observed Rémusat, 'was outstanding, not because it was *piquant* or gracious, but because it was direct, simple, elevated. He held to his reputation and indeed thought of history. He had courage, boldness, patriotism. What a pity that it was all spoilt and sometimes destroyed by habits of softness and of secret corruption!' But even the last part of that impression will, doubtless, have added to Talleyrand's fascination in a society where Regency, not yet high Victorian, values held sway.

The Prince was thus a perfect ambassador in the eyes of most of his diplomatic colleagues and English hosts; but he soon seemed far from perfect when viewed from the Foreign Ministry back in Paris. He knew how to flatter French politicians when necessary, but he had no intention of subordinating his judgement to theirs. Instead, he pursued a personal diplomacy agreed with Louis-Philippe, with whom he communicated on matters of substance via personal letters to Mme Adélaïde or their mutual friend the princesse de Vaudémont. Molé, as Foreign Minister, was furious. He complained to Talleyrand that all he received from him were reports full of trivia. In a petulant letter to the King he even threatened to resign.[10] Talleyrand wrote back, in an elaborately affectionate style – often a warning sign – to make amends: 'We know one another, we like one another, we want the same things, we understand them in the same way, our starting point is the same, our goal is the same. Why, en route, do we not agree?'[11]

He then carried on very much as before. And he did not forgive Molé, whom he blamed for failing to have his elegant speech to William IV published in the French press. When Molé was removed in favour first of Marshal Maison, and later of the much more amenable Sébastiani, Talleyrand wrote contemptuously about his shortcomings.[12]

From the start, there were substantial points of contention between Paris and its ambassador. Talleyrand was still regarded by many as, in Villèle's expression, an '*anglomane*'.[13] Molé was one of the group who thought that Russia was a more suitable ally for France – a difference of view which went back to the time of the Congress of Vienna.

When the decision was made to summon a conference to discuss the future of Belgium – at which Britain, France, Prussia, Russia and the Netherlands would be represented – the French government pressed hard for it to be held in Paris. Talleyrand dutifully advanced the case; but he did not believe in it. He feared the influence of Pozzo di Borgo and Russia over the negotiations, at which the Prince himself intended to represent France as he saw fit. He also worried that the upheavals that racked Paris at this time would threaten the orderly transaction of business. In any case, Wellington insisted, and Talleyrand obtained Louis-Philippe's acceptance: the conference would be held in London.[14]

Although Britain was the dominant power at the conference, Talleyrand made up for France's weakness by his own personality – much as at the Congress of Vienna. By the time of the first meeting, on 4 November, he had not even received any instructions; but this never bothered him.[15] According to the account in the memoirs, he followed a consistent course throughout the intricate and apparently endless negotiations. This is an exaggeration. But what is true is that he had a coherent policy, which was to minimize the risk of war while going as far as he could in securing French strategic interests.

At the end of November the comte de Flahaut, Talleyrand's illegitimate son, arrived in London. Representing the new Foreign Minister, Sébastiani, he brought with him a plan to partition Belgium. Talleyrand was highly critical. The proposal was to divide the disputed territory between the Netherlands, Prussia and France, while Britain would be awarded Antwerp and the mouth of the Scheldt.[16] Talleyrand's objection to the plan did not, in truth, rest on any great attachment to the idea of Belgian statehood. He considered the Belgians, much as he had considered the Poles, as impossible people. In conversation with Princess von Lieven, he said that the Belgians were not a nation and never would be. What he doubted was the value of partition when judged by his key criterion of maintaining the peace. Moreover, he was very strongly against allowing the British to gain possession of Antwerp, which would constitute a permanent threat to France. He became quite agitated about it, hit the floor with his stick and then the table with his fist, so that the teacups rattled and everyone looked round.[17]

In any case, the compromise of partition no longer seemed to make sense. The task of persuading the northern powers to abandon the Netherlands, and to accept Belgian independence, was greatly assisted by the revolt that now broke out in Poland. Austria, Prussia and, above all, Russia were henceforth keen to have done with Belgian matters in order to concentrate on those in their own back yard. On 20 December the conference accordingly voted for the future independence of Belgium, on conditions (to be established) that safeguarded the interests and security of the other powers, and 'European equilibrium'. Pressed by the duchesse de Dino, who harboured a *penchant* for the Poles, Talleyrand also urged the French government to offer to mediate in Poland. He argued, as he had done so many years before, that an independent Poland would be an effective barrier against Russia in Europe. But the proposal won no support from the other powers, and the following September the Russians re-took Warsaw.

At least, though, the Belgian crisis appeared to be nearing solution. On 20 January 1831 the conference agreed that Belgium should be a neutral state, its status guaranteed by the five powers. This was an important success for Talleyrand and for France. It meant that the great fortresses erected against its northern frontier would now no longer be accessible to its enemies. The news was warmly welcomed in Paris, where Louis-Philippe described it as 'a great *coup* by M. de Talleyrand'.[18]

Other matters also occupied the Prince and his fellow diplomats – the future of Greece, dissension in Portugal and, of course, the Polish revolt – but it was repeatedly Belgium that haunted their discussions. The Belgians now provoked the powers by electing Louis-Philippe's younger son, the duc de Nemours, as their King. Talleyrand strongly urged Louis-Philippe to reject the plan, which he did, despite nationalist pressures in Paris. The Prince had no time for such childishness. France could afford to wait. He had never believed in the viability of the Kingdom of the Netherlands erected in 1815, and he does not seem to have reckoned much for Belgium's chances either.[19] Writing to the princesse de Vaudémont he exposed the roots of his thinking: 'There is no support to be derived from scatter-brained, rowdy people like the Belgians. Belgium will come to us perhaps, but later. Today it is a secondary interest. The direction of events drives it towards

France. But we must make France; and France cannot be made well and securely except by dealing with the great powers, which today *applaud* it; for that is where I have brought matters.'[20]

In this, Talleyrand was developing the approach he had adopted fifteen years earlier in Vienna. Participation as a trusted member of the European community of nations was more important to France in its vulnerable state than national aspirations or short-term national interests. Nor is this the only instance of his recapitulating his earlier positions. For example, in a despatch to Sébastiani of the previous November, he argues, as he had done back in 1792, against formal alliances as the basis upon which French policy should rest. Rather, 'we should seek to grow closer to those governments where civilization is most advanced'. This meant, above all, Britain, and it also meant siding against the powers of the Holy Alliance, especially Russia and Austria: '[The latter] sustain their Divine Right with cannon. We and England shall sustain public opinion with principles. Principles are propagated everywhere, and the cannon has no greater reach than that which is well known.'[21]

On 4 June 1831 Leopold of Saxe-Coburg was elected King of the Belgians. Although he was not Talleyrand's first choice, the Prince soon considered him an excellent one. Unfortunately, the Belgians still opposed the territorial limits proposed for the new state, and, in his exasperation, Talleyrand was temporarily attracted by partition.[22] Then in August a Dutch army invaded Belgium. It was a mark of the confidence that Talleyrand commanded in London that the British government quickly agreed that a French army should also enter Belgium to repel the invasion. In fact, on two occasions French military intervention was authorized and its objectives successfully accomplished – though not until 1839 did the Netherlands finally accept the new *status quo*. Where, asked one of Talleyrand's English friends, Lord Alvanley, did all this leave the much vaunted strategy of 'non-intervention'? The Prince, who in his early days in London had made much of the concept, now cynically explained that non-intervention was 'a metaphysical and political expression that means more or less the same thing as intervention'.[23]

Alvanley was only one of many wealthy, aristocratic English acquaintances who helped to make Talleyrand's and his niece's lives agreeable: the Duke of Wellington acted as Dorothée's guide to see the curiosities of the city; Lady Jersey entertained them at her house amid fabulous luxury.[24] The Prince, too, entertained in great style. His dinners were gastronomic events; but they proved ruinously expensive, since the cost of living in London was much greater than in Paris. Talleyrand was remunerated well enough by his government, receiving the equivalent of his old salary as Grand Chambellan even after the post was abolished, as well as a salary as ambassador. But his expenses exceeded his income.[25] The aftermath of the Paravey bank collapse also continued to trouble him. He wrote to Dalberg to complain: 'I haven't a sou.'[26] In such circumstances, he was more reliant on his English admirers than perhaps they realized.

Of these, the most faithful were undoubtedly the Hollands. In his letters, Talleyrand signs as 'T' or 'Talley' – the nickname by which he was known in London – and Lord Holland is 'My dear friend' (in English) or even, less correctly but more affectionately, 'Dearest'. On departing for one of his annual periods of leave in France, Talleyrand explained his reluctance to leave: 'The truth is that I greatly miss England. People show me continual marks of kindness. The life I live there suits me. Even the climate during winter does me no harm. I am especially fond of a number of people there, and you top the list.'[27]

Lord Holland was a member of the Whig ministries of Lord Grey (whom Talleyrand admired) and later Lord Melbourne (whom, by then at a distance, he heartily despised). Holland served as a useful, informal contact with the government of the day, allowing Talleyrand to circumvent the Foreign Secretary, Palmerston. He was entrusted with private explanations and sometimes shown despatches from Paris intended only for the Prince.[28] On occasion, Talleyrand went so far as to provide an unflattering gloss on his sovereign's more grandiloquent observations. For example, when a French force landed at Lisbon and Louis-Philippe announced that 'the tricolour is flying on [*sur*] the walls', the Prince slyly observed that the King had substituted 'on' for 'under' (*sous*) 'in his enthusiasm'.[29]

Talleyrand's relations with the great Whig families, such as Holland and Lansdowne, reached back to his first stay in England. He liked to reminisce over dinner about the eighteenth-century celebrities whose acquaintance he had made at that time, the actor Garrick and playwright Sheridan among them.[30] But having known the English for so long, his affection for them was qualified by his grasp of the other side of their character. Thus he described them privately as 'egotists'.[31]

Dorothée's first impressions were very favourable. And as the months passed, she became an increasingly enthusiastic anglophile. She loved the capital with its verdant, blossom-filled squares and its balconies and façades covered with climbing plants; she was entranced by the country houses with their fine views; she found herself in awe of this 'complex' and 'colossal' Britain.[32] The English themselves were difficult to get to know, but 'when they have adopted you, they are the best, simplest, most sensible and most constant friends, delightful to live with and always perfectly *comme il faut*'.[33] Their peculiarities included that of suffering in the summer months from a curious ailment called 'hay fever', quite unknown on the Continent. The English women had beautiful complexions and beneath their shy exteriors were honest and refined, though they lacked grace. The men too were good-hearted, despite their stilted conversation.[34]

Talleyrand's public standing remained high throughout his time in England. He was fortunate to have in the Duke of Wellington a guarantor whose good faith could not be doubted. On 29 September 1831 the Prince's malign influence over the Whig government was the subject of an intemperate speech in the House of Lords by the Marquis of Londonderry, the former Lord Stewart, half-brother of Talleyrand's late collaborator Castlereagh. Wellington at once intervened in the debate to state his 'conscientious belief that no man's public and private character had ever been so much belied' as that of the Prince. This sincere, if exaggerated, praise moved Talleyrand to tears. He told Alvanley that Wellington was 'the only statesman in the world who had ever said anything good of [him]'.[35] The Prince was also strongly attacked the following year by the Tory opposition for leaking to the French press the contents of secret discussions over Belgium. On this occasion, he took no notice at all.[36] It was, however, much more difficult to cope with the ill-will of the Whig Foreign Minister, Lord Palmerston.[37]

Palmerston had first met the Prince in 1829 and they had had a long and apparently friendly conversation. They later proved capable of cooperation when common interests required, as when Palmerston persuaded a reluctant British Cabinet to support French military action against the Dutch in 1832.[38] But there was a temperamental antipathy. Palmerston had no nostalgic memories of Talleyrand or, indeed, of others from the old diplomatic school. Princess von Lieven, for example, received similarly rude treatment, despite the fact that she played an important part in keeping Russia and Britain close together during the Belgian crisis and thus, incidentally, making life more difficult for Talleyrand.[39] The truth is that Palmerston had no intention of showing any more regard for French sensitivities than British self-interest required, and possibly not even that. Moreover, as Talleyrand shrewdly notes in his memoirs, though the observation could apply almost equally to himself: '[For Palmerston] each political question complicates itself more or less with a personal question; and in appearing to defend the interests of his country, it is almost always those of his hatred or his vengeance that he serves. He applies great skill in hiding this motivation under what I could call an appearance of patriotism.'[40]

Talleyrand's popular standing seems to have irritated Palmerston, part of whose genius was a well-developed instinct for public opinion. The Prince remained a great celebrity right up until the time of his departure. When he alighted from his carriage in Kensington one day in May 1834, for example, Dorothée was struck by how women were lifted up by their husbands to gain a better look at him. Scheffer's engraving of Talleyrand, displayed in a window beside a print of William Pitt the Younger, attracted a crowd of curious spectators. Dorothée heard somebody say, looking at Pitt's portrait: 'There is someone who fashioned great events. That one [looking at Talleyrand's] knew how to foresee them and wait on them with profit.'[41] More personally wounding to Palmerston, though, must have been the popularity of a caricature entitled 'The Lame leading the Blind'. Talleyrand was, naturally, the Lame and Palmerston the Blind. The message, that the French ambassador had successfully duped the British Foreign Secretary and was directing British foreign policy, was no less unwelcome for being incorrect.

Yet there was more to the differences between Talleyrand and Palmerston than pique and personality. Talleyrand's diplomatic successes, after the destruction of Napoleonic France, always depended upon maximizing the role of influence and minimizing the role of naked power in international relations. There were, though, limits to the possibilities of such an approach. The Prince must quickly have realized that these had been reached when he came up against Palmerston. The trouble was that France could no longer bring sufficient benefits to a close alliance with Britain in order to deal on equal terms. Palmerston's brutal manner destroyed even the façade of equality, and this offended Talleyrand's sense of his own and his country's dignity. Despite his long-standing enthusiasm for a close relationship with Britain, what would soon come to be known as an Entente Cordiale, he was increasingly uneasy about how or even whether it could be managed.[42] Yet at the very time when he was becoming disillusioned with British policy, the government in Paris led by the duc de Broglie pressed hard for a formal alliance with Britain. Talleyrand complied with these wishes and eventually succeeded after a fashion; but the difficulties he faced illustrate the fundamental soundness of his analysis.

Britain had now begun to adopt a unilaterally determined interventionist approach to the affairs of the Iberian Peninsula, designed to uphold the constitutional régimes of Spain and Portugal – and thus British interests – against reactionary insurrections.[43] Eventually, Talleyrand had Palmerston's triple alliance with Spain and Portugal enlarged to a quadruple alliance, to include France as an equal partner. But in reality Britain retained a free military hand and also enjoyed commercial privileges denied France in Latin America. When the Prince returned to Paris his advice to Louis-Philippe was to distance France from Britain – perhaps by establishing links with Austria as a make-weight. For a time he even toyed with the idea of accepting the post of ambassador to Vienna, scene of his earlier triumphs, so as to pursue this objective.[44] Talleyrand's critics in England and in France assumed that his shift of approach was wholly attributable to personal dislike of Palmerston.[45] This was unjust, though the resentment was real enough.

Palmerston had treated him discourteously; in fact, he had treated him as if he were merely another ambassador, on one occasion keeping him waiting for a long period in his ante-chamber.[46]

This is how the British Foreign Secretary often behaved, but it did not make the rudeness any more tolerable.[47] When in 1834 the duchesse de Dino found William IV's attitude markedly less warm than in previous years, as she and the Prince departed England, she put it down to 'Palmerstonian influences'. At the farewell dinner organized for Talleyrand by Palmerston that August it was noticeable that not a single distinguished Englishman and not one friend of the Prince's were invited.[48] Such breaches of etiquette were in Talleyrand's book truly unforgivable; and he did not forgive them.

Talleyrand probably understood Britain better than any Frenchman of his time, but he also saw the country through French eyes. Perhaps because of his Revolutionary past, he had become mistrustful of radical reforms that might introduce the disasters of revolution. So, despite his sympathies with the Whigs, he shared all the Tories' unease about the Great Reform Bill of 1832, which he likened to the calling of the Estates General of 1789.[49] Speaking of the British Constitution, he was heard to say: 'What used to be unshakable is so no longer. That is all I would say, but I say it.'[50]

The continuing agitation for further institutional reform only confirmed his anxieties. He confided to Mme Adélaïde that he considered England 'strangely changed' and did not think it could stop 'in the new course it is pursuing'.[51] He regarded the resignation of Lord Grey as leader of the Whigs in 1834 as 'the end of the old England in which he had confidence'.[52] He hoped that Peel's – in fact short-lived – Conservative ministry of 1835 would last.[53] When his Whig friends learned of his opinions they were appalled. The impetuous Lady Holland described Talleyrand to anyone who would listen as, that worst of insults, 'a Tory'. The Prince wrote back an ironic letter, which put his own position more exactly:

> Today I know all too well that I am in [Lady Holland's] eyes a covert Tory [*un tory déguisé*]. I should think that a liberal conservative [*conservatif libéral*] would be more correct, for at my age one wants to be free and to conserve what has been gained. That is why I do not allow to be cut down a single one of the century-old trees which cover with their vast shade Pauline's young head. . .My most tender respects to the *hostile* Lady Holland.[54]

Talleyrand's interest in British politics did not at any point distract him from the political scene in France, of which he frequently despaired. He was exasperated by the disorder that marred the early part of Louis-Philippe's reign. Dorothée was particularly outraged by the desecration of the church of Saint-Germain-l'Auxerrois on the occasion of a memorial mass for the late duc de Berry.[55] Talleyrand disliked and distrusted the politicians on the left who were known as '*le Mouvement*'. He strongly backed Casimir Périer in repressing riots and attempts at revolt.[56] He described the French President of the Council to Lamartine, who visited him in London, as 'the most necessary of all men, the axis of the world'; he was 'a great pilot'.[57] But the pilot suddenly died of cholera in May 1832. Talleyrand greatly regretted his passing, as he told Sébastiani, and his advice was unqualified: 'Follow [Casimir Périer's] system.'[58] In fact, a figure of authority was required to take the helm, and some now looked to the Prince.

Charles de Rémusat was accordingly despatched by the Doctrinaires to persuade Talleyrand either to become President of the Council himself or at least to provide support for whomever was nominated to fill the post. The Prince was clearly tempted, asking numerous questions about the political figures in Paris. He said that he would support a Cabinet that continued the policies of Périer, but he would not commit himself to playing an active role. Eventually, the duchesse de Dino told Rémusat that Talleyrand did not want to be leader of a ministry, and that if he had wanted it she would have stopped him. The Prince was thus spared the unpleasantness of turning down the offer himself.[59] In truth, he knew he was too old to take on such an exhausting task. As he confided to Dalberg, he had absolutely no wish to return to government.[60]

But he retained a close interest in French politics. He had, indeed, been heavily involved in Parisian politicking during the long periods he spent on leave every year from his British mission. And once he finally departed London in August 1834 – though he did not formally resign his post until November – he had even more time to interfere. The results of his interventions were generally unhappy. His opposition to Broglie and then his championing of Thiers against Guizot helped break up the alliance of moderate opinion on which the July Monarchy's fragile foundations rested.[61] Moreover, the Prince's motivations were clearly personal rather than, in the wider sense, political; and in the end his protégé, Thiers, proved an unguidable weapon. When Thiers resigned as Foreign Minister in 1836, his one-time admirer Dorothée wrote to rebuke him for doing so over 'that hateful Spain', where Thiers's interventionism was anathema to Talleyrand.[62] Rémusat suggests that it was from this point on that Thiers conceived a deep enmity towards his old patron. This was to adopt a particularly distasteful form after Talleyrand's death – a topic that had begun increasingly to preoccupy him.[63]

17

The Final Curtain

THE CIRCUMSTANCES OF Talleyrand's death have created almost as much controversy as the more notorious events in his life. Naturally, many contemporaries were extremely doubtful about the sincerity of his deathbed 'conversion'. And it is, indeed, legitimate to question whether his intentions were as pure as the abbé Dupanloup, who received his last confession, believed, or his repentance as complete as Rome demanded. The combination of self-control and self-abandonment that the former bishop of Autun demonstrated in his final days perplexed many of those who witnessed it. The fact remains that Dupanloup, who was neither a fool nor a charlatan, and the duchesse de Dino, who was biased but extremely well informed of her uncle's state of mind, have provided accounts which establish that Talleyrand's reconciliation with the Church was no charade. By and large, those keenest to doubt or to scoff were also those who knew least of what was happening in his last years at Valençay and in the rue Saint-Florentin, behind the façade of Talleyrand's manner. Modern accounts usually refrain from reaching a conclusion on the matter. Unfortunately, this renders their portrayal of the old man in his last years less than psychologically coherent and convincing.[1]

The signs that Talleyrand shared the worries about death that have prompted many others of his age to think about religion are not far to seek. Despite his bad foot, and despite taking very little exercise, he had for most of his life enjoyed excellent health. He had not over-indulged in food or drink and he did not over-work; but, beyond that, he was also blessed with a very strong constitution. Although he had been seriously ill in 1827, perhaps with a heart attack, he recovered completely.[2] He demonstrated remarkable energy and stamina during his time in Britain. By 1833, however, observers thought that his health was finally breaking.[3] He complained that December that his 'legs, always bad, [were] becoming detestable'.[4] Two years later he was again seriously ill. Molé thought he would soon be dead, what with his bad heart and the debilitating treatments prescribed for it.[5]

Talleyrand affected unconcern about his ailments. When, at Bourbon-l'Archambault, he was involved in some kind of accident, he reported ironically to Lord Holland: 'I have learned during my stay here that nimble people like us can fall seven feet into a ditch without doing ourselves the slightest harm: it is always good to know.'[6] But as his health worsened and when he lacked the distraction of public affairs, he began to fret and showed signs of hypochondria. He complained of palpitations; his arms hurt, because he had to use them to take the weight that his legs could no longer bear; he became lethargic; he took to reading medical books and looked up ailments of the heart. The arrival of visitors or the need to embark on business pulled him out of his reveries, but black thoughts returned. He suffered from insomnia. He worried about death.[7]

The Prince was also depressed by the fate of his ageing friends. The Countess Tyszkiewicz suffered several strokes before she died in 1834. Talleyrand wrote to Lord Holland: 'Mme de Tyszkiewicz concluded yesterday her sorrowful career. Twenty-seven years of continual concern for us, of absolute devotion, make her death very real for me. A long illness, a lot of suffering, weakness that grew each day, made one foresee her imminent end. But nothing prepares one for the eternal separation.'[8]

The death of Baudois came in 1835. The doctor, who had previously been looking after Talleyrand, went to minister to Montrond, who was seriously ill at home. But it was Bourdois who died there, while Montrond recovered.[9] The episode may have helped lead to a reconciliation, for Talleyrand and the duchesse de Dino had fallen out with Montrond the previous year. The Prince had tired of his sarcasm, and Dorothée, who always disliked him and considered him a bad influence on her uncle but feared his tongue, demanded that he leave Valençay. This humiliation was all the greater because the duc d'Orléans was shortly expected.[10] Montrond sulked and even refused to acknowledge Talleyrand when their paths crossed in Paris. The Prince observed out loud: 'Oh! It is clear that I brought him up badly.' The ice was broken and the friendship, though dented, resumed.[11]

But by now even Paris had begun to pall. When Talleyrand and the duchesse de Dino returned to the capital in August 1834 after their final departure from England they were very well received. But the Prince complained that he knew nobody, that he was bored and that everyone he came across was old and worn out.[12] His unfavourable impression of Paris society became even stronger as the years passed, though he still spent his winters at the rue Saint-Florentin, entertained, listened to gossip, and dabbled in politics. His growing dissatisfaction with the world around him found expression in reflections, or 'maxims', which owed much to the tradition of La Rochefoucauld or, more recently, Chamfort, whom he had known.[13] He wrote down his thoughts on scraps of paper that he kept in his coat pocket or his red leather briefcase or pushed into the drawer of his desk at Valençay. They were discovered after his death.

> What will become of the world? I do not know at all. What I see is that nothing is replaced. . .
>
> Why does the future seem so uncertain? It is because the present has no self-confidence.
>
> The present century has an octogenarian character. For me, it is the image of old age – impotence and self-love.[14]

As the last of these maxims suggests with its implicit self-reference, Talleyrand was also reflecting on his own past, and this too without much pleasure. On his birthday he wrote:

> 2 February 1837. That makes eighty-three years that have passed! I do not know if I am satisfied when I recall the course of so many years. How much useless agitation! How many fruitless endeavours! Irritating complications, exaggerated emotions, worn-out strengths! Gifts wasted, ill-will inspired, equilibrium lost, illusions destroyed, tastes exhausted! And with what result? That of moral and physical fatigue, a complete despondency about the future and a profound disgust for the past. There are a mass of people who have the gift, or the deficiency, never to be self-aware. I have, in all too great a degree, the contrary misfortune; it increases along with the seriousness that the years bring with them.[15]

Such world-weary reflections on the futility of existence do not, of course, necessarily lead to religion. In Talleyrand's case, however, other influences combined to ensure that they did. Perhaps the most important of these was the social and cultural conservatism which, even as a Revolutionary, had remained a part of his outlook. He continued to value the institutional legacy of the Revolution. But from the time of his exile as a young man in England and America, and with increasing force during the last few years of his life under Louis-Philippe, he detested the disorders that the Revolutionary outlook itself engendered. Indeed, he came to see the roots of the Revolution as social and cultural.

Recommending the memoirs of Saint-Simon to Lord Holland in 1830, he noted: 'It seems to me that they are of great interest. I find there already the first germs of the Revolution, and I find them there because the Revolution had to be fashioned by manners [*moeurs*] and to be social before it was political.'[16] He returned to the point in one of his maxims: 'Envy, the guiding principle of the French Revolution, takes on the mask of a ridiculous equality. It casts its level over everyone's head, so as to destroy those innocent superiorities which social distinctions establish.'[17]

'Social distinctions' were one foundation of the *ancien régime*. The Catholic Church was the other. The Church had, indeed, in large measure consecrated those distinctions. Both the aristocracy and the priesthood had borne the brunt of the Revolution. But with the restoration of the Bourbons, a revivified Catholicism had made great inroads. Conversions and a return to devotion were common, particularly among the upper classes with whom Talleyrand mixed. The Prince himself was not immediately affected by this. For most of his life he had been (at best) a religious sceptic. Moreover, as a determined supporter of Gallicanism, he was suspicious of papal claims and hostile to clerical ambitions. But by his last years the political environment had changed significantly. The last obstacle to his acquiring a greater sympathy for Catholicism was overcome, paradoxically, with the overthrow of Charles X. Once the ultra ideology, which combined absolutism with ultra-montanism, had been defeated, it was natural that Catholicism should appeal to an increasingly conservative Talleyrand – initially as a force for order and tranquillity in society, and finally to resolve his own doubts and fears in the face of death.

It would not have occurred, however, without the duchesse de Dino. Born a Protestant, she had become a Catholic in 1811 and, more recently, and despite her numerous sexual encounters, she had developed a profound religious fervour. She was now determined that the Prince should be reconciled with the Church. He was anyway open to that suggestion, but particularly when it came from her, for as he wrote, with simplicity: 'You are everything for me; the little time I have left to live is consecrated to you.'[18] It would be strange if Talleyrand's posthumous reputation had not entered into Dorothée's calculation. France under Louis-Philippe was less overtly Catholic than under Charles X. But if Talleyrand had openly refused reconciliation with the Church, and so been forbidden a funeral mass and burial in consecrated ground, it would still have been a scandal. This was what had happened on the death of the abbé Grégoire, and it would be the case with Sieyès, who died shortly before Talleyrand. For the duchesse de Dino and her sons such an outcome would have been painful, and it is reasonable to suppose that Talleyrand wished to spare them this pain. Indeed, Colmache simply states that this was the motive of his 'conversion', and other contemporaries certainly assumed it.[19]

Yet, although the avoidance of scandal may have been one factor, it does not seem to have been a decisive or even, as it turned out, a particularly important one. Talleyrand was not, as the Church authorities recognized, in the same position as Grégoire or Sieyès. Although he had been responsible for perpetuating the schism represented by the Constitutional Church, and although he had contracted an illicit marriage, he was widely – albeit mistakenly – considered to have been sympathetic to the re-establishment of Catholicism under the Concordat. He was not a regicide. Rather, he was one of the authors of the Bourbon Restoration which had allowed the Church to flourish. He was also well known as a generous donor to ecclesiastical causes, and not only at Valençay. For example, he had made a large subscription to the cost of reinstituting theological studies at the Sorbonne.

More than that, he was a practising, if necessarily not a communicant, Catholic. He attended mass, not just at court and when in Paris, but every Sunday at Valençay, where he read Bossuet's sermons or the

Imitation of Christ during the liturgy, as was then the custom. He never lost a fondness for items of devotion. In February 1814 he had sent the duchesse de Courlande, a Protestant, a little picture of Our Lady to protect her in those troubled times.[20] He even had pronounced tastes in the matter of formal prayers. Thus he taught the duchesse de Dino the 'Salve Regina', which he thought more beautiful than the 'Pater Noster'. He was personally touched by the attention of friends concerned for his spiritual well-being, long before he paid heed to their arguments. He carried around with him a Marian medal which Mme de Marbeuf, now a nun, had sent him. This may merely have reflected the superstitious side of his character, but it showed his ease with the trappings and symbols of devotion. He was also, after his death, found to be carrying in his wallet a letter from the duchesse de Montmorency urging him to return to the faith.[21]

Not just the French hierarchy but Rome too recognized that he was in some respects a friend of the Church. In 1835, in answer to a request from the archbishop of Paris addressed to the Vatican for instructions about the attitude to take towards Talleyrand, Gregory XVI insisted on repentance and 'sufficient reparation' for his misdeeds. But, the letter continued: 'In any case, if the dying man does not openly refuse the sacraments, it is believed that he could not be refused an ecclesiastical burial.'

The duchesse de Dino and Talleyrand would almost certainly have known this. The threat of a scandalous refusal of Church rites was not, therefore, as great as it has often been represented. By contrast, the scandal that would erupt in the liberal, anticlerical circles in which Talleyrand had moved for most of his life was bound to be enormous in the event of his reconciliation with the Church. This prospect, which he also understood, was doubtless important in determining the timing and manner of his deathbed retraction and confession.

Barante believed that the turning point for Talleyrand occurred soon after his final return from his mission in London.[22] This is almost certainly correct. The Prince had not, after all, taken very seriously earlier suggestions that he should mend fences with the Church. He must have been under a degree of subtle pressure from his uncle, Alexandre-Angélique, whose company he frequented. After the latter's death in 1821, the new archbishop of Paris, Hyacinthe de

Quélen, felt an obligation, following his predecessor's wishes, to press Talleyrand on the matter. This he did to no great effect. Quélen was, in any case, an unsubtle man. He seems to have regarded Talleyrand as a potential 'catch', but the former bishop of Autun was too wily and too proud to allow himself to become a trophy of ecclesiastical politics. Talleyrand had other grievances. He considered that the archbishop had failed to defend his reputation at the time of the scandal caused by Savary's memoirs in 1823. Quélen just wrote him a pompous and unctuous letter, urging his reconciliation with the Church. It received no reply.[23]

Twelve years later, on 12 December 1835, Quélen wrote again, along the same lines. The archbishop had just received the last confession of Talleyrand's wife, the Princess having made an impressively devout end after a lifetime of notoriety. Talleyrand seemed unmoved by her death. Yet perhaps he was already thinking about his own return to the Church, because when told the news by Dorothée he remarked: 'This greatly simplifies my position.'[24] On the other hand, he was annoyed once more at the archbishop. Quélen had foolishly allowed himself to become a party to a dispute about the princesse de Talleyrand's legacy. He had accepted two boxes in safe-keeping from the dying woman, which were then claimed by the duchesse d'Esclignac, the Princess's niece and companion. Talleyrand had to threaten a lawsuit to get them back, which resulted in a full-blown public scandal, much to the archbishop's embarrassment. The duc Decazes acted as Talleyrand's intermediary in the matter. Finally, the duchesse d'Esclignac received a substantial sum and Talleyrand obtained the boxes, which probably contained compromising material along with the acknowledged bonds and jewels. This time, the Prince sent a brief reply to Quélen's letter, explaining that he was ill. The next day he wrote again, promising to visit the archbishop within a week. But he never did so.[25]

One result of the reopening of contacts with Quélen was, however, that the latter decided to establish precisely how Talleyrand's reconciliation with the Church might be accomplished. Having received advice from Rome, the archbishop in January 1836 assembled a group of theologians and friends of the Prince to draw up a form of words by which Talleyrand should make 'reparation' for his offences. The result was a text that was very explicit about the Prince's 'illicit' marriage which he had had the 'misfortune' to contract, and about his participation in the 'schism of the Civil Constitution'. The text begged God's pardon for 'all the faults and scandals of [his] life'. It is doubtful whether Talleyrand would have signed such a document. Fortunately for all concerned, it was never presented to the Prince, though a copy was given to Dorothée and to the curé of the Madeleine, their parish church.[26]

Talleyrand was not, in any case, likely to be swayed by politically conscious prelates. The duchesse de Dino and her daughter Pauline, whom the Prince adored and referred to as 'the good angel of the house', would alone be capable of touching his emotions. They were assisted by his prejudices. Although the Prince was a sceptic, as an aesthete he disliked both Protestantism – which he considered cold and lacking in consolation – and, even more so, atheism. Godlessness was uncultivated, and in particular it offended his idea of femininity. In 1834, when Pauline asked for a blessing from her 'uncle' ('*bon oncle*'), he exclaimed: 'How touching is the piety of a young girl, and how unnatural is unbelief among women!'[27] Three years later, in December 1837, when Dorothée fell gravely ill at Rochecotte and asked for a priest, Talleyrand was at first surprised: 'So you are at that point?' She explained her reasoning, but he interrupted: 'It is true, there is nothing less aristocratic than unbelief.'[28] It was a significant extension.

Dorothée was already trying, as often as she dared, to bring her conversations with Talleyrand back to the state of his soul. It was not easy. She spoke on one occasion of the need to make proper preparation for a good death. But he said nothing and just continued with his *piquet*.[29] The most important change in the Prince's attitude, however, was that resulting from his contact with the abbé Dupanloup.

Alongside Lacordaire, Dupanloup was already one of the most brilliant, fashionable and well-regarded young priests of his day.[30] He was now director of the *petit séminaire* of Saint-Nicolas du Chardonnet, having previously served at the Madeleine, where he had begun instructing Pauline in preparation for her first communion. Dupanloup remained her spiritual director after his move to Saint-Nicolas, and Talleyrand made his carriage available to take her there. Sometimes he went himself and waited outside. When asked what he was doing, he would smile and say that he was visiting 'our confessor'. He had begun by mistrusting Dupanloup's influence, thinking that the priest might try to turn his niece against him. But he was reassured by what she told him of the abbé's attitude. In May 1837 the duchesse de Dino brought Dupanloup to the rue Saint-Florentin to discuss the reopening of the church of Saint-Germain-l'Auxerrois, in which they shared an interest. Talleyrand liked what he heard of the priest and resolved on some suitable occasion to make his acquaintance.

The Prince and his family departed for Valençay as usual that autumn. In October there was a family play, with Pauline taking two parts. Talleyrand was delighted, and La Besnardière, who was visiting, claimed it was better than the Comédie-Française. Thiers and his wife and mother-in-law came to stay. Talleyrand and his family spent Christmas and New Year at Rochecotte. Only ill-health intervened to spoil the festivities, Dorothée suffering from migraines and Talleyrand complaining of his legs, which he could now hardly use. On 6 January the Prince and Pauline left in his carriage for Paris, with Dorothée following, braving the snow, a few days later. The usual round of entertaining resumed. But on 27 January, at a reception at the British embassy, as Talleyrand was giving his arm to Princess von Lieven, he tripped and fell. He was lifted back on to his feet, and he tried to carry on as if nothing had happened. But he was shaken, he had sprained his foot, and once he was out of sight in his carriage he groaned out loud with the pain.[31]

Perhaps the shock made him think again about his relations with the Church. His interest in meeting Dupanloup revived. He asked Barante, a practising Catholic, about the abbé. His friend replied that Dupanloup was cultivated, intelligent, liberal and open-minded – in fact, exactly the sort of cleric that was most likely to appeal to the Prince.[32] At Talleyrand's request, the duchesse de Dino therefore invited Dupanloup to dinner on Talleyrand's birthday. To her chagrin and the Prince's annoyance, the priest refused. Talleyrand acidly remarked: 'He has less intelligence than I thought, for he ought to have wished, both for his sake and for mine, to come here.' In fact, Dupanloup had succumbed to an attack of nerves. He was privately repelled by Talleyrand, appalled by his reputation, uneasy at where the invitation might lead.[33] But when the Prince's reaction was relayed to them, it was immediately clear to Dupanloup and Quélen what an error had been made. They discussed with the duchesse de Dino how to repair the damage.

It proved easier than expected. A new invitation was sent and this time it was accepted. Twenty people were at the dinner table, but the Prince had time only for Dupanloup. He talked about ecclesiastical affairs, reflected fondly on Saint-Sulpice, and threw in for good measure some attacks on Protestantism and on the egotism of the English. In fact, he exerted all his old charm and by the end of the evening the abbé, who could hardly believe his ears, was altogether under his spell. Talleyrand was equally pleased. 'I like your abbé: he knows how to live,' he later told Dorothée.[34]

The Prince, though, now had other matters on his mind. Learning of the death of comte Reinhard, he had resolved to deliver the eulogy at the Académie. His family and friends thought that in his precarious state of health it was madness, but he would not be dissuaded. His doctor, Cruveilhier, solemnly warned him that if he went ahead he would not answer for it. 'And who asked you to answer for it?' snapped the Prince. It was, he later explained, 'my farewell to the public'. He knew the risks, but he also knew that he had little time left; and he wanted one more appearance on the public stage.[35] Dorothée helped him with the draft, but the thoughts were all his own. As has been observed, it was in truth less a tribute to Reinhard than to his own virtuosity as a diplomat, and was understood as such. Some found the contents of the eulogy, when they read it, disappointing. The press reviews were mixed. But the impact of the Prince's appearance was immense. He had been seriously ill in recent days. He was so weak that he had to be carried in by his nephews. But he then proceeded to speak for half an hour in his full, deep voice without hesitation, and with complete self-possession. He was elevated by the experience. But a few hours later he almost collapsed under the strain. For some days, there were renewed fears for his life.[36]

Talleyrand had included in the eulogy a phrase, 'the religion of duty', which he hoped would please Dupanloup. The Prince sent him a copy of his speech, and Dupanloup used this as an opportunity to visit. It was the first meeting between the two men alone. But Talleyrand steered the conversation away from difficult spiritual questions on to other matters, in particular his poor health.

By now the duchesse de Dino, Quélen and Dupanloup were all becoming alarmed that the Prince would die without the last rites. The abbé accordingly tried a new approach. He sent Talleyrand a copy of a book he had written consisting of extracts from Fénelon, whom the Prince admired as a stylist as well as a religious author. He also enclosed a letter which contained subtle but clear allusions to the state of Talleyrand's own soul. The Prince asked Dorothée to read it out to him. At one point she broke down with emotion. 'Finish the letter,' he said sharply. 'It isn't something to become emotional about, it's a serious matter.'

The duchesse de Dino knew that Talleyrand was most unlikely to agree to the proposed wording of the 'retraction' of his errors, particularly as it was to be made public. She had been to see the archbishop to have this stipulation removed, but he was inflexible. However, he invited her to produce her own draft, which she had done. It was much less specific, but Dupanloup approved and Quélen was favourable. She now left it with Talleyrand.[37] He gave no reaction. But he replied to Dupanloup's letter with another invitation and enclosed a copy of the *Imitation of Christ* which originally came from his library as bishop of Autun.

He had now, in fact, resolved on the course to take. He went to see his notary and changed the wording of his Declaration. He wrote at the beginning: 'First, I declare that I die in the faith of the Catholic, Apostolic, Roman Church.' He also amended the reference to his laicization to read: 'I believed myself to be free' to marry.

On 28 April the Prince's younger brother, Archambaud, died. Dupanloup came to convey his condolences. The ensuing conversation was about death and faith, but as usual Talleyrand conveyed his thoughts through reflections and anecdotes. Dupanloup was impressed but frustrated.

In fact, the Prince had been preparing his own initiative. He had been secretly writing an alternative statement, which he hoped would be taken as sufficient 'retraction' for the purposes of his reconciliation with Rome. He gave a copy to Dorothée to take to Quélen. But it was not at all what was required, being a justification rather than a repudiation. The archbishop's rejection of the document was inevitable. Even the more emollient Dupanloup was disappointed by what it revealed of the Prince's attitude. Tactfully, Dorothée explained its insufficiency to her uncle. Talleyrand was surprised and displeased. But he agreed that an alternative document – or, following the Prince's own suggestion, two separate documents – should be prepared. One would be a declaration of submission to the Church and the other an explanation addressed to the Pope. The drafting would be entrusted to Dupanloup and Quélen.

Talleyrand was, in truth, still unhappy with the procedure. His health had temporarily improved and he even thought of going to Rome to try to negotiate directly with the Pope. But this hopeless venture was postponed when his condition again deteriorated. In any case, from the Prince's viewpoint the best possible option had already been found. Leaving the documents to be drawn up in France, rather than Rome, ensured that the wording was more sensitive to his feelings. The contents would be influenced not only by Dorothée but also by Talleyrand's friends, who were again summoned to work with theological advisers in the process, and then to act as witnesses. Moreover, Quélen was not the intellectual match of Dupanloup – and the abbé was now determined, within the limits laid down by Rome, to do all in his power to help Talleyrand make a Christian end. The two documents were finally entrusted on 9 May to Dupanloup for the Prince's signature.[38]

But the right occasion never seemed to present itself. Talleyrand was certainly in no hurry to sign anything. He was still meditating a journey to Rome, when he suddenly fell ill. On the evening of Saturday, 12 May he was entertaining his friends at the rue Saint-Florentin, when he started complaining that he felt cold. At table he recovered. Then they went back into the *salon*, where a fire was now burning. He leaned forward in his chair to try to get warm. Suddenly a tremor ran through him, his face was contorted with pain. He refused to go to bed and sat with his head in his hands for half an hour. Then he agreed to be wheeled into his room, where he was overcome by vomiting and struggled for breath. But he managed somehow to carry on a conversation through the open door about Lamartine's latest book.

He passed a quiet night. The following day he felt better and received guests, though he had a pain at the base of his back. In the evening he developed a temperature. His doctor was called. He found a large tumour, decided that an urgent operation was required, and summoned the well-known surgeon Marjolin. Talleyrand was completely conscious throughout. At one point he said: 'You know, you are putting me in great pain!' As soon as it was over, he insisted on being taken back into the *salon* and spoke for a while to his secretary Bacourt. He smiled as he recounted how his dog Carlos had bitten the surgeon and had had to be removed.[39] Later, in conversation with Montrond and other visitors, he referred to what he had undergone as 'the tickling of the scalpel'.[40]

The following day he was unable to get up. A messenger was sent to the abbé Dupanloup, who hurried to the Hôtel Talleyrand, passing the doctor on the stairs. Cruveilhier whispered that there was little time left. When Dupanloup entered, the Prince was sitting on the side of his bed. His head kept falling forward on to his chest. He said: 'M. l'abbé, it is a long time since we met. You find me very ill.' Dupanloup tried to hand him the two re-drafted documents. At first, the Prince insisted that he had said all he wanted to in his own earlier versions. But Dupanloup explained that it was important to avoid any subsequent misrepresentation and that this required some changes. Talleyrand said he understood. Dupanloup offered to read the documents out, but the Prince said that he would read them himself, and proceeded to do so.

The declaration or retraction was now couched in very general terms. It condemned 'the excesses' of the times in which the Prince had lived and the 'grave errors which during this long succession of years [had] troubled and afflicted the Catholic, Apostolic and Roman Church' in which he had had 'the misfortune to participate'. He submitted himself entirely to the 'doctrine and discipline' of the Church. In self-justification, he asserted that since his laicization he had served the interests of the clergy and had never ceased to consider himself a 'child of the Church'. The letter to the Pope was even more general. In justification of the actions of his lifetime, he referred Gregory XVI to his memoirs, which, however (he added), would not appear for thirty (in practice fifty) years after his death. He asked that whatever he had done be set against 'the general abandonment of the times'. Referring to his lack of religious vocation, he added that all his youth 'had been spent following a profession to which [he] had not been born'. Finally, he abandoned himself to the indulgence and justice of the Pope.

These two documents reflected the extraordinary degree to which the Prince's sensibilities had been respected by the draughtsmen. They contained no disavowal of any particular act, no regret for the schism, and no mention of his marriage, though these could all be read into the wording. No wonder that Talleyrand now pronounced himself 'very satisfied'. But instead of immediately appending his signature, he folded the papers up and put them in his pocket, saying that he wanted to reread them.

During the rest of that day (Tuesday) the illness was in remission. Talleyrand talked to his visitor, the duc de Noailles, about poetry and wine. The ensuing night was also tolerable. But at four o'clock in the morning he woke with palpitations and unable to breathe. The doctor now told him that it was time for him to put all his affairs in order. Dupanloup then arrived and was introduced by Pauline. The abbé summoned up courage to speak more directly than hitherto about the need for the Prince to pay his debt to the Church. Talleyrand interrupted, declaring that he wanted to do just that. Then he asked to see Dorothée, saying that he wanted to add something to his retraction. Dupanloup stayed in the house all day, but the Prince still did not sign. Royer-Collard expressed confidence that Talleyrand would finally do what was required: 'Have no fear: he who has always been a peacemaker will not refuse to make peace with God before dying.' When the Prince was told of this, he protested: 'I am not refusing! I am not refusing!' But still he did not sign.

At eight o'clock that evening Dupanloup entered the room. He said that he was going to see the archbishop: would Talleyrand now sign the documents? The Prince simply told him to thank Quélen for his concern and to rest assured that everything would be done. 'But when, Uncle?' interrupted Pauline. 'Tomorrow morning, between five and six o'clock,' Talleyrand answered. This took everyone by surprise. Dupanloup interjected: 'I can, therefore, offer the hope. . .' 'Do not say, hope. It is certain,' said the Prince firmly. But would he last that long? Had he some secret knowledge of when exactly he would die? Or was it a delaying tactic intended to avoid signing at all? Later that night, Bacourt persuaded Pauline to present the papers again for the Prince's signature. But he was not to be deceived, nor hurried. He said: 'But it is not yet six o'clock. Go away, Pauline. Be still. I have never done anything fast, and yet I have always arrived on time.'[41]

He passed a very difficult night, twisting and groaning with pain. At about five o'clock, the witnesses arrived: the duc de Poix (who the Prince said looked like an undertaker), Royer-Collard, Molé, Barante and the comte de Saint-Aulaire. They stayed outside in the *salon*, the door of Talleyrand's bedchamber remaining open. Dupanloup stood with the family by the bed. Talleyrand opened his eyes and asked what time it was. Someone said it was six o'clock, but the abbé corrected him: 'Prince, it is barely more than five.' He was clear that there must be no room for subsequent charges of manipulation. So Talleyrand waited and the others waited with him. As a further stratagem, Dorothée had persuaded Marie, the Prince's great-niece, daughter of Charlotte (and thus also, almost certainly, his own granddaughter), to come and ask for his blessing. She was dressed in white, ready to go and make her first communion. He blessed her, and when she left he remarked: 'You see both extremities of life: she is going to make her first communion. . .and I!'

At last it was six o'clock. The Prince sat up on the edge of his bed. He was held up on one side by Bacourt and on the other by the duc de Valençay. Dorothée, Pauline and Dupanloup stood near. The doctor looked on. So did the oldest of the Prince's servants, whom he had summoned to be present at this solemn moment to bear witness for the rest of his household. The formal witnesses observed proceedings through the open door. Pauline said: 'Uncle, it is now six o'clock. Shall I present the papers that you have promised to sign?' Talleyrand reached out and took the pen from her. Dorothée, equally determined that there should be no confusion, offered to read out the documents and he asked her to do so. By the time she had finished, the ink on his pen was dry. The Prince dipped it again, put on his spectacles, and then signed the retraction with a firm, clear hand. He then signed the letter to the Pope as well. Echoing Royer-Collard's thought, he remarked with more than a touch of vanity: 'It is my big signature, the one I have placed at the bottom of all the peace treaties of France. I must place it at the foot of this last treaty, that of my peace with Holy Church.'

He knew that others would subsequently pretend that he had signed without knowing what he was doing. So he had the documents dated 10 March, a week after his eulogy at the Académie, when everyone had seen that he was in full possession of his faculties. It was a final act of deception.[42]

Exhausted, Talleyrand lay back, while the witnesses appended their signatures as well. It was suddenly announced that the King had arrived. While Dupanloup hurried off to celebrate a mass of thanksgiving, Louis-Philippe entered accompanied by Mme Adélaïde. The King was not at ease. He muttered: 'I am unhappy to see you ill.' Talleyrand, who was again sitting on the side of his bed, replied: 'Sire, you are present at the last moments of a dying man. It is a great honour that Your Majesty does to this house to come today.' He proceeded formally to introduce the monarch to all those present, including his servant. After a short while Louis-Philippe left, but his sister stayed. She squeezed Talleyrand's hand, and he murmured affectionately: 'I am very fond of you.' Then she too departed.[43]

His strength was now almost completely gone. Those around were increasingly anxious lest he should die without the last rites. But Dupanloup returned. The Prince was still propped up on the side of his bed. The others now withdrew, so he held himself up by gripping the priest's arms. He then made his confession. So tight was his hold that Dupanloup found it difficult to break his hand away to give the absolution. The Prince now fell back. He could barely speak. He tried to say something about the archbishop. Dupanloup, with the kind of sentimentality that Talleyrand had never liked, repeated how Quélen had said that he would willingly give his life for him. The Prince smiled faintly and said: 'He has better things to do with it.'

Dupanloup then administered extreme unction. But when he was about to place the chrism oil on the dying man's palms, Talleyrand turned his hands over so that it could be placed on their backs, murmuring: 'Remember: I am a bishop.' The priest gave the viaticum. The room was now full of family and friends. They wept and kissed the Prince's hand. The litany of the saints was said by Dupanloup and all those present joined in. At the invocation of 'St Maurice' and 'St Charles' Talleyrand distinctly nodded.[44] He died at half past three.

Outside the bedroom, the mood was altogether different. In one corner sat Montrond, with his head in his hands, devastated by the approaching loss of his mentor, appalled at the popish nonsense to which the Prince was submitting. Some fashionable young men gathered around a beautiful woman lying on a chaise-longue. The irreverent laughter of another group of aristocratic ladies earned them an occasional rebuke. As soon as it was learned that the Prince had finally died, people hurried away to spread the news.[45]

The reaction to the Prince's deathbed reconciliation with the Church was generally hostile. As Rémusat put it, there was 'a singly cry from the world of Voltaire'. Montrond's sarcasm knew no bounds, certainly not those of taste. He blamed Talleyrand's family for what had happened. Thiers was even more abusive and contemptuous. He now talked of Talleyrand, his former friend and protector, with bitterness, accusing him of 'betraying the eighteenth century' by this act of 'monkery' ('*capucinade*'). Montrond and Thiers even used such language to Pauline in the salon adjoining where Talleyrand lay dead. She tried to explain but finished by denouncing them as 'slanderers'. The duchesse de Dino never spoke to Thiers again.[46]

One might have expected the clerical party and the Church itself to trumpet a success. But there was instead an embarrassed silence. There was doubt, at least outside the circle of those immediately concerned, about Talleyrand's sincerity. More seriously, perhaps, there was confusion about whether the formal act of retraction that he had signed sufficiently fulfilled the demands laid down by Rome. It was rumoured that other, more demanding, instructions arrived after the Prince's death.[47] This is not so. But what is true is that the Pope, on receiving copies of the documents, and while welcoming what had occurred, also noted that the language of the Prince's retraction was 'weaker' than he had hoped. This reaction, contained in a papal brief, would now have to be published alongside the text of the Prince's statements. Rome's coolness did not, of course, imply that Talleyrand's reconciliation and reception of the last rites were invalid. But it did immediately make Quélen very reluctant to publish anything at all, because he might appear to have been rebuked by Gregory XVI for exceeding his instructions.[48]

In any case, whatever the formalities, the legitimist Catholic party was as happy to pursue Talleyrand beyond the grave as were the liberals. And no one more so than Chateaubriand:

> The crowd watched open-mouthed at the final hour of the Prince, three-quarters rotten, a gangrenous opening in his side, his head falling on to his chest despite the bandage that held it, disputing minute by minute his reconciliation with heaven, his niece playing beside him a role prepared long since with a deluded priest and a deceived girl. . .Pride has never shown itself more wretched, admiration so stupid, piety so credulous.[49]

Others, though, were simply anxious to give the affair as little publicity as possible. The government was fearful of providing an excuse for an anticlerical demonstration in the Chamber by those claiming that the retraction was forced or fraudulent. Molé, President of the Council, Sébastiani, ambassador to Britain, and Dupin, President of the Chamber, all pressed the papal Internuncio, Mgr Garibaldi, at least to delay publicizing Talleyrand's retraction and conversion. Garibaldi was persuaded, and he in turn persuaded Rome.[50] Finally, to avoid a riot by anticlerical elements, the procession bearing the Prince's (now embalmed) body from the rue Saint-Florentin to the nearby church of the Assumption was diverted to a different route at the last moment. The disappointed crowds complained that Talleyrand had 'even deceived them in death'.[51]

But the funeral mass in Paris was not the end of the road for Talleyrand's remains. He had decided that he should be buried at Valençay alongside his brother Archambaud and his great-niece Yolande, who had died at the age of three. Accordingly, on the night of 3–4 September, a cortège bearing the Prince's coffin, with the crested ducal crown of the Talleyrands resting upon it, entered the gates of the château. The *cour d'honneur* was brightly lit by torches held by the local guard. The carriage circled the courtyard and stopped at the main steps, where the duc de Valençay climbed up on to it. (Dorothée and Pauline, as was the custom, had stayed away to grieve.) Then the cortège set out again through the dark to the parish church, followed by the château's staff and others from the neighbourhood. The coffin was placed before the altar. Hundreds of candles were lit to create a *chapelle ardente*. During the night the bodies of Archambaud and Yolande arrived, to be placed beside that of the Prince.

The requiem mass on 5 September was a local affair, after which 1,200 loaves of bread were distributed to the poor of Valençay. The coffins were brought to the chapel of Saint-Maurice, adjoining the alms house kept by the sisters of charity. Then, to the sound of musket-fire, the coffins were lowered, one by one – Charles-Maurice first, then Archambaud, then the tiny casket of Yolande – into the vault below. No representative of the archbishopric of Bourges or of the *préfecture* was present. The religious and secular authorities alike preferred to forget the Prince.[52]

18

Politician, Diplomat, Statesman

~·~

TALLEYRAND WAS NOT easy for his contemporaries to understand. By the time of his death he had argued so many cases and served so many régimes, he had lived so long in the public gaze, that there seemed no other explanation of his behaviour than opportunism. This was part of the truth, though it was not the whole truth. Talleyrand's genius was to reflect in his behaviour and decisions the changing and contradictory currents that marked the history of France between the times of Louis XV and Louis-Philippe. Vitrolles observed of Talleyrand's character: 'It seems to me that one will do him no injustice in accepting him for what he claimed to be: the type, the representative, of the times in which he lived. But, good God! What times!'[1]

That was a back-handed way of saying that Talleyrand was a superb politician, and since the point is sometimes overlooked it is worth emphasizing. It was only because he was politically able that he could act as a diplomat and indeed a statesman, those more distinguished roles for which he wanted to be known and admired. The Prince's most commonly mentioned political gift, then and since, was his foresight. Various anecdotes were told of it, such as one mentioned by Thomas Raikes. This has Jaucourt meeting Talleyrand shortly before 18 Brumaire and asking what he was doing. Talleyrand is meant to have answered: 'Me? I am doing nothing, I am waiting.'[2] But, if the account is accurate, Talleyrand was lying, because he was very actively involved in the plot. It is, therefore, misleading. The same could be said of the myth underlying the story. Talleyrand was certainly patient, did not waste effort and affected idleness but, as Guizot noted, he was bold and energetic when necessary. He was also more politically fortunate than gifted with exceptional foresight. None of the three occasions on which he lost or resigned office – as the Directory's Foreign Minister in 1799, as that of Napoleon in 1807, and as President of the Council in 1815 – suggests such a gift. The first instance was the result of disgrace, the second preceded Napoleon's fall by no less than seven years, and the third kept him out of front-line politics until he was seventy-six.

Talleyrand's political strengths were, in truth, less original but more important. Above all, he was quick to see and then bold to seize opportunities. In his eulogy of the Prince, Barante stressed that he had been an expert in the 'science of events' (*la science des événements*): 'He never despaired or became discouraged, because his superior intelligence perceived a means and an expedient where others just saw obstacles, and showed that – according to his maxim – there was always a better course to take. What was important was to see it, which is a matter of cleverness, and to take it, which is a matter of character. It is the second rather than the first that most people lack.'[3]

This insight helps explain what made Talleyrand so successful, and so different from those of his contemporaries who were lost when political conditions changed. He also possessed other useful attributes. He was capable of extraordinary personal charm, which he exerted through his distinctive speech and bearing, and which he particularly applied to well-connected women. Though only a passable public speaker, he was a good draughtsman and excellent propagandist, and throughout his career knew how to improve and adapt the work of others, while his ability to attract and to motivate younger colleagues and staff was legendary. Partly because of his upbringing, but more because of his inner reserves of self-confidence, he possessed, right up to the end of his life, 'a wonderful talent to impose himself', as the comtesse de Boigne expressed it.[4] He filled a room, especially when it was his own.

Talleyrand succeeded as a politician not just thanks to his aptitude but also as a result of his effort. He was remorseless. It has often been said, and rightly, that throughout his political life he pursued his financial interests. But the converse is also true. Money was essential to his style of politics. It allowed him to maintain his position, and on that position depended his political influence. Even when he was in society, and when he appeared to be talking about food or poetry or cards, he was almost invariably engaged in politics at some level. To his last days, he interfered in the make-up of governments, and his favourite guests at Valençay were those involved, in some sense at least, in public life.

In politics, Talleyrand embraced no consistent programme throughout his long career. But he did espouse certain political ideas and values. He supported, whenever he could afford to do so, the causes of freedom of speech and freedom of thought. He was, indeed, the enemy of censorship even when his government, in 1815, might have benefited from it.

He had been one of the group around Mirabeau who looked to Britain as a political model. Throughout his life he advocated a constitution that dispersed power rather than concentrated it, whether in an over-powerful executive or in a chaotic legislative assembly. As a very moderate Revolutionary, he favoured the royal veto and a second chamber. Under the Restoration, he again argued strongly for a hereditary Upper House, on the grounds that it would entrench the propertied interests behind the monarchy.[5] The Revolution of July 1830 finally introduced a system that corresponded more or less to the one he advocated, but the circumstances of its arrival had fatally undermined its stability, as he recognized and privately lamented.

To call Talleyrand a liberal constitutionalist does not, however, adequately describe his politics. He was more conservative than that, and as the years went by he became more conservative still. He had always been a proponent of social hierarchy, a believer in order, an enemy of demagogues, an advocate of property rights. These are, of course, the traits of a classical liberal, and they were shared by the younger Doctrinaires, of whom Talleyrand should be seen as the precursor. But the Prince was also entirely happy with the practice of organized violence in the name of *raison d'état*, which no liberal would approve. He had no problem with *coups d'état* as long as they could be turned to his own interest. His quarrels with Napoleon were more about foreign than domestic policy, though he would certainly have preferred a less dictatorial régime. The most significant demonstration of his approach to state violence is, however, his role in the execution of the duc d'Enghien. Because he consistently lied about his involvement, he was never in a position honestly to justify it. But there is no doubt that he shared Napoleon's view that it was a necessary measure to protect the state; indeed he used that argument in his written advice.[6]

For all his talents, Talleyrand's claims to that most elusive quality, statesmanship, are hard to sustain in domestic politics. He came closest to showing it in the change of régime between Napoleon and the Bourbons. His management of the first Restoration was acclaimed by contemporaries as a political *tour de force*, demonstrating his great reserves of shrewdness, ingenuity and boldness.

Had Talleyrand then been trusted by Louis XVIII to pursue the policies he wished, he might have created the basis for a stable monarchy – though whether that was truly possible can be questioned. At least he understood, as the returning *émigrés* could not, how deep were the scars and fierce the passions that remained from the Revolution. Only a liberal monarchy stood a chance of achieving a political consensus between the discordant – and very illiberal – factions and traditions of Restoration France.[7] But certainly the forces of ultra reaction would first have had to be faced down. This could only have been done with the personal support of the King, and Louis withheld it. That was partly the result of the monarch's personal pettiness. But the Prince's background was also heavily against him. After the assassination of the duc de Berry in 1820 and the reaction it provoked, the project of a liberal monarchy in any case became an impossibility.

It is, therefore, mainly in foreign policy that Talleyrand's claims to statesmanship must be assessed. Charles de Rémusat professed not to like the Prince personally, but admitted: 'I regard him as one of the superior men of my time, perhaps the only one of my French contemporaries who deserves the title of statesman.'[8]

The judgement is fair.

Talleyrand's historical reputation, in France at least, is mainly as a diplomat and French diplomats themselves have written in glowing terms of his achievements. One recent biography is even subtitled 'Prince of Diplomats'.[9] Within limits – the limits of diplomacy itself – this judgement is also fair. Napoleon valued Talleyrand for his poise and polish, his capacity to keep his own counsel and draw out another diplomat's secret thoughts, his ability to balance delay with speed in executing the Emperor's orders. The Prince's inscrutability and deportment contributed as much to the legend of his diplomatic finesse as any particular achievement. He was clearly able to conduct detailed and complicated negotiations with great skill, as in the creation of the Confederation of the Rhine (1806), at the Congress of Vienna (1814–15) and in London during the crisis over Belgium (1830–32). But he was also keen to cultivate his image. His eulogy of Reinhard shortly before his death was the culmination of that exercise.

It was, of course, as Napoleon's Foreign Minister that Talleyrand's reputation was established. But, as he himself recognized, diplomacy under such a ruler and in the circumstances of almost continual warfare was bound to be of secondary importance in shaping events. In reality, Talleyrand stood out among his contemporary diplomats for reasons both good and bad that had little directly to do with diplomacy in its narrowest sense.

The bad side of Talleyrand's exceptionalism was the extraordinary degree of corruption that accompanied his negotiations. It is impossible to gauge exactly how much he received from foreign powers in the course of his career. But from the XYZ scandal in 1798 right up to his last days, when he was (probably wrongly) alleged to be in the pay of the Russian government, his name was synonymous with venality on a scale that made even venal contemporaries blush.[10] Whether this had any adverse effect on French interests is debatable. Perhaps the bribes, by increasing his resources and so his influence, even led under Napoleon to marginally more sensible, less bellicose policies. Nor did his corruption necessarily affect the general course he pursued. He was, for example, well paid by Austria; but he genuinely also believed at this time that a Franco-Austrian alliance was in France's interests. At Erfurt and later, he was working for Russia and would expect to be paid for it; but he was primarily working to rid France of Napoleon, and for reasons that were French not Russian. Later still at the Congress of Vienna he was well rewarded by the Bourbons of Naples; but in serving their interest he was also pursuing the policy of Louis XVIII.

The second, and more commendable, reason why Talleyrand holds an exceptional position in the diplomatic pantheon is through his leadership of the French Foreign Ministry. He was an excellent administrator, rewarding and promoting talent, insisting on depth of knowledge and on the highest standards of competence. His well-known comments about the need to discourage 'zeal' reflect not a perverse promotion of idleness but rather a commitment to orderliness. Talleyrand worked to Napoleon's instructions, and he relied heavily on others, especially Hauterive, for the detail. But he deserves the lion's share of the credit for creating – or more accurately re-creating – the ethos and *esprit de corps* of the French diplomatic service. He restored the tradition of the *ancien régime* within the Napoleonic framework. This was recognized at the time and is recognized still. Today's Quai d'Orsay and the diplomats it sends out to protect French interests around the world owe much to Talleyrand's legacy.

But Talleyrand's historical claims to statesmanship – in the sense meant by Rémusat – must be assessed in areas beyond those of diplomacy or administration. They are strongest in the realm of ideas. Talleyrand was unusual in being an intellectual whose intellect was primarily applied to foreign policy. Through his reflection on international affairs he arrived at what today seem some remarkably modern insights.

Talleyrand had a view of history and of the political process within history that was more subtle and more realistic than that of most of his contemporaries. He believed that the course of history was set by social, cultural and ideological currents over which politicians had little control. Their role was to stay afloat, to preserve or improve when possible, to use the opportunities that occurred. This was, of course, in part an excuse for treason. But it was certainly a useful basis upon which to conduct a pragmatic and intelligent foreign policy.

He also understood very clearly the close connection between politics and economics. Sound finances were, in Talleyrand's view, essential for stable government and for the effective pursuit of foreign goals. Similarly, free trade and open markets were the best basis both for prosperity and for peaceful international cooperation.

This led him to a further insight into the future of colonialism. Talleyrand observed how Britain within a few years of an end to hostilities with the American colonies had once more achieved close relations through opening up its markets. By contrast France, which had fought alongside the rebels, was no longer close to them because of its protectionism. In his suggestions for the acquisition of new colonies, Talleyrand therefore urged an enlightened colonialism based not on simple exploitation but on shared mutual benefit. The fact that his preferred colony, Egypt, had other fatal drawbacks does not minimize the importance and originality of his argument.

Talleyrand similarly argued, from the time of his earliest diplomatic apprenticeship under the Revolution onwards, for an enlightened – and unusual – approach to treaties or what he called 'alliances'. Rather than regard relations between France and its neighbours as being a choice between domination or hostility, he urged the use of influence and building friendship and mutual confidence as the basis of satisfactory relations. He, therefore, urged respect from the Revolutionaries for other European peoples' self-determination, and restraint rather than conquest upon Napoleon. True, he was not always consistent in this approach. His attachment to 'peace' rather than war can be exaggerated, and he liked to exaggerate it himself. When necessary he saw war as useful and the threat of war – as with the Triple Alliance of January 1815 – even more so. But his conception of international relations was fundamentally peaceful.

The Prince has been hailed as the founder of the Anglo-French Entente Cordiale. That is in some respects true, but his attitude was both more subtle and more ambiguous than the formulation might suggest. His admiration for the British constitutional and political system was immense, as has been noted. He had close English friends, even if he disliked some English attitudes. He believed that Britain as a commercial power with interests around the globe and France as an agricultural economy with interests focused on Europe should be able to exist in harmony. But the main impulse behind his advocacy (until the very end of his career) of close relations with Britain was his understanding of the fundamental connection between systems of government and the behaviour of states. His foreign policy thus took into account values as well as interests. He regarded Britain as the leading liberal power in Europe, opposed to autocracy and authoritarianism. It was, therefore, desirable for the kind of France he envisaged – whether a moderate republic, or a liberal empire, or a constitutional monarchy – to rely upon Britain as an ally. The tragedy from

Talleyrand's point of view was that he was for so long unsuccessful in achieving the sort of régime that he wanted. The French Republic was committed to continual revolution; the Emperor was far from liberal; the Bourbons could not live with a constitution. And finally when a constitutional monarchy, built on Anglo-Saxon lines, did emerge, Talleyrand found that the scope for alliance with Britain was reduced because France was so obviously the junior partner in the relationship. That said, Talleyrand certainly stands out as the most intelligent and persistent advocate of the Franco-British alliance in his era.

His absorption of British political and economic ideas, as well as his personal experience in exile, encouraged him to formulate extremely perceptive conclusions about the United States. He understood the degree to which, despite the War of Independence, America was and would remain an offshoot of British society because of bonds of culture, institutions and language, all reinforced by economics, and he would not have been surprised by the modern consequences of those links. He even envisaged that America would eventually become a great power, one capable of intervening in Europe with effects that he, as a Frenchman, feared.[11]

As has been observed, Talleyrand was not insensitive to a wider internationalism. While in exile he had toyed with the idea of an international order of mutually respectful sovereign states, whose good relations were underpinned by free trade. But he soon forgot such projects and concentrated instead on determining and asserting France's place in Europe.

In his Declaration he writes that 'the real interests of France. . .are never in opposition with the real interests of Europe'. This was more than a rhetorical device, although it was a convenient elision to make. Talleyrand's conception of Europe has, of course, little in common with that espoused by modern devotees of a United States of Europe. On the other hand, his calculations about how to advance French interests in a European context have been largely shared by modern French politicians since (and including) de Gaulle. They, like Talleyrand, have regarded acceptance of some constraints within Europe as worth while, because the European framework itself allows France to limit the power of its rivals and to exert greater international influence.[12]

That said, Talleyrand had a conception of Europe that was quite distinctive – not least in relation to Europe's geographical and cultural limits. He thus regarded Russia as fundamentally non-European, synonymous with brutality and barbarism, and he wished to keep it out of European politics, preferably behind the wall of an independent, autonomous or at least anti-Russian Poland. His observations would do credit to a Cold War hawk.

His view of Europe was, naturally, one of independent states. But he was not by temperament a nationalist, though he claimed to be, and in a fashion was, a French patriot. He did not deny the force of nationalism. In the case of Germany he feared it. He was much more at ease with Austria than with Prussia, because the former was so nationally divided that it was a force for conservation rather than aggression in Europe. Napoleon accused Talleyrand of embracing the foreign policy of 'the old France', and the Prince did not demur.[13] Talleyrand held to the policy of alliance with Austria that had been pursued by Choiseul, though he would have liked if possible to reverse the partitions of Poland which had, in his view, upset the European balance. He was also prepared to invoke, as he did at the Congress of Vienna, the traditional concept of a European-wide 'public law' in order to resist the rule of force.

Talleyrand's adherence to the thinking that prevailed in foreign policy before the Revolution did not, however, reflect nostalgia. Rather it acknowledged what he saw as underlying European realities, realities that the Revolution had not changed. By the time of the death of Louis XIV, it was clear that while France remained the single most powerful European state, and although a Bourbon was now seated on the throne of Spain, France could not prevail without alliances with one or more other powers. The precise implications of this were debatable; but once the analysis was accepted, the conclusion must also be drawn that French interests required careful management, rather than attempted domination, of the other states of Europe. Napoleon refused to accept this. He believed that French feats of arms could preserve French dominance with a 'grand empire'. In this, he saw himself as the continuator of Louis XIV, 'le Grand Roi'. Talleyrand, whose admiration for 'le grand siècle' was mainly cultural not military, radically disagreed, and this disagreement underlay the early political tension and the later personal clashes between them.

Once defeat came, and Napoleon was deposed, the argument was clearly over. Between then and Talleyrand's death in 1838 France was always in a weak position, indeed doubly so: it was feared because of the recent past, yet it was no longer capable of imposing itself militarily or economically. To compound the problem, most Frenchmen did not understand the fact. In these circumstances, it was indeed true, as Talleyrand argued, that France's 'real' interests lay in working with, not against, the rest of Europe.

This, though, would not be easy. Hence the policy that he pursued at the Congress of Vienna. He decided that the long view required short-term accommodation. He made a virtue of the fact that France alone demanded nothing of the other powers. And he made what his critics saw as risky sacrifices of French strategic interest, particularly in the form of accepting Prussian expansion in the Rhineland close to France's border. In order to break the common front of the allied coalition against France he also took the risk of outraging Russia. The benefits he expected from this approach were twofold: France would be back at the top table of European powers, allied with Britain and Austria and an equal of Prussia and Russia; and within Europe itself a balance of power, leading to stability and peace, would be created. But the unexpected return of Napoleon from St Helena wrecked the strategy. France was once more a pariah; nothing was gained from the sacrifices made; and Russia, assisted by Prussia, was able to exact revenge.

Talleyrand's strategy of protecting France's position within Europe after the Restoration also depended upon the promotion of the idea of legitimacy as the basis of a European order. Of course, this was in origin a way of asserting the rights of the Bourbons. But it was Talleyrand, not Louis XVIII or any of the other figures at the Congress of Vienna, who invested it with its wider implications. He saw it as a way of underpinning not just monarchy but what made monarchies stable, namely constitutional government. He even envisaged that a liberal Bourbon monarchy first in France but also in Naples and Spain should embody and popularize the concept throughout Europe.[14] Nor were its benefits to be limited to rulers but rather extended to peoples, legitimacy being (as he put it) 'the most solid and

I dare to say the only guarantee of the existence and continuance of nations'.[15] In an age that has known genocide that judgement still has resonance.

Original and sophisticated conceptions of international relations, therefore, distinguished Talleyrand's statesmanship. But it was also marked by practical failure. He was, of course, unlucky, because he saw his achievements at Vienna nullified by the hugely destructive Hundred Days. Yet the judgement he reached at Vienna upon the balance between France's narrow strategic interest and its wider political influence reflects a weakness that was of long standing. This was his poor judgement in military matters.

On every occasion when Talleyrand chose to advise on the conduct of war he was wrong, though he usually covered his tracks. It began with the ill-fated expedition to Egypt in 1798, which he himself had helped conceive. Similarly, the strategy that he urged upon Napoleon in his famous memorandum of 1805, involving peace with Austria and hostility to Russia, might have made sense in the long term. But in the short term it did not, because he underestimated Russian military power and exaggerated that of Austria. Again, there is no evidence that he grasped the rationale, flawed as it was, of Napoleon's Continental Blockade, so he had no reason to support the disastrous invasion of Spain, which can in retrospect be seen as truly marking 'the beginning of the end'. Yet Talleyrand urged the enterprise upon Napoleon, from a mixture of self-interested opportunism and thoughtlessness about the military implications. Subsequently, he claimed that he had opposed the plan. But this was untrue. The misjudgements continued. At the Congress of Vienna he urged Louis XVIII to mobilize for a war against Russia and Prussia in defence of Saxony and Poland which the country could not have fought and which the régime would not have survived. True, the bluff worked. Russia and Prussia backed down. But war was a real possibility and it would have been disastrous for France.

Finally, and with the gravest long-term implications, Talleyrand underestimated Prussia, which he hated and despised but did not sufficiently fear. He was not unaware of the danger that a powerful Prussia might pose, and, as has been noted, he was also aware of the power of German nationalism. But he did not think through the dangers of the two coinciding to threaten French security. So at the Congress of Vienna he was more interested in keeping Prussia weak as a power within Germany, by preventing its consolidation in the north through absorbing Saxony, than in keeping it as far away as possible from France. In fact, the unsustainable territorial formation of the Prussian state only increased its desire to dominate Germany as a whole, and so become the focus and exploiter of German nationalism. It took Napoleon III's further misjudgements to lead to France's military humiliation, but Talleyrand's misreading of threats helped pave the way.

So while Rémusat was right to award Talleyrand the accolade of statesmanship, he was also right to add: 'What will damage his historical reputation is that he founded nothing. Nothing remains that comes from him.'[16] As a result, Talleyrand is today remembered more for *bons mots* that he may never have uttered, poses that were often affected, and a foresight that was most evident in retrospect, than for the shrewdness, intelligence, wisdom, courage and persistence that placed him at the forefront of French society and politics for half a century. Whether he would have been surprised, or even disappointed, is another matter. As he explained to a friend in 1789: 'People always say too much ill or too much good of me; I enjoy the honours of exaggeration.'[17]

Chronology[*]

1754   Birth of Charles-Maurice de
Talleyrand-Périgord (2 February)

1758   T's stay at Chalais (till 1760)

1762   T enters the Collège d'Harcourt

1769   T stays with his uncle,
Alexandre-Angélique, in Reims

1770   T enters the seminary of Saint-Sulpice

1774   Accession of Louis XVI (10 May)

1775   T ordained sub-deacon, incorporated   Coronation of Louis XVI
in Reims diocese (1 April); T   (11 June)
appointed promoter of the French
clergy

1778   France declares war on
Britain (10 July)

1779   T ordained priest (18 December)

1780   T appointed agent general of the French
clergy (10 May)

[*] For a fuller chronology on which this is in part based, see that compiled by André Beau, 'Le parcours de Charles-Maurice de Talleyrand-Périgord', on the excellent website of Les Amis de Talleyrand (www.amis-talleyrand.asso.fr).

1783		Peace of Versailles between France, Britain and American colonies (3 September)
1784	Attempt by Mme de Brionne to have T made a cardinal (August)	
1785	T presents his report as agent general (July)	The 'Affair of the Necklace'
1787		Assembly of Notables meets (22 February)
	T now advising Calonne	
1789	T consecrated bishop of Autun (4 Jan)	Opening of Estates General (5 May)
	T urges a royal coup in discussion with the comte d'Artois (16/17 July) T proposes confiscation of Church property (10 October)	
1790	T urges introduction of the metric system (10 March) T celebrates Mass of the Federation in the Champs-de-Mars (14 July) T takes oath to Civil Constitution of the Clergy (28 December)	
1791	T resigns as bishop (13 January)	Death of Mirabeau (2 April)
	T negotiates for power with the monarchy (April–May)	Arrest of French royal family at Varennes (20 June)
	T's report on public education (10 September)	Constituent Assembly dissolved, replaced by Legislative Assembly

1792	T's diplomatic mission to London (January–July)	France declares war against Austria and other German states (20 April)
		Crowds invade the Tuileries (20 June)
	T resigns from the Paris Directory (20 July)	Royal family imprisoned in the Temple (12 August)
		The September Massacres (2–6 September)
	T flees Paris for London (arrives 18 September)	Opening of National Convention (20 September)
		Declaration of the French Republic (22 September)
	T's memorandum on relations between France and the other states of Europe (25 November)	
	T placed on official list of suspects by Convention (5 December)	
1793		Execution of Louis XVI ('Louis Capet') (21 January)
		France declares war on Britain, Holland and Spain (1 February)
	Sale of T's library in London (April)	
	T on published list of émigrés (29 August)	
1794	T ordered to leave Britain under the Alien Act (28 January)	
	T arrives in Philadelphia (mid-April)	Robespierre and the 'Mountain' overthrown (27 July)
	T's expeditions into Maine and New York State (summer–autumn)	

1795   T's petition to Convention seeking his
return (16 June)
T's name removed from list of *émigrés*
(4 September)

Constitution of the
Year III ratified in
plebiscite (23 September)
Beginning of rule by
the Directory (October)

1796   T arrives in Hamburg (31 July), en route
to Paris (arriving 20 September)

1797   T's lecture on Anglo-US commercial
relations (4 April)
T's lecture on need for new colonies
(3 July)
T appointed Minister of Foreign
Affairs (16 July)

Directorial coup of
18 Fructidor
(4 September)
Treaty of Campo-
Formio signed by
Bonaparte (27 October)

T's first meeting with Bonaparte
(6 December)
T's speech introducing Bonaparte to the
Directors (10 December)

1798   T's reception for Bonaparte at the Ministry
of Foreign Affairs (3 January)
T's first report to the Directory urging
invasion of Egypt (27 January)
T's second report on Egypt (14 February)
The 'XYZ Affair' scandal (April–May)

Bonaparte's expedition
to Egypt (May)

1799   The Jorry Affair (April–July).
T's resignation accepted as Foreign
Minister (20 July)

Coup of 18/19 Brumaire
overthrows the
Directory, establishing
the Consulate (9/10
November)

T appointed Minister of Foreign
Affairs (22 November)

1800   T's reorganization of his department's
personnel (January)
T acquires the Hôtel de Créqui in the   Approval in plebiscite of
rue d'Anjou   Constitution of the Year
    VIII (February)
    Napoleon escapes
    assassination by bomb in
    the rue Saint-Nicaise
    (24 December)

1801   Peace of Lunéville with
    Austria (9 February)
T's ball at Neuilly for the King and   Concordat agreed
Queen of Etruria (8 June)   with the Pope (July)

1802   Peace of Amiens with
    Britain (27 March)
    Napoleon Bonaparte
    elected First Consul for
    Life by plebiscite (May),
    proclaimed in
    August

T marries Catherine Verlée in civil
ceremony (10 September), (invalid)
church marriage the following day

1803   T purchases the château and estates of
Valençay (May)

1804   Execution of the duc
    d'Enghien (20 March)
    Napoleon endorsed as
    hereditary Emperor of
    the French (May), then
    crowned in Notre-
    Dame (2 December)

T appointed the Emperor's Grand
Chambellan (11 July)

1805		Third Coalition against France (August)
	T addresses memorandum on foreign policy to Napoleon (17 October)	Battle of Trafalgar (21 October) Battle of Austerlitz (2 December) Peace of Pressburg with Austria (26 December)
1806	T appointed Prince of Benevento (prince de Bénévent) (5 June)	Creation of the Confederation of the Rhine (July) and abolition of the Holy Roman Empire (August), following Recess of Ratisbon Fourth Coalition against France (July) Battle of Jena (14 October) Beginning of Continental Blockade, by Berlin Decrees (21 November)
	T in Warsaw (from December until May 1807)	
1807		Peace Conference of Tilsit with Russia (7–9 July)
	T resigns as Foreign Minister (9 August) T appointed Vice-Grand Elector (17 August)	Beginning of Peninsula War (November)

1808	T's acquisition of the Hôtel Monaco, rue de Varenne (March) Arrival of the Spanish royal princes at Valençay (18 May) T's involvement in the Conversations of Erfurt (September–October)	
1809	T dismissed as Grand Chambellan (27 January) 'The Scene' with Napoleon (29 January) Marriage of Edmond de Périgord and Dorothée de Courlande (22 April)	Fifth Coalition against France (April) Napoleon's divorce of Joséphine (December)
1810	T seeks funds (in vain) from the Tsar (September), and in following March	Napoleon's marriage to Marie-Louise (April)
1811	Purchase by the state of T's houses, the Hôtel Monaco and La Muette (at Passy) (December)	Birth of the King of Rome (20 March)
1812	Purchase by T of the Hôtel de l'Infantado (later Hôtel Talleyrand) in the rue Saint-Florentin (March) T briefly appointed to act as Napoleon's agent in Warsaw, then rescinded (March)	Invasion of Russia (June) Battle of Borodino (7 September) Beginning of Retreat from Moscow (October)

1813

Sixth Coalition (August)
Battle of Leipzig (16–19
October)

T refuses on three occasions Napoleon's
request that he return as Foreign
Minister (October–November)

1814

Allies cross the Rhine
(January)

T's final meeting with Napoleon
at Council of War (25 January)

End of peace
negotiations at Châtillon
(19 March)

T gives advice to Council of Regency
prior to the Empress's departure
(28 March)

Fall of Paris to the allies
(31 March)

T appointed president of a provisional
government by the Senate (2 April)

Abdication of Napoleon
(6 April)

T and the provisional government
greet Monsieur at the Barrière de
Bondy (12 April)

First Restoration of
Louis XVIII (1 May)

T appointed Foreign Minister (13 May)
T signs Treaty of Paris with the
allies (30 May)

Proclamation of the
Constitutional Charter
(La Charte) (4 June)

T arrives in Vienna for the Congress
(23 September)

1815 T signs defensive alliance with Britain
and Austria (3 January)

Napoleon re-enters Paris
(20 March)

T signs final act of the Congress of
Vienna (9 June)

Battle of Waterloo
(18 June)

T appointed President of the Council
and Foreign Minister (9 July)
T resigns as President of the Council
and Foreign Minister (21 September?)
T becomes Grand Chambellan
(27 September)

1816   T completes first version of his
memoirs (August)
T insults the government and is
disgraced (17 November)

1820

Assassination of the duc
de Berry (13 February)

1821

Death of Napoleon on
St Helena (5 May)

T's speech against press censorship in
Chamber of Peers (24 July)
Death of the duchesse de Courlande
(20 August)
T's eulogy of Bourlier, bishop of
Évreux (13 November)
Death of Mme de Rémusat
(16 December)

1822   T's second major speech against press
censorship (26 February)

1823   T prepares speech against war with
Spain (printed but not delivered)
(3 February)
T justifies himself to Louis XVIII in
the affair of the duc d'Enghien
(8 November)

1824

Death of Louis XVIII
(16 September)

1825

Coronation of Charles
X (29 May)

1827   Maubreuil's 'coup de poing' as
T leaves memorial service for
Louis XVI (20 January)

1830	T writes to the duc d'Orléans, urging him to come to Paris (29 July)	Coronation of Louis-Philippe (9 August)
	T appointed French ambassador to Britain (6 September)	London conference on Belgium begins (4 November)
1831	T signs treaty fixing borders of Belgium (15 November)	
1834	T signs the Quadruple Alliance between France, Britain, Spain and Portugal (22 April) T receives the duc d'Orléans at Valençay (26–29 October) Death of Countess Tyszkiewicz (2 November) T resigns as ambassador (13 November)	
1835	Death of the princesse de Talleyrand (10 December)	
1838	T delivers his eulogy of Reinhard (3 March) Signature of 'retraction', reconciliation with the Church, and death of Talleyrand (17 May) Burial of Talleyrand's body at Valençay (5 September)	

Notes

PREFACE

1. *Revelations of the Life of Prince Talleyrand edited from the Papers of the late M. Colmache private secretary to the Prince* (London: Henry Colburn, 1850), p. 153.
2. Henry Lytton Bulwer, 'Talleyrand: The Politic Man', in *Historical Characters* (London: Macmillan, 1900), p. 3.
3. References here are to Duff Cooper, *Talleyrand* (London: Phoenix Press, 2001).
4. Jack F. Bernard, *Talleyrand: A Biography* (New York: Collins, 1973).
5. Perhaps the most influential early study is that of the great French historian, Sainte-Beuve, who declaimed against Talleyrand's venality and mendacity, while appreciating his abilities (C.-A. Sainte-Beuve, *Monsieur de Talleyrand* (Paris: Michel Lévy, 1870)). The tone of moral disapprobation was combined with disapproval of Talleyrand's diplomatic strategy, once France was faced with three disastrous conflicts with its Eastern neighbour. For Louis Madelin, the Prince should be understood as an eighteenth-century figure 'lost in the nineteenth' (Louis Madelin, *Talleyrand* (Paris: Flammarion, 1944), p. 435). Jean Orieux's lengthy study of Talleyrand similarly presents him as a civilized cynic, Voltaire in an age of upheaval, though the author is not very discriminating with sources – no references are given (Jean Orieux, *Talleyrand ou le Sphinx incompris* (Paris: Flammarion, 1970)). By constrast, the works of Michel Poniatowski are more notable by the wealth of valuable source material summarized and analysed than by obviously new conclusions (See: Michel Poniatowski, *Talleyrand aux États-unis 1794–1796* (Paris: Perrin, 1976), *Talleyrand et le Consulat* (Paris: Perrin, 1986), *Talleyrand et le Directoire* (Paris: Perrin, 1982), *Talleyrand et l'ancienne France* (Paris: Perrin, 1988), *Les Années occultées 1789–1792* (Paris: Perrin, 1995)).

6. References here, however, are to the revised single volume, Georges Lacour-Gayet, *Talleyrand* (Paris: Payot, 1990).
7. 'Talleyrand's exceptional reputation in history is largely accounted for by the greatness of the events in which he was involved' (ibid., p. 1314).
8. Philip G. Dwyer, *Talleyrand* (London: Pearson Education, 2002). See also Dwyer's introductory essay in *Charles-Maurice de Talleyrand 1754–1838: A Bibliography*, compiled by Philip G. Dwyer (Westport: Greenwood Press, 1996).
9. Emmanuel de Waresquiel, *Talleyrand, le Prince immobile* (Paris: Fayard, 2003).
10. 'Better than anyone else, he understood the upheavals of his time' (ibid., p. 15). Talleyrand had a 'truly European vision' (ibid., p. 273).
11. For example, the very favourable judgement of Talleyrand by France's former Foreign Minister, Hubert Védrine, reviewing Waresquiel's book ('Pour Talleyrand', *Le Nouvel Observateur*, 25 September 2003).
12. For fuller discussions of the history of Talleyrand's memoirs, see *Talleyrand, Mémoires 1754–1815*, ed. Paul-Louis et Jean-Paul Couchoud (Paris: Plon, 1982), pp. 10–15, and Waresquiel, *Talleyrand*, pp. 734–6.
13. Lacour-Gayet, *Talleyrand*, p. 1047. It is one of the 'maxims' he noted down towards the end of his life.

CHAPTER 1: A VOCATION OF CONVENIENCE

1. Waresquiel plausibly suggests that resentment at his father's lack of means compared with that of the latter's half-brother, Gabriel-Marie de Talleyrand, helped mould Charles-Maurice's outlook (Waresquiel, *Talleyrand*, pp. 31, 33).
2. *Mémoires complets et authentiques de Charles-Maurice de Talleyrand prince de Bénévent. Texte conforme au manuscrit originel. Contenant les notes de Monsieur Adolphe Fourier de Bacourt légataire des manuscrits de l'Auteur*, I (Paris: Bonnot, 1967), p. 3. – henceforth referred to as Talleyrand, *Mémoires*. All references are to this version of the memoirs, unless otherwise specified. It has the merit of containing the documents relating to Talleyrand's spell as ambassador to London between 1830 and 1834. But use is also made of the apparatus of the best critical edition, *Talleyrand, Mémoires 1754–1815*, ed. Paul-Louis and Jean-Paul Couchoud (Paris: Plon, 1982).
3. Literally 'lad'.
4. Lacour-Gayet, *Talleyrand*, pp. 11–15.

5. Poniatowski, *Talleyrand et l'ancienne France*, pp. 15–27. Talleyrand, like his successors, pronounced his name 'Talran'. Whether through ignorance or impertinence, Napoleon pronounced it in what was in fact its older version, 'Tailleran'.

6. *Souvenirs intimes sur M. de Talleyrand recueillis par Amédée Pichot* (Paris: 1870), pp. 87, 96.

7. Waresquiel, *Talleyrand*, pp. 26–8.

8. Lacour-Gayet, *Talleyrand*, p. 11: '*Les Talleyrand ne se trompent que d'une lettre dans leurs prétensions: ils sont du Périgord, et non de Périgord.*'

9. Waresquiel, *Talleyrand*, p. 31.

10. Poniatowski, *Talleyrand et l'ancienne France*, pp. 32–8.

11. Lacour-Gayet, *Talleyrand*, p. 14.

12. Benjamin Constant, *Portraits, mémoires, souvenirs*, ed. Éphraïm Harpaz (Paris: Champion, 1992), p. 37.

13. Poniatowski, *Talleyrand et l'ancienne France*, pp. 41–3; Waresquiel, *Talleyrand*, pp. 40–1.

14. His beloved friend and on occasion dupe, Mme de Rémusat, faithfully repeats in her memoirs the account of his childhood, upbringing and early youth that Talleyrand wished to have believed (*Mémoires de Madame de Rémusat 1802–1808*, ed. Paul de Rémusat, III (Paris: Calmann-Lévy, 1880), pp. 325–6). Henry Fox, Lord Holland, first met Talleyrand in 1791 and was quickly informed by the alleged victim of how he had been mistreated by his family due to his affliction and been forced into the priesthood (Henry Richard, Lord Holland, *Foreign Reminiscences*, ed. Henry Edward, Lord Holland (London: Longman, Brown, Green and Longmans, 1850), p. 34). See also Dumont de Genève's account below.

15. Talleyrand, *Mémoires*, I, pp. 7–8. On Talleyrand's great-grandmother, Marie-Françoise de Rochechouart, princesse de Chalais, see below.

16. Waresquiel, *Talleyrand*, pp. 34–7.

17. Chateaubriand's *Mémoires de ma vie*, the predecessor of his *Mémoires d'outre-tombe*, focus on life in the family château of Combourg in Brittany.

18. Talleyrand, *Mémoires*, I, pp. 8, 10–12.

19. Ibid.

20. Étienne Dumont de Genève, *Souvenirs sur Mirabeau et sur les deux premières assemblées législatives*, ed. J. Bénétruy (Paris: Presses universitaires de France, 1951), p. 193.

21. *Mémoires et relations politiques du baron de Vitrolles*, ed. Eugène Forgues, III (Paris: Charpentier, 1884), pp. 448–9.

22. Talleyrand, *Mémoires,* I, pp. 14, 34. The Collège was in the rue de La Harpe and had been founded in the late thirteenth century for the benefit of poor Norman university students.

23. Ibid., pp. 15–16.

24. Ibid., p. 16.

25. See p. 176 for another such resident.

26. Talleyrand, *Mémoires,* I, p. 20.

27. Sainte-Beuve, *Monsieur de Talleyrand,* p. 36.

28. *Mémorial de J. de Norvins,* ed. L. de Lanzac de Laborie, I (1769–93) (Paris: Plon, 1896), p. 47 and note 3; Lacour-Gayet, *Talleyrand,* p. 29.

29. Louis S. Greenbaum, *Talleyrand, Statesman Priest: The Agent-General of the Clergy and the Church of France at the End of the Old Régime* (Washington DC: Catholic University of America Press, 1970), pp. 9–10.

30. Poniatowski, *Talleyrand et l'ancienne France,* p. 62.

31. Greenbaum, *Talleyrand, Statesman Priest,* pp. 11–12.

32. *Mémoires inédits de Madame la comtesse de Genlis sur le dix-huitième siècle et la Révolution française depuis 1756 à nos jours,* II (Paris: Ladvocat au Palais-Royal, 1825), pp. 87–8. Stéphanie-Félicité Ducrest de Saint-Albin, comtesse de Genlis (1746–1830).

33. Jean-Jacques Olier (1608–57).

34. Poniatowski, *Talleyrand et l'ancienne France,* p. 202.

35. Duchesse d'Abrantès, *Histoire des salons de Paris,* IV (Paris: Garnier, n.d.), p. 176.

36. [Charles-Maxime de Villemarest] *Monsieur de Talleyrand,* I (Paris: Roret, 1834), pp. 19–24.

37. Olivier Blanc, *L'Amour à Paris au temps de Louis XVI* (Paris: Perrin, 2002), pp. 221–4.

38. *Revelations of the Life of Prince Talleyrand,* pp. 110–22.

39. Talleyrand, *Mémoires,* I, p. 22.

40. Poniatowski, *Talleyrand et l'ancienne France,* pp. 77–82. She died in 1830 at the age of eighty-three.

41. Talleyrand, *Mémoires,* I, p. 20.

42. Ibid., p. 21.

43. *Revelations of the Life of Prince Talleyrand,* p. 128.

44. Bernard de Lacombe, *La Vie privée de Talleyrand: Son Émigration – son mariage – sa retraite – sa conversion – sa mort* (Paris: Plon, 1910), pp. 283–4.

45. Waresquiel, *Talleyrand,* p. 54.

46. Jean Gorsas, *Talleyrand: Mémoires, lettres inédites et papiers secrets* (Paris: Albert Savine, 1891), pp. 37–42. According to Talleyrand, this episode

was 'perhaps the only sin [he] committed at seminary against the ninth commandment' and it was certainly only a 'venial one' (ibid., p. 40).

47. Poniatowski, *Talleyrand et l'ancienne France*, pp. 85–7.
48. Lit. 'lords surety of the sacred phial'.
49. *The Diary of Philipp von Neumann 1819 to 1850*, ed. E. Beresford Chancellor, I (London: Philip Allan, 1928), p. 271. The recollection is of 12 May 1832.
50. Talleyrand, *Mémoires*, I, pp. 23–4. For Mme de Laval see pp. 77, 181–2.

CHAPTER 2: THE PATH TO PREFERMENT

1. Poniatowski, *Talleyrand et l'ancienne France*, pp. 94–115.
2. Greenbaum, *Talleyrand, Statesman Priest*, pp. 17–19.
3. Talleyrand, *Mémoires*, I, p. 23.
4. Ibid., p. 33.
5. Lacour-Gayet, *Talleyrand*, pp. 57–8.
6. *Mémoires d'Aimée de Coigny*, ed. Étienne Lamy (Paris: Calmann-Lévy, n.d.), p. 192.
7. Poniatowski, *Talleyrand et l'ancienne France*, p. 122.
8. *Revelations of the Life of Prince Talleyrand*, p. 232.
9. Talleyrand, *Mémoires*, I, p. 35.
10. Lacour-Gayet, *Talleyrand*, p. 59.
11. Waresquiel, *Talleyrand*, p. 76.
12. Talleyrand, *Mémoires*, I, p. 35.
13. Ibid., p. 159.
14. The physiocrat school of economists believed that all national wealth originated with land. But it was their commitment to absolute free trade that had most impact, including upon Talleyrand's own thinking.
15. Holland, *Foreign Reminiscences*, p. 6.
16. Waresquiel, *Talleyrand*, p. 99.
17. Lacour-Gayet, *Talleyrand*, p. 140
18. *Revelations of the Life of Prince Talleyrand*, pp. 129–37. According to this highly coloured, but in other respects credible, account from Colmache, Mirabeau died in Talleyrand's arms. That is not true: but did the untruth come from Talleyrand, Colmache, or later literary embellishment?
19. '*Qui n'a pas vécu dans les années voisines de 1789 ne sait pas ce que c'est que le plaisir de vivre*' (M. Guizot, *Mémoires pour servir à l'histoire de mon temps*, I (Paris: Michel Lévy, 1858), p. 6). The phrase '*douceur de vivre*', which

is commonly quoted, is thus strictly speaking inaccurate. But one might add that *douceur* – lit. 'sweetness' but used in a sense closer to pleasure, with echoes of comfort, gentleness – was a favourite word of Talleyrand's and the expression might well have crossed his lips.

20. *Souvenirs de Madame Louise-Élisabeth Vigée-Lebrun*, I (Paris: H. Fournier, 1835), p. 288.

21. It might even have affected his own sex too, at least in the case of the bisexual Barras; see p. 91.

22. The problem with the anecdote is the date, since Talleyrand did not actually receive his first benefice until 1775. So perhaps he added that part subsequently to demonstrate the worth of his wit (Lacour-Gayet, *Talleyrand*, pp. 40–1).

23. Waresquiel, *Talleyrand*, pp. 62–3.

24. *Mémoires de Madame de Rémusat*, I, pp. 46–9.

25. Louise, princesse de Vaudémont (*née* de Montmorency) (1764–1832). For her *salon* under the Empire and the Restoration see below, p. 181.

26. Talleyrand, *Mémoires*, I, pp. 45–9.

27. Ibid., p. 23 note 2. Waresquiel dismisses this note added by Bacourt to the memoirs but without good reason, and the letter he subsequently cites from Talleyrand's mother (mentioned above) suggesting Talleyrand's satisfaction with his 'new estate' in any case relates to an earlier date, i.e. not the solemn moment of ordination.

28. Lacour-Gayet, *Talleyrand*, p. 54.

29. Poniatowski, *Talleyrand et l'ancienne France*, pp. 100–101, 133–47.

30. Greenbaum, *Talleyrand, Statesman Priest*, pp. 67–8.

31. Poniatowski, *Talleyrand et l'ancienne France*, pp. 133–5.

32. Ibid., pp. 164–6. Boisgelin later perished in the September massacres.

33. Greenbaum, *Talleyrand, Statesman Priest*, pp. 175–8, 203.

34. Talleyrand, *Mémoires*, I, p. 51.

35. Ibid., pp. 53–4.

36. Poniatowski, *Talleyrand et l'ancienne France*, pp. 153–62; Greenbaum, *Talleyrand, Statesman Priest*, p. 150.

37. Poniatowski, *Talleyrand et l'ancienne France*, pp. 191–6.

38. In answer to a question from Louis XVIII as to how he had brought down first the Directory and then Bonaparte: *'Mon Dieu! Sire, je n'ai vraiment rien fait pour cela: c'est quelque chose d'inexplicable que j'ai en moi et qui porte malheur aux gouvernements qui me négligent'* (*Monsieur de Talleyrand*, IV, p. 355).

39. Étienne-François, duc de Choiseul (1719–85).

40. Artaud de Montor, *Histoire de la vie et des travaux politiques du comte d'Hauterive* (Paris: Adrien Le Clere, 1838), pp. 15–17.
41. The biographical essay is included as an appendix in the first published version of the memoirs (*Mémoires du prince de Talleyrand*, ed. le duc de Broglie, V (Paris: Calmann-Lévy, 1891), pp. 515–91).
42. *The Greville Diary Including Passages Hitherto Withheld from Publication*, ed. Philip Witwell Wilson, I (London: Heinemann, 1927), p. 89.
43. Waresquiel, *Talleyrand*, p. 91⁾.
44. *La Mission secrète de Mirabeau à Berlin 1786–1787*, ed. Henri Welschinger (Paris: Plon, 1900), pp. 37–8, 225–6.
45. Ibid., pp. 322–6.
46. The costs of the war with England and of the assistance given to the American rebels had left France hugely in debt. These debts were covered by Necker, during his term as director of the treasury and then director general of the finances, from 1776 to 1781, by open-ended loans contracted at high rates of interest.
47. Charles-Alexandre, vicomte de Calonne (1734–1802).
48. Talleyrand, *Mémoires*, I, p. 89.
49. Anne-Robert-Jacques Turgot, baron de Laune (1727–81).
50. Talleyrand, *Mémoires*, I, p. 56; Waresquiel, *Talleyrand*, pp. 95–7; Poniatowski, *Talleyrand et l'ancienne France*, pp. 296–302.
51. Waresquiel, *Talleyrand*, p. 102.
52. Talleyrand, *Mémoires*, I, p. 104.
53. Lacour-Gayet, *Talleyrand*, p. 84.
54. On Talleyrand's association with d'Orléans, see below.
55. Jacques Necker (1732–1804).
56. Waresquiel, *Talleyrand*, p. 87. Perhaps in later life he came to regret this, at least on grounds of taste. Lord Holland found him 'generally somewhat averse to retailing anecdotes disparaging of the Royal Family of France' (Holland, *Foreign Reminiscences*, pp. 18–19 note).
57. The duc de Chartres had succeeded to the title duc d'Orléans in 1785.
58. Talleyrand recounts the incident: 'A cold manner, an apparent reserve, had caused some people to say that I was witty. Mme de Gramont, who did not like reputations that she had not made, was of some use to me by trying to cause me embarrassment. I was having supper for the first time at Auteuil at the house of Mme de Boufflers, placed at the end of the table, scarcely talking to my neighbour. Mme de Gramont, in a loud and raucous voice, asked me, calling out my name, just what had so struck me on entering the *salon*, where I had followed her, that I had said: Ah! Ah!

'"Madame la duchesse," I replied, "did not hear me correctly. It was not Ah! Ah! It was Oh! Oh!" This wretched response provoked laughter.'

In other words, presumably, it was not appreciation but rather shock that Talleyrand had expressed (Talleyrand, *Mémoires*, I, pp. 43–4).

59. Abrantès, *Histoire des Salons*, III, pp. 391–5.
60. *Mémoires inédits de Madame la comtesse de Genlis*, V, pp. 202–3.
61. Talleyrand, *Mémoires*, I, p. 163.
62. François de La Rouchefoucauld, duc de Liancourt (1747–1827), was master of the royal wardrobe and would be a useful ally of Talleyrand's; see p. 43. Pierre Choderlos de Laclos (1741–1803) was an Orléanist propagandist, as well as the author of the notorious novel *Liaisons dangereuses*. Lacour-Gayet asserts that Talleyrand was definitely a freemason, while Poniatowski, without evidence, is equally emphatic that he was not (Lacour-Gayet, *Talleyrand*, p. 87; Poniatowski, *Talleyrand et l'ancienne France*, p. 520 note 1).
63. Talleyrand, *Mémoires*, I, p. 167.
64. Ibid., pp. 145–215.
65. Waresquiel, *Talleyrand*, p. 81.
66. Lacourt-Gayet, *Talleyrand*, pp. 90–1.
67. Ibid., pp. 92–4.
68. Élie Méric, *Histoire de M. Émery et de l'Église de France pendant la Révolution*, I (Paris: Charles Poussielgue, 1895), p. 187.
69. *Lettre pastorale de Mgr. l'évêque d'Autun au clergé séculier et régulier et aux fidèles de son diocèse, 26 janvier 1789* (Autun: Imprimerie Dejussieu, 1789).

CHAPTER 3: BISHOP AND REVOLUTIONARY

1. Paul Montarlot, 'L'Épiscopat de Talleyrand', *Mémoires de la société éduenne*, nouvelle série, XII (1894), pp. 87–8.
2. Ibid., p. 89.
3. *Cahiers des paroisses et communautés d'Autun pour les États généraux de 1789*, ed. A. de Charmasse (Autun: Imprimerie Dejussieu, 1895), pp. 364, 366, 371.
4. Ibid., p. 356.
5. He sums up these proposals in a significant phrase as '*les principes conservateurs de la propriété et de la liberté*' (ibid., p. 357).
6. Ibid., pp. 357–60.
7. Montarlot, 'L'Épiscopat de Talleyrand', p. 90.

8. Daniel L. Wick, *A Conspiracy of Well-Intentioned Men: The Society of Thirty and the French Revolution* (New York: Garland, 1987), pp. 1–3, 35, 43–4, 304, 318–20.

9. Talleyrand, *Mémoires*, I, p. 114. Cf. 'Judge, Sir, of my surprise, when I found that a very great proportion of the Assembly (a majority, I believe, of the members who attended) was composed of practitioners in the law' (Edmund Burke, *Reflections on the Revolution in France* (Indianapolis: Liberty Fund, 1999), p. 131).

10. Lacour-Gayet, *Talleyrand*, pp. 108–9, 111.

11. This is, indeed, exactly how Talleyrand was accustomed to read from his days at the seminary, as he notes in his memoirs. 'So my ideas remained my own: books enlightened me, never enslaved me' (Talleyrand, *Mémoires*, I, p. 21).

12. A.V. Arnault, *Souvenirs d'un sexagénaire*, IV (Paris: Duféy, 1833), pp. 19–20.

13. *La Galerie des États généraux et des dames françoises* (n.p., 1790), pp. 49–50.

14. The appendix of volume I of the memoirs contains a letter from Vitrolles to Bacourt stating that the comte d'Artois had confirmed Talleyrand's account of these conversations of which there were 'several', the most important being that of 16/17 July 1789: on that discussion, see below (Talleyrand, *Mémoires*, I, pp. 137–41).

15. Poniatowski, *Les Années occultées*, pp. 29–30.

16. Lacour-Gayet, *Talleyrand*, I, pp. 120–23.

17. Disorder would also affect Burgundy and Talleyrand's bishopric. On 29 July the local peasantry burned down the château of Senozan, belonging to Archambaud, comte de Talleyrand-Périgord, Charles-Maurice's brother (Montarlot, 'L'Épiscopat de Talleyrand', p. 90).

18. Waresquiel, *Talleyrand*, p. 125.

19. Poniatowski, *Les Années occultées*, p. 52.

20. Talleyrand, *Mémoires*, I, pp. 123–9.

21. *Motion de M. l'évêque d'Autun, sur la proposition d'un emprunt, faite à l'Assemblée nationale, par le premier ministre des Finances, et sur la consolidation de la dette publique, jeudi 27 août 1789* (Paris: Baudouin, 1789).

22. Waresquiel, *Talleyrand*, p. 121.

23. Waresquiel places Talleyrand's speech in a strictly financial context, too strictly (ibid., p. 134).

24. Gallicanism has its roots in jurisdictional clashes between the Pope and French kings at the end of the Middle Ages but by the late seventeenth century it had acquired a panoply of political and theological theory. The 'liberties' of the Gallican Church were consistently perceived as

threatened by papal but not secular power and thus served as a useful device to increase the pressure on the Church to pay tax.

25. *Motion de M. l'évêque d'Autun sur les biens ecclésiastiques, du 10 octobre 1789* (Versailles: Baudouin, 1789). The thought invested in Talleyrand's plan is further evinced by the fact that at the end of the speech on his motion he appended articles to be contained in the Assembly's *arrêté* on the subject.

26. Lacour-Gayet, *Talleyrand*, pp. 1303–4.

27. The measure was, at this early stage, still seen as an extreme one. Thus Dumont de Genève considered that Talleyrand's view was 'that of the left and of all the *parti populaire*' (Dumont de Genève, *Souvenirs*, p. 131).

28. Montarlot, 'L'Épiscopat de Talleyrand', p. 101.

29. *Mémorial de Norvins*, I, p. 203.

30. Montarlot, 'L'Épiscopat de Talleyrand', pp. 105–23.

31. Waresquiel, *Talleyrand*, pp. 129, 134.

32. *Opinion de M. l'évêque d'Autun sur la question des biens ecclésiastiques* (Paris: Baudouin, 1789).

33. Poniatowski, *Les Années occultées*, p. 100.

34. *Opinion de M. L'évêque d'Autun sur les banques et sur le rétablissement de l'ordre dans les finances prononcé à l'Assemblée nationale le vendredi 4 décembre 1789* (Paris: Baudouin, 1789). Again he was not called to deliver the speech: he had it printed and circulated instead.

35. *Opinion de M. l'évêque d'Autun sur les assignats forcés le jeudi 15 avril 1790* (Paris: Imprimerie nationale, 1790).

36. *L'Assemblée nationale aux François* (Chartres: Le Tellier, 1790).

37. Charles-Maurice claimed to have acquired this dislike of jargon from listening to his mother's nuanced, yet clear conversation: 'I do not believe in the wit or the learning of people who know no equivalents and are always defining: it is only through memory that they know anything, and that they know badly' (Talleyrand, *Mémoires*, I, p. 45).

38. *Proposition faite à l'Assemblée nationale sur les poids et mesures par M. l'évêque d'Autun* (Paris: Imprimerie nationale, 1790). The proposal was accepted and a decree passed. But, despite British interest, as an international venture it was stillborn. Indeed, even France only acquired its national metric system in 1840. As regards weights, Talleyrand proposed that a (new) *livre* be established following the procedure devised by the eminent scientist Lavoisier to determine the weight of a cubic (new) foot of water at a temperature of 14 degrees and four-tenths on the Réaumur thermometer.

39. Waresquiel, *Talleyrand*, pp. 105–6.

40. The physical oddness of this *ménage* must have been increased by the fact that while Talleyrand had a club foot, Morris had a crippled arm.

41. *A Diary of the French Revolution by Gouverneur Morris 1752–1816*, ed. Beatrix Cary Davenport, I (London: Harrap, 1939), 250.

42. Ibid., p. 259.

43. The diary entry for 1 January 1790 records that Charles-Maurice shamelessly observed to Gouverneur Morris that the 'American debt would furnish a good speculation'. Morris, who was in France to re-negotiate it for his government, equally shamelessly replied that he was 'already engaged in it' (ibid., p. 355).

44. Ibid., p. 355.

45. Ibid., pp. 261, 292.

46. Lacour-Gayet, *Talleyrand*, p. 113.

47. *Mémoires du chancelier Pasquier*, ed. duc d'Audiffret-Pasquier, I (Paris: Plon, 1893), p. 247.

48. Arnault, *Souvenirs*, IV, p. 21.

49. Gorsas, *Talleyrand*, pp. 71–4.

50. *Mémoires de Vitrolles*, III, p. 451.

51. Gorsas, *Talleyrand*, pp. 74–5. Doubts have been raised as to the authenticity of this and the following letter. But, unfortunately, they ring true.

52. Ibid., p. 342.

53. Montarlot, 'L'Épiscopat de Talleyrand', pp. 130–41; Gorsas, *Talleyrand*, pp. 76–7.

54. Talleyrand, *Mémoires*, I, p. 136.

55. Gorsas, *Talleyrand*, pp. 80–81.

56. Poniatowski, *Les Années occultées*, pp. 257–61.

57. Dumont de Genève, *Souvenirs*, pp. 199–200.

58. *Diary of the French Revolution by Gouverneur Morris*, II, pp. 123–4.

59. Lacour-Gayet, *Talleyrand*, p. 139. While interdicting holy communion, primitive excommunication also forbade human association, hence sharing 'fire and water' with the excommunicated; hence also the proposed supper of cold meat and of wine on crushed ice.

CHAPTER 4: APPRENTICE DIPLOMAT

1. *Diary of the French Revolution by Gouverneur Morris*, II, p. 108.

2. Gorsas, *Talleyrand*, p. 76.

3. Dumont de Genève, *Souvenirs*, p. 162.

4. '*Il faut s'endormir*' (Poniatowski, *Les Années occultées*, p. 300).

5. *Mémorial de Norvins*, I, p. 254.

6. Dumont de Genève, *Souvenirs*, p. 170.

7. *Diary of the French Revolution by Gouverneur Morris*, II, pp. 151–2.

8. 'Mettez un roi d'un caractère ferme et décidé à la place de Louis XVI, et la révolution n'aurait pas eu lieu' (Dumont de Genève, *Souvenirs*, p. 185).

9. Ibid., pp. 125–7, 171.

10. *Recollections of the Life of Prince Talleyrand*, p. 130.

11. Waresquiel, *Talleyrand*, pp. 151–2.

12. Lacour-Gayet, *Talleyrand*, p. 142.

13. *Liberté des cultes religieux. Rapport fait au nom du Comité de constitution, à la séance du 7 mai 1791, relatif à l'arrêté du département de Paris, du 6 avril précédent, par M. de Talleyrand, ancien évêque d'Autun* (Paris: Imprimerie Lottin, 1791).

14. It met under the leadership of Antoine Barnave in the old Feuillant (Cistercian) convent in the rue Saint-Honoré. In March 1792 the Feuillant ministry was overthrown. After the fall of the monarchy in September that year it would be suppressed by the resurgent Jacobins.

15. C. Hippeau, *L'Instruction publique en France pendant la Révolution* (Paris: Didier, 1881), Part II, Rapport de Talleyrand, pp. 40, 42, 44, 182.

16. Talleyrand, *Mémoires*, I, pp. 220–21. The Feuillant Foreign Minister, Antoine Valdec de Lessart, had an unhappy end. He was accused in March 1792 on the motion of Brissot, the leader of the Girondin war party, and taken to Orléans to be tried. Ordered back to Paris, he was massacred en route, on 9 September 1792.

17. The project was originally unearthed more than fifty years ago by Nussbaum, but its significance in understanding the background to Talleyrand's mission to England has been highlighted more recently by Waresquiel (F.-L. Nussbaum, 'L'arrière-plan de la mission de Talleyrand à Londres en 1792', *Assemblée générale de la commission de recherche et de publication des documents relatifs à la vie économique de la Révolution*, II (1939), pp. 445–84; Waresquiel, *Talleyrand*, pp. 157–8).

18. *Correspondance diplomatique de Talleyrand: La Mission de Talleyrand à Londres, en 1792. Correspondance inédite de Talleyrand avec le Département des affaires étrangères, le général Biron etc. Ses Lettres d'Amérique à Lord Lansdowne*, ed. G. Pallain (Paris: Plon, 1889), no. xx, pp. 47–58.

19. Dumont de Genève, *Souvenirs*, p. 194.

20. *Correspondance diplomatique de Talleyrand: La Mission de Talleyrand à Londres*, no. xxiii, pp. 58–62; no. xxvi, pp. 69–72; no. xxix, p. 88.

21. John Ehrman, *The Younger Pitt: The Years of Acclaim* (London: Constable, 1969), p. 111.

22. Holland, *Foreign Reminiscences*, p. 35.

23. Dumont de Genève, *Souvenirs*, p. 195; *The Greville Diary*, p. 89.

24. Grenville had already received from Lessart a letter of introduction which described Charles-Maurice as a man of wit and talent and a distinguished participant in the National Assembly, which, however, meant that he could play no official diplomatic role (*Correspondance diplomatique de Talleyrand: La Mission de Talleyrand à Londres*, no. xv, pp. 40–1).

25. Ibid., no. xxxii, pp. 98–109.

26. Ibid., no. xxxvi, pp. 124, 126.

27. Ibid., no. xxxvii, pp. 133–43; no. xxxviii, pp. 144–6.

28. William Petty Fitzmaurice, second Earl of Shelburne, first Marquis of Lansdowne (1737–1805). He was briefly Prime Minister in 1783 and was perhaps the most consistently liberal British statesman of his day.

29. This was also, according to Dumont, why another man of letters, Jean-Antoine Gauvain, who wrote under the pseudonym Gallois, accompanied the mission. Gallois would later serve as president of the Napoleonic Tribunat.

30. Dumont de Genève, *Souvenirs*, pp. 196, 220–22. Talleyrand would pronounce Reinhard's eulogy in 1838.

31. Poniatowski, *Années occultées*, pp. 428–9.

32. *Correspondance diplomatique de Talleyrand: La Mission de Talleyrand à Londres*, no. lxiv, pp. 215–19.

33. Ibid., no. lxx, p. 256.

34. Sir Samuel Romilly (1757–1818) was also a strong supporter of the Revolution.

35. *Correspondance diplomatique de Talleyrand: La Mission de Talleyrand à Londres*, no. lxxx, pp. 289–306.

36. Ibid., no. lxxxi, pp. 307–8; no. lxxxv, pp. 317–18; no. xci, pp. 344–6.

37. Talleyrand, *Mémoires*, I, p. 222. Like so many others, Jérôme Pétion de Villeneuve was consumed by the Revolution whose ephemeral hero he had been. Proscribed and hunted, he was found dead in a field at Saint-Émilion in 1794.

38. Waresquiel, *Talleyrand*, p. 162; P.-L. Roederer, *Chronique de cinquante jours, du 20 juin au 10 août 1792* (Paris: Imprimerie de Lachevardière, 1832), p. 384.

39. Talleyrand, *Mémoires*, I, pp. 224–5.

40. Perhaps the most obvious example of this characteristic is his assertion near the end of his life that he had, through laicization, received permission from the Pope to marry. See pp. 140–1, 318.

41. Georges-Jacques Danton (1759–94).

42. *Correspondance diplomatique de Talleyrand: Le Ministère de Talleyrand sous le Directoire*, ed. G. Pallain (Paris: Plon, 1891), pp. v–ix.

43. Lacour-Gayet, *Talleyrand*, pp. 168–9.

44. *Mémoires de B. Barère*, ed. Hippolyte Carnot and David (d'Angers), II (Paris: Jules Labitte, 1842), pp. 25–6. Bertrand Barère de Vieuzac had not yet acquired his later notoriety, as a bloodthirsty and unscrupulous member of the Convention and Committee of Public Safety. He out-lived Talleyrand, dying in poverty in 1841.

45. Moreau de Saint-Méry, *Voyage aux États-Unis de l'Amérique, 1793–1798*, ed. Stewart L. Mims (New Haven: Yale, 1913), p. 103; Émile Dard, *Un Confidant de l'Empereur: Le Comte de Narbonne* (Paris: Plon, 1943), p. 124.

46. *Diary of the French Revolution by Gouverneur Morris*, II, pp. 538, 541. In fact, Morris decided to stay on.

47. BN, Fichier Charavay, 167, TAB-TAT: letter of 18 September (1792). Sainte-Foy had been superintendent of the finances of the comte d'Artois, and from then on enjoyed a shady reputation. The baron de Breteuil christened him '*Sainte-Foy sans foi*' (Michel Missoffe, *Le Coeur secret de Talleyrand* (Paris: Perrin, 1956), p. 104).

CHAPTER 5: EXILE

1. Waresquiel, *Talleyrand*, pp. 170–1.

2. *Correspondance diplomatique de Talleyrand: le Ministère de Talleyrand sous le Directoire*, pp. xliii–liii.

3. Ibid., pp. liii–lv.

4. There also appeared in *Le Moniteur universel* a long justificatory note defending Charles-Maurice's reputation and actions, signed 'D' – perhaps Desrenaudes (Lacour-Gayet, *Talleyrand*, p. 175).

5. Talleyrand, *Mémoires*, I, pp. 83–4; *Revelations of the Life of Prince Talleyrand*, pp. 82–8; *Diary of Philipp von Neumann*, I, p. 226.

6. See pp. 329–30.

7. *Lettres de Talleyrand à Lord Lansdowne 1792–1795* in *Correspondance de Talleyrand: La Mission de Talleyrand à Londres*, no. 99, pp. 419–20.

8. Waresquiel, *Talleyrand*, pp. 173–4.

9. *Diaries and Letters of Madame d'Arblay, edited by her Niece*, V (London: Hurst and Blackett, 1854), p. 255. Fanny Burney, later Mme d'Arblay, diarist and novelist (1752–1840).

10. Ibid., p. 284.

11. Ibid., p. 315.

12. *Mémoires de Madame de Genlis*, IV, p. 351.

13. *Madame de Staël, ses amis, ses correspondants. Choix de lettres (1778–1817)*, ed. Georges Solovieff (Paris: Klincksieck, 1970), no. 42, p. 83.

14. Madame de Staël, *Lettres à Narbonne*, ed. Georges Solovieff (Paris: Gallimard, 1960), no. 13, p. 84.

15. *Diaries and Letters of Madame d'Arblay*, V, pp. 329, 333.

16. Ibid., p. 334.

17. Ibid., p. 336.

18. Ibid., pp. 348–9.

19. Staël, *Lettres à Narbonne*, no. 104, p. 328.

20. *Madame de Staël, ses amis*, no. 55, pp. 97–8.

21. '*C'est une maison finie pour la France que la maison de Bourbon. Voilà de quoi penser*' ('Lettres de M. de Talleyrand à Madame de Staël', part I, ed. duc de Broglie, in *Revue d'histoire diplomatique* (Year 4/1: 1890), p. 89).

22. Staël, *Lettres à Narbonne*, no. 86, pp. 278–80; no. 91, pp. 287–8.

23. Talleyrand, *Mémoires*, I, pp. 229–30. Mme de Staël specifically blamed the Austrian ambassador to Britain for the decision (*Madame de Staël, ses amis*, no. 69, p. 110).

24. Lord Fitzmaurice, *Life of William Earl of Shelburne, afterwards First Marquess of Lansdowne*, II (London: Macmillan, 1912), pp. 394–5. This is revealed by the contents of Lansdowne's letter of introduction of Talleyrand to Washington of 2 March 1794, on which see below.

25. *Diaries and Letters of Madame d'Arblay*, VI, pp. 14–15.

26. Gorsas, *Talleyrand*, p. 118.

27. Ibid., pp. 119–20. Jeanne, vicomtesse de Laval (1748–1839). In fact, Mme de Laval later escaped from the prisons of Paris with her life. She died, at the age of ninety, a few weeks after Talleyrand.

28. Fichier Charavay, 167, TAB-TAT: letter to Windham (1750–1810) of 29 January 1794.

29. By 1796 Talleyrand was, apparently, speaking English as well as any Englishman (Waresquiel, *Talleyrand*, p. 647, note 4 to page 171).

30. *Diaries and Letters of Madame d'Arblay*, VI, pp. 16–17.

31. *Revelations of the Life of Prince Talleyrand*, pp. 338–9.

32. See below, pp. 305, 329–30.

33. Talleyrand, *Mémoires*, I, p. 231.

34. Ibid., p. 232.

35. *Diary of the French Revolution by Gouverneur Morris*, II, p. 353.

36. When Hamilton resigned to return to practising law so as to increase his income Talleyrand could not believe it. One evening in New York, on his way to a dinner party, he saw Hamilton still at his desk, and remarked in shock: 'I have seen a man who made the fortune of a nation labouring all night to support his family' (Ron Chernow, *Alexander Hamilton* (New York: Penguin, 2004), p. 549).

37. Poniatowski, *Talleyrand aux Etats-Unis*, pp. 103–12.

38. Moreau de Saint-Méry, *Voyage aux États-Unis*, pp. xx, 102.

39. Ibid., p. 139.

40. Montor, *Histoire de la vie*, p. 77. Antoine-René, comte de La Forest (1756–1846). He would join Talleyrand at the Ministry of Foreign Affairs, helping bring order to the department's finances, and still later act as his deputy under the Restoration.

41. *Madame de Staël, ses amis*, no. 80, pp. 116–17.

42. *Talleyrand in America as Financial Promoter 1794–1796*, tr. and ed. Hans Huth and Wilma J. Pugh (Washington: US Government Printing Office, 1942), pp. 9–10, 14, 28.

43. Ibid., pp. 10–13, 28–33.

44. Ibid., pp. 33–57.

45. Ibid., pp. 69–86.

46. Philip Schuyler (1733–1804) was a general in the American Revolution and served as a US Senator for two terms.

47. Gorsas, *Talleyrand*, pp. 125–6.

48. Marquise de La Tour du Pin, *Journal d'une femme de cinquante ans, 1778–1815*, ed. Aymar de Liedekerke-Beaufort, II (Paris: Berger-Levrault, 1925), pp. 29–33.

49. *Talleyrand in America as Financial Promoter*, pp. 86–91.

50. Cf *Mémoires de Vitrolles*, III, pp. 450–51.

51. Morris's speculations later went disastrously wrong. He was imprisoned for debt in 1801.

52. *Talleyrand in America as Financial Promoter*, p. 22; Poniatowski, *Talleyrand aux États-Unis*, p. 394.

53. *Talleyrand in America as Financial Promoter*, p. 95.

54. Talleyrand, *Mémoires*, I, p. 235.

55. Ibid., p. 234.

56. François de Chateaubriand, *Mémoires d'outre-tombe*, ed. Jean-Claude Berchet, I (Paris: Garnier, 1989), p. 459. Unlike Talleyrand, Chateaubriand was received by Washington.

57. Talleyrand, *Mémoires*, I, pp. 238–9.

58. Ibid., p. 236.

59. *Correspondance diplomatique de Talleyrand: La Mission de Talleyrand à Londres, en 1792. Lettres d'Amérique à Lord Lansdowne,* no. 110, pp. 421–44.
60. *Mémoire sur les relations des États-Unis avec l'Angleterre par Talleyrand, lu à l'Institut National le 15 germinal An V, suivi d'un Essai sur les avantages à retirer de colonies nouvelles dans les circonstances présentes par le même auteur, lu à l'Institut le 15 messidor An V* (London: J. Dean, 1806), pp. 1–30.
61. Talleyrand, *Mémoires,* I, pp. 242–4.
62. *Mémoires du comte de Moré (1758–1837),* ed. Geoffroy de Grandmaison and comte de Pontgibaud (Paris: Picard, 1898), pp. 155–6. Of Talleyrand's dogs, Pirame is mentioned at the rehearsal for the Mass of the Federation (see p. 52) and Carlos, an English spaniel, was his constant companion at the end of his life.
63. Constantin-François de Chasseboeuf, comte de Volney (1757–1820), was an expert on the Middle East and a moderate Revolutionary politician, imprisoned by the Jacobins. He had come to the US in 1795 and was expelled as a French spy in 1798.
64. Moreau de Saint-Méry, *Voyage aux États-Unis,* pp. 223–4.
65. Ibid., pp. 215–16.
66. Talleyrand, *Mémoires,* I, p. 247.
67. Paul-François-Jean-Nicolas Barras (1755–1829).
68. Jean-Lambert Tallien (1767–1820).
69. Marie-Joseph Blaise de Chénier (1764–1811), poet and playwright, also wrote the patriotic song 'Chant du départ'. He was the younger brother of the more famous André Chénier, a victim of the Terror.
70. Poniatowski, *Talleyrand aux États-Unis,* pp. 425–34.
71. Moreau de Saint-Méry, *Voyage aux États-Unis,* p. 217.
72. Poniatowski, *Talleyrand aux États-Unis,* pp. 468–9.
73. *Mémoires du comte de Moré,* p. 158.
74. Moreau de Saint-Méry, *Voyage aux États-Unis,* pp. xxvii, 225, 226, 232, 234–5, 244, 247–8, 260–64.
75. Constant, *Portraits,* p. 38.
76. *Revelations of the Life of Prince Talleyrand,* pp. 21–4.

CHAPTER 6: THE DIRECTORY

1. 'Lettres de M. de Talleyrand à Madame de Staël', II, pp. 209–21.
2. Moreau de Saint-Méry, *Voyage aux État-Unis,* pp. 232, 234–5; Gorsas, *Talleyrand,* pp. 133–4.
3. Waresquiel, *Talleyrand,* pp. 200–201.

4. Benjamin Constant (1767–1830). Charles-Maurice had already written to Mme de Staël about Constant, claiming to have read and admired the latter's latest publication. Or was it, perhaps, just seductive flattery? Even perhaps double flattery, since he claimed to find in Constant's writing similarities to those of Narbonne, Germaine de Staël's previous lover ('Lettres de M. de Talleyrand à Madame de Staël', II, p. 219).

5. Poniatowski, *Talleyrand et le Directoire, 1796–1800*, p. 66.

6. *Mémoire sur les relations des États-Unis avec l'Angleterre par Talleyrand, lu à l'Institut National le 15 germinal An V, suivi d'un Essai*, pp. 31–47. For the Egypt expedition, see below.

7. Talleyrand, *Mémoires*, I, p. 249. Though never delivered, the substance of the lecture finds its way into the memoirs, pp. 59–67.

8. *Monsieur de Talleyrand*, II, pp. 205–6.

9. *Mémoires de Barras, Membre du Directoire*, ed. George Duruy, II (Paris: Hachette, 1895), pp. 232–3.

10. Waresquiel, *Talleyrand*, p. 205. On 7 May 1797 Charles-Maurice dropped Barras a note, excusing himself from a dinner engagement; its tone suggests well-established friendly relations.

11. His contemporary, Thibaudeau, noted Reubell's use in conversation of 'violent manners which sat badly with the dignity with which he was clothed' (A.C. Thibaudeau, *Mémoires sur la Convention et le Directoire*, II (Paris: Baudouin, 1824), p. 7).

12. Lacour-Gayet, *Talleyrand*, p. 234.

13. Ibid., pp. 170–72.

14. Ibid., pp. 235–6.

15. *Mémoires de Barras*, II, p. 455.

16. Talleyrand, *Mémoires*, I, p. 250.

17. *Mémoires de Barras*, II, pp. 460–61.

18. '*Il faut faire marcher les femmes dans les circonstances importantes*' (Lacour-Gayet, *Talleyrand*, p. 238).

19. Talleyrand, *Mémoires*, I, pp. 250–52. Talleyrand's allusion to Barras's (well-known) homosexuality finds a kind of echo in Barras's own (obviously baseless) suggestion that the very heterosexual Talleyrand had tried physically to seduce him (*Mémoires de Barras*, III, p. 408). But in such competitive slander Talleyrand makes Barras appear a mere novice.

20. In fact, the post under the Directory and under Napoleon – despite Talleyrand's efforts to change its title – was termed Minister of External Affairs. It only reverted to Minister of Foreign Affairs under the Restoration. But to avoid confusion 'Foreign Affairs' and 'Foreign Minister' are here used for the whole period.

21. It reads better in the original French: '. . .*une fortune immense, une immense fortune, une immense fortune, une fortune immense*' (*Mémoires de Barras*, II, pp. 475–8). In society, Charles-Maurice affected greater nonchalance. The La Tour du Pins met him at the house of Mme de Valence. He casually let them know that he had just been made Foreign Minister, then took up his hat, made his excuses, and left (La Tour du Pin, *Journal*, II, p. 140).

22. Talleyrand, *Mémoires*, I, p. 257.

23. *Mémoires de Barras*, III, pp. 134, 186–7.

24. Talleyrand, *Mémoires*, I, pp. 252–3.

25. Poniatowski, *Talleyrand et le Directoire*, pp. 303–25; Raymond Guyot, *Le Directoire et la paix de l'Europe des traités de Bâle à la deuxième coalition (1795–1799)* (Paris: Félix Alcan, 1912), pp. 440–51.

26. *Preussen und Frankreich von 1795 bis 1807. Diplomatischen Correspondenzen*, ed. Paul Bailleu, I (Leipzig: Hirzel, 1881), no. 120, pp. 142–3; no. 121, p. 143. David Alfons von Sandoz-Rollin (1740–1809).

27. Thibaudeau, *Mémoires*, II, pp. 243–50.

28. *Mémoires de Barras*, III, pp. 23–5.

29. *Correspondance diplomatique de Talleyrand: Le Ministère de Talleyrand sous le Directoire*, p. 140 note 1: letter of 24 July 1797.

30. AN, 215 AP 1 (Papiers Talleyrand), dossier 1, unnumbered cahier: letter of 5 August 1797.

31. *Correspondance de Napoléon 1er publiée par ordre de l'Empereur Napoléon III*, III (Paris: Plon, 1869), no. 2307, pp. 390–92: letter of 18 October 1797.

32. Poniatowski, *Talleyrand et le Directoire*, pp. 336–77.

33. Ibid., p. 378.

34. *Mémoires du comte Miot de Mélito*, ed. général Fleischmann, I (Paris: Michel Lévy, 1858), pp. 180, 185.

35. 215 AP 1, dossier 1, unnumbered cahier: letter of 22 August 1797.

36. Louis-Antoine de Bougainville (1729–1814).

37. Talleyrand, *Mémoires*, I, pp. 259–60. The comte de Lille was the more 'correct' term to use of the Pretender; Napoleon had no wish to be correct and harboured no Jacobin prejudice either. His uncle, Joseph Fesch (1763–1839), would become archbishop of Lyon and a cardinal.

38. *Mémoires de M. de Bourrienne, Ministre d'état, sur Napoléon*, ed. Désiré Lacroix, I (Paris: Garnier, n.d.), pp. 214–17.

39. *Mémoires de Barras*, III, p. 120.

40. *Mémoires de Bourrienne*, I, pp. 218, 220.

41. Ibid., p. 221; *Mémoires de Barras*, III, pp. 170–71.

42. The building is now owned by the Italian government and serves as a consulate and cultural centre.

43. Frédéric Masson, *Le Département des affaires étrangères pendant la Révolution 1787–1804* (Paris: Plon, 1877), pp. 413–15.

44. Bélanger was paid 12,700 livres for the expenses he incurred (ibid., annex VIII, pp. 527–8).

45. *Mémoires de Madame la duchesse d'Abrantès. Souvenirs historiques sur Napoléon, la Révolution, le Directoire, le Consulat, l'Empire et la Restauration*, I (Paris: Garnier, n.d.), p. 391; BN, Fichier Charavay, vol. 167, TAB-TAT: letter to (the banker) Jean-Frédéric Perregaux of 31 December 1797.

46. Arnault, *Souvenirs*, IV, pp. 24–7.

47. *Mémoires de Bourrienne*, II, p. 143.

48. *Mémoires de Madame de Chastenay 1771–1815*, ed. Alphonse Roserot, I (Paris: Plon, 1896), p. 420.

49. Talleyrand, *Mémoires*, I, pp. 260–61.

50. Arnault, *Souvenirs*, IV, p. 29.

51. *Mémoires de Barras*, III, pp. 143–4.

52. *Mémoires du comte Miot de Mélito*, I, p. 231 and note 2.

53. *Mémoires de Bourrienne*, I, p. 230.

54. Ibid., p. 225.

55. Lacour-Gayet, *Talleyrand*, pp. 319–20.

56. Ibid., pp. 161–7.

57. C. de La Jonquière, *L'Expédition d'Égypte 1798–1801*, I (Paris: Henri Charles-Lavauzelle, n.d.), pp. 154–68.

58. It is not, though, true, as Talleyrand alleges in his memoirs, and as has been asserted by others wishing to spread the blame for the expedition more widely, that the Directory's aim throughout was to get rid of Bonaparte from France: cf Talleyrand, *Mémoires*, I, pp. 262–3.

59. *Mémoires du comte Miot de Mélito*, I, pp. 234–5.

60. Moreau de Saint-Méry, *Voyage aux États-Unis*, pp. 260–61.

61. *Correspondance de Napoléon 1er*, IV, no. 2608, p. 117.

62. Ibid., no. 2703, p. 172.

63. Ibid., no. 2834, p. 254.

64. Ibid., no. 3183, p. 436.

65. For a full analysis of the business, see: William Stinchcomb, *The XYZ Affair* (Westport: Greenwood Press, 1980). The relationship with the decision not to send Talleyrand to Constantinople is examined in: Carl Ludwig Lokke, 'Pourquoi Talleyrand ne fut pas envoyé à

Constantinople', *Annales historiques de la Révolution française*, X (1933), pp. 153–9.

66. *Preussen und Frankreich*, I, no. 144, p. 168.

67. Ibid., no. 152, pp. 173–4; no. 156, pp. 178–9.

68. Ibid., no. 159, p. 182.

69. Ibid., no. 178, p. 211.

70. Waresquiel, *Talleyrand*, p. 219.

71. *Correspondance diplomatique de Talleyrand: Le Ministère de Talleyrand sous le Directoire*, no. 27, pp. 243–346.

72. Ibid., no. 69, pp. 439–51.

73. *Preussen und Frankreich*, I, no. 162, p. 185.

74. Ibid., no. 234, p. 272.

75. Ibid., no. 256, p. 304.

76. Talleyrand, *Mémoires*, I, p. 213. Benjamin Constant's assessment is remarkably similar: 'After hatred, Sieyès's most lively passion was fear' (Constant, 'L'Abbé Sieyès', *Portraits*, p. 32).

77. *Monsieur de Talleyrand*, II, p. 319.

78. *Preussen und Frankreich*, I, no. 260, p. 306.

79. *Éclaircissemens donnés par le citoyen Talleyrand à ses concitoyens* (Paris: Laran, 1799). There ensued a series of polemical exchanges between Talleyrand and Delacroix in the pages of *Le Moniteur* as a result of which the latter clearly had the better of the argument (Lacour-Gayet, *Talleyrand*, pp. 363–4).

80. *Mémoires de Barras*, III, p. 412.

81. *Mémoires du comte Miot de Mélito*, I, pp. 261–2.

82. Talleyrand, *Mémoires*, I, p. 272 note 1.

83. *Mémoires de Barras*, III, pp. 49–56. Barras's self-serving account cannot, though, be taken at face value.

84. P.L. Roederer, 'Notice de ma vie pour mes enfants', *Oeuvres du comte P.L. Roederer*, ed. baron A.M. Roederer, III (Paris: Firmin Didot, 1854), pp. 296, 301.

85. *Mémoires de Barras*, III, pp. 79–81.

86. Missoffe, *Le Cœur secret de Talleyrand*, p. 121.

87. Arnault, *Souvenirs*, IV, pp. 391–5; *Mémoires et souvenirs du comte Lavalette publiés par sa famille et sur ses manuscrits*, I (Paris: H. Fournier, 1831), pp. 352–3.

88. *Mémoires de Bourrienne*, II, p. 334.

89. Roederer, 'Notice de ma vie pour mes enfants', p. 301; Arnault, *Souvenirs*, IV, p. 395.

CHAPTER 7: BONAPARTE'S FOREIGN MINISTER

1. *Mémoires de Madame de Rémusat*, I, pp. 109–10.

2. Talleyrand, *Mémoires*, II, p. 133.

3. Lacour-Gayet, *Talleyrand*, pp. 1192–3. This passage does not occur in the version published in Talleyrand's memoirs but was provided by the duchesse de Dino for the abbé Dupanloup.

4. Holland, *Foreign Reminiscences*, p. 289.

5. See below pp. 147, 213–14.

6. *A Portion of the Journal Kept by Thomas Raikes Esq.*, II, p. 381.

7. Waresquiel, *Talleyrand*, p. 267.

8. *Preussen und Frankreich*, I, no. 298, p. 349.

9. Talleyrand, *Mémoires*, I, p. 276. Talleyrand referred to the three Consuls as Hic, Haec and Hoc. Napoleon was Hic (masculine – the real power); Cambacérès was Haec (feminine – a reference to his widely rumoured homosexuality); and Lebrun was Hoc (neuter – a nonentity).

10. *Mémoires de Bourrienne*, II, pp. 216–17.

11. *Mémoires du chancelier Pasquier*, I, p. 253 note 1.

12. Chateaubriand, *Mémoires d'outre-tombe*, IV, p. 563.

13. Lacour-Gayet, *Talleyrand*, pp. 441–2.

14. *Mémoires de Madame de Rémusat*, I, pp. 229–230. There may also have been an element of revenge. Talleyrand had apparently been annoyed because he only heard about the successful conclusion of preliminary negotiations for the peace the previous autumn, when cannon-fire announced it to the whole of Paris (*Mémoires de la Reine Hortense, publiés par le prince Napoléon*, ed. Jean Hanoteau, I (Paris: Plon, 1927), pp. 102–3).

15. Ibid., p. 249. In other words, he had speculated on Bonaparte's successful coup.

16. *Mémoires de Madame de Rémusat*, III, p. 174.

17. Cambacérès, *Mémoires inédits*, ed. Laurence Chatel de Brancion, I (Paris: Perrin, 1999), pp. 468–9.

18. Comte de Las Cases, *Le Mémorial de Sainte-Hélène*, ed. Marcel Dunan, I (Paris: Flammarion, n.d.), p. 103. On St Helena, Napoleon, in recounting the tale, took pleasure in adding that Talleyrand had not had time to take a copy of the essay. But, as usual, he was wrong. Another copy existed and it was eventually published (ibid., p. 103 note 2).

19. Lacour-Gayet, *Talleyrand*, p. 407.

20. 215 AP 1, dossier 1, unnumbered cahier: letter of 4 September 1804.

21. MAE, Mémoires et documents, France, 1776, no. 29: letter of 24 August 1805.

22. Ibid., no. 36.

23. Ibid., nos 2, 5, 8.

24. *Lettres inédites de Talleyrand à Napoléon 1800–1809*, ed. Pierre Bertrand (Paris: Didier Perrin, 1889), no. 6, pp. 4–5: letter of 28 June 1801.

25. Ibid., no. 8, pp. 7–8: letter of 9 July 1801.

26. Ibid., no. 9, p. 8: letter of 19 July 1801.

27. Ibid., no. 12, p. 11: letter of 13 September 1801.

28. La Tour du Pin, *Journal*, II, p. 143.

29. Chateaubriand, *Mémoires d'outre-tombe,* IV, p. 563. Chateaubriand's modern admirers repeat the charge. Thus Marc Fumaroli states that 'Talleyrand could not write memoirs' and that the 'fragments he read in the *salons* are not of his own hand.' He adds that 'such a depraved human being' (as Talleyrand) could not have recorded his life in any tolerable manner (Marc Fumaroli, *Chateaubriand: Poésie et terreur* (Paris: Fallois, 2003), p. 74). On the authenticity of Talleyrand's memoirs see pp. x–xi.

30. Latouche, *Album perdu* (Paris: chez Marchands de nouveautés, 1829), p. 103.

31. Baron Claude-François de Méneval, *Mémoires pour servir à l'histoire de Napoléon Ier depuis 1802 jusqu'à 1815*, III (Paris: Dentu, 1894), pp. 441–4.

32. In later life, Talleyrand was anxious to counter the idea that he had merely taken dictation from Napoleon. In fact, he told Lord Holland that Napoleon could not dictate at all, which was clearly false (Holland, *Foreign Reminiscences*, pp. 292–3).

33. *Mémoires de Vitrolles*, III, p. 445.

34. Lytton Bulwer, 'Talleyrand', p. 227. Bacourt, Talleyrand's secretary, described the process to Lytton Bulwer.

35. *Lettres inédites de Talleyrand à Napoléon*, pp. xviii–xxi.

36. *Monsieur de Talleyrand*, III, pp. 181,183.

37. Ibid., pp. 182–3.

38. *Mémorial de Norvins*, II, pp. 267–70. Roux de Laborie (Roux de Rochelle was his literary name) (1769–1840).

39. *Monsieur de Talleyrand*, III, pp. 159–70; Masson, *Le Département des affaires étrangères*, pp. 472–84.

40. *Mémoires de Barras*, IV, pp. 257–63.

41. *Monsieur de Talleyrand*, III, pp. 159–60.

42. *Mémoires de Vitrolles*, III, p. 447.

43. Casimir de Montrond (1768–1843). Rémusat, *Mémoires de ma vie*, p. 272 note 1; Lacour-Gayet, *Talleyrand*, p. 296; Missoffe, *Le Coeur secret de Talleyrand*, pp. 107–8; Waresquiel, *Talleyrand*, pp. 226–31.

44. See p. 309.

45. Masson, *Le Département des affaires étrangères*, pp. 408–9.

46. Lacour-Gayet, *Talleyrand*, p. 318.

47. Masson, *Le Département des affaires étrangères*, pp. 448–50.

48. Ibid., p. 451.

49. *Éloge de M. le comte Reinhard prononcé à l'Académie des Sciences morales et politiques, par M. le prince de Talleyrand, dans la séance du 3 mars 1838* (Paris: chez Gabriel Warée, 1838).

50. Las Cases, *Le Mémorial*, I, p. 500.

51. Méneval, *Mémoires*, III, p. 443.

52. *Éloge de M. le comte Reinhard*.

53. Waresquiel, *Talleyrand*, p. 273.

54. Poniatowski, *Talleyrand et le Consulat*, pp. 111–31.

55. *Preussen und Frankreich*, II, no. 6, pp. 10–11.

56. Ibid., no. 31, pp. 39–40. A despatch from Lucchesini of 24 April 1801 reporting Talleyrand's proposals.

57. Ibid., no. 34, p. 43 note 1.

58. Ibid., no. 48, pp. 61–3.

59. See the next chapter.

60. For example, instructions to the French envoy in Berlin of 18 December 1801 (*Preussen und Frankreich*, II, no. 49, pp. 63–4).

61. The treaty established a Franco-Austrian alliance that would continue until the end of the *ancien régime*.

62. *Preussen und Frankreich*, II, no. 104, pp. 148–51.

63. On both of which, see the next chapter.

64. Talleyrand, *Mémoires*, I, p. 286.

65. Jean Tulard, *Napoléon, ou le mythe du sauveur* (Paris: Fayard, 1987), pp. 110–12.

66. Ibid., p. 280.

67. Ibid., p. 290.

68. *Mémoires de G.-J. Ouvrard, sur sa vie et ses diverses opérations financières*, I (Paris: Montardier, 1826), p. 59.

69. Chateaubriand, *Mémoires d'outre-tombe*, IV, p. 560.

70. Émile Dard, *Napoléon et Talleyrand* (Paris: Plon, 1935), p. xiii.

71. I am grateful to Professor Jeremy Black for illuminating my understanding of these matters.

72. See the argument of Jean Tulard in his introduction to *Talleyrand, Mémoires, L'époque napoléonienne*, ed. Jean Tulard (Paris: Imprimerie nationale, 1996), p. 25.

CHAPTER 8: POLITICAL FORTUNES

1. *An Englishman in Paris 1803. The Journal of Bertie Greathead,* ed. J.P.T. Bury and J.C. Bury (London: Geoffrey Bles, 1953), p. 9.
2. *'Quand M. de Talleyrand ne conspire pas, il trafique'.*
3. Chateaubriand, *Mémoires d'outre tombe,* IV, pp. 562–3.
4. *Mémoires de Madame de Rémusat,* II, p. 381.
5. *Monsieur de Talleyrand,* III, pp. 51–3.
6. *Souvenirs intimes sur M. de Talleyrand,* p. 65. The remark is by Talleyrand's friend, baron von Gagern, referring specifically to the re-ordering of German states.
7. *Mémoires du duc de Rovigo, pour servir à l'histoire de l'Empereur Napoléon,* VII (Paris: Bossange, 1826), pp. 45–9. Barras gives other details of subsidies paid by Godoy to France and creamed off by Talleyrand (*Mémoires de Barras,* IV, pp. 260–61).
8. Méneval, *Mémoires ,* I, pp. 60–61.
9. The final (Franco-Russian) plan was adopted on 24 March 1803, by which the Holy Roman Empire was abolished; all the ecclesiastical princes (bar two) were dispossessed; most of the Imperial Cities lost their autonomy, and the Habsburg Holy Roman Emperors became Emperors of Austria.
10. *Mémoires du chancelier Pasquier,* I, p. 249.
11. *Mémoires de Barras,* IV, pp. 257–9; Méneval, *Mémoires,* I, pp. 362–4.
12. *Monsieur de Talleyrand,* III, pp. 99–100.
13. *Mémoires de Madame de Rémusat,* II, p. 181.
14. *Mémoires de Vitrolles,* III, p. 450.
15. *Monsieur de Talleyrand,* II, p. 293.
16. *Souvenirs intimes sur M. de Talleyrand,* pp. 57–8.
17. *Monsieur de Talleyrand,* III, p. 198.
18. Lacour-Gayet, *Talleyrand,* pp. 448–9. Joseph-Dominique Louis (1755–1837) had begun life like Talleyrand as a cleric and even served at the bishop of Autun's celebration of the Mass of the Federation. He was made a baron of the Empire in 1809.
19. Duchesse de Dino, *Notice sur Valençay* (Paris: Crapelet, 1848), pp. vii–viii; André Beau, *Talleyrand: Chronique indiscrète de la vie d'un prince – Consulat, Empire, Restauration* (Paris: Royer, 1992, pp. 30–5).
20. *Revelations of Prince Talleyrand,* p. 28.
21. For these and other details about Valençay, see: R. Crozet, *Le Château de Valençay* (Paris: Henri Laurens, 1930).

22. André Beau, *Talleyrand: L'Apogée du Sphinx – La Monarchie de Juillet* (Paris: Royer, 1998), p. 16.

23. Crozet, *Le Château de Valençay*, pp. 497–8, 503; Duchesse de Dino, *Chronique de 1831 à 1862*, ed. princesse de Radziwill née Castellane, I (Paris: Plon, 1909), p. 264 note 1.

24. Dino, *Chronique*, II, pp. 57–8. Just possibly the dog's name may also have been an allusion to the Duke of San Carlos who had lived at Valençay and was the lover of the princesse de Talleyrand. But would even Talleyrand have stooped to that? A few weeks before his death Talleyrand went to see his notary and had a provision added to his will whereby Carlos was entrusted to the care of his great-niece Pauline's governess (Lacour-Gayet, *Talleyrand*, note to page 1234, quoting an account of the duchesse de Dino in the Archives de Broglie).

25. BL, Add. Ms. 51,635 (Holland House Papers), fos 135r–137r: letter to Lord Holland of 30 January 1837.

26. For his wife's seduction by the Duke of San Carlos, imprisoned in Valençay, see below.

27. *Mémoires de Madame de Rémusat*, II, p. 179.

28. *Revelations of the Life of Prince Talleyrand*, pp. 296–300; *Souvenirs intimes sur M. de Talleyrand*, pp. 58–60.

29. *Mémoires de Madame de Rémusat*, II, p. 183.

30. Waresquiel, *Talleyrand*, pp. 250–51.

31. *Mémoires de Barras*, III, p. 173.

32. Barry Edward O'Meara, *Napoleon at St Helena*, II (London: Richard Bentley, 1888), p. 2; *Monsieur de Talleyrand*, III, p. 221.

33. *Mémoires de Barras*, IV, p. 263.

34. *Revelations of the Life of Prince Talleyrand*, p. 284; Waresquiel, *Talleyrand*, pp. 310–12.

35. *Mémoires de Madame de Chastenay 1771–1815*, ed. Alphonse Roserot, II (Paris: Plon, 1896), p. 52. Mme de Chastenay, though, disliked Talleyrand and so was perhaps inclined to magnify the merits of his put-upon wife.

36. As is shown by Waresquiel, *Talleyrand*, pp. 310–11.

37. *Dinde* = turkey, also used to mean a stupid woman.

38. Thus confusing the River Seine (Paris) with the River Saône (Lyon) (*Revelations of the Life of Prince Talleyrand*, p. 306). The question of how stupid, or more precisely how ignorant, she was is difficult to resolve. In some cases her appalling orthography would suggest barely rudimentary education. For example, a note addressed to someone inviting him to witness the registration of her civil marriage contract with Charles-Maurice: '*Mon cher voizein le notaire vas venier de bhonneur ce*

matein pour vous fere siegner le nouvelle acte. Ie vous fere avertire ausitau ille ira ausitau le fere enregistre, et nous dira a quelle heur nous irons a la municipalité ou je vous meneré' (Fichier Charavay, 167, TAB-TAT: undated). Or, to an unknown recipient, describing the loss of some leather and silk goods: '*Vous vous en ales toujour sens me voir cela nes pas bien et Ovie vous contera ces desastre il ma portois troi morseau de peax pour quelque desue de soulier et quelque mouchois de soixe le tous lui a été prie a Boulogne*' (ibid., undated). But André Beau has shown me the text of an elegantly written letter bearing her signature, dated 1 July (1818?). The historical jury remains out.

39. *Mémoires du chancelier Pasquier*, I, p. 251.
40. *Souvenirs intimes sur M. de Talleyrand*, p. 145.
41. *Monsieur de Talleyrand*, III, pp. 298–9.
42. Marquis de Noailles, *Le Comte Molé 1781–1855. Sa Vie–ses mémoires*, I (Paris: Champion, 1922), p. 255. (Henceforth cited as: Molé, *Mémoires*.)
43. *Mémoires de Madame de Rémusat*, II, pp. 176–8. Lacour-Gayet was wrong to deduce that no church marriage could have taken place from the fact that Pope Pius VII would not receive her on his visit to Paris in 1804. Mme Grand had since 1798 been divorced from her former husband, but she had not obtained an annulment. Still more of an obstacle, Talleyrand was not permitted to marry, despite his 'laicization'. See below. Mme de Talleyrand was not, therefore, in the eyes of the Church his wife at all, and the church 'marriage' only added to the scandal (cf. Lacour-Gayet, *Talleyrand*, p. 475). Waresquiel sums up the evidence in *Talleyrand*, p. 307 note 1.
44. Lacour-Gayet, *Talleyrand*, pp. 475–8.
45. See below p. 207.
46. See below p. 213.
47. *Mémoires de la comtesse Potocka (1794–1820)*, ed. Casimir Stryienski (Paris: Plon, 1897), p. 212.
48. Waresquiel, *Talleyrand*, pp. 308–9.
49. BN, N. Acq. fr. 24,346, nos 25–28: letters from Roux to Mme de Talleyrand of 26 July, 17 August and 19 October 1815.
50. Dino, *Chronique*, II, pp. 232–3.
51. Talleyrand, *Mémoires*, I, p. 284.
52. Lacombe, *La Vie privée de Talleyrand*, p. 311.
53. Talleyrand, *Mémoires*, I, p. 284.
54. Cambacérès, *Mémoires inedits*, I, p. 618.
55. For example, Talleyrand wrote in the margin of Consalvi's initial proposals addressed to the First Consul: 'The memorandum of Cardinal

Consalvi sets the negotiation back much further than all the documents that preceded it' (*Mémoires du cardinal Consalvi, sécretaire d'état du pape Pie VII*, ed. J. Crétineau-Joly, I (Paris: Plon, 1864), pp. 331, 337).

56. Poniatowski, *Talleyrand et le Consulat*, pp. 296–7.

57. As suggested by Waresquiel, *Talleyrand*, p. 299.

58. On Napoleon's court, see Philip Mansel, *The Court of France 1789–1830* (Cambridge: Cambridge University Press, 1991), pp. 48–89.

59. *Lettres inédits de Talleyrand à Napoléon*, no. 4, pp. 3–4.

60. Waresquiel, *Talleyrand*, p. 337.

61. *Mémoires de Madame de Rémusat*, III, p. 20.

62. Charles de Rémusat, *Mémoires de ma vie*, ed. Charles H. Pouthas, I (Paris: Plon, 1958), p. 52.

63. Méneval, *Mémoires*, II, p. 17.

64. *Mémoires du chancelier Pasquier*, I, p. 244.

65. Las Cases, *Le Mémorial de Sainte-Hélène*, I, p. 243; idem, II, p. 42.

66. Méneval, *Mémoires*, II, p. 12; Waresquiel, *Talleyrand*, p. 286. Narbonne became Napoleon's favourite aide-de-camp.

67. [Comte Mollien], *Mémoires d'un ministre du Trésor public 1780–1815*, I (Paris: Fournier, 1845), p. 384. (Henceforth cited as: Mollien, *Mémoires*.)

68. Las Cases, *Le Mémorial de Sainte-Hélène*, I, p. 242 note 2.

69. Talleyrand, *Mémoires*, I, pp. 299–300.

70. *Monsieur de Talleyrand*, III, p. 392.

71. *Mémoires de Bourrienne*, II, p. 172.

72. Pierre Garat (1764–1823); Auguste Vestris (1760–1842).

73. Jean-François de La Harpe (1739–1803).

74. Mme Grassini (1773–1850) was Napoleon's favourite opera singer and lover. She first slept with him in 1800. She was also one of the Duke of Wellington's Parisian conquests in 1814 (Andrew Roberts, *Napoleon and Wellington* (London: Weidenfeld and Nicolson, 2001), pp. 124–30).

75. *Mémoires de la Reine Hortense*, I, pp. 64–5. Hortense de Beauharnais (1783–1837), often known as Queen Hortense, married Napoleon's brother, Louis, later King of Holland, and is the mother of Napoleon III.

76. Joseph Esménard (1770–1811). Later that year he would depart as secretary to General Leclerc on the expedition to recapture Santo Domingo.

77. *Mémorial de Norvins*, II, p. 279.

78. Girolamo Crescentini (1766–1846), a famous castrato, was another of Napoleon's favourite singers.

79. *Mémorial de Norvins*, II, p. 286.

80. The Kingdom of Etruria was short-lived. Louis of Bourbon-Parma died in 1803, the throne passing to his son with his widow acting as

regent. It was abolished in 1807 and annexed by France. After the Congress of Vienna, as the duchy of Tuscany, it passed to a Habsburg.

81. Las Cases, *Mémorial de Sainte-Hélène*, I, p. 502.

82. Louis Madelin, *Fouché 1759–1820*, I (Paris: Plon, 1901), pp. 33, 320, 380, 381, 382, 386, 387, 389, 405, 409, 415, 416; idem, II, pp. 77, 87.

83. *Mémoires de Bourrienne*, II, pp. 356–7.

84. A. Aulard, *Paris sous le Consulat*, II (Paris: Léopold Cerf, 1904), p. 16.

85. *Mémoires de Madame de Rémusat*, II, p. 187; *Mémoires du chancelier Pasquier*, I, pp. 154–5.

86. Madelin, *Fouché*, I, p. 353.

87. Waresquiel, *Talleyrand*, pp. 320–21.

88. Talleyrand, *Mémoires*, I, pp. 274–5.

89. *Mémoires de Madame de Rémusat*, I, p. 195.

90. *Mémoires de Barras*, III, p. 509.

91. *Mémoires du général de Caulaincourt, duc de Vicence, grand écuyer de l'Empereur*, ed. Jean Hanoteau, II (Paris: Plon, 1933), p. 253.

92. The best overall treatment of this affair is that of Maurice Schumann, *Qui a tué le duc d'Enghien?* (Paris: Perrin, 1984).

93. Armand, marquis de Caulaincourt (1773–1827), duc de Vicence (Vicenza) from 1808.

94. Anne-Jean-Marie-René Savary (1774–1833), duc de Rovigo from 1808. Savary's account and supporting material are to be found in: *Mémoires du duc de Rovigo*, I, pp. 47–75, 337–479.

95. Talleyrand, *Mémoires*, I, p. 292.

96. Ibid., III, pp. 301–22.

97. *Mémoires de Madame de Rémusat*, I, p. 296.

98. *Journal du comte P.-L. Roederer*, p. 245; O'Meara, *Napoleon at St Helena*, I, p. 302. On the other hand, Napoleon lied when he accused Talleyrand of holding back an alleged letter from d'Enghien offering to serve him, which had he received it in time would have prevented the duc's death. But perhaps, as the demons did their work on St Helena, Bonaparte had convinced himself it was true (ibid., pp. 198, 350)?

99. *Mémoires de Caulaincourt*, II, pp. 253–6.

100. Las Cases, *Mémorial de Sainte-Hélène*, II, appendix xvi, p. 627.

101. *Mémoires du chancelier Pasquier*, I, pp. 178–9. The council was, though, held on 8 March, not the following day as Pasquier says.

102. Chateaubriand, *Mémoires d'outre tombe,* II, p. 200. Méneval confirms that it escaped Talleyrand's 'auto da fe' of incriminating documents in 1814 (Méneval, *Mémoires*, I, pp. 305–6).

103. Holland, *Foreign Reminiscences*, p. 227: '*Le vin est tiré; il faut le boire.*'

104. *Mémoires du chancelier Pasquier*, I, p. 181; Schumann, *Qui a tué le duc d'Enghien?*, p. 63. Schumann concludes that Savary bears principal responsibility.

105. Molé, *Mémoires*, IV, p. 348. This judgement is, for example, accepted by Lacour-Gayet, *Talleyrand*, p. 510.

106. Villemarest says it was Fouché (*Monsieur de Talleyrand*, III, p. 358). But Talleyrand was certainly using the expression, albeit in another context, in London in 1830 as if it were his own (*Diary of Philipp von Neumann*, I, p. 226).

107. Méneval, *Mémoires*, I, p. 291.

108. *Mémoires du chancelier Pasquier*, I, p. 176.

109. *Mémoires de Vitrolles*, I, p. 236.

110. *Mémoires du chancelier Pasquier*, I, p. 199.

111. Untranslatable, but roughly: 'That's business' or, in this context, 'That's politics' (Montor, *Histoire du comte d'Hauterive*, p. 113). Three days later, Talleyrand very publicly organized a ball (*Mémoires du comte Miot de Mélito*, II, p. 159).

CHAPTER 9: RE-SHAPING EUROPE

1. *Monsieur de Talleyrand*, IV, p. 5.

2. *Mémoires du général de Caulaincourt, duc de Vicence, grand écuyer de l'Empereur*, ed. Jean Hanoteau, I, (Paris: Plon, 1933), p. 251.

3. Cambacérès, *Mémoires*, II, pp. 74–5.

4. *Preussen und Frankreich*, II, p. 276. Though relayed by the Prussian ambassador, Lucchesini, the account probably came to him from Talleyrand with whom he was on friendly terms.

5. *Mémoires de Madame de Rémusat*, I, p. 359.

6. *Lettres inédites de Talleyrand à Napoléon*, no. 82, p. 116: letter of 28 August 1804.

7. Lacour-Gayet, *Talleyrand*, pp. 538–9.

8. *Mémoires du baron Fain*, ed. P. Fain (Paris: Plon, 1908), p. 223.

9. Jean-Baptiste de Gouey, comte de La Besnardière (1765–1843).

10. Masson, *Le Département des affaires étrangères*, pp. 486–7.

11. Talleyrand, *Mémoires*, I, pp. 295–6. On this occasion Talleyrand's memoirs are to be preferred as a source. Mme de Rémusat's account, though doubtless also from Talleyrand, is suspiciously highly coloured. One cannot really imagine Napoleon grasping Joséphine and Talleyrand and saying: 'It is, though, painful to leave the two

people that one loves the most' (*Mémoires de Madame de Rémusat*, II, p. 61).

12. Montor, *Histoire du comte Hauterive*, p. 117.

13. Ibid., p. 118.

14. *Lettres inédites de Talleyrand à Napoléon*, no. 111, pp. 156–74: letter of 17 October 1805. Talleyrand also appended a draft treaty encapsulating his proposals.

15. Albert Vandal, *Napoléon et Alexandre 1er*, I (Paris: Plon, 1891), p. 9.

16. Talleyrand, *Mémoires*, I, pp. 296–7.

17. Montor, *Histoire du comte Hauterive*, pp. 119–22.

18. *Lettres inédites de Talleyrand à Napoléon*, no. 121, p. 185: letter of 12 November 1805.

19. Montor, *Histoire du comte Hauterive*, pp. 125–6.

20. Ibid., p. 127.

21. Ibid., pp. 131–2.

22. *Lettres inédites de Talleyrand à Napoléon*, no. 138, pp. 209–19: letter of 5 December 1805.

23. 215 AP 1, dossier 1, unnumbered cahier, p. 17: letter from Napoleon to Talleyrand of 3 December 1805 (the day after Austerlitz).

24. Montor, *Histoire du comte Hauterive*, pp. 147–8.

25. Talleyrand, *Mémoires*, I, p. 303; *Mémoires de Vitrolles*, III, p. 452. Vitrolles suggests, not improbably, that Talleyrand was financially rewarded by the Austrians for his leniency.

26. Talleyrand, *Mémoires*, I, p. 302.

27. *Mémoires de Barras*, IV, p. 262.

28. O'Meara, *Napoleon at St Helena*, I, pp. 197–8.

29. *Monsieur de Talleyrand*, IV, p. 29.

30. *Mémoires de la comtesse Potocka*, p. 211.

31. Talleyrand, *Mémoires*, I, p. 303.

32. MAÉ, Personnel, 1ère série, vol. 3848, 'Talleyrand-Périgord, prince de', unnumbered cahier (Accounts for Benevento 1814–1815).

33. A.M.P. Ingold, *Bénévent sous la domination de Talleyrand et le gouvernement de Louis de Beer 1806–1815* (Paris: Pierre Téqui, 1916), pp. 114–27, 150–76.

34. *Preussen und Frankreich*, II, no. 299, p. 401; no. 320, pp. 419–22; no. 321, pp. 422–4.

35. Ibid., Appendix II (Aus dem Briefwechsel Talleyrands mit Hauterive), p. 612.

36. *Mémoires, documents et écrits divers, laissés par le prince de Metternich*, ed. prince Richard de Metternich, I (Paris: Plon, 1880), p. 54.

37. Talleyrand, *Mémoires*, I, pp. 307–8. Manuel de Godoy (1767–1851), known as Principe de la Paz, Chief Minister of Spain, 1792–7.

38. *Lettres inédites de Talleyrand à Napoléon*, no. 216, pp. 282–3.

39. Talleyrand, *Mémoires*, I, p. 310.

40. On the walls of this room were also hung a portrait of Napoleon, again by Gérard, and in later years one of Louis-Philippe, by Hersant (Dino, *Notice sur Valençay*, p. 31).

41. *Monsieur de Talleyrand*, IV, pp. 123–4.

42. Ibid., pp. 124–5.

43. Ibid., p. 137.

44. Ibid., p. 167.

45. *Mémoires de Madame de Rémusat*, III, p. 53.

46. *Mémoires de la comtesse Potocka*, pp. 124–5; *Diary of Philipp von Neumann*, I, p. 271.

47. *Lettres inédites de Talleyrand à Napoléon* (unnumbered), pp. 468–9: letter of 18 June 1807.

48. Ibid., nos 219–312, pp. 286–463: letters of 27 December 1806 to 3 May 1807.

49. *Mémoires de la comtesse Potocka*, pp. 142–3; *Mémoires du chancelier Pasquier*, I, pp. 310–11 note 1. Emmerich von Dalberg, created duc de Dalberg (1773–1833).

50. Talleyrand, *Mémoires*, I, p. 308.

51. Ibid., p. 316.

52. *Mémoires de la comtesse Potocka*, pp. 158–9; *Monsieur de Talleyrand*, IV, pp. 145–51.

53. On the financial crisis of 1805 and the economic crisis of 1806–7, see Tulard, *Napoléon*, pp. 270–72. Reverting to his former role as financial expert, on 11 January 1806 Talleyrand sent Napoleon a proposal for the reform of the Banque de France (*Lettres inédites de Talleyrand à Napoléon*, no. 152, pp. 232–3).

54. Talleyrand, *Mémoires*, I (unpaginated introduction).

55. Apparently, Napoleon had already given his agreement in principle to Talleyrand's resignation while at Tilsit (Waresquiel, *Talleyrand*, p. 373).

CHAPTER 10: THE BUSINESS OF PLEASURE

1. 'Now is the time to drink' (*Monsieur de Talleyrand*, IV, p. 144).

2. Lacour-Gayet, *Talleyrand*, p. 490.

3. *Lettres inédites de Talleyrand à Napoléon*, no. 7, p. 7: letter of 9 July 1801.

4. Ibid., no. 34, p. 45: letter of 9 August 1803.

5. Ibid., no. 68, pp. 93–4: letter of 27 July 1804.

6. *Monsieur de Talleyrand*, IV, pp. 342–3.

7. Holland, *Foreign Reminiscences*, p. 39 note.

8. It should be observed that the word *'esprit'*, as used particularly by Talleyrand, has numerous English equivalents – not just wit, but also intelligence, intellect, genius, character – and, for that reason, it is ultimately untranslatable.

9. *Revelations of the Life of Prince Talleyrand*, pp. 260, 269. Louis-Adolphe Thiers (1797–1877).

10. *The Greville Diary*, p. 86.

11. Talleyrand, *Mémoires*, I, p. 44.

12. *Mémoires de la Reine Hortense*, I, pp. 269–70.

13. *Mémoires du chancelier Pasquier*, I, p. 250. For Pasquier's experience of one of Talleyrand's outbursts see below, p. 276.

14. *Souvenirs intimes sur M. de Talleyrand*, p. 190.

15. La Tour du Pin, *Journal*, II, p. 35.

16. *Mémoires de Vitrolles*, III, p. 445.

17. Molé, *Mémoires*, I, p. 272.

18. A. de Lamartine, *Cours familier de littérature*, II (Paris: Firmin Didot, 1856), pp. 307–8.

19. George Sand, 'Le Prince', *Revue des Deux Mondes*, 15 October 1834; Dino, *Chronique*, I, pp. 246–8, 268–9.

20. '*Est-ce quelqu'un?*' (Latouche, *Album perdu*, p. 150).

21. *Revelations of the Life of Prince Talleyrand*, pp. 14–48. It was almost certainly to the one-eyed princess that Talleyrand reputedly replied, in answer to a question about his situation: 'As you see, Madame.'

22. Michel-Louis-Étienne, comte Regnault de Saint-Jean d'Angély (1761–1819).

23. *Monsieur de Talleyrand*, IV, pp. 335–41.

24. Rémusat, *Mémoires de ma vie*, I, pp. 269–73. The account refers to 1816, that is the early Restoration period shortly after Talleyrand left office. Charles-Maurice had followed the practice of a public *lever* for many years. He would only abbreviate (never suspend) it, partly through decrepitude, partly because of a more simplified style of dress, and partly perhaps through modesty (at least in England) at the very end of his life (ibid., p. 271 note 1). For Molé's account, apparently from the period when Talleyrand was still President of the Council, see Molé, *Mémoires*, I, pp. 287–9.

25. Lacour-Gayet, *Talleyrand*, p. 732.

26. *Mémoires de la Reine Hortense*, II, p. 4.

27. Prosper Mérimée, *Correspondance générale*, ed. Maurice Parturier, I (Paris: Le Divan, 1941), p. 210. Prosper Mérimée, playwright (1803–70). Lady Sarah Fane (1786–1867) married George Child Villiers, 5th Earl of Jersey.

28. *Souvenirs intimes sur M. de Talleyrand*, p. 235.

29. *Revelations of the Life of Prince Talleyrand*, p. 312.

30. Abrantès, *Mémoires*, III, p. 151.

31. *Mémoires de Bourrienne*, II, p. 401.

32. Marie-Antoine (known as Antonin) Carême (1784–1833).

33. Philippe Alexandre and Béatrix de l'Auloit, *Le Roi Carême* (Paris: Albin Michel, 2003), pp. 24, 95, 97, 100, 104, 108, 112, 128.

34. Antonin Carême, 'Souvenirs de la Table et du Régime', in *Les Classiques de la table*, ed. F. Fayot (Paris: Béthune-Plon, 1843), p. 454.

35. *Lettres inédites de Napoléon I*, ed. Léon Lecestre, I (Paris: Plon, 1897), no. 361, pp. 247–8: letter of 26 October 1808.

36. Introduction to *Classiques de la table*, p. iv.

37. *A Portion of the Journal Kept by Thomas Raikes Esq.*, II, pp. 103–4.

38. *Souvenirs intimes sur M. de Talleyrand*, pp. 131–5, 142–3; Waresquiel, *Talleyrand*, pp. 540–41; Eric Schell, *Talleyrand en verve* (Paris: Horay, 2002), pp. 59–60; Molé, *Mémoires*, I, p. 273; M. Isid Bourdon, in *Classiques de la table*, p. 520; Lacour-Gayet, *Talleyrand*, pp. 1154–5; Gorsas, *Talleyrand*, pp. 37–8.

39. *Récits d'une tante: Mémoires de la comtesse de Boigne née Osmond*, ed. Charles Nicoullaud, I (Paris: Plon, 1908), p. 432.

40. *Mémoires de Madame de Chastenay*, II, p. 92.

41. The term was commonly used: both Molé and Countess Potocka record it (Molé, *Mémoires*, I, p. 289; *Mémoires de la comtesse Potocka*, p. 124).

42. Philip Mansel, *Paris Between Empires (1814–1852)* (London: Phoenix, 2003), pp. 120–40.

43. *Mémoires d'Aimée de Coigny*, pp. 164–5.

44. Ibid., p. 205; *Mémoires de Madame de Rémusat*, III, p. 196.

45. *Mémoires d'Aimée de Coigny*, p. 200.

46. *Mémoires du comte de Rambuteau*, ed. Georges Lequin (Paris: Calmann-Lévy, 1905), pp. 24–6. François, comte, later marquis, de Jaucourt (1757–1852) would serve as Navy Minister in Talleyrand's government.

47. Waresquiel, *Talleyrand*, pp. 404–6. Charles-Maurice had no prejudice on racial or indeed any other matters. His black mistress in Philadelphia has already been mentioned; see p. 84.

48. *Mémoires de la comtesse Potocka*, p. 240.

49. Gaston Palewski, *Le Miroir de Talleyrand. Lettres inédites de la duchesse à Courlande pendant le Congrès de Vienne* (Paris: Perrin, [1976]), p. 15.
50. Molé, *Mémoires*, I, p. 290.
51. The description of the benefits of whist reads better in the original French: '*Le jeu occupe sans préoccuper et dispense de toute conversation suivie*' (*Souvenirs intimes sur M. de Talleyrand*, p. 196).
52. Ernest d'Hauterive, *La Police secrète du Premier Empire. Bulletins quotidiens adressés par Fouché à l'Empereur*, IV (Paris: Perrin, 1963), pp. 13, 21.
53. Waresquiel, *Talleyrand*, pp. 407–8; Missoffe, *Le Cœur secret de Talleyrand*, pp. 139–41.
54. Talleyrand, *Mémoires*, I, p. 49.
55. All three – the Czech Jan Ladislav Dusík (Dussek), Philippe Libon and Jean-Henri Naderman – were well-known instrumentalists. But Dussek (1760–1812), who worked for Talleyrand during his time in France from 1807 until his death, was also a talented composer (*Mémoires de Madame de Chastenay*, II, p. 87).

CHAPTER 11: TREASON AND DISGRACE

1. *Mémoires de Vitrolles*, III, p. 454.
2. Méneval, *Mémoires*, II, pp. 45, 115, 122.
3. Lacour-Gayet, *Talleyrand*, p. 607.
4. Cambacérès, *Mémoires*, II, p.160.
5. Marshal Berthier also became Vice-Constable at this time.
6. Lacour-Gayet, *Talleyrand*, p. 609.
7. *Mémoires du chancelier Pasquier*, I, p. 312.
8. Jean-Baptiste Nompère de Champagny, duc de Cadore (1756–1834).
9. *Souvenirs de M. de Champagny, duc de Cadore* (Paris: Paul Renouard, 1846), p. 2.
10. *Mémoires du chancelier Pasquier*, I, p. 312.
11. Méneval, *Mémoires* II, pp. 135–6.
12. Cambacérès, *Mémoires*, II, p. 181.
13. *Mémoires du général de Caulaincourt*, I, p. 323.
14. Marcel Dunan, *Napoléon et l'Allemagne: Le Système continental et les débuts du royaume de Bavière, 1806–1810* (Paris: Plon, 1942), p. 219.
15. Talleyrand, *Mémoires*, I, pp. 400–401.
16. *Monsieur de Talleyrand*, III, pp. 54–5. Reading between the lines of Champagny's own account, one can also sense there Napoleon's exasperation (*Souvenirs de Champagny*, pp. 113–17, 173–86).

17. Talleyrand, *Mémoires*, I, pp. 307–8, 328–9.
18. *Mémoires de Champagny*, pp. 96–7.
19. Tulard, *Napoléon*, pp. 338–9.
20. Cambacérès, *Mémoires*, II, p. 186.
21. *Mémoires du général de Caulaincourt*, II, p. 243.
22. See p. 147.
23. The Treaty of Utrecht in 1713, concluding the War of Spanish Succession, recognized the former duc d'Anjou as Philip V of Spain, while precluding union of the two crowns.
24. *Mémoires du chancelier Pasquier*, I, p. 329.
25. *Mémoires de Madame de Rémusat*, III, appendix (by Charles de Rémusat), p. 401.
26. Méneval, *Mémoires*, II, pp. 135–6. Champagny exactly confirms this account (*Mémoires de Champagny*, p. 98). Talleyrand told Napoleon to avoid doing things 'by halves'.
27. *Mémoires du chancelier Pasquier*, I, pp. 328–9.
28. Mollien, *Mémoires*, II, p. 295.
29. Talleyrand, *Mémoires*, I, p. 385.
30. Geoffroy de Grandmaison, *L'Espagne et Napoléon* (Paris: Plon, 1908), p. 211 (Napoleon's instructions of 9 May), p. 213 (Talleyrand's reply of 13 May).
31. *Revelations of the Life of Prince Talleyrand*, p. 49.
32. *Mémoires de Madame de Rémusat*, III, appendix, p. 395.
33. Talleyrand, *Mémoires*, I, pp. 381–6.
34. *Mémoires du chancelier Pasquier*, I, p. 330.
35. *Mémoires de Madame de Rémusat*, I, p. 327.
36. 'Lettres de Talleyrand à Caulaincourt', part II, ed. Jean Hanoteau, *Revue des Deux Mondes,* Year 105 (1 November 1935), pp. 142–3, 145, 155. Caulaincourt finally gained Napoleon's permission to marry her, which he did on 24 May 1814.
37. Talleyrand, *Mémoires*, I, pp. 408–13.
38. Ibid., pp. 413–20, 422–4, 438–40, 447–57.
39. Dard, *Napoléon et Talleyrand*, pp. 198–200.
40. *Mémoires de Metternich*, II, no. 127, p. 248.
41. Holland, *Foreign Reminiscences*, p. 172 note.
42. Lacour-Gayet, *Talleyrand*, pp. 644–9.
43. *Mémoires de Vitrolles*, III, pp. 444–5.
44. *Mémoires de Madame de Rémusat*, III, p. 107.
45. *Mémoires du chancelier Pasquier*, I, p. 339.
46. Dunan, *Napoléon et l'Allemagne*, pp. 220, 608 note 59.

47. *Mémoires de Metternich*, II, no. 127, p. 244.

48. Ibid., I, p. 70.

49. Ibid., II, no. 125, pp. 234, 237.

50. Ibid., no. 130, pp. 261–3.

51. Montor, *Histoire du comte Hauterive*, pp. 269–70.

52. *Mémoires du chancelier Pasquier*, I, pp. 352–6. Antoine-Marie Chamans, comte de Lavalette (1769–1830) was Director General of the Post from 1804 to 1815.

53. Fouché had been able to tip off Talleyrand about the Emperor's imminent return (Dard, *Napoléon et Talleyrand*, p. 222).

54. Mollien, *Mémoires*, III, p. 7.

55. Waresquiel, *Talleyrand*, pp. 399–400.

56. Martin-Michel-Charles Gaudin, duc de Gaëte (Gaeta) (1756–1841); Vice-Admiral Denis Decrès (1761–1820).

57. *Mémoires de Bourrienne*, II, p. 139.

58. Accounts of the great scene differ, though not in their assessment of its violence or its impact. Of the memoirists, Cambacérès does not mention it, doubtless through embarrassment. Nor does Talleyrand. The others were not, themselves, present. Pasquier learned what had happened through Mme de Rémusat – repeating what she had heard from Talleyrand – and from Admiral Decrès.

59. Mollien, *Mémoires*, III, pp. 9–11.

60. *Mémoires du chancelier Pasquier*, I, p. 358; Méneval, *Mémoires,* II, p. 227.

61. It is not reproduced in any contemporary account. Sainte-Beuve derived it indirectly from General Bertrand, but the latter was not present at the scene (cf. C.-A. Sainte-Beuve, 'Essai sur Talleyrand par Sir Henry Lytton Bulwer', *Nouveaux Lundis*, XII (Paris: Michel Lévy, 1870), p. 30 note 1). The phrase was in use, however, in military circles – on one occasion by the rough-tongued Marshal Lannes when in conversation with Talleyrand (Méneval, *Mémoires,* II, p. 244). It is, therefore, just possible that Napoleon said it and that all concerned were too ashamed to reproduce it.

62. Lady Morgan, *France*, II (London: Henry Colburn, 1818), p. 261.

63. Comte Anatole de Montesquiou, *Souvenirs sur la Révolution, l'Empire, la Restauration et le règne de Louis-Philippe*, ed. Robert Burnand (Paris: Plon, 1961), p. 155. Montesquiou (1788–1867) was present because he had just been appointed Grand Chambellan in place of Talleyrand. Improbably, he suggests that the session lasted three hours. Louis-Philippe, comte de Ségur (1753–1830), was a diplomat, historian and, at this point, a member of the Corps législatif.

64. Mollien, *Mémoires*, III, pp. 12–13.

65. *Mémoires de Madame de Rémusat*, III, appendix, p. 399 and note.

66. *Mémoires de la Reine Hortense*, II, pp. 28–30.

67. Méneval, *Mémoires,* II, pp. 229–30.

68. Mollien, *Mémoires*, III, pp. 29–30.

69. Méneval, *Mémoires,* II, p. 228.

70. *Mémoires du baron Fain*, p. 297.

71. *Journal du comte P.-L. Roederer*, p. 244.

72. *Mémoires de Madame de Chastenay*, I, p. 367.

73. Lacour-Gayet, *Talleyrand*, pp. 388–9.

74. Léonce Pingaud, *Un Agent secret sous la Révolution et l'Empire: Le comte d'Antraigues* (Paris: Plon, 1893), pp. 246–56.

75. *Mémoires de Madame de Rémusat*, III, p. 269.

76. Dard, *Napoléon et Talleyrand*, pp. 227–32; Dunan, *Napoléon et l'Allemagne*, p. 608 note 59.

77. Dard, *Napoléon et Talleyrand*, p. 233.

78. Talleyrand, *Mémoires*, II, p. 321. Count Karl Robert von Nesselrode (1780–1862).

79. *Lettres et papiers du chancelier comte de Nesselrode 1760–1850*, ed. comte A. de Nesselrode, III (Paris: A. Lahure, 1904), p. 139.

80. Ibid., p. 225.

81. Dard, *Napoléon et Talleyrand*, pp. 249–51.

82. *Lettres du chancelier comte de Nesselrode*, III, p. 269.

83. *Mémoires du chancelier Pasquier*, I, pp. 391–5.

84. Lacour-Gayet, *Talleyrand*, pp. 686–7.

85. Ibid., pp. 688–91.

86. *Lettres du chancelier comte de Nesselrode*, III, pp. 341–2.

87. *Memoiren der Gräfin Kielmannsegge über Napoleon I*, ed. Gertrude Aretz (Dresden: Paul Aretz Verlag, 1927), pp. 67– 8, 80–81.

88. Ibid., p. 322.

89. *Mémoires de Madame de Rémusat*, pp. 305–14; Lacour-Gayet, *Talleyrand*, pp. 683–4.

90. *Mémoires du chancelier Pasquier*, I, p. 377.

91. Mollien was sent by Napoleon to sound out public opinion and discovered that Princess Marie-Louise would be regarded as a 'sort of mediatrix' to absolve France in the eyes of Europe for the fate of Marie-Antoinette (Mollien, *Mémoires*, I, p. 123).

92. Talleyrand, *Mémoires*, II, pp. 7–10.

93. *Correspondance de Napoléon Ier*, XXI, no. 16850, p. 79.

94. Tulard, *Napoléon*, pp. 371–83.

95. *Monsieur de Talleyrand*, III, pp. 211–13.

96. *Lettres du chancelier comte de Nesselrode*, III, p. 351 (June 1811). In other words, he could neither attend the *lever* nor the *coucher* of the Emperor, nor see him in the Empress's *appartements* in the evening. In terms of court protocol, this was a considerable humiliation. (I am grateful to Philip Mansel for elucidating this matter.)

97. Méneval, *Mémoires,*, II, p. 396.

98. *Memoiren der Gräfin Kielmannsegge*, pp. 77–8.

99. Ibid., p. 79.

100. *Mémoires de Vitrolles*, I, p. 249. Vitrolles, though, improbably adds this insult to the end of the others in the scene of 1809.

101. Napoleon originally demanded the return of 680,000 francs (*Lettres inédites de Napoléon I*, ed. Lecestre, II, no. 826, pp. 140–41).

102. Waresquiel, *Talleyrand*, pp. 415–17.

103. *Mémoires du général de Caulaincourt*, I, pp. 322–5.

104. Ibid., II, pp. 65, 221.

CHAPTER 12: RÉGIME CHANGE

1. Lacour-Gayet, *Talleyrand*, pp. 705–7.

2. *Mémoires du chancelier Pasquier*, II, pp. 12–40.

3. *The Greville Diary*, I, p. 90.

4. *Memoires d'Aimée de Coigny*, p. 210.

5. Lacour-Gayet, *Talleyrand*, pp. 706–7.

6. *Mémoires d'Aimée de Coigny*, pp. 239–51. These were, indeed, precisely the means that Talleyrand would proceed to employ; see below.

7. *Monsieur de Talleyrand*, IV, pp. 233–5.

8. Ibid., p. 252.

9. Ibid., pp. 236–9.

10. '*C'est le commencement de la fin*'. The observation is frequently connected with the arrival of Napoleon in Paris after his retreat from Moscow. But it appears to have been made later, and was, therefore, rather less prophetic (*Mémoires de Madame de Chastenay*, II, p. 260). Metternich specifically associates it with the defection of France's ally, Bavaria (Dard, *Napoléon et Talleyrand*, p. 315). Of course, like others of Talleyrand's *bons mots*, it was probably used on more than one occasion.

11. *Monsieur de Talleyrand*, IV, pp. 242–3.

12. *Mémoires d'Aimée de Coigny*, p. 190.

13. *Mémoires du chancelier Pasquier*, II, p. 141.

14. *Monsieur de Talleyrand*, IV, p. 253.

15. *Mémoires de Madame de Rémusat*, I, pp. 107–8.

16. *Mémoires du duc de Rovigo*, VI, pp. 250–51.

17. *Souvenirs intimes sur M. de Talleyrand*, p. 93.

18. *Mémoires du général de Caulaincourt*, I, pp. 160–69; *Mémoires du duc de Rovigo*, VI, pp. 228–9.

19. Mollien, *Mémoires*, III, p. 360.

20. Las Cases, *Mémorial de Sainte-Hélène*, II, p. 186; *Mémoires du général de Caulaincourt*, III, p. 392.

21. *Correspondance de Napoléon Ier*, XXVII, no. 21210, pp. 131–3.

22. La Tour du Pin, *Journal*, pp. 339–40.

23. *Monsieur de Talleyrand*, IV, p. 255; Talleyrand, *Mémoires*, II, p. 134.

24. *Mémoires du duc de Rovigo*, VI, p. 304.

25. *Talleyrand intime d'après sa correspondance avec la duchesse de Courlande* (Paris: Ernest Kolb, n.d.), p. 44: letter of 20 January 1814 to the duchesse de Courlande.

26. Robert Stewart, Viscount Castlereagh, 2nd Marquis of Londonderry (1769–1822).

27. *Mémoires du chancelier Pasquier*, II, p. 194.

28. Talleyrand, *Mémoires*, II, p. 149 note 2.

29. Count Karl August von Hardenberg (1750–1822).

30. *Mémoires de Vitrolles*, I, pp. 50–148; *Mémoires du chancelier Pasquier*, II, pp. 178–80.

31. Emmanuel de Waresquiel and Benoît Yvert, *Histoire de la Restauration 1814–1830: Naissance de la France moderne* (Paris: Perrin, 1996), pp. 25–31.

32. Guillaume de Bertier de Sauvigny, *Metternich* (Paris: Fayard, 1986), p. 193.

33. Alan Palmer, *Alexander I: Tsar of War and Peace* (London: Phoenix, 1997), p. 279.

34. *Mémoires de la Reine Hortense*, II, p. 183.

35. *Mémoires du chancelier Pasquier*, II, p. 215.

36. *Mémoires du duc de Rovigo*, VI, pp. 367, 371.

37. *Mémoires du général de Caulaincourt*, I, p. 86.

38. Talleyrand, *Mémoires*, II, p. 135.

39. *Mémoires du chancelier Pasquier*, II, pp. 217–18.

40. *Talleyrand intime*, p. 162. It is one of the few occasions that he dared write anything dangerous in the correspondence. No wonder he urged Mme de Courlande to burn the letter. But he also joked, for the benefit of the

censors, about the delay their interception caused his letters (ibid., p. 173: letter of 20 March).

41. *Mémoires du général de Caulaincourt*, III, p. 116.

42. *Monsieur de Talleyrand*, IV, p. 267.

43. Rémusat, *Mémoires de ma vie*, I, p. 135.

44. *Mémoires du chancelier Pasquier*, II, pp. 231–2; 'Mémoires inédites de M. le comte de Semallé, commissaire du roi en 1814', in L.-G. Michaud, *Histore politique et privée de Charles-Maurice de Talleyrand* (Paris: Bureau de la biographie universelle, 1853), p. 194.

45. *Lettres du chancelier comte de Nesselrode*, II, pp. 114–15.

46. Palmer, *Alexander I*, pp. 280–1.

47. Ibid., pp. 273–8.

48. *Mémoires de Bourrienne*, V, pp. 303–7.

49. Talleyrand, *Mémoires*, II, p. 164.

50. *Mémoires du général de Caulaincourt*, III, pp. 85–6, 93–9, 108.

51. Lacour-Gayet, *Talleyrand*, p. 768.

52. *Monsieur de Talleyrand*, IV, pp. 298–9; *Mémoires et correspondance du comte de Villèle*, I (Paris: Perrin, 1888), p. 228.

53. 'Mémoires de Semallé', pp. 195–6.

54. *Mémorial de Norvins*, p. 267.

55. *Mémoires du comte Beugnot (1779–1815)*, ed. Robert Lacour-Gayet (Paris: Hachette, 1959), pp. 245–6.

56. Pierre-Paul-Nicolas, baron Henrion de Pansey (1743–1824); General Pierre Dupont de l'Étang (1765–1839), whose capitulation at Bailén on 22 July 1808 Napoleon could not forgive; Pierre-Victor, baron Malouet (1740–1814); comte Jules Anglès (1778–1828). Louis-Antoine-Fauvelin de Bourrienne (1769–1834) had been Bonaparte's secretary before being disgraced for corruption and becoming close to Lavalette and Talleyrand.

57. *Mémoires du général de Caulaincourt*, III, pp. 291–3; *Lettres du chancelier comte de Nesselrode*, II, pp. 117–18.

58. Not that he was alone in such bizarre demonstrations. As a cruel joke, Talleyrand persuaded his colleague, the gullible Pradt, to run through the streets of Paris waving a white handkerchief and shouting '*Vive le Roi!*' The archbishop of Malines, predictably, ran into into a gang of Bonapartists and had to flee for his life (*Mémoires du comte Beugnot*, pp. 255–6).

59. Talleyrand, *Mémoires*, III, pp. 319–22.

60. *Mémoires du chancelier Pasquier*, II, pp. 373–5.

61. The reference is specifically to Henri IV, assassinated by a religious fanatic in 1610 (*Mémoires de Vitrolles*, I, p. 58 note 1).

62. Chateaubriand, *Mémoires d'outre tombe*, IV, pp. 559–60; A. Thiers, *Histoire du Consulat et de l'Empire*, XVIII (Paris: Paulin Lheureux, 1860), pp. 635–44; Lacour-Gayet, *Talleyrand*, pp. 804–7.

63. *Talleyrand intime*, p. 237.

64. Ibid., p. 281. The Peace of Paris also contained secret provisions, which bear on the subsequent Congress of Vienna. See p. 234.

65. Charles Webster, *The Foreign Policy of Castlereagh 1812–1815: Britain and the Reconstruction of Europe* (London: G. Bell, 1950), p. 267.

66. Charles Dupuis, *Le Ministère de Talleyrand en 1814*, I (Paris: Plon, 1919), pp. 283–5.

67. Webster, *Foreign Policy of Castlereagh*, pp. 270–72.

68. *Monsieur de Talleyrand*, IV, p. 322.

69. Webster, *Foreign Policy of Castlereagh*, p. 251.

70. *Mémoires du chancelier Pasquier*, II, p. 396.

71. *Monsieur* was the title traditionally given to the heir to the French throne.

72. *Mémoires de Vitrolles*, I, pp. 342–3.

73. Ibid., I, p. 135, III, p. 241.

74. Ibid., I, pp. 351, 367–74.

75. *Monsieur de Talleyrand*, IV, pp. 309–10.

76. *Mémoires du comte Beugnot*, p. 260.

77. Waresquiel, *Talleyrand*, p. 737. Of course, one very damaging document escaped; see pp. 149–50.

78. *Mémoires de Vitrolles*, I, pp. 380–405, II, pp. 2–15; Waresquiel and Yvert, *Histoire de la Restauration*, pp. 48–50.

79. *Mémoires du chancelier Pasquier*, II, p. 354.

80. *Mémoires de Vitrolles*, II, p. 27.

81. *Monsieur de Talleyrand*, IV, pp. 345–9.

82. Talleyrand, *Mémoires*, II, pp. 169–70; *Mémoires du chancelier Pasquier*, II, p. 403.

83. *Mémoires du chancelier Pasquier*, II, pp. 399–405; *Lettres du chancelier comte de Nesselrode*, II, p. 118.

84. Robert Tombs, *France 1814–1914* (London: Longman, 1996), p. 333.

85. Waresquiel, *Talleyrand*, p. 459; Lacour-Gayet, *Talleyrand*, p. 811. The expression also was open to ridicule. In June 1814 a caricature was being sold in Paris showing someone reading a book with the title, *Histoire des dix-neuf glorieuses années du règne de Louis XVIII*. The pages were blank (Philip Mansel, *Louis XVIII* (Stroud: Sutton, 1999), p. 200).

86. Talleyrand, *Mémoires*, II, pp. 171–2.

87. *Mémoires du comte de Villèle*, I, p. 234.

88. *Mémoires du comte Beugnot*, p. 287.

89. *Correspondance diplomatique du comte Pozzo di Borgo, ambassadeur de Russie en France, et du comte de Nesselrode*, ed. comte Charles Pozzo di Borgo, I (Paris: Calmann-Lévy, 1890), no. 17, p. 40.

90. *Mémoires du comte de Ferrand, ministre d'état sous Louis XVIII*, ed. vicomte de Broc (Paris: Alphonse Picard, 1897), pp. 80–81.

91. *Mémoires du chancelier Pasquier*, III, p. 68.

92. *Monsieur de Talleyrand*, IV, pp. 314, 344–5.

93. Talleyrand, *Mémoires*, II, pp. 210–14

CHAPTER 13: THE CONGRESS OF VIENNA

1. *Mémoires du chancelier Pasquier*, III, pp. 67–8.

2. Talleyrand, *Mémoires*, II, p. 202.

3. Talleyrand also, under the rubric of 'legitimacy', supported the house of Savoy in Piedmont, whose independence protected France against Austria.

4. Pozzo di Borgo notes the success of the strategy. Talleyrand obtained and retained Blacas's crucial support (*Correspondance diplomatique du comte Pozzo di Borgo*, I, no. 26, pp. 59–60).

5. Talleyrand, *Mémoires*, II, pp. 214–54.

6. Ibid., pp. 237–43.

7. Ibid., pp. 243–4.

8. Ibid., pp. 247–8.

9. Ibid., p. 253.

10. Charles Stewart (1778–1854) had just become Baron Stewart and would succeed Castlereagh on the latter's death in 1822 as 3rd Marquis of Londonderry.

11. Webster, *Foreign Policy of Castlereagh*, pp. 320–37.

12. *Monsieur de Talleyrand*, IV, p. 370.

13. Comte A. de La Garde-Chambonas, *Souvenirs du Congrès de Vienne 1814–1815*, ed. comte de Fleury (Paris: H. Vivien, 1901), pp. 221–2, 227–8.

14. M.-H. Weil, *Les Dessous du Congrès de Vienne*, I (Paris: Payot, 1917), no. 172, pp. 135–6; no. 504, p. 369; no. 509, pp. 372–3.

15. La Garde-Chambonas, *Souvenirs*, p. 113. Jean-Baptiste Isabey (1767–1855).

16. Micheline Dupuy, *La Duchesse de Dino, princesse de Courlande, Égérie de Talleyrand* (Paris: Perrin, 2002), pp. 7–8, 171, 208.

17. The dates during which Edmond and Dorothée cohabited seem compatible with his having been the child's father. Moreover, the assertion – based on third-hand clerical gossip – that the abbé Dupanloup had in his old age frequently asserted that Pauline was Talleyrand's child can surely be dismissed (cf. Casimir Carrère, *Talleyrand amoureux* (Paris: France-Empire, 1975), p. 392). For a contrary view, see Philip Ziegler, *The Duchess of Dino* (London: Collins, 1962), pp. 147–50.

18. Dino, *Chronique*, III, pp. 81–2.

19. Wenzel Anton Graf von Kaunitz-Rietberg (1711–94).

20. Weil, *Les Dessous du Congrès de Vienne*, I, no. 111, p. 96.

21. *Tagebücher von Friedrich von Gentz*, I (Leipzig: F.A. Brockhaus, 1873), p. 314.

22. Talleyrand, *Memoires*, II, pp. 278–82.

23. This was true of Austria which had signed an alliance with Murat in January 1814.

24. Talleyrand, *Mémoires*, II, p. 329.

25. Harold Nicolson, *The Congress of Vienna: A Study in Allied Unity, 1812–1822* (London: Constable, 1946), pp. 138–40.

26. Enno E. Kraehe, *Metternich's German Policy*, II: *The Congress of Vienna, 1814–1815* (Princeton: Princeton University Press, 1983), pp. 138–42; Webster, *Foreign Policy of Castlereagh*, pp. 339–41.

27. Talleyrand, *Mémoires*, II, no. 3, pp. 327–8; no. 4, p. 346.

28. Gaston Palewski, *Le Miroir de Talleyrand. Lettres inédites à la duchesse de Courlande pendant le Congrès de Vienne* (Paris: Perrin, [1976]) no. 7, p. 48.

29. For example, Talleyrand's hurtful remark to Alexander that it would be necessary 'to withdraw from him the fine title of Liberator of the World, that had been bestowed on him, and give him another instead' (Weil, *Les Dessous du Congrès de Vienne*, I, no. 293, p. 234).

30. Ibid., no. 344, pp. 271–2.

31. Ibid., no. 648, p. 452; Philip Mansel, *Prince of Europe: The Life of Charles-Joseph de Ligne 1735–1814* (London: Weidenfeld and Nicolson, 2003), p. 257.

32. La Garde-Chambonas, *Souvenirs*, p. 53.

33. Webster, *Foreign Policy of Castlereagh*, pp. 343–53.

34. Henry Kissinger, *A World Restored: Metternich, Castlereagh and the Problems of Peace 1812–1822* (London: Weidenfeld and Nicolson, 1957), p. 147. Henry Kissinger significantly underrates Talleyrand's role at Vienna, overlooking his contribution to the diplomatically fruitful concept of 'legitimacy', on which see below pp. 336–7.

35. '*Sa philosophie est devenue bien conquérante*' (Palewski, *Le Miroir de Talleyrand*, no. 16, p. 70: letter to the duchesse de Courlande of 17 November 1814).

36. Nicolson, *The Congress of Vienna*, pp. 15–152, 164–71.

37. Bertier de Sauvigny, *Metternich*, pp. 226, 233–4.

38. Talleyrand, *Mémoires*, II, no. 4, p. 342.

39. La Garde-Chambonas, *Souvenirs*, pp. 52–4, 60.

40. Talleyrand, *Mémoires*, II, no. 24, p. 31.

41. Mansel, *Prince of Europe*, p. 259.

42. Palmer, *Alexander I*, pp. 311–12.

43. Talleyrand, *Mémoires*, II, no. 9, p. 410.

44. Palmer, *Alexander I*, pp. 308–9.

45. Talleyrand, *Mémoires*, II, no. ii, pp. 435–9: letter from the comte de Blacas to Talleyrand of 9 November 1814.

46. Ibid., no. 12, pp. 457–73.

47. Ibid., pp. 255–6.

48. *Correspondance du comte de Jaucourt, ministre des affaires étrangères, avec le prince de Talleyrand pendant le Congrès de Vienne* (Paris: Plon, 1905), p. 75.

49. Talleyrand, *Mémoires*, II, no. 12, p. 466; no. 13, pp. 483–92.

50. Ibid., no. 14, p. 500.

51. Nicolson, *The Congress of Vienna*, pp. 173–6.

52. Talleyrand, *Mémoires*, II, no. 16, p. 529.

53. *Mémoires de Metternich*, II, no. 194 (annexe to no. 192), pp. 509–14.

54. Talleyrand, *Mémoires*, II, no 21 bis, p. 539.

55. Ibid., no. 18, pp. 543–4.

56. Ibid., III, no. 27, p. 75.

57. Ibid., no. 19, p. 556.

58. Webster, *Foreign Policy of Castlereagh*, p. 371.

59. Talleyrand, *Mémoires*, III, no. 23, p. 24.

60. La Garde-Chambonas, *Souvenirs*, pp. 296–9.

61. *Mémoires de Talleyrand*, ed. Broglie, V, p. 570.

62. Talleyrand, *Mémoires*, II, no. 6, p. 368.

63. *Mémoires du chancelier Pasquier*, III, pp. 85–90.

64. Weil, *Les Dessous du Congrès de Vienne*, I, no. 312, pp. 247–8.

65. Talleyrand, *Mémoires*, III, no. 29, pp. 80–83; no. 32, pp. 98–9; Alan Palmer, *Metternich* (London: Weidenfeld and Nicolson, 1972), p. 146.

66. Talleyrand, *Mémoires*, III, no. 32, p. 101.

67. Ibid., II, no. 5, p. 352; no. 3 ter, pp. 382–4.

68. Weil, *Les Dessous du Congrès de Vienne*, I, no. 1870, p. 320.

69. Talleyrand, *Mémoires*, III, no. 32, p. 100.

70. Palewski, *Le Miroir de Talleyrand*, no. 36, p. 138: letter to the duchesse de Courlande of 15 March 1815.

71. Pozzo di Borgo wrote to Nesselrode on 12 May from Ghent telling him to send Talleyrand: his presence by the King's side was indispensable (*Correspondance diplomatique du comte Pozzo di Borgo*, I, no. 56, pp. 114–15).

72. O'Meara, *Napoleon at St Helena*, II, pp. 20–21.

73. Waresquiel, *Talleyrand*, p. 494.

74. Palewski, *Le Miroir de Talleyrand*, no. 34, p. 130: letter to the duchesse de Courlande of 3 March 1815; *Revelations of the Life of Prince Talleyrand*, pp. 275–9.

75. Palewski, *Le Miroir de Talleyrand*, no. 38, p. 152: letter to the duchesse de Courlande of 30 March 1815.

CHAPTER 14: PRESIDENT OF THE COUNCIL

1. Talleyrand, *Mémoires*, III, no. 52, pp. 167–79.

2. Waresquiel and Yvert, *Histoire de la Restauration*, pp. 85–90.

3. Guizot, *Mémoires*, I, p. 103.

4. Talleyrand, *Mémoires*, III, pp. 214–19: 'Report made to the King during his Journey from Ghent to Paris'. The 'three distinct wills' are, of course, in British terms, those of King, Lords and Commons.

5. *Diary of Philipp von Neumann*, I, p. 260.

6. Marquis de La Maisonfort, *Mémoires d'un agent royaliste sous la Révolution, l'Empire et la Restauration 1763–1827* (Paris: Mercure de France, 1998), p. 273.

7. Talleyrand, *Mémoires*, III, p. 227. Metternich wrote to Talleyrand urging him to hold fast to his idea of keeping the King away from Paris (*Mémoires de Metternich*, II, no. 199, pp. 519–20: letter of 24 June 1815).

8. Chateaubriand, *Mémoires d'outre-tombe*, II, pp. 692–3.

9. *Mémoires du comte Beugnot*, p. 317.

10. *Correspondance diplomatique du comte Pozzo di Borgo*, I, no. 74, pp. 173–5.

11. *Mémoires du chancelier Pasquier*, III, pp. 293–6.

12. Talleyrand, *Mémoires*, III, pp. 230–32.

13. *Mémoires du comte Beugnot*, pp. 322–3.

14. *Journal du maréchal de Castellane*, I (Paris: Plon, 1895), p. 297.

15. Chateaubriand, *Mémoires d'outre-tombe*, II, p. 578.

16. *Journal du maréchal de Castellane*, III, p. 166.

17. Lacour-Gayet, *Talleyrand*, pp. 676–7.

18. Chateaubriand, *Mémoires d'outre-tombe*, II, p. 171.

19. Chateaubriand, *Correspondance générale*, ed. Pierre Riberette, III (Paris: Gallimard, 1982), no. 683, pp. 34–5.

20. Ibid., no. 684, p. 35: letter to Talleyrand of 6 May 1815.

21. Chateaubriand, *Mémoires d'outre-tombe*, II, p. 692.

22. Talleyrand, *Mémoires*, III, p. 233.

23. *Mémoires du comte Beugnot*, p. 333.

24. *Correspondance diplomatique du comte Pozzo di Borgo*, I, no. 83, pp. 190–93; no. 84, pp. 193–200.

25. Chateaubriand, *Mémoires d'outre-tombe*, II, p. 703.

26. Lacour-Gayet, *Talleyrand*, pp. 855–6.

27. Emmanuel de Waresquiel, *Le Duc de Richelieu 1766–1822: Un sentimental en politique* (Paris: Perrin, 1990), pp. 228–30.

28. *Mémoires de Vitrolles*, III, p. 127; Rémusat, *Mémoires de ma vie*, I, p. 293. Élie, comte (later duc) Decazes (1788–1860). Decazes worked to undermine Fouché (*Mémoires de Vitrolles*, III, pp. 192–5).

29. *Mémoires du chancelier Pasquier*, III, pp. 376, 424–5.

30. Molé, *Mémoires*, I, p. 332.

31. Guizot, *Mémoires*, I, pp. 36–7.

32. Molé, *Mémoires*, I, p. 289–90. Molé, like Chateaubriand, owed Talleyrand a large political debt, in this case for having him appointed to the Chamber of Peers despite suspicions of his loyalty during the Hundred Days. Also like Chateaubriand, he quickly forgot it (Talleyrand, *Mémoires*, III, p. 253).

33. *Mémoires du chancelier Pasquier*, III, pp. 377–8.

34. *Mémoires du comte de Ferrand*, p. 148.

35. Talleyrand, *Mémoires*, III, pp. 243–50; Fichier Charavay, 167, TAB-TAT: memorandum from Talleyrand to Louis XVIII of August 1815.

36. *Mémoires de Vitrolles*, III, pp. 204–9.

37. *Journal du maréchal de Castellane*, I, p. 299.

38. *Souvenirs du baron de Barante*, ed. Claude de Barante, II (Paris: Calmann-Lévy, 1892), pp. 177–9.

39. *Monsieur de Talleyrand*, IV, pp. 354–5.

40. *Mémoires du comte de Villèle*, I, p. 323.

41. *Souvenirs du baron de Barante*, II, p. 206. Joseph Lainé (1767–1835) represented Bordeaux, which he had helped turn into a royalist bastion. He was elected President of the Chamber in 1815 and would hold ministerial positions.

42. Talleyrand, *Mémoires*, III, p. 251; *Mémoires du chancelier Pasquier*, III, p. 390.

43. *Mémoires du chancelier Pasquier*, III, pp. 385–7; *Mémoires de Vitrolles*, III, p. 187.

44. *Journal du maréchal de Castellane*, I, p. 301; *Mémoires du chancelier Pasquier*, III, pp. 392–3.

45. *Mémoires du chancelier Pasquier*, III, pp. 419–20; *Mémoires de Vitrolles*, III, pp. 199–200.

46. *Mémoires de Vitrolles*, III, pp. 222–4.

47. Guillaume de Bertier de Sauvigny, *Metternich et la France après le Congrès de Vienne*, I (Paris: Hachette, 1968), pp. 50, 53.

48. *Journal du maréchal de Castellane*, I, p. 297.

49. *Mémoires du comte Beugnot*, pp. 339–43.

50. Talleyrand, *Mémoires*, III, pp. 265–74; Gentz, *Tagerbücher*, I, p. 410.

51. *Mémoires du chancelier Pasquier*, III, p. 411.

52. Ibid., pp. 397–400.

53. Lacour-Gayet, *Talleyrand*, p. 880. This seems to disprove Vitrolles's account of Talleyrand's 'stupefaction' when his offer of resignation was accepted – an account which, oddly, Lacour-Gayet himself accepts (ibid., pp. 878–9).

54. *Mémoires du chancelier Pasquier*, III, pp. 421–2.

55. Talleyrand, *Mémoires*, III, pp. 277–96.

56. The main sources are: Talleyrand, *Mémoires*, III, p. 297; *Mémoires du chancelier Pasquier*, III, pp. 426–7; *Mémoires de Vitrolles*, III, pp. 227–8. Pasquier says that he had already informed the King of Talleyrand's decision before the Prince arrived.

57. *Mémoires du général de Caulaincourt*, III, p. 246.

CHAPTER 15: OPPOSITION AND VINDICATION

1. *Mémoires de Vitrolles*, III, p. 230.

2. *Mémoires du chancelier Pasquier*, III, p. 422; IV, pp. 27, 100.

3. *Souvenirs intimes sur M. de Talleyrand*, p. 106.

4. Rémusat, *Mémoires de ma vie*, I, p. 238.

5. *Mémoires du chancelier Pasquier*, IV, p. 100 note 1.

6. Waresquiel, *Le Duc de Richelieu*, pp. 247–59, 350–51.

7. *Talleyrand und der Herzog von Dalberg: Unveröffentlichte Briefe (1816–1832)*, ed. Eberhard Ernst (Frankfurt am Main: Verlag Peter Lang, 1987), no. 48, p. 142: letter to Dalberg of 5 March 1831.

8. *Mémoires du chancelier Pasquier*, IV, pp. 100–101.

9. It was a piece of wordplay. Decazes was thus *'suffisant et insuffisant'* (*Souvenirs intimes sur M. de Talleyrand*, p. 106).

10. Molé connects the episode to Talleyrand's frequently indiscreet remarks after dinner, resulting from his habit of drinking without having eaten anything earlier in the day (*Mémoires du comte Molé*, II, p. 290). Sir Charles Stuart, later Baron Stuart de Rothesay (1779–1845), was British ambassador in Paris 1815–24 and 1828–31.

11. *Mémoires du comte de Villèle*, II, p. 99.

12. *Mémoires du chancelier Pasquier*, IV, pp. 136–9; *Mémoires du comte Molé*, II, pp. 290–2; Waresquiel, *Talleyrand*, p. 526; Fichier Charavay, 167, TAB-TAT: letter to Louis XVIII of 22 November 1816.

13. Lacour-Gayet, *Talleyrand*, pp. 904–7.

14. Ibid., pp. 909–10.

15. *Monsieur de Talleyrand*, IV, p. 367.

16. Lacour-Gayet, *Talleyrand*, pp. 893, 922.

17. *Mémoires de Barras*, IV, p. 261.

18. The details of these complex and secret transactions have been laid bare by Emmanuel de Waresquiel (Waresquiel, *Talleyrand*, p. 489 and note 3 to p. 489 on p. 711); also, Ingold, *op.cit.*, pp. 360–6.

19. *Mémoires du comte de Villèle*, II, p. 99.

20. *Mémoires de la comtesse de Boigne*, II, pp. 359–60.

21. *Mémoires du comte de Villèle*, II, p. 105.

22. *Correspondance diplomatique du comte Pozzo di Borgo*, II, no. 198, p. 29; no. 210, p. 86.

23. Ibid., no. 218, pp. 112–13.

24. Ibid., no. 272, pp. 333–4; no. 284, pp. 389–98.

25. *Mémoires de Vitrolles*, III, pp. 254–5.

26. *Correspondance diplomatique du comte Pozzo di Borgo*, II, no. 287, p. 405.

27. Rémusat, *Mémoires de ma vie*, I, p. 366.

28. *Mémoires de Vitrolles*, III, pp. 456–8.

29. Guy Antonetti, *Louis-Philippe* (Paris: Fayard, 1994), pp. 532–5; Waresquiel, *Talleyrand*, pp. 556–8.

30. Ernest Daudet, *La Police politique: Chronique du temps de la Restauration 1815–1820* (Paris: Plon, 1912), pp. 254–5.

31. Gorsas, *Talleyrand*, pp. 231–46.

32. *Mémoires du comte Molé*, IV, p. 214.

33. *Mémoires du comte de Villèle*, II, p. 250.

34. *Mémoires du comte Molé*, IV, p. 201.

35. Waresquiel, *Talleyrand*, p. 530.

36. *Mémoires du comte Molé*, V, p. 31.

37. Jean-Baptiste-Guillaume-Joseph, comte de Villèle (1773–1854).

38. Lacour-Gayet, *Talleyrand*, pp. 954–5.

39. Ibid., pp. 965–6. Guillaume-Chrétien de Lamoignon de Malesherbes (1721–94). Malesherbes was also admired by the ultras because he had bravely undertaken Louis XVI's defence and had perished on the scaffold.

40. Schell, *Talleyrand en Verve*, p. 74.

41. Fichier Charavay, 167, TAB-TAT: letter of (July) 1832.

42. Achille-Léonce-Victor-Charles, duc de Broglie (1785–1870); Amable-Guillaume-Prosper Brugière, baron de Barante (1782–1866); Pierre-Paul Royer-Collard (1763–1845).

43. '*Monsieur, vous avez des abords bien sévères.*' The English translation does not, in fact, do Talleyrand justice, because his wordplay was both on '*abords*' (i.e. approaches and manner) and '*sévères*' (i.e. physically testing and personally forbidding) (Lacour-Gayet, *Talleyrand*, p. 972).

44. *Souvenirs du baron de Barante*, II, p. 75.

45. *Opinion de M. le prince de Talleyrand sur le projet d'adresse en réponse au discours du Roi à l'ouverture de la session* (Paris: Tastu, 1823).

46. Chateaubriand, *Mémoires d'outre-tombe*, IV, p. 558.

47. Sainte-Beuve, *Monsieur de Talleyrand*, p. 110.

48. Talleyrand, *Mémoires*, III, pp. 316–19.

49. *Mémoires de la comtesse de Boigne*, II, p. 79.

50. *Talleyrand und der Herzog von Dalberg*, no. 4, p. 25: letter of 20 November 1823. Interestingly, Talleyrand also suggests that Dalberg contact Chateaubriand, then Foreign Minister, about the matter. This shows that Chateaubriand at this time cannot have had in his possession the damning letter that shows Talleyrand's involvement in the matter, mentioned earlier (see p. 149).

51. *Souvenirs intimes sur M. de Talleyrand*, pp. 105, 107.

52. *Diary of Philipp von Neumann*, I, p. 250.

53. *Souvenirs du baron de Barante*, II, p. 221: letter from the duchesse de Dino of 18 September 1824; p. 245: letter from the duchesse de Dino of 11 June 1825.

54. *Revelations of the Life of Prince Talleyrand*, p. 30.

55. *Talleyrand und der Herzog von Dalberg*, no. 10. p. 44: letter to Dalberg of 1 February 1826.

56. *Souvenirs du baron de Barante*, II, pp. 289–92: letter from the duchesse de Dino of 7 November 1825; pp. 316–18: letter from the duchesse de Dino of 31 January 1826.

57. Ibid., pp. 329–30: letter from the duchesse de Dino of 23 June 1826.

58. BL, Add. Ms. 51,635, fo 97r-v: letter from Talleyrand to Lord Holland of 16 October 1832. The gift was sent at the suggestion of his great-nephew Louis, who said that the fish must be 'excellent'.

59. Ibid., pp. 350–1: letter from Barante to Mme Anisson du Perron of 30 September 1826.

60. Lacombe, *La Vie privée de Talleyrand*, p. 238.

61. Lacour-Gayet, *Talleyrand*, p. 1153; Dino, *Notice sur Valençay*, p. xi.

62. Dino, *Notice sur Valençay*, pp. ix–x.

63. BN, N. Acq. fr., 24,346, no. 93: letter of 2 March 1831 to Bourdois; no. 95: letter of 11 April to Bourdois; no. 97: letter of 30 May to Bourdois. Talleyrand was a governor for life of the Royal Jennerian Society, founded to promote the ideas of Edward Jenner (1749–1823), the pioneer of vaccination against smallpox.

64. 215 AP 1, dossier 2, no. 13: letter of 1836 (no date) to Pierre-César Labouchère, the British-based banker.

65. *Souvenirs du baron de Barante*, II, pp. 455–6: letter of 5 July 1828.

66. Add. Ms. 51,635, fos 85r-86r: letter of 11 September 1832.

67. Lacour-Gayet, *Talleyrand*, p. 1163: letter of April 1835.

68. 21 January was a Sunday, so the memorial requiem was transferred.

69. *Journal du comte Rodolphe Apponyi*, ed. Ernest Daudet, I (Paris: Plon, 1926), pp. 42–4.

70. 'Sire, c'etait un coup de poing' (*Souvenirs intimes sur M. de Talleyrand*, p. 115).

71. Add. Ms. 51,635, fos 3r-4r: letter from Talleyrand to Lord Holland of mid-February 1827.

72. Lacour-Gayet, *Talleyrand*, pp. 1024–8.

73. *Talleyrand und der Herzog von Dalberg*, no. 9, pp. 40–41: letter to Dalberg of 14 January 1826.

74. *Journal du comte Rodolphe Apponyi*, I, pp. 105–6.

75. *Talleyrand und der Herzog von Dalberg*, no. 16, pp. 61–2: letter to Dalberg of 26 November 1828. He may, though, have lost just one million (Waresquiel, *Talleyrand*, p. 562).

76. Ibid., no. 19, pp. 68–9: letter to Dalberg of 30 June 1829.

77. Talleyrand seems to have had a haemorrhage in the eyes, perhaps as the result of a stroke. Molé attended him in his illness and his usually critical attitude towards his former colleague was suspended, as Charles-Maurice appeared to be approaching his end: 'He attracts me as I am attracted by everything that escapes, that threatens to disappear for ever'

(*Souvenirs du baron de Barante*, II, pp. 526–7: letter from Molé to Barante of 27 November 1829).

78. *Souvenirs intimes sur M. de Talleyrand*, p. 179.
79. Ibid., p. 106. According to Roman mythology, the cackling of the sacred geese in the Capitol alerted guards to the approach of the Gauls and thus saved the city.
80. Ibid., p. 121.
81. Ibid., p. 110.
82. Jean-Baptiste-Sylvère Gay, vicomte de Martignac (1778–1832). Known as a fine orator with flexible convictions, he had been elected a deputy in 1821.
83. *Revelations of the Life of Prince Talleyrand*, p. 31.
84. Jules-Auguste-Armand-Marie, prince de Polignac (1780–1847). Polignac had been implicated in the Cadoudal conspiracy of 1804 and was imprisoned until 1813. Appointed on 8 August 1829 as Foreign Minister, he became President of the Council formally in November. After the Revolution of 1830 he was condemned to perpetual imprisonment, but benefited from an amnesty in 1836. Talleyrand thought that he had made a poor impression at his trial by claiming merely to have been following Charles X's orders (*Diary of Philipp von Neumann*, I, p. 225).
85. Talleyrand, *Mémoires*, III, p. 326.
86. Adolphe Thiers (1797–1877).
87. Waresquiel, *Talleyrand*, p. 561.
88. Add. Ms. 51,635, fos 13r–15v.
89. Lacour-Gayet, *Talleyrand*, p. 1063.
90. *Revelations of the Life of Prince Talleyrand*, p. 37.
91. *Souvenirs (1775–1870) de feu le duc de Broglie*, I, (Paris: Calmann-Lévy, 1886), pp. 55–6.
92. *Mémoires du chancelier Pasquier*, VI, pp. 290–91.
93. Antonetti, *Louis-Philippe*, p. 583.
94. Waresquiel, *Talleyrand*, p. 566.
95. *Diary of Philipp von Neumann*, I, p. 225.
96. *Revelations of the Life of Prince Talleyrand*, pp. 36–7.
97. Dino, *Chronique*, I, p. 184.
98. *Diary of Philipp von Neumann*, I, pp. 228–9. Dorothea von Benckendorff, Princess von Lieven (1785–1857). Talleyrand provides a slightly different account of the exchange in his memoirs (Talleyrand, *Mémoires*, III, p. 405).
99. Talleyrand, *Mémoires*, III, p. 234.

100. Add. Ms. 51,635, fos 13r–15v: letter of March 1830.
101. Ibid., fo 16r: letter of 6 September 1830.

CHAPTER 16: AMBASSADOR IN LONDON

1. Talleyrand, *Mémoires*, III, p. 332.
2. 'Lettres de la duchesse de Dino à Adolphe Thiers (1830–1837)', part 1, *La Revue de Paris* (1 April 1923), no. 1, pp. 248–50: letter of 1 October 1830.
3. Talleyrand, *Mémoires*, III, appendix, pp. 451–2: letter to Mme Adélaïde of 2 October 1830.
4. *The Times*, Thursday, 7 October 1830.
5. Talleyrand, *Mémoires*, III, p. 393; Dino, *Chronique*, I, pp. 108–9.
6. *Talleyrand und der Herzog von Dalberg*, no. 33, pp. 103–4: letter of 11 October 1830.
7. Lacour-Gayet, *Talleyrand*, p. 108.
8. 'Lettres de la duchesse de Dino à Adolphe Thiers', part I, no. 4, pp. 255–6: letter of 7 October 1830.
9. Rémusat, *Mémoires de ma vie*, II, pp. 574, 578; *The Greville Diary*, I, pp. 86, 89; Chateaubriand, *Mémoires d'outre-tombe*, IV, p. 561; *A Portion of the Journal Kept by Thomas Raikes Esq.*, I, p. 74.
10. *Mémoires du comte Molé*, V, pp. 132–4.
11. Talleyrand, *Mémoires*, III, pp. 344–5: letter of 8 October 1830.
12. Waresquiel, *Talleyrand*, p. 580.
13. *Mémoires du comte de Villèle*, II, p. 250.
14. Talleyrand, *Mémoires*, III, pp. 346–8.
15. Ibid., p. 373.
16. Ibid., pp. 410–11.
17. *Lettres du chancelier comte de Nesselrode*, VII, p. 235.
18. Lacour-Gayet, *Talleyrand*, p. 1113.
19. Talleyrand, *Mémoires*, II, p. 297.
20. Ibid., IV, p. 106: letter to the princesse de Vaudémont (undated but of March 1831).
21. Ibid., III, pp. 412–17.
22. *Diary of Philipp von Neumann*, I, p. 256.
23. *A Portion of the Journal Kept by Thomas Raikes Esq.*, I, p. 64.
24. *Souvenirs du baron de Barante*, IV, pp. 9–10: letter from the duchesse de Dino of 13 October 1830.
25. Ibid., pp. 11–12: letter from the duchesse de Dino of 27 October 1830.

26. *Talleyrand und der Herzog von Dalberg*, no. 36, pp. 112–14: letter of 8 November 1830.

27. Add. Ms. 51,635, fo 90r–91r: letter of 23 September 1832.

28. *The Holland House Diaries, 1831–1840: The Diary of Henry Richard Vassall Fox, third Lord Holland*, ed. Abraham D. Kriegel (London: Routledge & Kegan Paul, 1977), p. 115.

29. Ibid., p. 18.

30. *Diary of Philipp von Neumann*, I, p. 226.

31. Talleyrand, *Mémoires*, III, appendix, pp. 451–2: letter to Mme Adélaïde of 2 October 1830.

32. *Souvenirs du baron de Barante*, IV, pp. 9–10: letter from the duchesse de Dino of 13 October 1830; pp. 101–3: letter from the duchesse de Dino of 23 February 1831; Dino, *Chronique*, I, pp. 75, 79.

33. *Souvenirs du baron de Barante*, IV., pp. 445–8: letter from the duchesse de Dino of 11 February 1832.

34. Dino, *Chronique*, I, pp. 66, 75–6.

35. *Hansard: House of Lords*, 29 September 1831, cols. 792–7, 807–8; *The Greville Diary*, I, p. 87; *A Portion of the Journal Kept by Thomas Raikes Esq.*, I, p. 83.

36. *Holland House Diaries*, p. 114.

37. Henry John Temple, Viscount Palmerston (1784–1865).

38. James Chambers, *Palmerston 'The People's Darling'* (London: John Murray, 2005), pp. 123, 157.

39. John Charmley, *The Princess and the Politicians: Sex, Intrigue and Diplomacy, 1812–1840* (London: Viking, 2005), pp. 202–3, 205–6.

40. Talleyrand, *Mémoires*, III, p. 407.

41. Dino, *Chronique*, I, p. 64.

42. For a powerful defence of Talleyrand's consistency, see: Maurice Schumann, 'Talleyrand, Prophet of the *Entente Cordiale*' (The Zaharoff Lecture for 1976–7) (Oxford: Clarendon Press, 1977).

43. Maria II of Portugal and Isabella II of Spain (in effect her mother, the regent Maria-Cristina) were faced by insurrections led respectively by Dom Miguel and Don Carlos.

44. Rémusat, *Mémoires de ma vie*, III, p. 141.

45. *A Portion of the Journal Kept by Thomas Raikes Esq.*, I, p. 198; *Holland House Diaries*, p. 338.

46. Rémusat, *Mémoires de ma vie*, III, p. 141.

47. One of his biographers notes: '[Palmerston's] unpunctuality did not spring from fecklessness or from a slapdash inability to plan his affairs. . .[but] from arrogance and lack of consideration for others'

(Jasper Ridley, *Lord Palmerston* (London: Constable, 1970), p. 117).

48. Dino, *Chronique*, I, pp. 198, 214.

49. *A Portion of the Journal Kept by Thomas Raikes Esq.*, I, p. 98.

50. Rémusat, *Mémoires de ma vie*, II, p. 579.

51. Talleyrand, *Mémoires*, V, p. 475: letter of 12 November 1834.

52. Rémusat, *Mémoires de ma vie*, III, p. 141.

53. *Journal du comte Rodolphe Apponyi*, III, p. 11.

54. Talleyrand's use of '*conservatif*' not the more usual but more general '*conservateur*' shows that he was thinking about British party politics, not just making a philosophical point (Add. Ms. 51,635, fos 129–130: letter of 22 June 1835).

55. *Diary of Philipp von Neumann*, I, p. 242.

56. Casimir-Pierre Périer (1777–1832).

57. Lamartine, *Cours familier de littérature*, II, p. 306, X, p. 390.

58. Fichier Charavay, 167, TAP-TAT: letter of 18 May 1832.

59. Rémusat, *Mémoires de ma vie*, II, pp. 575–7.

60. *Talleyrand und der Herzog von Dalberg*, no. 58, pp. 176–7: letter of 13 April 1832.

61. *Souvenirs du baron de Barante*, IV, pp. 293–8: letter from Molé of 22 February 1836.

62. 'Lettres de la duchesse de Dino à Adolphe Thiers', part I, no. 38, pp. 818–19: letter of 29 August 1836.

63. Rémusat, *Mémoires de ma vie*, III, p. 235. See p. 324.

CHAPTER 17: THE FINAL CURTAIN

1. Dupanloup's account, written in 1839, is published as an appendix in Lacombe, *La Vie privée de Talleyrand*, pp. 343–432. Lacombe also had access to other material from Dupanloup's archives. The duchesse de Dino's account is contained in her *Chronique*, II, pp. 85 *et seq.* After Talleyrand's death, and on reading Dupanloup's account, she sent the abbé a long letter supplementing and endorsing what he had written (pp. 226–45). The account given by Barante – though written much later and having the express purpose of refuting anticlerical arguments about the circumstances of Talleyrand's death – is also reliable because it comes from one of the old man's confidants in religious matters and a witness at his deathbed 'retraction' (Baron de Barante, *La Conversion et la mort de M. de Talleyrand: Récit de l'un des cinq témoins*, ed. Baron de Nervo (Paris: Librairie ancienne Honoré Champion, 1910)). By con-

trast, although informative and useful in many respects, the accounts of Raikes (probably derived from Montrond), Apponyi (some details from Pauline de Périgord) and the comtesse de Boigne (information from Pasquier, among other gossip) are less reliable and authoritative as sources (*Récits d'une tante*, IV, pp. 204–32). Waresquiel suggests that Catholicism has led in French historiography to a diabolization of Talleyrand's life; but it is equally evident that a certain degree of latent anti-Catholicism, or at least liberal scepticism, continues to lead to distortion of the circumstances of his death (cf. Waresquiel, *Talleyrand*, p. 17).

2. *Récits d'une tante*, IV, p. 204.
3. *A Portion of the Journal Kept by Thomas Raikes Esq.*, I, p. 98.
4. *Souvenirs du baron de Barante*, V, p. 93: letter from Talleyrand of 13 December 1833.
5. Ibid., p. 220: letter from Molé of 9 December 1835.
6. Add. Ms. 51,635, fos 81r–82r: letter to Lord Holland of 9 August 1832.
7. Dino, *Chronique*, I, pp. 365–75; Lacombe, *La Vie privée de Talleyrand*, p. 245.
8. Add. Ms. 51,635, fo 123r-v: letter to Lord Holland of 4 November 1834.
9. Ibid., fo 133r–134r: letter to Lord Holland of 15 December 1835.
10. Dino, *Chronique*, I, pp. 249–52.
11. Lacour-Gayet, *Talleyrand*, p. 1170.
12. Dino, *Chronique*, I, p. 231.
13. François de La Rochefoucauld, prince de Marcillac (1613–80); Nicolas Chamfort (born Nicolas Sébastien-Roch) (1741–94). Talleyrand made a collection of extracts from Chamfort's *Maximes*. Two of his favourites were: 'Public opinion is a tribunal that an honest man must never recognize completely, but which he should never reject', and 'To be agreeable in the world, one must allow oneself to learn what one knows' (Fichier Charavay, 167, TAB-TAT: extracts (undated)). Colmache also mistakenly attributes to Talleyrand himself another of Chamfort's maxims, one that the Prince obviously liked to the extent of making it his own: 'What I have been taught, I have forgotten; what I know, I have guessed' (*Revelations of the Life of Prince Talleyrand*, p. 358).
14. Lacombe, *La Vie privée de Talleyrand*, p. 246.
15. Ibid., p. 250.
16. Add. Ms. 51,635, fo 13r–15v: letter to Lord Holland of January–March 1830.
17. Lacombe, *La Vie privée de Talleyrand*, p. 246.
18. Waresquiel, *Talleyrand*, p. 602.

19. *Revelations of the Life of Prince Talleyrand*, p. 341.

20. *Talleyrand intime*, p. 69: letter of 7 February 1814.

21. Dino, *Chronique*, II, pp. 230, 233, 236.

22. Barante, *La Conversion et la mort de M. de Talleyrand*, p. 14.

23. Lacombe, *La Vie privée de Talleyrand*, pp. 258–65.

24. Dino, *Chronique*, II, pp. 232–3. In fact, it did not simplify Talleyrand's position in the eyes of the Church, since he had never been validly married and he had not lived with his wife for twenty years. But the Prince's understanding of the status of his marriage remained curiously defective for someone educated in canon law.

25. Lacombe, *La Vie privée de Talleyrand*, pp. 270–73; *Journal du comte Rodolphe Apponyi*, III, pp. 158–60; *Récits d'une tante*, IV, p. 219; *Souvenirs du baron de Barante*, V, pp. 224–6: letter from the duc Decazes of 15 December 1835. Talleyrand had become reconciled with Decazes, who visited him at Valençay.

26. Lacombe, *La Vie privée de Talleyrand*, pp. 275–6.

27. Dino, *Chronique*, II, p. 227.

28. Ibid., p. 238.

29. Dino, *Chronique*, I, pp. 85–6.

30. Félix-Antoine-Philibert Dupanloup (1802–78); Jean-Baptiste-Henri Dominique Lacordaire (1802–61).

31. Dino, *Chronique*, I, p. 208; *Récits d'une tante*, IV, p. 223.

32. Barante, *La Conversion et la mort de M. de Talleyrand*, p. 16.

33. Lacombe, *La Vie privée de Talleyrand*, pp. 347–9.

34. Ibid., pp. 296–7.

35. *Récits d'une tante*, IV, p. 222.

36. Dino, *Chronique*, II, pp. 214–18; ibid., p. 242.

37. Ibid., pp. 219–24.

38. Lacombe, *La Vie privée de Talleyrand*, pp. 303–20.

39. Ibid., pp. 321–3.

40. *Récits d'une tante*, IV, p. 225; *A Portion of the Journal Kept by Thomas Raikes Esq.*, II, p. 93.

41. *Récits d'une tante*, IV, pp. 227–8.

42. Lacombe, *La Vie privée de Talleyrand*, pp. 323–6; Barante, *La Conversion et la mort de M. de Talleyrand*, pp. 21–5.

43. *Récits d'une tante*, IV, p. 230; *Revelations of the Life of Prince Talleyrand*, pp. 343–4; *Journal du comte Rodolphe Apponyi*, III, p. 326.

44. Barante, *La Conversion et la mort de M. de Talleyrand*, pp. 25–6; *Journal du comte Rodolphe Apponyi*, III, p. 327; Lacombe, *La Vie privée de Talleyrand*, pp. 338–9, 409–11.

45. *Revelations of the Life of Prince Talleyrand*, pp. 346–7.
46. *Journal du comte Rodolphe Apponyi*, III, pp. 324–5.
47. *Récits d'une tante*, IV, p. 231.
48. Léon Noël, *Énigmatique Talleyrand* (Paris: Fayard, 1975), pp. 164, 166, 179–80.
49. Chateaubriand, *Mémoires d'outre-tombe*, IV, pp. 565–6.
50. Noël, *Énigmatique Talleyrand*, pp. 172–6.
51. *A Portion of the Journal Kept by Thomas Raikes Esq.*, II, p. 98.
52. Beau, *Talleyrand: l'Apogée du sphinx*, pp. 179–85.

CHAPTER 18: POLITICIAN, DIPLOMAT, STATESMAN

1. *Mémoires de Vitrolles*, III, p. 450.
2. *A Portion of the Journal Kept by Thomas Raikes Esq.*, I, p. 414.
3. 'Discours du duc de Barante sur M. de Talleyrand', in Alexandre Sallé, *Vie politique du prince Charles Maurice de Talleyrand* (Paris: Hivert, 1838), pp. 5–16.
4. '. . .[L]e talent merveilleux de M. de Talleyrand pour s'imposer'. She was referring to the delivery of his eulogy of Reinhard in March 1838 (*Récits d'une tante*, IV, p. 222).
5. Fichier Charavay, 167, TAB-TAT: letter of August 1815 from Talleyrand to Louis XVIII.
6. See above pp. 150–1.
7. The historian of the Restoration and July Monarchies observes: 'The failure of constitutional monarchy goes back to the fundamental illiberalism of French culture. It is for that reason that the almost metaphysical opposition between monarchy and republic was of such importance in French political life in the nineteenth century' (Pierre Rosanvallon, *La Monarchie impossible: Les Chartes de 1814 et de 1830* (Paris: Fayard, 1994), p. 179).
8. Rémusat, *Mémoires de ma vie*, III, p. 236.
9. Waresquiel, *Talleyrand*, p. 17; Georges Bordenove, *Talleyrand, Prince des diplomates* (Paris: Pygmalion/Gérard Watelet, 1999).
10. *Journal du comte Rodolphe Apponyi*, III, p. 225.
11. Or at least he did if the document reproduced by Gorsas is not a forgery (Gorsas, *Talleyrand*, p. 25).
12. Of course, the willingness of the French political élite to sacrifice French sovereignty within Europe greatly increased after the reunifica-

tion of Germany in 1990.

13. Talleyrand, *Mémoires*, I, p. 440.

14. Fichier Charavay, 167, TAB-TAT: letter from Talleyrand of 11 August 1820, calling for a 'new era' of Bourbon constitutional monarchy.

15. Ibid.: letter of 25 July 1820.

16. Rémusat, *Mémoires de ma vie*, III, p. 236.

17. Lacour-Gayet, *Talleyrand*, p. 1355. Extract of a letter to the comtesse de Brionne of 9 October 1789.

Bibliography

I list here only those sources that I found of direct use for the writing of this book and to which, therefore, reference is made in the notes. For fuller bibliographies, one can turn to the essay on sources in Waresquiel's *Talleyrand*, pp. 739–68, and to Philip G. Dwyer, *Charles-Maurice de Talleyrand 1754–1838: A Bibliography* (Westport: Greenwood Press, 1996).

PRIMARY SOURCES

a) Manuscript

British Library
    Additional Manuscripts, 51,635 (Holland House Papers)
Archives Nationales
    215 AP 1, 'Papiers Talleyrand'
Bibliothèque Nationale
    Nouvelles Acquisitions françaises, 24,346 'Recueil de pièces concernant le prince et la princesse de Talleyrand'
    Fichier Charavay, 167, TAB-TAT (Extracts of sales catalogues of ms. letters)
Ministère des Affaires Étrangères
    Personnel, 1ère série, vol. 38348 'Talleyrand-Périgord, prince de'
    Mémoires et documents, France, vol. 1776 'Lettres et ordres de l'Empereur au Ministère des relations extérieures'

b) Published

i. Works by Talleyrand
Éclaircissemens donnés par le citoyen Talleyrand à ses concitoyens (Paris: Laran, 1799)
Éloge de M. le comte Reinhard prononcé à l'Académie des Sciences morales et poli-

tiques, par M. le prince de Talleyrand, dans la séance du 3 mars 1838 (Paris: chez Gabriel Warée, 1838)

Gorsas, Jean, *Talleyrand: Mémoires, lettres inédites et papiers secrets* (Paris: Albert Savine, 1891)

L'Assemblée nationale aux françois (Chartres: Le Tellier, 1790)

Lettre pastorale de Mgr. L'évêque d'Autun au clergé séculier et régulier et aux fidèles de son diocèse, 26 janvier 1789 (Autun: Imprimerie Dejussieu, 1789)

Liberté des cultes religieux. Rapport fait au nom du Comité de constitution, à la séance du 7 mai 1791, relatif à l'arrêté du département de Paris, du 6 avril précédent, par M. de Talleyrand, ancien évêque d'Autun (Paris: Imprimerie Lottin, 1791)

Mémoire sur les relations des États-Unis avec l'Angleterre par Talleyrand, lu à l'Institut National le 15 germinal An V, suivi d'un Essai sur les avantages à retirer de colonies nouvelles dans les circonstances présentes par le même auteur, lu à l'Institut le 15 messidor An V (London: J. Dean, 1806)

[Talleyrand,] *Mémoires complets et authentiques de Charles-Maurice de Talleyrand prince de Bénévent. Texte conforme au manuscrit originel. Contenant les notes de Monsieur Adolphe Fourier de Bacourt légataire des manuscrits de l'Auteur*, 5 vols. (Paris: Bonnot, 1967)

Mémoires du prince de Talleyrand, 5 vols., ed. duc de Broglie (Paris: Calmann-Lévy, 1891–2)

Motion de M. l'évêque d'Autun sur la proposition d'un emprunt faite à l'Assemblée nationale par le premier ministre des Finances et sur la consolidation de la dette publique, jeudi 27 août 1789 (Paris: Baudouin, 1789)

Motion de M. l'évêque d'Autun sur les biens ecclésiastiques, du 10 octobre 1789 (Versailles: Baudouin, 1789)

Opinion de M. l'évêque d'Autun sur la question des biens ecclésiastiques (Paris: Baudouin, 1789)

Opinion de M. l'évêque d'Autun sur les assignats forcés le jeudi 15 avril 1790 (Paris: Imprimerie nationale, 1790)

Opinion de M. l'évêque d'Autun sur les banques et sur le rétablissement de l'ordre dans les finances prononcé à l'Assemblée nationale le vendredi 4 décembre 1789 (Paris: Baudouin, 1789)

Opinion de M. le prince de Talleyrand sur le projet d'adresse en réponse au discours du Roi à l'ouverture de la session (Paris: Tastu, 1823)

Proposition faite à l'Assemblée nationale, sur les poids et mesures, par M. l'évêque d'Autun (Paris: Imprimerie nationale, 1790)

Talleyrand, *Mémoires 1754–1815*, ed. Paul-Louis and Jean-Paul Couchoud (Paris: Plon, 1982)

Talleyrand, *Mémoires, L'époque napoléonienne*, ed. Jean Tulard (Paris: Imprimerie nationale, 1996)

ii. Memoirs, Letters, Documents

Abrantès, duchesse d', *Histore des salons de Paris*, 4 vols. (Paris: Garnier, n.d.)

An Englishman in Paris 1803. The Journal of Bertie Greathead, ed. J.P.T. Bury and J.C. Bury (London: Geoffrey Bles, 1953)

A Portion of the Journal Kept by Thomas Raikes Esq. from 1831 to 1847. Comprising reminiscences of social and political life in London and Paris during that period, 2 vols. (London: Longman, Brown, Green, Longmans, and Roberts, 1858)

Arnault, A.V., *Souvenirs d'un sexagénaire*, 4 vols. (Paris: Librairie Duféy, 1833)

Barante, Baron de, *La Conversion et la mort de M. de Talleyrand: Récit de l'un des cinq témoins*, ed. baron de Nervo (Paris: Librairie ancienne Honoré Champion, 1910) (see also *Souvenirs du baron de Barante* and 'Discours du duc de Barante' below)

Cahiers des paroisses et commaunautés d'Autun pour les États généraux de 1789, ed. A. de Charmasse (Autun: Imprimerie Dejussieu, 1895)

Cambacérès, *Mémoires inédits*, ed. Laurence Chatel de Brancion, 2 vols. (Paris: Perrin, 1999)

Carême, Antonin, 'Souvenirs du Table et du Régime', in *Classiques de la table*, ed. F. Fayot (Paris: Béthune-Plon, 1843), pp. 154–64 (also M. Isid Bourdon, untitled, in *idem*, pp. 518–20)

Chateaubriand, François de, *Correspondance générale*, ed. Pierre Riberette, 5 vols. (Paris: Gallimard, 1979–86)

——, *Mémoires d'outre-tombe*, ed. Jean-Claude Berchet, 4 vols. (Paris: Garnier, 1989)

Constant, Benjamin, *Portraits, mémoires, souvenirs*, ed. Éphraïm Harpaz (Paris: Champion, 1992)

Correspondance de Napoléon Ier publiée par ordre de l'Empereur Napoléon III, 32 vols. (Paris: Plon, 1858–70)

Correspondance diplomatique de Talleyrand: La Mission de Talleyrand à Londres, 1792. Correspondance inédite de Talleyrand avec le Département des affaires étrangères, le général Biron etc. Ses Lettres d'Amérique à Lord Lansdowne, ed. G. Pallain (Paris: Plon, 1889).

Correspondance diplomatique de Talleyrand: Le Ministère de Talleyrand sous le Directoire, ed. G. Pallain (Paris: Plon, 1891)

Correspondance diplomatique du comte Pozzo di Borgo, ambassadeur de Russie en France, et du comte de Nesselrode, ed. comte Charles Pozzo du Borgo, 2 vols. (Paris: Calmann-Lévy, 1890, 1897)

Correspondance du comte de Jaucourt, ministre des affaires étrangères, avec le prince de Talleyrand pendant le Congrès de Vienne (Paris: Plon, 1905)

Diaries and Letters of Madame d'Arblay, edited by her Niece, 7 vols. (London: Hurst and Blackett, 1854)

Diary of the French Revolution by Gouverneur Morris 1756–1816, A, ed. Beatrix Cary Davenport, 2 vols. (London: Harrap, 1939)

Diary of Philipp von Neumann 1819 to 1850, The, ed. E. Beresford Chancellor, 2 vols. (London: Philip Allan, 1928)

Dino, duchesse de, *Chronique de 1831 à 1862*, ed. princesse de Radziwill née Castellane, 2 vols. (Paris: Plon, 1909)

'Discours du duc de Barante sur M. de Talleyrand', in Alexandre Sallé, *Vie politique du prince Charles Maurice de Talleyrand* (Paris: Hivert, 1838)

Dumont de Genève, Étienne, *Souvenirs sur Mirabeau et sur les deux premières assemblées législatives*, ed. J. Bénétruy (Paris: Presses universitaires de France, 1951)

Galerie des États généraux et des dames françoises, La (n.p., 1790)

Greville Diary Including Passages Hitherto Witheld from Publication, The, ed. Philip Witwell Wilson, 2 vols. (London: Heinemann, 1927)

Guizot, M., *Mémoires pour servir à l'histoire de mon temps*, 8 vols. (Paris: Michel Lévy, 1858–67)

Hauterive, Ernest d', *La Police secrète du Premier Empire. Bulletins quotidiens adressés par Fouché à l'Empereur*, 5 vols. (Paris: Perrin, 1909–12, 1963–64)

Holland, Henry Richard, Lord, *Foreign Reminiscences*, ed. Henry Edward, Lord Holland (London: Longman, Brown, Green and Longmans, 1850)

Holland House Diaries, 1831–1840, The: The Diary of Henry Richard Vassall Fox, third Lord Holland, ed., Abraham D. Kriegel (London: Routledge & Kegan Paul, 1977)

Journal du comte Rodolphe Apponyi, ed. Ernest Daudet, 4 vols. (Paris: Plon, 1913–26)

Journal du maréchal de Castellane, 5 vols. (Paris: Plon, 1895–7)

La Garde-Chambonas, comte A. de, *Souvenirs du Congrès de Vienne 1814–1815*, ed. comte de Fleury (Paris: H. Vivien, 1901)

La Tour du Pin, Marquise de, *Journal d'une femme de cinquante ans, 1778–1815*, ed. Aymar de Liedekeke-Beaufort, 2 vols. (Paris: Berger-Levrault, 1925)

Las Cases, comte de, *Le Mémorial de Sainte-Hélène*, ed. Marcel Dunan, 2 vols. (Paris: Flammarion, n.d.)

'Lettres de la duchesse de Dino à Adolphe Thiers', part I, *La Revue de Paris* (1 April 1923), pp. 241–60

'Lettres de M. de Talleyrand à Madame de Staël', part I, ed. duc de Broglie, *Revue d'histoire diplomatique* (Year 4/1: 1890), pp. 779–94

'Lettres de Talleyrand à Caulaincourt', part II, ed. Jean Hanoteau, *Revue des Deux Mondes*, Year 105 (1 November 1935), pp. 142–80

Lettres et papiers du chancelier comte de Nesselrode 1760–1850, ed. comte A. de Nesselrode, 11 vols. (Paris: A. Lahure, 1904–12)

Lettres inédites de Napoléon Ier, ed. Léon Lecestre, 2 vols. (Paris: Plon, 1897)

Lettres inédites de Talleyrand à Napoléon 1800–1809, ed. Pierre Bertrand (Paris: Didier Perrin, 1889)

Madame de Staël, ses amis, ses correspondants. Choix de lettres (1778–1817), ed. Georges Solovieff (Paris: Klincksieck, 1970)

Memoiren des Gräfin Kielmannsegge über Napoleon I, ed. Gertrude Aretz (Dresden: Paul Aretz Verlag, 1927)

Mémoires d'Aimée de Coigny, ed. Étienne Lamy (Paris: Calmann-Lévy, n.d.)

Mémoires de Barras, Membre du Directoire, ed. George Duruy, 4 vols. (Paris: Hachette, 1895)

Mémoires de B. Barère, ed. Hippolyte Carnot and David (d'Angers), 4 vols. (Paris: Jules Labitte, 1842–3)

Mémoires de G.-J. Ouvrard, sur sa vie et ses diverses opérations financières, 3 vols. (Paris: Montardier, 1826–7)

Mémoires de la comtesse Potocka (1794–1820), ed. Casimir Stryienski (Paris: Plon, 1897)

Mémoires de la Reine Hortense, publiées par le prince Napoléon, ed. Jean Hannoteau, 3 vols. (Paris: Plon, 1927)

Mémoires de Madame de Chastenay 1771–1815, ed. Alphonse Roserot, 2 vols. (Paris: Plon, 1896)

Mémoires de Madame de Rémusat 1802–1808, ed. Paul de Rémusat, 3 vols. (Paris: Calmann-Lévy, 1880)

Mémoires de Madame la duchesse d'Abrantès. Souvenirs sur Napoléon, la Révolution, le Directoire, l'Empire, et la Restauration, 12 vols. (Paris: Garnier, n.d.)

Mémoires de M. de Bourrienne, Ministre d'état, sur Napoléon, ed. Désiré Lacroix, 5 vols. (Paris: Garnier, n.d.)

Mémoires, documents et écrits divers, laissés par le prince de Metternich, ed. prince Richard de Metternich, 8 vols. (Paris: Plon, 1880–4)

Mémoires du baron Fain, ed. P. Fain. (Paris: Plon, 1908)

Mémoires du cardinal Consalvi, secrétaire d'état du pape Pie VII, ed. J. Crétineau-Joly, 2 vols. (Paris: Plon, 1864–6)

Mémoires du chancelier Pasquier, ed. duc d'Audiffret-Pasquier, 4 vols. (Paris: Plon, 1893–4)

Mémoires du comte Beugnot (1779–1815), ed. Robert Lacour-Gayet (Paris: Hachette, 1959)

Mémoires du comte de Ferrand, ministre d'état sous Louis XVIII, ed. vicomte de Broc (Paris: Alphonse Picard, 1897)

Mémoires du comte de Mélito, ed. Général Fleischmann, 3 vols. (Paris: Michel Lévy, 1858)

Mémoires du comte de Moré (1758–1837), ed. Geoffroy de Grandmaison and comte de Pontgibaud (Paris: Picard, 1898)

Mémoires du comte de Rambuteau, ed. Georges Lequin (Paris: Calmann-Lévy, 1905)

Mémoires du duc de Rovigo, pour servir à l'histoire de l'Empereur Napoléon, 8 vols. (Paris: Bossange, 1826–8)

Mémoires du général de Caulaincourt, duc de Vicence, grand écuyer de l'Empereur, ed. Jean Hanoteau, 3 vols. (Paris: Plon, 1933)

Mémoires et correspondance du comte de Villèle, 5 vols. (Paris: Perrin, 1888–90)

Mémoires et relations politiques du baron de Vitrolles, ed. Eugène Forgues, 3 vols. (Paris: Charpentier, 1884)

Mémoires inédits de Madame la comtesse de Genlis sur le dix-huitième siècle et la Révolution française depuis 1756 à nos jours, 10 vols. (Paris: Ladvocat au Palais-Royal, 1825)

'Mémoires inédits de M. le comte de Semallé, commissaire du roi en 1814', in L.-G. Michaud, *Histoire politique et privée de Charles-Maurice de Talleyrand* (Paris: Bureau de la biographie universelle, 1853)

Mémorial de J. de Norvins, ed. L. de Lanzac de Laborie, 3 vols. (Paris: Plon, 1896–7)

Méneval, baron Claude-François de, *Mémoires pour servir à l'histoire de Napoléon 1er depuis 1802 jusqu'à 1815*, 3 vols. (Paris: Dentu, 1894)

Mérimée, Prosper, *Correspondance générale*, ed. Maurice Parturier, 6 vols. (Paris: Le Divan, 1941–7)

Mission secrète de Mirabeau à Berlin 1786–1787, La, ed. Henri de Welschinger (Paris: Plon, 1900)

[Mollien, comte,] *Mémoire d'un ministre du Trésor public 1780–1815*, 4 vols. (Paris: Fournier, 1845)

Montesquiou, comte Anatole de, *Souvenirs sur la Révolution, l'Empire, la Restauration et le règne de Louis-Philippe*, ed. Robert Burnand (Paris: Plon, 1961)

Montor, Artaud de, *Histoire de la vie et des travaux politiques du comte d'Hauterive* (Paris: Adrien Le Clere, 1838)

Moreau de Saint-Méry, *Voyage aux États-Unis de l'Amérique, 1793–1798*, ed. Stewart L. Mims (New Haven: Yale, 1913)

Morgan, Lady, *France*, 2 vols. (London: Henry Colburn, 1818)

Noailles, Marquis de, *Le Comte Molé 1781–1855. Sa Vie et ses mémoires*, 6 vols. (Paris: Champion, 1922–30)

Oeuvres du comte P.L. Roederer, ed., baron A.M. Roederer, 6 vols. (Paris: Firmin Didot, 1853–7)

O'Meara, Barry Edward, *Napoleon at St Helena*, 2 vols. (London: Richard Bentley, 1888)

Palewski, Gaston, *Le Miroir de Talleyrand. Lettres inédites à la duchesse de Courlande pendant le Congrès de Vienne* (Paris: Perrin, 1976)

Preussen und Frankreich von 1795 bis 1807. Diplomatisches Correspondenzen, ed. Paul Bailleu, 2 vols. (Leipzig: Hirzel, 1881 and 1887)

Récits d'une tante: Mémoires de la comtesse de Boigne née d'Osmond, ed. Charles Nicoullaud, 4 vols. (Paris: Plon, 1908)

Rémusat, Charles de, *Mémoires de ma vie*, ed. Charles. H. Pouthas, 5 vols. (Paris: Plon, 1958–67)

Roederer, P.-L., *Chronique de cinquante jours, du 20 juin au 10 août 1792* (Paris: Imprimerie de Lachevardiere, 1832)

Souvenirs (1775–1870) de feu le duc de Broglie, 4 vols. (Paris: Calmann-Lévy, 1886)

Souvenirs de Madame Louise-Élisabeth Vigée-Lebrun, 3 vols. (Paris: H. Fournier, 1835–7)

Souvenirs du baron de Barante, ed. Claude de Barante, 8 vols. (Paris: Calmann-Lévy, 1890–1901)

Staël, Madame de, *Lettres à Narbonne*, ed. Georges Solovieff (Paris: Gallimard, 1960)

Tagebücher von Friedrich von Gentz, 4 vols. (Leipzig: F.A. Brockhaus, 1873–4)

Talleyrand in America as Financial Promoter 1794–1796, tr. and ed. Hans Huth and Wilma J. Pugh (Washington: US Government Printing Office, 1942)

Talleyrand intime d'après sa correspondance avec la duchesse de Courlande (Paris: Ernest Kolb, n.d.)

Talleyrand und der Herzog von Dalberg: Unveröffentlichte Briefe (1816–1832), ed. Eberhard Ernst (Frankfurt am Main: verlag Peter Lang, 1987)

Thibaudeau, A.C., *Mémoires sur la Convention et le Directoire*, 2 vols. (Paris: Baudouin, 1824)

iii) Other

Hansard, 29 September 1831

The Times, 7 October 1820

SECONDARY SOURCES

Alexandre, Philippe, and l'Auloit, Béatrix de, *Le Roi Carême* (Paris: Albin Michel, 2003)

Antonetti, Guy, *Louis-Philippe* (Paris: Fayard, 1994)

Aulard, A., *Paris sous le Consulat*, 4 vols. (Paris: Léopold Cerf, 1903–9)

Beau, André, *Talleyrand:Chronique indiscrète de la vie d'un prince – Consulat, Empire, Restauration* (Paris: Royer, 1992)

—— *Talleyrand: L'Apogée du sphinx – La Monarchie de Juillet* (Paris: Royer, 1998)

Bernard, Jack F., *Talleyrand:A Biography* (New York: Collins, 1973)

Bertier de Sauvigny, Guillame de, *Metternich et la France après le Congrès de Vienne*, 3 vols. (Paris: Hachette, 1968–71)

——, *Metternich* (Paris: Fayard, 1986)

Blanc, Olivier, *L'Amour à Paris au temps de Louis XVI* (Paris: Perrin, 2002)

Bordenove, Georges, *Talleyrand, Prince des diplomates* (Paris: Pygmalion/ Gérard Watelet, 1999)

Carrère, Casimir, *Talleyrand amoureux* (Paris: France-Empire, 1975)

Chambers, James, *Palmerston 'The People's Darling'* (London: John Murray, 2005)

Charmley, John, *The Princess and the Politicians: Sex, Intrigue and Diplomacy, 1812–1840* (London: Viking, 2005)

Chernow, Ron, *Alexander Hamilton* (New York: Penguin, 2004)

Cooper, Duff, *Talleyrand* (London: Phoenix Press, 2001)

Dard, Émile, *Napoléon et Talleyrand* (Paris: Plon, 1935)

——, *Un Confidant de l'Empereur: Le Comte de Narbonne* (Paris: Plon, 1943)

Daudet, Ernest, *La Police politique: Chronique du temps de la Restauration 1815–1820* (Paris: Plon, 1912)

Dino, duchesse de, *Notice sur Valençay* (Paris: Crapelet, 1848)

Dunan, Marcel, *Napoléon et l'Allemagne: Le Système continental et les débuts du royaume de Bavière 1806–1810* (Paris: Plon, 1942)

Dupuis, Charles, *Le Ministère de Talleyrand*, 2 vols. (Paris: Plon, 1919)

Dupuy, Micheline, *La Duchesse de Dino, princesse de Courlande, Égérie de Talleyrand* (Paris: Perrin, 2002)

Dwyer, Philip G., *Charles-Maurice de Talleyrand 1754–1838: A Bibliography* (Westport: Greenwood Press, 1996)

——, *Talleyrand* (London: Pearson Education, 2002)

Ehrman, John, *The Younger Pitt: The Years of Acclaim* (London: Constable, 1969)

Fitzmaurice, Lord, *Life of William Earl of Shelburne, afterwards First Marquess of Lansdowne*, 2 vols. (London: Macmillan, 1912)

Fumaroli, Marc, *Chateaubriand: Poésie et terreur* (Paris: Fallois, 2003)

Grandmaison, Geoffroy de, *L'Espagne et Napoléon* (Paris: Plon, 1908)

Greenbaum, Louis S., *Talleyrand, Statesman Priest: The Agent-General of the*

Clergy and the Church of France at the End of the Old Régime (Washington DC: Catholic University of America Press, 1970)

Guyot, Raymond, *Le Directoire et la paix de l'Europe des traités de Bâle à la deux-ième coalition (1795–1799)* (Paris: Félix Alcan, 1912)

Hippeau, C., *L'Instruction publique en France pendant la Révolution* (Paris: Didier, 1881)

Ingold, A.M.P., *Bénévent sous la domination de Talleyrand et le gouvernement de Louis de Beer 1806–1815* (Paris: Pierre Téqui, 1916)

Kissinger, Henry, *A World Restored: Metternich, Castlereagh and the Problems of Peace 1812–1822* (London: Weidenfeld and Nicolson, 1957)

Kraehe, Enno H., *Metternich's German Policy*, II: *The Congess of Vienna, 1814–1815* (Princeton: Princeton University Press, 1983)

Lacombe, Bernard de, *La Vie privée de Talleyrand: Son Émigration – son mariage – sa retraite – sa conversion – sa mort* (Paris: Plon, 1910)

Lacour-Gayet, Georges, *Talleyrand* (Paris: Payot, 1990)

La Jonquière, C. de, *L'Expédition d'Égypte 1798–1801*, 5 vols. (Paris: Henri Charles-Lavauzelle, n.d.)

La Maisonfort, Marquis de, *Mémoires d'un agent royaliste sous la Révolution, l'Empire et la Restauration 1763–1827* (Paris: Mercure de France, 1998)

Lamartine, A. de, *Cours familier de littérature*, 26 vols. (Paris: 1856–68)

Latouche, Henri, *Album perdu* (Paris: chez Marchands de nouveautés, 1829)

Lokke, Carl Ludwig, 'Pourquoi Talleyrand ne fut pas envoyé à Constantinople', *Annales historiques de la Révolution française*, X (1933), pp. 153–9

Lytton Bulwer, Henry, 'Talleyrand: The Politic Man', in *Historical Characters* (London: Macmillan, 1900)

Madelin, Louis, *Fouché 1759–1820*, 2 vols. (Paris: Plon, 1901)

——, *Talleyrand* (Paris: Flammarion, 1944)

Mansel, Philip, *The Court of France 1789–1830* (Cambridge: Cambridge University Press, 1991)

——, *Louis XVIII* (Stroud: Sutton, 1999)

——, *Prince of Europe: The Life of Charles-Joseph de Ligne 1735–1814* (London: Weidenfeld and Nicolson, 2003)

Masson, Frédéric, *Le Département des affaires étrangères pendant la Révolution 1787–1804* (Paris: Plon, 1877)

Méric, Élie, *Histoire de M. Émery et de l'Église de France pendant la Révolution*, 2 vols. (Paris: Charles Poussielgue, 1895)

Missoffe, Michel, *Le Coeur secret de Talleyrand* (Paris: Perrin, 1956)

Monsieur de Talleyrand, 4 vols. (Paris: Roret, 1834–5)

Montarlot, Paul, 'L'Épiscopat de Talleyrand', *Mémoires de la société éduenne*, nouvelle série, XII (1894), pp. 83–156

Nicolson, Harold, *The Congress of Vienna: A Study in Allied Unity, 1812–1822* (London: Constable, 1946)

Noël, Léon, *Énigmatique Talleyrand* (Paris: Fayard, 1975)

Nussbaum, F.-L., 'L'Arrière-plan de la mission de Talleyrand à Londres en 1792', *Assemblée générale de la commission de recherche et de publication des documents relatifs à la vie économique de la Révolution*, II (1939), pp. 445–84

Orieux, Jean, *Talleyrand ou le Sphinx incompris* (Paris: Flammarion, 1970)

Palmer, Alan, *Metternich* (London: Weidenfeld and Nicolson, 1972)

——, *Alexander I: Tsar of War and Peace* (London: Phoenix, 1997)

Pingaud, Léonce, *Un Agent secret sous la Révolution et l'Empire: Le comte d'Antraigues* (Paris: Plon, 1893)

Poniatowski, Michel, *Talleyrand aux États-Unis 1794–1796* (Paris: Perrin, 1976)

——, *Talleyrand et le Directoire* (Paris: Perrin, 1982)

——, *Talleyrand et le Consulat* (Paris: Perrin 1986)

——, *Talleyrand et l'ancienne France* (Paris: Perrin, 1988)

——, *Les Années occultées 1789–1792* (Paris: Perrin, 1995)

Revelations of the Life of Prince Talleyrand edited from the Papers of the late M. Colmache private secretary to the Prince (London: Henry Colburn, 1850)

Ridley, Jasper, *Lord Palmerston* (London: Constable, 1970)

Roberts, Andrew, *Napoleon and Wellington* (London: Weidenfeld and Nicolson, 2001)

Rosanvallon, Pierre, *La Monarchie impossible: Les Chartes de 1814 et de 1830* (Paris: Fayard, 1994)

Sainte-Beuve, C.-A., *Nouveaux Lundis*, 13 vols. (Paris: Michel Lévy, 1863–72)

——, *Monsieur de Talleyrand* (Paris: Michel Lévy, 1870)

Sand, George, 'Le Prince', *Revue des Deux Mondes* (15 October 1834)

Schell, Eric, *Talleyrand en verve* (Paris: Horay, 2002)

Schumann, Maurice, *Qui a tué le duc d'Enghien?* (Paris: Perrin, 1984)

Souvenirs intimes sur M. de Talleyrand recueillis par Amédée Pichot (Paris: Dentu, 1870)

Stinchcomb, William, *The XYZ Affair* (Westport: Greenwood Press, 1980)

Thiers, A., *Histoire du Consulat et de l'Empire*, 21 vols. (Paris: Paulin Lheureux, 1845–69)

Tulard, Jean, *Napoléon, ou le mythe du sauveur* (Paris: Fayard, 1987)

——, *Nouvelle Bibliographie critique des mémoires sur l'époque napoléonienne* (Geneva: Droz, 1991)

Vandal, Albert, *Napoléon et Alexandre 1er*, 3 vols. (Paris: Plon, 1891–96)

Védrine, Hubert, 'Pour Talleyrand', *Le Nouvel Observateur*, 25 September 2003

Waresquiel, Emmanuel de, *Le Duc de Richelieu: Un sentimental en politique* (Paris: Perrin, 1990)

——, *Talleyrand, le Prince immobile* (Paris: Fayard, 2003)

Waresquiel, Emmanuel de, and Yvert, Benoît, *Histoire de la Restauration 1814–1830: Naissance de la France moderne* (Paris: Perrin, 1996)

Webster, Charles, *The Foreign Policy of Castlereagh 1812–1815: Britain and the Reconstruction of Europe* (London: Bell, 1950)

Weil, M.-H., *Les Dessous du Congrès de Vienne*, 2 vols. (Paris: Payot, 1917)

Wick, Daniel L., *A Conspiracy of Well-Intentioned Men: The Society of Thirty and the French Revolution* (New York: Garland, 1987)

Ziegler, Philip, *The Duchess of Dino* (London: Collins, 1962)

Index

In the index the abbreviation CMT stands for Charles-Maurice de Talleyrand-Périgord

Aboukir Bay, Battle of (battle of the Nile, 1798), 102, 105
Abrantès, Laure, duchesse d' (*née* Permon), 11, 33
Adams, John, 102
Adélaïde, Mme (Louis-Philippe's sister), 292, 294, 297, 305, 323
Aix-la-Chapelle, Congress of (1818), 275
Alexander I, Tsar: in Berlin, 164; maintains enmity with France, 165; meets Napoleon at Tilsit, 168; alliance with Napoleon, 185, 193, 243; Napoleon negotiates Erfurt treaty with, 192–4; arranges marriage of Edmond and Dorothée de Tallyrand-Périgord, 195; and French victory over Austria, 203; CMT requests financial aid from, 204, 206; hostility to Bourbons, 215, 256–7; advocates allies' advance on Paris, 217; CMT negotiates with on entry into Paris, 219–21, 237; meets Napoleon's representatives, 224; and Maubreuil affair, 225; and d'Artois' post as lieutenant general, 229; relations with Louis XVIII, 231–2; on new French constitution, 232; leaves Paris, 233; and acquisition of Poland, 237, 242–4, 246–7, 251; at Congress of Vienna, 242–6, 251, 254; differences with CMT at Congress of Vienna, 242–4; learns of 1815 Triple Alliance, 253; marriage alliance with France denied, 253; leaves Vienna, 255; and Louis XVIII's government, 265; opposes CMT's recall to government, 274
Algiers: France occupies, 295
Allies: enter Paris, 219; demands on France, 271–2; occupation of France ends, 275

Alvanley, Richard Pepper Arden, 3rd Baron, 300, 302
Amiens, Peace of (1802), 112, 126–9
Anglès, Jules, comte, 223
Angoulême, Louis-Antoine, duc d', 216
Angoulême, Marie-Thérèse Charlotte, duchesse de, 214
anticlericalism, 48
Antigny, Joseph-François de Damas, marquis d' (CMT's maternal grandfather), 3, 17
Antigny, Marie-Judith, marquise d' (CMT's maternal grandmother), 3
Antonio, Don, 191
Antwerp, 128, 295, 298
Arblay, Alexandre d', 75
Argus, The (journal), 121
Arnault, Antoine-Vincent, 40, 52, 98, 109
Arnold, Benedict, 78
Arnouville, 263
Artois, Charles, comte d' *see* Charles X, King of France
assignats: CMT opposes, 49
Auerstadt, Battle of (1806), 164
Augereau, General Pierre, duc de Castiglione, 93
Aumale, Henri-Eugène-Philippe-Louis d'Orléans, duc d', 279
Austerlitz, Battle of (1805), 129, 143, 156, 161, 164
Austria: French negotiations with (1797), 94, 103–4; Prussian hatred of, 125; treaty with France (1756), 126; fears French threat over Italy, 154; prepares for war against France (1805), 155; in Third Coalition against France, 156; in CMT's 1805 policy memoranda, 157–61, 337; and Treaty of Pressburg, 162, 164;

Austria (*cont.*)
Napoleon's hostility to, 193–4; payments
to CMT, 195, 202–3; CMT opens direct
relations with, 202, 208; France defeats
(1809), 203; CMT proposes Napoleon's
dynastic marriage into, 205–6; position
in Italy, 236; and Congress of Vienna,
244–9, 254; fear of Russia, 245; in Triple
Alliance (1815) with Britain and France,
250; Prussia defeats (1866), 252; and
Murat's machinations in Naples, 254;
and Napoleon's escape from Elba, 255;
CMT proposes alliance with, 304;
CMT's favourable view of, 335–6
Autun: CMT's bishopric of, 35–40; chapter
protests at CMT's speech on Church
property, 47; opposition to CMT in,
53–4; CMT resigns bishopric, 54

Babeuf, François-Noël, 90
Bacourt, Adolphe de, 294, 320, 322
Bagration, Princess Katharina, 246
Barante, Amable-Guillaume-Prosper
Brugière de, 282, 286–7, 313, 316, 322,
328
Barbier du Bocage, Jean-Denis, 120
Barère, Bertrand, 68
Barras, Paul: receives copy of CMT's
petition to Convention, 85; favours
CMT, 89–92; and Fructidor coup, 93;
quarrel with Carnot, 93; CMT and
Bonaparte support, 94; and reception of
Napoleon, 96; and CMT's demands for
payment from US envoys, 103; and
coups of 30 Prairial and 18 Brumaire,
106–7, 109; interest in money, 107;
internal exile, 109; on CMT's faults, 131;
CMT seeks release of Catherine Grand
by, 138; and CMT's benefits from
negotiating Confederation of Rhine,
163; on CMT's rewards from Naples
Bourbons, 277
Barry, Marie-Jeanne du (*née* Bécu), 20, 32
Barthélemy, François de, 90–2, 94
Bassano, duc de *see* Maret, Hugues-Bernard
Bassano, duchesse de, 208–9
Bastille: falls (1789), 43
Batavian Republic: created, 132–3
Bavaria: payments to CMT, 195–6; and
Triple Alliance, 250
Beauharnais, Eugène de, Prince, 186,
197
Beauharnais, Hortense de, 98, 144, 173–4,
177, 200, 217
Beaumetz, Bon-Albert Briois de: friendship
with CMT, 34; and CMT's flight from
France, 69; exile in London, 70;

accompanies CMT to America, 78–81;
dies in India, 86
Beer, Louis de, 163
Bélanger, François-Joseph, 97
Belgium: revolt against Holland (1830),
295–6, 331; London conference on
future of, 298–9; Dutch invade, 300;
Leopold elected King, 300
Bellechasse, Paris, 16–19
Bellegarde, Adélaïde and Aurore de, 181
Benevento, 163, 277
Berlin: Napoleon in, 164
Berlin Decrees (1806), 165
Bernadotte, Marshal Jean-Baptiste (*later*
King Charles XIV John of Sweden), 220
Bernier, abbé, 141
Berry, Charles-Ferdinand, duc de, 253, 261,
281, 306, 330
Berthier, Marshal Alexandre, 94–5, 153,
168
Bertrand, M. (CMT's tutor), 176
Beugnot, Claude, comte, 223, 228, 260–1,
264, 282
Beurnonville, Pierre de Riel, comte de,
222
Biron, Armand de Gontaut, duc de (*earlier*
duc de Lauzun): friendship with CMT,
18, 20, 33; and CMT's
excommunication threat, 56;
accompanies CMT on mission to
England, 62
Bismarck, Prince Otto von, 159
Blacas d'Aulps, Pierre, comte de, 228, 230,
232–3, 235, 257, 259, 262, 267
Blacons, Henri-François, marquis de, 79,
84, 86
Boigne, Adèle, comtesse de, 278, 283
Boisgelin, Bruno, marquis de,
209–11
Boisgelin, Pierre-Daniel, abbé de, 23–4
Bonaparte, Jérôme, 169
Bonaparte, Joseph: signs treaties, 112; as
King of Naples, 162, 169; nominated
successor to Napoleon, 168; relinquishes
office of Vice-Grand Elector, 186; as
King of Spain, 189; Napoleon complains
of ingratitude, 201; CMT converses
with, 213; Napoleon warns against
CMT, 214; and allies' advance on Paris,
217
Bonaparte, Louis, 169
Bonaparte, Lucien, 109, 146, 153
Bonaparte, Pauline *see* Borghese, Princess
Pauline
Bonneuil, Laure, comtesse de, 175
Borbón, Carlos María Isidro de, 191
Bordeaux: royalist coup (1813), 216

Bordeaux, Henri, duc de (Henri V), 292
Borghese, Princess Pauline (*née* Bonaparte; Napoleon's sister), 114
Bossuet, Jacques-Bénigne, 312
Boucher (*chef de service*), 178
Boufflers, Marie-Charlotte Hippolyte, comtesse de, 32, 87
Bougainville, Louis-Antoine de, 95
Bourbon family: Napoleon's treatment of, 144–5; restoration, 146, 210–11, 214–17, 220, 222–3, 227, 230–3, 330, 336; and d'Enghien's death, 151; CMT's hostility to, 189, 210; Alexander I's hostility to, 215, 256–7
Bourbon, Louis-Henri Joseph, duc de (Enghien's father), 279
Bourbon-l'Archambault, 115, 136, 171–2, 175–6, 209, 280, 285, 291, 309
Bourdieu, Choller and Bourdieu (bankers), 61
Bourdois de la Motte, Dr (CMT's physician), 286, 309
Bouret, Étienne-Michel, 50
Bourlier, Jean-Baptiste, bishop of Évreux, 13, 24
Bourrienne, Louis-Antoine Fauvelet de, 112, 223
Brionne, Louise de Rohan, comtesse de, 21, 32, 46, 256
Brissot, Jacques-Pierre, 65
Britain: commercial treaty with France (1786), 27–8, 61; CMT's exile in, 34, 70–2, 74–5; CMT's missions to (1792), 61–7; hostility to France, 69; CMT on France's relations with, 72, 104, 333–4; France declares war on (1793), 75; relations with America, 83, 87; negotiations with French at Lille, 92; French invasion threat to, 100, 155; Jay Treaty with USA, 102; and Peace of Amiens, 112, 126, 128–9; CMT criticizes as disturber of peace, 124; renews war with France (1803), 126, 129–30, 154; as threat to French interests, 128–9; French blockade of, 129–30, 165, 169; in Third Coalition against France, 156; in CMT's strategic policy memorandum, 157, 159–60; CMT passes information to, 201, 204; and restoration of Louis XVIII, 227; CMT seeks alliance with, 237; and Congress of Vienna, 237, 244, 247–9, 254; in Triple Alliance (1815) with Austria and France, 250, 254; CMT copies constitution in proposed political programme, 258, 267, 333; CMT's ambassadorship to, 293, 294, 301–2;

CMT's view of governance, 304, 333–4; CMT's understanding of, 305–6
Broglie, Victor, duc de, 282, 291, 304, 306
Bruix, Admiral Eustache, 108
Brün (Brno), Battle of (1805), 162
Brunswick, Karl Wilhelm Ferdinand, Duke of, 69
Burke, Edmund: *Reflections*, 40
Burney, Fanny (Mme d'Arblay), 74–5, 77

Cadore, duc de *see* Champagny, Jean-Baptiste de
Cadoudal, Georges, 147
Caillard, Antoine-Bernard, 120
Calonne, Charles-Alexandre de, 19, 28–31
Cambacérès, Jean-Jacques: as Minister of Justice, 112; and Napoleon's view of CMT, 114; pleads for duc d'Enghien, 149; appointed Grand Chambellan to court, 153; on CMT's creation of imperial court, 153; and decline of Prussian power, 164; as gourmand, 178; salary, 185; and CMT's resignation as Foreign Minister, 186; supports CMT's application for post of Archichancelier d'état, 187; on Treaty of Fontainebleau, 189; attends Napoleon's council meeting, 198; intercedes for CMT with Napoleon, 211; and allies' advance on Paris, 217
Cambrai, Declaration of (1815), 268
Campo-Formio, Treaty of (1797), 94, 99, 104
Canisy, Adrienne de Carbonnel, comtesse de, 192, 279
Carême, Antonin, 178–80, 221
Carignan, Marie-Thérèse Louise de Savoie, princesse de, 21
Carlos, Don *see* Borbón, Carlos María Isidro de
Carnot, Lazare: mistrusts CMT, 90; in Directory struggle, 91; and CMT's attendance at Lille negotiations, 92; quarrel with Barras, 93–4
Castellane, Boniface de, 92
Castlereagh, Robert Stewart, Viscount: negotiates at Châtillon, 215–16; and capitulation of Paris, 219; differences with CMT at Congress of Vienna, 236, 238, 243–4, 246–50, 256; visits Paris, 238; agrees to Triple Alliance with Austria and France, 249–50; and exile of Napoleon, 255; and treatment of France after 1815, 270; founds Travellers Club, 297
Cateau-Cambrésis, Le, 260
Catherine, Grand Duchess of Russia, 194

Catherine of Württemberg, Queen of Westphalia, 224

Caulaincourt, General Louis de, duc de Vicence, 148, 150, 189, 192, 194, 202, 211, 213, 215, 221, 224, 279

Cavanac, Mme de (Mlle de Romans), 24

Cazenove, Theophilus, 79–80, 121

Celles, Poitou: CMT granted abbey, 35

censorship: CMT and liberal opposition to, 281, 289–90, 329

Cercle Constitutionnel, 90

Chalais, Daniel de Talleyrand, prince de, 2

Chalais, Marie-Françoise de Rouchechouart, princesse de (CMT's great-grandmother), 4–6

Chambonas, Victor-Scipion de la Garde, marquis de, 67

Chamfort, Sébastian Roch Nicolas de, 33

Champ-de-Mars: Messe de la Fédération celebrated in, 52

Champagny, Jean-Baptiste de, duc de Cadore, 113, 163, 186–8, 190, 192, 213

Championnet, General Jean Étienne, 95

Charlemagne, Mlle (governess), 5, 17

Charles IV, King of Spain, 189

Charles X, King of France (formerly comte d'Artois; Monsieur): and CMT's title claim, 2; takes Louise Contat as mistress, 11; and CMT's benefice of abbey of Celles, 35; and outbreak of French Revolution, 44; and comtesse de Flahaut, 50; emigrates, 58; and succession to Napoleon, 210, 215–16; and Bourbon restoration, 222, 233; relations with CMT, 228, 230; returns to Paris, 228–30; relies on own advisers, 233; and Congress of Vienna, 238; influence on Louis XVIII, 257, 259–60; removed from Council, 261; supports Fouché's inclusion in government, 263; and Talleyrand dynasty's privileges, 277; favours alliance with CMT, 278–9; accession, 284–5; enquires about Maubreuil's attack on CMT, 288; and government changes, 289–90; reactionary stance, 289; overthrown, 290, 292, 295, 311

Charles, Archduke of Austria, 157

Charlotte Sophia, Queen of George III, 63

Chartres, duc de see Louis Philippe Joseph, duc de Chartres

Chastenay, Victorine, comtesse de, 138, 201

Chateaubriand, René, vicomte de: clerical career, 9; on America, 82; on CMT as Foreign Minister under Napoleon, 112, 116; on Napoleon's mistakes, 128; on CMT's venality, 131; and CMT's advice

on d'Enghien affair, 149; condemns CMT's peace terms with allies, 225; on CMT's encounters with Louis XVIII after Waterloo, 259; with CMT in Mons, 260; animosity to CMT, 262; resigns over d'Enghien's execution, 262; on Fouché's inclusion in government, 263–4; on CMT's opposition to Spanish war, 282–3; condemns press censorship, 289; on CMT's expression of contempt, 296; on dying CMT, 325

Châtillon, 215–16

Chaumont de la Galaizière, Barthélemy de, bishop of Saint-Dié, 9

Chaumont, Treaty of (1814), 234

Chauvelin, François de, 65–6

Chavagnac, Mme Gentil de, 13

Chénier, Marie-Joseph, 85, 89, 90

Chernyshev, General Z., 205

Chevaliers de la Foi, 222, 289

Choiseul, Étienne-François, duc de: CMT's relations with, 25–6, 29; political record, 26; and CMT's clerical career, 34; on delegating work, 117; treaty with Austria (1756), 126, 335; attends salons, 181

Choiseul-Gouffier, Auguste, comte de: friendship with CMT, 7, 30, 20; diplomatic career and travels, 17–18, 26; exile and financial ruin, 18; on CMT's ordination as priest, 22

Chouans, 126, 144, 147

Civil Constitution of the Clergy, 53–5, 59

Clam-Martinitz, Count von, 239, 256

Clancarty, Richard le Poer Trench, 2nd Earl of, 257

Clarke, Marshal Henri, duc de Feltre, 260, 264

Clavière, Étienne, 65

Club de Chichy, 90

Cobenzl, Ludwig, Count von, 141

Coigny, Aimée de: on CMT's conversing in library, 17; Montrond saves from death, 121; friendship with Mlles de Bellegarde, 181; and plots against Napoleon, 209–10

Collège d'Harcourt, 6–7

Collot, Jean-Pierre, 109

Colmache, Charles, 12, 138, 292, 312

colonialism: CMT's views on, 88, 332–3

Committee of the Constitution, 43

Committee of Public Safety, 76

Concordat (1801), 141–2

Condé, Louis-Henri-Joseph de Bourbon, prince de, 279

Confederation of the Rhine: formed, 162–3, 331; Saxony joins, 165; see also Rhineland

Congrégation (Catholic organization), 289
Consalvi, Cardinal Ercole, 141
Conseil d'État: formed, 230
Conseil des Anciens, 90, 108
Conseil des Cinq-Cents, 90, 108–9
Conservateur, Le (journal), 90
Constant, Benjamin: on CMT's feet, 4;
    relations with Mme de Staël, 87; in
    Cercle Constitutionnel, 90; lobbies for
    CMT's promotion, 91–2
Contat, Louise, 11
Continental Blockade, 129–30, 165, 169,
    188–9
Council of Regency, 214, 217
Council of War (January 1813), 213
Courlande, Dorothea von Medem, duchesse
    de, 182, 205, 218, 225, 239, 243, 256,
    264, 271, 313
Courtiade, Joseph, 77–8, 80, 121, 177
Crawford, Quintin, 183
Crawford, Mrs Quintin, 111, 183
Crescentini, Girolamo, 144
Cruveilhier, Dr Jean, 317, 320

Dalberg, Emerich von: as CMT's confidant,
    121, 176, 215; considers succession to
    Napoleon, 168; favours Bourbon
    restoration, 215; and Vitrolles, 215–16;
    and Tsar's arrival in Paris, 219–20; in
    CMT's provisional government (1815),
    222; opposes censorship, 233; in Vienna,
    238; and Treaty of Paris, 272; and
    CMT's defeat of Savary, 283; co-founds
    Paravey bank, 288; and CMT's
    ambassadorship in London, 295; and
    CMT's financial difficulties, 301; and
    CMT's declining political office, 306
Dambray, Charles-Henri, 260, 264
Danton, Georges Jacques, 71
David, Jacques-Louis: depicts Napoleon's
    coronation, 154
Davout, General Louis-Nicolas, 164
Decazes, Élie, duc, 265, 271, 275–6, 280–1,
    314
Decrès, Denis, 198
Delacroix, Charles, 89–91, 100, 122
Denon, Vivant, 118, 138
Desrenaudes, Martial-Borie, abbé: relations
    with CMT, 24; on peace mission to
    Britain with CMT, 65; and coup of 18
    Brumaire, 109
Dessolle, General Jean-Joseph Paul Auguste,
    230
diamond necklace affair, 32
Dino, Dorothée, duchesse de: dislikes
    Montrond, 122, 309; at Valençay, 135–6,
    287; relations with CMT, 140–1, 239,

256, 265; George Sand offends, 175;
    marriage to Edmond, 182, 195, 206–7;
    on Napoleon's return from Russia, 210;
    accompanies CMT to Congress of
    Vienna, 239, 245; infatuation with
    Clam-Martinitz, 239, 256; informs
    CMT of Napoleon's escape, 254;
    acquires title, 277; visits Royer-Collard,
    282; concern for CMT's health, 284;
    accompanies CMT to Midi and Pont-
    de-Sains, 285–6; and CMT's
    improvements to town of Valençay, 286;
    acquires Rochecotte, 287; meets Thiers,
    291; with CMT in London, 294, 296,
    301–3; takes Bacourt as lover, 294;
    favours settlement for Poland, 299; on
    William IV's cooler attitude, 305; on
    CMT's declining offer of Presidency of
    Council, 306; outraged at desecration of
    church of Saint-Germain-l'Auxerrois,
    306; rebukes Thiers for resigning over
    Spain, 307; and CMT's deathbed
    reconciliation with Church, 308; returns
    to Paris from England, 310; religious
    beliefs and influence, 312–13, 315–17,
    319; ill health, 315–16; and Quélen's
    document of apologia for CMT, 315;
    and CMT's impending death, 318–19,
    321; and CMT's dying signature, 322;
    refuses to speak to Thiers, 324; absent
    from CMT's funeral, 325
Dino, Edmond, duc de (CMT's nephew),
    119, 182, 195, 206, 239, 277
Directory (French): in power, 89–94; and
    Napoleon's reception in Paris, 96–7, 99;
    and Napoleon's Egyptian expedition,
    100–1; and CMT's foreign policy, 104–5;
    and coup of 18 Brumaire, 108
Doctrinaires, 281–2, 306
Du Barry, Mme see Barry, Marie Jeanne du
Duchesne, Henri-Gabriel, 24
Dumont de Genève, Étienne: on CMT's
    sense of rejection by parents, 6; and
    death of Mirabeau, 57; on fate of Louis
    XVI, 58; accompanies CMT to Paris
    from London, 64–5
Dumouriez, General François, 64–5,
    148
Dupanloup, Félix Antoine Philibert, abbé,
    308, 315–23
Dupin, André Marie Jean Jacques, 325
Dupont de l'Étang, General Pierre, 223
Dupont de Nemours, Pierre: friendship
    with CMT, 19; on CMT's diplomatic
    manner, 62; and Bourbon restoration,
    222
Duport, Adrien, 39

Duquesnoy, Adrien, 109
Duras, Amedée Bretagne Maio, duc de, 259
Duroc, General Christophe, 189, 198
Du Roveray, Jacques-Antoine, 64
Dussek, Jan Ladislav, 183
Duvoisin, Jean-Baptiste, Bishop, 24

Egypt: French expedition to, 88, 99–101,
    105, 337; CMT favours as colony, 333
Elba: Napoleon exiled to, 224; Napoleon
    escapes from, 254
Eliot, Edward James, 63
Émery, Jacques-André, 13, 35
Enghien, Louis de Bourbon-Condé, duc d':
    execution, 147–52, 192, 194, 199, 229,
    262, 283, 329
Erfurt, 192–6, 331
Esclignac, Georgine de Talleyrand-Périgord,
    duchesse d', 314
Esménard, Joseph, 144
Estampes, Jacques d', 135
Estates General: demands for, 31, 37–9;
    CMT elected clerical representative to,
    39; composition, 40
Eylau, Battle of (1807), 167–8

Fauchet, Joseph, 78
Faye, Dr, 176
Fénelon, François de Salignac de La
    Mothe-, 318
Ferdinand IV, King of Naples, 162, 235,
    277
Ferdinand VII, King of Spain (formerly
    Prince of Las Esturias), 188–9, 191, 282
Feuchères, Adrien-Victor, baron de, 279
Feuchères, Sophie, baronne de (née Dawes),
    279
Feuillants, 60–1
Fitz-James, Marie, duchesse de, 14
Flahaut, Adélaïde, comtesse de (later Souza),
    50–3, 57, 71, 181; Adèle de Senanges, 71
Flahaut, Charles-Joseph, comte de (CMT's
    son), 51, 71, 298
Fleury, Cardinal André-Hercule de, 12, 26
Floret, chevalier de, 203
Fontainebleau, Treaty of (1807), 188–9
Foreign Ministry (French): reforms under
    CMT, 122–3
Fouché, Joseph, duc d'Otrante: clerical
    career, 9; and coup of 30 Prairial, 108;
    background and position, 145–6; CMT's
    hostility to, 146; uncovers duc d'Enghien
    conspiracy, 147, 151; on decline of
    Prussian power, 164; and CMT's
    purchase of Hôtel Monaco, 183; on
    CMT's vices, 186; joins CMT in
    opposition to Napoleon, 197–200, 206;
    retains position as Minister of Police,
    200; dismissed, 204; and Châtillon
    meeting, 216; and return of d'Artois,
    229; in Louis XVIII's government,
    263–5, 268–9; CMT removes from
    government, 269–71
Fox, Charles James, 129
France: Church authority in, 9–10, 15;
    commercial treaty with Britain (1786),
    27–8, 61; public finances under ancien
    régime, 28–30, 38, 45, 49; public
    education, 60; proposed agreement with
    Britain (1792), 61–3; and war threat
    (1792), 64; European powers declare war
    on (1792), 67; monarchy abolished, 68;
    clergy flee to England, 69; exiles in
    Britain, 70–4; CMT's view on foreign
    relations, 71–2; list of emigrants issued,
    73; declares war on Britain (1793), 75;
    under Terror, 76; relations with
    America, 83; Thermidor coup (1794),
    84; new Constitution (1796), 86;
    negotiations with British at Lille, 92;
    Fructidor coup (1797), 93–4; coup of 18
    Brumaire, 95, 108–9; invasion threat to
    Britain, 100, 155; military conquests and
    expansion in Europe, 103–5, 128; coup
    of 30 Prairial (1799), 106–7; renews war
    with Britain (1803), 126, 129–30, 154;
    British threat to, 128–9; aristocracy
    restored, 142–4; Bourbon restoration,
    221–3; provisional government, 223; and
    terms of Paris Peace Treaty (1815),
    225–7, 234; fortresses demobilized, 226;
    Senate drafts new constitution (Charte
    constitutionnelle, 1815), 227–8, 234;
    discussed at Congress of Vienna, 234–6;
    rearms, 246–7; status enhanced at
    Congress of Vienna, 248, 250; in Triple
    Alliance (1815) with Austria and Britain,
    250; and Prussian dominance, 252; lacks
    bargaining power, 266; amendments to
    Charte, 267; electoral system, 267;
    Upper Chamber, 267; political
    composition of Chambers, 268–9;
    royalist sentiments in provinces, 268;
    allies' demands on after 1815, 271–2;
    allies' occupation ends, 275; war with
    Spain (1823), 282–3; and balance
    between monarch and Chambers, 289;
    1830 revolution, 290, 329; Villèle's
    government falls (1827), 290; and Low
    Countries border fortresses, 295–6, 299;
    intervenes in Belgium (1831), 300;
    campaign against Dutch (1832), 303; in
    Quadruple Alliance with Britain,
    Portugal and Spain, 304; international

position, 334–6; *see also* Bourbon family;
    French Church
Francis I, Emperor of Austria, 247, 251
Francis, Sir Philip, 137
Franco-Prussian War (1870), 252
Frederick II (the Great), King of Prussia,
    126, 158
Frederick Augustus, Elector (King) of
    Saxony, 165, 169–70, 235, 243, 248, 251,
    255
Frederick William III, King of Prussia, 125,
    132, 164, 168, 219–21
freemasonry: CMT and, 33
French Church: power and authority, 9–10,
    15; assemblies of clergy, 15, 23, 25;
    relations with King, 25; property and
    land, 38, 46–8; oath of loyalty under
    Civil Constitution, 53–5; and Concordat
    (1801), 141–2; and political divisions,
    289; revival, 311–12; and social values,
    311
French Revolution: effect on Church, 10;
    outbreak, 43–4; and confiscation of
    Church property, 46; CMT's differences
    with ideals, 73, 311; and Terror, 76
Friedland, Battle of (1807), 167–8

Gallifet, Hôtel, 183
Garat, Dominique-Joseph, 65, 90, 143
Garibaldi, Antonio, 325
Garrick, David, 301
Gaudin, Martin, 198
Gaulle, Charles de, 334
Genlis, Stéphanie Felicité Ducrest de St
    Aubin, comtesse de, 10, 33, 74, 143
Gentil de Chavagnac, Marie-Madeleine de
    Verniquet, 13
Gentz, Frederick von, 240–1
George III, King of Great Britain, 63, 66
George IV, King of Great Britain (*earlier*
    Prince Regent), 237, 270
Germany: reorganized under Recess of
    Ratisbon, 132; and formation of Rhine
    Confederation, 162–4; Napoleon's 1813
    campaign in, 211; Prussia's position in,
    236–7, 252, 338; Federation proposed,
    249; nationalism, 253, 335, 337–8
Gerry, Elbridge, 102–3
Girondins, 60, 64–5
Gobel, Jean-Baptiste Joseph, archbishop of
    Paris, 55
Godoy, Manuel (príncipe de la Paz), 132,
    164, 188–9
Gohier, Louis-Jerôme, 107–8
Goldsmith, Lewis, 121
Gouvion Saint-Cyr, Marshal Laurent,
    264

Grand, Catherine *see* Talleyrand, Catherine
    de
Grand, George-Francis, 137
Grassini, Giuseppina, 144
Greathead, Bertie, 131
Greece, 299
Grégoire, Henri, abbé, 53, 312
Gregory XVI, Pope, 313, 320, 325
Grenville, William Wyndham, Baron,
    62–4
Grey, Charles, 2nd Earl, 301, 305
Grignols family, 2
Grimaldi, Louis-André de, bishop of
    Noyon, 35
Guerry-Maubreuil, comte de *see* Orvault,
    marquis d'
Guizot, François Pierre Guillaume, 20, 260,
    265–6, 282, 306, 327
Gustav III, King of Sweden, 32

Habsburg dynasty, 125
Hague Treaty (1790), 64
Hamburg, 86–7, 207
Hamilton, Alexander, 78, 84
Hanover: CMT offers to Prussia, 125, 164;
    and Triple Alliance, 250
Hardenberg, Karl August, Prince von, 216,
    241, 248–9
Hardi, abbé, 7
Hartwell, England, 211
Haut-Brion, château de, 179
Hauterive, Maurice Blanc d': early
    friendship with CMT, 26; in America,
    79; and CMT's reluctance to write,
    116–17; heads Second Division in
    CMT's Ministry, 120, 122; and reform of
    Foreign Ministry, 123; and d'Enghien's
    execution, 152; in Paris during CMT's
    travels, 156; and CMT's proposals for
    alternative European policy, 157–8; and
    proposed treaty with Austria, 160; and
    CMT's view of Trafalgar defeat, 161;
    and CMT's absence on Napoleon's
    campaigns, 162; on decline of Prussian
    power, 164; accompanies CMT to
    Bourbon l'Archambault, 171; arranges
    reconciliation between CMT and
    Fouché, 197; investigates CMT and
    Fouché for Napoleon, 204; *L'État de la
    France à la fin de l'an VIII*, 124–5
Henri, Colonel, 191
Henrion de Pansey, Pierre Paul Nicolas,
    baron, 223
Hohenlinden, Battle of (1800), 126
Hohenzollern family, 125
Holland, Elizabeth, Lady, 121, 136, 286–7,
    301, 305

Holland, Henry Richard Vassall Fox, 3rd
  Baron, 172, 286–8, 291, 293, 301, 309
Hüber, Barthélemy, 61
Huidekoper, Jan, 80
Hulot, M. (tutor), 7
Humboldt, Wilhelm von, 242
Hundred Days (1815), 253, 258, 337
Huningue, 272

Île de France: ceded to Britain, 226
Infantado, Hôtel de l' *see* Talleyrand, Hôtel,
  Paris
Institut National des Sciences et des Arts,
  87–9, 104
Isabey, Jean-Baptiste, 238–9
Italy: Napoleon's peace terms (1797), 94;
  Napoleon's ambitions in, 104, 160;
  French domination of, 126; Napoleon
  proclaimed King, 154; CMT proposes
  French withdrawal from, 159–60; gains
  in Treaty of Pressburg, 162; Austria's
  position in, 236, 254
Izquierdo, Don Isidor, 189

Jacobin Club: formed, 39; breaks up, 59
Jacobinism, 94, 105, 146, 269
Jaucourt, François, marquis de, 70, 74, 181,
  222, 233, 238, 247, 253, 264, 327
Jay Treaty (US-Britain), 102
Jena, Battle of (1806), 164
Jersey, Frances Villiers, Countess of, 177,
  301
Jesuits, 289–90
Jorris (Swiss porter), 121
Jorry, Lieutenant Sébastien, 105
Joséphine, Empress of Napoleon I: praises
  CMT, 95; and Napoleon's 1797
  reception in Paris, 97–9, 114; intercedes
  for Catherine Talleyrand, 139; attends
  Archambaud Talleyrand's ball, 144;
  divorce from Napoleon, 172, 194
Jourdan, General Jean-Baptiste, comte, 90,
  228
July Monarchy, 282, 293, 306
Juniper Hall, Mickleham, Surrey, 74

Kaunitz, Wenzel Anton, Prince of, 240
Kielmannsegge, Auguste Charlotte,
  Countess of, 205
Kléber, General Jean-Baptiste, 90
Königgrätz (Sadowa), Battle of (1866),
  159

La Bedoyère, General le comte Charles,
  269
La Besnardière, Jean-Baptiste de Gouey,
  comte de, 238, 316, 345

La Billarderie, Alexandre-Sébastien de
  Flahaut, comte de, 50
La Bouchardie, Eugénie de, 85
Labrador, Don Pedro, 240
La Châtre, Charlotte, comtesse de, 70, 74
La Châtre, Louis-Claude, duc de, 267
Laclos, Pierre Ambroise François Choderlos
  de, 33
Lacordaire, Henri-Dominique, abbé, 315
Lacour-Gayet, Georges, 225
Lafayette, Marie-Joseph Gilbert du Motier,
  marquis de, 39
La Forest, Antoine, comte de, 79, 223
La Garde-Cambonas, Auguste, comte de,
  245
La Harpe, Jean-François de, 143
Lally-Tollendal, Trophime-Gérard, marquis
  de, 70, 260
Lamartine, Alphonse de, 175, 306, 319
Lameth, Alexandre, 39
La Motte Valois, Jeanne de, comtesse, 32
Landau, 272
Landry, M., 12
Lange, Mlle (Mme Michel Simons), 109
Langlois, M. (tutor), 7
Lannes, Marshal Jean, 123
Lansdowne, William Petty, 1st Marquis of:
  Dumont serves, 64; and snubs to French
  in London, 66; and CMT's exile in
  London, 68, 73; and CMT's expulsion
  from England, 77; gives letter of
  recommendation to CMT for
  Washington, 78; and CMT's views on
  America, 83; CMT's relations with,
  301
Laporte, Arnaud de, 58, 73
La Révellière-Lépaux, Louis-Marie, 89, 91,
  99
La Roche-Aymon, Charles-Antoine, comte
  de, archbishop of Reims, 8, 10, 14, 15,
  22
La Rochefoucauld, François, duc de, 310
La Tour du Pin-Gouvernet, Fréderic
  Séraphin, marquis de, 80, 238
La Tour du Pin-Gouvernet, Henriette,
  marquise de, 80–1, 116, 174, 181, 214
Lauzun, duc de *see* Biron, Armand de
  Gontaut, duc de
Laval, Bonne-Charlotte, duchesse de, 122
Laval, Jeanne, vicomtesse de, 14, 18, 70, 77,
  152, 181, 205, 208
Lavalette, Antoine-Marie Chamans, comte
  de, 197, 215
Law, Thomas, 80
Lebrun, Charles-François: as Finance
  Minister, 112; salary, 185; attends
  Napoleon's council meeting, 198; and

allies' advance on Paris, 217; and redrafted constitution, 227

Leclerc, General Victor-Emmanuel, 114

Legendre de Luçay, Jean-Baptiste-Charles, 135

Legislative Assembly: formed, 60; emergency powers, 67

Leipzig, Battle of (1813), 211

Lemercier, Népomucène, 139

Leoben, 94

Leopold I, King of the Belgians, 300

Lessart, Antoine Valdec de, 60–2, 64, 137

Letourneur de La Marche, Charles, 90

Liancourt, François de La Rochefoucauld, duc de, 33, 43, 47, 67, 70

Libon, Philippe, 183

Liechtenstein, Prince Johann von, 220

Lieven, Dorothea, princesse de (née von Benckendorff), 293, 298, 303, 316

Ligne, Charles-Joseph, prince de, 243, 245

Lille: Anglo-French negotiations at, 92

Lisbon: falls to French, 188

Livingston, Robert, 133

Locke, John, 38

Loménie de Brienne, Cardinal Étienne-Charles de, archbishop of Toulouse, 31

London: French exiles in, 70–1, 74; CMT's ambassadorship in, 293, 294–5

Londonderry, Charles William Stewart, 3rd Marquis of (earlier Lord Stewart), 238, 249, 302

Lorraine, princesse de, 21

Louis XIII, King of France, 2

Louis XIV, King of France, 158, 335

Louis XVI, King of France: coronation, 14; accession celebrated by French clergy, 15; and Calonne's financial proposals, 30; appoints CMT bishop of Autun, 35; addresses National Assembly, 43–4; dismisses Necker, 43; accepts Civil Constitution of the Clergy, 53; attempted flight and capture, 59; CMT delivers letter from to George III, 66; seized and imprisoned, 67–8; documents incriminating CMT discovered, 72–3; execution, 74–5, 99, 148; memorial requiem mass in Vienna, 251; annual memorial masses, 276, 287

Louis XVIII, King of the French (earlier comte de Provence): mocks CMT's title, 3; CMT's rumoured negotiations with, 89; eating habits, 178; as successor to Napoleon, 214–15; restoration, 221–3, 227; demands incorporation of Belgian territory in France, 226; returns to France, 227, 230–2; attitude to CMT, 230–1; resists constitutional monarchy, 232; restricts CMT's influence, 232–3; and CMT's role at Congress of Vienna, 235, 240, 246–8, 250, 253–4, 257–8, 331, 337; and memorial requiem mass for Louis XVI in Vienna, 251; and Napoleon's escape from Elba, 254; favours sending Napoleon to Azores, 255; withdraws to Ghent, 256, 257; allies demand commitment to constitutional government from, 257; reactionary government, 258; CMT sees after Waterloo, 259; second restoration and government, 259–60, 263–5; proclamation at Cateau-Cambrésis, 260; CMT drafts apology for, 261; agrees to inclusion of Fouché in government, 263; and composition of Upper Chamber, 267; on deputies serving without salary, 268; CMT advises, 271; accepts CMT's resignation, 272–3; and allies' demands on France, 272; opposes CMT's return to government, 274; suspends CMT from Grand Chambellan's position, 276; grants princedom of Talleyrand on CMT, 277; and Richelieu's resignation, 280; sees CMT's private letters, 280; and charges against CMT over d'Enghien's death, 283–4; CMT attends during illness and death, 284; concern for formality, 284; estrangement from CMT, 284; mistrusts CMT's policies, 330; and France's international position, 336

Louis of Bourbon-Parma, King of Etruria, 144

Louis, Dominique, Baron (earlier abbé), 134, 219–20, 223, 258, 260, 264–5, 285

Louis-Philippe, King of France (earlier duc de Chartres; then duc d'Orléans): in Hamburg, 87; and succession to Napoleon, 210, 256–7; visits dying CMT, 210, 256–7, 323; Chateaubriand proposes as head of army, 262; and recall of Sophie de Feuchères, 279; accession, 292–3; and CMT's London ambassadorship, 295, 297, 299; CMT advises to distance France from Britain, 304; disorder in early reign, 306

Louis-Philippe Joseph, duc de Chartres (later duc d'Orléans; 'Philippe Égalité'): and Mme de Genlis, 10; marriage to marquise de Montesson, 21; CMT's relations with, 22, 26, 31–3, 40; CMT's biographical essay on, 34; CMT abandons biography of, 74; household in exile in England, 74

Lucchesini, marquis Girolamo, 125, 164

Lunéville, Treaty of (1801), 112, 126, 144

Luynes, Élisabeth de Montmorency-Laval, duchesse de, 14
Luzy, Dorothée, 12

Macdonald, General Etienne-Jacques, 224
Mack von Leiberich, General Karl, Baron, 156
Maison, Marshal Nicolas Joseph, 297
Malesherbes, Guillaume-Chrétien de Lamoignon de, 281
Malet, General Claude de, 209
Malouet, Admiral Pierre-Victor, 223
Malta: Napoleon captures, 101; British retain troops in, 130
Mannay, Charles, bishop, 24
Marbeuf, Alexandre de, bishop of Autun, 34
Marbeuf, Mme de, 313
Marengo, Battle of (1800), 126–7
Maret, Hugues-Bernard, duc de Bassano, 90, 208, 212–13
Mareuil, Durant de: heads First Division in CMT's ministry, 120; and payment for creation of Batavian Republic, 133; attends CMT, 176
Maria Louisa de Bourbon, Queen of Etruria, 144, 188, 236
Marie-Antoinette, Queen of France, 32, 206
Marie-Louise, Empress of Napoleon I: marriage, 206; and son's regency, 210, 214; and allies' advance on Paris, 217–18; crown jewels recovered from, 229; Austria seizes Italian possessions, 254
Marjolin, Jean-Nicolas, 320
Marmont, General Auguste, duc de Raguse, 219, 223–4, 228
Marseilles, 285
Marshall, John, 102
Martignac, Jean-Baptiste Gay, vicomte de, 290
Marx, Karl, 291
Matignon, Hôtel, 183
Maubreuil, comte de see Orvault, marquis d'
Maury, Jean-Sifrein, abbé (later archbishop and cardinal), 47
Médavy, Charles d'Osmond de, bishop of Comminges, 8–9
Melbourne, William Lamb, 2nd Viscount, 301
Méneval, Claude, baron de, 117, 123, 132, 149, 166, 185, 190
Mérimée, Prosper, 177
Merlin, Mme, 99
Merlin de Douai, Philippe-Antoine, comte, 90, 93
Messe de la Fédération, 52–3

Metternich, Prince Klemens Wenzel Lothar von: on Prussian mobilization against France, 164; and Talleyrand's meeting with Alexander I at Erfurt, 194; as Austrian ambassador in Paris, 196; and CMT's favouring Austria, 196; CMT opens direct relations with, 202; as Foreign Minister, 203; discusses Bourbon restoration at Châtillon, 216–17; and capitulation of Paris, 219; at Congress of Vienna, 238, 240, 243–9; and Russian threat, 245; and divisions in France, 265–6; and treatment of France after 1815, 270; supports CMT's recall to government, 274
Meudon, 109, 134
Miot de Mélito, comte André François, 94–5
Mirabeau, Honoré Gabriel Riqueti, comte de: friendship with CMT, 19, 33; mission to Berlin (1786–7), 27; and CMT's hopes of archbishopric, 34; in Society of Thirty, 39; and duc d'Orléans, 40; supports CMT's speech on Church property, 47; acts as CMT's server for mass, 52; as constitutional monarchist, 57–9; death, 57; CMT succeeds to political posts, 59
Miroudot du Bourg, Jean-Baptiste, bishop of Babylon, 55
Molé, Louis-Mathieu, comte: on duc d'Enghien's death, 151; on CMT's conversation, 174; on CMT's daily routine, 176, 266; and allies' advance on Paris, 217; on CMT's presidency of council, 267; and CMT's disgrace, 276; Pozzo aims to separate from CMT, 278; and CMT's ambassadorship in London, 297; on CMT's health decline, 309; attends dying CMT, 322; and CMT's religious retraction, 325
Mollien, Nicolas-François, comte, 190, 199
Monaco, Hôtel, Paris, 183, 206–7
Moncey, Marshal Bon-Adrien Jeannot de, 230
Monge, Gaspard, 94
Moniteur universel, Le, 72, 85
Monsieur see Charles X, King of France
Montesquieu, Charles-Louis de Secondat, baron, 95
Montesquiou, Anatole, comte de, 198
Montesquiou, François-Xavier, abbé de, 211, 222, 230, 233
Montesson, Charlotte Béraud, marquise de (later duchesse de Chartres), 21, 33
Montmorency, Caroline, duchesse de, 313

Montmorency, Mathieu, duc de, 70, 74

Montrond, Casimir, comte de, 109, 121–2, 138, 176, 256, 285, 309, 324

Moreau, General Jean-Victor, 147

Moreau de Saint-Méry, Médéric, 78, 84, 86, 126–7

Morris, Gouverneur: CMT lends book to, 17; and Adélaïde de Flahaut, 51; and CMT's consecration of bishops, 55; and CMT's appointment as administrator of Paris *département*, 57; CMT urges to flee Paris, 69; reports on CMT to Washington, 78

Morris, Robert, 82

Moulin, General Jean, 107–8

Mounier, Jean-Joseph, 42

Mouvement, le, 306

Murat, Marshal Joachim: and coup of 18 Brumaire, 109; on CMT's inscrutability, 123; and duc d'Enghien affair, 150; Fouché writes to, 197; and Napoleon's exile in Elba, 224; in Naples, 235, 236, 238, 241, 247, 254; and Napoleon's escape, 255

Musset, Alfred de, 175

Naderman, Jean-Henri, 183

Nantes, 192

Naples: in Third Coalition against France, 156; transferred to Joseph Bonaparte, 162; and Congress of Vienna, 235–6, 241–4, 247, 254; and Bourbon monarchy, 336

Napoleon I (Bonaparte), Emperor of the French: behaviour towards women, 21; CMT's relations with, 93, 110–16, 126, 133, 190, 201, 212–14, 329–30; and Fructidor coup, 93; offers generous terms to Austria (1797), 94; and 18 Brumaire coup, 95, 108–9; CMT's impression of, 95–6; praises CMT, 95; European ambitions, 96–7; reception in Paris (1797), 96–9; expedition to Egypt, 99–101; invasion threat to England, 100, 155; returns from Egypt, 107; and Sièyes, 107; authority as First Consul, 111–12; reappoints CMT Foreign Minister, 111–12, 114; on CMT's diplomatic supremacy, 123–4; and *L'État de la France à la fin de l'an VIII*, 125; made First Consul for Life, 127, 146; and Marengo outcome, 127; military ambitions after Peace of Amiens, 127, 129–30; rejects accommodation with Britain, 129; and CMT's venality, 132; and creation of Batavian Republic, 132–3; and CMT's acquisition of

Valençay, 135; and CMT's marriage, 137–40; Concordat with Pius VII (1801), 141–2; restores social-hierarchical and aristocratic culture, 142–3; assassination attempts on, 146; and duc d'Enghien conspiracy, 148–51, 330; proclaimed Emperor, 153; coronation, 154; as King of Italy, 154; expedition against Austria in Germany, 155; epileptic fit, 156; and CMT's proposed alternative strategy, 157–9, 161; military victories, 158, 160–1, 164–5, 167; on Treaty of Pressburg, 162; on dismissing CMT, 163; reaches Berlin, 164; pursues Russians in eastern Prussia, 165–6; and Marie Walewska, 167; conditions at Tilsit, 168–9; and Dalberg, 168; appoints family members to European thrones, 169; CMT's disenchantment with, 169, 195; divorce from Joséphine and marriage to Austrian princess, 172, 194, 205–6; CMT entertains for, 178–9; eating habits, 178; and CMT's resignation as Foreign Minister, 185–7; forms Russian alliance, 185, 193, 243; appoints Champagny Foreign Minister, 187; Spanish policy, 188–91, 197–8, 201, 204; negotiates with Tsar at Erfurt (1808), 192–5; CMT and Fouché oppose, 197–9; abuses and humiliates CMT, 199–201; rages, 200–1, 212; CMT's opposition to grows, 201–2, 205, 209–10; humiliates CMT's family, 206–7; refuses CMT personal access, 206; payments to CMT, 207–8; campaign and defeat in Russia (1812), 208–10; unaware of CMT's contacts with Austria and Russia, 208; plots for succession to, 209–11; threatens CMT, 211–12; offers Foreign Ministry to CMT (1812–13), 212–13; disbelieves CMT's early treason, 214; negotiates with allies (1813), 215; and allies' advance on Paris, 217–18; orders evacuation of Marie-Louise and son, 217; abdication and exile in Elba (1814), 224; at Fontainebleau, 224; and Maubreuil's supposed assassination attempt, 225; escape from Elba and progress through France, 254–5, 336; alleges CMT offers services on return to France, 256; Waterloo defeat, 258; CMT expresses hatred for, 264; exile and death on St Helena, 264; art plunder restored, 270–1; predicts CMT's ejection by Bourbons, 272; on CMT's foreign policy, 335

Napoleon II, King of Rome (*later* Duke of Reichstadt; Napoléon-François-Joseph-Charles Bonaparte), 210, 215, 217–18, 221

Napoleon III, Emperor of the French: and Prussia, 252, 338

Narbonne, Louis, comte de: friendship with CMT, 18, 20, 33; removed from Ministry of War, 64; and CMT's flight from France, 69; exile in England, 70, 74–6; on CMT's deference to Napoleon, 112; financial constraints, 134; relations with Napoleon, 143; lives with vicomtesse de Laval, 181

Nassau-Orange, William V, Prince of, 132

National (Constituent) Assembly: composition, 40–1; CMT joins, 43, 48–50; Louis XVI addresses, 43–4; and Civil Constitution of the Clergy, 53; dissolved (September 1791), 60

National, Le (newspaper), 291

Necker, Jacques, 31, 40, 43, 49, 60

Nelson, Admiral Horatio, Viscount, 160

Nemours, Louis Charles d'Orléans, duc de, 299

Nesselrode, Count Karl von, 203–5, 216, 219–20, 242

Netherlands: French invasion threat to, 64; as ally of France, 92; Napoleon refuses to evacuate, 130; and Triple Alliance, 250; teritorial claims after 1815, 270–1; Belgium revolts against (1831), 295; and London conference on Belgium's future, 298–9; kingdom established (1815), 299; invades Belgium, 300; France acts against (1832), 303

Neufchâteau, François de, 93

Neukomm, Sigismund von, 238, 251

New York, 79, 82

Ney, Marshal Michel, 156, 224, 268

Nicholas I, Tsar, 295

Noailles, comte Alexis de, 13

Noailles, Just, duc de (prince de Poix), 321–2

Noailles, Louis Marie, vicomte de, 79, 84, 238

North German Confederation, 164

Nye Prove, Den (Danish ship), 86

Ordener, General Michel, 150

Orléans, Louis-Philippe, duc d' *see* Louis-Philippe, King of France; Louis-Philippe Joseph, duc de Chartres

Orvault, Marie-Armand, comte de Guerry-Maubreuil, marquis d', 224–5, 287–8

Ottoman Empire: and French expedition to Egypt, 100–2; Russian relations with, 156, 192; Louis XIV's policy on, 158; and CMT's proposed European strategy, 159; Napoleon's policy towards, 166

Oudinot, Marshal Nicolas-Charles, 230

Ouvrard, Gabriel, 127, 204, 271

Palmerston, Henry John Temple, 3rd Viscount, 301–5

Panchaud, Isaac: friendship with CMT, 19; financial speculation, 27–8

Paravey, Pierre-François, 288

Paris: CMT resides in as young abbé, 16–17; *salons*, 20–2, 180–2; allies advance on (1792), 68; under Terror, 76; allies advance on (1813), 217; capitulates to allies, 219; in revolution of 1830, 291; CMT's disenchantment with, 310

Paris, Peace of (1800), 133

Paris, Treaties of (1815): first, 225, 234, 238, 241, 248, 271–2, 275; second, 275

Pasquier, Étienne-Denis, duc de: on CMT's religious performance, 52; on payment to CMT at Recess of Ratisbon, 132; and duc d'Enghien conspiracy, 149; on CMT's move towards treason, 168; on CMT's *bons mots*, 173–4; on Champagny, 187; and CMT's views on Spanish alliance, 190; and CMT's payments from Austria, 195; on CMT's presence at Council of Regency meeting, 217–18; and allies' advance on Paris, 218; and CMT at Congress of Vienna, 234, 253–4; in Louis XVIII's government, 264; on CMT's obsession with duchesse de Dino, 265; on weakness of CMT's government, 266; and Fouché's removal from government, 269; and CMT's attack on Decazes, 275–6; in new ministry, 275–6; Pozzo aims to divide from CMT, 278; and CMT in 1830 revolution, 291; and accession of Louis-Philippe, 292

Paul I, Tsar: treaty with Napoleon, 119

Peel, Sir Robert, 305

Périer, Casimir, 306

Perrey, Gabriel, 229

Pétion, Jérôme, 67

Petit-Andilly, Le, near Montmorency, 285

Philadelphia, 78–9, 82, 84

Phillips, Susanna, 74–5

Pichegru, General Jean-Charles, 147

Piedmont: Napoleon annexes, 129

Pinckney, Charles, 102

Pitt, William, the Younger, 62–3, 66, 303

Pius VI, Pope, 32, 53, 59

Pius VII, Pope, 141, 154
Poix, prince de *see* Noailles, Just, duc de
Poland: CMT and Napoleon's view of, 166–7; CMT proposes Russian kingdom of, 205; discussed and partitioned at Congress of Vienna, 235, 237, 242–4, 246–9, 251–3, 337; discussed at London conference, 299
Polignac, Jules, prince de, 290–1
Pompadour, Jeanne Antoinette Poisson, marquise de, 26
Poniatowski, Józef Antoine, Prince, 167, 290
Pont-de-Sains château, 285
Portier des Chartreux, Les (book), 17
Portugal: French intervention in, 165; partitioned under Treaty of Fontainebleau, 188; dissension in, 299; British intervention in, 304
Potocka, Countess Zofja, 163, 168, 181–2
Poznan, 165
Pozzo di Borgo, General Carlo, 220, 260, 263–6, 278, 298
Pradt, Dominique de, archbishop of Malines, 208, 214, 219–20
press: censorship, 281, 289–90
Pressburg (Bratislava), Treaty of (1805), 162, 168, 196
Prussia: and CMT's diplomatic principles, 125–6, 158; defeated at Jena and Auerstadt, 164; and reform of Germany, 164, 236; and Treaty of Tilsit, 168–9; and Napoleon's 1812 Russian campaign, 208; at Congress of Vienna, 236–7, 241–2, 244, 246, 248–50; CMT mistrusts, 236, 335; dominance in Germany, 236–7, 252, 338; British friendship with, 244; claims on Saxony, 249, 251, 253; losses and gains at Congress of Vienna, 251–2, 337; CMT misjudges power, 252–3, 337; demands on France after 1815, 270–1; Rhineland acquisitions, 295

Quadruple Alliance (Britain-France-Portugal-Spain), 304
Quélen, Hyacinthe de, archbishop of Paris, 313–14, 317–19, 321, 323–4
Quid Aliquantum (Pius VI's brief), 55

Radix de Sainte-Foix, Maximilien, 69, 109, 121
Raikes, Thomas, 327
Rastadt, 95
Ratisbon, Recess of (1802–3), 126, 132

Réal, Pierre-François, 108, 150
Reform Bill (Britain, 1832), 305
Regnault de Saint-Angély, Michel-Louis-Etienne, comte, 175
Reims: CMT in, 8, 14, 15–16; Louis XVI crowned in, 14
Reinhard, Charles-Frédéric (Karl-Friedrich), comte: as confidant of CMT, 65; succeeds CMT as Foreign Minister, 106, 111, 120, 123; death and eulogy by CMT, 123–4, 317, 331
Rémusat, Augustin de, 142, 156; connives at CMT remaining in Paris on arrival of allies, 218–19; barred from office under CMT (1814), 233
Rémusat, Charles de: on CMT's working routine, 176; and CMT's attack on Richelieu, 274; visits CMT during London ambassadorship, 296–7; and CMT's declining political office, 306; and Thiers' hostility to CMT, 307; on CMT's deathbed reconciliation, 324; judgement of CMT as statesman, 330, 332, 338
Rémusat, Claire de ('Clari'): CMT's description of, 21; on Napoleon's forcing CMT to marry, 137, 139; on CMT's belief in monarchy, 147; and d'Enghien conspiracy, 149; on CMT's unease at Napoleon's becoming Emperor, 153; and CMT's growing hostility to Napoleon, 195, 201; recruits Hortense de Beauharnais to plead with Napoleon for CMT, 200; on allies' advance to Paris, 217; *salon*, 218, 274
Reubell, Jean-François, 89–93, 99, 105–6
Rhineland: and Congress of Vienna, 251–3, 295, 336; *see also* Confederation of the Rhine
Richelieu, Armand-Emmanuel, duc de, 264–5, 272, 274–6, 280–1
Robert (chef/restaurateur), 180
Robespierre, Maximilien, 81, 84, 89
Rochecotte, château, near Langeais, 287, 291
Roederer, Pierre-Louis, 85, 107–9, 146, 201
Roederer, Tony, 119
Roger Ducos, Pierre, 107–8
Rohan, Prince-Cardinal Louis de, 32
Rohan-Lorraine family, 31
Roland de la Platière, Jean-Marie, 72
Romilly, Sir Samuel, 66
Rouen, Achille, 238
Roux de Laborie (or Roux de Rochelle; CMT's secretary), 119–20, 140, 220, 222–5

Roveray, Jacques-Antoine du see Du
    Roveray, Jacques-Antoine
Rovigo, duc de see Savary, General Anne-
    Jean-Marie
Royer-Collard, Pierre, 282–3, 289, 321–2
Russia: French hostility to, 125; in Third
    Coalition against France, 156; in CMT's
    1805 policy memoranda, 157–61, 337;
    desire for peace, 164; and Continental
    Blockade, 165, 169; Napoleon's 1806
    campaign against, 165–6; and Treaty of
    Tilsit, 169; forms alliance with
    Napoleon, 185, 193, 243; and Erfurt
    negotiations (1808), 192–4; Napoleon
    proposes new treaty with (1808), 192–3;
    CMT gives information and advice to,
    201, 203–5, 208, 331; Napoleon's
    campaign and defeat in (1812), 208–10;
    claims on Poland, 237, 242, 248, 251–3,
    299, 337; British mistrust of, 244; and
    Congress of Vienna, 244–5, 247–9, 253,
    336; demands on France after 1815, 270;
    influence on Richelieu's government,
    274; mistrusts CMT, 278; CMT regards
    as non-European, 335

Saar, 272
Sagan, Duchess Wilhelmina von, 246
Saint-Aulaire, Louis de Beaupoil, comte de,
    322
Saint-Brice, 207, 277
Saint-Denis abbey, Reims, 16
Saint-Florentin, Hôtel see Talleyrand, Hôtel
St Lucia, 226
Saint-Nicolas-du-Chardonnet church, Paris,
    14
Saint-Ouen, Declaration of (1815), 231–2
Saint-Simon, Louis de Rouvroy, duc de,
    311
Saint-Sulpice seminary, Paris, 10, 12–14
Sainte-Beuve, Charles-Augustin, 8
Salieri, Antonio, 251
salons, 20–2, 180–2, 218, 274
Sand, George, 175
Sandoz-Rollin, David Alfons von, 93,
    103
Sardinia, 236, 272
Savary, General Anne-Jean-Marie, duc de
    Rovigo, 148, 150, 166, 211, 214,
    217–18, 283
Savoy, 272
Saxony, 165, 235–6, 242–4, 246–9, 251–4,
    337–8
Scheffer, Ary, 296, 303
Scheldt, river, 128, 295, 298
Schuyler, General Philip, 80–1
Schwarzenberg, Karl, Prince zu, 220–1, 247

Sébastiani, Horace, comte, 297–8, 300, 306,
    325
Second Coalition, 105
'Secret Note' (1817), 278
Ségur, General Philippe-Paul, comte de,
    199
Semallé, Jean-René-Pierre, comte de, 222
Sémonville, Charles Tristan, 133
Senate: and restoration of Bourbons, 220–2;
    drafts new constitution, 227–8, 231; and
    d'Artois' lieutenant general post, 229;
    presented to Louis XVIII, 231
Sheridan, Richard Brinsley, 302
Sieyès, Emmanuel Joseph, abbé: in Society
    of Thirty, 39; and duc d'Orléans, 40;
    and formation of National Assembly, 41,
    43; on Messe de la Fédération, 52; as
    constitutional monarchist, 57; in Cercle
    Constitutionnel, 90; serves on Directory,
    105–8; character, 106; and coup of 18
    Brumaire, 108; death, 312
Silhouette, Étienne de, 134
Simons, Michel, 109, 134, 206, 286
slave trade: phased out, 226
Société du Palais-Royal, 40
Society of Thirty, 39
Souham, General Joseph, 224
Soult, Marshal Nicolas Jean-de-Dieu, 282
Souza, Adélaïde de see Flahaut, comtesse de
Spain: colonies in New World, 62, 71; as
    ally of France, 92, 155; war with France
    under Napoleon, 164–5, 188;
    Napoleon's policy in, 188, 195, 201, 204;
    Joseph Bonaparte made king, 189; war
    with France (1823), 282–4; British
    intervention in, 304; Bourbon monarchy
    in, 336
Stadion, Prince Johann, 216, 247, 270
Staël, Anne-Louise-Germaine Necker,
    baronne de: as Narbonne's lover, 18;
    CMT's relations with, 51, 173; and
    CMT's flight from France, 69; helps
    Jaucourt to exile, 70; exile in England,
    75; and CMT's expulsion from England,
    76–7; and Franco-British war, 76; and
    CMT's relations with La Tour du Pins in
    America, 81; receives copy of CMT's
    petition to Convention, 85; and CMT's
    return from exile, 87; relations with
    Benjamin Constant, 87; on Delacroix's
    stomach tumour, 91; lobbies for CMT's
    promotion, 91; and Fructidor coup, 93;
    idealises Napoleon, 95–8; CMT
    abandons, 98–9; effect on CMT, 139;
    Delphine, 173–4
Stewart, Charles William, Baron see
    Londonderry, 3rd Marquis of

Strasbourg, 156
Stuart, Sir Charles, 275, 278, 291
Sully, Maximilien de Béthune, duc de, 116
Switzerland: and French expansion, 103–4

Talleyrand family: status and genealogy, 1–2
Talleyrand, Hôtel, rue Saint-Florentin, Paris
    (*formerly* Hôtel de l'Infantado and Hôtel
    Saint-Florentin), 207, 219–20, 222–4,
    229, 277
Talleyrand, Alexandre de (CMT's cousin),
    267
Talleyrand, Alexandre-Angélique de,
    archbishop of Reims (*later* cardinal
    archbishop of Paris; CMT's uncle): and
    CMT's clerical career, 8–10, 14, 15–16,
    22, 36; and CMT's political reform
    proposals, 42; refuses to take oath of
    loyalty, 54; and return of Bourbons, 211;
    and CMT's religious reconciliation in
    old age, 313
Talleyrand, Alexandre-François-Jacques de
    (CMT's elder brother): birth, 3; death, 4
Talleyrand, Alexandrine-Victoire-Eléonore
    de (CMT's mother), 3, 6, 139
Talleyrand, Alix de, duchesse de Valençay
    (*née* Montmorency), 277
Talleyrand, Archambaud de (CMT's
    brother): displaces CMT as father's heir,
    5; returns from exile, 144; death and
    funeral, 318, 325–6
Talleyrand, Auguste de (CMT's cousin), 206
Talleyrand, Catherine de (*earlier* Grand;
    princesse de Bénévent; *then* princesse de
    Talleyrand; *née* Verlée or Worlée; CMT's
    wife): background and character,
    137–40; corruption, 138; separated from
    CMT, 140; and CMT's title of Prince of
    Benevento, 163; in Bourbon-
    l'Archambault, 171; entertaining, 180;
    exiled to Belgium, 207; relations with
    Duke of San Carlos, 207; death, 314
Talleyrand, Charles-Daniel, comte de
    (CMT's father): background and career,
    1; CMT separated from as child, 6;
    attends Louis XVI's coronation, 14;
    death, 35; requests bishopric for CMT,
    35
Talleyrand, Charles-Maurice, prince de:
    biographies of, ix–x; memoirs, x–xi;
    birth, 1, 3; family background, 2–4;
    childhood and upbringing, 4–6;
    deformed right foot, 4–5; education,
    6–7, 16; sense of rejection by parents,
    6–7; smallpox as schoolboy, 7; clerical
    training and career, 8–14, 15–16, 22–5,
    31–2, 34; in Reims, 8; reputation for

immorality, 11–12, 48; romantic liaisons
    and mistresses, 14, 33; libraries, 17, 74;
    social circle at Bellechasse, 18–21;
    appearance, 20, 41, 296; women's
    influence on, 21, 181; ordained, 22;
    financial investments and speculation,
    27–8, 61, 79–80, 82; on commission to
    reform discount bank, 28–9, 31; interest
    in public finances, 29, 49; freemasonry,
    33; exile in England, 34, 70–2, 74; as
    bishop of Autun, 35–40; on rights and
    liberty, 38; view on taxation, 38–9;
    qualities as politician, 41; and origins of
    French Revolution, 42; and proposals
    for legislature, 42; composes Louis XVI's
    speech to National Assembly, 43–4;
    serves on Committee of the
    Constitution, 43; declines to leave
    France, 44–5; supports raising of new
    state loan, 45; weak oratory, 45, 58, 328;
    speech on Church property, 46–8;
    liaison and child with Adélaïde de
    Flahaut, 50–1; religious practices, 52,
    312–13; and establishment of Civil
    Constitution of the Clergy, 53;
    gambling, 53; resigns as bishop of
    Autun, 54, 57; consecrates bishops, 55;
    monarchist sympathies, 58–9, 67; speech
    to Assembly on religion, 59; succeeds to
    Mirabeau's political posts, 59; proposes
    reforms of public education, 60;
    missions to England (1792), 61–7; flees
    France, 68–9; letter to Danton on
    foreign relations, 71; declared traitor,
    72–3; denies connections with royal
    court, 72–3; disagreements with French
    Revolution, 73–4, 76; constitutionalist
    politics, 76; expulsion from England and
    exile in USA, 76–84; Convention
    withdraws accusations against, 84–5;
    return to France from exile, 85–7; public
    lectures, 87–8; seeks appointment from
    Directory as minister, 90–1; appointed
    Minister of Foreign Affairs by Barras,
    91–4; negotiates with Britain at Lille,
    92–3; relations with Napoleon, 93,
    110–16, 126, 133, 190, 201, 212–13,
    329–30; and Napoleon's peace
    settlement with Austrians, 94–5;
    impression of Napoleon, 95–6; and
    Napoleon's reception in Paris (1797),
    96–9; collaborates with Napoleon on
    Egyptian expedition, 99–101; offered
    ambassadorship in Constantinople,
    101–3; demands payments from US
    envoys, 102–3; concern for stability in
    Europe, 103–5; seeks nomination to

Talleyrand, Charles-Maurice (*cont.*)
Directory, 103; resigns as Foreign
Minister (1807), 106–7, 170, 184, 185–6;
self-justification, 106; and coup of 18
Brumaire, 108–9; properties, 109, 134–6,
207, 285–6; returns as Foreign Minister
under Napoleon, 111–12, 114, 116–18;
measured approach, 113; takes cure at
Bourbon-l'Archambault, 115, 136,
171–2, 175–6, 280, 285, 291;
entertaining, 116, 133, 143–4, 177–81;
working methods and organisation of
office, 116–22, 124; circle of cronies and
confidantes, 121; delivers eulogy of
Reinhard, 123–4, 317, 331;
inscrutability, 123, 199; diplomatic style
and policies, 124–7; on Peace of
Amiens, 126–7; judgement of
Napoleon's mistakes, 127–8; venal and
corrupt practices, 131–3, 195–6, 207,
277, 331; money needs and
extravagance, 133–4; marriage, 136–7,
139–40; liaison with duchesse de Dino,
140–1, 239, 256, 265; secularization by
Vatican, 140–1; on Church-state
relations, 141; and Napoleon's social-
aristocratic pretensions, 142–3; relations
with and attitude to Bourbons, 146–7;
and duc d'Enghien conspiracy, 148–52,
229, 283, 329–30; and Napoleon's
appointment as Emperor, 153–4;
accompanies Napoleon on military
campaigns, 155–6, 161, 165–7; attends
Napoleon during epileptic fit, 156;
proposes alternative European strategy to
Napoleon, 157–61; benefits from
negotiating Confederation of Rhine,
163; made Prince and Duke of
Benevento, 163; considers resignation,
165; activities in Warsaw, 167; at Tilsit,
168; disenchantment with Napoleon,
169–70; *bons mots* and conversation,
172–5; suggests Napoleon divorce and
remarry, 172, 194, 205; daily routine,
176–7, 266; eating and drinking habits,
177–80; attends *salons*, 181; love affair
with duchesse de Courland, 182; love of
whist, 182–3; financial fluctuations,
183–4, 204–6, 273; moves to Hôtel
Monaco, 183; income, 186; as Vice-
Grand Elector, 186; and Treaty of
Fontainebleau, 189; cares for Spanish
royal prisoners, 191; and Napoleon's
negotiations with Tsar at Erfurt, 192–5;
promotes Austrian interests, 195–6;
Fouché joins in opposition to Napoleon,
197–9; Napoleon abuses and humiliates,

199–201; opposition to Napoleon
hardens, 201–2, 205, 209–10, 213–14;
Napoleon refuses personal access to, 206;
in Paris during Napoleon's 1812 Russian
campaign, 208–9; plots succession to
Napoleon, 210–11; rejects Napoleon's
offers of Foreign Ministry (1812–13),
212–13; appointed to Council of
Regency, 214, 217; and Napoleon's
negotiations with allies, 215; advises
Marie-Louise remain in Paris on allies'
entry, 217; in Paris during allies'
advance, 218–19; negotiates with Tsar
on entry into Paris, 219–21, 224; and
restoration of Bourbons, 220–2;
establishes provisional government,
222–3; and Maubreuil's claimed
assassination attempt on Napoleon, 225;
negotiates peace terms, 225–7; and
Charte constitutionnelle ('la Charte'),
227, 231–3; and return of comte
d'Artois (Monsieur), 228–9; as Foreign
Minister under restoration, 230;
influence restricted by Louis XVIII,
232–3; attends Congress of Vienna,
233–42, 246, 248, 250–3, 255, 300, 331,
336–8; and German nationalism, 253;
policy at Congress of Vienna criticized,
253–4; and Napoleon's escape from Elba
and arrival in Paris, 254–6; informs
Louis XVIII of Tsar's grudges, 257;
proposes political programme after
Congress of Vienna and Waterloo,
258–9; Wellington supports at second
Restoration, 260; takes control of
Council, 261–2; Chateaubriand's
animosity to, 262; as President of
Council under Louis XVIII, 264–5;
administrative qualities, 265–6, 332; and
constitutional reforms, 267; and allies'
demands on France after 1815, 269–72;
property seized by Prussians, 270; resigns
as President of Council, 272;
reappointed Grand Chambellan, 273;
disgraced after attack on Decazes, 276;
granted dukedom in Two Sicilies, 277; as
prince de Talleyrand, 277; sells property
and art works, 277; relations with ultras,
278–9; under surveillance, 280; swings to
liberal camp, 281; attends dying Louis
XVIII, 284; pays visit to Midi, 285;
assaulted by Maubreuil, 287; financial
crisis (1826), 288; illness (1829), 289; and
accession of Louis-Philippe, 292–3; as
ambassador in London, 293, 294–8,
301–5; limp in later years, 296; portrait
by Scheffer, 296, 303; at London

conference on Belgium, 298–300; overspends in London, 301; differences with Palmerston, 303–5; declines offer to succeed Périer as President of Council, 306; maintains interest in French politics, 306; resigns post as London ambassador, 306; preoccupation with death and religion in old age, 307, 308–10, 314–15; health decline, 309, 316–17, 319–20; composes maxims, 310; social/cultural conservatism, 311, 329; Dupanloup visits, 316–18; documents on religious state while dying, 318–22, 324; signs documents on deathbed, 322–3; given last rites, 323; death, 324; final religious conversion questioned, 324; funeral, 325–6; achievements and qualities, 327–38; political ideas, 329; Declaration on interests of France, 334

Talleyrand, Charlotte de (baroness Alexandre; CMT's daughter): CMT adopts, 140; in Bourbon-l'Archambault, 171

Talleyrand, Daniel-Marie-Anne, comte de Grignols (CMT's grandfather), 1

Talleyrand, Gabriel-Marie, comte de Périgord (CMT's uncle), 1, 4

Talleyrand, Louis de, duc de Valençay (CMT's great-nephew), 119, 136, 277, 287, 322, 325

Talleyrand, Marie-Thérèse de (CMT's granddaughter), 322

Talleyrand, Pauline de, marquise de Castellane (Dorothée's daughter), 239, 315–16, 321–2, 325

Talleyrand, Sabine, comtesse de (CMT's sister-in-law), 81

Talleyrand, Yolande de (CMT's great-niece), 325–6

Talleyrand-Périgord, Dorothée de see Dino, Dorothée, duchesse de

Talleyrand-Périgord, Edmond de see Dino, Edmond, duc de

Tallien, Jean-Lambert, 85

Talon, Omer, 79, 84

Tessier, M. (of Foreign Ministry), 120

Thiers, Adolphe: and art of conversation, 172; condemns CMT's peace terms with allies, 225; CMT meets, 291; CMT champions against Guizot, 306–7; forms enmity towards CMT, 307; stays at Valençay, 316; scorns CMT's final religious conversion, 324

Third Coalition, 156

Third Estate (commoners), 40–2

Thurn und Taxis, Princess Theresa of, 194

Tilsit, Treaty of (1807), 166, 168–9, 192–3

Times, The, 293, 294

Tobago, 61, 64, 226

Toulon: surrenders to British fleet, 6

Trafalgar, Battle of (1805), 160

Travellers Club, London, 296

Triple Alliance (Austria-Britain-France, 1815), 249–50, 253, 333

Tuileries: mob invades, 67–8

Turgot, Anne-Robert-Jacques: clerical career, 9; economic reform, 28; Encyclopédie article on 'foundations', 46

Tyszkiewicz, Maria Theresa, Countess, 167, 175, 285, 309

Ulm, Battle of (1805), 156, 160

United States of America: CMT's exile in, 77–83; CMT's views on, 82–3, 334; relations with Britain, 83, 87; France attacks shipping, 102; Talleyrand demands payment from envoys, 102–3

Valdec de Lessart, Antoine see Lessart, Antoine Valdec de

Valençay (château): CMT occupies, 135–6, 175, 179–80, 286, 329; Spanish princes detained in, 191–2, 207; Spanish princes leave, 212; CMT's final years in, 308; CMT buried at, 325

Valençay (town): CMT's improvements as mayor, 286–7

Valois, Club de, 40

Varennes, 59

Vaudémont, Louise, princesse de (née Montmorency), 21, 181, 291, 297, 299

Vendée, 126, 144

Vergennes, Charles Gravier, comte de, 30

Vestris, Auguste, 143

Vicence (Vicenza), duchesse de (Mme de Caulaincourt), 279

Vienna: Napoleon seizes, 156, 203; CMT in, 161–2; Kaunitz Palace, 240; memorial requiem mass for Louis XVI (1815), 251

Vienna, Congress of (1815): CMT attends, 182, 233–44, 246, 248, 250–3, 255, 300, 331, 336–8; aims, 234; organization and conduct of, 241–2; on law and power, 242; and formation of Triple Alliance, 250; decisions, 251–2; CMT reports on to Louis XVIII, 257

Vigée-Lebrun, Elisabeth-Louise, 20, 137

Villèle, Jean-Baptiste-Guillaume-Joseph, comte de, 281, 289–90, 297

Villemarest, Maxime de: on CMT's working methods, 118–19; Monsieur de Talleyrand, 131–2

Vincent, Charles, baron de, 196
Vitrolles, Eugène-François d'Arnauld, baron de: on CMT's lack of true friends, 6; and formation of National Asssembly, 42; and CMT's Messe de la Fédération, 52; and CMT's working methods, 118; on CMT's cronies, 121; and CMT's need for money, 134; on CMT's conversation, 174; on CMT's resignation as Foreign Minister, 185; and CMT's role at Erfurt, 195; and Napoleon's negotiations with allies, 215–16; and restoration, 228; modifies d'Artois' speech to Senators, 230 appointed minister-secretary of state, 230; drafts Declaration of Saint-Ouen, 231; supports inclusion of Fouché in government, 263; and removal of Fouché, 269; as Monsieur's spy, 271; and CMT's curiosity about new government, 273; Pozzo's anxieties over, 278; on CMT's character, 327
Voltaire, François-Marie Arouet de, 73

Wagram, Battle of (1809), 203
Walewska, Marie, Countess, 167
Walpole, Horace, 138
Warsaw: CMT in, 165, 167, 171; Grand Duchy of, 166, 251; Russia reoccupies, 299
Washington, George, 78, 82

Waterloo, Battle of (1815), 258, 263
weights and measures: reform of, 50, 60, 67–8
Wellesley, Lord Arthur (Wellington's son), 294
Wellington, Arthur Wellesley, 1st Duke of: and CMT's reaction to Napoleon's death, 111; CMT suggests bribing, 212; visits Louis XVIII, 246; replaces Castlereagh at Congress of Vienna, 254; leaves Vienna to confront Napoleon, 255; and Louis XVIII's return after Waterloo, 259–60; supports Fouché's appointment to government, 263, 269; and treatment of France after 1815, 270; supports CMT's recall to government, 274; on CMT's outbursts, 275–6; organizes royalist ball in Paris, 278; and CMT's ambassadorship in London, 294, 302; and conference on Belgium, 298; as guide to duchesse de Dino in London, 301
Wilberforce, William, 63
William I, King of the Netherlands, 295
William IV, King of Great Britain, 296–7, 305
William Penn (ship), 77–8
Wycombe, John Petty, Earl of, 71

Zoé (Mme de Laval's black servant), 182